POSIDONIUS

II. THE COMMENTARY:

(i) Testimonia and Fragments 1–149

I. G. KIDD

Emeritus Professor of Greek,
University of St Andrews

CAMBRIDGE UNIVERSITY PRESS

CAMBRIDGE

NEW YORK NEW ROCHELLE
MELBOURNE SYDNEY

Published by the Press Syndicate of the University of Cambridge
The Pitt Building, Trumpington Street, Cambridge CB2 1RP
32 East 57th Street, New York, NY 10022, USA
10 Stamford Road, Oakleigh, Melbourne 3166, Australia

First published 1988

Printed in Great Britain at
The Alden Press, Oxford

British Library cataloguing in publication data

Posidonius.
Posidonius. – (Cambridge classical texts
and commentaries).
Vol. 2, The commentary
1. Greek literature
I. Title II. Kidd, I.G.
888'.0108 PA4399.P2

Library of Congress cataloguing in publication data

Posidonius.
(Cambridge classical texts and commentaries, 13–)
Greek and Latin text; pref. and introd. in English.
Includes bibliographical references.
Contents: v. 1. The fragments – v. 2. The
commentary: i. Testimonia and fragments 1–149;
ii. Fragments 150–293.
I. Edelstein, Ludwig, 1902–1965, ed. II. Kidd, I. G.,
ed. III. Series: Cambridge classical texts and
commentaries; 13, etc.
PA399.P2 1972 188 77-145609

ISBN 0 521 35499 4 THE SET
ISBN 0 521 20062 8 II (i)

AL

For my wife Sheila

CONTENTS

Preface *page* ix

VOLUME II(i): TESTIMONIA AND FRAGMENTS 1–149

PART I: TESTIMONIA

T1–72	Life and influence	3
T73–107	Characteristics of his philosophy	58
T108–15	Dubia	90

PART II: FRAGMENTS AND TITLES OF NAMED BOOKS

F1–3		99
F4–28	Physics	102
F29–41	Ethics	151
F42–5	Logic	189
F46–83	Sciences and History	205
F84–6	Dubia	336

PART III: FRAGMENTS NOT ASSIGNED TO BOOKS

F87–91	Divisions and Content of Philosophy	349
F92–149	Physics	368

VOLUME II(ii): FRAGMENTS 150–293

PART III: FRAGMENTS NOT ASSIGNED TO BOOKS (*cont.*)

F150–87	Ethics	553
F188–94	Logic	684
F195–251	Sciences	699
F252–91	History	861
F292–3	Miscellaneous	983

References 989

Indices 1009

Index of passages cited or discussed 1010
Index of proper names 1036
Subject index 1047

PREFACE

The purpose of this Commentary is primarily to explicate and understand the attested fragments as listed in volume I.

At the outset, I asked myself what were the major problems confronting a Posidonian commentator, and two of these in particular have affected my procedure, organisation and presentation. The first is obvious: that we are dealing with a reported fragmentary tradition. Study of the fragments has confirmed my view that ancient authors are not, any more than modern writers, mere reporters or tape-recorders of predecessors to whom they refer. Authors such as Cicero, Strabo, Seneca and Galen use Posidonius for their own purposes. Therefore the general context of a 'fragment' is important, and I have always tried to make this clear in the Commentary. But the matter is more complicated, for the actual argument or method of presentation in which the report is embedded raises problems, not only of the extent of a fragment, but also to what degree it has been coloured, reinterpreted or distorted. This applies not only to highly individual discursive writers such as Cicero and Plutarch, but to the doxographies as well; the presentations of Diogenes Laertius and Arius Didymus, for example, are quite different. For these reasons, I am sceptical of the value of the purely horizontal collocation of supposedly parallel passages on their own as a basis for Posidonius, although they must always be examined. The reporter is as important as the report. In order to understand one Posidonian 'fragment' in Seneca, one should have read the whole of Seneca, to equip oneself for the interpretation of Posidonius through his spectacles. Since there are some sixty reporters who actually name Posidonius, apart from those who used him without acknowledgement, this is no easy matter, and much more work is required on individual authors; there is, for example, still no detailed examination of Diodorus and Posidonius from this point of view. I can only claim to have wrestled with the problem as best I could, to bring it continually to the attention of the reader. For I am convinced that this is a fundamental principle of some importance for the future of Posidonian studies.

The second problem which I would briefly mention concerns the vast range of Posidonius' writing over the philosophies, sciences and historiography, the formative background of which a commentator must take into account. This affects comment both in general and in detail: in general, because Posidonius regarded all these different disciplines as an interrelated organic whole in his intellectual enquiries. Thus in examining the historical fragments one may not forget that they are the account of a philosopher historian, a factor which becomes a key for the understanding of the notoriously lavish presentation of the tyranny of Athenion (F253). So too his work *On Ocean* requires some knowledge of his posited relationship between natural philosophy and a whole range of sciences to explain the behaviour of natural phenomena and human anthropology.

But also the problem at issue frequently depends on detailed knowledge, not only of the history of philosophy, but of ancient theories of sciences such as mathematics, mathematical geography, astronomy, meteorology, hydrology, seismology, mineralogy, and indeed of the history and geography of the whole Graeco-Roman world of the period. Thus the reader will hardly be aware of the significance of Posidonius' definition of parallel lines (F197) without being apprised of the mathematical debate on Euclid's notorious fifth postulate. The realignment of the mapping of India (F212) cannot be appreciated without knowledge of the common disorientation of the continent. Explanation of the adventures of Eudoxus of Cyzicus (F49) depends to some extent on the history of the monsoon trade routes. Zonal theory cannot be understood without astronomical background, nor Posidonius' measurement of the earth without an examination of the methods available to him. The details of Athenion's coup demand knowledge of the situation at Athens in 88 B.C.; and so on. Such a range puts considerable strain on a single commentator's competence, and I am very conscious that there will be readers much more expert than I in the various specialised disciplines involved. But it is surely true that we cannot begin to assess the importance and relevance of Posidonius' contribution without confronting such additional evidence, so I have always tried to raise this larger contextual problem in the hope that it may be investigated further.

These two principles have tended to make my commentary discursive rather than descriptive. They have also strengthened my belief that I must concentrate for the discovery of Posidonius first on the attested fragments, in which much is still uncertain, and I have examined possible unattested material mainly in relation to them. In those respects above all readers will note that my approach is different from that of Theiler. I have merely attempted to supply a tool with which future scholars may let in more light and gain more enlightenment in this fascinating and important area.

It will now be obvious that my obligation to other scholars in a work of this scale is enormous, and this I hope is acknowledged in my references and bibliography. I have been privileged to consult Edelstein's notes, and although these were inchoate, fragmentary and by now out of date, I have always learned from them. In the exact sciences I owe a special debt to Dr Otto Neugebauer, who with kind and patient forbearance in the Institute for Advanced Study at Princeton stretched a helping hand to a callow amateur. For the historical fragments much was gained from the learned and meticulous work of Dr Jürgen Malitz. More friends than I can mention, and in particular my long-suffering colleagues at St Andrews, have responded generously to importunate requests. But, as in the first volume, I wish most of all to record my gratitude to Professor Harold Cherniss who initiated this project and, with more confidence than seemed justified, sustained it with continual encouragement; and to Professor C. O. Brink and Professor F. H. Sandbach who spent many hours over the typescript attempting to cleanse it with pertinent criticism. To the scholarship of these three friends I owe more than I can adequately express. It is a pleasure to have the opportunity to thank my own university, St Andrews, an alma mater indeed, for study leave, and the Institute for Advanced Study at Princeton for supplying an ideal haven for its pursuit. Again Cambridge University Press have prepared the book with courteous efficiency and unfailing skill. To my wife, who in quite different and no less important maieutic ways fostered my gestation, this volume is dedicated.

I. G. KIDD

University of St Andrews
September 1986

PART I
TESTIMONIA

LIFE AND INFLUENCE

T1a, b Suda, *s.v.* Ποσειδώνιος, 2107–10; *s.v.* Πολύβιος, Codex A, *in marg.*

The Suda appears to have taken material from Hesychius of Miletus (6th c. A.D.) some of which in turn derived from Demetrius of Magnesia, the friend of Atticus (1st c. B.C.) (Adler, *RE* IVA (Suidas), 706f; Leo, *Griechisch-römische Biographie*, 30f, 39ff; Schühlein, *Studien zu Posidonius* 4f, *Zu Posidonius Rhodius* 2). But the Suda article is extremely garbled and confused.

It is arranged under four entries:

(i) **1–4** Posidonius the Stoic philosopher from Apamea in Syria or Rhodian citizen. The double designation was significant, and both or either is used as identification (T2).

2 His nickname was Ἀθλητής. This occurs nowhere else, but we have no reason to doubt it. It has been taken literally, that Posidonius was an athlete before turning philosopher (F. A. Wright, *History of Later Greek Literature* 415), presumably from such anecdotes on Cleanthes (πύκτης, D.L. VII.168), Chrysippus (δόλιχον ἤσκει, D.L. VII.179), Pythagoras (D.L. VIII.48), or Hierocles of Hyllarima (Steph. Byz., p. 647 Meineke). But ἐπεκλήθη refers to a nickname, and nicknames were common, like Eratosthenes' Beta. I suspect that the Chrysippus anecdote may derive from a nickname which would well suit him. The comparison or metaphor of ἀθλητής for philosophers goes back at least to Plato (*Phil.* 41b 8). Strabo uses the metaphor of Posidonius himself: τῷ . . .

περὶ πρωτείων ἀγωνιζομένῳ (F49.292f). It probably means something like 'The Champion'.

2–3 That Posidonius taught for most of his life in Rhodes is borne out by the other testimonies (T2). He was a pupil of Panaetius at Athens (T9), but to say that he was the διάδοχος of Panaetius is at the least confusing. He was not Panaetius' successor as head of the School at Athens. The tradition may have meant that after Panaetius' death, Posidonius was the spiritual διάδοχος as the most important Stoic. Presumably the shift of power in the School moved at this time from Athens to Rhodes.

4–5 'He also went to Rome in the consulship of Marcus Marcellus.' The old conjecture of Μαρίου for Μάρκου arose from Posidonius' embassy in 87/86 B.C. (T28); but Μαρκέλλου remains. Wilamowitz (*Der Glaube der Hellenen*, II.397 n. 1) held that it refers to M. Cl. Marcellus (*RE* no. 226), Marius' legate in 102 (Broughton, *Magistrates*, I.569), and the legate of the consul L. Iulius Caesar in 90 (Broughton II.28; cf. *Add.* p. 16) (F258 comm.). But the date should have some significance for Posidonius' life. Also ἐπί should imply 'in the consulship of'. The consulship of M. Claudius Marcellus (*RE* no. 229) was 51 B.C. (Broughton, II.240), which was also the date when Rhodes reaffirmed her treaty with Rome (Cic. *Fam.* 12.15.2), in connection with which Posidonius may have been at Rome (F86e, F258). If so, he was at least 80 (T4 comm.). But it must also have been about the time of his death (T4 comm.), so it has been conjectured that a verb of dying has been omitted: Ῥώμην ⟨ἐπὶ Μαρίου καὶ ἐτελεύτησεν⟩ ἐπὶ Jacoby; Ῥώμην ⟨ἅμα τελευτήσας⟩ ἐπὶ Reinhardt (*RE* col. 564); Μαρκέλλου ⟨καὶ ἐπανιὼν ἐτελεύτησε⟩. Theiler.

4 'He wrote much.' But surprisingly no titles are given, and worse, two of his major works are assigned to other Posidonii below.

(ii) 5–10 Posidonius of Alexandria; Stoic philosopher and pupil of Zeno of Citium (so also D.L. VII.38). But he is credited with the impossibility of writing a *History* continuing

Polybius. However, the epitomator opines that the books assigned to the Alexandrian should be credited to Posidonius of Olbia in the next entry. That this includes not only the rhetorical works but also the *History* is supported by his entry under *Polybius* (T1b). Nevertheless, despite the doubts of Bake and others (*Posidonii Rhodii Reliquiae Doctrinae* 250f; cf. Pozzi, *RFIC* 41 (1913), 58–67), the *History* is certainly that of Posidonius of Apamea. The coincidence that two Posidonii wrote a continuation of Polybius' *History* on that scale (of which we only know one) is too outrageous to contemplate. That the Suda defines the *History* as τὴν μετὰ Πολύβιον, while Athenaeus always refers to it simply as '*The History*', is not surprising; he is giving an indication of its beginning, size and extent. Strabo can refer to his own *History* in the same way (F282). Our evidence for the content of the *History* supports the claim that it began from where Polybius finished (146/145 B.C.). The Suda adds that it consisted of 52 books and continued 'to the Cyrenaic war and Ptolemy'. This latter phrase is devoid of meaningful significance. On the difficulties arising from the number of books and from the reference of termination, see F51 comm. The emendations arising out of these difficulties in no way solve the problems. Pozzi argued that ἕως τοῦ πολέμου τοῦ Κυρηναϊκοῦ καὶ Πτολεμαίου should be referred to the Λιβυκά of Posidonius of Olbia; but this is not convincing.

(iii) 11–14 Posidonius of Olbia (at the mouth of the Hypanis or Bug and near that of the Borysthenes or Dnieper), sophist and historian. Jacoby, *FGrH* 279 puts him in the 2nd c. A.D. This writer, clearly popular with the epitomator, is also credited with Περὶ τοῦ ὠκεανοῦ καὶ τῶν κατ' αὐτόν. This again must be the Περὶ ὠκεανοῦ of Posidonius of Apamea, which Strabo knew (F49). To debate whether the fuller or shorter form of the title is the 'correct' form (Malitz, *Die Historien des Poseidonios* 6 n. 12) is a modern preoccupation.

(iv) 15–17 Another Posidonius (about whom the epitomator knows nothing: only the proper name, ὄνομα κύριον, is given) wrote a work on augury or divination based on involuntary twitching (παλμικόν). See F86b, F113 comm. for the evidence as to whether or not Posidonius of Apamea may have written on this subject.

The confusion of the Suda article is a salutary warning that even the ancients at a later period had difficulty distinguishing different Posidonii, and deciding who wrote what. It should not be forgotten that Posidonius was a common name. Even in the surviving literature, we can pick out several more in addition to those listed by the Suda: (1) the Spartan at the battle of Plataea (Hdt. IX.71, 85); (2) the engineer who constructed a siege engine (ἑλέπολις) for Alexander (in Biton's *Instruments of War*); (3) the Posidonius who turns up in Lycon's will (3rd c. B.C.; D.L. V.73); (4) the distinguished pupil of Anniceris (early 3rd c. B.C.; Suda, *s.v.* Anniceris); (5) Aristarchus' reader (2nd c. B.C.; T109, T110); (6) Posidonius Λαμπτρεύς and (7) Posidonius Πειραιεύς (both in *I.G.* II^2, 1938, 59, 60; Cichorius, *RhM* 63 (1908), 198; mid-2nd c. B.C.); (8) the legate of Nicanor, the general of Demetrius Soter (Bake, *Posidonii Rhodii Reliquiae Doctrinae* p. 255); (9) Posidonius of Corinth, who wrote on angling, and was probably a grammaticus about the end of the 2nd c. B.C. (Athenaeus, I.13B); (10) Posidonius of Ephesus, a distinguished silver chaser at the time of Pompey (Pliny, *NH* 33.156; 34.91); (11) probably a doctor and fellow-pupil of Zopyrus with Apollonius of Citium, i.e. 1st c. B.C. (but see T112); (12) certainly other doctors of the name Posidonius (T113, T114; Christ–Schmidt–Stählin, *Geschichte der griechischen Litteratur*, II.925); (13) Posidonius Ἀπολλωνιάτης (Tzetz. *Comm. on Iliad* Δ. 10); (14) a minor Latin poet (T115); and (15) a friend of Apsyrtus, the veterinary surgeon at the time of Constantine (*Corpus Hippiatricorum Graecorum* I.198.12).

In addition the name continually appears in inscriptions, for example: *SEG* VIII.574 (Egypt), 794 (Egypt); IX.102, 103, 132, 478 (Cyrenaica), 908; XI.414 (Epidauria); XII.101

(Attica), 128, 176 (Attica), 230 (Macedonia); XIII.497 (Ionia); XIV.631 (Trieste); XV.697 (Ephesus); XVIII.36A (Attica), 456 (Ionia), 512 (Ionia); XIX.459 (Moesia), 736a, b (Pisidia), 734; XX.741a.51 (Cyrene), 740b; XXI.480 (Attica), 603 (Attica), 614 (Attica), 884 (Attica).

T2a, b; T3 Strabo, XIV.2.13; Athenaeus, VI.252E; Cicero, *Tusculanae Disputationes*, V.107

Posidonius was born at Apamea on the Orontes in Syria. There has therefore been speculation about 'oriental' origins and influences (Pohlenz, 'Stoa und Semitismus', *Neue Jahrb.* 2 (1926), 257–69; cf. *Die Stoa* I.208, II.116; Wilamowitz, *Der Glaube der Hellenen* II.403; Cumont, *CAH* XI.642; cf. Wendland, *Die hellenistisch-römische Kultur* 84f). But Apamea had a strong hellenic element of population including Macedonian colonists (Strabo, XVI.2.10; A. H. M. Jones, *The Cities of the Eastern Roman Provinces* 241–3). Posidonius had a Greek name, wrote in Greek, had his higher education in Greece, and lived the whole of his adult life in Athens and Rhodes, where he clearly felt at home. He retained an unsentimental and critical view of his birthplace (F54). Whether his philosophy or writing betrays any influence from the environment of his early unformed boyhood years is likely to lead to circular argument, but there is nothing in it which cannot be explained by the hellenistic intellectual, philosophical and scientific background of his time (see also Reinhardt, *RE* 628, 36ff; Laffranque *Poseidonios d'Apamée*, 49ff; Malitz, *Die Historien des Poseidonios* 8).

After an education in Athens with Panaetius, he settled in Rhodes, became a citizen (ἐπολιτεύετο, T2a.1), indeed an active one (T27, T28), made his living there (χρηματίσας, T2b), and, according to Cicero, never returned to live in Apamea (T3). This is hardly surprising. Syria remained very unsettled, and although the hellenistic intellectual world was cosmopolitan, Syria did not feature highly in it (Bevan, *House of Seleucus* I.224ff). But why not Athens? Possibly because he wanted to set up on his own, and the Athenian Stoa was dominated by Panaetius until his death, *c.* 110 B.C., and Panaetius was succeeded by Mnesarchus as Head of the School in Athens. Also, Rhodes was a free city, prosperous, and above all had become one of the major intellectual centres in science (Hipparchus) as well as philosophy (Strabo, XIV.2.5ff). But we do not know precisely when he settled there and was awarded citizenship.

T4 Ps.-Lucian, *Longaevi* 20, 223

The *Longaevi* (Μακρόβιοι), falsely ascribed to Lucian, gives Posidonius' age as 84.

This compilation, whose Greek suggests a period certainly later than Lucian, is of uncertain reliability, and the compiler's figures do not always tally with other estimates, even those given by authors to whom he refers. We have no control over the statement.

Our dates for Posidonius' birth and death are conjectural. The last certain datable reference to him alive is 60 B.C. (T34). He was dead by 43 (the siege of Rhodes by Cassius; see Scheppig, *De Posidonio Apamensi* 12) and most probably by 45 (the date of Cicero's *Tusculans* (T3)). He was a pupil of Panaetius (T9, T10) who died *c.* 110 B.C. (van Straaten, *Panétius*, 23–5), so it is unlikely that he was born much if at all later than *c.* 130 B.C.

If ἐπὶ Μάρκου Μαρκέλλου (T1a.4) refers to the consulship of M. Claudius Marcellus in 51 B.C., and *if* this contained an allusion to Posidonius' death (T1a comm.), and *if* Ps.-Lucian reported his age correctly, then Posidonius was born in 135 B.C. This sort of chronological bracket is at least consonant with all our other evidence. But the dates 135–51 B.C. have passed into the vulgate of Posidonian literature. It is important to remember that the precise dates rest on very hypothetical and insecure evidence.

T5 Strabo, VI.2.11

There are two possible dates for this event:

(i) 126 B.C.; Pliny, *NH* 2.203; Julius Obsequens 29. In this year Titus Quinctius Flamininus (cos. 123 B.C.) was almost certainly praetor (Broughton, *Magistrates*, 508f; *RE* XXIV, Quinctius (47), 1100). It would be an easy change in line 6 to read Φλαμινῖ⟨ν⟩ον. Compare Nissen, *Italische Landeskunde* I.251; JACOBY, *Kommentar* 202.

(ii) 90/89 B.C. (cf. Holm, *Geschichte Siciliens* III.521; *RE* VI Flaminius (5), 2502) when Pliny, *NH* 2.238 records a similar eruption in the Social War, *donec legatio senatus piavit*. These words recall F227.15–17. But Titus Flaminius, the supposed praetor of Sicily as given in Strabo's codices, is otherwise unknown and does not fit into the praetor list of that time (Broughton, *Magistrates*). Also the praenomen Titus suits a Quinctius better than a Flaminius.

Unfortunately the phrase κατὰ τὴν ἑαυτοῦ μνήμην used of Posidonius is ambiguous. It might mean either 'in his own lifetime' (a Latinism? cf. *maiorum nostrorum memoria*, F228.1), or 'in his own memory'. The second seems more likely in Greek. If so, it would be an odd phrase for *c.* 90 B.C., when Posidonius was well over 30. On the other hand, in 126 B.C. Posidonius would only be a young boy, probably still in Apamea.

μνήμη does not imply autopsy, and the story may have been one of his early memories. Joannes Lydus, *De mensibus* IV.115 (p. 153 Wuensch), in a passage on volcanic and seismic activity mentions Panaetius for the sea area between Lipara and the mainland (van Str. F136); Posidonius may have picked up further details from him (cf. Grilli, *RFIC* 84 (1956), 266–72). Although Pliny assigns purificatory rites to the later eruption, it is unlikely that formal rites were not also performed on the earlier occasion.

On balance, the reference to 126 B.C. and to Titus Quinctius Flamininus seems more likely. Therefore in line 6 Du Theil's emendation Φλαμινῖ⟨ν⟩ον should be adopted, and we may suppose an early recollection on the part of the young Posidonius, to be fully documented later (F227).

T6 Athenaeus, VI.275A

Posidonius says that 'even in my time still' Roman parents brought their sons up frugally (F267). But καὶ καθ' ἡμᾶς ἔτι is a vague statement. Athenaeus' chronology in his context for Frs. 265–7 is so confused (see comm.) that we have no clear indication of when Posidonius thought the decline of ancient Roman virtues began or became prevalent. K. Bringmann (*A & A* 23 (1977), 37–40) argued that Posidonius dated it to the time of the Cimbric war, but his case is unproved. The form of the phrase, καὶ . . . ἔτι, suggests an early date in Posidonius' life, but then presumably he could not himself have observed such frugality in Italy. But the phrase does not demand personal observation, and on the whole an early date is likely. See Frs. 265–7.

T7 Athenaeus, XII.549D–E

Athenaeus confused Posidonius with Panaetius as the companion of Scipio Aemilianus on the famous diplomatic visitation to Egypt in 140/139 B.C. See F58.

T8 Athenaeus, XIV.657E

The passage occurs in Athenaeus' section on hams (πέρναι).

The only thing certain about this garbled account is that Athenaeus repeats (5f) the same mistake, confusing Posidonius and Panaetius, that he committed in T7.

Athenaeus refers to Strabo III.4.11, reporting on the excellence of Spanish hams, adding ἀνὴρ οὐ πάνυ νεώτερος (1–2). This is followed by an explanatory parenthesis, λέγει γὰρ . . . τὴν Καρχηδόνι ἑλόντι (2–6). Athenaeus (or his epitomator) then resumes (δ'οὖν) with a supposed quotation from Strabo, which in fact wrongly conflates the end of III.4.10 on Pompelon (or Pompeiopolis) with the end of III.4.11 on comparison of ham regions, incidentally confusing the proper names in each case. This simply confirms the total unreliability of the whole passage.

The parenthesis (2–6) appears to maintain that Strabo says, in Bk VII of the same work (F58b Meineke, F60 Jones), that αὐτόν (3) knew Posidonius. But who is αὐτόν? Kaibel suggested Pompey who was mentioned in Strabo, III.4.10. But that depends on further conflation of Bk III; the parenthesis refers to Bk VII. Gercke (*RhM* 62 (1907), 116.1) inserted ⟨Πολύβιος καὶ⟩ Στράβων in line 1, but not only does the book objection hold, but it makes nonsense of the reference to hams. R. Philippson (*RhM* 78 (1929), 340 n. 2) rewrote the passage extensively to bring in a reference to Panaetius, than whom Posidonius is younger, and whom Posidonius said he knew. But this is no more than imaginative guesswork.

Editors have therefore followed Schweighaeuser in emending to αὐτός. ἀνὴρ οὐ πάνυ νεώτερος would then have to mean, 'not belonging to recent times', explained (γάρ) in the following sentence: Strabo himself says that he knew Posidonius who accompanied Scipio. But could Strabo have known Posidonius? Not in Rome, because that would extend Posidonius' life into the later forties. Is it conceivable that

Strabo was taken as a young boy to see Posidonius in Rhodes before his death, possibly in 51 B.C. (T1, T3, T4)? But ἐγνωκέναι would then be a strange claim (so also Malitz, *Die Historien des Poseidonios* 30).

I also find the sense assigned to οὐ πάνυ νεώτερος difficult. I would have expected it from the context of the following sentence to mean 'not much younger'; and the position of αὐτόν/αὐτός before ἐν τῇ ἑβδόμῃ . . . is confusing. I have therefore wondered whether the troublesome αὐτόν should be deleted. Since the parenthesis explains (γάρ) οὐ πάνυ νεώτερος, the sense must then be 'a man hardly younger than Posidonius', admittedly a very careless shorthand prolepsis. For Strabo in Bk VII said that he knew Posidonius. Since Strabo was at least seventy years younger than Posidonius, the first statement is a gross exaggeration, and is not significantly improved by Kaibel's οὐ πολύ. It is hardly helped either by Athenaeus' belief that Posidonius accompanied Scipio to Egypt; but this merely underlines the fact that Athenaeus had very little sense of chronology. The second statement is open to the deepest doubts. Nevertheless, in neither case does that mean that Athenaeus could not have written them.

T9, T10 Cicero, *De Officiis* III.8; Cicero, *De Divinatione* I.6

Cicero, who ought to know, is quite clear that Posidonius was a pupil of Panaetius (so also T1a.3). This must have been at Athens, where Panaetius was (if not at Rome) from at least 148/7 B.C. (*I.G.* II². 1938; Meritt, *Historia* 26 (1977), 184), until his death, *c.* 110 B.C., having succeeded Antipater as Head of the School in 129 B.C.

It is not known exactly when Posidonius studied under Panaetius at Athens, but the problem has been confused by an influential article by Philippson (*RhM* 68 (1929), 338), followed by Pohlenz (*RE* XVIII.2, Panaitios, 425). Philippson argued that Cic. *De Off.* III.8 shows that Panaetius lived for thirty years after the publication of Περὶ τοῦ καθήκοντος; but *De Off.* I.90 implies that the work was written after the death of Scipio Aemilianus (in 129 B.C.). Therefore Panaetius was alive at least in 99 and probably later. Therefore when Crassus in his visit to Athens (109 B.C. at the latest) heard Panaetius' pupil Mnesarchus, but not Panaetius (Cic. *De Or.* I.45), this only implies that Panaetius was no longer Head of the School, but not that he was dead. In fact Cic. *De Off.* I.90 is not evidence that Περὶ τοῦ καθήκοντος was written after the death of Scipio, and the natural interpretation of *De Or.* I.45 is that Panaetius was dead by 109 B.C. But even if Philippson were right, if Posidonius was a pupil of Panaetius, it would be while he was the active Head of the Athenian School, and therefore before 110 B.C. We do not know how long before, as there is no evidence that Posidonius was a pupil when Panaetius died. But it is now clear from Posidonian chronology (T4 comm.) that Posidonius must have gone to Athens from Apamea as a young man for his education.

T11 Ps.-Galen, *Historia Philosopha* 3 (*Dox. Gr.* p. 600, 10–11)

The *Historia* maintains that Posidonius heard the lectures of (was a pupil of, ἠκροᾶτο) Antipater of Tarsus. This is impossible. Antipater, who succeeded Diogenes of Babylon as Head of the School in Athens, died in 129 B.C. (van Straaten, *Panétius* 19).

Either there was a confusion between Posidonius and Panaetius arising from the kind of formulation found in Cicero, T10, or we should assume a lacuna from the miscopying of the *Historia*'s source(s). Codex B omits δὲ Ποσειδώνιος ἠκροᾶτο. The context is a list of the Stoic succession from Zeno of Citium, and it is very surprising that Panaetius' name is missing. Perhaps the source had something like: τούτου δὲ ⟨Παναίτιος μετειλήφει τῶν λόγων ὧν⟩ Ποσειδώνιος ἠκροᾶτο (cf. *Dox. Gr.* 600.8). Posidonius was of course familiar with and interested in Antipater's work (F170.45ff; and see vol. 1, Index *s.v.* Ἀντίπατρος).

T12 Ps.-Plutarch, *Pro Nobilitate* 18 (Bernardakis, *Mor.* VII, p. 260.20ff)

This is a strange and puzzling reference to Posidonius discoursing to Tubero supposedly περὶ εὐγενείας.

The problem is the source. For the Ps.-Plu. *Pro Nob.* see Sandbach, Plu. *Mor.* Loeb vol. XV, p. 405f. Whoever made the forgery had a weak hold on Greek, the date is unknown and the history of the text mysterious. The forger incorporated passages lifted from Stobaeus.

Ch. 18 (Bernardakis) begins allegedly with Philo, but in fact quotes Stob. IV.29 A24 which Stobaeus gives as ἐκ τοῦ Ἀριστοτέλους Περὶ εὐγενείας (F91 Rose³, 68 Gigon; Arist. *Fr. Sel.* p. 57 Ross). This is in dialogue form raising the problem whom we should call οἱ εὐγενεῖς and refers to the disparagement of εὐγένεια by Lycophron the sophist. The forger then inserts: 'It is not surprising that this has been written by an ignoble (ἀγένους) sophist. Whom shall we oppose to him? Posidonius, I think, a much respected philosopher discoursing the following to Tubero: . . .'. Then resumes another long passage from Stob. IV.29 A25 which Stobaeus also ascribes to Aristotle's Περὶ εὐγενείας (ἐν ταὐτῷ; F92 Rose³, 69 Gigon; Ross, p. 57f), continuing with an examination of definitions of εὐγένεια from Socrates and Simonides, again in a dialogue form of a very Platonic or Socratic style.

So the quotation is not from Posidonius. Is it possible that Posidonius somewhere quoted Aristotle and was mistakenly taken to be the author? This is hardly unknown in doxographic collections; an opinion given by Aristotle as Pythagorean is attributed to Aristotle himself in Diels, *Dox. Gr.* 316.11. And the subject was of interest to the Middle Stoa; Diogenes of Babylon wrote a book Περὶ εὐγενείας, *SVF* III Diog. F52. But the exact reproduction of the Stobaean quotations of Aristotle both before and after the naming of Posidonius suggests that the forger took them from Stobaeus or from his source. So any explicit evidence for a Posidonian Περὶ εὐγενείας is removed (F86a).

On the other hand the sudden reference to a discourse from Posidonius to Tubero is so unusual and strange in such a late forgery that it can hardly have been invented out of thin air. There must have been some earlier source for this, whatever its context or content. The candidates for Posidonius' correspondent could be either Q. Aelius Tubero, the pupil and friend of Panaetius (Frs. 137–9 van Str.), or L. Aelius Tubero, the friend of Cicero (Cic. *Lig.* 10) and legate of Quintus Cicero in Asia. There is also, however, the possibility that Posidonius has been confused with Panaetius as elsewhere (T7).

T13 Cicero, *De Officiis* III.10

P. Rutilius Rufus (*FGrH* IIIC 815; *RE* 34), *c.* 155–75 B.C., serious pupil of Panaetius (also Cic. *Brut.* 114), member of the Scipionic circle, served under Scipio at Numantia, legate of Metellus in Numidia, cos. 105 (Broughton, *Magistrates* I.555), legate of Scaevola in the reorganisation of Asia in 97 (Broughton, II.8), and after a notorious trial repetundarum, retired in exile to Asia in 92, eventually taking citizenship of Smyrna. A good example of the type of eminent Roman Posidonius must have met as a young man among the older associates of Panaetius, and of the society to which Panaetius introduced him. The association between the two men clearly persisted throughout Rutilius' lifetime. They had several points of contact (*doctus vir et Graecis litteris eruditus, Panaetii auditor, prope perfectus in Stoicis*, Cic. *Brut.* 114). Rutilius was known as a strict Stoic in outlook and practice (e.g. Athen. VI.274C, where he is coupled with Mucius Scaevola and Aelius Tubero (T12)). They also shared literary interests, since Rutilius also wrote a Roman history of his times in Greek (cf. F78; *FGrH* 815). The year of Rutilius' consulship saw one of the most dangerous of the Cimbrian invasions in south Gaul and Spain, with the victory of Orange. Perhaps Posidonius gained information on the Cimbri from him (F272 comm.; Norden, *Germanische Urgeschichte* 69, n. 3).

T14–18

Posidonius' famous Grand Tour to the West is most likely to have taken place in the nineties (cf. Laffranque, *Poseidonios d'Apamée* 65–7; Malitz, *Die Historien* 12ff). This was the most settled period for such ventures, after the Cimbrian invasions and the Second Sicilian Slave War. It is also likely to have been posterior to the last voyage of Eudoxus of Cyzicus (F49.227–32 comm.), and to the voyages and accounts of Artemidorus, criticised by Posidonius. Moreover, time was needed after his education at Athens to further his own researches into the sciences, and above all to establish himself at Rhodes. For such long, dangerous and expensive journeys, Posidonius must have needed support and backing (cf. Strabo II.4.2 on Pytheas), both financial (Rhodian?) and certainly from Roman influence. If they took place in the nineties, Posidonius was in his late thirties to early forties. For all these reasons, such an undertaking in the last decade of the 2nd C. B.C. is unlikely. After the nineties Posidonius became politically involved (T28), the Mithridatic War involved Rhodes, and above all he must have settled to writing; for the travels were clearly the major collecting pot for Περὶ ὠκεανοῦ.

In the later part of his life, we have the strong impression that he remained at Rhodes, where others visited him. It is not known how many journeys he undertook, and their extent is unclear. His visit to Massilia and Gaul was not directly from Spain, because he sailed from Cadiz to Italy (T21, T22). His travels must have been prolonged; the return voyage from Spain to Italy took three months (T22). Since Posidonius valued autopsy (T26, T85), we have an unusual number of self-testimonies for his travels.

Spain was one of the countries which interested Posidonius most, because of tidal phenomena, natural resources and environmental ethnology. He was at Cadiz in mid-summer (T14) to check on Seleucus' tidal theory (F218), and stayed at least a month (T15), in order to check the monthly cycle, which he observed correctly (F217). But he was not there for a year, because he mistakenly relied on the people of Cadiz (T17, F217) and on Seleucus (F218) for the annual cycle. He also used the opportunity there to check personally Eudoxus' observations of Canopus as a method of establishing the Rhodes/Cadiz klima (T16, F204), and to make observations on natural history (F241). The floating bricks he claims to have seen personally in Spain (T18) were probably those mentioned by Vitr. II.3.4 and Pliny *NH* 35.171 at Maxilua and Callet (F237 comm.), probably in north Baetica in the Sierra Morena. For the extent of Posidonius' travels in Baetica/Turdetania, see T20. It is highly unlikely that he travelled beyond Baetica. But Strabo regards Posidonius as an expert on Spain (F237 comm., T25).

T19 Strabo, IV.4.5

Posidonius said that he himself had seen Gallic head trophies. He could have seen them quite near to Massilia, in Gallia Narbonensis, where he stayed (T23), because archaeological finds have produced head trophy evidence at various places in the Bouches-du-Rhône area at Entremont, Roquepertuse and Les Pennes-Mirabeau (F274.5–7 comm.). There is no evidence whatsoever that he penetrated into northern Gaul, and this is unlikely in the extreme.

T20 Strabo, III.2.9

The implication of this passage is that when Posidonius was at Cadiz he took a trip into the hinterland where he saw something of the mining operations in the Rio Tinto sector of the southern Sierra Morena, probably a large number of small-scale operations (F239; J. S. Richardson, *JRS* 66 (1976), 141). It may have been the same occasion when he was north of Seville, observing flooding at Ilipa (T14, F218). He had also been as far east as New Carthage (Cartagena, F241).

T21 Strabo, XVII.3.4

The interest of this testimony lies in the fact that Posidonius returned from his famous visit to Cadiz and Spain, not by land through Spain and Gaul, but directly to Italy by sea. Therefore, if he visited Gaul and Massilia it was on some other occasion (Malitz, *Die Historien* 98). The observation of apes on the coast of Mauretania was accordingly by chance. Yet even from the misfortunes of this voyage he recorded detail which was later written up with personal reactions (F245) in his books.

T22 Strabo, III.2.5

This is the same voyage as T21. On the return from Spain to Italy, Posidonius was blown off course by etesian easterlies both towards the Balearic Islands (αἱ Γυμνησίαι, 4) and Sardinia, and again towards parts of the African coast opposite them, and so was hard put to it to reach Italy in three months.

Posidonius recorded this as a peculiarity (ἴδιον, 1). His surprise must have been occasioned not by the encounter of etesian winds, but by the fact that they were easterlies. Εὖροι (2) should strictly be E-S-E winds (F137a). He was interested in such winds (F137), and living in the eastern Mediterranean, knew that there they were northerlies (F137; F49.122; F210.36).

In fact the wind systems in the western Mediterranean are more complex and variable. In summer, the build up of heat on the Spanish plateau draws in easterlies, which can remain constant for periods. But there are also crosswind northerlies and south winds which would explain Posidonius' being swept both north to the Balearics (although the usual route from Cadiz was towards Sardinia), and southwards to the African coast: J. Rougé, *Recherches*, 31ff, 93.

But the ancients were struck by the easterlies and thought them etesian. Pliny *NH* 2.127 records that the etesians in Spain are easterlies. Columella's paternal uncle on the coast of Baetica had to protect his vines from them (5.5.15; 3.12.6). No doubt it was they which helped to blow Colaeus eventually all the way through the Straits of Gibraltar in Hdt. IV.152. Strabo, just before this passage, talked of the ease of trading between Rome and Spain, because of the good shipping routes through the regularity (τάξιν) of the winds in the open sea. But the trouble with etesian winds is that they are splendid in one direction, but a problem for the return (Casson, *Travel in the Ancient World*, 151f). It may have been possible to reach Cadiz from Ostia within seven days (Pliny, *NH* 19.4). The return journey was a different matter. The ancients thought of the etesians as summer winds, particularly occurring about the rising of the Dog Star (Sen. *NQ* v.10; Columella, 5.5.15).

T23 Strabo, III.4.17

When in Massilia, Posidonius stayed with a host with the Greek name of Charmoleon. The arrangement may have originated from Rhodes. It is unlikely that he went east into Liguria, because the anecdote based on it was told him by his host (F269; cf. F268). He probably remained in the area of Massilia, with an expedition to the Stony Plain of La Crau near the mouth of the Rhône (F229), and a visit to nearby head trophies (T19, F274). It is improbable that he penetrated further west to Tolosa (F248); the story of its treasure could easily have come from Massilia and elsewhere from his Roman friends. It has been argued that he was taken to see the Cimbrian battlefields (Norden, *Germanische Urgeschichte* 69f). It is certainly unlikely that he went north into Celtic Gaul (T19 comm.). He no doubt used Massilia as a centre to collect material about the Celts and the north.

T24 Athenaeus, IX.401A

The voyage from Dicaearcheia (Puteoli) to Naples was a short hop round the cape into the bay of Naples. Strabo informs us (III.2.6) that Dicaearcheia was a regular destination port for merchantmen sailing from Spain to Italy, so it is possible that Posidonius found himself there after his adventurous return voyage from Spain (T21, T22). Although the distance was small there was regular coastal traffic from the port of Dicaearcheia.

T25 Strabo, II.4.2

Strabo begins to examine Polybius as a geographer at II.4.1. Polybius cannot understand why Eratosthenes believed

Pytheas' stories, when even Dicaearchus disbelieves them. Strabo agrees about Pytheas, who was one of his pet hates (F49.289; F208.24), but scornfully says that to bring in Dicaearchus as a criterion is a laugh. He now contrasts Eratosthenes and Dicaearchus with Polybius and Posidonius: the first two have some excuse because of their ignorance of the West and North, regions they never set eyes on. But who could pardon Polybius and Posidonius if they go wrong, because they have seen and been there?

But Strabo is being rhetorical (for the form of the sentence, cf. T46) and inexact. Polybius had been to Spain, and so had seen the West; but although he had crossed the Alps, he hardly knew 'the North', as Strabo was well aware. With respect to Pytheas, 'the North' for Strabo means Britain and northern Gaul (II.4.1–2; III.4.4), but we must not infer from that either that he believed that Posidonius any more than Polybius had personally visited northern Gaul and Britain: T19, T23, T26 comm.

T26 Priscianus Lydus, *Solutiones ad Chosroem*, p. 72.2–12 (Bywater)

Priscianus' remark that Posidonius was a personal investigator of tidal phenomena (9ff) must refer to his well-known observations at Cadiz. For the reference to rivers in Spain (6), see F218. It is virtually certain that he had not visited the Rhine estuary (5), nor the river Thames (6ff) (F219.71–80 comm.). For the problems concerning Priscianus' sources, see T71, T72, F219.

T27 Strabo, VII.5.8

The prytany

Apart from the nauarchia, the prytany was the most

important office in Rhodes (Livy, 42.45.4; Appian *BC* iv.66.282). Plutarch *Mor.* 813D groups it with the strategia at Athens and the boiotarchia. The prytaneis were more powerful than most Greek magistrates in that they seem to have combined presidential and executive functions (J. L. O'Neil, *Athenaeum* 59 (1981), 471ff; F. Gschnitzer, *RE* Supplb. xiii.766–9; van Gelder, *Geschichte der alten Rhodier* 239ff). There were 5, or perhaps 6 (Holleaux, *Hermes* 28 (1903), 638f; Gschnitzer, 766) holding office for half a year (Plb. 27.7.2; Busolt, *Gr. Staatsk.* i.419, n. 4). It is remarkable, and no doubt exceptional, that Posidonius, who had first to gain Rhodian citizenship, attained this office, although his countryman, the sculptor Plutarch of Apamea, also became prytanis after rising through the customary ladder of office (Malitz, *Die Historien* 15, n. 86). But there is no indication that Posidonius held lower political office, and it seems unlikely that he would have committed himself so fully to a political career. His prytany is mentioned solely in connection with the discovery of bituminous 'vine-earth' at Rhodes, reflecting his practical scientific interest (F235). Malitz (15) may be right that his election was due to the practical recognition of his relationship with leading Romans; but it also probably reveals his relationship with the few wealthy families which really ruled Rhodes (Strabo xiv.2.5; O'Neil, 468ff). They could no doubt assess his usefulness without feeling threatened by a philosopher. There is no evidence as to date. It is generally put before the embassy to Rome in 87/6 (T28), and therefore in the early eighties or late nineties; but this is quite uncertain. Of the two honours, perhaps the prytany was the greater. It was quite within Greek tradition to send famous intellectuals and philosophers on embassies to Rome.

T28 Plutarch, *Marius* 45.7

Posidonius' embassy

The date of the embassy is fixed by Marius' last consulship

of 86 B.C. and his terminal illness reported as pleurisy by Posidonius (F255). The embassy probably went to Rome in the late sailing season of 87, but Posidonius may not have seen Marius until he assumed office as consul in January 86. The subject of the embassy was presumably the relationship between Rome and Rhodes, which had successfully resisted Mithridates' siege in 88. But the situation was dangerous and delicate with Sulla in Greece and a vindictive Marius in Rome, where the political climate was highly unstable. Posidonius must have been much trusted by the Rhodians, deeply interested in the political situation or fascinated by Marius to undertake such an office. His name only is mentioned in discussion with Marius, but although he may have been the leader of the embassy, it is likely that there were others. It has been claimed from Cic. *Brut.* 307 (A. E. Douglas, Comm., *ad loc.*) that Apollonius Molon was a member, but *Brut.* 312 may indicate that Cicero misremembered (Badian, *Historia* 18 (1969), 455f), and at one point confused this embassy with that to Sulla in Rome in 82/1 when Molon was an ambassador. Posidonius was not present on that occasion.

T29 Plutarch, *Cicero* 4.5

In 79 B.C. Cicero, because of a deterioration of health and voice which may have bordered on an incipient breakdown (Plu. *Cic.* 3.5), set off for Athens where he spent six months and heard the lectures of Antiochus (Plu. *Cic.* 4.1). He then toured Asia Minor with Quintus, attending the lectures (συνεσχόλασεν, 3) of the most famous oratorical teachers (2–3), before ending up at Rhodes to study rhetoric with Apollonius Molon and philosophy with Posidonius (4–5). He was 28/9 years old at the time. He departed for Rome in 77 B.C. When Cicero himself refers to his visit to Rhodes in *Brutus*

316, he mentions only Molon, but this is not surprising because of the oratorical subject of *Brutus*. But see T30.

T30 Cicero, *De Fato* 5–7

Cicero is disagreeing with Posidonius on the thesis that everything happens by fate (F104), but he treats him with the utmost respect and gratitude due to his teacher. The tone of the context (cf. line 3) suggests that *pace magistri dixerim* means 'with all due respect to my Professor', and refers to his study in Rhodes; although presumably *magistri* could also mean 'The Maestro'.

T31 Cicero, *De Natura Deorum* 1.6

Cicero stresses that he has been devoted to philosophy continually from his early youth (1–4). He cites as evidence for this (a) his intimacy (*familiaritates*) with the most learned men who always graced his household (5–6), and (b) the leading authorities or masters (*principes*) by whom he was trained or educated. In this last group Posidonius is listed with Diodotus the Stoic, Philon of Larissa and Antiochus of Ascalon.

The classification is slightly odd. Posidonius correctly is not in (a) (household intimates), but Diodotus did become one. Presumably Cicero is elevating Diodotus to the category of *princeps*. Cicero had attended Antiochus' lectures in Athens in 79 B.C. (Plu. *Cic.* 4.1), as he had those of Posidonius in Rhodes in 78/7. Philon was dead by 79. But Cicero had studied with him and knew him earlier in Rome (Plu. *Cic.* 3.1), for Philon, because of a quarrel with Antiochus, had left the Headship of the Academy in Athens in 88 B.C., and spent the rest of his life in Rome. So the list does imply personal acquaintance as well as the recognition that these four men were the great mainsprings of his education in the Academy and Stoa.

T32 Cicero, *De Finibus* I.6; *De Natura Deorum* II.88; *Tusculanae Disputationes* II.61; *De Natura Deorum* I.123

Posidonius did not enjoy that degree of *familiaritas* with Cicero marked by household intimacy (T31). But Cicero refers to him as *familiaris noster*. The range of *familiaris* can be wide, as Cicero's *Epistulae ad Familiares* reveal. Cicero obviously cannot be claiming the close intimacy of *Socrates . . . dicens Critoni suo familiari* (*De Div.* I.52), but the word should convey more than mere acquaintance. Cicero may be playing up his relationship with the great man, although he thought he knew him well enough to ask him to write up his consulship (T34). Posidonius' friendship with leading Romans is indicated elsewhere (with Marcelli, for example, F258 comm., F86e); and in *ND* I.123 (T32d), Cicero claims Posidonian *familiaritas* with Gaius Cotta (the nephew of Rutilius, T13, and a leading Academic), Gaius Velleius (claimed to be the chief Roman Epicurean of the time, *ND* I.15) and Q. Lucilius Balbus (a Stoic, but not a Posidonian). Cicero uses the term elsewhere of philosophical relationship: *Peripatetici, familiares nostri* (*Tusc.* III.22).

T33 Cicero, *Hortensius* F50 Grilli, 44 Mueller (Nonius Marcellus, *De Doctorum Indagine*, p. 527M)

The characters in the *Hortensius* were Lucullus, Catulus, Hortensius and Cicero.

The tone of this fragment seems quite different from T38. Here Posidonius, 'the greatest of all the Stoics', is said when in pain from gout to have been no whit braver than Nicomachus of Tyre, Cicero's host. Nothing is known of Nicomachus, but he is clearly an ordinary man contrasted with a great Stoic philosopher.

Since F2 (Mueller) proves that in the dialogue, philosophy was attacked by Hortensius and defended and praised by Cicero, the strong presumption is that this sentence comes from the character Hortensius. Recently L. Straume-Zimmerman (*Ciceros Hortensius* 69f) and Malitz (*Die Historien* p. 22, n. 146) have argued that it could not be assigned to Hortensius for whom there is no evidence that he was ever in Rhodes (*vidi*, 1), and Cicero's silence in *Brutus* 317–33 is proof against it. So it was spoken by Lucullus, who was certainly in Rhodes in 85 B.C. But our evidence for Posidonius' gout is much later than 85, and the argument from silence in the case of Hortensius is particularly weak.

In any case, the main point is that Posidonius' fortitude in pain from gout was a well-known story (T38), no doubt familiar to all four leading Romans.

T34 Cicero, *Ad Atticum* II.1.2

The date is 60 B.C., probably about 3rd June (Shackleton Bailey).

Cicero had sent to Atticus a *commentarius* on his consulship in Greek, and had received from Atticus a similar effort on the same subject (later published, Nep. *Att.* 18.6). He says that he had also sent a ὑπόμνημα to Posidonius, in the hope that he would compose something more elaborate (*ornatius*) on the same topic. Posidonius declined. Cicero admitted that the draft he had sent to Atticus used, in contrast to Atticus' plain style, all the rhetorical tricks of an Isocrates and Aristotle (II.1.1). So by *ornatius* (3) Cicero must have expected something very elaborate indeed from Posidonius.

Malitz (*Die Historien* 28) suggested that Cicero's hopes may have been raised by the publication already by Posidonius of monographs on Pompey and Marcellus. But the existence of such monographs is doubtful (F79, F86e). The action does however strongly underline Cicero's admiration for Posidonius, and not least the power of his style (T103–6), in entrusting to him the record for posterity of his precious consulship. He believed no doubt that a monograph from Posidonius would make a literary impact particularly on the Greek world.

Political reasons have been suggested for Posidonius' refusal, for example that Cicero's interference in the trial of Clodius in 61 antagonised the Claudii, which in turn may have cooled literary Greeks who were fully conscious of the powerful patronage of the Claudii (Wiseman, *Cinna the Poet* 146). Cicero goes on to say that he seems to have dumbfounded the whole Greek community who before had been pestering him for material to write up. But it is more likely that Posidonius was not interested in the subject, and simply did not want to do it. He was, after all, about seventy-five at the time.

Posidonius clearly declined tactfully. Cicero's colossal egotism seems to have persuaded him that Posidonius said no, because he had been frightened off by the mastery of Cicero's own composition.

For Lambinus' *deterritum*, emending *perterritum* of the codices, see Shackleton Bailey's commentary on this passage, and add Cic. *Brut.* 262.

T35 Strabo, XI.1.6

The date is 66 B.C., for Pompey was engaged in the sweep against the pirates, and had not yet embarked on his Caucasian campaign against Mithridates (2). His reason for being in Rhodes was no doubt to increase the numbers of his fleet (Florus, 1.41.8), so in that sense his opportunity to sit in on a Posidonian lecture was fortuitous (παρατυχεῖν, 3).

There is no means of telling whether the two had met before, but there are already clear signs of respectful liking on both sides: the powerful Pompey on leaving asked whether Posidonius had any instructions for him, and Posidonius answered with the famous advice from father to son (Posidonius was nearing seventy, Pompey was forty at the time) that occurs twice in the *Iliad*, from Peleus to Achilles (XI.783), and from Hippolochus to Glaucon (VI.208). So Strabo was justified in taking this anecdote as evidence to prove (γοῦν, 1) friendship between the two, φίλος Πομπηΐῳ γεγονώς (F206.24).

The story (φασί, 1) probably came from Theophanes of Mytilene, Pompey's historian.

See F206 for the use Strabo makes of the anecdote.

T36, T37 Pliny, *Naturalis Historia* 7.112; Solinus, *Collectanea Rerum Memorabilium* I.121

I.121

The date is 62 B.C., when Pompey was returning from his Asiatic campaigns (1), and enjoying the triumph of his success. He was at the height of his reputation (4), and the dipping of the fasces before Posidonius' door (3) was a remarkable gesture of honour and respect, not only to Greek philosophy in general (cf. Marcellus, F261), but to Posidonius personally.

The extract in Solinus was clearly derived from Pliny.

T38 Cicero, *Tusculanae Disputationes* II.61

This anecdote also refers to Pompey's visit to Posidonius in 62 B.C., after his command in the east (3); *quod solebat narrare Pompeius* (2) may indicate an oral tradition, and suggests that

Pompey liked to parade his acquaintanceship with the great philosopher. But the terms of greeting both from Pompey (*honorificisque verbis prosecutus esset*, 7) and from Posidonius (*tantus vir*, 10) suggest formal regard rather than intimate friendship.

Pompey may have been hoping for commendation on the fulfilment of the Homeric instruction received in 66 before setting out on his campaigns (T35). What he got was a lecture on *nihil est bonum nisi quod est honestum*, and the demonstration in person from the gout-ridden philosopher that pain was not an evil.

Cicero tells the story because he can contrast Posidonius, the true Stoic, with the renegade Dionysius of Heracleia, who, unable to bear pain, confessed it an evil (*Tusc.* II.60). Posidonius agreed with Chrysippus (*SVF.* III.574). Posidonius to Cicero was an orthodox Stoic. *Honestum* is the only *bonum*. For the importance of this evidence, see Frs. 170–3.

T39 Plutarch, *Pompeius* 42.5

The date is still 62 A.D., when Pompey was making his way back to Rome after the successful conclusion of the Mithridatic war in the east. He attended and generously rewarded lectures from all the 'sophists' in Rhodes. Posidonius later published his. On the content of Posidonius' lecture, see F43. The subject chosen by Posidonius has caused surprise (Malitz, *Die Historien* 19; Wilamowitz, *Hermes* 35 (1900), 17; Kroll, *Die Kultur der ciceronischen Zeit* II.123). But to choose a topic where Posidonius through the means of a contemporary debate within rhetoric (the educative and philosophical standing of Hermagoras' θέσεις, or training debates on general questions) clarified his views on the subordinate relationship of rhetoric to philosophy was hardly surprising before a great Roman statesman with intellectual pretensions, especially since Pompey had been going the rounds of the 'sophists' in Rhodes, presumably both rhetors and philosophers.

T40 Suda, *s.v.* Ἰάσων 52

The Suda records that Posidonius had a grandson, Jason, through his daughter who married a Menecrates from Nysa. Jason was a philosopher, a pupil of his grandfather, and succeeded him in his School at Rhodes.

A. Gercke (*RhM* 62 (1907), 116–22) argued that Jason's father belonged to the family of the Menecrates of Nysa who was a pupil of Aristarchus of Samothrace. Strabo (XIV.1.48) says that he himself studied with the son of that Menecrates, Aristodemus, when he was a very old man. The family had a School both in Nysa and in Rhodes. Strabo mentions another cousin, also Aristodemus, a teacher of Pompey the Great. If there is a connection, which is not improbable, the exact relationship remains conjectural. Strabo does not mention Jason.

We can, however, infer from the Suda notice that Posidonius' 'School' in Rhodes continued after his death under his grandson, presumably at least until the time of Augustus. What its character was is another matter; Jason's list of works, which included *Lives of Famous Men*, *Successions of Philosophers* and a book on Rhodes, indicates that he was a very pale reflection of his grandfather, in spite of being his pupil.

T41a, b Seneca, *Naturales Quaestiones* II.26.6; Seneca, *Naturales Quaestiones* VI.17.3

Seneca knew Asclepiodotus as a pupil of Posidonius (*auditor Posidonii*), and refers to him five times in *NQ*. Apart from F228 (T41a) and T41b, he is cited in II.30.1 for a theory that thunder and lightning may also be produced by the collision of certain solid bodies; in v.15.1, he is an authority for a story that Philip II of Macedon sent men down an old mine to examine its condition. They found large rivers and great lakes in underground caverns; compare F230 comm. for his theory in vi.22.2 on falling rocks creating shock waves.

The theory has been advanced that Seneca in *NQ* did not use Posidonius' *Meteorology* directly, but knew him only through the transmission of Asclepiodotus (Schmekel, *Die Philosophie der mittleren Stoa* 14, n. 5; cf. Diels, *Dox. Gr.* 19, 225; Rusch, *De Posidonio* 18.48; Susemihl, *Geschichte der griechischen Literatur* I.138; Oldfather, *Asclepiodotus* (Loeb), Introd. p. 236). This is not borne out at all by the evidence. Seneca cites both separately, sometimes in the same passage (e.g. F228), and Posidonius more often than Asclepiodotus. It is clear that Posidonius is one of Seneca's main sources (among others) for the principal theories and problems of meteorological phenomena, although he is independent of him (T54); Asclepiodotus is rather brought in for additional detail (e.g. F228). We cannot tell to what extent Asclepiodotus followed and how far he departed from Posidonius' meteorological writing and lectures (cf. Oder, *Philologus*, Supplb. vii (1899) 302f), but the Senecan evidence strongly suggests that he wrote his own book(s) on the subject, and did not merely summarise or abridge his master's work.

T41b (*NQ* vi.17.3) seems to give the title of one of Asclepiodotus' books. At this point in his review of previous theories on the cause of earthquakes (see F12), Seneca considers an anonymous hypothesis that they are caused by *spiritus vitalis* (ch. 16f), i.e. vital active air, which has its own natural movement. This is why (ch. 17.3) when an earthquake occurs, if only some part of the earth is broken open, a wind blows from there for many days, as is reported to have happened in the quake which Chalcis suffered. 'You will find this in Asclepiodotus, the pupil of Posidonius, *in his ipsis quaestionum naturalium causis*.'

Unfortunately these last six words are very difficult to interpret. Either (i) they refer to a book of Asclepiodotus, which one would expect after *quod apud Asclepiodotum invenies . . . in. . . .* But if so, there is something wrong with the Latin. (a) Asclepiodotus' book may have been entitled Αἰτίαι Φυσικαί or Αἰτιῶν Φυσικῶν Ζήτησις but could not have had the title Ζητήσεων Φυσικῶν Αἰτίαι. Also (b) *his ipsis* would seem to indicate subject matter rather than the volume (but cf. perhaps *hic ipse Panaetius*, Cic. *De Off.* II.60). Attempts have been made to improve the text, either by deleting *quaestionum* (Gercke, Müller), or more fundamentally: *in ipsius rerum naturalium causis* (Warmington, Loeb, vol. II p. 178, n. 1; thinking *quaestionum* to be a gloss on *rerum*). This has the merit of recognising the difficulty of *his ipsis* as well as that of *quaestionum*, but is not otherwise convincing. Or (ii), the reference is not to a book title but to subject matter, and *causis* means 'circumstances' or 'situation': 'in these very situations in natural questions to which we have been making reference'. But *causis* in that sense and context is odd. Compare Oltramare, Budé vol. II, p. 272, n. 1. It seems more natural therefore to accept the book reference, and assume that a mistake has been made in translating the title into Latin. Obelise therefore *in . . . causis*.

In fact the concept of Asclepiodotus as a mere epitomiser of Posidonius springs not from Seneca, but from his monograph on tactics. There is no reason to doubt that the work which has survived under the title 'Ασκληπιοδότου φιλοσόφου τακτικὰ κεφάλαια should be assigned to our Asclepiodotus: Müller, *RE*, Asklepiodotus (10), 1637ff; Oldfather, Introduction to Loeb edition. This is a brief, dry, antiquarian account in twelve chapters of the different branches of the army, the equipment, numbers and drill manoeuvres of the hellenistic phalanx. It is so sparse and elementary that it looks like a summary. It was used by Aelian in his *Tactica*, and then subsequently by Arrian in *De Tactica*; yet in their introductory lists of previous writers on the subject both record that

Posidonius wrote a Τέχνη Τακτική (Frs. 80, 81), but nowhere mention the name of Asclepiodotus. It is therefore commonly suspected that Asclepiodotus' monograph was known to be an epitome or abridgement of Posidonius' work (Müller, *RE*, and Oldfather, Loeb edition). The word κεφάλαια in the title also lends colour to this view (cf. τὰ κεφάλαια, F41a.10). We know that other admirers of Posidonius published epitomes of his work (Geminus, T42) or transcriptions of his lectures (Phanias, T43); cf. also T44. It is very possible then that Aelian and Arrian knew Posidonius' *Tactics* through an epitome of Asclepiodotus. But that is no argument for thinking that the same situation held good with respect to Seneca, Posidonius and Asclepiodotus on meteorology.

T42 Simplicius, *In Aristotelis Physica* II.2

A Geminus wrote an Epitome of Posidonius' *Meteorology*, known to Alexander of Aphrodisias (F18) and to Priscianus Lydus (T72). He also wrote on optics and on mathematics; it is probable that Proclus, who quotes him frequently in the *Commentary on Euclid*, gained his references to Posidonius on mathematics through Geminus (F195 comm.). The only work of his which survives is an elementary *Introduction to Astronomy* (the *Isagoge*), which contains basic concepts of astronomy, mathematical geography and the calendar.

About Geminus himself, his nationality, where he lived, and when, we know nothing. Because of his interest in Posidonius' work, it has come to be assumed that he was a pupil of Posidonius in Rhodes. His latest editor, Germaine Aujac (Budé, XIX–XXIV), wishes to identify him with the addressee of Dionysius of Halicarnassus' *Letter to Cn. Pompeius Geminus*. On the strength of this, she conjectures his dates to be *c.* 80–10 B.C., that he was a pupil of Posidonius, lived at Rhodes, received Roman citizenship from Pompey and wrote the *Isagoge* *c.* 55 B.C. and the *Epitome* of Posidonius *c.* 45 B.C. As

Aujac herself admits, this is no more than speculation, and based on a single doubtful identification; because apart from the plurality of Gemini, the exclusively rhetorical content of Dionysius' *Letter* fits ill with Geminus' concentration on scientific subjects.

Neugebauer (*History of Ancient Mathematical Astronomy* II. 579–81) attempted a date from a much-discussed (Aujac, XIX, n. 1) passage in *Isag.* VIII.20–4. Here Geminus criticises the naive opinion that the Isis festival according to the Egyptians, and the winter solstice according to Eudoxus would always coincide, simply because '120 years ago', it happened that the Isis festival was celebrated at the winter solstice. Neugebauer constructed a corresponsion table over the 1st c. B.C. and 1st c. A.D. parameters for Geminus' date, '120 years earlier', the winter solstice, and the Egyptian calendar, which reveals that if Geminus' date was in the 1st c. B.C., the winter solstice of 120 years earlier would correspond with dates in the Egyptian month Athyr, while if his date was in the 1st c. A.D., the corresponsion would be with Egyptian Khoiak. The Denderah texts (Porter–Moss *Topographical Bibliography* VI. 94, 96) place the Osiris festival at Khoiak 12–30 (cf. Grenfell–Hunt, *Hibeh* 27). Plutarch, *De Is.* ch. 13 (cf. chs. 39, 42 and Griffiths, *Plutarch's De Iside* ad loc.) dates seemingly identical rites as Athyr 17–20, but his addition, 'when the sun moves through Scorpio', shows that he is using the Alexandrian calendar; and for the probable date of *De Is.* Alexandrian Athyr 17 corresponds to Egyptian Khoiak 22/3. So if the Isis festival referred to took place in Egyptian Khoiak, Geminus was writing in the 1st c. A.D. This argument seems to me to be cogent, although some doubts may remain about which Isis festival is meant (Aujac, XIX). It is still the most likely evidence we have for Geminus, until something better turns up.

Neugebauer therefore put Geminus in mid-1st c. A.D., but this is no more than to put him in the centre of his parameters. Neugebauer himself says (II.579) that it would be strange for a Greek to say that ' "Greeks until our time" were not aware of the rotation of the Egyptian calendar, a century after the Augustan reform . . .' (pointed out to me in correspondence by Bruce Eastwood). So if Neugebauer's arguments are correct, they would rather indicate Geminus writing the *Isagoge* at the very beginning of the 1st c. A.D. If so, he was not a pupil of Posidonius, but he was living at a time in the later 1st c. B.C. when the memory of Posidonius and the interest in his works was still fresh.

Geminus' *Epitome* was a published work, probably for the general reader. It thus differed from individual summaries of convenience such as Athenodorus sent to Cicero at his request in 44 B.C. (τὰ κεφάλαια, T44), or that made by Galen for his own exposition (F166.1–7 comm.).

T43 Diogenes Laertius, VII.41

Diogenes referred (F91) to a certain Phanias, 'an acquaintance (γνώριμος) of Posidonius', who had published his lectures (σχολῶν), in more than one volume. We know nothing more about this Phanias. The evidence suggests that apart from Posidonius' own works, other published material survived of his oral lectures, perhaps of the nature of Arrian's record of Epictetus.

T44 Cicero, *Ad Atticum* XVI.11.4

Strabo, XIV.5.14 records two Stoics of the name Athenodorus known in Rome in the 1st c. B.C. Two also are named immediately after Posidonius in the Stoic index of D.L. One called Cordylion was brought to Rome (from the Pergamene Library as an old man, Plu. *Cat. min.* 10) by Cato Uticensis to live in his house, the other, of Tarsus, son of Sandon, became tutor and friend of Augustus, and gained a great reputation. T. W. Allen (*CQ* 7 (1913), 35n) attempted to identify Athenodorus Calvus with Cordylion, a suggestion adopted by Shackleton Bailey (*Letters to Atticus* 420.4); it is more likely that Athenodorus of Tarsus is meant. Strabo (XIV.5.14) says of Cordylion: συνεβίωσε Μάρκῳ Κάτωνι καὶ ἐτελεύτα παρ' ἐκεινῷ. Cato died in 46 B.C., Cicero was writing for notes on Posidonius' Περὶ καθήκοντος in 44 B.C., when Athenodorus of Tarsus would be in Rome with Octavian. Athenodorus of Tarsus (? *c.* 85–*c.* 3 B.C.; Philippson, *RE* Supplb. v col. 47ff) was much the more famous of the two as a public figure and as an author. Strabo, who knew him well (XVI.4.21), refers to him without the need of qualification, and associates him closely with Posidonius on ocean and tides (T79, Frs. 114, 115). It is reasonable to suppose that Athenodorus had been a pupil, certainly an admirer, of Posidonius, which would lead Cicero to write to him for information on Posidonius' works or Commentarii (F41C.12), as Posidonius was by now dead. It seems to me certain from the Latin that the reference throughout this exchange is to Posidonius, not to Panaetius (as Philippson, *RE* suggests; cf. Shackleton Bailey, *Letters to Atticus* 420.4). Another possible common interest between Athenodorus and Posidonius was divination (F7). Perhaps this was a further reason for Cicero referring Appius Claudius Pulcher to him (*Fam.* III.7).

The simplest explanation of Calvus is that a nickname, 'the Bald', was given to Athenodorus of Tarsus in Rome to distinguish him from Athenodorus Cordylion ('the man with the tumour') (so Pohlenz, *Die Stoa* I.242).

For Athenodorus of Tarsus in general: Jacoby, *FGrH* IIIC 746; Philippson, *RE* Supplb. v, cols. 47–55; Zeller, *Die Philosophie der Griechen* III.i, p. 607n; Pohlenz, *Die Stoa* I.242f, II.124f.

For other difficulties in this passage see F41.

T45 Plutarch, *De Animae Procreatione in Timaeo* 22, 1023B

The phrase οἱ περὶ ᾿A is ambiguous (K. Lehrs, *Quaestiones Epicae* (Regimontii Prussorum, 1837), 28 n.).

(a) It can refer simply to the person A himself: D. A. Russell, '*Longinus' On the Sublime* 117, on 13.3; B. Einarson (*CP* 52 (1957), 201) on Plutarch, *De Musica* 1134C. Compare also D.H. *Thuc.* 51; S.E. *PH* III.218; Epict. II.19.2. Diogenes Laertius appears to incline to this usage (II.77; I.12; I.30; II.38; II.62; II.105; II.134; IV.40). Therefore it is dangerous to infer 'followers' from F89, F117, F126, F180, F288.

(b) It could refer to the followers of A (e.g. Xen. *An.* I.5.8), which is the way Laffranque (*Poseidonios d'Apamée*, 379 n. 37) interprets οἱ περὶ Ποσειδώνιον in Plu. 1023B.

(c) The phrase often means 'A *and* his followers' (Kühner–Gerth, I.269ff; Schwyzer, II.416f). Cherniss (Plu. *Mor.* Loeb vol. XIII, Part I, p. 217 n. g) argued strongly for this interpretation of Plu. 1023B from a comparison with οἱ περὶ τὸν Κράντορα at 1012F.

But in any case the phrase is vague. In one sense Posidonius' 'School' at Rhodes was continued by his grandson Jason (T40), although there is no evidence for it thereafter. Also there is no evidence for the perpetuation of a distinctive Posidonian sect within the Stoa after his death. Indeed mainstream Chrysippean Stoicism continued to predominate, particularly in ethics. But the School remained, as it had been in Posidonius' time, a single School, in which it was recognised that there were differences of opinion on particular issues. Posidonius, like Chrysippus, was regarded as a leading member, and, like the others, particular elements of his philosophy and writing found both adherents and critics. See also T54, T81.

T46 Strabo, II.3.5

The general context is Strabo's review, in his introductory survey of previous geographers, of Posidonius' contribution in Περὶ ὠκεανοῦ (T49, F49). The immediate reference is to Posidonius' account of the voyages to India of Eudoxus of Cyzicus and the attempted circumnavigation of Africa, which Strabo regarded as a severe lapse into the fabulous or gullible (F49.233–93). Strabo elsewhere (I.3.1; II.4.2; F49.236f) groups Antiphanes of Berge and Euhemerus of Messene as romancers of pure fiction (no doubt a contemporary debate, since e.g. Diodorus Siculus VI appears to have used Euhemerus as fact), unfortunately classifying with them the reports of Pytheas (II.4.1–2; cf. F208); and Eudoxus was put into the same category. But the passage underlines Strabo's high valuation and admiration of Posidonius. His outrage, and the length and detail of criticism on this point (F49.233–7 for details), is provoked by his general belief in Posidonius' scientific credentials and methodology, a savant relying on demonstrative proof (ἀποδεικτικῷ καὶ φιλοσόφῳ) and contending for the highest honours (T47).

ἀποδεικτικός is a characteristic label for Posidonius, T83, T84.

Strabo discusses his interpretation and valuation of φιλοσοφία in the geographer at I.1.1, T75; his valuation of authorities, and 'Bergaean' lapses in main authorities (Eratosthenes), at I.3.1; II.4.1.

For the antithetical form of the argument, see T25.

T47 Strabo, I.2.1

Strabo gives his reasons for writing on a subject, geography, which has been treated by many before him. Advances in knowledge enable him to criticise his predecessors. But if he is compelled in places to oppose the very men whom elsewhere he follows above all, he should be forgiven. This is because it is the best who deserve criticism: the rest can be ignored. οὐδὲ πρὸς ἅπαντας φιλοσοφεῖν ἄξιον (5f): Strabo is clearly using φιλοσοφεῖν in a broad sense, cf. T46.4. He names his big four, clearly implying that they have been the greatest influence on him, because they have been for the most part right (4f), and so he has followed them in many places (1f). They are Eratosthenes, Posidonius, Hipparchus, Polybius, and it is in fact these four whom he reviews and criticises in his general Introduction in Bks I–II. The order of the names is certainly not chronological, but may well be in order of importance for him.

Strabo reviews the general contribution of Posidonius' Περὶ ὠκεανοῦ at F49; he criticises Posidonius e.g. at Frs. 49, 239, 217.

T48 Strabo, XVI.2.10

Strabo after dealing with the geography of Apamea records Posidonius as one of its famous sons. Strabo knew him as 'the Stoic' (in spite of Aristotelian tendencies, T85), and as τῶν καθ' ἡμᾶς φιλοσόφων πολυμαθέστατος.

πολυμάθεια is one of Strabo's main requirements in the geographer (I.1.1; T75) and so a most complimentary term (although πολυμαθία was not always regarded as an unmixed blessing; cf. Pl. *Laws* 819a; Heraclitus B40 Diels). It clearly refers to range (e.g. Athenaeus 398E on Aristotle) which in Posidonius was both remarkable and obvious, particularly to his immediate successors. No doubt Strabo, originally a student of Aristotelianism (XVI.2.24), also consulted the *History*, and probably other works.

φιλόσοφος may be used by him in a fairly wide sense: at I.1.1, the term embraces Homer, Hecataeus, Ephorus and Polybius (see T75).

καθ' ἡμᾶς, 'in my time', should indicate at least an overlap with the writer's own lifetime, and indeed has been regarded as a technical term in Strabo for this (e.g. by Schwartz, *RE* VI, Eusebius of Caesarea (24), 1370, 35ff); thus Strabo, XVI.2.24: τὰ μὲν οὖν παλαιὰ ἐάσθω· καθ' ἡμᾶς δὲ ἐκ Σιδῶνος μὲν ἔνδοξοι φιλόσοφοι γεγόνασι Βοηθός τε, ᾧ συνεφιλοσοφήσαμεν ἡμεῖς τὰ 'Αριστοτέλεια . . .; cf. Galen, T60. But it seems that sometimes the expression was used rather loosely: Wyttenbach in Bake, *Posidonii Rhodii Reliquiae Doctrinae* 263; Zeller, *Die Philosophie der Griechen* III.1.593 n.6; *CAH* VII.319. Nevertheless in this context it is unlikely that Gulick (Athenaeus, vol. VII (Loeb), p. 27 n. f. on 657F) is correct in suggesting that it may refer to 'equal origin (Asia Minor) and to the same Stoic school of thought'. We are entitled to assume until it is proved otherwise that according to Strabo Posidonius was still alive in his (Strabo's) lifetime, but not (at least from this evidence) that Strabo had met or seen him. On this latter point see T8.

T49 Strabo, II.2.1

These words introduce the section on Posidonius in Strabo's general introduction reviewing the most important writers on geography before himself: F49. This is evidence that Strabo used Posidonius as a major source (cf. T47), and above all his Περὶ ὠκεανοῦ, which he must have considered the principal work on geography. It is also clear from Strabo's programme of use, namely an immediate preliminary survey of some topics (τὰ μὲν νῦν, i.e. F49), followed by scattered detail when the occasion arose (τὰ δ'. . . κτλ), that he knew and possessed for consultation the whole book. Apart from the initial lengthy survey of F49, there are some sixty other passages throughout the *Geography* where Strabo actually names Posidonius (see Index of Sources), and we cannot tell how often he used him without acknowledgement.

Sometimes Posidonius is used for detail or evidence (as Frs. 227, 226, 221, 207), sometimes for theory (as Frs. 229, 208, 49, T79). Strabo's use was not uncritical, however, e.g. T46, T76, Frs. 49, 216, 217. Indeed Strabo's conception of geographical study and content was hardly that of Posidonius: T76; Reinhardt, *Poseidonios* 59.

T50 Vitruvius, *De Architectura* VIII.3.26–7

Vitruvius names Posidonius with six others as his authorities for Bk VIII, which is concerned with water supply, its sources and transport. The list is very odd (13–15). Apart from Theophrastus, it consists of historians: Timaeus, Hegesias (the 3rd c. B.C. Milesian author of the highly rhetorical *History of Alexander*, *FGrH* 142), Herodotus (presumably the historian and not the author of the work on figs in Athen. III.75F, 78D), Aristides (probably the author from Miletus of historical works cited frequently by Ps.-Plu. *Parall. min.*, *FGrH* 286, whether or not he is the same man as the Aristides who wrote the scandalous Μιλησιακά about the turn of the 2nd and 1st centuries B.C.), and Metrodorus (the 1st c. B.C. historian from Scepsis in Mysia, connected with Mithridates, *FGrH* 184). But we should recall that Vitruvius demanded a liberal education for the architect (I. ch. 1), regarding his profession as a liberal art as well as a science (F. E. Brown, 'Vitruvius and the Liberal Art of Architecture', *Blucknell Review* 11 (1963), 99ff). Since the list is heavily weighted with historians, the question arises whether it was Posidonius' *History* with which Vitruvius was acquainted. But his list of characteristics, *locorum proprietates, regionum qualitates, aquarum virtutes ab inclinatione caeli ita esse distributas* (16–17), suggests rather Περὶ ὠκεανοῦ; cf. Vitr. I.1.7 on *physiologia* and water-supply.

Since Posidonius is here named, inevitably much of Vitruvius has been claimed for him (Oder, *Philologus Supplb.* VII.304ff, 337ff; Reinhardt, *Poseidonios* 112ff). Jacoby printed as *Anhang* F123, Vitr. VIII.3.1–19 as well as 26–7; Theiler F79 prints VIII.3.12–13. But Posidonius is only one 'authority' among others in the heterogeneous list, and we can hardly now distinguish with any certainty, although we may speculate, which elements in particular may be due to him. Vitruvius presents his own popular mélange of literary, scientific and philosophical resources available to him. It is certainly dangerous to build theories for Posidonius on Vitruvius as K. Schmidt (*Kosmologische Aspekte im Geschichtswerk des Poseidonios*) did on the mistaken basis that Vitr. VI.1.1–12 is Posidonian evidence for the mean as an ideal κρᾶσις for both temperature and moral behaviour, leading to the divine mastery of the Roman race (see Kidd, *Gnom.* 54 (1982), 186). Again it is noticeable and revealing that Vitruvius, who is not backward about naming authorities, makes no mention of Posidonius in the Preface or body of Bk IX, a book concerned with astronomy and gnomonology (planetary periods and motions, lunar phases, description of the major constellations, Chaldean astrology and Greek parapegma calendars, clocks). Yet again, Posidonius has been taken to be a source, which should be treated with scepticism (cf. Soubiran, Budé, IX.xlvii ff). We have no reason to see Posidonius in particular here. Nevertheless, it is interesting to know that Posidonius' work was consulted by an educated practical professional like Vitruvius in the 1st c. B.C.

T51 Galen, *De Causis Contentivis* 2.1

Galen says that Athenaeus, the founder of the Pneumatist School of medicine, was a pupil of Posidonius, but there has been controversy over the date of Athenaeus.

Wellmann, 'Die pneumatische Schule', *Phil. Unters.* 14 (1895), 8 and *RE* (followed by Edelstein, *OCD*), put him in the time of Claudius (41–54 A.D.), mainly because Celsus makes no mention of the Pneumatist School. In which case either Galen was wrong, or *conversatus fuit* in the translation of Nicolaus of Rhegium may have had a looser sense of being acquainted with Posidonius' works (cf. Gal. *De Caus. Procat. CMG* Suppl. 2. p. 49.35, 50.13). But the latter argument fails, because the Arabic translation of *De Caus. Cont.* (*CMG* Suppl. Or. II.54) says explicitly that he was a pupil and disciple of Posidonius. F. Kudlien, (*Hermes* 90 (1962), 419ff; *RE* Supplb. XI.1097ff), has put forward a number of arguments to show that Galen was right, and that the Pneumatist School was founded in the 1st c. B.C. Although the lack of mention in Celsus remains surprising, this may be correct.

In any case, there is little doubt that Posidonius influenced Athenaeus and causal theory in the medical pathology of the Pneumatist School: F190. His influence may have been still wider, but Kudlien's arguments in 'Poseidonisches bei Pneumatikern' in *RE* Supplb. XI.1104–6 should be treated with reserve and caution, since they are based on unattested evidence mainly from theories of Reinhardt which have been under attack.

T52 Seneca, *Naturales Quaestiones* IVb.3.2

Seneca, Posidonius and the *Naturales Quaestiones*.

This testimony is double-edged. It is uncertain whether Seneca is being sceptical of Posidonius here, and denying any responsibility for the latter's statements, or whether he is stressing Posidonius' authority as likely to increase the credibility of the statements (details in F136 Context). There is certainly at least jocular reference later in the passage to Posidonius' assurance (F136); on the other hand the assumption behind the playfulness of the passage is that Posidonius was a great authority and would be recognised as such by the reader.

The ambivalence of treatment in this passage is not

untypical of Seneca's use of Posidonius in *NQ*. There is little doubt that he was one of Seneca's main authorities on the subject, and the extent of this influence cannot now be measured (cf. F121). But he was only one among other influences, and while sometimes Seneca may be basically in agreement with Posidonius (F135), and at others influenced but independent (F134), there is at least one clear case (F132) where Seneca disagreed absolutely, and did not hesitate to use Posidonius for his own purposes.

T53 Seneca, *Epistulae* 90.20

This is explicit evidence that Seneca, although frequently disagreeing with Posidonius, in this case on the subject of the Golden Age as an account of human social and cultural development, nevertheless regarded him as one of the major influences in the history of philosophy. That ought to mean that Posidonius' works were still very much alive in this period. Seneca certainly knew the philosophical works and the *Meteorologica*, but the content of the Golden Age would imply that he also knew the *History*.

T54 Seneca, *Epistulae* 33.3–4

Seneca is discouraging Lucilius from picking out purple patches (*flosculi*, 33.1) for study. Such isolated maxims are characteristic of the Epicureans, who attribute them all to Epicurus (33.2). The Stoa does not go in for such eye-catching aphoristic *sententiae*. To whom should they be attributed anyway – Zeno, Cleanthes, Chrysippus, Panaetius, Posidonius? 'We are not ruled by a king. Each is his own man' (7–9). So one must not skim or extract, but read them whole (33.5).

The point of this is that Posidonius is regarded by Seneca

as an equal and individual authority with Zeno, Cleanthes, Chrysippus and Panaetius, the leading Stoic writers who are to be studied in his time. No one of these is to be given more authority than another.

T55 Seneca, *Epistulae* 108.36–8

Seneca has been arguing that the study of philosophy is different from that of literature. Philosophy is not about language, but about action (108.3–35). Philosophy is not to be practised for a commercial trade. Such teachers are useless steersmen in the storms of life. Anything they say in their lectures, tossed to their crowded audiences, is not their own, but comes from Plato, Zeno, Chrysippus, Posidonius and the rest. The only way they can prove their words to be their own is to turn them into action.

This implies that not only for Seneca, but in general for the professional teaching of philosophy in his time, Posidonius was a major figure in the lecture rooms.

T56 Pliny, *Naturalis Historia* 1.2, 4, 5, 6, 11

It has been suggested that Pliny did not know Posidonius first-hand, but derived information through intermediaries like Varro (Malitz, *Die Historien des Posidonios* 57 n. 175; cf. Jacoby, *Kommentar* 200; Beaujeu, Pliny *NH*, Budé vol. 2, xv–xviii). This seems unlikely. He had a high opinion of Posidonius (T36), and named him explicitly as one of his sources for Bks 2, 4, 5, 6 and 11. It is, however, true that it is now impossible for the most part to trace precisely what use Pliny made of him, and too much has been claimed in the past for this (so Beaujeu, Budé vol. 2, xv–xviii). It is also true that where Pliny actually names Posidonius (F120, F212) the report is somewhat hasty, partial and inaccurate. Περὶ ὠκεανοῦ would be an obvious work of reference for Pliny and Frs. 120, 212 may derive from it, although F120 might come from a meteorological work. In *NH* 1.5 Pliny names a chorographical work of the *Periplus* or *Periegesis* category. For this see F50.

T57 Cleomedes, *De Motu Circulari* II.7.126 (p. 226.24ff Ziegler)

Cleomedes concludes his work with a tailpiece: 'Enough has been said about these matters for the present. These lectures do not comprise the opinions of the author himself, but have been gathered from works both ancient and more modern. The greater part of what has been said has been taken from the works of Posidonius.'

The last two sentences have been doubted and excised (Ziegler), but are rightly defended by Goulet (*Cléomède*, 15, and n.127). There is a similar ending to Bk. I, see F19.

σχολαί (2, cf. ἐν τῷ πρώτῳ τῶν σχολικῶν, II.2, p. 168.20 Z) suggests that the *De Motu* was a course of lectures on elementary astronomy (ἐν τοιαύτῃ εἰσαγωγῇ, F19.4), originally given by Cleomedes, perhaps as a teacher of Stoic philosophy, to his students, which may help to explain the elementary content and exposition (Goulet, 15ff), and also the disclaimer of originality. But Posidonius, although the chief, was only one of the sources used (T57, F19; cf. Neugebauer, *History of Ancient Mathematical Astronomy* II.959), which included his opponents (F210.27). F210 (comm.) shows detailed criticism of Posidonius. F115 is followed (146.18–150.23 Z) by another method of estimating the size and distance of the sun, which does not seem to be from Posidonius (F115 comm. Yet Theiler F290a prints the whole of 120.7–168.10 Z). It cannot therefore be assumed that where Posidonius is not named (as in Frs. 19, 114, 115, 123,

202, 210), the source is Posidonius rather than some other, or even if prompted from Posidonius, to what extent modified or simplified in a general account of the period. The whole tract is orientated from a general base of Stoic natural philosophy, and is virulently anti-Epicurean.

Unfortunately nothing is known of Cleomedes apart from this monograph, and his date remains controversial with guesses running from the 1st to the 4th centuries A.D. (Goulet, 5–8; W. Schumacher, *Unters. zur Datierung des Astronomen Kleomedes*). Certain features of the tract, such as complete ignorance or disregard of Ptolemy, the strong attacks on Epicureanism, the pejorative use of the term Jew, and style, have led to suggestions of a bracket between 1st to mid-2nd centuries A.D. (Schumacher). But in a compilation of this kind, such criteria can be very far from precise or even relevant. On the other hand, Neugebauer (*History of Mathematical Astronomy* II.960, cf. *AJPh* 85 (1964), p. 418 n. 1, following a lead from Letronne, *Oeuvres* II.1, p. 249ff), argued that the information given by Cleomedes (p. 106.25–108.5 Z) on the stars Aldebaran (α Tauri) and Antares (α Scorpii) could be calculated from Ptolemy's Catalogue of Stars in the Almagest by the ancient constant of precession of 1° per century to date Cleomedes at 370 ± 50 A.D. But Cleomedes (who could not of course have observed personally the phenomenon, as the stars have the same longitude but not the same latitude) betrays no knowledge either of Ptolemy or of the 1° per century theory of precession which would enable him to make Neugebauer's calculation. He may have done so, but it remains open that he simply took the supposed information about the two stars from a source using other unknown criteria. On our present evidence, the date of Cleomedes remains speculative.

T58 Galen, *De Sequela, Scripta Minora*, vol. II, pp. 77.17–78.2

See F35 comm. for the context of this statement in Galen's argument on the cause and origin of evil.

Galen is following Posidonius in criticism against Chrysippus and other Stoics in general (2–6). Moreover it is implied by ταῦτ' αὐτά (1), that he was following him closely. He gives two reasons for according Posidonius the highest praise (2): (a) he was πάντων ἐπιστημονικώτατος (1–2). By that Galen appears to refer to Posidonian scientific methodology, apodeictic proof from factually true premisses (see T84, F35 comm.). (b) Whereas all other Stoics would prefer to betray their country rather than Chrysippean doctrine, Posidonius would betray School dogma rather than the truth (4–6). (a) and (b) are complementary. Galen was therefore well acquainted with the works of Chrysippus, Posidonius and subsequent Stoic writers, but of them all Posidonius was the most influential for him.

T59 Galen, *De Placitis* IV.390, p. 362.11–13 M, 258.23–5 De Lacy

Just about all the other Stoics somehow or other put up with following Chrysippus' mistakes rather than choosing the truth; cf. T58.

The context is psychology, and is probably restricted to that. Although the statement reflects Galen's own attitude to Chrysippus and Posidonius, it is also a historical statement, which would certainly include the Stoics of Galen's own period (mid-2nd c. A.D.), and probably Stoics after Posidonius in general. Independent evidence indicates that Stoicism remained basically Chrysippean. Posidonian psychology did not seem to catch on, at least among the Stoics themselves; perhaps it was regarded as too Platonic or Academic.

T83 and T99 intervene.

T60 Galen, *De Placitis* IV.402–3, p. 376.7–13 M, 270.3–8 De Lacy

For context, see F164.

Galen expresses unqualified approval of Posidonius' arguments as corresponding to the evidence of observed fact (cf. F164.21, 25). This is the common attitude of Galen in *De Plac.*, where Posidonius is used as a principal authority in ethical psychology against Chrysippus. He can, however, on a rare occasion criticise Posidonius on a matter of medical analysis or mathematical logic (F163). It is more interesting that Galen refers to Stoics contemporary with himself, of considerable numbers and standing, who knew Posidonius' work well enough to engage in problems of such complexity as those raised in F164. But Galen implies that they tried to argue against Posidonius, and so were more likely to be supporters of Chrysippus' theories.

T61, T62, T63 Galen, *De Placitis* IV.427, p. 403.2–12 M, p. 290.20–7 De Lacy; Galen, *De Placitis* V.430, pp. 405.14–406.5 M, p. 292.25–294.3 De Lacy; Galen, *De Placitis* V.479, pp. 459.15–460.3 M, p. 336.7–11 De Lacy

These three testimonies link together to mark the particular section of *De Plac.* where Galen has used Posidonius constantly in his attack on Chrysippus' psychology and theory of emotions.

T61 occurs in the summing-up passage at the end of Bk IV, in which Galen had attacked Chrysippus' mistaken statements about πάθη (emotions) and still more fundamentally the δυνάμεις (faculties, powers) which produce them (1–3). Although that is no doubt sufficient (ἱκανὰ μὲν οὖν ἀμέλει, 1), he is to continue to discuss this subject in Bk V, concentrating on contradictions and inconsistencies with observed fact (3–8). In this he will mention still (ἔτι) in addition (καὶ) Posidonius' criticisms of Chrysippus (8f). So Posidonius is to be used as a principal source and aid in Bk V, as he was used in Bk IV (ἔτι).

This is confirmed by T62, which occurs in the introduction to Bk V. Galen tried to give briefly the most important of Posidonius' many statements in relation to a proof of the ancient doctrine (i.e. Plato, against Chrysippus) at the end of Bk IV (1–4). In the previous books (I–III), he relied on his own account, αὐτὸς ἐπ' ἐμαυτοῦ διῆλθον, not waiting for an external accuser (4–7). The claim for independence in Bks I–III puts more weight on the reliance on Posidonius in IV–V.

Galen then in Bk V proceeds with a detailed direct attack on Chrysippus which in fact contains much named material from Posidonius, until p. 334.16 De Lacy, where he decides to end the polemic against Chrysippus (F151), and return to his main subject, Hippocrates and Plato (334.33ff). He is being as brief as he can (336.1ff). After all, Chrysippus wrote four large tomes, each twice the length of Galen's (T63.1–3), and Galen included in less than two books (Bks IV and V, up to this point) Posidonius' comments on Chrysippus' Περὶ παθῶν (T63.3–6). Galen then passes on to Plato (336.16ff).

Four points seem to follow:

(1) Galen used Posidonius principally and extensively in Bks IV–V (336.15). There are no passages in Bks I–III.

Fragments and testimonia do occur after Bk v, p. 336.15 De Lacy, but they are mostly in relation to Plato. But note T64.

(2) The main use of Posidonius was criticism of Chrysippus' Περὶ παθῶν. Therefore a considerable section of Posidonius' Περὶ παθῶν was engaged in explicit criticism and attack on Chrysippus' work.

(3) Was Galen simply following Posidonius in this section, or using him for his own purposes?

(a) T61–3 all suggest the latter, however extensive and basic the use.

(b) Although T61.6–8 proclaims two targets, self-contradiction and inconsistency with observed fact, which are certainly Posidonian procedures against Chrysippus (T83), we can infer nothing from that. It is clear from the rest of Galen's work that they are also characteristic methods of his. Anyway, attack on self-contradiction was a well-established practice, as Plutarch *De SR* shows, and indeed goes back to Socrates.

(c) It would be difficult to establish from the Posidonius fragments an order of development in Posidonius' Περὶ παθῶν.

Bk IV includes three main long passages: F34 on emotions and judgement, and Posidonius' argument against Chrysippus on the cause of emotions; F164 concerns criticism of Chrysippus that the cause of emotion can be ascribed to degrees of magnitude of presentations or to weakness of soul, and is also concerned with education and training; F165 asks why emotions arise and abate in time, and raises the importance of time and habit in the treatment of emotion.

The sequence of major fragments in Bk v involves, for example: F163 on the condition of soul of φαῦλοι, with a detailed analogy of health and sickness; F167 in the context of explaining how one can heal πάθη when they occur, or prevent them from occurring; F169 on the cause of evil; F31 on education and virtues; F187 with a compendious summary of Posidonius' views on ethics and education arising from his psychology related to πάθη, and including a wide range of topics.

There is a good deal of overlapping between the two books, and ἀπορίαι occur in each which can be supplemented by the other: in general, Kidd, *Problems* 202.

(4) Therefore if Galen used Posidonius to the extent that he did, and as appositely for his own purposes, it is likely that he had the complete work of Posidonius' Περὶ παθῶν before him.

T64 Galen, *De Placitis* VII.589, pp. 583.15–584.10 M, 430.7–16 De Lacy

At the beginning of Bk VII of *De Plac.* Galen returns to questions concerning τὸ ἡγεμονικόν. At this point, he recalls his earlier attack in Bks IV–V on Chrysippus' theory of πάθη, which included Posidonius' arguments against Chrysippus in support of the 'ancient doctrine' (2–8). One of the συγγράμματα referred to in line 6 was Posidonius' Περὶ παθῶν; T61–3 show the range and extent of its use. Galen also now mentions using Posidonius on the difference in virtues (8f). In fact he proceeds immediately with criticism of Chrysippus on this topic in a passage (584.10–596.3 M) in which he was probably following another book of Posidonius, possibly Περὶ τῶν ἀρετῶν; see comm. on Frs. 38, 182, 31.29–47.

T65 a, b, c

Athenaeus

Posidonius is assumed as familiar reading in the circle of Athenaeus' dining sophists. In F65c his frequent mention is addressed in the dramatic context to Masurius, but presumably reflects on Athenaeus. The only book of Posidonius apparently quoted by Athenaeus is the *History*, to which he can refer by book number. Yet Athenaeus never refers to Posidonius as 'the historian', but as 'the Stoic' or 'the philosopher' (F65c). F71.1, ἀναγιγνώσκων τὴν ὀγδόην καὶ εἰκοστὴν τῶν Ποσειδωνίου Ἱστοριῶν, ought to imply that he had actually read the *History* and not merely extracts. It would in any case be difficult to imagine a compendium of the *History* based on the quotations produced by Athenaeus. Although he betrays an awareness of the general character of Posidonius' *History* as being in tune with his philosophy in its addiction to ethnography (T80), he never uses it for historical or philosophical purposes, but infuriatingly extracts snippets germane to the particular literary or antiquarian topic of the dinner table.

T66 Diogenes Laertius, *Index in Parisino gr.* 1759 (P), *et in Laurentiano* 69.13 (F)

On the first folio of codex P of Diogenes (and in F) is listed a register of Stoic Lives for Bk VII. The list omits Ariston, Herillus, Dionysius and Sphaerus, who actually appear in Bk VII, and after Chrysippus names twenty other Stoics, including Posidonius, from Zeno of Tarsus to Cornutus. The name κάτων given before Posidonius must be Ἑκάτων. The suggestion appears to be that there was a Life of Posidonius.

It is worth noting here the very mixed report on Posidonius in Bk VII by Diogenes or his sources, as displayed by the references.

Thus under logic, the section on criterion of truth (VII.54) comes from a Posidonian doxography (F42 comm.), but the major section on logic (55–83) owes nothing to him, with Chrysippus in the lead with 8 citations, closely followed by his pupil, Diogenes of Babylon, with 7. The mysterious figure of

Crinis (4 citations) outnumbers better known 2nd c. figures. Posidonius has only 2 (60, F44; 62, F188).

On the other hand, in the section on cosmos (137–42), Posidonius is the major authority, cited for standard Stoic doctrine (twice alone, Frs. 8, 14). Here his citations number 9 (Frs. 4, 6, 8, 13, 14, 20, 21, 23, 99) against Chrysippus 6, Antipater and Apollodorus 3 each, Zeno and Cleanthes 2 each, and Apollophanes, Panaetius and Boethus 1 each.

Yet in the section on ethics (84–131) the situation is reversed: Chrysippus is cited more than twice as often as anyone else (21), and after Zeno (9) and Cleanthes (6), it is Hecaton (10) who is cited most of the later Stoics. After the comprehensive doxography on classification of ethics (84, F89) and on τέλος (86–7, F185), and the two mini-doxographies on virtue (91, F2; 92, F180), mention of Posidonius is insignificant: twice briefly on minor points (124, F40; 129, F1, F39), and twice, highly dubiously, for alleged unorthodoxy (103, F171; 128, F173). Still odder is the section on meteorology (152–4), where one would have expected Posidonius to be a major authority; yet he is only cited thrice (Frs. 11, 135, 136). See F11 Context for this section.

In other words there is a marked lack of homogeneity in the report by Diogenes' sources on Posidonius, as indeed on other Stoics. This suggests a multiplicity of sources.

The relationship of the register of T66 to Bk VII of Diogenes is discussed by J. Mansfeld in *Elenchos* 7 (1986), 310–12.

T67 Eusebius Hieronymus, *Commentarii in Danielem, Praefatio* 622A–B (Migne, 25.516)

In the Preface to his *Commentary on Daniel*, Jerome gives a list of Greek historians, which includes Posidonius, as necessary for the understanding of the Book of Daniel. He adds that Porphyry says that he had followed them.

It is virtually certain that Jerome himself had not read Posidonius (Courcelle, *Les lettres grecques*[1], 64). His reference elsewhere to a Posidonian *consolatio* is derived from Cicero (F37 comm.), and Courcelle (47ff) has shown that Jerome's parade of learning in Greek authors appears to be second-hand and often shameless plagiarism of intermediary writers. He did however read Porphyry (Courcelle, 61f). Later in the *Commentary* (11.21, 36) he asserts that he found quotations he gives from Callinicus Sutorius, Polybius and Diodorus Siculus in Porphyry. However, Porphyry's Κατὰ Χριστιανῶν was proscribed, so that Jerome may have been familiar with that particular work principally through refutations of it such as that of Eusebius of Caesarea. Even so, the list of historians must go back to Porphyry, and there is no reason to doubt that Porphyry used Posidonius' *History* in Κατὰ Χριστιανῶν, where he employed historical criticism to prove the lateness of the Book of Daniel.

T68 Macrobius, *Commentarii in Ciceronis Somnium Scipionis* 1.15.7

Macrobius' sources were not homogeneous, but complex (Flamant, *Macrobe et le néo-platonisme latin* 476ff). The citations of Posidonius indicate clearly that Macrobius did not know him first-hand. In the *Somnium* he occurs in two doxographies, on the Milky Way (F130) and on definitions of soul (F140, which reveals ignorance), and in a very confused comment on Posidonius' estimate of the size of the sun and method of measurement (F116). The two references in the *Saturnalia* arise from allegorical interpretations from Cornificius Longus, bringing in a theory of the sun's path explained by ocean (F118), and the etymology of δαίμων (F24, naming a book, *On Heroes and Daimons*). At least some of Macrobius' information on Posidonius seems to have come from Porphyry's *Commentary on Timaeus*, but there were no doubt other sources.

It is clear, however, that Posidonius' name and reputation were still very much alive in the early 5th c. A.D. (A. Cameron, *JRS* 56 (1966), 25ff; Flamant, 96ff on the controversy over the identification and date of Macrobius), and that not only aspects of his metaphysics of interest to Neoplatonists, but also traces of his scientific and geographical works, still filtered through in the intellectual conglomerate of the time.

T69 Augustine, *De Civitate Dei* v.5

To Augustine Posidonius is still a name of great authority, but there is no evidence that he had actually read him. In the only instance where he is cited (F111), Augustine appears to have culled his evidence from Cicero, almost certainly from *De fato*. On this question see H. Hagendahl, *Augustine and the Latin Classics* II.526f; Schmekel, *Die Philosophie der mittleren Stoa* 165; A. Lörcher, *De compositione et fonte libri Ciceronis qui est de fato*, Diss. phil. Halenses vol. 17, part 4 (1907), p. 346; Yon, *Introd.* XXXVIII. The case of Lactantius (F155) is comparable.

Augustine cites Posidonius as an astrologer, which is his own context. The Ciceronian context was doubtless Stoic εἱμαρμένη. He also knows him as a philosopher, but he uses *philosophi* earlier in v.1 (F111, context) with reference to stars as portents. Whether or not he understood Posidonius' attitude to astrology in the strict sense (T74), he clearly thought of Posidonius mainly as an authority on that subject (cf. T70).

T70 Boethius, *De Diis et Praesensionibus* 20.77, p. 395

Boethius suggests that Posidonius and Julius Firmicus Maternus were regarded as the two main authorities of his age on astrology; F112. The evidence is insufficient to show whether he himself had actually read him, or had culled his information from Cicero (cf. Augustine, T69, and Lactantius, F155) or from some other intermediate source. He, like Augustine (F111), classified Posidonius with the stricter adherents of an astrology which regarded the stars as influencing human lives, not merely displaying signs for interpretation and prediction of future events (F112); but he shows no understanding of how astrology could be fitted into the pattern of Posidonius' (or Stoic) physical philosophy (T74).

T71, T72 Priscianus Lydus, *Solutiones ad Chosroem* VI, p. 69.29–31 (Bywater) = F219.12–15; Priscianus Lydus, *Solutiones ad Chosroem, Prooemium*, p. 42.8–11 (Bywater)

Priscianus was a pupil of Damascius who, on Justinian's ban on pagan teaching, quit Athens and accepted an invitation *c.* 531 A.D. from the Persian king, Chosroes I, but returned after peace between Rome and Persia. The 'Explanation of Problems for King Chosroes' survives only in a Latin translation (probably 9th c.) of extreme barbarism (F219), but it is clear from ch. VI (T71, T26; F219) that in the 6th century Posidonius was regarded as the main authority for the causal explanation of tidal behaviour. In the *Prooemium* (41f, Bywater) Priscianus lists his bibliography from Plato and Aristotle to Proclus. Posidonius is not mentioned individually, but Strabo's *Geography*, Geminus' *Commentary on Posidonius' Meteorology* and Arrian's *Meteorology* (cf. A. G. Roos, *Arrianus* (Teubner), vol. II) are. Chapter VI of the *Solutiones*, which features Posidonius, may be an amalgam from these three and other sources such as Aristotle. So it remains uncertain whether Priscianus had read Posidonius himself: F219 comm. See also W. Capelle, *RE* XXII, col. 2348; *RE* Supplb. VI, col. 323; 'Zur Geschichte der meteorologischen Literatur', *Hermes* 48 (1913), 347ff.

CHARACTERISTICS OF HIS PHILOSOPHY

T73 Simplicius, *In Aristotelis Physica* II.2 (193 b 23), p. 292.29–31 Diels

Simplicius has just quoted a passage from Geminus' *Epitome of Posidonius' Meteorology*, a passage which Simplicius correctly summarises as Posidonius' teaching on the distinction between φυσιολογία (natural philosophy) and ἀστρολογία (the science of astronomy). The fragment is crucial for the understanding of Posidonius' interest in the sciences and for their relationship to philosophy. Science and philosophy are different, and distinguished in subject matter (although this overlaps), and in methodology. Above all science is hypothetical and descriptive, philosophy apodeictic and explanatory. Nevertheless they are complementary, and while science depends on philosophy for principles and final adjudication, the sciences are necessary tools for the philosopher concerned with the physical universe. Thus Posidonius' scientific works are germane to his natural philosophy, in the same way as his *History* is to his ethical philosophy. His output is not simply the result of πολυμάθεια (T48, Strabo), but an organic whole directed by philosophy. For details see *Commentary* on Frs. 18, 90, 134.57ff; Kidd, *A & A* 24 (1978), 7–15.

Simplicius adds that Posidonius took his starting points

from Aristotle (3). This is Simplicius' opinion. Whether Posidonius consciously did so himself is controversial (Sandbach, *Aristotle and the Stoics*, 61), but one can understand why Simplicius said so.

T74 Augustine, *De Civitate Dei*, v.2

Augustine and Boethius (F112) give the only explicit evidence that Posidonius was regarded (in their time) as having been devoted to astrology. But it is important and difficult to distinguish between different 'astrological' attitudes in relation to Posidonius.

Augustine and Boethius clearly believed that Posidonius represented the strongest sense whereby the life of a human being is determined by the influence of the position of the stars at birth (Frs. 111, 112). It is more likely that he held a more limited and modified position. Cicero's *De Div.* indicates that at least he believed the weaker thesis that the stars offer signs for the prediction of the future, and are part of the science of divination (Frs. 109, 110). So some (as A. Lörcher, *De compositione et fonte libri Ciceronis qui est de fato*, Diss. phil. Halenses vol. 17, part 4 (1907), p. 347) think that Augustine and Boethius confused the Stoic doctrine of *contagio naturae* and συμπάθεια, or the reciprocal interaction of all parts of the universe, with a theory of astrology.

That there is misunderstanding on the part of Augustine and Boethius is virtually certain (Frs. 111, 112). Also ἀστρολογία can mean for Posidonius something more akin to theoretical astronomy (F18). He also took account both of natural factors such as environment in physiognomy (F169), and of other methods of prediction from signs in nature (Frs. 106–10). But the combination of the Stoic doctrine of fate with συμπάθεια, and a belief, according to Cicero, in a *vis fatalis* (Frs. 104.4; 106.28; cf. 111.8) is likely to have developed some interest in astrology. The cases cited at the beginning of F104 presume the *influence* of the heavens on terrestrial events, and F111 shows that they must have been investigated at greater length in the missing part of Cicero's *De fato*. One must remember that divination and astrology are commonly regarded as sciences in the ancient world (E. Pfeiffer, *Studien zum antiken Sternglauben, Stoicheia* II (1916); F. Boll, *Die Erforschung der antiken Astrologie, N. Jahrb.* 1908, 103ff = *Kleine Schriften* 1ff; esp. 5f), accepted by scientists such as Hipparchus (Pfeiffer, 115), and with a respectable philosophical pedigree from Plato on (id. 46f).

We cannot therefore dismiss Posidonius' interest in astrology. But it is unlikely that he simply accepted the Chaldean version; cf. the case of Diogenes of Babylon in Cicero, *De Div.* II. 90. With his interest in causes (F18), Posidonius probably tried to investigate it scientifically as one possible form of the interaction between heavenly and terrestrial phenomena. But a *vis fatalis* goes much further than a theory of lunar periodicity of tides.

T75 Strabo, I.1.1

At the very beginning of the *Geography*, Strabo defends the academic respectability of his subject, by claiming it to be a branch of philosophy. He gives three reasons:

(1) From the earliest times geography has been touched on by men of a philosophic cast. Thrcc groups are given as examples; early: Homer, Anaximander, Hecataeus; middle: Democritus, Eudoxus, Dicaearchus, Ephorus and many more; later (modern?): Eratosthenes, Polybius, Posidonius (classed as φιλόσοφοι, 9).

(2) πολυμάθεια, the essential requisite for geography (9f), is the qualification of the man who examines τὰ θεῖα καὶ τὰ ἀνθρώπεια, the knowledge of which is said to be philosophy.

(3) The manifold utility (ὠφέλεια) arising from geogra-

phical knowledge related to the politics, climate, environment and habitat of various peoples and nations of the world provides the tracery (ὑπογράφει, 16) for the man who cares for the art of life, and so happiness (i.e. the philosopher) (12–17).

Since Posidonius features as an example in Strabo's list, indeed the most modern and latest in line, the question arises whether this estimate of geography in relation to philosophy might derive from him or be taken to be characteristic of him. There are superficial resemblances, but the statement is surely Strabo's and fits Strabo's views.

It is clear from the list in (1) that Strabo is using 'philosophy' in a wider sense than Posidonius would. There is no reason to suspect that the list derives from Posidonius; indeed, it is only Eratosthenes who is cited as evidence (6).

It is true that πολυμάθεια is a general characteristic of Posidonius, certainly in Strabo's opinion (T48), but Posidonius would not have maintained that it was the *only* (μόνης, 9) qualification for the geographer; and while he may have regarded it as a necessary characteristic of the philosopher it would be misleading to think of it as a key concept for his philosophy (F18).

Philosophy as the science of things human and divine (10–12) simply echoes a common Stoic definition of σοφία (*SVF* II.35f) which no doubt Posidonius followed (cf. T81.8; Kidd, 'Posidonius and Logic' 275), as he followed a similar Stoic definition of κόσμος (F14), but neither definition is exclusively his. (But for geographical ἀνθρώπεια cf. F49.49ff.)

It is certain that Posidonius believed that geography (Περὶ ὠκεανοῦ), history (T80) and the sciences in general were 'useful' as the 'tools' for philosophy, but he did not regard them as parts of philosophy, but as subordinate (F90; Kidd, 'Philosophy and Science in Posidonius'). Also Strabo himself is critical of Posidonius precisely on the grounds of utility and is sceptical of the practical contribution of some of Posidonius' arguments (F49.315; cf. T76). In fact while both men believed in a relationship between geographical studies and philosophy, it is doubtful whether their concepts of philosophy, geography or indeed of the precise liaison between the two were similar. Strabo's chorography and ethnography lean more to Polybius, and he neither understood nor approved of Posidonius' mathematical and scientific side. It is noticeable that Hipparchus is missing from this list. Strabo, of course, was well aware of the difference of approach: T76, T77.

T76a, b Strabo, II.2.1; II.3.8

Both at the beginning and at the end of Strabo's general review of Posidonius' Περὶ ὠκεανοῦ (F49) the reader is warned that besides what Strabo regarded as proper geographical material there was also content which merged more into the territory of mathematics and natural philosophy (μαθηματικώτερον, φυσικώτερα); the latter Strabo will either ignore or examine elsewhere. This honest statement will surprise no one familiar with both Strabo and Posidonius.

For a clarification of Strabo's position, cf. II.5.34: τοῖς δὲ γεωγραφοῦσιν οὔτε τῶν ἔξω τῆς καθ' ἡμᾶς οἰκουμένης φροντιστέον, οὔτ' ἐν αὐτοῖς τοῖς τῆς οἰκουμένης μέρεσι τὰς τοιαύτας καὶ τοσαύτας διαφορὰς [*sc.* ἐν τοῖς οὐρανίοις] παραδεκτέον τῷ πολιτικῷ· περισκελεῖς γάρ εἰσιν. And later: ὁ δὲ γεωγράφος ἐπισκοπεῖ ταύτην μόνην τὴν καθ' ἡμᾶς οἰκουμένην. For this reason Strabo at II.5.34 limits his account of *klimata* in Hipparchus of which his understanding is imperfect; also T77.

One would very much like to know what we have lost in Posidonius because of this attitude. It would also affect topics with which Strabo deals. For example, zones are clearly regarded by Strabo as οἰκεῖα (F49.8ff), but Posidonius' theory of zones was φυσικῶς and mathematical, and Strabo's account of it is fudged. Again Strabo merely mentions Posidonius' measurement of the earth's circumference (F49.33); this time we are fortunate to have the mathematics preserved in Cleomedes (F202). But in general F18 shows the importance for Posidonius of natural philosophy and mathematics. It is in this area where scientist and philosopher meet for him (see also T85 comm.), and this is where much of our evidence is missing, thanks to distortions and omissions caused by attitudes like Strabo's (Kidd, 'Philosophy and Science in Posidonius' p. 11). See also F49.357 comm.

T77 Strabo, VIII.1.1

At the beginning of Bk VIII, Strabo summarises his progress from the west (the inner and outer seas (2) are the Mediterranean and the Atlantic), across Europe north of the Mediterranean, and turns to Greece. He classifies three types of earlier geographical writing on Greece, apart from Homer (5):

(1) Separate monographs with such titles as (ἰδίᾳ . . . ἐπιγράψαντες) *Harbours* (Λιμένας, also 1.1.21), *Coastal Voyages* (or *Charts*, Περίπλους; as those of Skylax, Agatharchides, Artemidorus, Arrian, the *Periplous of the Red Sea*) or *Tours* (or *Maps*, Περιόδους γῆς; cf. Hdt. 4.36; 5.49; Aristoph. *Clouds* 206; Arist. *Rhet.* 1360a 34).

(2) General histories, containing separate sections on the topography of the continents, as Ephorus' and Polybius'.

(3) 'Others attached some of these (geographical) topics as well to the field of natural philosophy and mathematics, like Posidonius and Hipparchus.'

Strabo adds delightfully: the rest are easy to comment on, but Homer needs critical investigation, because of his poetical language and early date.

The general classification is clear. Strabo puts Posidonius in the same category as Hipparchus; his geographical work is scientific rather than descriptive. But does Strabo mean that Posidonius' geographical works were 'physical' and mathematical in character, or that Posidonius' contributions to geography came in books which were primarily devoted to natural philosophy and mathematics? Since for Strabo, Posidonius' major geographical treatise was Περὶ ὠκεανοῦ (F49), that book must fall under category (3). Topics which we know occurred in it (see F49), as zones, the question of a world circumambient ocean, alterations and variations in the earth's surface, theory of tides, were all unquestionably subjects thought proper to ancient geography (as indeed was the title, cf. Pytheas (F9a Mette), and Strabo, II.5.17), but equally (and certainly for Posidonius), they were relevant to the study of Φυσική and its mathematical aids. So which τόπος a work like Περὶ ὠκεανοῦ is ascribed to depends on the individual's point of view. Strabo did not himself wish to exclude from geography all mathematical and astronomical background (I.1.21). There is a different emphasis from T76, but this is understandable in context. It is possible of course that Strabo also found geographical material in indisputably 'physical' books, see e.g. F12 from Φυσικὸς Λόγος.

Strabo's general classification does not rule out influence from the other two categories either. He certainly knew Posidonius' *History* for example. There is also the question of Pliny's source Περίπλους ἢ Περιήγησις (F50). This has been identified with Περὶ ὠκεανοῦ (as by Jacoby, *Kommentar* 163.29), but would be a very strange title indeed for it (as Jacoby admitted, *ibid.* 171.19f), especially as the Περὶ ὠκεανοῦ is categorised here. If quite separate, its title (Περίπλους) should put it in category (1). As a general characterisation, however, Strabo is clearly right about Posidonian geography, and this is valuable evidence for Περὶ ὠκεανοῦ.

T78 Strabo, x.3.5

In a diversion caused by criticism of Ephorus on the early history of Aetolia (x.3.1–4), Strabo opines that no writer on geographical topics is infallible or final, and that if Ephorus could make such a mistake (τοιοῦτος ὤν, 1), yet he is better than others. But one must expect improvement and greater accuracy in successors. So although Ephorus was acknowledged by Polybius to be the best in Greek history on foundings of cities, kinships, migrations, founding fathers (3–5), Polybius claimed to be more up-to-date on topography and distances (5f) (most germane for chorography, 6); he coined the phrase 'popular statements' for Eratosthenes' and Dicaearchus' distances (7f). Yet Polybius too submits to correction from Posidonius, Artemidorus and many others (9f).

The implication is that it is Polybius' statements of distances which were corrected or reduced to greater accuracy by Posidonius, Artemidorus etc., which at first sight might be another aspect of Strabo's mathematical characterisation of Posidonian geography (T76, T77). But this point of view is unlikely in this context where Posidonius is coupled with Artemidorus. This is Artemidorus of Ephesus (Frs. 119, 217, 223, 246, 247; Berger, *RE* II.1.1329f; *Erdkunde* 526ff; Bunbury, *A History of Ancient Geography*, II.61ff; Thomson, *History of Ancient Geography*, 210), who flourished *c.* 100 B.C., and was not a mathematical geographer, but a writer of Περίπλους and the like, that is, a more typical example of Strabo's category (i) of T77. He certainly made careful statements of distance, and Strabo used him (e.g. III.2.11, Artemidorus contradicts Eratosthenes on distance).

It is possible that Posidonius' mathematical interest in κλίματα led to a correction of distances (e.g. F249); but distances between places were more typical of descriptive geography and chorography (Strabo *passim*). Since Strabo specially mentions Posidonius in this context, one wonders whether Pliny's source, Περίπλους ἢ Περιήγησις (F50), was a separate chorographic work. The accurate calculation of distances was notoriously difficult, particularly by sea.

Strabo is not making judgements on different kinds of geographical writing here (as in T77), but on the progressive accuracy of geographical evidence. For all his excellence, Ephorus was improved by Polybius, and Polybius in turn by Posidonius and Artemidorus. Strabo continues that he himself should not be blamed for mistakes in material he has taken over from his predecessors, and that he will be content if his researches improve for the most part what has already been said, or include what has been omitted through ignorance. Strabo is not talking about theory, but about factual content. That Posidonius has been included in such a context is interesting.

7 τὰς λαοδογματικὰς ἀποφάσεις: Tyrwhitt's emendation for τάλας ὁ δογματικὰς *DxCs* (τὰς τῶν ἄλλων δογματικὰς *Bk* being an effort to make sense of the tradition) is guaranteed by VII.5.9 *fin.* (again criticism of Eratosthenean distances) and by II.4.2 as the phrase used by Polybius in criticism of the distances of Eratosthenes and Dicaearchus (Plb. 34.1.6; 5.14; 12.2); but in turn Polybius' distances are attacked in II.4.3–5 (from a Posidonian or Artemidoran base?).

9 καί διαδοὺς *BCDx*: καὶ διαδιδοὺς *no*. But a main verb is needed. Yet καὶ is difficult with the simple καὶ δίδως. Tyrwhitt's νὴ Δία δίδως or Groskurd's καὶ αὐτὸς δίδως are perhaps preferable.

T79a, b Strabo, I.1.9; I.3.12

It is clear that one of the main features of Posidonius' Περὶ ὠκεανοῦ was his detailed theory of tidal phenomena (Frs. 138, 214–20). This aspect of his work was immediately recognised, for Athenodorus of Tarsus (T44) must have adopted the main features of Posidonius' theory (perhaps, although not necessarily, in a Commentary) to be bracketed so closely with Posidonius by Strabo, although Athenodorus differed in some details (F217 comm.). For Strabo, Posidonius was the established authority on the subject (for ἱκανῶς διακρατήσαντας, see F214 comm.) to whom readers may merely be referred. Strabo only mentions details of the theory incidentally to combat Posidonius' explanation of the wells at Cadiz (F217). The theory was too involved in physics for Strabo's conception of geography (ἐχόντων καὶ αὐτῶν φυσικώτερον λόγον . . .T79b; cf. T76b, T77, F138). Posidonius probably explained the phenomena of refluent strait currents in similar fashion (F219), but it seems that Strabo did not follow him as an authority on this subject also (T79b, F215 comm.). For the later influence of Posidonius' theory see Frs. 138, 217–19.

T80 Athenaeus, IV.151E

Athenaeus expressly characterises Posidonius' *History* as being composed in tune with his philosophy. οὐκ ἀλλοτρίως . . . φιλοσοφίας must be taken with συνέθηκεν, and so is a general characteristic, not with the following participial phrase as Gulick (F67 comm. *B*). But the general statement is further particularised by 'reporting many habits and customs of many peoples', i.e. ethnography. There is little doubt that this is an accurate statement as far as it goes. Posidonius saw history as the descriptive canvas of ethics, as the sciences were for natural philosophy. Ethnography was essential to this description, but Athenaeus gives no sign of understanding why. In fact what follows these introductory lines, part of the account of eating and drinking habits from Posidonius' Celtic ethnography, shows no connection with or relation to philosophy, Stoic or otherwise (F67). So one wonders whether this introductory statement was picked up from an original profession in Posidonius. Ethnography was important for Posidonius not for its own sake, but because the habits and customs of a nation revealed their character, and their character (which is a form of ethics) governed their actions. So ethnography was an aetiological key for historical analysis and explanation (cf. comm. on Frs. 253, 272, 240). Posidonian reporters show little appreciation of this, in separating snippets from the ethnographies from their context (see F67 comm. *A*). Posidonius was the first major philosopher to write history, and Athenaeus generally refers to him as 'the Stoic' or 'the philosopher', never as 'the historian'. Galen noted the reverse of the coin, that Posidonius in a philosophical book (Περὶ παθῶν) would use historical examples (F164.51f). On the comparable relationship between scientific writing and philosophy: F18, F90 (Kidd, *A & A* 24 (1978), 7–15); and see F49.357–60 for Strabo on geography and philosophy in Posidonius. See also Kidd, 'Posidonius as Philosopher-Historian', in *Philosophia Togata*, edd. Miriam Griffin and Jonathan Barnes, Oxford, 1988.

T81 Seneca, *Epistulae* 104.21–4

The Letter is prompted by Seneca, sick with fever, withdrawing to the country. He takes the opportunity to point out that travel or change of air will not of itself make a better man of you, because your maladies and passions travel with you. You cannot run away from vice; it is within you, your travelling companion (104.1–20). Therefore if you want to get rid of vice, you must move into better company (1–3). So live with the Catos, Laelius (the close friend of Scipio Aemilianus), Tubero (T12) (4); or if you prefer Greek society, with Socrates and Zeno; the first will teach you how to die if you have to, the second how to die before you have to (4–7). Live with Chrysippus, with Posidonius. They will impart to you the knowledge of things human and divine; they will instruct you to go into action, not merely to talk smart and toss off words for the delectation of an audience, but to steel your spirit and raise it up against what threatens (7–11). What they teach as the only port of salvation in the storm of life (11f) is:

(1) Not to fear what will happen, but to stand with fortitude, four-square and prepared, to meet the arrows of fate (12–14).

(2) To cultivate what nature has given us (i.e. the peculiar natural constitution of human beings in comparison with animals), a mind for great things (*magnanimos*, 14), i.e. a proud and lofty spirit which seeks not where we may most safely live, but where we may live most morally (14–18).

(3) This spirit (*spiritus*, πνεῦμα, λόγος) is most like the universe, which it strives to follow, as far as human steps may take it (*quantum mortalium passibus licet* 18f). It is master of all, above all, indomitable (18–21).

Seneca's exemplars are Socrates and Zeno on the one hand, and Chrysippus and Posidonius on the other. Socrates and Zeno are examples by their way of death. Chrysippus and Posidonius are the great writers and teachers; they are whom you read. But their teaching is not mere words and clever argument, but how to act and live well, i.e. morally (*honestissime*). Seneca groups Chrysippus and Posidonius together. He sees no opposition between them. They are the two Stoic writers to study.

No doubt Seneca is transposing into his own language, and perhaps into his own images. *Tela fortunae* (13) is a popular topic of his, although Posidonius may have used it (F105 comm.). But this much is clear: he believed that Posidonian ethics was an ethic for action not theory; but it is not understandable merely on the human level. It involves knowledge of both human and divine (the common Stoic definition of σοφία, *SVF* II.35f; cf. Kidd, 'Posidonius and

Logic' 275), a knowledge of the universe to which the human λόγος is organically related. This in particular reflects Posidonius' formulation of the τέλος (F186); and compare commentary on F161, F187.

T82 Seneca, *Epistulae* 121.1

Archedemus (*SVF* III. v. Arch. F17) and Posidonius will take up the challenge if Lucilius, when he hears the subject which has been causing Seneca perplexity for long enough, should threaten to have the law on him on the grounds that it has nothing to do with morality (1–6). But Seneca argues that ethics is wider than Lucilius thinks: you will only understand what to do and avoid, when you have learnt what you owe to your own nature (121.2–3).

The question, which Posidonius would defend as a part of ethics, is whether all animals are conscious of their own natural constitution (*constitutionis suae sensus*, 121.5). It is not true that animals only act through the negative impulse of fear, they positively strive to fulfil their own nature (§7). Seneca gives examples from babies and animals (§8). Although babies and animals do not understand that constitution which is the relationship between the *principale animi* and the *corpus*, yet they are consciously aware of themselves and of their natural constitution and consequent natural impulses (§§10–13). Seneca goes on to propound the different *constitutiones* for different periods of life: baby, boy, adolescent, old age (14ff). *Primum sibi ipsum conciliatur animal* (§17), and this is true for all animals. We can learn this from animals, and so better understand nature and ourselves.

It is impossible to know how much of this is Seneca and how much Posidonian influence, or indeed due to Archedemus of Tarsus. The list of different age *constitutiones* is probably Senecan, although it may have had a wider general Stoic background (Kidd, *Problems* 166). But the emphasis on the relevance of babies and animals almost certainly derived from Posidonius, who used them in arguments against Chrysippus: babies, F169.10ff, F159; animals, F33, F169.14ff. So the enquiry into ethics for Posidonius not only extended upwards to the relationship of human nature with the universe (T81), but downwards to its relationship with animals and infants, leading to his consequent arguments with respect to irrationality, πάθη and οἰκείωσις. See F159 comm. For criticism of supposedly Posidonian theories built on this Letter by Reinhardt (*Poseidonios* 356ff), Pohlenz (*Hermes* 76 (1941), 1ff) and Jaeger (*Nemesios*), see F159 comm.

T83, T84 Galen, *De Placitis* IV.390, p. 362.5–9 M, 258.19–22 De Lacy; Galen, *De Placitis* VIII.652, p. 653.14f M, 482.33ff De Lacy

Galen calls Posidonius the most scientific of the Stoics (ἐπιστημονικώτατος, T84; also F35.8) because he was trained in mathematics (T84, T83); with this is linked the statement that Posidonius was accustomed to follow ἀποδείξεις more than any other Stoic (T83). Because of these qualities, Posidonius was ashamed of the conflict with evident facts and the self-contradiction to be found in Chrysippus (T82).

Galen is clearly referring to axiomatic deduction typical of mathematical methodology. That Posidonius was himself committed to this view of mathematics is plain from his impassioned attack on Zeno of Sidon's Epicurean mathematics in Frs. 46, 47. His treatment of the relational syllogism in F191 shows that he formed the closest methodological link in this between mathematics and logic. It is clear that this apodeictic method was extended to ethics (F157, cf. F165.

177ff), and above all it is characteristic of the natural philosopher (F18). Galen therefore appears to be right that this methodology characterises and is fundamental to his whole philosophy.

ἀπόδειξις however is not only valid reasoning (S.E. *Adv. Math.* VIII.123), but is always both valid and true (S.E. *Adv. Math.* VIII. 412); therefore it must start from premisses which are true. Galen too makes this point in *De Plac.* VII.1.8, p. 430.5–7 De Lacy: 'It was also shown that the argument itself is not satisfied with generally accepted beliefs (ἐνδόξοις) as its starting points, but uses premisses that are scientific (ἐπιστημονικοῖς), which is the distinctive feature of the apodeictic method (ἀποδεικτικῆς μεθόδου).' Compare also Galen, *De Plac.* VIII.1.19ff, p. 484.17 De Lacy, where Galen emphasises the importance of this method for philosophy. But whereas for Galen apparently such premisses are established by science (*De Plac.* VII.1.5f, p. 428.23ff De Lacy), for Posidonius they are established by φυσιολογία (F18). But they must also be seen to be in tune with clear fact, and so (as Galen says) Posidonius continually criticises Chrysippus for holding premisses in conflict with evident facts (e.g. F164.11–15 comm.; F159) and for self-contradiction (e.g. F34.20ff; F165.121; F164.87–93), which cannot be the result of an apodeictic method (cf. Galen, *De Plac.* p. 314.16–17 De Lacy).

For extended argument on the importance of this methodology for Posidonius' philosophy, see Kidd, 'Posidonius and Logic' 277–82.

T85 Strabo, II.3.8

At the end of his general survey of Posidonius as a geographer in II.2–3 (F49), Strabo characterises him as having an abundance of τὸ αἰτιολογικόν. The context indicates what Strabo means by this. He says that geographical elements from Περὶ ὠκεανοῦ will receive attention in his later detailed account, but all that relates more to natural philosophy (ὅσα δὲ φυσικώτερα) he will deal with elsewhere, or even not bother about. '*For* (γάρ) there is much enquiry into causes in him, that is (καί), "Aristotelizing", a thing which our School (the Stoics) sheers off from because of the concealment of causes.' So αἰτιολογικόν in Posidonius is (a) specifically connected with φυσιολογία; but (b) accused of intruding into other disciplines; (c) criticised as being indulged to an extent more than other Stoics thought possible; and (d) is characterised as aping Aristotle.

All this is borne out by the fragments:

(1) F18 shows that aetiology was the prime characteristic of the natural philosopher.

(2) F18, F90 also show, however, that although explanation of causes was the prerogative of the natural philosopher, the investigation of causes descended necessarily into the sciences and arts because of the complementary relationship between them and philosophy (T73 comm.).

(3) The normal Stoic withdrawal into admitting that we cannot know all causes, because of their obscurity to the human mind (*SVF* II.973, 351; cf. the criticism of Alexander, *De fato* XXV, *SVF* II.949), was not accepted by Posidonius. He wished to discover the whole chain of intermediate causation, and in his criticism of Chrysippus relentlessly pursued the question against him: 'But what is the αἰτία of this?'; and condemns Chrysippus for being unable to answer (F165. 75–102). For an exposition of this whole question see Kidd, *Problems* 210f; *A & A* 24 (1978), 13–15.

(4) The Aristotelian connection with thorough investigation of causes in this way is echoed precisely in D.L. V.32 on Aristotle: ἐν δὲ τοῖς φυσικοῖς αἰτιολογικώτατος πάντων ἐγένετο μάλιστα, ὥστε καὶ περὶ τῶν ἐλαχίστων τὰς αἰτίας ἀποδιδόναι. See T100 for 'Αριστοτελίζον and Posidonius.

Tied in with the investigation into causes and the apodeictic method of pursuing them (T83, T84), which was also recognised as characteristic of Posidonius, filtering down even to Priscianus Lydus, and which relates closely to his view of the relationship of philosophy and science, is another factor: any αἰτία must square with the facts. Much of Posidonius' aetiological criticism of Chrysippus' explanations of psychological behaviour is based on showing that they are in contradiction to observed fact, τήν τε πρὸς τὰ σαφῶς φαινόμενα μάχην (T83.3). So F164.11–25 (ὅπερ οὐχ ὁρᾶται γιγνόμενον). For τὰ ἐναργῶς φαινόμενα employed thus against Chrysippus see Frs. 156, 158, 159, 165.143–50, 169.45; and cf. Frs. 164.25–37, 165.165, 166.20, 169.1–18, T60. But Posidonius' use of this criterion was general; it was also employed, for example, in the rejection of historical theory and explanation (e.g. Frs. 272, 273). With this corresponds Posidonius' own respect for observed fact, and his stress on autopsy in his investigations (e.g. of the tides). For the importance of this factor and its place in his methodology, see Kidd, *Problems* 212; *A & A* 24 (1978), 13.

T86 Cicero, *De Natura Deorum* II.88

Cicero, arguing for the providential government of the world, uses the old art/nature analogy. Since any product of art is at once assumed to be a rational construction, so nature and its structure must be seen to be the result of reason. He chooses as an example of an immediately recognisable rationally constructed product of art, Posidonius' planetarium, 'recently' (*nuper*) constructed. Even if a traveller took it to the barbaric limits of the world (Scythia or Britain), no one would doubt for a moment that it was a product of a rational being. It displayed in each revolution the positions of sun, moon and five planets for each separate day and night. Cicero goes on to mention also Archimedes' σφαῖρα.

Cicero was much struck by such planetaria. In *Rep.* I.21f he has a detailed reference to the two famous planetaria of Archimedes, one in the Temple of Virtue in Rome, the other owned by the Marcelli, which had been taken by Marcellus as booty from the captured city of Syracuse (cf. Plu. *Marc.* 19.6). There is no mention here of Posidonius, but there is a lacuna in the text. Archimedes' σφαῖρα is referred to again in *Rep.* I.28 and *Tusc.* I.63.

Cicero's description indicates that Posidonius' planetarium was similar to that of Archimedes. It may well have been inspired by inspection of it. Neugebauer (*History of Ancient Mathematical Astronomy* II.652) is somewhat scornful about the elementary efficacy of such devices, but it demonstrates a mechanical interest in Posidonius to translate theory into an operating model.

This looks like an isolated reference by Cicero. It is dangerous either to build from the Posidonius/Archimedes link a wider Posidonian source for Plu. *Marc.* (Gigon, *Studia I. H. Waszink* 162ff; F86e), or to print the whole of *ND* II. 81–8 as Posidonius (Theiler F361). Cicero probably mentions the less well-known planetarium of Posidonius as the most recent and modern example (*nuper*, 2) of such devices. But *nuper* is an elastic term; by the time *ND* was written (45 B.C.), Posidonius must have been dead for five years. But it was *nuper* compared with Archimedes, and may have been a product of his later years.

T87 Galen, *De Placitis* V.502, p. 487.3–10 M, 356.28–358.3 De Lacy

For the context of this testimony, the extent of Posidonian reference, and for the importance of ἔνδειξις in relation to πάθη, see comm. on F156.

The passage arose as criticism of Chrysippus' use of

quotation (F156). Chrysippus was notorious for the quantity of his quotations (D.L. VII.180–1). Posidonius too was no mean quoter (see Index), but this passage is concerned with the proper function of quotation in argument, concerning (a) timing and (b) subject matter. Under (a) it is recommended that quotations should not occur at the beginning of an argument, but only after one has adequately proved what is proposed; for then their function is μαρτυρία, not ἀπόδειξις (formal proof). As for (b), the subject of quotations should not be the completely non-evident, but clear fact (φαινόμενα ἐναργῶς), or a subject which admits of ἔνδειξις, the immediate recognition of fact by inspection. For the technical meaning of ἔνδειξις, see F156. Both (a) and (b) are characteristic of Posidonius.

Appeals to φαινόμενα ἐναργῶς and ἔνδειξις are frequent in Posidonius, as F169 *init.*; F164.11–15, comm. *B*; F164.25–37, comm. *C*; F159; Frs. 169.45; 158; 165.165; 166.20 (cf. T85). And it is in this area that Posidonius uses quotation: F164.56–86, comm. *H*; F165.133ff. Quotations are used as μαρτυρία, not ἀπόδειξις, at F164.50–2 (comm. *F*, and T104); and a quotation of verses from Cleanthes is produced at the very end of a long argument and as an ἔνδειξις at F166.21ff.

T88 Strabo, VII.3.2

In several places Strabo uses the word εἰκάζειν of Posidonius when he is reporting a hypothesis or argument derived from certain evidence: e.g. with regard to conjecture from Homeric evidence (F216.11, F277a.9); hypotheses of the cause of the Cimbric migrations (F49.303, F272.32): the hypothesis of a common etymology for the names of the peoples of Mesopotamia (F280.19). Other allied words are sometimes used: στοχάζεσθαι of explicit conjecture on the extent of the torrid zone (F49.20); ὑπονοεῖν of surmise on the consequences of the length of the inhabited world (F49.305);

τεκμαίρεσθαι on the identification of Canopus at Cadiz (F204; cf. Galen on a Posidonian inference in T91). Apart from the Galenic example, all this comes from Strabo, but it looks as if he is taking care to echo guarded statements on the part of Posidonius on the strength of certain hypotheses from evidence. The most instructive example is F217.51, where with εἰκάζει δὲ αὐτός . . . Posidonius is reported as distinguishing precisely between autopsy, reported information and consequent hypothesis with regard to the analysis and theory of tidal cycles.

T89 Strabo, I.2.34

Posidonius followed the Stoic devoted interest in etymology (F102) in the apparent belief that the linguistic form of a word gave some natural indication of its true meaning, explanation or reference (*SVF* II.146); thus Chrysippus wrote two books on the subject (D.L. VII.200).

Some examples follow the traditional School style, even when he disagrees with the established explanation (F102, F193); indeed in some he shows origins from an earlier Platonic base(F24, F193). Even in these more traditional examples (Ζεύς (Δι-), F102; ὄψις, F193; δαίμων, F24), it is noticeable that the etymologies in fact derive from his natural philosophy; so it would be in tune with his belief that if etymology is a 'science', the right explanation would have to come from the physical philosopher, not the scientist (F18). This is developed in a more interesting and original way in the examples from the *History*, where the etymology of proper names is derived from the philosopher's study of ethnology: the Cimmerian Bosporus from the Cimbri, F272.34–6; the Ἄβιοι from Thracian ethnography, F277a.41ff; and the Ἐρεμβοί from the ethnography of the Mesopotamian peoples, F280.19–24. The last example is the most instructive, because here the etymology of naturally grouped ethnic names is contrasted with the popular etymology of Ἐρεμβοί from εἰς τὴν ἔραν ἐμβαίνειν. For details see F280.

T90

In spite of the efforts of much modern scholarship to impute heterodoxy to Posidonius, he was invariably regarded in the ancient world simply as a Stoic without qualification.

T91 Galen, *De Placitis* v.478, pp. 458.9–459.5 M, 334.23–33 De Lacy

The context is the explanation of emotions (F151). Chrysippus was criticised for his psychology (one faculty, the rational); Posidonius was right in adopting a Platonic plurality of faculties, as did Cleanthes (T92, T93). It seems that the position of Zeno was in doubt (2 ff), but if he held that emotions supervene on judgements (instead of *being* judgements, as Chrysippus held), then he occupied an intermediate position between Chrysippus and Posidonius.

This is interesting as regards Zeno, because Posidonius maintained that Chrysippus differed from Zeno (T93), but Galen is uncertain (2). Explicit written evidence from Zeno may have been indecisive; at F165.4 Chrysippus is said to have taken over in his writing *verbal* statements by Zeno. Zeno's doctrines were such apparently that they could be interpreted in different ways by his successors, e.g. by Ariston and Chrysippus. Posidonius usually gives the impression that he is going back to a correct interpretation of Zeno, who was distorted by Chrysippus (T93).

Posidonius added Pythagoras as a forerunner of Platonic psychology: cf. Cic. *Tusc.* IV.10, Plu. *Mor.* 441E (from Posidonian influence?). Or rather he was careful to state that he inferred that (τεκμαιρόμενος; T88) from Pythagoreans, there being no work of Pythagoras extant. See also T95, T101. The revival of interest in Pythagoreanism was marked in the 1st c. B.C. (e.g. Dillon, *The Middle Platonists* 117ff). It may well have received a major impetus from Posidonius.

T92 Galen, *De Placitis* VIII.653, p. 654.2 M, 484.3–4 De Lacy

Posidonius, according to Galen, claimed agreement with Cleanthes in his opinion, directed against Chrysippus, that we are governed by three distinct powers or faculties (δυνάμεις), the desiring, spirited and rational: F32.

The only evidence we have to substantiate this also comes through Galen from Posidonius, who interprets some verses which he quotes from Cleanthes, representing a dialogue between Anger (Θυμός) and Reason (Λογισμός), as implying distinct rational and irrational faculties (F166.19–31).

It may be argued that since this relies on an interpretation, there was no positive clear statement from Cleanthes for Posidonius to produce; and also that, since Posidonius in general was concerned to show that he was developing early Stoic theory which had been distorted by Chrysippus, his interpretation may not have been without bias. And so it is most commonly held that Cleanthes' verses were merely employing a rhetorical device misinterpreted by Posidonius (e.g. Zeller, *Die Philosophie der Griechen* III.1.203 n.1; Kerferd, 'Origin of Evil in Stoic Thought', 486). On the other hand, Posidonius had no doubt about the implication of the verses (ἐναργῶς, F166.28); he may have chosen them for vivid rhetorical reasons, and we have no right to assume that he, who had more of Cleanthes available than we do, had no other supporting evidence. Galen also clearly believed that Cleanthes followed a kind of Platonic psychology (T91). Of course one may argue that it would have been inconsistent for Cleanthes to hold such a view (Kerferd, 486), but there is no other evidence against Posidonius' positive statement.

The case for Zeno is quite different: T91.

T93 Galen, *De Placitis* v.475, pp. 455.16–456.4 M, 332.18–22 De Lacy

1 **τῶν τοιούτων:** The reasons why emotions abate in time: F166.

Posidonius' basic disagreement with Chrysippus was that the latter did not recognise an irrational 'emotional' power (faculty) or powers, distinct and separate from reason. From this stemmed a different theory of explanation not only of πάθη, but of all ethical dogmas (F150). Much of Posidonius' Περὶ παθῶν was engaged in extended criticism of Chrysippus from this base (T61–3 comm.). Part of the grounds of criticism alleged a contradiction between Chrysippus' theory and observed fact (τοῖς φαινομένοις, 4): F167 comm. end; but Posidonius also claimed that Chrysippus distorted earlier Stoicism (5) which he, Posidonius, believed that he was developing.

For Zeno and Cleanthes: T91, T92.

T94 Galen, *De Placitis* v.434, p. 410.14 M, 296.27f De Lacy

This testimony has little value. It occurs in a passage, F163.30–52, where for once Galen criticises Posidonius, on his analogy of health and sickness of the soul. Galen thinks that the mistake he supposes Posidonius to make arises through an agreement with Chrysippus (F163.20ff), which Galen excuses by supposing that Posidonius was cautious not to be caught out disagreeing with Chrysippus in everything. In fact, it is Galen who misunderstands Posidonius (F163 comm.). The testimony tells us more about Galen than about Posidonius. Of course, Posidonius did not disagree with Chrysippus about everything. εὐλάβεια was used technically by the Stoics as a form of εὐπάθεια, that is, an emotion properly felt by the σοφός, the counterpart of the πάθος, φόβος (D.L. VII.115 = *SVF* III.431; cf. F259.9). Could Galen be cracking an academic joke?

T95 Galen, *De Placitis* IV.425, p. 401.11–15 M, 290.1–5 De Lacy

The context is criticism of Chrysippus on the causes of emotions rising and abating, faculties of soul, the conflict of reason and emotions and the treatment of emotions by habituation (F165). Plato is admired particularly for his psychology, but also for his advances in the whole area of ethical philosophy (T97); Aristotle in this ethical field for psychology (F142, T96; cf. *De An.* 414b 2, 432b 4–7), perhaps for his recognised devotion to aetiology (T85, T100; Chrysippus was attacked for declaring ignorance of αἰτίαι in this context, F165.75–102 comm.), and possibly for his development of ἠθική and διανοητική ἀρετή. For Pythagoras (or Pythagoreans, T91), Posidonius probably had in mind the doctrine of purification of the soul by cultivating the divine element and subduing the earthly.

For Posidonius' reference to such a list of earlier philosophers, and use of doxographies in general, see T101.

T96 Galen, *De Placitis* V.481, pp. 462.12–463, 6 M, 338.11–18 De Lacy

For context see Frs. 144, 183. Galen is discussing Plato, *Rep.*

IV, and in this passage is concerned to show the basic similarity in psychology of Posidonius, Plato and Aristotle against Chrysippus (4–6, 9), while reminding the reader that there are differences of detail between the three (6–8).

Galen is choosing his words with care to avoid misunderstanding. It was enough for Plato's purposes to have demonstrated three distinct *faculties* (δυνάμεις) of soul (3–4). To that extent at least (οὕτω γοῦν, 4) Posidonius took him up, and departed from Chrysippus (5), and preferred to follow Aristotle and Plato (6, cf. F143). He puts Aristotle before Plato, because Posidonius like Aristotle insisted on *faculties* of soul, and refused Plato's *parts* (μέρη) of soul (Frs. 142, 145, 146). Also all three differed on the virtues (7–8). Posidonius remained distinctively a Stoic (cf. F31 comm.).

Galen's language implies that Posidonius was consciously influenced by both Plato and Aristotle. This is proved for Plato by the fact that Posidonius adopts some of Plato's imagery (F31). For further details of the relationship between Posidonius, Plato and Aristotle in psychology, see Frs. 142–6.

T97 Galen, *De Placitis* IV.421, pp. 396.15–397.5 M, 284.33–286.4 De Lacy

That Galen was himself a great admirer of Plato is evident from *De Placitis* in general (but in particular 812.2f M); but the reconstruction of Posidonian argument in e.g. Frs. 165 and 31 is enough to show that Galen was not merely transferring his own enthusiasms. There is no reason to doubt that Posidonius gave Plato the first rank in philosophy, or that he called him divine. Panaetius had already done so, according to Cicero (F56 van Str.), and such an epithet cannot have been uncommon in the 1st c. B.C. (cf. Cic. *ND* II.32).

The main context of approval of Plato in F165 is the

psychology of the tripartite soul, but the immediate reference of this fragment (ταῦτα, 1) is to the treatment of emotions, to prevent them rising, and healing them once they occur (F165.88f). Posidonius could have derived support on this subject from *Republic*, *Phaedrus*, and *Laws*, all books with which he was familiar. But perhaps we should remember that Greeks of this period tended to look for and expect to find answers to all problems in Plato; Walzer, *Greek into Arabic* 149f.

T98 Galen, *De Placitis* V.429, p. 405.9–11 M, 292.20–2 De Lacy

The context this time is the explanation of the nature and origin of πάθη (F152). Posidonius, in rejecting Chrysippus' view that πάθη are κρίσεις (F151), both praised and attached himself to Plato's opinion that they are motions (κινήσεις) of irrational powers, which Plato named ἐπιθυμητική and θυμοειδής. There is no doubt that Plato was a stimulus to Posidonius' problems over πάθη, and that he discussed the Platonic psychology of *The Republic* in Περὶ παθῶν.

T99 Galen, *De Placitis* IV.390, p. 362.9–11 M, 258.19–23 De Lacy

This fragment completes T83, where Posidonius was said to be ashamed of Chrysippus' self-contradiction and conflict with plain facts, because of his training in mathematics and devotion to apodeictic proof. Galen adds that he tried to move not only himself towards the Platonists but Zeno of Citium as well.

One should bear in mind that Galen may have overemphasised Posidonius' 'Platonism' for his own polemical purposes in *De Plac.*, but he is also careful at times to mark the limits and differences (T96 comm.). His comment about Zeno is perceptive. It is clear that some of Zeno's positions were open to speculation, and Posidonius claimed that Chrysippus distorted them, while he (Posidonius) was interpreting them correctly (T93, T91 comm.); so too with Cleanthes (T91–3). Galen remained sceptical about Zeno (T91).

T100

Aristotle

Twice in his *Commentaries* on Aristotle, Simplicius asserts that Posidonius has taken material from Aristotle. In one case probably (F93), and in the second certainly (F18), the information comes through Alexander. The first is embedded in a discussion of *De Caelo* 310b 1 (F93), and the second of *Phys.* 193b 23 (F18, T43, T73). In neither case can Simplicius mean that Posidonius simply took over passages from Aristotle (F18, F93 comm.); but only that he took his impulse from Aristotle (τὰς ἀφορμὰς λαβών, F18.52, T73).

Galen unquestionably saw a relationship between Aristotle and Posidonius' ethical psychology and its developments. His language implies that it was a conscious influence. He coupled in this connection Aristotle and Plato, the latter of whom Posidonius certainly used directly. Indeed, Galen suggests that Aristotle was the closer influence in some respects (T96, Frs. 141–6). Compare also F155 comm. (anger), F165.168 comm. (conflict between reason and affection), F169.95 comm. (physiognomy and character), F183 comm. (virtues).

Strabo accused Posidonius of 'Aristotelising', by which he meant indulging in aetiological explanation more than one would expect in a Stoic; in Strabo's case, in geography (see T85 for details). Sandbach (*Aristotle and the Stoics*, p. 80 n. 123) produces evidence that -ίζειν suffixes in verbs tend to indicate conscious imitation.

Cumulative evidence strongly suggests that Posidonius knew and was influenced by Aristotle's *Meteorologica*: F49.14ff (terrestrial zones), F121.15 (mock suns), F131a (comets), F229 (Stony Plain at la Crau). Compare also Commentary on F137a.11 (winds), F129/130 (Milky Way), F135 (thunderstorms). Other mention of Aristotle must derive from other Aristotelian works, such as F222 ('On the Nile Risings') and F220 (on tides). Some of these are now lost to us, such as the *Problemata Physica* (Sandbach, 60). Obviously a major part of the problem is not knowing what was available to Posidonius. Posidonius himself records (F253.150) that Apellicon had recently purchased the library of Aristotle. He does not say what the content of it was, but it is hard to believe that if Posidonius knew of the existence of such a collection, he did not take steps to familiarise himself with it.

Sandbach (*Aristotle and the Stoics*) has cast a cold salutary eye on the paucity of evidence of Aristotle for the earlier Stoics, and in the case of Posidonius on the difficulty of knowing which books, apart from *Meteor.*, Posidonius had actually read; but this is not an argument that Posidonius was not directly acquainted with and influenced by what was available to him of Aristotle. Apart from the confusion concerning the contemporary Aristotelian corpus, and the difficulty of our fragmentary evidence of Posidonius, the meteorological and ethical evidence shows that in any case Posidonius did not simply reproduce Aristotle, but formed his own theories stimulated from an Aristotelian base. And given his penchant for doxographies, and above all his view of philosophy and science as a conscious progression from the works of the great thinkers of the past (οἱ παλαιοί, T101, T102), of whom Aristotle was one, it is difficult to credit that he did not seek to read as much as he could of him, although precisely what that was may not be clear. Even if it is true that the earlier Stoics were comparatively uninterested in Aristotle, this could hardly be so for Posidonius with his strong scientific interests; and indeed he continually criticised Chrysippus for ignoring the previous theories of Plato and Aristotle. So Strabo, Galen, Alexander and Simplicius were probably right to think that Posidonius was consciously influenced by Aristotle, although the precise bibliographical details of this are now impossible to verify, as Sandbach rightly stressed. My own impression is that although Aristotle was an influence in ethics (Galen), he was not nearly so important both immediately and fundamentally as the much-admired and much-read Plato. But in certain scientific areas, such as meteorology, Aristotle had the greatest influence. Above all, Posidonius' passion for aetiological explanation from top to bottom, so uncharacteristic of the Stoa, but which pervaded and characterised the methodology of the whole of his philosophy and thought, derived, as Strabo complained, from Aristotle.

T101, T102 Galen, *De Placitis* IV.420, pp. 395.11–396.3 M, 284.18–24 De Lacy; Galen, *De Placitis* IV.377, p. 348.16 M, 248.6 De Lacy

Galen frequently refers to Posidonius' enthusiasm for 'the ancients', where παλαιός may qualify φιλόσοφοι, λόγος or δόγμα. Chrysippus departed from 'the ancients' (F34.3), whereas Posidonius praised and accepted what they said (F165.77, F182), indeed said much with regard to proving (ἀπόδειξις) their teaching (F157, T62), and so criticised Chrysippus by this method (F182); indeed Chrysippus is blamed for blind or wilful contrariness for ignoring their theories (F158). The context in Galen is the emotions, their cause, operation and treatment, their relation to ethical behaviour in general, but above all to the assumption of a tripartite psychology necessary to understand them.

παλαιός in Greek simply means 'earlier'; so F165.186 of a person abandoning his earlier opinion (τὴν παλαιὰν δοξαν). 'Earlier' in the case of οἱ παλαιοί is defined by (a) before Chrysippus (*passim*) and (b) F160, before Epicurus. But the dominant theme of psychology (F34.12, F157, T62), and more specifically F160, F169.34: 'the earlier philosophers were the only ones who saw the natural affinities of the three parts of the soul', show that Posidonius had Plato mostly in mind (especially F165.171f), but Pythagoras and Aristotle are also specifically included (F165.168ff).

Although the phrase occurs almost exclusively in Galen, it indicates an important attitude of Posidonius to the natural progression of philosophy and science in which the understanding of earlier theories could contribute to one's own development of problems; thus, according to Strabo (F285), he investigated the origins of the παλαιὸν δόγμα of the atomic theory. This strong historical sense of the development of ideas led him to incorporate doxographies in his books. For traces of doxographies see Commentary on Frs. 31, 49.10ff, 129, 130, 131, 137, 139, 149, 165.164ff, 200, 216, 222, 246, 285. Compare Diels, *Doxographi Graeci*, *Prol.* 225, and Kidd, *Problems* 213.

T103 Strabo, III.2.9

For the rhetorical details of this passage see F239 comm. Strabo refers to Posidonius' customary rhetorical style, but it is clear in this instance that Posidonius was deliberately writing up a purple passage to match the richness of Spain's mineral wealth, and secondly that at least some of the rhetorical devices came from Demetrius of Phalerum. Nevertheless it is evident that in that rhetorical age, Posidonius was noted for his highly coloured style. This is corroborated by

Cicero, who expected a Posidonian version of his consulate to be even *ornatius* than his own very rhetorical draft (T34 comm.), and by Seneca (T106). Even in the fragmentary state of filtered fragments, enough has survived to reveal the power of Posidonius' style, and to increase regret that a complete work has not survived as an example of its full force.

It is admittedly dangerous from the nature of the evidence to specify precise features of this style, but here are a few instances of probable characteristics: a love of compound words (some of which occur nowhere else), leading sometimes to a rhetorical play on verbs with different prefixes (Frs. 59.7–8; 239.9; 240a.41; 253.66, 112f, 123–31); some compounds are coined for technical use (εὐεμπτωσία, Frs. 163, 164; προενδημεῖν, F165.25); an inclination to neuter singular generalisations (F164.53f; F165.25ff); strings of diminutives in scornful invective (F54); asyndeton (F253.12, 30, 34, 44, 53, 72, 110, 154); balance (F68.4ff; F253.97ff); chiasmus (Frs. 55a.6; 67.40f; 68.10f; 70.2f; 253.97ff); order (F64.5–7); density of participles (F253.64ff; F257); repetition (F72); indignant expletives (Frs. 18.7; 165.166; 168.8); highly coloured poetic phrases and words (F62a.11f); analogy (Frs. 31; 85; 117; 163; 166.11ff; 219.89ff); comparisons (Frs. 243; 244; 250; 252); similes (T105 comm.); metaphor (F239.8, 32; F253.21); play on meaning of words (F261; cf. Frs. 170.46ff; 175; 277a; 293); puns (Frs. 58.9f; 239.11); anecdote (Frs. 168.8ff; 253.149ff; 269; 287); riddles (F239.21ff); a vivid pictorial eye for detail, expressed in precise compressed vignettes often of biting sarcasm (Frs. 54; 57; 61; 67.41–53; 77; 253; 257). A good general impression of his style may be gleaned from Frs. 253, 257 and 54.

T104 Galen, *De Placitis* IV.399, p. 372.12–13 M, 166.22–3 De Lacy

At F164.50 Galen, in the middle of an account of Posidonian

criticism of Chrysippus on πάθη, says that Posidonius went on at this point to offer quotations from the poets and from history as witnesses in support of his arguments. Clearly Posidonius was fond of using quotations from the poets, in this instance too liberally for Galen to quote. He used them however not as authorities in the way Plato criticises, but as illustrations which enlivened and gave rhetorical point to his arguments. A good example is the 'sleepless Agamemnon' quotations from *Il.* x in F164.58–86. They present vividly a psychological phenomenon which he is probing, but they do not in themselves constitute an argument; the argument proper follows in 79–86. Their function is that of μαρτυρία, and in that limited capacity may be used as illustrative evidence, F165.134ff. Elsewhere (F156) Posidonius criticised Chrysippus, a notorious quoter (D.L. VII.180 = *SVF* II.1), for the wrong use of quotation. See T87 comm. for Posidonius' own dialectical employment of quotations, and his reasons for doing so. He also, of course, used quotations which had become stock examples (F164.99). In the extant fragments quotations from Homer outnumber others by far.

T105 Strabo, III.4.13

Posidonius made fun of Polybius with a witty simile (F271). He certainly possessed a sardonic humour, of which the story of Nicias of Engyium (F257) is a good example. He was also addicted to similes (e.g. Frs. 34.19; 88; 108.8; 114; 149.10; 166.11ff; 200–1; 230; 253.168), and could attack a simile of Chrysippus (F163.6f). In spite of Strabo's comments on Posidonius' rhetorical style (T103), he clearly appreciated his wit (F268).

T106 Seneca, *Epistulae* 90.20–3

Seneca accuses Posidonius of being carried away by the

charm of his own oratorical style from the truth, and also that the power of his eloquence (*nec minus facunde*) misleads others. Seneca himself in this is using a rhetorical device in his criticism of Posidonius' account of the Golden Age in a Letter in which his own rhetorical style is very marked. Nevertheless, it is further evidence that the force of Posidonius' eloquence and style impressed such an expert judge no less than the content of his philosophy.

T107 Cicero, *De Officiis* I.159

Cicero's context (F177) is not related to style. He himself is arguing that in choice of appropriate acts (*officia*), primacy should be given to duties of society (*communitas*). But there are some acts so vile and infamous that the wise man would not do them to save his country. He claims that Posidonius made a large collection of such acts; but it is highly likely that, if such a collection existed, Cicero had never set eyes on it (F177 comm.). Nevertheless Cicero is shocked even at the thought of the expression (*dictu*, 2) of such foul and disgusting language (*obscena*, *turpia*), from a writer whose dignity (*Tusc.* II.61, T38) he respected. But Posidonius was perfectly capable of deliberately vulgar language in indignant invective, as in his scathing picture of Athenion 'farting' (σιληπορδῶν) round Attica (F253.46).

DUBIA

T108 *IG* XII.I.127

It is tempting to relate this inscriptional reference to a Posidonius, son of Posidonius, of Rhodes, either to Posidonius himself (H.v. Gaertringen, *RE* Supplb. v, Rhodos, col. 801; Laffranque, *Poseidonios d'Apamée* 71), or to a son of his (Theiler, *Poseidonios* II.3; cf. T40). But it must be remembered that Posidonius was a common name (T1a comm.), and there is nothing more to nail this evidence to the philosopher Posidonius.

T109, T110 Eustathius, *Commentarii ad Homeri Iliadem* VI.511; XVII.75

This is certainly not our Posidonius. The term ἀναγνώστης refers to a specific office, that of a slave in wealthy and intellectual households, whose duty was to read aloud for his master; thus Cic. *Ad Att.* I.12.4, *nam puer festivus anagnostes noster Sositheus decesserat*; compare the slaves who read aloud (ἀναγνῶσται) for Crassus (Plu. *Crass.* 2) and for Callisthenes (Plu. *Alex.* 54).

Both fragments sound like learned anecdotes. In T109, when Aristarchus' reciter came to *Il.* VI.511 (ῥίμφα ἑ γοῦνα φέρει . . .), he said ῥίμφαε in one trisyllabic word: the ε being redundant, says he. That is, the reader made a mistake running ῥίμφα and ἑ together, and then attempted to justify it. Again, in T110, at *Il.* XVII.75 (Ἕκτορ, νῦν σὺ μὲν ὧδε θέεις ἀκίχητα διώκων / ἵππους Αἰακίδαο δαΐφρονος), the reciter made a slip of repetition after ἀκίχητα (-ητα· εἶτα), and Aristarchus accepted it; that is hard to swallow, but perhaps the anecdote meant that Aristarchus did not notice the slip or let it pass.

It is nonsense to attempt to foist Frs. 45 and 192 on to this comic reciter of Eustathian anecdote, as Christ–Schmidt–Stählin, *Geschichte d. griechischen Litteratur* II.1.443, Theiler, *Poseidonios* II.414 and others. Frs. 45 and 192 are concerned with the philosophy of language, and belong to the Stoic Posidonius.

T111 Scholium on Homer, *Iliad* XXII.325

The line refers to the exposed gap at Hector's throat: λαυκανίην, ἵνα τε ψυχῆς ὤκιστος ὄλεθρος. The scholiast first quibbles about Homer's knowing that the ψυχή is immortal, and therefore is talking of its disappearance and its parting from the body. He then brings in remarks from Praxagoras and Posidonius; the latter says that in the passage of food the windpipe is protected by the epiglottis. Cicero has a similar remark in *ND* II.136, where he is describing the providential structure of the human body. So the reference could be to Posidonius of Apamea (Theiler, *Poseidonios* F366). Of course the structure and function of the epiglottis was common knowledge both to philosophers and medical writers from at least the 4th c. B.C. (e.g. Aristotle; Hipp. *Cord.* 2). The Praxagoras reference (the famous anatomist of the second half of the 4th c. B.C.) is to his *Anatomy*, and gives a description of the mouth and the two passages leading from it; it ends: 'between the windpipe and the tongue is the epiglottis, ἐπιπωματίζουσα τοῦ φάρυγγος τὸ στόμα'. The coupling of Praxagoras and Posidonius leaves open the possibility that the reference is to another physician (cf. T114). But ῥιπή is an odd word in this connection; on the one hand it may be poetical with strong Homeric associations; on the other it seems to have passed into common usage in later Greek and κοινή.

T112 Apollonius Citiensis, *De Articulis* I, *CMG* XI.1.1, p. 12.1–5

Apollonius of Citium was an Alexandrian physician of the middle of the 1st c. B.C. The reference occurs in the introduction of his commentary on Hipp. *On Joints*, addressed to Ptolemy. Apollonius gives his credentials: '... on reduction of limbs, some I set myself, others I observed when I attended Zopyrus in Alexandria. That Zopyrus in the case of fractures and the surgery of dislocations for the most part followed the treatment of Hippocrates, Posidonius, who had spent time with this same doctor, would bear witness for us.'

Zopyrus was a physician at Alexandria of the Empirical School, *c.* 100 B.C., famed for pharmacology as well as surgery; see *RE*[2] XA (1972) (15). It would hardly be surprising for Apollonius to know Posidonius of Apamea, the outstanding intellectual figure of the previous generation. It would be still less so for him to advance the great man's name when ingratiating himself with Ptolemy (Auletes?), to whom our Posidonius would be a greater reference than some otherwise unknown doctors. The disturbing factor is συνδιατετριφώς (6). Posidonius probably had some interest in medical science (T51, F190), and may well have attended Zopyrus' surgery in Alexandria, but this is technical surgery whose relationship to philosophy is unclear, and it is unlikely that Posidonius was a pupil of Zopyrus. But Apollonius may have been exaggerating. In general, Kudlien, *Hermes* 90 (1962), 427f.

T113 Oribasius, *Collectiones Medicae* XLIV.14.2 (*CMG* VI.2.1, p. 132.4ff)

A tantalising fragment which surfaces in Oribasius' *Medical Compendium*, but derived from Rufus of Ephesus, of the time of Trajan. The subject is bubonic plague, and we are told that outbreaks are seen occurring especially in Libya, Egypt and Syria. Dioscurides and Posidonius have given most details in the work on the plague that occurred in Libya in their time (1f). Rufus continues with the symptoms of the plague.

The reference must be to before the time of Trajan. Kudlien (*Hermes* 90 (1962), 428f) argues against Dioscurides of Anazarbus, who although well-travelled, was a pharmacologist. He suggests rather the physician Dioscurides Phakas

(*RE* v (10), 1129f), who lived at Alexandria at the time of Cleopatra and Antony, and was in good standing with Ptolemy Auletes. He left twenty-four books on medicine. This identification had already been made by Wellmann in *RE*. Posidonius then could be Posidonius of Apamea, for such an event would be of interest to a historian and scientist; but this remains no more than a possibility. For πλεῖστα διεληλύθασιν in the context would suggest full medical details.

T114 Aetius Amidenus 6.2ff, *CMG* VIII.2, p. 125.4ff.

Aetius' date is the first half of the 6th c. A.D., and in the first half of Bk 6 of the *Iatrica* a Posidonius is frequently mentioned as an authority for mental disorders. Kudlien (*Hermes* 90 (1962), 422ff) argued a tempting case for Posidonius of Apamea. He points out that many of the specific subjects mentioned in this passage were of philosophical interest to the Stoa, e.g. *SVF* III.237, 238, 239 for μελαγχολία, κάρος, λήθαργος, σκότωσις; that the name of Posidonius is coupled several times with Archigenes of Apamea, a pupil of Agathinus, who was himself a pupil of Athenaeus, the pupil of Posidonius and founder of the Pneumatist School of medicine (T51). This School was itself interested in mental disorders (Kudlien, p. 423 n. 2), and while Posidonius was hardly likely himself to have written technical medical handbooks on these subjects, he may have been cited and adopted by the School as a philosophical source, as Galen cited him on πάθη. But the context and detail of Aetius' account is against this reconstruction. Posidonius is named here as a chief medical authority for medical disorders, and it is impossible to separate the Posidonius cited from the lengthy medical detail of pharmacological treatment, e.g. in p. 147.1–151.8. H. Flashar, *Melancholia und Melancholiker*, 118–26, has argued more convincingly, that the Posidonius here in question is the physician of the second half of the 4th c. A.D. mentioned by Philostorgius (*Hist. Eccl.* VIII.10) as his contemporary.

To the medical evidence may be added a curious reference from Abū 'l-Ḥasan, 'Alī b. Riḍwān b. 'Alī b. Ja'far of Egypt, court physician to the Fatimid caliph al-Ḥākim. 'Alī, who died between 1061 and 1068, was a noted writer on medical themes, including numerous commentaries on the medical writings of Greek authors, among them Galen and Hippocrates. He also wrote on astrology, logic and public health questions (Brockelmann, *Geschichte der Arabischen Literatur* I.484; *Suppl.* I.886). 'Alī is stated to have composed a *ta'liq*, that is, a supplement to a medical treatise by Posidonius entitled 'Delicious potions for healthy persons'.

This information is to be found in 'Uyūn al-Anbā' fī Ṭabaqāt al-Aṭibbā', the celebrated biographical dictionary tracing the lives and works of the most famous physicians by Abū 'l-'Abbās, Aḥmad b. al-Qāsim b. Khalīfah b. Yūnus, known as ibn abī Uṣaibi'ah (ed. Nizār Riḍā, Beirut, 1965, p. 566). Aḥmad's dates are 1203–70 (Brockelmann I.325; *Suppl.* I.560).

Whether this Posidonius was Posidonius of Apamea, or another medical writer of the same name, we have no further means of establishing. See also Jadaane, *L'Influence du Stoïcisme sur la pensée musulmane* 81.

T115 *Anthologia Latina* XLIII.547 (*Poetae Latini Minores* IV, p. 440 Baehrens)

There is nothing to be said for this fragment, apart from having a name, Posidonius, attached to it. Posidonius was interested in the rhetorical theory of poetry (F44), and his prose style was sometimes thought to be 'poetic'; but there is no evidence that he wrote poetry, and if he had done so, it would not have been in Latin.

PART II

FRAGMENTS AND TITLES OF NAMED BOOKS

F1 Diogenes Laertius, VII.129

CONTENT

Disagreement is no reason for standing aloof from philosophy, for on that reasoning one would abandon one's whole life. Posidonius made this point in *Exhortations*.

CONTEXT

This is in the middle of a miscellany of Stoic tenets (ἀρέσκει αὐτοῖς).

COMMENT

Diogenes records this as a general Stoic conviction (δοκεῖ δ' αὐτοῖς), but takes his reference from Posidonius (ὡς καὶ Ποσειδώνιός φησιν . . .). It is a view not only suitable for an introductory work to philosophy, such as *Exhortations* probably was, but an essential point to establish at the beginning for a dogmatic School of the period. For the Sceptics formulated διαφωνία, i.e. contradictory views on a subject put forward by different Schools or held in popular belief, as one of their main τρόποι of scepticism leading to ἐποχή, suspension of judgement (S.E. *Hyp.* I.165, D.L. IX.88; and compare *SVF* II.120).

προλείψειν ὅλον τὸν βίον cannot mean 'commit suicide'. There were circumstances which could lead a Stoic σοφός to suicide, but disagreement among philosophers was not one of them. Either then it means abandoning living in the sense of being reduced to indecision and inactivity, or being unable to fulfil one's proper life as a human being.

1 *BPF* have μήτε τὴν διαφωνίαν. διά (Bake) is easily supplied. If μήτε is kept (Edelstein), a lacuna must be inferred, but its content remains mysterious. So, μηδὲ διὰ Hicks. But μηδέ 'not even' is odd; perhaps: μὴ δεῖν διὰ. The sense at least is clear.

F2 Diogenes Laertius, VII.91

CONTENT

Virtue is teachable, referred to Posidonius' book *Exhortations*.

CONTEXT

Preceded immediately by F29 and followed by F180.

COMMENT

This view was held by all Stoics. As Seneca put it: *dociles natura nos edidit et rationem dedit imperfectum, sed quae perfici posset* (*Ep.* 49.11 = *SVF* III.219). Virtue itself was a τέχνη (*SVF* II.96; III.214). Individual Stoics could differ, however, on how to teach virtue. Since Posidonius adopted a different psychology from Chrysippus, his παιδεία was peculiar to him: F31, Frs. 163–9.

The proof of the teachability of virtue is said to be obvious from the fact that people become good from being bad (ἐκ φαύλων). Since Posidonius is only cited second last in a named list of four Stoics, one cannot be certain that this proof is to be referred particularly to him. It would be consonant with the type of τεκμήριον proof that is assigned to him elsewhere (e.g. F7, F29), where an empirical appeal to fact is cited as evidence for a conclusion. It is in any case a bad proof, as there could be other reasons for bad men becoming good. As it stands, neither Posidonius nor any other Stoic could have offered it. F. H. Sandbach has suggested to me in correspondence that the participle διδασκομένους has fallen out, which is convincing.

F3 Papyrus Milanensis, I.11

CONTENT

In a list of book titles, Posidonius' Περὶ τοῦ προτρέπεσθαι is named.

COMMENT

Reported by A. Vogliano, *Papiri della Real. Università di Milano*, Florence, 1935, vol. I, Nr. 2, p. 31ff. But see U. Wilcken, *Archiv für Papyrusforschung* 12 (1937), 80f; E. G. Turner, *JEA* 38 (1952), 91.

It is an Oxyrhynchus of the time of Hadrian, from Theon to Heracleides, described as φιλόσοφος, and runs: 'As I put all my energy into procuring books which are of service and relevant above all to conduct, so I think you should not be inattentive in reading them. To those in earnest to profit by them no ordinary benefit will accrue. What I have sent by Achillas is set out in the following list. Farewell, I am myself well. Greet all whom it may concern.' Then follows the list of books 'written in Alexandria': Boethus Περὶ ἀσκήσεως γ'δ', Diogenes Περὶ γάμου, Diogenes Περὶ ἀλυπίας, Chrysippus Περὶ γονέων χρήσεως, Antipater Περὶ οἰκετῶν χρήσεως α'β', Posidonius Περὶ τοῦ προτρέπεσθαι γ'.

προτρεπτικοὶ λόγοι by sophists to stimulate interest in their subject of teaching are referred to by Isocrates I (*Dem.*), 3. Ueberweg, p. 161, traces the tradition back to Antisthenes. Books with the actual titles of Προτρεπτικοὶ Λόγοι (or a similar form) are common from Aristotle and Epicurus (D.L. X.28) on. In the Stoa itself, the title is preserved for Ariston of Chios (*SVF* I.333), Persaeus (*SVF* I.435), Cleanthes (*SVF* I.481), and Chrysippus (*SVF* III p. 203.20–8).

Reinhardt (*RE* 768) suggests that the letter gives the exact title of Posidonius' work (*der genaue Titel*) as against Frs. I and 2. But titles were not exact in ancient times, but variable.

Both Προτρεπτικοί and Περὶ τοῦ προτρέπεσθαι were equally 'correct'; cf. the variations for Chrysippus' book (*SVF loc. cit.*).

There were at least three volumes of Posidonius' work, since Theon sent vol. III. So too with Chrysippus. The other books in Theon's list are instructive in giving the level of reading in which Posidonius' *Protrepticus* is grouped. Its topics probably included non-specialist, general themes, such as those in Frs. 1 and 2. We should be chary of assigning other extant fragments to it; but cf. Reinhardt, *RE* 768–70; W. Gerhäusser, *Der Protreptikos des Poseidonios.*

PHYSICS

F4 Diogenes Laertius, VII.143

CONTENT

Posidonius, *Natural Philosophy*, Bk 1 is given as a reference for the statement that the universe (κόσμος) is one. References are also given to Zeno, Chrysippus and Apollodorus.

CONTEXT

It is curious that this comes as a kind of addendum right at the close of Diogenes' section on the cosmos, which runs from §§137–43, and in which Posidonius features prominently (F99a comm.). The unity of the universe had been mentioned earlier (140; see F8 and below). This fragment is preceded by F99a. After it Diogenes passes to the account of the heavenly bodies, where the first reference is F17 (D.L. VII.144) from Posidonius' Περὶ μετεώρων.

COMMENT

The reference to the 'oneness' of the universe in F8 (D.L. VII.140) is assigned to Bk 5 of *Natural Philosophy*, and in this fragment to Bk 1. Since they also occur in different places in the same doxography and possibly from the same source (F99a comm.), the question arises whether the two references have the same meaning. In F8 ἕνα possibly means 'one' in the sense of 'unity'. It is possible that εἷς in F4 means 'one' in the sense of 'single'. The Stoics believed in a single, one-and-only universe, in opposition to those who entertained a plurality of universes (Stob. *Ecl.* 1.22.3^b = 1. p. 199.10ff W = *SVF* 1.97; also *SVF* II.542 (Galen); 620 (Philo); 528). In Bk 1, Posidonius may in a doxographical passage have sided on this question with Plato (*Tim.* 31a–b) against the Epicureans (*SVF* 1.97; II.542; II.620). But of course, we cannot be sure. Proclus (*SVF* II.533, *In Tim.* p. 138E) in a context of 'single' (Pl. *Tim.* 31b) refers to the 'unity (ἡνῶσθαι) of substance of the 'one' cosmos of the Stoics.

See also Frs. 13, 14, 20, 21, 23, 99a for cosmos.

F5 Diogenes Laertius, VII.134

CONTENT

'It is the Stoics' opinion that there are two principles (ἀρχάς) of all that there is (τῶν ὅλων), the active and the passive. The passive principle is unqualified substance, matter; the active is the *logos* (rational organisation) in matter, namely god. For the latter, being eternal, fashions through the whole of matter each separate thing (ἕκαστα). This view is laid down by Zeno of Citium in *On Substance*, Cleanthes in *On Indivisibles*, Chrysippus near the end of Bk 1 of *Physics*, Archedemus in *On Elements*, and by Posidonius in *Natural Philosophy*, Bk. 2. They say (he says, F^{ac}) that principles are different from elements (στοιχεῖα). Principles are not subject to generation or destruction; elements are destroyed in the conflagration (ἐκπύρωσις). But also principles are bodies (so *codices*; 'incorporeal' *Suda*) and without form (ἀμόρφους), elements are enformed (μεμορφῶσθαι).'

CONTEXT

The passage follows immediately after Diogenes' classifications of the topics of Stoic physical philosophy (for which see F99a comm.). It is followed by a passage on body (σῶμα), to which is attached F16.

COMMENT

The list of references (5–9) is remarkable for its length and precision. For the possible bearing of this on the question of Diogenes' source: F99a and J. Mejer, 'Diogenes Laertius and his Hellenistic Background', *Hermes, Einzelschr.* 40 (1978), 6. It is clear that Posidonius is cited as an authority for standard Stoic doctrine on this topic (F99a comm.). As far as the context of this fragment is concerned, Posidonius is not thought of as holding divergent views on the first principles (as Edelstein, *AJPh* 57 (1936), 290ff, and Reinhardt, *RE* 642f maintained). But see also F92 comm.

2–4 The identification and description of the two Stoic principles is entirely normal; in general, *SVF* I.85; II.229ff.

For Posidonius' interpretation of the passive principle as τὴν ἄποιον οὐσίαν τὴν ὕλην, F92 comm.

4 It is tempting to see behind ὄντα, the stock participle in such phrases, διήκοντα (Frs. 21, 100; cf. F102), but emendation is perhaps unnecessary. For δημιουργεῖν, which no doubt derives ultimately from *Tim.*, cf. *SVF* II.323a, p. 116.11–13 Arn.

ἕκαστα: λόγος is also the individuating principle. For Posidonius on this divine rational principle, see Frs. 21, 100, 101, 102.

10–13 The principles are distinguished from the elements.

(1) The elements are destroyed in the ἐκπύρωσις (and therefore are recreated again afterwards). This contradicts explicitly Edelstein's strange theory that Posidonius denied 'the creation of elements from matter' and held that 'the elements exist always as the material principle' (Edelstein, *AJPh*, p. 291). On the contrary, Posidonius appears to have subscribed to the doctrine of conflagration (Frs. 13, 97); nor do his theories of substance and of change (Frs. 92, 96) invalidate this statement.

On the other hand the principles are not subject to generation and destruction, for in the conflagration they persist as god-enformed matter in the purest form as αἰθήρ (cf. Plu. *Comm. Not.* 1077Df, *SVF* II.1064; F92 comm.).

(2) The elements are enformed; the principles are without form. For οὐσία being ἄμορφος as ὕλη, and the difficulties involved in this, see F92 comm.; and for the divine rational enforming principle being itself without form, F101.

There is however, a major crux at line 12. A second characteristic is given to the principles as well as ἀμόρφους. The codices of Diogenes give it as σώματα (bodies), but the Suda preserves this same passage under the entry ἀρχή, and the text there is ἀσωμάτους (incorporeal). At first sight it might be thought that in these lines (10–14), we are being offered contrary and opposing qualities distinguishing principles and elements, and so in this case since elements are unquestionably σώματα as well as μεμορφῶσθαι, principles should be ἀμόρφους and ἀσωμάτους (cf. exactly for form, 10–13). So the Suda's version, ἀσωμάτους, has been adopted by Lipsius, Cobet, Hirzel, v. Arnim (*SVF* II.299), R. F. Hicks (Loeb edn.), J. Moreau, H. H. Long (OCT), G. Verbeke, and most recently defended at length by Graeser, *Zenon von Kition* 103ff (in general, 94–108). But ἀσωμάτους is difficult both historically and philosophically; historically, because the overwhelming surviving evidence gives as the typical view of the Stoics that the ἀρχαί were corporeal. So, ὕλη as σῶμα: *SVF* II.305, 310, 312, 325, 326; τὸ ποιοῦν/λόγος/θεός as σῶμα: *SVF* II.310, 313, 323; for both, where ὕλη and θεός are specifically referred to as ἀρχαί: *SVF* I.98 (Aristocles in Eusebius, *Praep. Evang.* XV, p. 816d), where οὗτος ἄμφω σώματά φησιν εἶναι (p. 27.13 Arn.) must refer to Zeno, and the following ἐκείνου to Plato.

Also philosophically, with regard to active and passive principles, only body can act or be acted upon (Plu. *Comm. Not.* 1073E; *SVF* II.363; cf. *SVF* I.90, 146; II.140, 387). And if the principles are seen as causes, cause (αἴτιον) also is a σῶμα for the Stoa (*SVF* I.89).

The case for σώματα against ἀσωμάτους, is argued by Baeumker, *Das Problem der Materie*, p. 332 n. 3; Schmekel, *Die Positive Philosophie*, p. 245 n. 4; J. Mansfeld, 'Zeno of Citium', *Mnem.* 31 (1978), 162, 167ff (in criticism of Graeser).

Nevertheless, although I cannot support some of Graeser's arguments (which are well criticised by Mansfeld), I still have some sympathy with some of the difficulties he raises in his general thesis.

F92 indicates that Posidonius may have tried to meet general criticism of the Stoic position that the ἀρχαί are σώματα ἄποια καὶ ἄμορφα. He appears to have taken the line that the principles never 'exist' separately on their own, but are only logically distinguishable. This is, of course, different from denying their corporeality. But it is not impossible that he took the argument further, and raised the question whether the principles, ὕλη and λόγος/θεός, as distinct from qualified substance in which they always corporeally concur, and which is all that there is, may purely *qua* ἀρχαί, that is as separate ἄποια that are the principles of qualifying and being qualified, be nothing more than logical concepts; see Commentary on F92, and Sandbach, *The Stoics* 73–4.

However, it must be admitted that this is no more than supposition. And even if it be granted that Posidonius may have debated the problem of the corporeality of the ἀρχαί, or that a certain confusion may have arisen from such a debate, there is no doubt that the standard accepted doctrine for the Stoa held that the principles were corporeal. The passage in Diogenes is presenting main-line doctrine, and therefore σώματα of the codices is to be preferred. If ἀσωμάτους were to be defended, it would be necessary to adopt φησιν (i.e. Posidonius) F^{ac} at line 10.

F6 Diogenes Laertius, VII.140

CONTENT

In a list which includes Chrysippus, Apollophanes and Apollodorus, Posidonius is cited precisely (Bk 2 of *Natural Philosophy*) as one of the Stoic authorities on void (τὸ κενόν).

CONTEXT

This passage occurs in the middle of an extended report by Diogenes on the Stoic cosmos (137–43). Some statements on void are introduced to help explain that the universe itself is εἷς and πεπερασμένος (F8). For void, which is infinite and incorporeal, extends only outside the circumference of the universe. There is no void in it. So the universe is itself a single unified whole (ἡνῶσθαι, F8 comm.). F6 is followed by a couple of sentences on time, as an interval of the movement of the universe (which is not Posidonian, F98 comm.). This in turn leads to the topic of the universe being φθαρτός and γενητός and F13.

COMMENT

This list of references is extraordinary for Diogenes in that it does not allude to a particular point, but offers general references for a whole topic (Jørgen Mejer, 'Diogenes

Laertius and his Hellenistic Background', *Hermes, Einzelschr.* 40 (1978), p. 6; cf. F13 (D.L. VII.142) and D.L. VII.136). Posidonius is cited not for any particular deviation or variant, but as a main-line authority on the topic.

F99a comm. discusses Diogenes' source on the topic of cosmos.

See also Frs. 97 and 8 for Posidonius on void.

F7 Diogenes Laertius, VII.149

CONTENT

Two statements are made: (a) 'What is more, Stoics say that divination exists in all its forms if it is true that providence exists; (b) and they prove it to be a science (τέχνη) as well through its results (ἐκβάσεις)'; for which are cited Zeno, Chrysippus, Athenodorus and Posidonius in *Natural Philosophy*, Bk 2 (or Bk 12).

CONTEXT

Diogenes' presentation in §§148–9 deals in order with god (F20), nature (φύσις), fate (F25), divination.

COMMENT

Diogenes' order of presentation is important. God, nature and fate are three different aspects of providence, and therefore divination naturally follows from their establishment. The general thesis that the existence of divination depends on establishing the existence of divine providence is a basis of argument in Cicero, *De Div.* I, e.g. I.9ff, 82ff, 110, 117. It is certainly Posidonian as well as Stoic. Posidonius seems to have defined the Stoic position more precisely by justifying the existence of divination by the triad of god, fate and nature, F107, F103. So Diogenes may be following a Posidonian order of presentation here. For the form of the argument cf. F29.

Quintus in Cic. *De Div.* I also frequently uses another argument to prove that divination exists, namely that we merely require to recognise the results (*eventa* = ἐκβάσεις). He asserts that the mere observation of agreement between sign and event in a very few or even in a single case without understanding the cause, is enough to establish the existence of divination (e.g. *De Div.* I.12ff, 35, 71, 86, 109, 124f, 127). This is not only unPosidonian in its disregard of causes, but nonsense and easily attacked by Cicero in Bk II. This fragment shows that it is a perversion of the Stoic position of Posidonius, who was arguing that the evidence of results confirmed that divination was a *systematic science* (τέχνη) (F109 comm.). For this method of approach compare Hipp. *VM*. The colourless word ἔκβασις is used, and not the astrological term ἀποτέλεσμα. For divination as a science cf. T74 comm.

The fact that Posidonius dealt with this question in his book on *Natural Philosophy* as well as in the separate work *On Divination* (Frs. 26, 27) shows his close association of divination with the natural principles of the universe. The reading $\overline{\iota\beta}$ (Bk 12) of the codices is probably due to an iota adscript, for iota numbers occur with suspicious frequency elsewhere in Diogenes; e.g. Frs. 13, 17, 21, 42.

Athenodorus (4) could conceivably be Athenodorus of Soli, the pupil of Zeno (*SVF* I.38, 39), but it is very much more likely that the reference is to Athenodorus of Tarsus, who was associated elsewhere with Posidonius (T44).

In this case Diogenes gives references for the main doctrine on divination, because he goes on to say that Panaetius denied the existence of divination. Panaetius' divergence gave more force to Posidonius' reaffirmation, and possibly led to the greater stress and schematisation of his presentation.

F8 Diogenes Laertius, VII.140

CONTENT

'The Stoics say that the universe is one, and this is finite, with a spherical shape; for such a shape is most suitable for its (τὴν) movement, as Posidonius says in *Natural Philosophy*, Bk 5, and Antipater (and his circle) in the books on Cosmos.'

CONTEXT

F23 precedes and F6 follows. For general characteristics of D.L. VII.137–43, on the cosmos: F99a comm., T66 comm.

COMMENT

This extract is immediately followed by a few remarks on τὸ κενόν, void. Since this is in the middle of a section (137–43) devoted to the universe (κόσμος), and void is not part of the universe but outside it, the insertion is likely to be explanatory of ἕνα and πεπερασμένον. So void is briefly explained: it is outside the universe, infinite and incorporeal. 'The universe has no void in it, but is itself a unified whole (ἡνῶσθαι); this necessarily happens from τὴν σύμπνοιαν καὶ συντονίαν of heavenly things in relation to things on earth.'

For ἕνα see F4 (where reference is made to Bk 1 of *Natural Philosophy*). It could mean either 'single' (references given under F4) or 'unity'. καὶ τοῦτον (1) may be slightly in favour of 'single', by separating ἕνα and πεπερασμένον (and cf. *SVF* II.528, p. 169.15 Arn., ἕνα μόνον εἶναί φασι καὶ πεπερασμένον), but the verb ἡνῶσθαι in the void addition shows that 'unity' is strongly in mind here. The two senses may have been closely associated; as *SVF* II.533, where Proclus (*In Tim.* 138E) in the context of a *single* universe (Pl. *Tim.* 31b) raises the *unity* of Stoic substance (ἡνῶσθαι τὴν οὐσίαν). The sense of 'unity' (ἡνωμένον) also occurs at S.E. *Adv. Math.* IX.79 = *SVF* II.1013. For πεπερασμένον, cf. *SVF* II.534, and II.528, p. 169.15 Arn. = Ar. Did. F29, where the explanation is added that in this universe all bodies are encompassed, and there is no void in it. So again: 'The universe is finite, the void is infinite' (D.L. VII.143 = *SVF* III.Apoll. 9). In general: *SVF* II.534–46. Posidonius on void: Frs. 6, 97.

For the unifying aspect of the universe (called here σύμπνοια καὶ συντονία): *SVF* II.447 (πνευματικὸς τόνος); II.448; II.546.

σφαιροειδές: cf. F49.7; F117; *SVF* II.547, 681, 1143. The sun also is spherical, analogous to the universe (F117); so is the moon (F122), and the earth itself (F18.20; F49.7).

All these characteristics of the universe are standard Stoic beliefs. The reference to Posidonius and Antipater was probably intended to cover them all, but is certainly directed in particular to the reason given for the spherical shape of the universe, namely that such a shape is most fitted for the movement of the universe. This presumably alludes to the movement of circumference around the centre. But this too was common Stoic doctrine: Stob. *Ecl.* I, p. 184.13ff W = Ar. Did. F31, *SVF.* II.527, p. 168.16ff Arn; compare also Plu. *De SR*, ch. 44, 1054E = *SVF* II.550; Ar. Did. F39, p. 471.11f Diels; Cic. *ND* II.115ff; Cleom. *De Motu* I.1, p. 16f Ziegler, and chs. 8 and 9. But perhaps the movement of the universe was a specific topic in Bk 5 of *Natural Philosophy*. Posidonius discussed void in Bk 2 of Φυσικὸς Λόγος (F6).

What is interesting is that Diogenes cites only Posidonius (and Antipater) for main-line Stoic doctrine on the universe, without mention of the earlier leading Stoics (T66 comm.). Since οἱ περὶ A. comes after Posidonius, it is just possible that the reference came from pupils of Antipater rather than from Antipater himself. But οἱ περὶ A. probably simply means Antipater (T45 comm.) as the book citation suggests, and there is no significance in the order of names (cf. F13). Since these two are the only authorities cited, Diogenes' source for the section on cosmos may have been near to Posidonius' time (F99a comm.).

For cosmos see also Frs. 4, 13, 14, 20, 21, 23, 99a.

F9 Diogenes Laertius, VII.144

CONTENT

Size of sun.

CONTEXT

The paragraph in Diogenes is complex. (a) Posidonius, Περὶ μετεώρων Bk VII is quoted for the composition of the sun (F17); (b) *Natural Philosophy*, Bk 6 for its size (F9.1–2); (c) οἱ περὶ Ποσειδώνιον on the shape of the sun (F117); Diogenes then adds information on (a), followed by further matter on (b) (this Fr. lines 2–5). Thus the arrangement is (a-b-c-a-b).

COMMENT

ις *B*: ςι *P*: *om.F*. It was a custom of *F* to omit such information (vol. I, *Introduction*, xxv). *BP*'s reading is probably due to an iota adscript; cf. Frs. 7, 13, 17, 21, 42.

μείζω τῆς γῆς See Frs. 19, 115, 116. There is a chapter on this vague comparison in Cleom. *De Motu* II.2. It is odd that the only general ascription of this formula to Stoics occurs in Aetius *Plac.* II.26.1 (*SVF* II.666), and that incidentally to a statement on the moon. Perhaps such a general comparison has significance in an anti-Epicurean context; cf. Cleom. *De Motu* II.1. But see F19 and F114, and in general Gilbert, *Griechische Meteorologie* 687; Zeller, *Die Philosophie der Griechen* III.1.193, 2. It does look, however, as though Posidonius was the Stoic who was known to have discussed the question.

Three reasons are given:

(1) All earth and indeed heaven are illuminated by the sun; cf. Cicero, *ND* II.40 (Cleanthes on the sun's radiance: *quippe qui inmenso mundo tam longe lateque conluceat*); Cleom. *De Motu* II.3.98 p. 178.2 Z (of the moon).

(2) Conical shadow. This is implied in Arist. *Meteor.* 345b 1–9 (cf. Alexander, *In Meteor.*, p. 38.7–23 and Philoponus, *In Meteor.* 104.18–23), and assumed by Aristarchus (*On Sizes and Distances*); but see especially Cleom. *De Motu* II.2.94, p. 170.11ff Z (but his other reasons in that chapter are different); Plu. *De Facie* 932E (cf. 923B); Pliny *NH* 2.51; Heraclitus, *Quaest. Hom.* §§45–6 (referring to οἱ μαθηματικοί, p. 68.6–7 Oelmann and κατὰ τὴν τῶν πλείστων φιλοσόφων ἔννοιαν, p. 69.1–2); F115 comm.

(3) Sun is seen from everywhere (πάντοθεν). I can find no exact parallel for this explanation, but again there is a hint of it in the Aristotelian argument of *Meteor.* 345b 1–9, and compare Philoponus, p. 105.9–14.

F10 Diogenes Laertius, VII.145

CONTENT

Φυσικὸς Λόγος, Bk 6. Moon.

CONTEXT

The Posidonian reference should probably be limited as in the fragment. D.L. VII.145 begins with the statement that the moon is γεωδεστέραν inasmuch as it is also προσγειοτέραν, which sounds a separate source from ἀερομιγῆ . . . πρόσγειον of the fragment. Then comes description of the nourishment of sun, moon and other stars. The fact that the other stars' being nourished from the earth is given after the Posidonian reference, and that the reference to the moon includes other information than about nourishment, shows that only the moon reference comes from Posidonius' *Natural Philosophy*.

COMMENT

ὡς P^3 is preferable to the emendation ὡς ὁ of *Vat. Urb.* 109, because Diogenes usually omits the article on such occasions.

For the moon being nourished from fresh water, sun from the sea, and the other stars from moisture from the earth, see F118. Add to the evidence there cited, Plu. *De Facie* 940D, and Stob. *Ecl.* I, p. 219.25 W (*SVF* II.677). See also F214 comm. *C.*

ἀερομιγής, i.e. a mixture of fire and air; F122 for evidence.

πρόσγειον. So already at the beginning of D.L. VII.145.

So also Cleom. *De Motu* II.3.99 (p. 178.26–180.20 Z), and Chrysippus, Stob. *Ecl.* I. p. 185.14ff W (Ar. Did. F31; *Dox. Gr.* 466). For distance, F120.

F11 Diogenes Laertius, VII.153

CONTENT

Φυσικὸς Λόγος, Bk 8. Snow.

CONTEXT

Diogenes' account of Stoic meteorology in chs. 152–4 is probably from mixed origins. Posidonius is cited by name three times, for rainbow, from *Meteorology*, for snow and for earthquakes from *Natural Philosophy* Bk 8. Immediately after this fragment Zeno, *On the Whole*, is cited for lightning, and certainly the theory of lightning and thunder given is not that of Posidonius (F135). Although the description of comets is not at variance with Posidonius (Frs. 131a, b, F132), and although no other named authority is given (apart from the single reference to Zeno), it must remain uncertain whether or to what extent the remainder of these meteorological chapters is dependent on Posidonius. For example, although we would expect accounts of hail and snow to stand together (F136), and although their description here appears parallel, the evidence and arguments in F136 leave it in doubt whether we can regard the definition of hail here as coming from Posidonius. The very sporadic nature of Diogenes' citations would advocate caution. See also T66 comm.

COMMENT

The account of snow is woefully brief, but seemingly individual in the stress on moisture (ὑγρόν) from the frozen cloud. All agreed with Aristotle (*Meteor.* I.11, 347b 23) that snow comes from a cloud that freezes, but the question remained what was the process of formation (cf. F136 for hail). Chrysippus (Ar. Did. F35 = Stob. *Ecl.* I. p. 245 W = *SVF* II.701) apparently said snow was a frozen cloud or the freezing of a cloud (i.e. the process is moisture → freezing). Compare *De Mundo* 394a 33ff, that snow occurs in the breaking up of condensed clouds which have split up *before the change to water*; and Arrian *ap.* Stob. *Ecl.* I, p. 247 W, that the cloud freezes into snow absolutely before it forms into water. It would appear that Posidonius thought rather of a frozen cloud liquefying (cf. again F136 on hail) until the moisture consistency of snowflakes was reached. That is still probably different from Anon. II, *Isag.* 8, p. 127 Maass, defining snow as rain drizzle (ὑετῶν ψακάς) *in* a frozen cloud.

F12 Diogenes Laertius, VII.154

CONTENT

The cause and classification of earthquakes.

CONTEXT

For the meteorological section in Diogenes §§152–4, see F11, Context. In §154 meteorological phenomena of wind, or air in motion (πνεῦμα), are being examined.

COMMENT

1 **πρηστήρ** is a hurricane or form of thunderstorm similar to but distinct from typhoon (τυφῶν). It cannot be assumed that this was Posidonius' rather than Chrysippus' definition; cf. *SVF* II.703, 705.

1–4 The text is very uncertain. Since after the reference to πρηστήρ we find ourselves in mid-sentence on earthquakes without introduction of subject, there must be an old lacuna which affected all the surviving codices. One solution is to accept that the new subject must be named, an alternative supplied to ἢ (2), and that the omission may have been due to the recurrence of the last word before the break. v. d. Mühll's ⟨σεισμοὺς δὲ γίνεσθαι εἰσδύοντος πνεύματος⟩ is an economical way of satisfying these conditions: 'earthquakes occur when wind enters the hollows of the earth, or when wind is shut up in the earth, as Posidonius says in the eighth book'. Even if this should be correct, the question remains whether the ascription to Posidonius refers to the whole sentence, or if alternatives are being offered, whether only the latter is assigned to Posidonius (as Reinhardt, *Poseidonios* 159 n. 1).

In Seneca's review of the history of the aetiology of earthquakes (*NQ* VI.5–21), which is different in comparable details from that in Arist. *Meteor.* II.7, theories which explained earthquakes by subterranean air in motion (πνεῦμα, *spiritus*) are dealt with in chs. 12–19 and 21ff. Although such theories may have agreed that the cause was the pressure of air forcing a way out, there were differences of opinion as to the actual operation, and also as to how the air got there in the first place. This is already in Aristotle, who criticised Anaxagoras on this point (*Meteor.* 365a 26ff), and himself held that the cause was dry exhalation, i.e. πνεῦμα, when the external exhalation flows inwards (366a 4), which can happen through porous places in the earth (366b 1, 367a 22ff).

In Seneca's review, the hypothesis of wind penetrating the earth from outside features in chs. 12.1 (Archelaus; Anaxagoras in Amm. Marc. 17.7.11), 13.4 (Strato), 14 (an anonymous analogy to the human body; and see esp. §3. The human analogy is already in Aristotle, *Meteor.* 366b 15ff), 15 (an anonymous theory of numerous perforations in the earth), 19 (Metrodorus of Chios), and later in ch. 23, Callisthenes (the nephew of Aristotle) is criticised for the hypothesis that air pours in through the porosity of earth and so creates pressure for the tilting kind of earthquake.

On the other hand, Seneca himself in ch. 24 rejects the theory of influx of air from above; he maintains that it is the subterranean air shut up in underground caverns (25) that is the cause. This narrower Senecan theory, which may be taken to correspond to the second alternative in Diogenes, was thought to be that of Posidonius by Reinhardt (*Poseidonios*), who attached to it also Seneca's earlier talk of *spiritus vitalis* in ch. 16. But while Seneca used Posidonius (Frs. 230, 232), he is certainly not simply reproducing him. He cites him on the classification of earthquakes (F230), but gives no indication whatsoever of Posidonius' stance on the details of the πνεῦμα theory. In fact the presentation of the objection to external influx of air is put in very personal terms in ch. 24.1–5; and Oltramare for example (Budé, *ad loc.*, p. 280 n. 2) thinks that Seneca was attacking Posidonius' theory, supposedly given in ch. 14.3; but this is equally speculation. Ps.-Arist. *De Mundo* 395b 30ff assumes both natural subterranean πνεῦμα *and* incursion of external air shut up in the hollows (κοιλώμασιν, cf. F12.2) of earth, but we cannot be certain that this is Posidonius either (as Gilbert, *Griechische Meteorologie* 317), although it may be.

Also, ἤ in line 2 offers a strange exclusive alternative, in that a theory of external influx could also hold a theory of trapped air. The Suda, *s.v.* σεισμός, quotes, obviously from the same source as Diogenes: πνεύματος εἰς τὰ κοιλώματα τῆς γῆς ἐγκαθειρχθέντος. Perhaps then ἤ is a corruption, and something like ⟨σεισμοὺς δὲ γίνεσθαι πνεύματος⟩ εἰς τὰ κοιλώματα τῆς γῆς ἐγκαθειρχθέντος [πνεύματος ἐν τῇ γῇ] is nearer the mark. At all events, Diogenes' evidence permits merely the conclusion that Posidonius thought that πνεῦμα trapped in subterranean caverns was the cause of earthquakes, and we can infer nothing further.

4 It is very strange that the number of Posidonius' book is given, ἐν τῇ ῆ, without the book itself. Bake, p. 83, suggested ἐν τῇ Μετεωρολογικῇ, presumably because of the feminine τῇ (cf. Capelle, *Neue Jahrbücher für das klassische Altertum* 21 (1908) 612. But Diogenes can use either τῇ or τῷ with a book number (e.g. F5.7; F13.2). It has been argued that the eighth book of Φυσικὸς λόγος is meant, since it had just been mentioned (D.L. VII.153 = F11). It is possible that Bk 8 of *Natural Philosophy* was devoted to the aetiology of natural phenomena (F11), but a further lacuna may be suspected, and therefore Posidonius' book remains in doubt.

4–6 For the explanation of the terms, and the classification of earthquakes: F230.

F13 Diogenes Laertius, VII.142

CONTENT

Posidonius, *On the Universe* Bk I, is cited as a general authority on the generation and destruction of the universe, in a list which names Zeno and Chrysippus before him, and Cleanthes and Antipater after.

CONTEXT

The passage occurs in the extended report by Diogenes (VII. 137–43) on the Stoic cosmos. It is immediately preceded by arguments for the destruction of the cosmos (141) and by an account of its generation (142). It is followed by the statement: 'But Panaetius declared that the universe is indestructible.' F6 comes before this section, and F99a follows.

COMMENT

A. The list

This list of authorities is remarkable on two counts:

(1) for its length. To name as many as five references is a practice in Diogenes found only in the Stoic doxography of VII.38–159. Mejer (*Hermes, Einzelschr.* 40 (1978), p. 6) argued that this pointed to a single common source for the whole doxography, such as Diocles of Magnesia. T66 comm. shows, however, that different sections of the main doxography have different characteristics.

Such lists usually are given in chronological order (but cf. F8); but here Cleanthes and Antipater are named after Posidonius. This may indicate that Posidonius was regarded as a principal authority on the same level as Zeno and Chrysippus. For the prominence of Posidonius in the section on cosmos (137–43): F99a comm.

(2) The list gives general references to a whole topic, not evidence for a particular statement, variant or deviation (cf. F6). That implies that Posidonius is not only a principal, but a main-line, orthodox authority on the topic of generation and destruction of the universe, a position reinforced by the addendum of a deviant opinion held by Panaetius. For the structure, cf. the addition of Boethus in F99a.

B. φθορᾶς τοῦ κόσμου

Since before the list general arguments are given that the

universe is subject to destruction, and since immediately after the list the precise objection is added: 'But Panaetius declared that the universe is indestructible' (cf. van Straaten, Frs. 64–9), it follows from A (1) and (2) above, that Posidonius, with the others in the list, believed the universe to be destructible. This is supported by F97, which discusses the void into which the cosmos disperses on destruction, and is not countered by F99b, where Posidonius' name has been unnecessarily and wrongly conjectured (see F99b comm.).

C. τῆς γενέσεως καὶ φθορᾶς τοῦ κόσμου

From A (1) and (2) it should also follow that the general remarks in 141–2 on generation and destruction were supported and even evidenced by Posidonius' book *On the Universe*.

They are:

(1) Arguments for destruction (141).

(a) Inasmuch as the world is γενητός it is also φθαρτός on the analogy (τῷ λόγῳ) of our concept of sensible things.

(b) That of which the parts are subject to destruction, is itself perishable as a whole. But the parts of the universe are perishable since they change into each other (εἰς ἄλληλα γὰρ μεταβάλλει; cf. F96); therefore the universe is φθαρτός. For this argument see also Philo, *SVF* I.106, p. 30.30ff Arn.

(c) If anything admits of change to the worse (a teleological argument?), it is perishable. But the universe dries up (ἐξαυχμοῦται; cf. Cic. *ND* II.118 = *SVF* II.593) and changes into a watery state; therefore it is perishable. In general cf. Alexander, *SVF* II.594.

(2) Generation (142)

The universe comes into being when its substance (οὐσία) turns from fire through air (ἀέρος) into water. Then (εἶτα), the thicker part contracts into earth, the finer part becomes airy and this refines further to generate fire.

(cf. *SVF* I.102; II.579; II.413)

(Or diagrammatically: fire→air→water
earth—┴—air
|
fire)

Then from mixture of these (elements) come plants, animals and all other kinds (γένη).

It would obviously be dangerous to assume that all these statements as reported were to be found in Posidonius' Περὶ κόσμου, but we are entitled to suppose that Diogenes' source believed that Posidonius supported such orthodox accounts of the generation and destruction of the universe.

D. ᾱ Περὶ κόσμου

πρώτῳ BP: τῷ F. *Cod.* F. is capricious in reporting precise bibliographical reference, and often omits it altogether (cf. lines 2–3, 4 app. crit.). Posidonius' work had more than one book. His remarks on cosmos were not of course confined to Περὶ κόσμου: Frs. 4, 8, 14, 20, 21, 23, 99a.

F14 Diogenes Laertius, VII.138

CONTENT

Posidonius' *Meteorology* is cited for a definition of the universe (κόσμος) as a systematic compound (σύστημα) composed from heaven (οὐρανοῦ) and earth and the natural constitutions (φύσεων) in them. An alternative version, which may or may not also be referred to Posidonius, is added: a systematic compound composed from gods and men and what has come into being for their sake.

CONTEXT

The passage occurs near the start of Diogenes' extended report on the Stoic universe (137–43; F99a comm.), which begins with a tripartition of usages of κόσμος: (1) god himself (cf. *SVF* I.88; I.163; II.1027); (2) διακόσμησις τῶν ἀστέρων (cf. *SVF* II.645; II.527); (3) the combination of (1) and (2) (e.g. *SVF* I.160; Ps.-Arist. *De Mundo* II.391b 11f). F14 follows. It is succeeded by a sentence on οὐρανός (heaven): heaven is the outermost circumference (ἡ ἐσχάτη περιφέρεια) on which is established all divinity (πᾶν τὸ θεῖον). Then comes F21.

COMMENT

1 The definition of κόσμος as the individually qualified being (ὁ ἰδίως ποιός) of the substance of the whole, echoes the first sense of κόσμος given in §137 (see Context), as god, τὸν θεὸν τὸν ἐκ τῆς ἁπάσης οὐσίας ἰδίως ποιόν. Cf. *SVF* II.528, p. 169.17 Arn.; *SVF* II.590; II.624; I.163. ἰδίως ποιός conveys the individuation of the whole of substance, F96 comm. This definition is not assigned to anyone in particular. We may assume that it was held by all Stoics including Posidonius.

2–3 On the other hand, it is surprising that Posidonius is singled out as evidence for the second definition, because the doxographers assign it to Chrysippus (Stob. *Ecl.* I. p. 184.9f W = Ar. Did. F31, p. 465.14f Diels = *SVF* II.527), or to the Stoa in general (Ar. Did. F29 (Eusebius), p. 464.18ff Diels = *SVF* II.528). It does however recur in authors or works which for various reasons have been associated with Posidonius; e.g. Cleomedes, *De Motu* I.1.1, p. 2.9f Ziegler = *SVF* II.529; Galen in *SVF* II.638; Ps.-Arist. *De Mundo* II.391b 9f (see Diels, *Dox. Gr.*, *Prol.* 77). So while it no doubt was a standard definition, it may have become particularly familiar through Posidonius' meteorological work. For the meaning of φύσεων (3): *SVF* II.527.

3–4 The third definition is again linked to the second as an alternative in Stob. *Ecl.* I, p. 184.10f W = *SVF* II.527; cf. also *SVF* II.528. There is no reason to believe that Posidonius did not also hold it, but the reference to *Meteorology* is more apt for the second than the third definition. The Suda's στοιχείων for θεῶν in line 3 can hardly be correct, and may have arisen from στοιχειώσει in the preceding line.

Rist (*Stoic Philosophy* 204) assumed that the following sentence, 'heaven is the outermost circumference on which is established all divinity', is also assigned to Posidonius. This may be true, but is by no means certain from the report of Diogenes. Elsewhere Posidonius followed Zeno and Chrysippus in saying that the whole of the universe (κόσμον) and the heaven (οὐρανόν) was the substance of god (F20; *SVF* I.163; II.1022). But he also thought that heaven was the ἡγεμονικόν of the universe (F23), and ἡ ἐσχάτη περιφέρεια has a Posidonian ring, so Rist may be right. But see F20 comm.

The title of the book is given as Μετεωρολογικὴ Στοιχείωσις, which is clearly the same as ἡ Μετεωρολογική of F15. But scholars are divided as to whether this is identical with (Susemihl, *Geschichte der griechischen Literatur* II.138, 189; Schmekel, *Philosophie der mittleren Stoa* 14, n.5; Laffranque, p. 100) or different from (Bake, 241ff; Zeller, *Die Philosophie der Griechen* III.1.194.3; Manitius, *Geminus* 239–45; Reinhardt, *RE* 568) the work referred to as Περὶ μετεώρων in Frs. 16, 17. Schmekel, Rehm (*Sitzungsberichte der Bayerischen Akademie* (1921), 46.5) and Laffranque also suggested that Μετ. Στ. may alternatively have been an abridgement or epitome of Περὶ μετ. Diogenes' source gives book numbers for Περί μετ. but not for Μετ. Στ. However, στοιχείωσις does not mean 'abridgement', but 'elementary treatise', and so it is probable that not only were the books not identical, but they were different in character. If so, it is likely that Μετ. Στ. was more popular with later readers, and it is noticeable that both Frs. 14 and 15 have echoes in the doxographies. See also F18.

For cosmos, also Frs. 4, 8, 13, 20, 21, 23, 99.

F15 Diogenes Laertius, VII.152

CONTENT

Μετεωρολογικὴ στοιχείωσις. Definition of rainbow.

CONTEXT

Diogenes is reeling off a succession of Stoic definitions of τῶν ἐν ἀέρι γινομένων. Rainbow follows winds, and is followed by comets.

COMMENT

Posidonius defines rainbow as an appearance in reflection (ἔμφασιν) of a section of sun or moon in a dewy cloud that is hollow and continuous in appearance, the impression being revealed as in a mirror as an arc of a circle. The wording is almost exactly reproduced in Ps.-Arist. *De Mundo* IV.395a 33ff. A similar phraseology occurs in Arius Didymus F14, *Dox. Gr.* p. 455.15f, but under the name of Aristotle.

For Posidonius' theory of rainbow in general, and other references, see F134.

ἔμφασιν: the effect was merely optical (κατ' ἔμφασιν) not substantial (καθ' ὑπόστασιν); F134.

σελήνης: Aristotle, *Meteor.* III.2.372a 22f acknowledged that rainbows could occur through the moon at night, but that this was rare and unknown to οἱ ἀρχαῖοι.

δεδροσισμένῳ: recalls Aristotle's theory, whereby the reflector was not the cloud as a whole, but the multiplicity of individual raindrops in it. *De Mundo* has νοτερῷ, and Posidonius can only have wished to call attention to the wetness of the cloud, rather than the drops in it.

κοίλῳ will refer to the theory of the shape of the cloud like a ball cut in half: F134.

συνεχεῖ πρὸς φαντασίαν: Against Aristotle, Posidonius wished to maintain the whole cloud as a single reflector: F134.

ὡς ἐν κατόπτρῳ: For the arguments for and against mirror reflection: F134, F133.

κατὰ κύκλου περιφέρειαν: Posidonius appears to have been more concerned to explain the shape of rainbows (how an arc can be a *reflection* of an orb), rather than its colours, which appears to have been of more interest to Aristotle: F134.

F16 Diogenes Laertius, VII.135

CONTENT

'Plane surface (ἐπιφάνεια) is the limit (πέρας) of body, or that which has length and breadth only, but not depth. This (i.e. surface) was admitted by Posidonius, in *Meteorological Phenomena*, Bk 5, to exist both in thought and reality.'

CONTEXT

The immediate context occurs in a section dealing with body (σῶμα). 'Body' is defined by Apollodorus (in *Physics*) as that which has three-dimensional extension, length, breadth and depth; this is also called solid body (στερεὸν σῶμα). Then comes F16. It is followed by a definition of line as limit of plane surface (or length without breadth, or that which has length only); and of point, which is the least possible sign (or mark or dot, σημεῖον), as limit of line.

The whole section appears in Diogenes' report on the physics, coming after the account of the principles (ἀρχαί) (F5). For questions on source and Posidonian influence: F99a comm.

COMMENT

Stoics defined body both in terms of acting and being acted upon, and as three-dimensional extension (cf. Ps.-Gal. *H. Phil*, ch. 23 = *Dox. Gr.* p. 612; S.E. *Hyp.* III.38–9 (but cf. *Adv. Math.* IX. 366–7, where the distinction is referred to Pythagoreans and οἱ μαθηματικοί); Mansfeld, 'Zeno of Citium', *Mnem.* 31 (1978), 158–67). For three-dimensional extension as σῶμα: *SVF* II.357; and for στερεὸν σῶμα: *SVF* II.358. But the Stoics also thought that mathematical limits (surface, line, point) were not corporeal (σώματα), but merely concepts (κατ' ἐπίνοιαν ψιλήν). This is clear from Plutarch (*Comm. Not.* 1080E = *SVF* II.487; cf. 1078E = *SVF* II.485 and Cherniss's notes in Loeb edn *ad locc.*), Proclus, *In Eucl.* (*SVF* II.488; II.365), and from the doxographies (Stobaeus, *SVF* II.482; cf. also Cleomedes, *De Motu* I.1.7, p. 14.2 Ziegler). In this the School was following the Aristotelian criticism of Plato and others (Arist. *Meteor.* III.5; VII.2).

Posidonius' move to regard plane surface as existing in reality as well as being conceptual is therefore heretical, and appears to have had no subsequent influence on the School. It may well have been stimulated by Plato (cf. *Tim.* 53c ff); but it appears to be closely connected with Posidonius' views on σχῆμα (shape or form), as the corporeal containing limit, which is the cause of definiteness, limitation and inclusion of that which is contained or limited (F196). Even this may have its roots in Plato: cf. *Meno* 76a, στερεοῦ πέρας σχῆμα εἶναι (Bréhier, 'Posidonius d'Apamée. Théoricien de la Géométrie', *REG* 27 (1914), 56 n. 2); cf. Aetius, *Dox. Gr.* 312a 9f, b 12f: σχῆμά ἐστι ἐπιφάνεια καὶ περιγραφὴ καὶ πέρας σώματος.

It has been thought (e.g. by Edelstein, *AJPh* 57 (1936), 303) that this ontological mathematical theory of Posidonius affected his definition and interpretation of soul. And it is true that Posidonius referred to soul as 'form' (F140), emphasised its containing function of body (F149), and was known to have defined it in mathematical terms (F141). But there are grave difficulties in pressing the connection too far, as in regarding soul as an enveloping πέρας, or as a two-dimensional existent; see commentary on Frs. 139–41, 149. Again, whether the theory affected Posidonius' concept of cosmic structure, with the οὐρανός as ἡ ἐσχάτη περιφέρεια, and so also his concept of the active principle of the universe (Rist, *Stoic Philosophy* 204ff) remains speculative; see Frs. 14, 20, 23 comm. But it is reasonable to think that there was some connection, since this information comes from Περὶ μετεώρων, and therefore must have had some relation to heavenly phenomena.

It should be noted that the evidence explicitly (ταύτην, 2) connects Posidonius' theory of mathematical reality with plane surface only, and not with all mathematical πέρατα or limits. After the interruption of the Posidonian reference to plane figures, Diogenes continues with line and point (see Context). The description of point as σημεῖον ἐλάχιστον is strange, however. So it is dangerous to build any theories on 'punctual existence' (as Edelstein, p. 302). Certainly, in his definition of time, Posidonius does not (*pace* Edelstein, 302 n. 66) employ the notion of punctual existence (F98 comm.).

The distinction between κατ' ἐπίνοιαν and καθ' ὑπόστασιν is used effectively by Posidonius in his examination of οὐσία and ὕλη: F92.

ἀπολείπει: cf. D.L. VII.54 = F42.

The fragment recurs in the Suda, *s.v.* ἐπιφάνεια (Adler, 1.2.391 n. 2739), but the reference to Posidonius is omitted, so that the last part runs: αὕτη δὲ κατ' ἐπίνοιαν καὶ καθ' ὑπόστασιν λέγεται.

F17 Diogenes Laertius, VII.144

CONTENT

Composition of sun.

CONTEXT

The paragraph in Diogenes is complex. (a) Posidonius Περὶ μετεώρων Bk 7 is quoted for the composition of the sun (this Fr.); (b) *Natural Philosophy*, Bk 6 for its size (F9.1–2); (c) οἱ περὶ Ποσειδώνιον on the shape of the sun (F117); Diogenes than adds information on (a) (F17.2), followed by further matter on (b) (F9.2–5). Thus the arrangement is (a-b-c-a-b).

COMMENT

ἐν ζ̄: see vol. I, *Introduction* xxv for F's omission. Numeralised iota adscripts are not uncommon in the codices of D.L., so perhaps we should read ἐν τῷ ζ̄ to explain *P*'s ιζ̄. *B* may be right, however; book numbers are not always accompanied by the article; cf. Frs. 16, 20.

εἱλικρινὲς πῦρ: also Chrysippus, *SVF* II.413 (Stobaeus). That the sun had a fiery composition was a common Presocratic view (Gilbert, *Griechische Meteorologie* 688ff). Aristotle, *De Caelo* II.7, maintained that the stars were not πύρινα, but were composed of a fifth element. The Stoics reaffirmed that the sun was πύρινος (of a vital organic kind of fire): Cic. *ND* II.40–1 (Cleanthes, *SVF* I.504; cf. Pos. F118 note); *SVF* II.677 (Plu. *De Facie* 940C), II.579 (Plu. *De SR* 1053A); compare the definition of sun as ἄναμμα νοερόν (Cleanthes, *SVF* I.501, accepted by Chrysippus, *SVF* II.652, 655; Pos. F118 comm.). Aristotle deliberately separated the fifth element, the celestial quality. Stoics in reverting to fire (even a πῦρ τεχνικόν, *SVF* I.120) do not admit any difference of kind between the celestial sphere and the terrestrial one.

εἱλικρινές is presumably used to distinguish sun from moon, which is ἀερομιγής (F10, F122). εἱλικρινής was a favourite word of Plato's. The phrase εἱλικρινὲς πῦρ occurs in *Tim.* 45b (and cf. *Tim.* 76b 2), but the adjective has special associations with the Forms in the sense of καθαρόν (*Symp.* 211e; *Phil.* 52d; Ast, *Lexicon*, and Des Places, *Lexique*, *s.v.*). Compare the composition of stars in general, F127.

F18 Simplicius, *In Aristotelis Physica* II.2 (193b 23); pp. 291.21–292.31 Diels

CONTENT

The distinction between physical philosophy (φυσιολογία) and astronomy (ἀστρολογία).

CONTEXT

Simplicius is commenting on Aristotle's distinction in *Phys.* B.2 between physics and mathematics.

The precise genealogy of the Posidonian extract is given (1–3). Simplicius found it in Alexander of Aphrodisias, who had taken pains (φιλοπόνως, 1) to set out a quotation from Geminus, which came from the latter's epitome of Posidonius' *Meteorology*. Whether Geminus is to be dated to the 1st c. B.C. or to the 1st c. A.D. (T42), he was certainly well acquainted at first hand with Posidonius' work. His abridgement of Posidonius' *Meteorology* probably became popular because Priscianus Lydus also knew Posidonius' meteorology through Geminus (T72). Μετεωρολογικά is a somewhat general title, and there is no evidence to clarify further which precise meteorological book (F14 comm.) or even combination of books Geminus may have gutted. Simplicius suspected (50) that this extract is a direct quotation from Posidonius. He is very probably correct. The style (νὴ Δία, 7; cf. Frs. 165.166; 168.8) and the detail of argument (e.g. 39 ff) smack of the real thing. The careful history of the tradition also seems to guarantee authenticity.

Simplicius maintains (3, 52) that Posidonius took the starting points of his exposition (ἐξηγήσεως (3) is probably to be taken with τὰς ἀφορμάς) from Aristotle. While Posidonius might well have made such a remark himself, this must be an expression of opinion on Simplicius' part, otherwise it would have been included in the extract, which as it stands is probably the whole of what Simplicius found in Alexander. Simplicius no doubt has *Phys.* B.2 in mind; but cf. also *De Respiratione* 193b 23ff on the relationship between physics and medicine. Posidonius also owes something to Plato's distinction between dialectic and the τέχναι at the end of Bk VI and in Bk VII of *Rep.* But Posidonius' exposition is distinctively Stoic in orientation in the first part, and from 30ff peculiarly his own.

COMMENT

A. Subject matter (5–18)

First, natural philosophy (φυσικὴ θεωρία) and astronomy (ἀστρολογία) are distinguished (μὲν . . . δέ, 5, 8) with reference to subject matter. It is the task of natural philosophy to examine (σκοπεῖν) in the case of heaven and stars their substance (οὐσία), power (δύναμις), quality and generation and destruction. By δύναμις probably ἡ ποιητικὴ δύναμις (26) is meant; i.e. the λόγος or active force in the universe. So the philosopher is dealing with the two principles of the universe in the heaven and heavenly bodies (cf. Frs. 20, 127, 128, 5, 92, 100–2). For γένεσις and φθορά: F13. Posidonius adds with emphasis (for the vivid νὴ Δία as characteristic of Posidonius' style, see Context) that the philosopher can even prove questions relating to their size, shape and order. The stress is on proof (ἀποδεικνύναι) as distinct from description (λέγει, 11), and the singulars μεγέθους etc. (7) contrast with the plurals in line 11. Fundamental general questions of size and shape are meant, rather than detailed individual calculations; e.g. F8. But already Posidonius is introducing common areas of investigation to be explained later (18ff). καὶ νὴ Δία . . . δύναται (7f) is parenthetical. Bake's νὴ Δία ⟨διὰ⟩ is tempting.

On the other hand, astronomy (i.e. the scientist) attempts

to talk about nothing of that kind (i.e. οὐσία, δύναμις κτλ); it proves the order or arrangement of the heavenly bodies, 'having declared that' (i.e. on the basis of the preliminary acceptance that) the heaven is really a cosmos (which it takes from philosophy). It talks about the shapes (plural), sizes and distances of the earth, sun and moon, about eclipses and conjunctions of the stars, and about the quality and extent of their movements. So, since it touches on the enquiry into how big, how much, what sort in relation to figure (σχῆμα), it naturally needs the sciences of number and measurement (ἀριθμητική, γεωμετρία). For what alone it claims to give an account of, it is capable of bringing about through mathematics. Cf. Plu. *De Facie* 942B.

B. Method (18–30)

Although there is a real distinction in subject matter, this is still inadequate because the area or field of investigation of philosopher and scientist can overlap. 'Often both natural philosopher and astronomer will propose proving the same point (κεφάλαιον): the sun is large, the earth is spherical; but (οὐ μήν, a strong adversative) they will not go by the same routes (or methods, ὁδούς)' (18–21).

The critique now concentrates on difference of method, which is further subdivided:

(i) The direction of argument is still allied to the proper subject matter. 'The philosopher will demonstrate each fact from (ἀποδείξει ἀπό) substance (οὐσία), or force (δύναμις), or value (ἄμεινον οὕτως ἔχειν), or generation and change (μεταβολή); the astronomer will establish them from the properties of the figures and magnitudes, or from the amount of the movement, and the time that is appropriate to it' (21–5). In other words the philosopher argues deductively from his fundamental universal principles or axioms; the scientist proceeds in his proofs from the observation and calculation of the properties of the particular phenomena which form his field of study.

(ii) But the basic difference lies in cause or explanation (αἰτία). 'The philosopher will often fasten on to (ἅψεται, 26) the cause, concentrating on (ἀποβλέπων εἰς; the phrase is strongly Platonic, often used by Plato for concentrating on the Forms, e.g. *Euth.* 6e 4, *Men.* 72c 8) the creative force (τὴν ποιητικὴν δύναμιν, 26; i.e. the λόγος). The astronomer however (a) whenever he proves facts from external conditions, is not an adequate observer of cause, e.g. when he states that the earth or the stars are spherical (27–9); and (b) sometimes he does not aim at grasping the cause at all, e.g. when he discusses eclipses' (29f). That is, science is mainly descriptive, and when it seems to deal with causes, the explanation is always inadequate.

C. The limitations of science and its dependence on philosophy (30–49)

So far the tenor of the argument is familiar from Plato and Aristotle, as Simplicius remarked, although the approach and framework is entirely Stoic (οὐσία in the Stoic sense, and ἡ ποιητικὴ δύναμις), and above all Posidonian with the stress on αἰτιολογία (T85). What follows attempts to be more precise about the limitations of scientific method, and is distinctively Posidonian. It does not seem to me that the implications of the argument have been clearly seen.

30–9 'Sometimes the scientist tries to find out (εὑρίσκει) by hypothesis, stating some ways (methods, τρόπους) by which, if established (ὧν ὑπαρχόντων), the phenomena will be saved. E.g. why do some heavenly bodies seem to move irregularly (with respect to the ecliptic, or with respect to the sun); if we suppose their circuits to be eccentric, or the stars to revolve in epicycles, their apparent irregularity will be saved; and it will be necessary to pursue the argument in accordance with *how many* ways (τρόπους) these phenomena can be produced; so that their study of the planets *is like* (ἐοικέναι) the enquiry into cause (αἰτιολογίᾳ) in respect of the *possible* method (κατὰ τὸν ἐνδεχόμενον τρόπον).' The scientist with his hypothetical method seems to save the phenomena by giving an explanation, but the point is that a number of alternative hypotheses (eccentric circles or epicycles or the like as suggested by scientists like Apollonius of Perge and Hipparchus) may accommodate the phenomena, and the scientist cannot tell which is *the* αἰτία, since he works only with possible ὑποθέσεις.

39–49 So it is easy to confuse scientific hypothesis with explanation, but if so one is confusing the spheres of science and philosophy. 'And that is why you actually have a man like Heraclides Ponticus coming forward and saying that even if (καί) the earth is moving somehow (πως) and the sun stands still somehow (πως), the apparent anomaly with regard to the sun is saved. For (γάρ, 42) it is not the job of the astronomer at all (ὅλως) to know what is at rest by nature or what sort of things are capable of motion; rather, introducing hypotheses, granting that some things stay still and others are in motion, he enquires which hypotheses celestial phenomena will accommodate. He must take principles (ἀρχάς) from the natural philosopher, that the movements of the stars are simple, uniform (ὁμαλάς) and orderly, and through these principles he will demonstrate that the rhythmic motion (χορείαν, cf. Pl. *Tim.* 40c) of all the stars revolves in a circular fashion, with some moving in parallel (i.e. the fixed stars) and others in ecliptic circles (i.e. the planets).'

39f Heath (*Aristarchus*, 275–83) showed clearly the difficulty of reconciling ἡ περὶ τὸν ἥλιον φαινομένη ἀνωμαλία (41) with Heraclides' theory of the rotation of the earth. For this reason he agreed with Tannery (*REG* XII (1899), 305–11) in deleting the words Ἡρακλείδης ὁ Ποντικός. It is true that Frs. 104–8 (Wehrli) of Heraclides refer to diurnal rotation of the earth, and that is a quite distinct problem from the movement of the planets, which has been in question since 32ff.

However, there was a tradition surviving in Simplicius (*In Ar. De Caelo*, Frs. 106, 108 Wehrli), which in general terms associated Heraclides with 'trying to save the phenomena' (cf. 32) by a hypothesis that the earth was in motion and the heavens at rest, and in F108 he is coupled with Aristarchus. This is not an argument for Posidonius believing that Heraclides had a heliocentric theory like Aristarchus; it merely establishes that Heraclides was well known for trying to save the phenomena with a hypothesis of earth being in motion in some way (cf. πως, 40). But why then did Posidonius not cite Aristarchus or Seleucus who were more apposite for the immediate problem of planetary irregularity? Perhaps because what is at issue here is simply a hypothesis παρὰ φύσιν, namely that earth is in motion in some fashion. This is where the philosopher will come in, according to Posidonius, and say that you must not hypothesise like that (42–5). He may have chosen Heraclides, and not Aristarchus or Seleucus, because they were scientists, but Heraclides was a philosopher, and as a φυσικός he should have known better than to challenge philosophical postulates of what moves and is at rest by nature. The ἀρχαί must come from natural philosophy, and be accepted by the scientist for his hypotheses (46–9). So τις (39) may be contemptuous (LSJ *s.v.* A6). See also Wehrli, F110 comm.

D. Posidonius' theory in relation to subsequent evidence

There are a number of echoes and reactions to the kind of position put forward by Posidonius. Diogenes Laertius (VII.132–3) in his account of the universe gives a generic section of φυσικὸς λόγος subdivided under the headings οἱ φυσικοί and οἱ ἀπὸ τῶν μαθημάτων (i.e. scientists). They are distinguished by subject matter, roughly on Posidonian lines. Another subdivision concerns τὸ αἰτιολογικόν, doctors researching into the ἡγεμονικὸν τῆς ψυχῆς and such matters, οἱ ἀπὸ τῶν μαθημάτων concerned with how we see, the explanation of mirror image, the composition of clouds, thunder, rainbows, haloes, comets. These are all Posidonian scientific subjects, but Diogenes betrays no knowledge of Posidonius' relationship between science and philosophy.

Strabo, II.5.2 is more interesting in accepting Posidonius' dependence of science on philosophy. In matters of the principles, geographers must rely on geometricians, who must depend on astronomers, who in turn must rely on natural philosophers. Physical philosophy is a kind of ἀρετή, in that it is ἀνυπόθετος, depends on itself and contains in itself its own principles and proofs. This is illustrated by a list of topics which depend on οἱ φυσικοί, which again is similar to Posidonius and includes the immobility of the earth. οἱ ἀστρονομικοί accept all these from οἱ φυσικοί, then work out τὰ ἑξῆς: namely movements, orbits, eclipses, magnitudes, respective distances and much else. οἱ γεωμέτραι adhere to the above in measuring the earth, and οἱ γεωγράφοι adhere to the findings of the γεωμέτραι.

But there are signs of a debate in progress between those who believed that science was dependent on deductions from a system of philosophy and those who insisted that the sciences must rest on observation and empirical experience. Diodorus of Alexandria, a contemporary of Cicero, repeats the gist of what Posidonius said (Achilles, *Commentariorum in Aratum Reliquiae* 2, p. 30.20ff Maass). On the other hand, Xenarchus, a teacher of Strabo, attempted in a pamphlet Πρὸς τὴν πέμπτην οὐσίαν (reported in Simplicius, *In Ar. De Caelo*) to demolish Aristotle's philosophical postulate of a fifth essence on scientific grounds. Dercyllides, a Platonist possibly of the time of Augustus, is said by Theon of Smyrna (199.9ff, Hiller) to have compared the methodology of astronomy with geometrical proof: unless you first lay down the hypotheses (he meant postulates in the sense of ἀρχαί of geometry), you cannot grasp the arguments which come after the ἀρχαί. Theon of Smyrna again (166.4–10, Hiller) records that Hipparchus said that it was worth the mathematician's attention to see the explanation (αἰτίαν) whereby from such different hypotheses as eccentric or homocentric circles or epicycles, the same results seem to follow. But the reply to this (188.19ff, Hiller) was that it was because Hipparchus was not equipped from natural philosophy for the journey (διὰ τὸ μὴ ἐφωδιάσθαι ἀπὸ φυσιολογίας) that he did not see that it was the task of the philosopher of nature to decide that question; cf. Plu. *De Facie* 921D. Finally Simplicius (*In Ar. De Caelo*, 1.2.17b 16ff, p. 32, 29ff Heiberg): 'Obviously, it is no matter of complaint or reproach that people differ on these hypotheses (i.e. of astronomy); for the subject matter (τὸ προκείμενον) is, on what hypothesis (τίνος ὑποτεθέντος) would the phenomena be saved. So it is no wonder if people tried to save the phenomena from different hypotheses.' Cf. in general, Duhem, *Le système du monde* 1.59ff.

To what extent Posidonius stimulated this controversy cannot now be judged, but his own position is quite clear. Epicurus said that all such alternative scientific hypotheses were equally true; Posidonius thought that they were equally inadequate. Philosopher and scientist investigated their own fields by their own distinctive methods. It was important that these should not be confused. Science was either descriptive or could work out possible lines of explanation only. This was like aetiology, but it was only philosophy which could give ultimate and decisive explanation, and arbitrate the hypotheses of the scientists. Science in its hypothetical method was subject to the principles of natural philosophy. But in a sense philosophy and science were complementary, and science too was necessary for physical philosophy (F90). For alternative possible hypotheses in Posidonius compare F138 and F219 (moon and tides), and F210 and F49 (cool equatorial strip).

For the general question of the relationship of philosophy and science in Posidonius: Kidd, *Antike und Abendland* XXIV (1978), 7–15.

F19 Cleomedes, *De Motu* I.11.65

CONTENT

A work by Posidonius on the size of the sun.

CONTEXT

The sentence comes at the end of *De Motu*, Bk I, introducing a subject and authorities for Bk II. Compare T67 for the sentence which ends Bk II.

COMMENT

περὶ μόνου τούτου συντάγματα πεποιηκότων must indicate monographs on the subject in question, and Posidonius is singled out as one of these authors.

Was the subject (περὶ μόνου τούτου) primarily an attack on the Epicurean view that the sun was, as it appeared, a foot in diameter, or was it a monograph on the size of the sun, in which Epicurean theories were incidentally attacked? For the first alternative: Frs. 46, 47; but the second seems more likely (cf. F22 in Περὶ θεῶν). In *De Motu* II.1 the criticism of Epicurus seems mainly the concern of Cleomedes, while the named references to Posidonius (Frs. 114, 115) concentrate on the size and distance of the sun.

Was the σύνταγμα a separate monograph (so Bake, p. 242), or perhaps a single book of a larger work (F. Boll, *Studien über Cl. Ptolemäus*, p. 138)? For the latter cf. F41a. Perhaps it was Bk 6 of the Φυσικὸς Λόγος, cf. F9. But this book also contained general observations on the moon (F10), and had no special title known to Diogenes Laertius. It is true that no title is given by Cleomedes either, but περὶ μόνου τούτου σύνταγμα suggests a separate monograph, as διὰ μεγάλης πραγματείας ἰδίᾳ γεγραμμένης of F38. Certainly it would be wrong to argue (as Susemihl) that since the subject is handled in Φυσικὸς Λόγος, Bk 6, it could not be the subject of a separate book. Compare the literary spread of Posidonius' treatment of mantics.

If Posidonius did write such a work, it is nevertheless possible that Cleomedes did not know it directly (cf. Reinhardt, *Poseidonios*, 185). F115 would presumably derive from it, and possibly F114 (which, however, relates to F119). The garbled evidence of F120 is of more uncertain provenance.

This fragment reveals that Posidonius was only one source for Cleomedes (in a collection of material?). Therefore the whole of *De Motu* II.1 must certainly not be taken as deriving from Posidonius.

F20 Diogenes Laertius, VII.148

CONTENT

'Zeno says that the substance (οὐσίαν) of god is the whole universe (κόσμον) and heaven (οὐρανόν); a similar version is given by Chrysippus, *On Gods*, Bk I, and by Posidonius, *On Gods*, Bk I. And Antipater, *On the Universe*, Bk 7, says that god's substance (οὐσίαν) is airlike (ἀεροειδῆ); Boethus, *On Nature* says that the sphere of the fixed stars is god's substance (οὐσίαν).'

CONTEXT

Section 147 begins Diogenes' report on god. God is a living creature, deathless, rational, perfect and intelligent in happiness, receptive of no evil, and provident for the universe and the things in the universe. He is not anthropomorphic. He is the artificer of all things together, as it were the father of all, both in general and that part of him which pervades everything, which is called many names according to different powers.

So far no references or deviations have been given, so what has been said is presumably regarded as common ground. F20 follows with the first variations on οὐσία θεοῦ. Diogenes then passes to φύσις, which is followed by fate, εἱμαρμένη, F25. For the order: F103.

COMMENT

Diogenes' note is confused and puzzling. In the first place, οὐσία with reference to the whole universe and heaven cannot be used in the same sense as Antipater's οὐσία qualified as airlike. The latter is in the same category as Posidonius' interpretation of god as πνεῦμα νοερόν (F100). Diogenes, or his source, appears to have been collecting occurrences of οὐσία θεοῦ, without regard to the particular reference.

Secondly, the whole universe and heaven is odd, because heaven should be a part of the whole universe. Again, although κόσμος can itself mean οὐρανός (Isocr. 4.179; Arist. *Met.* 339a 20), so that τὸν οὐρανόν could be explanatory of κόσμον, it can not be so of τὸν ὅλον κόσμον. Nor could τὸν ὅλον κόσμον be used in the sense of κόσμος as earth as opposed to heaven (Stob. *Ecl.* 1.49.44).

Therefore, καὶ τὸν οὐρανόν must be added with emphasis: 'and in particular, heaven' (Denniston, *Greek Particles*[2] 291). Posidonius wished to stress the immanent pervasiveness of god, or the rational active principle, through the *whole* of the universe, τὸν ὅλον κόσμον (Frs. 100, 101); but he also regarded heaven (οὐρανός) as the governing principle (τὸ ἡγεμονικόν) of the universe (F23), with the same importance and significance for him in a cosmic sense, as the rational power had a controlling factor in human psychology.

Rist (*Stoic Philosophy* 204ff) develops this line of thought, bringing in as peculiarly Posidonian the definition of οὐρανός as ἡ ἐσχάτη περιφέρεια ἐν ᾗ πᾶν ἵδρυται τὸ θεῖον (D.L. VII.138). But caution is necessary, because Cicero assigns to

Cleanthes: *ultimum et altissimum atque undique circumfusum et extremum omnia cingentem atque conplexum ardorem, qui aether nominetur, certissimum deum indicat* (*ND* I.37); and Achilles Tatius (*SVF* I.115) gives to Zeno the definition of οὐρανός as αἰθέρος τὸ ἔσχατον· ἐξ οὗ καὶ ἐν ᾧ ἐστι πάντα ἐμφανῶς· περιέχει γὰρ πάντα πλὴν αὑτοῦ· οὐδὲν γὰρ ἑαυτὸ περιέχει, ἀλλ' ἑτέρου ἐστὶ περιεκτικόν. And for Chrysippus: D.L. VII.139, F23 Context and Comm. See F23, F14 comm.

As far as this fragment is concerned, Posidonius is cited as a central orthodox authority on the subject, grouped with Zeno and Chrysippus.

F21 Diogenes Laertius, VII.138

CONTENT

'Stoics say that the universe is governed according to intelligence (νοῦν) and providence (πρόνοιαν), as Chrysippus says in Bk v of *On Providence*, and Posidonius in Bk III of *On Gods*, since intelligence pervades every part of it like soul in us; but actually (or perhaps 'further', ἤδη) through some parts it is more, through some less. For through some parts it has come as cohesion (ἕξις) as through bones and sinews; through others as intelligence, as through the governing principle (ἡγεμονικοῦ).'

CONTEXT

The passage occurs in Diogenes' report on the Stoic universe (137–43; F99a comm.). It is preceded by F14 and followed by F23.

COMMENT

Since νοῦς and πρόνοια are aspects of god (*SVF* II.1027; I.157; I.146; I.102; II.933; II.1118), it is not surprising that this reference occurred in Posidonius' book *On Gods*. The number of the book remains uncertain. *BP* have ἐν τοῖς ιγ̄; *F* followed his frequent practice of omitting the bibliographical information (*see* vol. I *Introd.* xxv), and ἐν τω ιΓ′ was supplied by a second hand; this becomes ἐν τῳ γ̄ in a minor codex. It is possible that there was a Bk XXIII, but it is suspicious how often iota occurs in a number in Diogenes' codices in the Stoic doxography, e.g. Frs. 6, 9, 13, 17, 42, where sometimes it could be due to an iota adscript (Frs. 9, 13, 42). Sandbach could be right that originally there was no number here, and that the corruption arose from τοῖc.

As indicated by the twin reference to Chrysippus, the first part at least is completely orthodox. For the cosmos being κατὰ νοῦν: *SVF* II.945 (p. 272.40 Arn.); I.111–14; II.618 (p. 188.11 Arn.); II.1013 (p. 303.8 Arn.); II.1015; II.641; Pos. F99a, F23. For πρόνοια: *SVF* III.657; I.172; II.528 (p. 169.35 Arn.); II.1127. The interest therefore lies in the fact that Posidonius is expressly cited with Chrysippus for standard Stoic doctrine. This suggests that the source used by Diogenes was fairly close to Posidonius in time; F99a comm.

But there seems to be a Posidonian twist in the latter part of the fragment. That the active rational principle (in the material form of πνεῦμα) permeates the whole of the universe, but in varying degree (i.e. τόνος, *SVF* II.439ff), is common doctrine. So are the extreme examples of degree, the governing principle at one end, and mere cohesion (ἕξις) at the other (for πνεῦμα holding body together: *SVF* II.368; II.473 (p. 155.29 Arn.); II.477 (p. 157.7 Arn.)). But the comparative analogy between cosmic νοῦς and human soul (4), leads to the ἕξις of bones and sinews being taken as part of our soul permeating the whole body. But the standard Stoic doctrine held that ἕξις was quite distinct from φύσις and ψυχή: *SVF* I.158; II.458; II.1013 (p. 302.36ff Arn.). It was Posidonius who was known to have maintained that soul was diffused even in our bones, F28.

Although in this passage it is indicated that the analogy

proceeds from the human soul to the cosmic soul (καθάπερ ἐφ' ἡμῶν ψυχῆς, 4), it is likely that for Posidonius the analogy went from the cosmic to the human soul. The diffusion of cosmic pneuma throughout the whole universe, including the manifestation of ἕξις, was normal Stoic doctrine (D.L. VII.139); it was this analogy which would lead Posidonius to ascribe ἕξις in bones to the human soul.

For the fragment as a whole cf. Atticus F8, 814 Aff (Dillon, *The Middle Platonists* 252) which shows the influence of the Stoa in this area on Middle Platonism.

For cosmos, see also Frs. 4, 8, 13, 14, 20, 23, 99.

F22a, b, Cicero, *De Natura Deorum* I.123; Lactantius, *De Ira Dei* IV.7

CONTENT AND CONTEXT

Posidonius, *On Gods*, Bk V, criticises Epicurus.

At *ND* I.121, Cotta attacks Epicurus for uprooting religion from the minds of men, by removing from the gods beneficence and benevolence, i.e. providential care. But what sort of animate being is it, asks Cotta, that cares for nothing (§123)? At this point he brings in Posidonius: Posidonius is nearer the truth in arguing that Epicurus does not believe in any gods; what he said about the gods was to avert unpopularity. There follows a sentence of scathing invective, which is tied as explanation to the Posidonian statement, and may well be closely modelled on Posidonius' rhetoric. 'For Epicurus could not have been so silly (*desipiens*: ἀνόητος) as to fashion god like a manikin (*homunculi*: ἀνθρωπαρίου or ἀνθρωπίσκου), a shell of an outline without solid build, endowed with all a man's limbs but without their slightest exercise, a drawn transparent sort of being, imparting nothing, favouring nothing, caring for nothing at all, doing nothing. A nature like that can be nothing; Epicurus saw that: he abolished gods in fact (*re*: ἔργῳ) and left them as a manner of speech (*oratione*; *verbis*, Lactantius: λόγῳ).' Cotta continues: in the second place, if that is god and he exists, Cotta does not want to know him.

COMMENT

There are pre-echoes of this passage at *ND* 1.85; *quamquam video non nullis videri Epicurum ne in offensionem Atheniensium caderet, verbis reliquisse deos, re sustulisse* (and cf. Plu. *Non Posse* 1102B). But R. Philippson, 'Des Akademikers Kritik der epikur. Theologie', *Symb. Osl.* 20 (1940), 42ff, pointed out that the background to this passage does not seem to be Posidonian, because it is there taken for granted that Epicurus did actually think that gods exist (1. 86).

Posidonius' criticism is directed to three points:

(1) Bad faith. Epicurus does not really believe in gods, and does not even stand by his own belief of truth, but puts out a story for political reasons. This appears to be the particular standpoint of Posidonius in what was a widely spread controversy.

(2) Childishness (*desipiens*), related to the form of god, ridiculed as the ghost of a manikin. Posidonius did not believe in anthropomorphic, but in physical theology. This was common Stoic ground (D.L. VII.147 = *SVF* II.1021), but the detailed invective may be Posidonian.

(3) The function of god (*officium*, Lactantius). God cannot exist without a function (cf. Seneca, *SVF* II.1059). What is at stake is the Stoic belief in providence (πρόνοια, cf. F21). This is the nub of the main general attack of the Stoics on Epicurus; Plu. *Comm. Not.* 1075E = *SVF* II.1126 = Epicurus F368, p. 248.11–14 Usener; cf. *De SR* 1051E, 1052B.

While Epicurean theology was a common target for Stoic

argument (Plu. *Comm. Not.* 1075E), Posidonius was noted for his general, and on occasion sharp, criticism of Epicurus: Frs. 46, 47, 149, 160, 288, 289.

Lactantius clearly took his information from Cicero. Ogilvie, *The Library of Lactantius*, discusses Lactantius' dependence on Latin authors.

F23 Diogenes Laertius, VII.139

CONTENT

The governing principle of the universe: 'They (i.e. Stoics) say that since in this way then (cf. F21) the universe (κόσμον) also taken as a whole is a living being (ζῷον) and ensouled (ἔμψυχον) and rational (λογικόν), it has the *aether* as its governing principle (ἡγεμονικόν), as Antipater of Tarsus says in *On Universe*, Bk 8. But Chrysippus in *On Providence*, Bk I and Posidonius in *On Gods* say that the heaven (οὐρανόν) is the governing principle of the universe, and Cleanthes says it is the sun.'

CONTEXT

The passage occurs in the extended report by Diogenes on the Stoic universe (137–43). It is preceded by F21. After the reference to Cleanthes, Diogenes adds a rather different (διαφορώτερον) version from Chrysippus in the same book (i.e. *On Providence*), namely that the ἡγεμονικόν is the purer part of the *aether*. This is followed by F8.

COMMENT

1–2 The argument follows closely from F21, where an analogy between cosmic intelligence and human soul was developed. So the universe too (οὕτω . . . καί, 1, i.e. like a human being) is a live, rational creature with a governing principle or ἡγεμονικόν. For ζῷον ἔμψυχον καὶ λογικόν, see F99a.

2–5 αἰθήρ may have been given as the first definition of cosmic ἡγεμονικόν not of course because Antipater said so, but because it was probably the first interpretation (*SVF* I.154) and in all likelihood continued to remain the most popular. So Chrysippus refined his general statement that it was the οὐρανός, to a more precise form: the purer part of the *aether* (τὸ καθαρώτερον τοῦ αἰθέρος) (Context, above). Diogenes says that this is διαφορώτερον, but in fact it is merely a reinterpretation of οὐρανός. In the same way, Posidonius too *may* have further defined οὐρανός, e.g. as 'the outermost circumference (ἡ ἐσχάτη περιφέρεια) on which is established all deity' (D.L.VII.138; F14; Rist, *Stoic Philosophy* 204).

Posidonius could not, however, have identified οὐρανός with the sun (ἥλιος); and the latter is expressly assigned to Cleanthes as ἡγεμονικόν, as distinct and different from Posidonius. The point has to be made because Cumont, *La Théologie solaire du paganisme romain* (*Mémoires de l'Académie des inscriptions et belles lettres* XII (1909) 2, 464 and 473–6), and more influentially Reinhardt (*Kosmos und Sympathie* 308–85), constructed a whole Posidonian theory of solar theology and eschatology, based on the importance of the sun for Posidonius and bolstered by dubious texts. The theory was attacked in detail by R. M. Jones, 'Posidonius and solar eschatology', *CP* 27 (1932), 113–35, and Cumont retracted (*Recherches sur le symbolisme funéraire des Romains* (1942), 199f). Reinhardt reiterated his position in *RE* 691ff; 778ff, but has not won support; for details, Hoven, *Stoïcisme et Stoïciens face au problème de l'au-delà* 95–102.

What is more interesting is that on a question where there is recorded variation of opinion of detail within the Stoa (there is even a testimony that Archedemus thought that the ἡγεμονικόν ἐν γῇ ὑπάρχει (*SVF* III. Arch. 15), whatever that might mean) Posidonius is grouped together with Chrysippus (cf. Frs. 13, 21). That is in accord with the whole section on cosmos in Diogenes, where Posidonius is referred to as a standard authority (F99a).

Since the ἡγεμονικόν was an aspect of god (D.L. VII.139, *SVF* II.634), it is a proper subject for Περὶ θεῶν. It is reasonable to suppose that this fragment came from the same book as F21, i.e. possibly Bk 3.

For cosmos: Frs. 4, 8, 13, 14, 20, 21, 99.

F24 Macrobius, *Saturnalia* I.23.7

CONTENT

Posidonius in his books *On Heroes and Daemons* gave an etymology of the word δαίμων: since the nature of δαίμονες is created and partitioned from the substance of *aether*, the word is derived from τὸ δαιόμενον either in the sense of burning (καιόμενον), or in the sense of being partitioned (μεριзόμενον).

CONTEXT

The passage is in the same section of Macrobius as F118, *q.v.* for general context. At this particular stage, Macrobius is pursuing the line of Cornificius Longus that Zeus is the sun, and the gods are stars. He cites in support Plato, *Phdr.* 246e 4–247a 2 (which he wrongly ascribes to *Tim.*). It is the Platonic phrase, τῷ δὲ (i.e. Zeus) ἕπεται στρατία θεῶν καὶ δαιμόνων, which leads to etymological speculation on δαίμονες. Macrobius' source for the whole passage may be Cornificius' *De Etymis Deorum*.

COMMENT

The first etymology, δαίμονες<δαήμονες i.e. 'knowing' the

future (2), comes from Plato himself, *Crat.* 398b 5–c 4. That passage is itself a commentary on Hesiod, *W & D* 121ff, and the context is the theory that when a good man dies, he becomes a δαίμων, which has nothing to do with δαίμονες as stars.

The form of the sentence: *nomen . . . coniungit aut quia . . . aut . . . quia* raises the question of whether Posidonius' etymological explanation was a commentary by him on the *Phaedrus* passage, or whether the conjunction was made by Macrobius or Cornificius. The former is certainly possible; cf. Frs. 290, 31, 86c. Indeed Posidonius may have quoted the Platonic etymology as well. All this could have been in an initial doxographical review in his book (T101 comm.).

Edelstein thought that this could indicate that Posidonius' own interpretation of the *Phaedrus* passage was astronomical or astrological, and this was because he himself understood ἥρωες and δαίμονες to be the stars (*AJPh* 57 (1936), 298 n. 51; 300 n. 57). But even if the first is granted, the second does not follow (cf. δαήμονες, above). At least such an interpretation of δαίμων would be incomplete and misleading for Posidonius. He certainly regarded the heavenly bodies as divine (F127), and therefore may have called them δαίμονες. But the human νοῦς is also a δαίμων (F187.6f), and the immortal souls who affect divinatory dreams when one is asleep (F108), cannot be the stars. Posidonius' theory of δαίμονες, no doubt expounded in this book, must have been more complex, but our evidence is too meagre to be more precise. For further argument: F108 comm. It seems likely that a major interest lay in the connection of δαίμονες with divination (F108). But this in turn was bound closely to his theology and to his theories of the physical structure of the universe; so δαίμονες probably had to be accommodated to his physical philosophy. One would expect all these themes to appear in the books which he devoted to the subject.

For Posidonius' interest in etymology: T89.

F25 Diogenes Laertius, VII.149

CONTENT

Posidonius said that everything happened by fate in *On Fate*, Bk 2.

CONTEXT

Preceded by F20 on the substance of god and by two sentences on φύσις without specific references. Frs. 7, 27 on divination follow. For the possible significance of the sequence, see Frs. 103, 7.

COMMENT

In this case the citations support the standard Stoic doctrine, and do not mark variations as in Frs. 20, 7. The order is curious: Chrysippus and Posidonius are given first (as the main authorities?), followed by Zeno and Boethus. It is surprising that such a fundamental statement should be postponed to Bk 2 of *On Fate*. Possibly Bk 1 was occupied with doxographies, definitions and the background of natural philosophy, while Bk 2 developed in detail the consequences of everything happening by fate (cf. F104).

Since Diogenes is giving common doctrine for which Posidonius is specifically cited, it would be natural to assume that Posidonius also accepted the definition of fate given in the next sentence: ἔστι δ'εἱμαρμένη αἰτία τῶν ὄντων εἰρομένη ἢ λόγος καθ' ὃν ὁ κόσμος διεξάγεται. This is also in line with Cicero, *De Div.* I.125–8, for which see F107 comm.

Posidonius on fate: Frs. 103–7.

F26 Cicero, *De Divinatione* 1.6

CONTENT

Posidonius published five books *On Divination* (cf. F27).

CONTEXT

Cicero begins his work with a brief gallop through the popularity of the belief in divination from early times. Sections 5–6 offer a curt doxography of Greek philosophers with §6 devoted to the Stoa: Zeno, Cleanthes, Chrysippus, Diogenes of Babylon, Antipater and Posidonius. The doubts of Panaetius are recorded.

COMMENT

Posidonius' five books *On Divination* were certainly used by Cicero (Pease, vol. 1, *Introduction* 178–82 (20–4); Frs. 106–110). Book 1 is likely to owe more to him than Cicero expressly acknowledged. The doxography in 1.5–6 may derive from him (T101), and there are reasons for thinking that Posidonius may have dominated the argument from 1.125–30 (Frs. 107, 110). It is likely that his books were read, not least for debating examples (cf. F104, F27). But there are many Roman examples in Bk 1, and the pervasive Roman colouring is stressed in 2.8. Cicero also alludes to collections from Chrysippus, Antipater and Stoics in general (F27), and there are sections where clearly Cicero is independent of Posidonius (F108, Context), or pursuing a line of argument which cannot be reconciled with Posidonius (F7, comm.). Therefore Posidonius' influence on Cicero's *De Div.* should not be overstressed (cf. Hoven, *Stoïcisme et Stoïciens face au problème de l'au-delà*, 59). But he was still regarded as a great authority on astrology by Augustine (F111) and Boethius (F112).

Remarks on divination appeared also in *Natural Philosophy* (F7).

F27 Diogenes Laertius, VII.149

CONTENT AND CONTEXT

See F7.

COMMENT

Perhaps the fifth book *On Divination* was devoted to a collection of the ἐκβάσεις referred to in F7, some of which surface in Cicero's *De Div.* and *De Fato.* Posidonius was not the only Stoic to compile such collections; Cicero in *De Div.* mentions Chrysippus (I.37, 39), Antipater (I.39) and simply Stoics (I.56).

F28a, b Scholia in Homerum (T), Ad Iliadem XII.386 (Dindorf, V.457, Erbse III.374); Eustathius, *Commentarii ad Homeri Iliadem* XII.386

CONTENT

In Homer's opinion, τὸ ψυχικόν (ψυχικόν τι πνεῦμα, Eustathius), i.e. soul spirit, is diffused also (even?) in our bones, as is also the opinion of Posidonius in *On Soul*, Bk 3 (the book number is not given in Eustathius). The scholium adds that Plato says that its (soul's) bonds are in the roots of the bone (*Tim.* 73b: this is the marrow (μυελός) that binds the body together).

COMMENT

That the soul is diffused even into our bones as ἕξις or cohesion, is not normal Stoic doctrine, which distinguishes ἕξις from φύσις and ψυχή (*SVF* I.158; II.458; II.1013, p. 302.36 Arn.). But this position of Posidonius is supported explicitly by F21. F149 also stresses that function of soul which συνέχει σῶμα.

Posidonius was fond of referring to Homer (Index, vol. I), and indeed had something to say on when it was proper to cite him (T87 comm.), so it is possible that Posidonius may have quoted this line in *On Soul*. It is also likely that he referred to *Tim.* 73b, as a precursor of his view. So Posidonius may have been the source bringing these passages together (F139 comm.). Would such a doxography also have included Xenocrates, who also held the opinion that the soul extended throughout the whole body (Lact. *De Op. Dei* 16.12)?

ETHICS

F29 Diogenes Laertius, VII.91

CONTENT

A proof of the existence of virtue in Bk I of *Ethics*, followed by a proof of the existence of vice.

CONTEXT

D.L. VII.89–93 discusses virtue and vice. F29 is followed by F2 and F180.

COMMENT

This is the only named reference we have to the Ἠθικὸς

Λόγος, which presumably corresponded to the Φυσικὸς Λόγος (Frs. 4ff), and like it comprised more than one book, since reference here is to Bk I. Pohlenz (*Die Stoa* II.120) suggested that the book referred to in F38 was the first book of Ἠθικὸς Λόγος, but this is unlikely (F38 comm.). It could however have been a source for Frs. 89, 170, 171, 173, 180, 186. Oddly, there is no record of any other Stoic book with this title.

There are two arguments:

(1) Evidence to prove (τεκμήριον) that virtue exists (ὑπαρκτὴν εἶναι) is that Socrates, Diogenes and Antisthenes were in a state of progression (γενέσθαι ἐν προκοπῇ).

(2) Vice exists (ὑπαρκτήν) because it is the opposite of (ἀντικεῖσθαι) virtue.

The two arguments are different in form. (1) depends on empirical observation of fact which serves as evidence to prove (τεκμήριον) the existence of virtue. (2) is a logical proof. That (2) is still Posidonius is shown by the indirect construction dependent on φησιν in l.1.

The τεκμήριον form of (1) presents no problems for Posidonius; compare exactly Frs. 2, 7. But the argument itself has caused puzzlement. Hirzel (*Untersuchungen* II.286ff) thought that the argument only proves the existence of the progressor, not the sage (σοφός), and that therefore Posidonius was replacing the σοφός by the προκόπτων, and interpreting ἀρετή in the light of the latter. But this is certainly not the meaning of ἀρετή in the context of Diogenes, and is against our other evidence for Posidonius. Bonhöffer (*Die Ethik des Stoikers Epictet* 217, n. 1), agreeing that the argument fails, proposed emending ὑπαρκτήν by διδακτήν. But Posidonius' proof that virtue is teachable follows in the next sentence in Diogenes, F2.

The argument is odd, but is no doubt compressed in Diogenes' report. It is true that evidence for the existence of progressors is not evidence for the existence of σοφοί (which was Hirzel's point); but that is different from saying that evidence for progression is evidence that virtue exists, which is more defensible. Stoics clearly felt able to claim the reality of virtue, that there is such a thing as virtue, without actually having to name a perfectly virtuous man. Which is just as well, since although it would have been better evidence to point to a σοφός, Stoics traditionally had difficulty in naming any such (Plu. *De SR* ch. 31, 1048E = *SVF* III.662, 668; *Comm. Not.* 1076B); and this created trouble in some of their arguments, as in S.E. *Adv. Math.* IX.13 = *SVF* III, Diog. 32. There is no doubt that Posidonius discussed the σοφός (Frs. 40; 163.15; 164.13, 28; 165.19), but given the conditions laid down by him (as in F163), it would have been difficult for him to point to an actual σοφός as empirical evidence for ἀρετή. It is noticeable that even the traditional great figures of Socrates, Diogenes and Antisthenes (οἱ περί here must be the periphrastic phrase, meaning simply the men themselves, T45 comm.) are represented merely as progressors, not σοφοί. However, the mere fact of progression (προκοπή), implied already for a Stoic the use of moral intelligence (F174), although this was not yet firm enough always to be right (which ἀρετή demanded); it also required a σκόπος at which to aim, and it is impossible even to aim without the existence of a target.

The logical form of argument (2) was used by Chrysippus with regard to good and evil (*SVF* II.1169). It derives from Pl. *Theaet.* 176a.

F30 Galen, *De Placitis* V.469, p. 448. 7–11 M, p. 326. 12–16 De Lacy.

CONTEXT

Preceded by F31 which ends with Posidonius' criticism of Chrysippus on virtues. Galen then says (326.9ff De Lacy) that he will return to the virtues later, because Chrysippus also abused Plato on the subject. He has brought them up here for logical reasons (ἐξ ἀκολουθίας τινος; see F31 comm. E) as the doctrine of virtues necessarily follows (i.e. logically, ἑπομένου) the doctrine of the emotions (πάθη), as Posidonius said. F30 follows immediately, and is followed in turn by F187.

CONTENT

Galen quotes Posidonius exactly from near the beginning of Book I of Περὶ παθῶν: 'I believe that the examination of things good and evil, of ends (τελῶν) and of virtues, depends on the correct examination of emotions (παθῶν).'

COMMENT

The context shows that Galen is concerned specifically with Posidonius (as distinct from Plato) through this section of *De Plac.*

1–2 Two points follow:

(1) Galen knew the Περὶ παθῶν itself well, which is amply borne out by the close familiarity shown elsewhere in *De Plac.* IV–V.

(2) Right at the beginning of his work *On Emotions*, Posidonius declared clearly the general importance of the subject, and probably the width and range of its contents (cf. F150a). The book is not a narrow specialised investigation on a single topic, but really a work on moral philosophy, based on an investigation of the problem of emotions.

3–5 The scope of subject and method of investigation in the extant fragments bears out the statement. In particular F187, which follows, surveys different sections of ethics in the light of the inquiry into emotions. It is nevertheless a startling statement that the main problems of ethics depend on the solution of the problem of emotions; but it is amplified and clarified by F150a, which reiterates the claim with an explanation.

F31 Galen, *De Placitis* v.446–8, pp. 444.11–448.2 M, 322.28–326.8 De Lacy

CONTENT

Posidonius' views in relation to Plato and Chrysippus on the education of children; related criticism of Chrysippus on virtues.

CONTEXT

Preceded by F169; followed by Frs. 30, 187. Immediately before (F169.106ff) Galen was discussing ἴασις τῶν παθῶν τῆς ψυχῆς and different psychosomatic conditions for its application and function (whether easy or severe), εἴ τις μέλλοι βελτιόνα τὸ ἦθος ἀποδείξειν τὸν ἄνθρωπον. οὕτω (1) looks back to the previous sentence (F169.114ff) where mention is made of the blunting of emotional movements by habitual good practices.

ANALYSIS

A. (1–6)

Galen praises Plato for his comprehensive and detailed account of how a human being should be moulded from the beginning, in relation to what is best. Chrysippus on the other hand left no adequate account of his own, and did not even leave his successors a starting point for investigation.

B. (6–11)

Posidonius too (i.e. as well as Galen) censured Chrysippus

and admired Plato on the nurture and education of children from the womb onwards. In Περὶ παθῶν, Bk 1, he included a sort of epitome of Plato's remarks.

C. (11–16)

(a) A Galenic paraphrase (11–14) from this 'epitome' on the purpose of children's education: that the emotional and irrational faculty of the soul display a proper proportion (or measure, σύμμετρον) in its movements, and obedience to the commands of reason.

(b) A quotation (14–16) from Posidonius (see F148): 'this is the best education for children, a preparation of the emotional faculty of soul so that it be most conformable to the rule of the rational faculty'.

D. (16–29)

Galen continues in indirect speech (i.e. from Posidonius): for the rational faculty, originally weak, only attains at the age of 14 strength and fitness to rule like a charioteer the horses of desire and anger, if they are in a proper submissive state to follow and obey the rational faculty in everything. But whereas the training and virtue of the rational faculty is knowledge of reality, which comes from rational instruction, the proper virtue of the irrational faculties (in which no knowledge occurs) derives from a kind of irrational habituation.

E. (29–47)

The account of the virtues too follows upon this directly (29f; for interpretation, see Comment below). There is a double error, whether one posits all the virtues to be kinds of knowledge, or all to be faculties (δυνάμεις) (31f); because:

(1) (μὲν γὰρ, 32) since the virtues of the irrational parts of the soul must be irrational, and that of the rational part only, rational, then it follows reasonably (εὐλόγως, 34; as Pos. εὐλόγως, F164.86), that the virtues of the former are

faculties; and of the latter only knowledge, 32–5; (i.e. the first mistake is the assumption that *all* virtues must be *either* δυνάμεις *or* ἐπιστῆμαι; neither supposition can be correct).

(2) (δὲ, 36) Chrysippus' major mistake lies not in failing to make any virtue a faculty, but in maintaining both a plurality of kinds of knowledge and virtues, and a single faculty of soul. For virtue is the perfect state (τελειότης) of the nature of each thing, and each thing can only have one perfect state; so there cannot be many virtues of a single faculty of soul (i.e. of a unitary soul) (36–43).

Ariston of Chios was more consistent in declaring a single virtue of soul, namely knowledge of things good and evil (43–7).

COMMENT

Structure and content in relation to Περὶ παθῶν, *Bk 1*

It is clear from the *Analysis* that the structural hub of this Fr. as far as source is concerned lies in B, the reference to the kind of epitome of Platonic views in the first book of Περὶ παθῶν. C must derive from this, and probably D. It will be argued below that E probably does not.

A at first sight seems to be Galen, not Posidonius (cf. 6). The subject is set by πλάττειν (1), which was a Platonic educational metaphor (e.g. *Laws* 671c 2, *Rep.* 377c 3, 500d 6, *Tim.* 88c 4; cf. Brink, *Horace on Poetry* III, App. 10; so of course is the use of τὸ βέλτιστον, the examples being too numerous to quote). ἐξ ἀρχῆς is explained by the omitted lines (2), which detail the care required for the physical and emotional state of the pregnant mother: conception, Pl. *Laws* 674b 5f; pregnancy, *Laws* 789a 8ff, 792e 2–7; in general, *Laws* 653b 1ff. It has however been suggested (Pohlenz, *Diss.* 596; De Lacy, *De Plac. ad loc.*) that the details go beyond Plato's account in *Laws*, and are derived from Posidonius. But Galen's references to Plato are general, and if he found them in Posidonius, the latter probably thought that they were implied by the *Laws*, as indeed they are. In any case it is highly likely that Galen was already writing from his Posidonian base. Although the main passages (Analysis C and D) refer to Posidonius on the education of children after birth, the 'epitome' also contained matter on the period of pregnancy (8); and the criticism of Chrysippus' unsound foundation in comparison with Plato surely derives from Posidonius. But it must remain uncertain whether the metaphor (5f) comes from Posidonius, although he had a taste for metaphor (Frs. 239.8, 32; 253.21; T103). After being common in 5th c. B.C. poetry, κρηπίς recurs in this usage in Maximus of Tyre 13.7, a contemporary of Galen.

B Epitome: there are strong indications that Posidonius with his historical sense of the development of ideas included doxographic accounts of predecessors in his physical books (T101,102 comm.). It is possible that there was such a section in Περὶ παθῶν A, after the initial statement of scope (F30). If so, it is likely to have included Aristotle, Pythagoras (F165.168ff), and probably Zeno (F34) and Cleanthes (F32) as well as Chrysippus. But Galen writes 'a kind of (οἷον) epitome', so this may not have been a formal doxography.

C (a) and (b) give a juxtaposition of paraphrase and quotation without warning, which is by no means uncommon in ancient critical literature; thus Plut. *De SR passim*. Here it is the προστάγμασιν εὔπειθές of the paraphrase which is most immediately illustrated by the quotation; but the concept of σύμμετρον is resumed below (20ff) in 'neither too strong nor too weak'. In spite of the careful chiasmus of the paraphrase, σύμμετρον ταῖς κινήσεσι must mean: in due measure *in* its movements. For παθητικαὶ κινήσεις: Frs. 153, 165, 169. For this παιδεία in general: F169, and R. Walzer, 'New Light on Galen's Moral Philosophy', *Greek into Arabic* 142–63 (originally in *CQ* 43 (1949), 82–96). There is a different παιδεία for τὸ λογιστικόν, 24ff.

D The whole of 16–29 is in indirect speech, which should

indicate that Galen intended it as a report of what Posidonius said. There are two reasons for accepting the natural assumption that Galen found the passage also in Bk I, directly after the quotation of 14–16.

(1) The argument is an explanation of the quotation, which indeed requires it. Posidonius is discussing the education of children in terms of a preparation (παρασκευή, 15) of the emotional faculty to be suitable for the rule of reason (14–16). This is necessary in any child because (γάρ, 16) the rational faculty does not develop appropriately (προσήκει, 19) for rule before the age of 14 (16–19). So a child's education must concentrate on training the irrational faculties to make them ready to follow and obey reason when it takes over command (23). This training and virtue cannot therefore be that of the rational faculty itself, which is knowledge (23f), but the training of the proper virtue of the irrational faculties, which is derived from a kind of irrational habituation (26–9).

(2) The imagery and language of the passage is peculiarly apposite to a context where Posidonius was arguing his own views against a Platonic background, the 'sort of epitome' of Plato's views in Bk I (9f). The analogy for the soul of the charioteer reason, and the two horses, ἐπιθυμία and θυμός (19f), is clearly taken from *Phaedrus* 246a 6ff, and the analogy persists throughout (25–7). For Posidonius' knowledge of *Phdr.*, see Frs. 290, 86c. Plato, too, probably thought that λόγος was at first weak, to be developed later to strength (thus *Tim.* 44b with A. E. Taylor's notes), so that children's first training was directed to their irrational faculties, ἐπιτηδεύματα, in the language of *Tim.* 87b 7, rather than μαθήματα; so *Rep.* II and *Laws* VII (793d 7ff). For Posidonius' knowledge of *Tim.*: Frs. 141, 85, 49, 291, 205, 149, 28a; for *Laws*: Frs. 178, 49.

But Posidonius, although starting from Platonic bases, images and words (note also apart from the analogy, σύμφυτος from *Phdr.* 246a 6, but the word is very apposite also for Posidonius' conception of soul as a natural whole (F146); and ἀποτελεῖν (17) is a favourite word in *Tim.*), soon slips into his own. His own simile (F166.11ff) is of a runaway horse (ἔκφορος, F166.11, 16; F31.22) carrying off its rider by force, until brought under control (κρατεῖν, F166.10, 13; cf. F165.139; F31.19). Posidonius' horse runs again in Arius Didymus' summary of Stoic ethics, Stob. *Ecl.* II.89.7–9 (Kidd, 'Euemptosia', 107ff). For εἰς ἅπαν ἑτοίμων ἕπεσθαι, F31.23, compare κατὰ πᾶν ἕπεσθαι, F187.6; for δυνάμεις of soul, Frs. 142ff; for the οἰκεία ἀρετή of the irrational faculties, Frs. 161, 160. It is noticeable that the irrational 'team' of the soul should not be too strong, but not too weak either (21). Posidonius was not aiming at the eradication of the irrational elements, which have their οἰκεία ἀρετή, but at their submission to reason (Frs. 161, 187); hence the importance of the education of children for him. The stress is on the directive role of reason based on scientific knowledge (ὥσπερ τοῦ ἡνιόχου τῶν ἡνιοχικῶν θεωρημάτων, 25f).

For θεώρημα in connection with rational in opposition to irrational training: F165.185 (and for θεωρηματικαὶ ἀρεταί, D.L. VII.90); in relation to scientific theory: F195.

In 16–18 Posidonius may have been siding with Plato against a Stoic dogma reported by Iamblichus (in Stob. *Ecl.* I.317.21ff W = *SVF* I.149, II.831) that λόγος did not straight away grow in humans, but only by the 14th year was consolidated from perceptions and appearances; or more probably, it was held that it was developed, filled out from προλήψεις at the age of 7 (Aetius, *Dox. Gr.* 400.23ff; *SVF* II.83), and reached maturity at 14 (τελειοῦται, D.L. VII.55 = *SVF* III, Diog. 17). But he was apparently sticking to the Stoic hebdomadal convention, which was of earlier origin (Solon 27, and Taylor on *Tim.* 44b). The change of emphasis lay in positing the early occurrence of logos in children, however weak, and was in line with his insistence on the recognition of πάθη in children (F159), which other Stoics denied.

E The provenance of 29–45 is more dubious than the earlier part of the Fr., which probably all derives from Bk 1 of Περὶ παθῶν. Much depends on whether ἕπεται (29) refers to positional sequence in Posidonius' book, or to logical connection of arguments. Pohlenz maintained the former (*NGG* 1921, 171; *GGA* 1922, 165; *GGA* 1926, 273), Reinhardt the latter (*Kosmos und Sympathie* 394, on *Pos.* 320; *RE*, col. 742). Reinhardt must be right, because Galen continues after F31: νυνὶ γὰρ ἐξ ἀκολουθίας τινὸς αὐτῶν (i.e. τῶν ἀρετῶν) ἐμνημόνευσα, τῷ περὶ τῶν παθῶν δόγματι καὶ τοῦ περὶ τῶν ἀρετῶν ἐξ ἀνάγκης ἑπομένου, ὥσπερ καὶ ὁ Ποσειδώνιός φησιν . . . F30 follows (p. 448.4–7 M). αὐτῶν ἐμνημόνευσα refers to F31.29–47; ἀκολουθίας and ἑπομένου clearly refer to logical connection. ἕπεσθαι in this sense: Galen, *De Plac.* 164.7 M; 189.9; 248.8 (all with ἐξ ἀνάγκης); εὐθὺς (F31.30): Galen, *De Plac.* 141.10 M; Arist. *Met.* 1004a 5. Since, then, Galen introduced the topic of virtue in F31.29ff, because of the relevance of Chrysippus' mistakes in that sphere to Posidonius' criticism of Chrysippus' psychology in the discussion of the education of children, it follows that we have no evidence that Galen found the source of these remarks in Περὶ παθῶν. The possibility that they came from a work Περὶ τῶν ἀρετῶν is discussed at F38.

On the other hand, Reinhardt must be wrong in holding that Galen was attacking both Chrysippus and Posidonius in F31.29ff. The 'double mistake' (31) cannot apply to Posidonius, who (a) believed in both virtues of irrational faculties and a virtue of knowledge in soul; and (b) derived a plurality of virtues from a plurality of faculties. The criticism is in fact based on Posidonian hypotheses (F31.24–9; F32; Frs. 142–6). Chrysippus is accused of a double mistake elsewhere in *De Plac.* (233.14ff, 422.4ff M).

The text is infuriatingly uncertain at line 31. *H* has αὐτὰς ἔχων; *L* is confused. If ἔχων is right, then ὁ περὶ τῶν ἀρετῶν λόγος must refer to Chrysippus (who made the double mistake), and not to any work of Posidonius (which did not).

But that would be an unexpected transition in the context (and cf. F38). Müller, to restore the reference to Posidonius, emended to αὐτοῦ ἐλέγχων, but the hiatus is offensive. I suspect that he is right, however, in thinking that the participle should refer to Posidonius, and that therefore the corruption conceals a participle denoting criticism. I suggest διελέγχων (as F181.3; F47.54); or perhaps: ἐλέγχων αὐτὸν σφάλμα διττόν, since τὸ seems rather odd. If, however, the specific reference is to a work of Chrysippus, almost certainly it would be to the four books Περὶ τῆς τῶν ἀρετῶν διαφορᾶς (F181); and in any case that work must have been implied (F182).

The argument of 26–43, and the reference to Ariston (43ff) show that Posidonius was attacking Chrysippus in the context of the polemical controversy between Chrysippus and Ariston on plurality and difference of virtues. Galen later (*De Plac.* 584.10–596.3 M) renews at greater length this very controversy in a passage prefaced by acknowledgement of Posidonius' criticism (F182). Therefore for an examination of the arguments as a whole, see Comment on F182.

For τελείωσις as a Stoic definition of ἀρετή (42): D.L. VII.90 (*SVF* III.197), a passage which gives no indication of Posidonius' difficulties.

F32 Galen, *De Placitis* VIII.652–3, pp. 653.12–654.3 M, 482.32–484.4 De Lacy

CONTENT

In the Περὶ παθῶν, Posidonius, the most scientific of the Stoics because of his mathematical training, departed from Chrysippus and shows that we are governed by three powers, the desiring and spirited and the rational; he showed that Cleanthes too was of the same opinion.

CONTEXT

For the general context of the beginning of *De Plac.* VIII, see F181 Context. At this point Galen is yet again excusing the length of his treatment. Chrysippus' continued popularity (653.6ff M) led him to bring in Posidonius also to the attack.

COMMENT

1–2 Rather odd. In fact in the first *three* books of *De Plac.*, Galen relied on himself, and used Posidonius extensively in Bks IV–V, as he says himself in T61, T62, T63.

3f See T84, T58. Shortly after this Fr., Galen expands on the importance of ἀπόδειξις ἐπιστημονική for philosophy (654.14ff M; 484.17ff De Lacy).

4–6 For the three powers, and Posidonius' fundamental disagreement with Chrysippus, see e.g. F144, F148, Frs. 158–60. This is the psychological basis of Posidonius' ethical and emotional theories: see F150.

5 **διοικουμένους**: F169.3 comm.

6 ἐπιθυμητικῆς and θυμοειδοῦς are linked by τε καί against λογιστικῆς.

6–7 For Cleanthes: T92. Posidonius was concerned to represent his philosophy as a development of the early Stoa before Chrysippus.

F33 Galen, *De Placitis* v.476–7, pp. 456.14–457.11 M, pp. 332.31–334.10 De Lacy

CONTENT

Posidonius argued at length in Περὶ παθῶν against Chrysippus, that animals are governed by desire and anger, and made a psychological classification of the animal kingdom.

CONTEXT

F166 immediately precedes, *q.v.* F166.11–15 contains an illustration of the training of young animals, as support for the simile used for the control of the passions, namely, a rider gaining control of a runaway horse.

COMMENT

1–2 Chrysippus does not think that the emotional aspect (τὸ παθητικόν) of the soul is distinct (ἕτερον) from the rational (τοῦ λογιστικοῦ), and so (καὶ) deprives irrational animals of emotions (τὰ πάθη). For Chrysippus πάθη presuppose reason (λόγος), which animals do not have. For Posidonius emotions can be quite distinct from reason, and so can occur even when reason is not present, as in children (F169.5) and animals.

3–4 'Although it is obvious (φανερῶς) that animals are governed by desire (ἐπιθυμίᾳ) and anger (θυμῷ), as Posidonius too (i.e. as well as Galen) goes through in detail (διεξέρχεται) at length (ἐπὶ πλέον).'

See also F158, F159.

For the importance of the governing power (διοίκησις) in animals and children for Posidonius: F169 *init.* Posidonius (and Galen) typically appealed to the obviousness of fact as evidence: F159; F156; F167 comm. *ad fin.*; F169.12–18 comm.; T85; T58.

That this question was not merely a side issue, but a basic factor in the two opposing psychologies, is indicated by the length and detail of Posidonius' treatment.

4–10 Posidonius' triple classification of ζῷα (ὅσα, κτλ):

(1) Those that are least mobile and are naturally attached like plants to rocks and the like, are governed by desire (ἐπιθυμίᾳ) alone.

Perhaps δυσκίνητ' ἔστι *H* is right, and the following καί is explanatory. This is reminiscent of Pl. *Tim.* 77b, where plants are said to partake of the third kind of soul, whose seat is between the midriff and the navel, ᾧ δόξης μὲν λογισμοῦ τε καὶ νοῦ μέτεστι τὸ μηδέν, αἰσθήσεως δὲ ἡδείας καὶ ἀλγεινῆς μετὰ ἐπιθυμιῶν (cf. Taylor, *ad loc.*). For the Stoa, however, plants are different: οἱ δὲ Στωϊκοὶ οὐδὲ ψυχὴν ὅλως ὀνομάζουσι τὴν τὰ φυτὰ διοικοῦσαν, ἀλλὰ φύσιν (Galen, *De Plac.* 509.1f M = *SVF* II.710); they are not ἔμψυχα (*SVF* II.708), nor do they have αἴσθησις (*SVF* II.177.32f), but are ἀόρμητα (*SVF* II.458). Also δυσκίνητος occurs quite frequently in *Tim.* (56a 2, 64b 1, 74e 7, 85c 6).

Posidonius probably had in mind sponges, and indeed σπόγγος appears in *Tim.* 70e in a simile. In any case, the expression employed became a stock usage for sponges; e.g. Plu. *De Soll. Anim.* 980B f of the sponge, ταῖς μὲν πέτραις, ὡς ἄλλα πολλά, προσπέφυκεν; and Jaeger (*Nemesios* 116) pointed to the phraseology in Nemesius p. 41: ἐρρίζωσε αὐτὰς ἐν τῇ θαλάττῃ δίκην φυτῶν, followed shortly by προσπεφυκότα ταῖς πέτραις, and σπόγγος occurring some lines on. Whether all this springs from Posidonius, we cannot say.

(2) *All* other irrational animals use both δυνάμεις, i.e. ἡ ἐπιθυμητική and ἡ θυμοειδής. δύναμις was Posidonius' term (F146); Galen, siding with Plato, preferred μέρη (μόρια) or εἴδη of the soul (F145), and tended sometimes to foist the terms on to Posidonius (thus F169.27f; cf. Clement in F186.15). But Posidonius adopted the Platonic usage ἐπιθυμητικόν, θυμοειδές, λογιστικόν.

(3) Only man uses all three (ταῖς τρισί), because he has acquired the rational ruling principle. ἀρχήν probably has the stress of a *ruling* principle; cf. the quotation from Posidonius in F148 (= F31.16), πρὸς τὴν ἀρχὴν τοῦ λογιστικοῦ; and the context in this fr. points to a governing power (διοικουμένων, 3).

προσειληφέναι: Pl. *Laws* 897b νοῦν μὲν προσλαβοῦσα ἀεί of the ψυχή that ἄγει all things in heaven and earth, in a context again of control and government. But Posidonius by λόγος here means not the wide Stoic sense of the fundamental active principle which is and enforms everything, but the narrower sense of human reason, which we 'acquire' at a later date (F169.5, F31.16ff). Note that in this classification there is no difference in kind between irrational δυνάμεις in animals and humans. Category (2) would include small children (F169, e.g. 12–18; F31).

10–11 The source is Posidonius' Περὶ παθῶν. More exact location is not possible. Galen says 'over the whole of the work', but the subject matter is somewhat ambiguous: 'that and very many other things'. However, considering the importance of the point for Posidonius' psychology and theory of emotions, and Galen's emphasis in line 4, it seems likely that Posidonius did return to the argument in several places in the work.

F34 Galen, *De Placitis* IV.377–9, pp. 348.5–350.13 M, pp. 246.36–248.32 De Lacy

CONTENT

Emotions and rational decision. Posidonius attempts to refute Chrysippus' theory that emotions are a kind of rational decision (κρίσις).

CONTEXT

Galen opens Bk IV of *De Plac.* with an attack on Chrysippus' psychology of faculties of soul. At 238.20 he turns to his view that emotions are rational decisions. To examine this, Galen starts with Chrysippus' definitions of emotion. He mentions the definition of 'fresh belief' (δόξα πρόσφατος) leading to a classification of emotions as impulses, beliefs and rational decisions (ὁρμαὶ καὶ δόξαι καὶ κρίσεις) which Galen says abandons the doctrine of 'the Ancients' (238.24–240.10), but he concentrates on the more commonly accepted definition of 'impulse in excess' (πλεονάζουσα ὁρμή), 240.11ff. This is reported at some length and includes Chrysippus' analogy of runners unable to stop when they want to. Some initial criticism and Galen's analysis of the problem follows (242.12–246.35). The section ends (246.33–5): 'So far, then, up to and including his explanation of the definitions (Galen must mean here, the definition of "Excessive impulse"), Chrysippus has said nothing contrary to the Ancients' (Plato is probably meant, cf. 244.11, and perhaps Zeno, cf. 240.1–10). F34 follows.

STRUCTURE

A. (1–12)

A triple classification of the views of Chrysippus, Zeno and Posidonius on the relationship between emotion and rational decision.

B. (12–20)

Posidonius' criticism and argument against Chrysippus.

C. (20–42)

Criticism by Galen, bringing in Posidonius.

COMMENT

A

1.(1–4) **ἐφεξῆς** Galen is turning from arguments related to the definitions of emotion by Chrysippus to the next question, namely the relationship between emotion and rational decision. Note that the question here concentrates on κρίσις. Chrysippus' definitions or analyses of πάθος also included ὁρμαί and δόξαι: *De Plac.* 238.26ff De L. The aspect of δόξα seems to be raised more in Frs. 163, 164, 165. For the problems concerning the theories of Zeno and Chrysippus on πάθη and κρίσεις: Lloyd, 'Emotion and Decision in Stoic Psychology' in *The Stoics*, ed. Rist, pp. 233–46; Rist, *Stoic Philosophy*, ch. 2 'Human Action and Emotion'; Pohlenz, 'Zenon und Chrysipp', *NAG*, phil.-hist. Kl. I.2.9 (1938), 188f; *Die Stoa* I.90f. κρίσις is usually translated 'judgement', but it is important to realise that it also conveys the sense of 'decision', e.g. Ar. *Ath. Pol.* 1275a 23 πολίτης ὁρίζεται τῷ μετέχειν κρίσεως καὶ ἀρχῆς.

πότερα . . . ἡγεῖσθαι. i.e. Chrysippus held the first (and worse, in Galen's opinion, φαυλότερον, 4) of the two alternatives, viz., that emotions were rational decisions (κρίσεις) of a sort (τινάς): *De Plac.* 238.20f De L; 336.2ff M, *SVF* III.461. He was departing from 'the older philosophers' (οἱ παλαιοί) in respect of both of the two alternatives. Presumably Galen has in mind Plato and Zeno in particular.

2. (4–8) Chrysippus thus contradicts Zeno, himself (*De Plac.* 234.24ff), and many other Stoics, who understand that the emotions of the soul are not the actual κρίσεις of the soul, but the irrational contractions (συστολαί), lowering abasements (reductions, ταπεινώσεις) and pangs (δήξεις), the rising elations (ἐπάρσεις) and relaxed diffusions (διαχύσεις), which come after (ἐπὶ) the κρίσεις.

The words used have in Greek physical, medical and emotional reference. They are discussed at F152. Clearly the first three terms are grouped against the last two to indicate feelings of depression and elation in emotions. As soul was material, they also had a physical connotation.

Galen implies (5) that many Stoics followed Zeno's account rather than that of Chrysippus. Certainly the doctrine that emotions were κρίσεις is identified as peculiarly Chrysippean in Galen and elsewhere (e.g. D.L. VII.111 = *SVF* III.456). It would not, and did not, debar Chrysippus from recognising descriptions such as συστολή, ἔπαρσις etc. (as in *De Plac.* 240.1–10 De L, 337 M), but he would disagree with ἐπὶ ταύταις (i.e. κρίσεσιν) (6f). But no doubt Chrysippus also had his supporters (13).

3.(9–12) Posidonius completely departed from both the previous views. He believed that emotions were not κρίσεις nor followed on κρίσεις, but were caused by the spirited and desiring power or faculty (δύναμις), thus following completely the old account (τῷ παλαιῷ λόγῳ). (See F152, F150.) This theory is of course closely linked to Posidonius' psychology; cf. Frs. 142–6.

For κατὰ πᾶν . . . λόγῳ: T102. Here ὁ παλαιὸς λόγος must refer to Plato (F152) and not include Zeno.

This theory of the *cause* of emotions did not prevent Posidonius from also holding the Zenonic description of πάθη in the stock physical terms of συστολή, διάχυσις (of 7f above); see e.g. F154.16 (διαχύσεις), F165.11, 13 (συστέλλει). But the context of the argument here is related to κρίσις.

B. (12–20) (cf. F157)

1. (12–15) Time and again (οὐκ ὀλιγάκις) Posidonius, in his work Περὶ παθῶν, asks Chrysippus and his sympathisers, what is the *cause* of the excessive impulse (τῆς πλεοναζούσης ὁρμῆς).

Galen wishes to stress this point (καὶ . . . γε), and makes it clear that it was important for Posidonius also, since it was repeatedly made in *On Emotions*. For that very reason there is no point in or evidence for attempting to locate the position of this statement in that book. Galen certainly used Posidonius' *On Emotions* to attack Chrysippus; but this and other passages show that much of *On Emotions* itself was an *ad hominem* attack on Chrysippus. τῶν περὶ τὸν X. may mean no more than Chrysippus, but it could include any others of his immediate persuasion (T45). It is also clear that Galen must be summarising the argument that follows in 15–20. But there is no reason to doubt the basic Posidonian question, or the spine of the argument. The question and argument are typical of Posidonius in two ways:

(a) the form of the question, 'what is the cause of. . . ?':

Frs. 161.2; 162; 164.86, 100; 165.10; 166.19; 168.1; 187.5, 10, 61; 169.51ff, 78f; 174; and e.g. in Physics, F94. To ask the question is the peculiar characteristic of the philosopher: F18.25ff, F90.27. τὸ αἰτιολογικόν is particularly associated with Posidonius: T85.

(b) The structure of the argument is characteristic, whereby Posidonius uses a 'School' definition, accepted by Chrysippus and by himself, as a basis for arguing against Chrysippus' theory; Frs. 165.6–8 comm.; 182 *fin.*; 31.39ff.

πλεονάζουσα ὁρμή as a definition of πάθος is used especially as a Chrysippean definition in the earlier context of this fragment, p. 240.13 De L (*SVF* III.462), and again after the fragment, p. 260.31ff De L (*SVF* III.479).

2. (15–20) Posidonius' argument follows (cf. F157).

(a) Agreed premiss (15f): λόγος (whatever else, μὲν *solitarium*) could not exceed (πλεονάζειν) its own acts (πράγματα) and measures (μέτρα).

This is somewhat reminiscent of Heraclitus, DK 22 B94, Ἥλιος γὰρ οὐχ ὑπερβήσεται μέτρα. But that of course is different. I cannot find any exact parallel in Stoicism, although the premiss is understandable in Stoic physics through the equation of λόγος and god and πρόνοια, and in epistemology, with ἐπιστήμη as a ἕξις ἀμετάπτωτος ὑπὸ λόγου (D.L. VII.46). Moreover the very nature of λόγος is limit (πέρας), and so it can have nothing to do with the limitless or indefinite. But it seems most likely from Galen's own evidence that Posidonius was arguing *ad hominem*; because in the passage leading up to this fragment, Galen quotes for criticism a passage from Chrysippus' *On Emotions*, Bk I, which he probably found in Posidonius' own book (*De Plac.* p. 240.10–242.11 De L = *SVF* III.462). Chrysippus, examining emotion as excessive impulse, wrote: συμμετρία γάρ ἐστι φυσικῆς ὁρμῆς ἡ κατὰ τὸν λόγον καὶ ἕως τοσούτου, [καὶ] ἕως αὐτὸς ἀξιοῖ. διὸ δὴ καὶ τῆς ὑπερβάσεως κατὰ τοῦτο καὶ οὕτως γινομένης πλεονάζουσά τε ὁρμὴ λέγεται εἶναι καὶ παρὰ φύσιν καὶ ἄλογος κίνησις ψυχῆς (p. 242.8–11 De L). Cf. διὰ τὸ τὴν καθ' αὑτοὺς καὶ φυσικὴν τῶν ὁρμῶν συμμετρίαν ὑπερβαίνειν (240.34f De L); πλεονάζει παρὰ (242.3 De L); διὰ τὸ τὴν κατὰ λόγον ὑπερβαίνειν συμμετρίαν (242.5f De L).

The Chrysippean provenance is strengthened by what follows.

(b) Conclusion (16–20): Therefore it is obvious that there is some other distinct faculty as cause of the impulse's exceeding the measures of λόγος, just as the cause of the running's exceeding the measures of choice is irrational (ἄλογος), namely the weight of the body.

The reference to running looks back also to the earlier Chrysippean quotation where Chrysippus illustrated his point by a comparison between walking and running (240.35f De L). When merely walking one can stop when one wishes, but runners are carried on beyond the point they wish to stop. Galen himself went on to argue (244.14ff De L) that the analogy of swift runners is much more complex. There is a δύναμις ἑτέρα παρὰ τὸν λογισμόν, irrational by nature, of the same description as the weight (βάρος) in the bodies of living creatures (244.26ff De L; cf. later, 260.31ff De L). *B.2* (b) shows that in the whole passage from 240.10–244 Galen is following Posidonius' detailed criticism of Chrysippus' *On Emotions* on this point.

C. (20–42)

It is Galen's comments which follow, but they help to bring out a core of Posidonius' criticism.

(1) Galen begins by saying that Chrysippus may be forgiven for contradicting a great number of people, and even for being wrong through human fallibility (20–3), but he expresses surprise on two counts. The first is that Chrysippus did not even attempt to resolve the statements of the 'Ancients' (τῶν παλαιῶν). In this context this must mean principally Plato (and perhaps Zeno) (*A.1*); and given

Posidonius' insistence on οἱ παλαιοί, Galen may be following Posidonius' cue here.

The second main criticism is that Chrysippus is self-contradictory. This is also a Posidonian line of attack on Chrysippus. Chrysippus contradicts himself in (a) at one point thinking that emotions arise without reason and judgement (ἄνευ λόγου καὶ κρίσεως) and (b) at another alleging that not only do they follow judgements, but that is just what is judgement (23–7).

(2) Galen now (27–33) offers an objection which might help Chrysippus (εἰ μὴ νὴ Δία βοηθῶν τις αὐτῷ φαίη): the word κρίσις has several meanings; so in Chrysippus' explanation of the definition (of πάθος as πλεονάζουσα ὁρμή, *De Plac.* 240.11ff De L) κρίσις was used in the sense of περίσκεψις so that 'without judgement' = 'without circumspection or consideration'. But when Chrysippus says that emotions are judgements (*A*.1), the objector would say that the word κρίσις is being applied to impulse *and assent* (τὰς ὁρμάς τε καὶ τὰς συγκαταθέσεις).

(3) Galen rejects this on two counts.

(a)(33–5) If then one were to accept that emotion will be an excessive assent (that is, if the formula of definition, πλεονάζουσα ὁρμή, is to contain a sense of κρίσις, as already stated by *De Plac.* 240.1 (*SVF* III.463), ὁρμὰς καὶ δόξας καὶ κρίσεις, so here that of συγκατάθεσις or assent), then *again* Posidonius will ask what is the cause of (τὴν αἰτίαν ὑφ' ἧς) the excess. In other words, the difficulty which Posidonius and Galen press is the implication of πλεονάζουσα.

(b)(35–42) There would be an additional (πρὸς τῷ . . .) very great mistake in exposition (κατὰ τὴν διδασκαλίαν). One would have every right to criticise Chrysippus if the crucial part of the doctrine lies precisely in distinguishing the ambiguity and so showing in what sense emotions are without κρίσις and in what sense they are κρίσεις, and yet Chrysippus has not made the point in a single one of his four books of *On Emotions*.

(4) It is by no means clear to what extent Galen may be following Posidonius in *C*. The general criticisms in *C.1* are characteristic of Posidonius. But the ambiguity objection of *C.2, 3* is expressed εἴπερ τοῦτό τις δέξαιτο . . . ὁ Ποσειδώνιος ἐρήσεται (33–5), which suggests that Posidonius did not actually pose the question in *On Emotions*. It is perhaps safer to assume that *C* is Galen's development of Posidonius' criticism; but it does bring out the emphasis of Posidonius' argument on πλεονάζουσα.

F35 Galen, *De Sequela* 819–20 (*Scripta Minora*, vol. II, pp. 77.9–78.19 M)

CONTENT

The cause and origin of evil.

CONTEXT

At pp. 74.21–77.1 Galen mounted an attack against the Stoics for thinking that all human beings are suitably or conveniently adapted for the possession of moral excellence, but are corrupted by their fellows. The context and argument are similar to the attack on Chrysippus' first explanation of moral corruption in F169.51, 55–7, which is also Posidonian (F169 *ad loc.*). At p. 77.1 Galen proceeds to argue against the view that we are corrupted by pleasure itself (the second explanation of Chrysippus in F169.51, 57ff). After F35, Galen returns (p. 79) to his theme that men's characters are related to physical temperaments or mixtures of the body, a theory of physiognomy similar to that of Posidonius in F169.84ff. It is noteworthy that the same overall sequence of argument occurs in both F35 (*De Sequela*) and F169 (*De Placitis*). Both are linked to Posidonius.

STRUCTURE

A. (1–7)

The view that we are corrupted by pleasure is attacked.

B. (7–18)

This was Posidonius' criticism of the Stoics.

C. (18–27)

Posidonius' explanation of the origins of evil.

COMMENT

A

The two sentences before F35 opens as printed are germane to the argument (*Scripta Min.* II, p. 77.1–9 M): 'Those are also very simple-minded who say that we are corrupted by pleasure and pain, the one pulling us to it, the other turning us away and rough. For if we all had a natural affinity (ᾠκειώμεθα) to pleasure, when it was not good, but as Plato said, the greatest bait (δέλεαρ; cf. δελεάζεσθαι, F169.60) of evil (*Tim.* 69d), then we are all by nature evil; but if not all but some have such an affinity, only they are naturally bad.'

What follows (F35.1–7) is very uncertain textually: Mueller, *Praef.* LIV. I now think that ἥτις (2) must refer, not to ἡδονῆς, but to ἑτέραν δύναμιν (1), and that therefore, my emendation ἀρετὴν (3) is wrong; ἡδονὴν of the codd. should be kept.

From 4f it is plain that Galen has in mind the case where there are (at least) two powers (δυνάμεις) in the soul, a better (κρείττων) and a rascally one (μοχθηρά), which may be stronger (ἰσχυροτέρα) or weaker (ἀσθενεστέρα) than the other. If we have the better power weaker, and the rascally one (i.e. the one leading to pleasure) stronger, we should *all* (stress on ἅπαντες) be bad (4–5; although Stoics say that all men have a natural affinity for the good); the alternative (reading εἰ δ' ἡ with Mueller, for ἤδη or ἤ codd., 5f) would be if the better were stronger; but then who persuaded the first human beings to be conquered by the weaker (i.e. pleasure)? In other words in this case we cannot be corrupted by pleasure itself, or the δυνάμις leading to it, which is weaker than the power leading to the good, so one must have been talked into it by others. But this alternative position, which Chrysippus also suggested (F169.51, 55–7, comm.), was already earlier refuted by Galen in pp. 74.21–77.1 M above.

Nevertheless, the first three lines of the fragment remain a puzzle. If ἥτις . . . δυνάμεως refers to ἑτέραν δύναμιν (1), the sense must be: 'If we have no power at all other than pleasure that makes itself at home in us, such a power that is stronger than the power leading us to pleasure . . .', where the stress of the negative has to be carried on to the ἥτις clause, i.e. if we had another power that was *weaker than* the power leading to pleasure. This ambiguity would be removed by my earlier suggestion of ἀρετὴν for ἡδονὴν in line 3 (the confusion reflected perhaps in the muddled conjecture notes of line 2); but the indefinite ἥτις counts against the reference to ἡδονῆς (2). There remains the confusion in line 2:

(1) ἡδονῆ μᾶλλον ἀρετὴν μᾶλλον is a confused note and should simply be excised. Alternatively: ᾠκειωμένην ἡδονῆ⟨ς⟩ μᾶλλον [ἀρετὴν μᾶλλον ἡδονῆς] ἥτις . . .

(2) ἀρετὴν should somehow be kept to forewarn κρείττων δύναμις, so: ᾠκειωμένην ⟨πρὸς⟩ ἀρετὴν μᾶλλον ἡδονῆς, De Lacy, *AJPh* 96 (1975), 102.

(3) Perhaps the double μᾶλλον conceals an amplification: ἡδονῆ⟨σ⟩ μᾶλλον ⟨τουτέστ'⟩ (cf. F187.5, Galen, *De Plac.* p. 326.20 De L) ἀρετὴν μᾶλλον ἡδονῆς. But the difficulty with this, and indeed with any reading of ἡδονῆς, is that neither ἀρετή nor ἡδονή is a δύναμις. The codices' φύσεως in line 3 may mark this, and may even be retained (cf. D.L. VII.148/9); but it does not help line 2, where δύναμις seems to be applied to pleasure and virtue themselves, not to

powers leading to them. In any case the whole argument is expressed through the term δύναμις. This difficulty and the ambiguity of the ἥτις clause may suggest a deeper corruption and lacuna.

The line of argument is, however, familiar from F169.51ff. There Chrysippus gives two explanations for the cause of moral corruption: (a) by communication from other people; (b) from the very nature of pleasure and the like. Galen criticises both at length (F169.54–77), adjoining Posidonius' name to the criticism. For details, F169 comm.

Similarly in *De Sequela*, Galen begins an attack on the Stoics at p. 74.21 M, first for thinking that human beings in spite of having a natural affinity for the good are corrupted by their fellows, and then at 77.1 M for believing that we are corrupted by pleasure itself. These views were important for Galen, and recurred in his *De Moribus*, on which see R. Walzer, 'New Light on Galen's Moral Philosophy' in *Greek into Arabic*, pp. 143–63 (especially 160f). It is clear from F169 that the line of attack was also Posidonian, and Galen himself emphasises this in the following section (F35.7–18).

B. (7–18)

This was Posidonius' criticism of the Stoics. Four points emerge:

(1) ταῦτ' οὖν αὐτά (7f) suggests that Galen was following (or agreeing with) Posidonius closely.

(2)(9–13) Posidonius' position was unorthodox. No other (τῶν ἄλλων, 10) Stoic followed him. In Galen's opinion their support of Chrysippus was total; they would have persuaded themselves (read ἔπεισαν ⟨ἂν⟩, 11?) to betray their country rather than the Chrysippean line; Posidonius preferred the truth to a School dogma.

(3) While Galen's admiration for Posidonius is obvious, why the expression ὁ πάντων ἐπιστημονικώτατος *here*? The phrase must refer to method and should be relevant to the

context. Perhaps a clue comes from the earlier passage, *De Sequela*, p. 75.21ff M, where Galen criticises the methods adopted by his opponents: 'If they were genuinely philosophising, they would be watching first just this, that the premisses (starting points) of proofs (τὰς ἀρχὰς τῶν ἀποδείξεων) be made from clearly observed fact (ἀπὸ τῶν ἐναργῶς φαινομένων).' The most ancient (παλαιότατοι) philosophers did not indulge in mere theorising, but based theory on fact and practice. This appears to be what 'scientific' means to Galen, and probably what he recognises in Posidonius. See T58.

(4) Galen gives his source for Posidonius: his Περὶ παθῶν (13–15). If Mueller's emendations, κατά τε (13) and κἂν (14) were right, Galen would also be referring here to a separate book Περὶ τῆς διαφορᾶς τῶν ἀρετῶν, as Reinhardt, *RE* 568, thought. But this is by no means certain, since the codd. reading is translatable with the phrase ἐν τοῖς . . . ἀρετῶν referring to subject matter, not title. There is, however, separate evidence that Posidonius wrote a book Περὶ τῶν ἀρετῶν: F38.

C. (18–27)

Posidonius' view of the origins of evil.

18–24 'Posidonius doesn't think either (οὐδὲ, like Galen; or perhaps 'not even Posidonius', i.e. although a Stoic) that vice comes in afterwards (ἐπεισ-) to human beings from outside, without a root (ῥίζαν) of its own in our souls, starting from which it sprouts (βλαστάνει) and grows big, but the very opposite. Yes, there is a seed (σπέρμα) even of evil in our own selves; and we all need not so much to avoid the wicked as to pursue those who will prune away (καθαρίσοντας) and prevent the growth of our evil.'

This is a graphically written passage with the metaphor of the root sustained throughout (βλαστάνειν, σπέρμα, καθαρίζειν which can have a horticultural sense of pruning). Surely it comes directly from Posidonius. This theory of the origin of evil derives from Posidonius' psychology, positing distinct irrational powers (δυνάμεις), which yet have their own οἰκειώσεις; a theory which in turn, according to Galen, arose from Posidonius' observation of the facts of children's behaviour: F169 for details. It is in direct opposition, root and branch, to Chrysippean Stoicism. So since the main danger lies within, the main remedy does not lie in avoiding bad associations as Chrysippus maintained (see F169). καθαρίζειν, to prune away evil, may look to the final state of the σοφός (ἀπαθῆ μὲν γὰρ γίνεσθαι ψυχὴν τὴν τοῦ σοφοῦ, F163.15), while 'hindering the growth' may refer rather to the φαῦλος and προκόπτων. F163 has another metaphor, that of health, in which Posidonius attacked Chrysippus, this time on his own grounds.

There is no evidence as to whether Posidonius believed he was developing pre-Chrysippean views of Zeno and Cleanthes. He held that they too accepted irrational powers, and Cleanthes' Hymn, line 13 (*SVF* I.537.13) might have been a straw to clutch at. The major impetus must be Plato and Aristotle, but Posidonius' theory is distinctively Stoic. Blatantly unorthodox at the time, it found no followers in the School. But cf. Plu. *De Virt. Mor.* 451C.

24–8 The connection (γὰρ) should indicate that this is still Posidonius. If so, it should be noted that the whole source of evil is not internal, but that a very minor influence may come from outside (e.g. perhaps environment, F196.84ff).

F36 Pap. Memph. 155, fr. 1, v.8.

CONTENT

In a list of book titles, Posidonius, *On Anger*, Bk I is named.

COMMENT

The papyrus from Memphis, dated to the beginning of the

3rd c. A.D., appears to be part of the catalogue of a (private?) library: Wilcken, *Chrest.*, n. 155, p. 182f; Pack 2089 for other references. Among other books listed are Aristotle, Περὶ ἀρετῆς; Theophrastus, Περὶ σωφροσύνης; Dion, Περὶ ἀπιστίας; Aristotle, Ἀθην. πολιτεία; Chrysippus, Τέχνης λόγων καὶ τρόπων α′.

Posidonius' book contained more than one volume, since Bk I is catalogued.

It is clear that monographs on *Anger* had become popular by the 1st c. B.C. Cicero, *Epistulae ad Quintum fratrem* 1.1.37 writes: *quare illud non suscipiam ut quare de iracundia dici solent a doctissimis hominibus, ea tibi nunc exponam, cum et nimis longus esse nolim, et ex multorum scriptis ea facile possis cognoscere.* Apart from Philodemus and later Seneca and Plutarch (Περὶ ἀοργησίας, and Lamprias Cat. n. 93, Περὶ ὀργῆς: Ziegler, *RE* XXI.1.774f) such a title can be ascribed to Bion of Borysthenes (Phil. I.16), Antipater (Athen. XIV.643F), Sotion (Stob. III.14.10, p. 427W), and in a more shadowy way Basilides and Thespis (Phil. V.21), Timasagoras (Phil. VII.7), Nicasicrates (Phil. XXXVII.5, XXXVIII.28), Hieronymus (Wehrli X, frs. 21–3), Quintus Sextius (Sen. *De Ira* II.36.1), Calvenius Taurus (Gell. I.26; cf. *PIR*²). The topic therefore spanned all the Schools, and common τόποι in argument and illustration can be traced.

It is easy to see why anger was singled out for special attention. It is the most common and most obvious of all the passions (Sen. *De Ira* I.1.7), and indeed controversial since some thought that it roused the spirit to bravery (e.g. Sen. *De Ira* I.7.1). It is possible that Posidonius was particularly interested in it because of physiognomy; cf. F169.84ff. It was commonly held that the physical marks of anger were especially noticeable (Sen. *De Ira* I.1.3–7).

See also F155.

F37 Eusebius Hieronymus, *Epistulae* LX.5.2–3

CONTENT

Posidonius is named in a list of *consolationes*.

CONTEXT

A *consolatio* to Heliodorus, bishop of Altinum, for the death of his nephew, Nepotianus, to be dated 396 A.D. The theme of §§1–6 is that death is not final. Examples for this are given from pagans (§5) and Jews (§6).

COMMENT

Courcelle, *Les Lettres grecques en occident*[1] 54f, shows that it is highly probable that Jerome's acquaintance with his impressive and rather bizarre list of writers of *consolationes*, comes from Cicero's lost *De Consolatione*. The authors mentioned are all also cited in *Tusc.*, including the reference just before our passage opens to Anaxagoras and the line assigned to Telamon: *sciebam me genuisse mortalem*, which recurs *Tusc.* III.58; III.28f. See for Crantor, *Tusc.* III.12; for Plato and Diogenes, I.103–4 (cf. III.56); for Clitomachus and Carneades: *legimus librum Clitomachi quem ille eversa Carthagine misit consolandi causa ad captivos cives suos . . . in eo est disputatio scripta Carneadis*, III.54; for Posidonius, cf. *Tusc.* II.61 = T38. There is no means of telling whether Posidonius ever used the examples of Pericles and Xenophon or not.

F176 explains the importance of *consolationes* in Posidonius' teaching.

F38 Galen, *De Placitis* VIII.653, 654.3–6 M, 484.4–6 De Lacy

CONTENT

Posidonius showed in a large work, which he wrote separately, that the account of the virtues is completed from a base of the principles established in his Περὶ παθῶν.

CONTEXT

The general context of the beginning of Bk VIII is explained at F181 under Context. Posidonius has just been praised (T84) for his criticism in Περὶ παθῶν of Chrysippus' psychology (F32, which immediately precedes this fragment).

COMMENT

Galen refers to Posidonius' criticism of Chrysippus' books Περὶ τῆς τῶν ἀρετῶν διαφορᾶς in Frs. 181–3; F31.29–47; F35.13–18. This fragment gives clear evidence that Posidonius wrote a separate (ἰδίᾳ) treatise on the subject, separate that is from Περὶ παθῶν just mentioned before (F32.4f). See in general Reinhardt *RE* 568, 754ff. This however (*pace* Reinhardt), is the only certain reference to a separate work. F35.13–18, on which Reinhardt relied (misled possibly by Müller's emendations), specifically cites the Περὶ παθῶν (13f); the phrase ἐν τοῖς περὶ τῆς διαφορᾶς τῶν ἀρετῶν (14f) refers to the subject matter, and the similar expression at line 17f to Chrysippus' book. In F31.29ff Reinhardt rightly against Pohlenz saw that the section on virtues referred to logical connection in the context rather than positional sequence in Περὶ παθῶν, but seems to have thought that ὁ περὶ τῶν ἀρετῶν λόγος (F31.30) indicated a book of Posidonius, although it merely alludes to Posidonius' account of or argument on the virtues, as in F38.1 (cf. F31 comm.). Other occurrences of the phrase 'on the difference of the virtues' refer to Chrysippus' work (F181), or to subject matter (Frs. 182, 183).

Nevertheless, F38 is sufficient evidence that Posidonius wrote a specific treatise on the subject. Pohlenz (*Die Stoa* II.120) suggested that it was the first book of the Ἠθικὸς λόγος (F29). This is unlikely because of the length (μεγάλης, F38.3) of the work, which might indicate more than one book.

On the other hand F35.13–18 shows that Posidonius also introduced the argument on the difference of the virtues in Περὶ παθῶν. The other evidence (F31.29ff; Frs. 181, 182) not only does not contradict that, but by constantly connecting the arguments on πάθη and difference of virtues, supports the probability. Indeed at the very beginning of Περὶ παθῶν the examination of virtues was stated to depend on the examination of πάθη (F30; so also F150, and in general for structure, F187).

The evidence can best be maintained if it is granted that Posidonius introduced arguments against Chrysippus on difference of virtues both in Περὶ παθῶν and in a separate work on the virtues. It remains uncertain what the title of the latter treatise was. It may simply have been Περὶ τῶν ἀρετῶν, which would follow the evidence of F38 and be appropriate to the size of the work. It is possible that the title was Περὶ τῆς τῶν ἀρετῶν διαφορᾶς, following Chrysippus' four books under that label (F181) and the subject discussed by Galen; but that particular aspect of the virtues was precisely what Galen reveals as relevant to the Περὶ παθῶν arguments. Galen may well have been familiar with the big monograph, but he may also have found most of what he needed in Περὶ παθῶν.

For the content of the arguments themselves, see Commentary on F182; also T64.

F39 Diogenes Laertius, VII.129

CONTENT

Like other Stoics, including Chrysippus, Posidonius held that there was no justice (δίκαιον) between humans and the other animals, because of their unlikeness (τὴν ἀνομοιότητα). The reference is to Περὶ καθήκοντος, Bk I.

CONTEXT

In a miscellaneous collection of Stoic dogmas.

COMMENT

Posidonius in this matter follows the usual Stoic line. On the other hand he differed from Chrysippean Stoicism in recognising πάθη in animals as well as in humans. This was because he believed that animals and men both shared an irrational factor of ψυχή. They do not however share rationality, and since morality depends on the rational, there can be no justice between men and animals because of this ἀνομοιότης. Cf. Frs. 159, 33. Posidonius is perfectly consistent in this area. Although animals have no rights, man's treatment of them can still be moral or immoral.

F40 Diogenes Laertius, VII.124

CONTENT

Posidonius is cited (from Περὶ καθηκόντων, Bk I) with Hecaton (*On Paradoxes*) for the common Stoic (φασίν) dogma that the wise man (σοφός) will pray, asking for goods (τὰ ἀγαθά) from the gods.

CONTEXT

§§121–5 contain a collection of Stoic *dicta* on the wise man. This is the only citation of Posidonius in this section.

COMMENT

φασίν (1) assigns this *dictum* to Stoics in general. But there was probably discussion on the point within the School. M. Aurelius (IX.40) raises and debates the question: 'Either the gods have no power or they have power. If they have no power, why pray? If they do, pray; but for freedom from fear or desire (i.e. from πάθη). But you may say, the gods have put these things *in my power*. Very well, use it. But, who told you that the gods do not co-operate with us even in what is in our power?' The difficulty for a Stoic was that god is within him (Sen. *Ep.* 41.1; Posidonius F187). *Quid votis opus est? fac te ipse felicem* (Sen. *Ep.* 31.5; cf. 31.8; 41.1f). Is this why the topic occurs in Hecaton's Περὶ παραδόξων?

What will the wise man pray for? M. Aurelius (*op. cit.*) unlike Socrates favours specific requests. It is noticeable that our fragment does not have τὸ ἀγαθόν, but the plural τἀγαθά, and the context is not περὶ ἀρετῶν but περὶ καθήκοντος, i.e. in the realm of appropriate acts. But the reference cannot be to external or physical 'goods', unless we have an inaccurate use of ἀγαθά. But the plural may refer to specific acts or situations, which for the wise man are not only right, but also appropriate (καθῆκον). Possibly religious observance, like πολιτεύεσθαι, lay for a Stoic within the sphere of καθήκοντα. To be sure the wise man will not only be εὐσεβής, but he alone will perform all religious ritual rightly (*SVF* III.604). But prayer seems different. Posidonius' definition of τέλος (F186) seems to imply some form of co-operation between man and what is beyond him. He had of course good precedents for prayer in earlier philosophers whom he admired, as Socrates and Aristotle (*EN* v.1129b 5f).

For this question in Epictetus: Bonhöffer, *Die Ethik des Stoikers Epictet* 75–85.

F41a, b, c Cicero, *Ad Atticum* xvi.11.4; *Ad Atticum* xvi.14.4; *De Officiis* iii.7–10

POSIDONIUS, CICERO AND THE *DE OFFICIIS*

Analysis

The sequence of events and key statements are as follows:

A

On 5 November 44 B.C. Cicero writes to Atticus (xvi.11.4 = F41a) that he has completed the first two books of his *De Officiis* covering the ground of Panaetius' three books Περὶ καθήκοντος. He now wishes (in his Bk iii) to deal with the third topic of Panaetius' tripartition of καθῆκον: how to judge in cases of apparent conflict between actions which are right and actions which are expedient (*honestum/utile*); but Panaetius had not written this subject up (F41a.1–8). Cicero now writes:

(1) Posidonius had followed that topic up (F41a.8). (How did Cicero know this? Was it true?)

(2) *eius librum* (i.e. Posidonius' book; which book?) *arcessivi* ('I have sent for' or 'I have had fetched'?). (F41a.9).

(3) I have written to Athenodorus Calvus to send me τὰ κεφάλαια (F41a.10),
quae exspecto (F41a.11). (What did Cicero intend by τὰ κεφάλαια? A résumé of Posidonius' book? 'Headings' from Athenodorus on the topic of *honestum/utile*? Does *quae* refer to Athenodorus' κεφάλαια only, or to the κεφάλαια and the book?)

(4) *in eo* (i.e. in Posidonius' book) *est* περὶ τοῦ κατὰ περίστασιν καθήκοντος (i.e. the topic: circumstantial duties) (F41a.12). (Did Cicero know this to be true, or did he just believe it to be so?)

B

On 12 (?) November 44 B.C. in a letter to Atticus (XVI.14.4 = F41b) Cicero writes that there is no need to prod Athenodorus further, since he has by now sent a *satis bellum* ὑπόμνημα. (But what is the form and content of this ὑπόμνημα? See *A* (3).)

C

In *De Officiis* III, Cicero, having complained that Panaetius neglected the topic of *honestum v. utile* (§7 = F41c.1–11), adds that

(i) he is surprised that this topic (*honestum/utile*) has been only briefly touched on by Posidonius in *quibusdam commentariis* (§8 = 11f) (What were these Commentarii? Had Cicero read them? How does this statement square with A(1)?);

(ii) especially since Posidonius had written that no topic was of such essential importance in the whole of philosophy (F41c.13f). (Where had Posidonius written this? Had Cicero read it himself, or been told of it?)

(iii) Posidonius, *in quadam epistula*, quoted (Cicero implies with approval) the remark of P. Rutilius Rufus that as no painter had ventured to finish Apelles' Venus of Cos, so no one had followed up Panaetius' excellent unfinished work (§10 = F41c.18–25). (What letter? How did Cicero know of it? Did he know the context?)

COMMENT

It is obvious from this analysis that Cicero's statements are so vague and ambiguous that we are left very much in the dark on questions of importance, such as: did Cicero ever at this time have access to a book of Posidonius which he consulted for *De Off.* III? If so, when did he get it, what were its title and contents? What was the nature of the material Cicero received from Athenodorus, and what evidence is it for Posidonius? Is any of Cicero's evidence for Posidonius on this topic first hand?

The book which Cicero sent for was almost certainly the Περὶ καθήκοντος (Frs. 39, 40). Whether Cicero knew or not that Περὶ τοῦ κατὰ περίστασιν καθήκοντος was a section of that book, he at least believed that it was (A(4)).

Whether Cicero already had Περὶ καθήκοντος when he wrote to Atticus and Athenodorus (F41a) depends on the interpretation of *arcessivi* (A(2)). Pohlenz ('Cicero de Officiis III', *NGG* I.1 = *Kleine Schriften* I, p. 253f; *Antikes Führertum* 7; *Die Stoa* II.120f) argued for the sense 'I have had fetched', explaining that Cicero had just got the book, seen that it contained something on κατὰ περίστασιν (A(4)), but not yet discovered that it did not deal with the conflict of *honestum* and *utile* as he had believed. Pohlenz further suggests that he did however find a section dealing with apparent conflict of *honestum* and *honestum* and used it for *De Off.* I.152–61.

This is a possible interpretation, but far from certain. If Cicero had the book, he was not only vague about its contents but ventured unnecessarily on an explicit false statement A(1), for A(1) is contradicted by C(i) and C(iii). Had he been misled by a memory of C(ii), which has no reference? A(4) could easily arise from hearsay, since he was obviously uncertain how relevant this section was for his purpose (cf. D.L. VII.109), and in the end it was never used or mentioned again (C(i); *Off.* III.34). Indeed the *liber* is never referred to again either to Atticus or in *Off.*, where Cicero is noticeably vague about Commentarii and a letter, although he criticises Panaetius' *liber*. Cicero's eagerness for Athenodorus' κεφάλαια (*quae* A(3) with reference to τὰ κεφάλαια only), and his urgent demands for its delivery (F41a.11), make more sense if he did not have Περὶ καθήκοντος, and did not know when he could expect it. So on the whole, 'I have sent for' seems a likely interpretation of *arcessivi*, and it remains an open question whether Cicero ever received Posidonius' book; or at least it may have arrived after Athenodorus' ὑπόμνημα (B), which dissuaded Cicero from the labour of reading the book for the purposes of *De Off.* III.

What did Cicero expect from Athenodorus under the label of τὰ κεφάλαια? The close juxtaposition of the reference to Posidonius' book would suggest some sort of résumé or epitome. It is known that some admirers and followers of Posidonius wrote such epitomes, e.g. Geminus' ἐπιτομή (F18, T42), the τακτικὰ κεφάλαια of Asclepiodotus (F80, T41), the Posidonian σχολαί of Phanias (T43). Athenodorus himself may have written a commentary on Περὶ ὠκεανοῦ (T79, Frs. 214, 215) of which Cicero could have known. In this case however something less elaborate and formal was perhaps expected. In any case Cicero must have specified the particular topic in which he was interested. On the other hand what Cicero expected and what he got from Athenodorus need not have been the same thing. He did not receive a résumé of Περὶ καθήκοντος as F41c (C(i)) shows, but information on the few remarks Posidonius had made on the topic of apparent conflict between *honestum* and *utile*, culled from certain Commentarii and perhaps other sources. Cicero was well pleased with the ὑπόμνημα (B), because it told him all he needed to know about Posidonius on the topic. It seems certain from the very vague reference to *quibusdam commentariis* (C(i)) that Cicero's knowledge of these merely derived from Athenodorus' ὑπόμνημα. The equally vague reference to the letter containing the cautionary remark of P. Rutilius Rufus (C(iii)) probably derives from the same source. It would follow that Cicero's knowledge of any Posidonian material suitable for *De Off.* III was second-hand from Athenodorus' ὑπόμνημα, did not derive from the book Περὶ καθήκοντος, and was so exiguous in amount and relevance that it played no part in Cicero's book; for he says in *De Off.* III.34, *hanc igitur partem relictam explebimus nullis adminiculis, sed ut dicitur Marte nostro. neque enim quicquam est de hac parte post Panaetium explicatum, quod quidem mihi probaretur, de iis quae in manus meas venerunt.*

But some evidence emerges, if only negative, for Posidonius' Περὶ καθήκοντος. We are entitled to infer from the ὑπόμνημα of Athenodorus, as filtered through Cicero, that the Περὶ καθήκοντος did not contain a discussion on the apparent clash between *honestum* and *utile*, but that Posidonius briefly touched on the topic in Commentarii. Also we have no reason to disbelieve Cicero that a section of Περὶ καθήκοντος was subtitled Περὶ τοῦ κατὰ περίστασιν καθήκοντος. Of the Commentarii there is no further evidence, and it is always possible that it is a vague phrase of Cicero's to cover scattered Posidonian sources from which material was culled and brought together by Athenodorus in his ὑπόμνημα; but they could have existed, although in what form is uncertain from the title itself, and been referred to by Athenodorus. The quotation in the Letter (C(iii)) is without context, but if, as is probable, it also is derived from Athenodorus' ὑπόμνημα, the context must be Posidonius' views on the apparent conflict between *honestum* and *utile*, and therefore further evidence, on Athenodorus' authority, that Posidonius did not write a separate treatise on this topic.

For Athenodorus Calvus: T44; for P. Rutilius Rufus: T13.

LOGIC

F42 Diogenes Laertius, VII.54

CONTENT

Posidonius, in his book *On Criterion*, said that some older Stoics recognised ὀρθὸς λόγος as a criterion.

CONTEXT

The account of Stoic logic in D.L. VII.41–83 comprises three distinguishable sections. 41–8 contain some general remarks on τὸ λογικὸν μέρος. 49–54 begin a more detailed account and are concerned with an exposition of φαντασία as the criterion of truth and the *sine qua non* of everything else that follows, and ends in 54 with a doxography of the criterion of truth. But this in turn is described as a prelude (προτάττειν, 49) to 'logic', and 55–83 make a new start with dialectic beginning with voice, and consist of the main account of Stoic logic. 49 opens with a quotation from the *Compendium of Philosophers* of Diocles of Magnesia, from which it has often been assumed that the whole of 49–83 is derived. I believe that the Diocles 'quotation' is confined to 49 (Kidd, 'Orthos Logos'). Mejer (*Diogenes Laertius and his Hellenistic Background* 5–7) argued that the whole of 38–159 must have been taken *in toto* from a single source. If so, that source itself must have had very mixed origins (T66 comm.). 54 then is the culmination of the continuous exposition of the section 49–54, in which there is Posidonian trace. But the main account of Stoic logic which follows in 55–83 owes nothing to Posidonius (T66 comm.). Mansfeld, in *Elenchos* 7 (1986), 351–73, argues that 49–53 are derived from Diocles.

COMMENT

Title

It may be by chance, but it is nevertheless remarkable considering the interest roused by this topic in Stoic philosophy, that this title is not evidenced elsewhere in surviving Stoic literature, not even in Chrysippus' voluminous bibliography (311 volumes on logic alone; D.L. VII.189ff). Graeser (*Zenon von Kition* 60–8) argued that the logical problem of a criterion of truth was an Academic and Sceptic characteristic, and that Stoics did not speak of a criterion of truth in that sense; but this fragment indicates that Chrysippus used the term for καταληπτική φαντασία. And Zeno could not have been unfamiliar with the technical implications of the term as the title Περὶ κριτηρίου ἢ Κανών is as early as Epicurus (D.L. x.27; Usener, p. 85, 104f). However, although the topic of φαντασίαι could be treated as a sub-section of Stoic dialectic, as in the initial general account of logic in D.L. vii.43, theory of knowledge was also regarded by Stoics as part of natural philosophy, being psychology (Sandbach, *The Stoics* 85); and Chrysippus dealt with the problem in the second book Περὶ φυσικῶν (line 3), rather than as a separate book on logic. Posidonius was interested enough and thought the topic of sufficient importance to devote a separate book to it under that title. As such it is contributory evidence, despite the paucity of surviving logical fragments, for the serious attention paid by Posidonius to logic as an organic part of philosophy (F88; in general, Kidd, 'Posidonius and Logic' 273ff).

Extent of fragment

The Posidonian reference may be limited to the last sentence on ὀρθὸς λόγος, but there is a reasonable probability from form, provenance and characteristics of content that the whole doxography comes from him.

The surviving evidence shows that doxographies were characteristic of Posidonius' works (T101/102 comm.), and it is likely that there was one in *On Criterion*; and if such a monograph was unusual for the Stoics, it would be a natural source for the compiler, with Posidonius' name coming last in the list. The list itself has a stress on 2nd c. Stoicism, containing the three names, Antipater, Apollodorus and Boethus, which recur most frequently in other Posidonian doxographies. The most important evidence is the comment on Chrysippus, διαφερόμενος πρὸς αὑτόν (7). *BPF* have πρὸς αὐτόν (i.e. Boethus), which makes nonsense of the relative dating of Chrysippus and Boethus (Zeller III.1.47 N. 2). πρὸς αὑτόν (von Arnim; already by Hirzel, *Untersuchungen* II.10) is clearly right, and alleges self-contradiction on Chrysippus' part. Such a side comment is most unusual in Diogenes (Mejer, 6 n. 14), but the charge of self-contradiction is at the very centre of Posidonius' attack on Chrysippus (T83, Frs. 34, 159, 164.87–93, 165.121). And when this is juxtaposed to a reference to 'the older Stoics', to whom Posidonius continually referred in the contextual accusation that Chrysippus had misinterpreted or ignored their views (T101, 102; Frs. 165, 166.19–31, 34), the likelihood of Posidonian origin becomes very strong. The doxography refers to 'the older Stoics', but has no specific entry for Zeno and Cleanthes, or for anyone before Chrysippus.

ὀρθὸς λόγος *and 'some other older Stoics'*

The ascription of ὀρθὸς λόγος as a criterion to some others of the older Stoics raises historical and philosophical problems which have been much debated.

Who are meant by ἄλλοι τινες τῶν ἀρχαιοτέρων Στωϊκῶν? Corssen's deletion of Στωϊκῶν should be disregarded in the context of this Stoic doxography. It has generally been assumed that the reference is to Zeno and Cleanthes (Hirzel, *Untersuchungen* II.14, 23; Pohlenz, 'Zenon und Chrysipp', 187, *Die Stoa* I.60f; Rist, *Stoic Philosophy* 138–47, *Les Stoïciens et leur logique* 397; Graeser, *Zenon* 63ff). But Pearson (*Fragments* 8f, 58, 40) voiced doubts, more cogently expressed by Sandbach (*Problems* 17), who found 'certain others of the older Stoics' strange language for the founder of the School. He also argued that Zeno must have accepted καταληπτικὴ φαντασία as the criterion of truth. This is a real difficulty which Pohlenz ('Zenon und Chrysipp', 175ff; *Die Stoa* I.60ff) had tried to counter by suggesting that the criterion for Zeno was κατάληψις (comprehension) in which ὀρθὸς λόγος was involved, whereas the exclusive emphasis on καταληπτικὴ φαντασία was first made by Chrysippus. This has been rightly rejected (Sandbach, Rist, Graeser), for in the extensive ancient criticism of Stoic epistemology, including Arcesilaus and Carneades in S.E. *Adv. Math.* VII.150ff, 227ff and elsewhere, there is no mention of any change of position or contradiction between Zeno and Chrysippus. Indeed, Arcesilaus' refutation of the early Stoa in S.E. *Adv. Math.* VII.151ff is based on the position that they do *not* relate κατάληψις to λόγος, but to the καταληπτική φαντασία (Kidd, 'Orthos Logos'). So there is a double difficulty about Posidonius' statement: (a) the curiously vague ascription to some older Stoics; and (b) the evidence suggests that it is historically incorrect; Zeno did not entertain right reason as a criterion of truth.

The best way to break through this impasse is to understand how Posidonius uses such references to οἱ ἀρχαιότεροι, especially in the context of polemic against Chrysippus, which appears to be the background here (διαφερόμενος πρὸς αὐτόν, 7). He frequently claims (T91, 92, 93, 101, 102, Frs. 32, 34, 151, 165.77, 166, 182) that Chrysippus departed from or distorted positions held by 'the ancients', or, more specifically, Zeno and Cleanthes, which he, Posidonius, on the contrary was correctly interpreting. But it is also clear that he was on occasion interpreting for his own purposes very uncertain, ambiguous (T93, 91.2 comm.), perhaps even hearsay (F165.4 comm.), evidence. The nature of Zeno's extant works were such that they could be interpreted differently by successors, as with Ariston and Chrysippus. Since Posidonius saw much of his own philosophy as a development from pre-Chrysippean philosophy, he was sometimes led, in order to support his own views, to impute to it positions which derived from interpretation or inference, but appear to be historically dubious or even wrong. For example, it is highly unlikely that the early Stoa meaningfully foreshadowed his own psychology, as he claimed. If this is the background for his statement on the criterion, the suspiciously vague ascription to some older Stoics becomes immediately understandable as confirming the lack of explicit evidence even for Posidonius, and we need not feel bound to consider it as historical evidence for Zeno or the early Stoa, but rather as Posidonian apologetics in controversy.

In other words, the real historical context shifts from the early Stoa to the controversies of the 2nd and 1st centuries B.C. It was in this period that the Stoa was reacting to hard criticism of the Chrysippean καταληπτικὴ φαντασία, forced to defend, explain and review the implications of καταληπτικὴ φαντασία, κατάληψις and the criterion. Recent modern scholarship has taken up the challenge and offered solutions in change of emphasis over different aspects of the problem (Watson, *Stoic Theory of Knowledge* 34–7), or in the complexity of the Stoic theory of cognition (Cic. *Ac.* I.40–2; II.145; Rist, *Stoic Philosophy* 138–47, *Les Stoïciens et leur logique* 395; Graeser, *Zenon* 60–8) involving φαντασία, καταληπτικὴ φαντασία, συγκατάθεσις, κατάληψις, πρόληψις, ἐπιστήμη, where each stage requires interpretation both in itself and in relation to others; and so ὀρθὸς λόγος has been associated with κατάληψις or ἐπιστήμη. But this has more to do with Stoic theory of knowledge than with the criterion, which depends for Stoics on validation from the 'real' world. Kerferd (*Les Stoïciens etc.* 258–60) attempted to relate ὀρθὸς λόγος to καταληπτικὴ φαντασία as a criterion 'involving the validation of φαντασίαι by reference upwards (to intelligibles) instead of downwards (to objects of the external world)'. But all this merely illustrates the difficulties and complexities of the post-Chrysippean controversy over the criterion. The Stoics never abandoned καταληπτικὴ φαντασία as *the* criterion of truth, but under the pressure of criticism, their explanations began to include other subordinate or related criteria, as a plurality is implied in the doxography under Boethus. D.L. VII.49–53, with which 54 is connected, repays careful study in this respect (Kidd, 'Orthos Logos'). φαντασία remains *generically* the criterion, but λόγος appears as a criterion in connection with φαντασίαι which are not αἰσθητικαί. In any case, ὀρθὸς λόγος would be *a* criterion for the wise man.

There is no doubt that Posidonius, like other Stoics, maintained that καταληπτικὴ φαντασία was *the* criterion of truth, but one can understand that he may have been sympathetic to an interpretation of καταληπτικὴ φαντασία which included the active aspect of λόγος as a criterion. His psychology stressed the active role of λόγος in cognition in the different areas of his philosophy: in physics (F85); in ethics, in the training of the λόγος as the knowledge of the nature of being (F31.24), and in his definition of happiness (F187.6ff; cf. the definition of τέλος, F186.12ff). In F164.41ff he argues against Chrysippus that the state of a person's λόγος is more critical than the objective presentation (φαντασία).

Kidd, 'Orthos Logos' gives a fuller discussion of the implications of this fragment, and the problems of ὀρθὸς λόγος and the criterion.

11 The use of ἀπολείπουσι gives no clue as to the status or characteristics of this criterion, despite the theories of Stein (II.259) and Hirzel (II.11 n. 1). The verb simply means 'maintain', 'recognise'; compare line 6; F16.3; D.L. VII.168; Plu. *De SR* 1043D; S.E. *Adv. Math.* VII.55.

F43 Plutarch, *Pompeius* 42.5

CONTENT

Posidonius actually wrote up the lecture he gave before Pompey in Rhodes on General Enquiry in an attack on Hermagoras the rhetor.

CONTEXT

See T39.

COMMENT

The subject of attack is Hermagoras of Temnos of the mid-2nd c. B.C., whose work on rhetoric was of great influence (Matthes, 'Hermagoras von Temnos', *Lustrum* 3 (1958), 58–214; Kennedy, *The Art of Persuasion* 303ff; *Classical Rhetoric* 88). What is being attacked under the title Περὶ τῆς καθόλου ζητήσεως is probably Hermagoras' theory of θέσις.

Hermagoras having defined the function of the orator as τὸ τεθὲν πολιτικὸν ζήτημα διατίθεσθαι κατὰ τὸ ἐνδεχόμενον πειστικῶς (S.E. *Adv. Math.* II.62; cf. Cic. *De Inv.* I.8), subdivided πολιτικὰ ζητήματα (for which see Matthes, 123) into θέσεις (*quaestiones*) and ὑποθέσεις (*causae*) (Matthes, 124ff). ὑποθέσεις (ζητήματα ὡρισμένα) argued particular cases of particular agents and events. θέσεις (ζητήματα ἀόριστα) argued general questions within the sphere of πολιτικὰ ζητήματα in a broad sense (Matthes, 129ff). Cicero's examples of such Hermagorean θέσεις in *De Inv.* I.8 are: *ecquid sit bonum praeter honestatem? verine sint sensus? quae sit mundi forma? quae sit solis magnitudo?* Whether or not there is some misunderstanding involved here (Matthes, 131f; Kennedy, *The Art* 305), Cicero's immediate reaction is explicit, that these questions are the business of the philosopher rather than fodder for the rhetor. In other words, the debate concerned the conflicting spheres of philosophy and rhetoric. F18 (cf. F90) shows that Posidonius' answer was complex, in that the subject matter of philosophy and the sciences and μαθήματα could overlap, but that the ultimate answers to such questions as causes were the responsibility of philosophy. The debate continued in rhetoric, and Cicero offered his own later compromise in *De Orat.* and *Or.*: Wehrli, *MH* 35 (1978), 90f; v. Arnim, *Dion v. Prusa* 92.

Posidonius elsewhere disagreed with Hermagoras on the technical subject of στάσις: F189.

F44 Diogenes Laertius, VII.60

CONTENT

Posidonius defined ποίημα and ποίησις in his *Introduction to Style.*

CONTEXT

This occurs in the expanded account of Stoic logic, in the classification φωνή (language) (F188 Context). It is immediately preceded (59) by the definitions of the five ἀρεταὶ λόγου (good Greek, lucidity, conciseness, appropriateness, artistry), and is followed by ὅρος, as defined by Antipater and Chrysippus.

COMMENT

The title and content show that Posidonius is engaged in the rhetorical division of Stoic logic; but context, and σημαντικόν (5), reveal the connections with the language (φωνή) subdivision of dialectic.

1–3 Posidonius defines ποίημα as a style of speech (λέξις) in metre or rhythm, done with artistry (or elaboration, μετὰ κατασκευῆς), and outstepping the form of prose.

2 **μετὰ σκευῆς** *BPF*. But κατασκευή is the rhetorical technical term for artistic treatment (ἡ ποιητικὴ κατασκευή – poetry as an art, Strabo, I.2.6) or elaboration (D.H. *Pomp.* 2); a Stoic definition was given in the previous paragraph (D.L. VII.59) as λέξις ἐκπεφευγυῖα τὸν ἰδιωτισμόν. Kaibel's emendation is therefore probable. But the fact that κατασκευή and λογοειδές recur in Str. I.2.6 is hardly sufficient grounds to claim that passage as a fragment of Posidonius, as Theiler does.

3f We are given an example for ἔνρυθμος, but not for

ἔμμετρος; so Brink, *Horace on Poetry* I.65 n. 3, tentatively suggested a lacuna; but, as he added, the change to indirect speech may indicate compression. Perhaps simply one example was felt to be enough. It is not very clear what the difference here between ἔμμετρος and ἔνρυθμος would be (cf. D.H. *Comp.* 11; but for ῥυθμός distinguished from μέτρον: Quint. *Inst.* IX.4.45, and E. M. Cope, *An Introduction to Aristotle's Rhetoric* (London, 1867), 389f).

τὸν should not be changed to τὸ with the *ed. princeps*, but deleted with Kaibel.

The Euripidean quotation is important, because it gives an example of a Posidonian ποίημα as distinct from ποίησις.

4f ποίησις is defined as a ποίημα which signifies, i.e. conveys a meaning (σημαντικόν), containing an imitation of things divine and human.

The most penetrating study of the literary context of this fragment occurs in Brink, *Horace on Poetry* I. ch. 1 (43–78). He illustrates the preoccupation with defining and relating the terms ποίημα and ποίησις in poetical theory in Neoptolemus (3rd c. B.C.), Lucilius (2nd c. B.C.), Posidonius, Varro and Philodemus. While there are interesting points of comparison and difference, Posidonius' treatment is idiosyncratic in that the distinction between the two terms depends on a Stoic logical term, σημαντικόν. As F189 shows, Posidonius was in the habit of importing Stoic dialectical classifications into contemporary debates on rhetorical technicalities (*vox*, *res* for *status*). So here σημαντικόν has a Stoic implication deeper than the Aristotelian use applied to nouns, verbs and phrases (*Int.* 16a 19, 16b 26; *Po.* 1457a 14), and reflects the division of dialectic into σημαίνοντα and σημαινόμενα (F188). Now ποίησις entails ποίημα, but not *vice versa*; so while ποίημα represents style, metre and artistic form, this is not sufficient for a ποίησις, or poetical work, because it is not σημαντικόν. γαῖα μεγίστη καὶ Διὸς αἰθήρ is a line of poetry in that it fulfils the formal artistic canons, but it conveys no complete sense. How Posidonius went on to elaborate the extent of scope of this principle of σημαντικόν in a poetic work we do not know, but a hint may come from the remainder of the definition. θείων καὶ ἀνθρωπείων ἐπιστήμη was the normal Stoic definition of σοφία (*SVF* II.35f; cf. for Posidonius, Kidd, 'Posidonius and Logic' 275). So perhaps Posidonius has in mind the philosopher–orator; or at least that σημαντικόν does not merely refer to significant meaning of words, phrases or even whole passages, but that poetry in its imitation of things human and divine should give significance to the objects or content of wisdom itself. And Posidonius may have used the phrase μίμησις θείων καὶ ἀνθρωπείων in reminiscence of Pl. *Rep.* x.607a 4ff, where imitative ποίησις is ideally restricted to hymns to the gods and praises of good men.

F45 Apollonius Dyscolus, *De Coniunctione* 214.4–20 Schneider

CONTENT

Posidonius in his book *On Conjunctions* was completely opposed to those who held that conjunctions merely join expressions; he maintained that they have a meaning of their own.

CONTEXT

This passage occurs immediately after Apollonius' introduction (213f Schneider), in which he briefly comments on the deficiencies of previous treatment of conjunctions. In particular the contribution of the Stoics is mentioned, with their propensity to import dialectical terms and approaches into the technical subject of grammar. Apollonius will not neglect Stoic doctrine, but will proceed by his own method.

COMMENT

Authorship

Most commentators (Reinhardt; Theiler II.414; Schneider, *ad loc.*; Uhlig, A.D. *Synt.* p. 488; Christ–Schmidt, *Geschichte der griechischen Litteratur* II.1.443; but not Pohlenz, *Die Stoa* II.26; cf. Camerer, *Hermes* 93 (1965), 202) assign this fragment to a different Posidonius, called 'Aristarchus' reciter' by Eustathius (T109f). But the strong Stoic context of Apollonius here makes Posidonius of Apamea by far the most likely candidate. Not only is the passage preceded by explicit reference to the importance of the Stoics, but it is followed by an argument based on stock Stoic propositions such as εἰ ἡμέρα ἐστί, φῶς ἐστί (214.23 Schneider). Besides, the Posidonian argument is ultimately philosophical rather than grammatical, with its emphasis on meaning rather than syntax, and is consonant with Posidonius' views. As a Stoic, Posidonius had a philosophical interest in grammar and rhetoric (esp. F192, and cf. Frs. 43, 44, 189). See also T109 for the inappropriateness of the subject matter for 'Aristarchus' reciter'.

Posidonius on conjunctions (1–8)

1–3 He criticises those who allege that conjunctions do not reveal anything (i.e. have not in themselves significant meaning) but merely join or bind the expression.

Those who are being attacked certainly include Stoics, because the stock Stoic definition of conjunction is μέρος λόγου ἄπτωτον, συνδοῦν τὰ μέρη τοῦ λόγου (D.L. VII.58; but against this view, Frede, 'Principles of Stoic Grammar', *The Stoics* 64ff). The word is closely linked to its derivation; Quint. I.4.18 prefers the translation *convinctiones* to the usual *coniunctiones*, because of the linking function, *ex* συνδέσμῳ. That a conjunction has no meaning by itself goes back to Arist. *Po.* 1456b 38ff, σύνδεσμος δέ ἐστι φωνὴ ἄσημος.

3–6 According to Apollonius, Posidonius argued for his view by saying that conjunctions differ (from each other, i.e. each is significant in itself) as ἐπιδοῦναι differs from ἀποδοῦναι, ἀπαιτεῖν from προσαιτεῖν and other such compound forms. He is confident that (or, he proves or guarantees it because) prepositions (or prefixes) and conjunctions are a single part of speech.

In line 3, Uhlig provides the simplest cure for ὡς διαφέρει of cod. *A*. ἤδη πιστούμενος ὅτι (5) may either report a claim on the part of Posidonius, or be an inference drawn by Apollonius from his statement or argument. But whatever the reading of (3) and interpretation of (5), it is clear that Posidonius was arguing for significant conjunctions on the analogy of significant prefixes.

In the first place, in common grammatical usage, the term πρόθεσις covered both prepositions and prefixes: A.D. *Synt.* 444.9ff Uhlig; cf. D.H. *De Comp.* VI.108.15ff Roberts, where κατ in κατιδών is regarded as a πρόθεσις. Secondly, σύνδεσμος was a wide term originally intended to include any connective elements of speech such as conjunctions, particles, prepositions, prefixes, and was thought of as merely expressing a relation of time, place, cause etc., of one thing to another without independent significance: in general Cope, *Introduction to Aristotle's Rhetoric* 371–4, 392–7; Schmidt, *Stoicorum Grammatica* 46ff. In the development of grammar Quintilian (I.4.18f) tells us that Aristotle had three parts of speech: nouns, verbs, σύνδεσμοι, which were gradually increased especially by the Stoics, first by the article and then by prepositions. The recognition of a separate category of prepositions was late (in spite of Galen, *De Plac.* 498.6f De L = *SVF* II.148), because the evidence is that the Stoics generally presented four parts of speech (noun, verb, conjunction, article, D.H. *De Comp.* II.70.15ff Roberts). Above all, Apollonius (*Synt.* 436.10ff Uhlig), commenting on prepositions deriving their name from being prothetic, says that this was the reason Stoics called prepositions προθετικοὺς συνδέσμους, thinking that the nomenclature came better from their particular construction, rather than from their meaning or sense (ἤπερ ἀπὸ τῆς δυνάμεως), like hypothetical conjunctions (συναπτικοί, i.e. εἰ etc.), copulatives (συμπλεκτικοί) and the rest (cf. Schol. Londin. in Dion. Th., 519.26 Hilgard; Prisc. *Inst.* XIV.18). It appears then that Posidonius accepted this wide Stoic definition of σύνδεσμοι, but used it to combat the Stoic denial of their independent significance. This would be a typical method of argument on his part, using a School definition to criticise a Chrysippean position; compare F34.

6–8 'At least (γοῦν, part proof of what has just been said) again in the same diametrically opposed reply to these people he sets out the natural conjunctions, saying that by their meaning (διὰ τὴν δύναμιν) . . .', the sense must be: 'they differ'.

δύναμιν is the last word of fol. 92 of *A*, and Schneider must be right that a lacuna follows, because 8–16 cuts in immediately with the remnants of Apollonius' criticism. The lacuna may be considerable, since *A* is again badly and deeply lacunose after the Posidonian passage (see Schneider, 214f).

The lacuna is particularly unfortunate, because Posidonius now abandoned the analogy of prepositions and prefixes (i.e. προθετικοὶ σύνδεσμοι), and turned his attention to 'natural' conjunctions, i.e. to conjunctions proper. This would inevitably bring him to Stoic propositional logic, which was concerned with and classified by arguments based on σύνδεσμοι such as εἰ, ἐπεί, καί, ἤτοι . . . ἤ, διότι (hypothetical/συνημμένον, inferential/παρασυνημμένον, conjunctive/συμπεπλεγμένον, disjunctive/διεζευγμένον, causal/αἰτιῶδες: D.L. VII.71f). If so, this would help to explain Apollonius' warnings against Stoic dialectical intrusion (Context), and his examination of some such arguments after this passage. And this was a common complaint against Stoic grammarians; thus D.H. *De Comp.* IV.96.12ff Roberts, protesting that Chrysippus' Περὶ τῆς συντάξεως τῶν τοῦ λόγου μερῶν was about the dialectical grouping of propositions, not about rhetoric. All we can say is that Posidonius vigorously opposed the syntactical approach to such conjunctions, and put forward instead some kind of semantic theory. For the possible significance of this step in Galen, *I.L.* IV: J. Brunschwig, 'Le modèle conjonctif', *Les Stoïciens etc.* 74f. For further evidence of Posidonius' linguistic interest in the conjunctions of Stoic propositional logic: F192 on ἐπεί.

For the characteristic vigour and passion of this attack (6f): Frs. 46, 47, 18.7, 165.166, 168.

Apollonius' criticism (8–16)

It is impossible to say how much of Apollonius' criticism has been lost, for there is no sign of an attack on Posidonius' basic position, that in philosophy of language a σύνδεσμος is a φωνὴ σημαντική. What survives contests his argument by analogy, by denying that prepositions or prefixes are conjunctions (15f).

8–12 Apollonius is in the middle of an illustration whereby he distinguishes different usages of ἵνα and ὄφρα by grammatical function. Both words can perform as final conjunctions (σύνδεσμος ἀποτελεστικός); but they also occur as adverbs of place or time (ἐπίρρημα τοπικόν *or* χρονικόν), in which case 'the expression forbids calling them conjunctions' (9). This last phrase shows that this argument comes from Apollonius against a missing statement from Posidonius that they are all natural conjunctions but distinguished in meaning. Apollonius repeats the same classifications of ἵνα and ὄφρα in *Conj.* 243.11–25, 244.6ff; *Adv.* 154.28ff; *Synt.* 485. He also uses the same examples from Homer, so it is likely that his illustration of the ἐπίρρημα τοπικόν for ἵνα, namely ἵνα τ' ἔτραφεν ἠδ' ἐγένοντο (*Od.* x.417) also occurred in the lacuna in our passage.

12 ἀποτελεστικός *Skrzeczka*: αἰτιολογικός *A*. Sk.

emended *A* because with σύνδεσμοι like ἵνα and ὄφρα, Apollonius distinguishes two conjunctive forms: causal (αἰτιολογική) and final (ἀποτελεστική): *Conj.* 243.19ff, 244.24ff; *Adv.* 154.31; *Synt.* 376f, 382, 388.9ff. But usually this is with reference to ἵνα, and αἰτιολογικός (or αἰτιώδης) may have been the common general term, especially in relation to Stoic logical grammar; see Dionysius Thrax 93 Uhlig.

13–16 Apollonius concludes (οὖν): according to this argument there is nothing to prevent parts of speech which have taken on themselves a meaning or function (δύναμιν) equal to conjunctions being called conjunctions homophonic (ὁμοφωνοῦντας) with prepositions, but by no means (οὐ μήν), as Posidonius thought, can prepositions (i.e. prefixes) of the sort given in ἐπιδοῦναι, ἀποδοῦναι be called conjunctions.

Apollonius' argument appears to be: in the case of ἵνα and ὄφρα you have words which are homophones but different in grammatical function (conjunctive and adverbial). So too you could say that there are cases where prepositions and conjunctions are homophones, but prepositions are not conjunctions, any more than adverbs are.

Apollonius proceeds immediately after the fragment (214.20–5) to say that he has not forgotten the argument that prepositions cannot be completely substituted for σύνδεσμοι, because an article has to be supplied. The examples come from Stoic propositional logic, e.g. with εἰ ἡμέρα ἐστί, φῶς ἐστί compare διὰ τὸ ἡμέραν εἶναι φῶς ἐστί. Whether this comes from the Posidonian context is unknown, because further lacunae follow in the text.

SCIENCES AND HISTORY

F46 Proclus, *In Euclidis Elementa*, pp. 199.3–200.6 Friedlein

CONTENT

Posidonius wrote a book against Zeno of Sidon, attacking his criticisms of Euclidean axiomatic geometry.

CONTEXT

Proclus has just turned from an examination of Euclid's principles (ἀρχαί) to the propositions which follow the principles. The fragment forms part of the introduction to the propositions. F47 returns to the subject after some intervening comment.

COMMENT

Proclus provides an important classification of those who attack geometry (i.e. Euclidean geometry) (1). There are two main divisions, of which the first is further subdivided.

A. (1–7)

'The greatest number (οἱ μὲν πλεῖστοι) have raised objections with regard to the principles (ἀρχαί), spending their efforts on showing the parts (τὰ μέρη) are without foundation (ἀνυπόστατα).'

In line 2, either ⟨ταῦτα⟩ τὰ μέρη should be read with Morrow, in which case 'these parts' refer to the principles; or τὰ μέρη means 'the single parts', i.e. the propositions and theorems (cf. S.E. *Adv. Math.* III.18), which would be ἀνυπόστατα if the principles were destroyed.

This class is now subdivided into:

(**a**) (**3–6**) **τῶν μέν**: 'those who try to destroy all knowledge like hostile troops doing away with crops from a foreign land, namely the one productive of philosophy. These are the Sceptics' (οἱ Ἐφεκτικοί).

(**b**) (**6f**) **τῶν δέ**: 'those who propose to overturn geometric principles only: Epicureans' (οἱ Ἐπικούρειοι).

B. (7–12),

οἱ δέ: 'others already even (καί, 8) concede the principles, but deny that what follows the principles (i.e. the propositions) are demonstrated without something else being admitted for them, which is not actually contained in the principles. It was this kind of controversy that Zeno of Sidon pursued, although (μὲν . . . δέ) he was an Epicurean. Posidonius wrote an entire (ὅλον, 12) book against him, showing that his whole conception was unsound.'

Proclus will return to the Zenonian controversy later; see F47.

The importance of the classification is that it distinguishes Zeno not only from the wholesale scepticism of the Sceptics, but also from the Epicureans who refuse Euclid's principles (so correctly, Vlastos, 'Zeno of Sidon as a Critic of Euclid', *The Classical Tradition*, ed. Wallach, 152f, against Crönert, *Kolotes und Menedemos* 109). But it is still (*pace* Vlastos, 154ff) an attack on the whole of Euclidean axiomatic geometry falling under Proclus' heading τῶν πρὸς γεωμετρίαν ἐνστάντων (1). But the thrust of the attack is different, it is directed against methodology: *even* (καί, 8) if you grant the principles (in any axiomatic system), what follows (i.e. the propositions and theorems) can not be demonstrated.

For the details and significance of this controversy, see F47. There is a trace of this position in S.E. *Adv. Math.* III.93, where after the ἀρχαί have been attacked in 1–91, Sextus says: ὅμως δὲ ἐπαγωνιζόμενοι πειρασόμεθα διδάσκειν ὅτι κἂν τῶν ἀρχῶν ἀποστῶμεν τῶν τῆς γεωμετρίας, οὐ δύνανται θεώρημα συστῆσαι οἱ γεωμέτραι οὐδ' ἀποδεῖξαι. But in fact Sextus does not proceed on these lines. Proclus clearly reveals the strength of Posidonius' feelings on this matter: he devoted an entire book to showing up the rottenness (σαθράν, 13) of Zeno's conception (and cf. F47.44ff, 64ff). Zeno was roughly a contemporary of Posidonius, and there may have been personal animosity between the two, but the heat of this controversy arises from the fundamental importance for Posidonius of the issue under debate; see F47 comm.

F47 Proclus, *In Euclidis Elementa*, pp. 214.15–218.11 Friedlein

CONTENT

Posidonius' refutation of Zeno of Sidon's criticism of the methodology of axiomatic geometry.

CONTEXT

After F46, Proclus, turning to Proposition I.I (On a given finite straight line to construct an equilateral triangle), offers some introductory distinctions relevant to the propositions in general and to Prop. I.I in particular, for example: the difference between problems and theorems, their structure, and the clarification of technical terms employed. In his exposition he is going to select the most elegant comments of οἱ παλαιοί, and what is most competent, reliable and fundamental. So he turns to the controversy between Zeno and Posidonius. He is clearly on the latter's side.

ANALYSIS

The Proposition under question is I.I: to describe an equilateral triangle on a straight line of given length.

A. Introduction (1–3)

'Since some have objected to the construction of the equilateral triangle, thinking that they were refuting (διελέγχειν) the whole of geometry, a brief answer will be given to them.'

This makes clear that the object of the attack is the whole of Euclidean geometry.

B. (3–17)

Zeno's methodological objection to Prop. 1.1. 'That Zeno who was mentioned before (F46) says: *even* if (κἂν, 4) one concedes the principles of geometry, what follows would not be established, unless it were admitted that two straight lines can not have a common segment. If that is not granted, the construction of the equilateral triangle is not demonstrated.' Cf. F46.8–10.

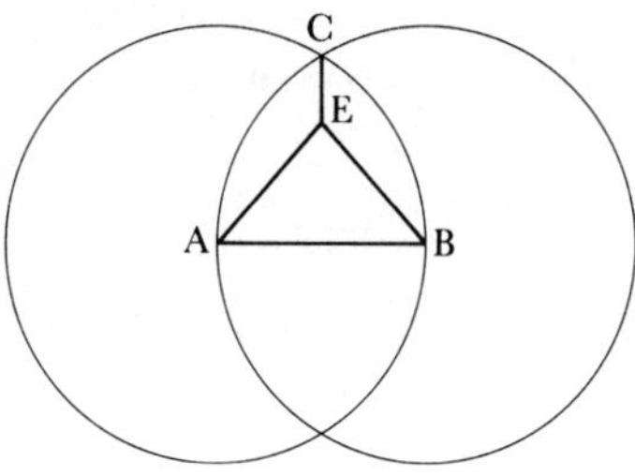

Fig. 1

7–14 Suppose CE to be the common segment of CEA and CEB. AE and BE would then be less than AB. Therefore the triangle is not equilateral (Fig. 1).

14–17 Therefore even (καί) granted the ἀρχαί, τὰ ἑξῆς do not follow, unless this too is first presupposed: neither circumferences nor straight lines can have common segments.

C. (18–29)

First answer: Zeno's missing presupposition is already given in the principles, (a) in the definition of straight line (20–6), and (b) from the postulates (26–9).

'Against this is must first be said (πρῶτον μέν, 18; the answering δέ comes at line 29) that this in a way (τρόπον τινα) *has* been presupposed in the first principles (ἀρχαί) (namely that no two straight lines have a common segment) (18–20). For the definition (ὁρισμός) of straight line already has this (i.e. Definition 4), if a straight line is a line that lies evenly with all the points on itself (20f). For, it is the fact that the interval between points is equal to the straight line between them that makes the line that joins them one and the shortest (21–3); so that if any line coincides with a part, it would coincide with the remaining part (i.e. the rest would coincide). For if stretched to the extremities, through being the shortest, the whole line must fall on the whole line (23–6); and furthermore because this has been evidently assumed in the postulates (αἰτήμασιν; in fact, Postulate 2). For the postulate that a finite straight line may be extended in a straight line, shows clearly that the extended line must be one single line and its extension result from a single motion' (26–9).

D. (29–35)

Second answer: we can prove this anyway.

'But if one must have a proof of this as if it were a lemma (i.e. a proposition invoked for the purpose of establishing another; see Proclus, 211.1ff Fr.):

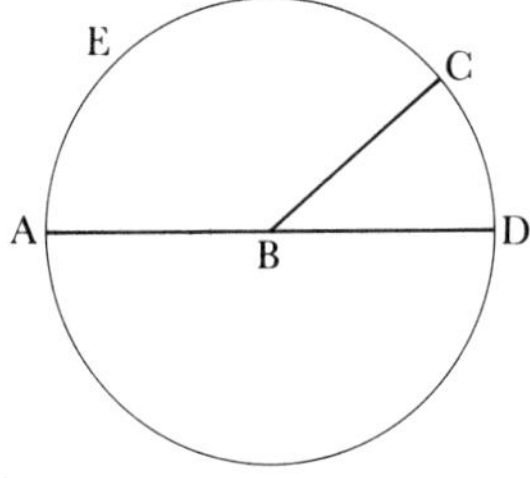

Fig. 2

Let AB be common segment, if possible, of AC and AD. With B as centre and AB as radius, describe circle ACD. Since ABC is a straight line through the centre, AEC is a semicircle. Since ABD is a straight line through the centre, AED is a semicircle. Therefore AEC = AED, which is impossible' (Fig. 2).

E. (36–43)

Zeno's riposte: this would still leave an undemonstrated assumption.

'To this proof Zeno could say: again that the diameter cuts the circle in half has been proved (157.10ff Fr.) only on our presupposition that two circles have no common segment. For we presupposed that one circle coincided thus with another, or, if it didn't coincide, it fell outside or inside. But, he says, there is nothing to hinder, if one circle does not wholly coincide with the other, that they may *partly* coincide. And as long as it has not been *proved* that the diameter cuts the circle in half, the proposition will not be proved either.'

It is to be noted that Zeno's complaint is that there is always something left *undemonstrated.*

F. (44–54)

Posidonius' answer: that can be refuted whichever assumption Zeno adopts.

'That objection Posidonius correctly met with a jibe at our sharp 'Epicurus' for not realising that even if the circles only in part coincide, the proof is valid.'

There is no need to change Ἐπίκουρον at line 45 to Ἐπικούρειον with Bake and Morrow; it is not uncommon practice to call the representative of a School the name of the Founder: so exactly Plu. *Mor.* 548A, 928E, and cf. Cherniss, Plu. *Mor.*, Loeb vol. XII.6; and the sarcasm of the whole phrase is patent.

47ff 'For at the part they do not coincide, one circle will be outside and the other inside, and the same absurdity results if the straight line is extended from the centre to the outside circle. For the lines from the centre will be equal,

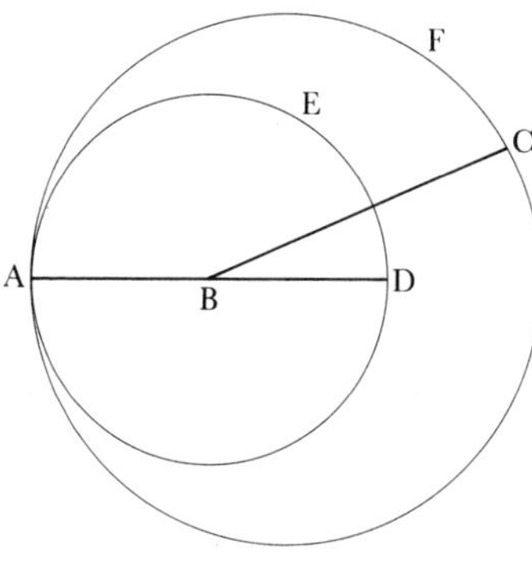

Fig. 3

both the line to the outer circle which is greater (BC), and the line to the inside circle which is less (BD).' That is, BC = BD as radii – B being the centre point of both circles; but BC is greater than BD, since AFC lies outside AED (Fig. 3).

'So *either*, one coincides wholly with the other and they are equal; *or*, one coincides partly and diverges for the rest; *or*, no part coincides with any part, and if so, either falls outside or inside. And all these are refuted in the same way' (51–4).

Posidonius' point is that Zeno's objection is refuted whichever of these assumptions you adopt; and you must adopt one of them, for they are exhaustive.

G. (55–64)

Zeno himself constructs a similar proof which he claims also in its turn demands an unproved assumption.

'But Zeno constructs another proof of this kind which he tries to discredit (διαβάλλειν).

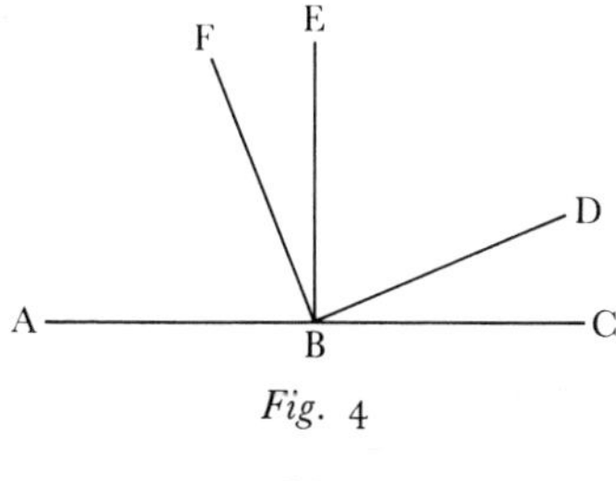

Fig. 4

Let two straight lines AC and AD have a common segment AB, and let BE be drawn at right angles to AC (Fig. 4). Then the angle EBC will be a right angle. Now if the angle EBD is also a right angle, the two angles will be equal, which is impossible. But if it is not a right angle, let BF be drawn at right angles to AD. Then the angle FBA will be a right angle. But the angle EBA is also a right angle. Therefore the two angles are equal, which is impossible. That is the proof. Zeno tries to discredit it on the grounds that it already contains an assumption which is only established later, namely that one can draw a line at right angles to a given straight line from a given point.'

H. (64–75)

Posidonius accuses Zeno of sharp practice here, but even this bad proof can be met.

'But Posidonius says that a proof like that nowhere occurs in any elementary treatise on mathematics, and that Zeno is adopting sharp practice (συκοφαντεῖν) against mathematicians of his own day by implying that they use a bad proof (64–7). But there is an account (λόγον) to give even of this proof. For, however you look at it (πάντως), there is a line at right angles to each of the two straight lines, for any two straight lines can form a right angle. And that was presupposed in the definition of right angle. For it is only from such an inclination that we establish a right angle. So let it be this one which we have erected (67–72).'

Posidonius adds (72–5) that Epicurus himself agrees and all other philosophers agree to entertain many hypotheses that are possible and many that are materially impossible in order to contemplate their consequences. Posidonius is using hypothesis here in the technical sense of definition which is conceded without demonstration, and so distinguished from postulate (αἴτημα) which requires proof (F195). He is accusing Zeno of treating hypotheses as if they were postulates, and so wrongly demanding their demonstration.

COMMENT

The passion of Posidonius' attack clearly arises from the fundamental issue at stake between him and Zeno. This has been obscured by Vlastos ('Zeno of Sidon as a Critic of Euclid', *The Classical Tradition*, ed. Wallach, 148–59), who thought that Zeno's methodological attack was directed against the incompleteness of Euclid's system: 'Zeno's complaint . . . could be met in full by simply *adding* some further propositions to Euclid's postulate-set.' This is a misconstruction. In the first place, Zeno is classified in F46 under the general heading of those attacking geometry (F46.1); this is strengthened in F47.2 by οἰόμενοι τὴν ὅλην γεωμετρίαν διελέγχειν, which must have a general reference of intention. The introduction of Zeno's position at F46.8–10 is a general statement covering anything following from any principle. We are not concerned merely with an unnamed assumption behind Prop. 1.1, but with a general attack on the method of axiomatic geometry. Secondly, the force of the repeated καί at F46.8, F47.4, F47.14f stresses that *even* if one concedes the principles, τὰ ἐφεξῆς could not be established: Zeno is out to destroy the whole structure of Euclidean geometry.

Thirdly, at F47.42 Zeno demands not only inclusion of an assumption, but proof of it, and however his objection is met, he can always show another unproved assumption behind the proffered refutation (F47.36ff). On the other hand, Posidonius meets this by trying to show that whatever additional assumption is demanded by Zeno, he can refute the objection; and at one point attempts to give an exhaustive list of alternative assumptions (F47.44–54).

Finally, Posidonius asserts (F47.67–75) that one has to accept some hypotheses, in the technical sense of definitions not requiring proof, and implies that Zeno was against accepting any at all. διαβάλλειν (F47.56) and συκοφαντεῖν (F47.66) are not words which supporters of Euclidean geometry, like Posidonius and Proclus, would use of a man who was trying to improve it by making it more watertight, but of a man who was attempting to destroy it by objecting to its whole formal structure. Zeno's aim was the same as other Epicureans' (Posidonius even calls him 'our sharp Epicurus', F47.45), the refusal of Euclidean geometry in favour of an empirical mathematics (cf. De Lacy, *Philodemus on Methods of Inference* 147f; Crönert, *Kolotes und Menedemos* 109–11). But while they attacked the base in the principles, he tried to show that even if you granted the principles, an axiomatic system would not work methodologically, because it would always involve additional unproved assumptions.

The interesting thing is Posidonius' anger. This is only explicable if not only Euclid was at stake, but also his own philosophical methodology. Apart from his clear interest in Euclidean mathematics (Frs. 195–8), in logic he stressed that the validity of relational syllogisms depended on 'the implied force of an axiom' (F191). But his whole philosophy (F18) depended on an axiomatic system of apodeictic proof. For the importance of this in an assessment of Posidonius: Kidd, 'Posidonius and Logic', 273–83; *A & A* 24 (1978), 7–15.

F48a, b Anonymus II, *Isagoga in Arati Phaenomena* 2.2 (p. 142f Maass; Anonymus II 3, p. 4f Martin); Anonymus II, *In Arati Phaenomena, Arati Genus* 3 (p. 249f Maass; *Vita III* p. 16f Martin)

CONTENT

Posidonius in a book, *On the Comparison of Aratus and Homer on Mathematics*, followed Hipparchus and Dionysius in accusing Aratus of relying completely on Eudoxus, and of being no mathematician (i.e. scientist). '"For," says he, "we don't make him a doctor because he wrote Medical Powers (δυνάμεις, prescriptions? cf. Oribasius, 10.33), so we shall not make him a scientist either, when he said nothing that falls outside (foreign to, ξένον) Eudoxus' work."'

COMMENT

The Latin version of the Introduction (F48a) is so barbarous that there seems little point in attempting to emend it (cf. Martin, pp. 4f). But the comparison of 48a.14–17 with 48b.6–10 shows that Posidonius' name has fallen out of the latter, and that the title, Περὶ συγκρίσεως Ἀράτου καὶ Ὁμήρου περὶ τῶν μαθηματικῶν belongs to him. *Praedicatio* in 48a.16 is a vaguer word, probably meaning no more than Propositions, Teaching. The Latin translator was also ignorant, because the Dionysius mentioned at 48a.15 is *manifeste* ⟨*non*⟩ *potius Thrax* in this scientific company. He is also probably not Dionysius of Heraclea, although the latter is associated with Aratus as a fellow student in *Vita I*, p. 8.18; *Vita II*, p. 11.7; *Vita IV*, p. 19.5 Martin. He may be Dionysius of Cyrene, the Stoic and pupil of Antipater of Tarsus, γεωμέτρης ἄριστος (*Index Stoicorum* 52; Pohlenz, *Die Stoa* I.245, II.127).

Aratus was fashionable in the 1st c. B.C., translated by Cicero (in early youth, *ND* II.104), Varro and Germanicus. So also Eudorus of Alexandria is mentioned here (48a.8). Posidonius was clearly familiar with the *Phaen.* (F202.31), interested in a Stoicising writer on a scientific subject. His own work was addressed to scientific content, not literary, as is shown by the quotation (48b.10–12), the context and the company listed (Hipparchus). The criticism that the *Phaen.* was merely dependent on Eudoxus and revealed an embarrassingly inadequate scientific grasp was an old story, exampled by the anecdote on Antigonus Gonatas (48a.10ff; 48b.1ff), and more explicitly by Hipparchus' *Commentary on*

Aratus and Eudoxus (1.2.1; 1.1.8 Manitius; Frs. 4, 5 Lasserre). It was common stock in the 1st c. B.C.: Cic. *Rep.* 1.22, *non astrologiae scientia, sed poetica quadam facilitate*; Cic. *De Orat.* 1.69, *etenim si constat inter doctos, hominem ignarum astrologiae, Aratum* . . .

Posidonius' sarcastic comment (48b.10–12) certainly implies that Aratus wrote medical poems, and Ὀστολογία and Κανών have been thought to be such; but the tradition has been doubted by Effe, *Hermes* 100 (1972), 500ff.

The title would suggest that Posidonius presented both Aratus and Homer as poets writing on scientific subjects without scientific knowledge. Homer was regarded as a kind of scientific source, e.g. Strabo, Bk I (cf. T75, T77), and he probably occurred in Posidonius' doxographies: F216, F222, F137.

Beros(s)us (48a.6) was the Babylonian author (350–270 B.C.; Schnabel, *Berossus*) whom Neugebauer (*History of Ancient Mathematical Astronomy*, 607) judges had little technical astronomical information to add to Babylonian cosmogony and mythological history.

F49 Strabo, II.2.1–3.8

CONTENT

Strabo's general examination and assessment of Posidonius' Περὶ ὠκεανοῦ.

CONTEXT

Strabo's first two books are introductory to the main work, reviewing the contribution of predecessors and stating his own basic positions. The first chapter of Bk II turns to mathematical geography: §§1–3 review Eratosthenes' parallels and distances; §§4–40 present Hipparchus' criticisms of

Eratosthenes, with Strabo's comments and adjudication. After summing up his attitude to Eratosthenes and Hipparchus in §41, Strabo turns his attention next to Posidonius in II.2–3.

STRUCTURE

A. Introduction (1–5)

Strabo reviews only Περὶ ὠκεανοῦ; the general characteristics of the work, and his own use of it.

B. Zones (5–145)

(1) Preconditions (5–9)

(2) Doxography and Posidonian criticism of early predecessors (Parmenides and Aristotle) on
- (a) extent of torrid zone (10–17), with Strabo's comments on Posidonius' argument (17–36);
- (b) the use of οἱ ἀρκτικοί as a zonal determinant (37–43).

(3) Posidonius' own division of zones in relation to (a) celestial phenomena (44–8) and (b) human geography (44–61).

(4) Polybius' division into six zones (62–4) is criticised by Strabo on the basis of the Posidonian division and theory:
- (a) General criticism of Polybius (64–96) for number of zones
    - (i) on grounds of natural philosophy
        - (α) in relation to celestial phenomena (67–70)
        - (β) in relation to atmospheric zones of temperature (71–80);
    - (ii) on geographical grounds, i.e. of habitable and uninhabitable zones (80–96).
- (b) Detailed criticism of Polybius:
    - (i) Definition of zones by arctic circles (97–101).
    - (ii) Tropics as boundaries of torrid zone (101f).
    - (iii) Division of torrid zone into two (102–18).

(iv) Temperate habitable equatorial strip (118–25)
 (α) supported on astronomical grounds by Posidonius (126–9).
 (β) Polybius' grounds, namely a high mountainous area, criticised by Posidonius (130–5).
 (γ) Posidonius criticised by Strabo for inconsistency (136–9), and for a conflicting theory of an equatorial ocean (139–45).

C. Eudoxus of Cyzicus and the attempted circumnavigation of Africa (146–293)

(1) Posidonius' account:
 (a) Doxography and criticism of earlier evidence (146–50).
 (b) First voyage to India (151–70).
 (c) Second voyage to India (170–90).
 (d) Third voyage attempting to reach India round Africa (191–219).
 (e) Fourth voyage attempting the same (219–26).
 (f) Posidonius' conclusion (227–32).
(2) Strabo's criticism of Posidonius (233–93).

D. Changes in earth levels (294–6)

(1) Atlantis (297–303)
(2) The cause of the Cimbrian migrations (303–5).

E. Length of the inhabited world (305–8)

F. (309–56)

Geographical divisions in relation to variations of fauna, flora, climate, race etc.: division by zones; division by continents. Human geography and environmental ethnography.

(1) Strabo accuses Posidonius of inconsistency (309–16)

(2) Strabo's criticism of natural zonal variations (316–26)
(3) Strabo attacks Posidonius' continental variations: the Ethiopians (326–56).

G. (357–62)

Strabo's summing up and general criticism of Posidonius' inclination to natural philosophy and addiction to causal explanation.

This analysis reveals that Strabo's review must be a very inadequate account of Περὶ ὠκεανοῦ. Strabo promised to take account elsewhere of the detail, of which there was clearly much; but for a general account there are major gaps, the theory of tides, for example, perhaps because it was too scientific and philosophical for Strabo; and D and E are mere tokens. Above all, the imbalance of what is reported is striking, sections D and E, for example, compared with C. Perhaps Strabo was picking on topics of current notoriety, so C becomes grossly inflated, and ludicrous illustrations of the important topic D are included. Strabo's inability or unwillingness (F) to take account of Posidonius' larger philosophical and scientific canvas can lead to petty criticism of detail (F.(3)) or obfuscation (B, F).

Yet the order of presentation, however lacunose and distorted, could reflect the general order of the items selected from Περὶ ὠκεανοῦ. Zones, the theory of which depended on axioms from natural philosophy, were themselves probably the basis of Posidonian geography, and B led naturally into C (see B.4.b.iv. γ) the problem of circumambient ocean. So it is quite likely that Posidonius' Περὶ ὠκεανοῦ culminated in a human geography resting on the causal nexus of his natural philosophy. The title, which can be traced back to Pytheas (F9a Mette) and adopts one of the most traditional terms of Greek geography (Berger, *Erdkunde* 551f), can clearly serve the whole field of geographical investigation. Indeed Posidonius' book appears to have covered an astonishing span, not only in content but also in form, ranging from mathematical theory to the vivid narrative of Eudoxus. Even the blurred and cracked image from Strabo suggests the analysis of detail, of which much no doubt came from his travels, and the philosophical synthesis of the whole, characteristic elsewhere of Posidonius. It was possibly one of the books which established his reputation, written certainly after the travels in the nineties and after the prytany (T27), published possibly in the eighties (after 88 B.C.) or even the seventies before he saw Pompey after his eastern campaigns (F206 comm.); in general: Reinhardt, *RE* 662f; Schühlein, *Untersuchungen* 5.

COMMENT

A. Introduction (1–5)

Posidonius had been mentioned earlier in the *Geography* (see Index of Sources), but in the general survey of Strabo's most important predecessors, Posidonius' Περὶ ὠκεανοῦ deserves general examination, because of its prevalent geographical material, although some of that was rather mathematical. Further reference will be made in particular sections of the main work.

Strabo's remarks imply:

(1) Περὶ ὠκεανοῦ was Posidonius' principal work on geography, and Strabo knew it directly (T49).

(2) It had an importance and influence which put Posidonius on a par with Eratosthenes, Hipparchus and Polybius for geographical studies (see Context).

(3) Περὶ ὠκεανοῦ was not completely about what Strabo would call geography (τὰ πολλά, 2). No doubt it also overlapped on natural philosophy (see 357ff) and astronomy (T76).

(4) Even in geography, parts are strictly so (οἰκείως, 2),

but other parts are rather mathematical (3): T76, and cf. Strabo's remarks about Hipparchus. Despite this disadvantage, Strabo agrees that it was not 'out of place' (ἄτοπον, 3) to discuss here in the Introduction some of Posidonius' arguments too (καί, 3; i.e. as well as those of Eratosthenes and Hipparchus). The topic of zones is obviously in mind here.

(5) Strabo will also discuss him on individual points as they come up in his *Geography* (4f); for Strabo's actual use: T49. Strabo adds that in doing so, he will stick to a kind of μέτρον (5). Strabo mentions such a μέτρον in II.1.37, but the context is quite different. It is not clear what Strabo has in mind here, unless he means that he will not overdo his reference to and reliance on Posidonius.

B. Zones (5–145)

B. (1) Preconditions (5–9)

One of the οἰκεῖα (i.e. proper elements) related to geography is the hypothesis that the whole earth, like the universe too, is spherical, and consequently so is the acceptance of all the conclusions that follow from that hypothesis; and one of these is that the earth has five zones.

For Strabo on the importance of the hypotheses that the universe and the earth are spherical: I.1.20–21; for Posidonius: F18.20 (γῆ); F8 (κόσμος). The establishment of the sphericity of the universe and earth was the responsibility of the natural philosopher, but the topic is shared with the scientist (F18).

The theory of zones depends on sphericity in that they are defined by the circular path of heavenly bodies. So the sun determined the tropics; the 'arctic' circle was either determined by the circle of stars which never set (in the latitude of Greece, the Great Bear, ἡ Ἄρκτος), or by the sun's shadow in revolution, see below. Such circles were both celestial and in projection terrestrial. For the relationship between celestial and terrestrial zones: Strabo, II.5.3; sphericity and zones, cf. Geminus, *Isag*. XV.1; on the five zones: Achill. Tat. *Isag*. 29, p. 62ff Maass.

B. (2) Doxography and criticism of early predecessors
(a) (10–36)

10–17 'Posidonius says that it was Parmenides who was the founder of the division into five zones, but that he represented the torrid zone as virtually double in width [the codices continue: 'the zone between the tropics falling beyond the tropics outwards and overlapping the temperate zones'] falling beyond the two tropics outwards and overlapping the temperate zones; but Aristotle, he said, called the zone between the tropics the torrid zone, and the zones between the tropics and the arctic circles Aristotle called the temperate zones.'

13 The reading of the codices, τῆς μεταξὺ τῶν τροπικῶν ὑπερπιπτούσης, adopted by Aly and Aujac (Budé *ad loc.*) creates severe difficulties for the consistency of the passage in Strabo. It does not, as Jones maintains (Loeb, p. 360, n. 4; cf. Berger, *Erdkunde* 208), make Posidonius say that the torrid zone is double the zone between the tropics; but it would have to represent the explanation of Parmenides' torrid zone being virtually double in width (what Posidonius thought it to be): the zone between the tropics (presumably Parmenides' conception of the zone between the tropics) falling beyond the two tropics (i.e. the two tropics as defined by Posidonius). This is at the least confusing, but it depends also on an assumption which the reader is expected to pick up without warning, that the torrid zone is the equivalent of the zone between the tropics. Not only was this not the case for Posidonius and Strabo, but the argument of the whole passage together with Posidonius' criticism demands that the two expressions and concepts, torrid zone and zone between the tropics, should be kept distinct. When they are equated by Aristotle (14–16), this is not only made explicit, but contrasted with Parmenides in a μὲν/δέ antithesis. What is at issue is the extent of the torrid zone; Parmenides extended it beyond the tropics, Aristotle equated it with the zone between the tropics. Posidonius and Strabo criticise both, and hold that the torrid zone occupies about half or a little more than half of the zone between the tropics. Therefore it is preferable to excise τῆς μεταξὺ τῶν τροπικῶν and to adopt Brequigny's ὑπερπίπτουσαν with Kramer, Meineke, Jones and Sbordone. There are signs of scribal confusion in this area, since in line 16 τὰς δὲ μεταξὺ τῶν τροπικῶν must be supplied as Casaubon saw.

Strabo below (29), using Eratosthenes' measurement of the circumference of the earth, calculates his (and Posidonius'?) torrid zone to be 17,600 stades. If Parmenides' zone is thought to be double that figure, then by calculating 700 stades for 1° (from the Eratosthenes/Hipparchus base of 252,000) it reaches over 25°, or beyond the tropic (tropic of Cancer ≈ 24°), that is, as Posidonius said, at the temperate zone (πρὸς ταῖς εὐκράτοις, 14).

10–13 Posidonius' expression, τῆς . . . ἀρχηγόν, is vague, and Strabo's phrasing implies that the honour was uncertain. Parmenides is again credited with inaugurating discussion on zones (no number specified) in Achilles Tatius *Isag.* 31, p. 67.27 Maass, but this too probably derives from Posidonius (F209). The doxographic tradition assigns the five zones to Thales and Pythagoras or Pythagoreans (Aet. II.12 = *Dox. Gr.* 340.7ff; Aet. III.14.1 = *Dox. Gr.* 378.21ff; Ps.-Galen, *H. Ph.* = *Dox. Gr.* 633.15ff; cf. Diels, *Dox. Gr.*, *Proleg.* 181), which reveals the inadequacy of Heidel's methodology (*Frame of the Ancient Greek Maps* 65ff) based on the assumption that Diels's *vetusta placita* are not only Theophrastan but 'Posidonian *areskonta*' (p. 65).

The latter two passages also credit the Pythagoreans with the related hypothesis of the sphericity of the earth. D.L. VIII.48 also names Pythagoras as the first to call οὐρανὸν κόσμον, καὶ τὴν γῆν στρογγύλην, but adds that according to

Theophrastus, it was Parmenides. Heidel (*Ancient Greek Maps* 70–6) and others (e.g. Frank, *Platon und die sogenannten Pythagoreer* 184–200) have maintained that στρογγύλην means not spherical but disc-like or curved; but cf. D.L. IX.21 of Parmenides: πρῶτος . . . τὴν γῆν ἀπέφαινε σφαιροειδῆ καὶ ἐν μέσῳ κεῖσθαι. In this context στρογγύλη must mean spherical as Pl. *Ph.* 97d shows, where Socrates expected to find from Anaxagoras whether the earth was πλατεῖα . . . ἢ στρογγύλη. Also neither Pythagoras nor Parmenides could have been thought to be the *first* to say that the earth was disc-like. The evidence of Posidonius and Strabo also implies sphericity. There seems no reason to deny the tradition that Parmenides conceived of the earth as spherical (cf. Tarán, *Parm.* 296–8).

As for the five zones, it only confuses the issue to think of the scientific theory of the determination of the tropics, developed through the obliquity of the ecliptic (probably Oenopides, despite Aet. II.12 = *Dox. Gr.* 340f) and the work of Eudoxus (Ninck, *Die Entdeckung von Europa durch die Griechen* 46) and Eudemus (Theon Smyrnaeus, p. 199). Posidonius' ἀρχηγόν implies a more archaic situation. His manner of concentration on the torrid zone (ἡ διακεκαυμένη) suggests that he may have inferred that Parmenides distinguished zones in relation to habitable and uninhabitable zones (cf. Ach. Tat. *Isag.* 31, p. 66f Maass); he apparently believed that he could calculate the extent of Parmenides' torrid zone, but we have no idea what the evidence for this was (Berger, *Erdkunde* 211; in general, pp. 204–13). There is the curious and puzzling statement in Aet. III.11.4 = *Dox. Gr.* 377.18f, where Parmenides is said to have first marked off the inhabited places of the earth under the two zones of the solstices (ὑπὸ ταῖς δυσὶ ζώναις ταῖς τροπικαῖς). There is no evidence in Posidonius for astronomically defined tropics for Parmenides (see above), but he may have understood Parmenides to have a rough delimitation of zones in relation to the path of the sun, and thus in a very elementary sense, to have been the founder of the division into five zones. So Posidonius' evidence should not be rejected out of hand on scientific grounds (as by Reinhardt, *Parmenides* 147 n. 1; *Kosmos und Sympathie* 361).

14–17 The statement about Aristotle is borne out by *Meteor.* II.5.362a 32ff:

(i) In this case it is clear that the zones are determined by celestial zones, the tropics and the 'ever visible circle'. The summer tropic is defined by shadow procedure (362b 6f). Unfortunately the 'ever visible circle' (i.e. of stars which do not set) is variable with the latitude of the observer, unlike the fixed arctic circle, and it is not clear whether Aristotle knew this (Thomson, *History of Ancient Geography* 117; Berger, *Erdkunde* 304ff).

(ii) Aristotle's approach is to determine the habitable and uninhabitable sectors of the earth, which he marks off by tropic and arctic circle. Beyond the tropic, where the shadow disappears or falls to the south, the land is uninhabitable because of the heat, while the lands beneath the Bear are uninhabitable through cold (362b 6ff; 362b 26ff). Therefore Posidonius is justified in equating Aristotle's 'torrid' zone (διακεκαυμένη) with the zone between the tropics.

17–36 Strabo approves of (δικαίως, 17) and comments on Posidonius' criticism of Parmenides and Aristotle on the extent of the torrid zone.

(i) 17f Torrid zone is defined as the uninhabitable zone, because of heat (καῦμα). This is not merely an etymological argument; it is also based on Aristotle's own hypotheses (see above on 14–17).

(ii) 18–36 An attempt is made to calculate the extent of the torrid zone relative to the breadth of the zone between the tropics.

Unfortunately an initial statement of the thesis is made (18f), which raises a textual crux (19): οἰκήσιμον *codd.*: ⟨οὐκ⟩ οἰκήσιμον *Kramer*; 'Of the zone between the tropics more than half of the breadth is ⟨unin-⟩habitable.' This must be considered after the analysis of what follows. The thesis is derived from:

(a) Conjecture (στοχαζομένοις, 20) from the Ethiopians beyond Egypt. For conjecture in relation to Posidonius: T88.

(b) Calculation. If it is granted that the equator divides the zone between the tropics into two equal parts (20f), the northern half can be calculated.

Syene (on the summer tropic) to Meroë is 5000 stades (the codd. have μύριοι, but 5000 is guaranteed elsewhere, e.g. II.5.7) (22f).

Meroë to the 'Cinnamon' parallel, which is the beginning of the torrid zone (cf. II.1.13, Hipparchus), is 3000 stades (23–5).

So far the distances are measurable by land and sea (25f). The next part up to the equator is shown by proportional calculation (λόγῳ δείκνυται, 27).

Eratosthenes' figure for the circumference of the earth is taken, i.e. a great circle of 252,000 stades, and from this it is calculated that the distance from the Cinnamon parallel to equator is 8800 stades (27–9; cf. II.1.13, Hipparchus).

II.5.7 shows how this was done: equator to tropic was 4/60 of the meridian, i.e. 16,800 stades; from this is subtracted 8000 stades for the distance from Syene to the Cinnamon parallel. Or to proceed by degrees: given Eratosthenes' measurement of the earth, 700 stades = 1°; the tropic lies at 24°; therefore the distance from equator to tropic is 24.700, i.e. 16,800 stades (cf. Geminus, *Isag.* XVI.7).

29ff So the ratio of the distance between the tropics to the breadth of the torrid zone is 16,800: 8800, i.e. 21 : 11. In fact on this calculation the uninhabited torrid zone is slightly larger than half of the zone between the tropics.

32–6 But Strabo continues: 'Even if, of the more recent measurements, the one that makes the earth smallest is introduced, like Posidonius' estimate of 180,000 stades, it renders the torrid zone as somewhere about half the zone between the tropics, or a little more than half, and by no means equal and the same.'

This is nonsense. Strabo was day-dreaming and had not done his arithmetic, nor apparently even seen that the torrid zone shrinks with the smaller circumference. 4/60 of 180,000 (or 500 stades to 1°) gives the distance between equator and tropic as 12,000 stades. This gives a ratio of 12,000:4000 or 3:1 for the zone between the tropics to torrid zone. Curiously, if the other Posidonian figure for the circumference of the earth given by Cleomedes (F202), 240,000 stades, be adopted, the ratio would be 2:1; i.e. the torrid uninhabitable zone would be exactly half the zone between the tropics. But this is irrelevant, since we must confine ourselves to the data given by Strabo here. For the same reason, it is not particularly helpful for Aujac (Budé, p. 142, n. 5) to point out that in I.4.2 Strabo makes Eratosthenes give 3400 stades for Meroë to the Cinnamon parallel. Aujac is arguing for the reading οἰκήσιμον (19), but even this figure makes the torrid zone exactly half of the zone between the tropics. Of course the distances between Syene, Meroë and the Cinnamon parallel are round figures and not exact (explicitly noted in II.5.7, where precisely the same calculation is made as here; and cf. the slightly different figure in Geminus, *Isag.* XVI.24); but we must use the specific figures Strabo gives us in this passage.

To return to the textual crux of 19: οἰκήσιμον *codd.*: ⟨οὐκ⟩ οἰκήσιμον *Kramer*. On Strabo's own calculations from Eratosthenes (20–32), and on his statement with regard to Posidonius' figure (34–6), the torrid uninhabitable zone is slightly larger than the habitable zone between the tropics. Therefore, if the statement is Strabo's statement, the manuscript reading is inconsistent and incorrect, and Kramer's emendation is more logical. On the other hand, Strabo was quite wrong about the results derived from Posidonius' figure of 180,000, where the habitable area is indeed more than half the width of the zone between the tropics. It is probable that

Posidonius held this to be the case (cf. Geminus, *Isag.* XVI.24, τὰ πλεῖστα οἰκήσιμα, but the sentence is vague), and the positive version of the codices, which might derive from a Posidonian statement, fits more smoothly with what precedes it (the criticism of Aristotle), although it would be at odds with Strabo's explanation which follows. Since neither reading is satisfactory in the context, one must conclude that the confusion lies in Strabo himself, caused probably by the interlacing of Posidonius' criticism and his own presentation. Anon. I, *In Arati Phaenomena*, p. 97.1ff Maass, notes that Panaetius and Eudorus held that the διακεκαυμένη was inhabited, but there are no details of extent or definition. It is, however, further evidence of contemporary debate on the subject.

B. (2)(b) (37–43)

Criticism of the use of οἱ ἀρκτικοὶ (κύκλοι) to determine limits of the temperate zones:

(a) They are not available to all observers (e.g. on the equator, Cleom. *De Motu* I.5.21).

(b) They are not the same everywhere.

Clearly οἱ ἀρκτικοί are the circumpolar stars which never set, or Aristotle's 'ever-visible circle' (*Meteor.* 362b 3), as opposed to stars and constellations which rise and set in relation to the horizon. Strabo rejects (a) as irrelevant πρὸς τὸν ἔλεγχον, presumably Posidonius' refutation of Aristotle. His reason is that they must be visible to all those who live in the temperate zone, with reference to whom alone 'temperate' is actually used. This strange argument is based on Strabo's conviction that 'geography' is concerned only with the study of the inhabited world. However, he admits the force of objection (b).

In fact the circumpolar circle tangential to the horizon varies with latitude, as the altitude of the celestial pole is the same as the latitude of the observer (Aujac, *Strabon et la science de son temps* 122ff). It is only to an observer on the tropic

($\varphi = 24°$) that the 'arctic circle' would correspond to our fixed circle ($\bar{\varphi} = 66°$). The Greeks knew about this variation (e.g. Geminus, *Isag.* v; Cleom. *De Motu* I.5; I.7.35 (p. 64 Z)), but arbitrarily fixed the 'arctic circle' at 6 parts of the sexagesimal system, i.e. 6/60 (36°) from the pole (thus Geminus, *Isag.* v.45f; XVI.10f: the quadrant being divided into 15 parts, the plotting of arctic circle and ecliptic on the meridian was expressed as $(6+5+4)^p = 90°$, the obliquity of the ecliptic thus taken as the round 24°; Neugebauer, *HAMA* 582, 733). Thus the 'arctic circle' was put at 54°, which is the circle for observers on the geographical latitude 36°, the latitude passing through Rhodes and the Pillars of Hercules, regarded as the basic band of latitude for Greece (cf. Achill. *Isag.* 26, pp. 59–60 Maass). Apart from the false figure for the arctic circle, the continued confusion between variable and arbitrarily fixed circle was highly unsatisfactory. But the main trouble is that in this case, unlike the ecliptic and tropics, the celestial circle did not produce a fixed terrestrial counterpart, and Posidonius and Strabo were right to criticise it.

B. (3) Posidonius' own division of zones (44–61)

(**a**) **44–8** There are five zones, useful πρὸς τὰ οὐράνια.

(i) περίσκιοι: two zones under the poles and up to those which have the tropics as arctic circles. The last phrase in fact defines our fixed arctic circle of 66°. At this latitude ($\varphi = 66°$), the arctic circle is the tropic ($\bar{\varphi} = 24°$). 'Periskian' describes where the shadow caused by the sun can go right round (περι-), as the sun does not set. Since the determination is by the path of the sun, it is a fixed arctic circle.

(ii) ἑτερόσκιοι: two zones next to the above zones up to those living under the tropics. Note that the reference is to people and habitation. 'Heteroskian' is where the shadow of the sun falls in one of two possible directions only, to the north in the northerly zone, and to the south in the southern.

(iii) ἀμφίσκιος: refers to a single zone in between the

tropics; the shadow of the sun falls on either side, to the north during one part of the year, to the south during the other part.

This is a division of five zones determined in relation to a celestial body (namely the sun) by fixed boundaries (cf. Strabo II.5.3). It avoids variable 'arctic circles' and the confusions of defining a torrid uninhabitable zone, which cannot be done πρὸς τὰ οὐράνια. Posidonius was responsible for the terms and classification: F208, where the terms are explained. Compare also Strabo II.5.43. The determination by shadow, and the technical labels (*Periskioi* etc.) are repeated in Cleomedes, *De Motu* I.7, p. 62 Z. On the other hand Geminus, *Isag*. XV.1–3 makes no use of this classification (Mette, *Sphairopoiia* 66; Aujac, *Géminos* 148).

(b) 49–61 Posidonius' zones are also related to human geography (πρὸς τὰ ἀνθρώπεια), which in turn is related to temperature, climatic factors, topography, geology. In addition to the five astronomical zones, two more subtropical zones are distinguishable by peculiarities of their own (τι ἴδιον . . . ἰδίως, 52). They lie under the tropics, narrow (στενάς, 49) strips cut in two by each tropic (51). As with the other zones, the corresponding southern hemisphere zone has to be inferred from the northern. The sun is directly overhead for about half a month each year (50, i.e. at the solstice) (cf. F210). They are peculiarly parched and sandy, produce nothing but silphium and some fiery burnt-up fruits. (For silphium in Libya and Cyrene: II.5.33; II.5.37; XVII.3.23. It was in danger of disappearing through destruction by invasion, XVII.3.22.) A topographical reason (γάρ, 54) is given: there are no mountains near for clouds to hit and produce rain, nor irrigation by rivers (F223). The result is (διόπερ, 56) a distinctive ethnic population: curly woolly hair (and animals with curly crumpled horns), protruding lips, flat noses (because their extremities contract or curl back on themselves). It is in these zones that the Fisheaters live (II.5.53; this is not thrown in as an extra piece of information, but is a generic ethnic classification: see below). Further evidence that all this is peculiar to a narrow sub-tropical zone is that the people to the south have a more temperate climate, and a country that is more fertile and better watered (58–61).

The Fisheaters were placed by Nearchus (Arrian, *Indica* XXIX) in the territory of Gedrosia at the top of the Erythraean Sea, i.e. the Makran coast of Baluchistan, Iran and Pakistan, a little south of the tropic (Bunbury, *History of Ancient Geography* I.53; Hyde, *Ancient Greek Mariners* 182f). But there were supposed to be Fisheaters on the west coast of the Red Sea at and below Berenice, which is roughly on the tropic, *Periplus of the Erythraean Sea*, §2 (cf. Hyde, 109). Compare also Hdt. III.19 for the Fisheaters from Elephantine, near Syene, on the tropic again. See Diod. III.15ff (probably from Agatharchides) for a general account (cf. Bunbury II.52). In one sense they represented primitive tribes living in very hot temperatures (Diod. III.16.1; 19.1). But for Posidonius they are the generic ethnic distinction of a particular latitudinal band or zone; for another example, compare the Ethiopians stretching along a whole band of latitude further south in Posidonius' human geography or ethnography: see 326ff below.

(a) and (b) are quite distinct from each other. (a) defines terrestrial zones by celestial projection. (b) is a particular exercise in human geography. Strabo no doubt abbreviates and contracts, but does not conceal the characteristic development of aetiological argument in each case. For a further development of (b); F49.309ff comm. below.

B. (4) Criticism of Polybius on zones (62–145)

Polybius adopted a six-fold division: 2 under the arctic circles, 2 between arctic circles and tropics, and 2 between tropics and equator (62–4).

(a) 64–96 General criticism of Polybius for choosing six instead of five zones.

The division into five zones (instead of six) is defended on the grounds of natural philosophy and geography (φυσικῶς ἅμα καὶ γεωγραφικῶς, 65).

(i) The argument from natural philosophy is itself twofold:

(α) in relation to celestial phenomena:

67–70 'Because it is by the periskian ⟨heteroskian⟩ and amphiskian zones (which would be the best way of determining the ⟨terrestrial⟩ zones) that the phenomena concerned with our observation of the stars are also (καί) determined with them (συν-), taking their variation by a sort of overall general (ὁλοσχερεῖ) division.'

This is obscure, but appears to assert a correspondence between terrestrial and celestial zones. In fact the terrestrial zones are determined by the sun, while the corresponding celestial zones refer to astral position. Cf. Aujac, Budé, *ad loc.* p. 144. A pentezonal system is determined by the movements of celestial bodies, and so is in accord with natural philosophy.

Since the argument relates to five zones, it seems necessary to add ⟨καὶ τοῖς ἑτεροσκίοις⟩ at line 68.

(β) in relation to atmospheric zones of temperature (τὴν τοῦ περιέχοντος κρᾶσιν):

71–5 'Because since the temperature of the atmosphere is judged in relation to the sun, there are three distinctions which are most fundamental and contribute to the constitution of animals and plants (cf. F169.92), and to the ? of everything else under the air (i.e. on earth) or in it itself (i.e. the air), namely excess, defect and mean of heat.'

74 **ἡμισυσταλεῖς** *codd.* made no sense to *E* either, which left a space. The position of τε (73) suggests another accusative parallel to συστάσεις (73), but no convincing emendation has been presented. Madvig's ἡμισυστάσεις has been supported as 'semi-organisations', e.g. seeds (Jones,

Loeb *ad loc.*, p. 369, n.3), but that seems remarkably limited for everything else under the air and in it. In fact, it is difficult to see what other category Strabo may have in mind apart from animals and plants.

75–80 'The temperature receives its proper determination by the division into the zones: the two frigid zones imply the defect of heat and combine into a single natural atmospheric condition, the temperate zones similarly are brought into a single characteristic, the mean, and the remaining zone, which is single and torrid, falls into the remaining characteristic.'

It is at first sight unclear why this is an argument for five, instead of six zones, since there are three differentiations of temperature. But the division is based on the path of the sun, and the ecliptic traverses a single zone, while the other zones are separated by the tropics into north and south. But astronomically defined zones and zones defined by temperature need not coincide, and in fact caused confusion: F208, F209; not least with the location of the 'torrid' zone, see below.

(ii) 80–92 The division into five zones is geographical. This is a division of habitable and uninhabitable zones: 'for geography seeks to define that section which is inhabited by us as consisting in one of the two temperate zones'.

But the genitive τῆς ἑτέρας (81) is difficult; a genitive of definition? Madvig's τῇ ἑτέρᾳ ('by one . . .') is possibly right. For the southern temperate zone: Geminus, *Isag.* XVI.19f.

The habitable zone(s) is (are) bounded to west and east by sea, but to the north and south by the air (ἀήρ, i.e. temperature): the air in the middle is temperate both for plants and animals (and so forms a habitable zone); to north and south it is harsh (δύσκρατος) through excess and lack of heat (82–6). So the three differentiations of temperature, together with the division into northern and southern hemisphere by the equator, fit the division into five zones (86–92).

64–92 So far, all three topics, correspondence between terrestrial and celestial zones (F208), temperature of atmosphere or environment (F169.92), and habitable and uninhabitable zones (F49.17ff), are known to have been of great interest to Posidonius. Indeed Strabo uses the Posidonian terms, Periskian etc. It is also highly likely that Posidonius, who held a five-zone theory and was interested in its history, criticised the six-zone theory of Polybius, especially since it was one of the most recent discussions. But it is impossible to say to what extent Strabo himself may have taken over in this defence of the pentezonal theory. In the second ((i)(β)) and third ((ii)) sections (80; 89f) Strabo introduces torrid zone as one of the five zones, and if the zones in (i)(β) and (ii) correspond to the zones in (i)(α), the torrid zone will be equated with the zone between the tropics, which was not Posidonius' theory (10ff, above). But Posidonius discussed zones both as celestially defined and as habitable and uninhabitable (in terms of torrid and temperate), and both could be categorised as five-zone systems. Strabo's definition of torrid zone in (ii) is far from clear (89f), and the passage remains too vague to decide whether Strabo is still basically following Posidonius or not. The distinction between the natural philosophy classification of (i)(α) and the geographical zoning of (ii) seems clear, but (i)(β) hovers rather uncomfortably between them.

92–6 It is noticeable that Strabo now returns to Posidonius explicitly, but simply as 'he' (ὁ δέ . . .) without benefit of proper name. While at first sight it looks like criticism, it may merely be a case of underlining a distinction. Posidonius' addition of his zones under the tropics (see 49ff) 'is not analogous to the five zones, nor is he using a like criterion; no, it is as if he were representing zones also by their ethnic differences, an Ethiopic zone, a Scythian and Celtic zone, and a third in between.'

Strabo is right to distinguish two separate methods for Posidonius (πρὸς τὰ οὐράνια . . . πρὸς δὲ τὰ ἀνθρώπεια, 45ff). It is uncertain with ὡς ἂν εἰ (94) to what extent Strabo is interpreting Posidonius on 'ethnic' zones; but 309ff below, and especially 326ff on the Ethiopians shows that there was a basis for Strabo's suggestion.

93. There is no need to emend ταύταις, the reading of the codd.

B. (4)(b) Detailed criticism of Polybius (97–145)

(i) 97–101 The definition of some zones by arctic circles, i.e. the circle of stars which do not set. But this is defining invariables (τὰ ἀμετάπτωτα) by variables (τοῖς μεταπίπτουσι σημείοις, 100) as has already been said (εἴρηται, 99); see 41–3. This is a Posidonian objection.

(ii) 101f The use of the tropics as boundaries of the torrid zone has also been objected to already (14ff). This is also a Posidonian objection.

(iii) 102–18 But the notion leading to a division of the torrid zone into two is not a bad one (102f; is this Strabo?), in that it rests on a division into hemispheres of three zones each, which would return to the six-zone theory (102–9). But this is an artificial division, because if a hemispherical division through the poles were adopted, the five zones would suffice (109–13). This is because both sections of the torrid zone are similar in character (ὁμοιοπαθές) and contiguous (συγκεῖσθαι), thus making the division superfluous, while the temperate and frigid zones, although similar in form, are not contiguous (113–16). So even if the whole earth be conceived from the point of view of such hemispherical division, five zones are enough (117f).

This ingenious argument substituting meridian hemispherical division for equatorial does not sound characteristic of Strabo, but rather of Posidonius' more mathematical mind.

(iv) 118–45 Temperate equatorial zone.

118–25 'But if the zone that falls under the equator is temperate, as Eratosthenes says (II.A.5 Berger; LXVIII Bernhardy), and as Polybius agrees (Polybius adds the additional reason that the ground is very high; because of this it is also rained upon, since the clouds from the north are driven in great number by the etesian winds against the rising ground there), then it is much better to make that a third temperate zone, a narrow one, than to introduce the zones under the tropics.'

This is clearly Strabo since it is designed to criticise Posidonius' sub-tropical zones.

Berger (*Fragmente des Eratosthenes* 83ff; *Erdkunde* 393f; cf. Thomson, *History of Ancient Geography* 163) doubted the correctness of the inclusion of Eratosthenes' name; there is no mention of an inhabited equatorial zone in the Hermes poem in Achilles, *Isag. in Arat.* 29, p. 63 Maass. But someone earlier than Polybius is required for him to agree with and add to (ὁμοδοξεῖ, προστίθησι δ', 120), and there is no real objection to Eratosthenes (cf. Schühlein, *Untersuchungen* 25ff).

It is clear that the habitability of the torrid zone and the possible existence of a temperate equatorial strip was much debated: Geminus, *Isag.* XVI.25ff; Achilles, *Isag. in Arat.* 29, p. 63 Maass; cf. Cleomedes, *De Motu* I.6. Among those who argued that the torrid zone was habitable were Panaetius (F135 van Str.; Anon, *Isag. in Arat.* p. 97 Maass), Eudorus of Alexandria (Anon. *loc. cit.*), and Posidonius himself (58–61 above; F210). But it is to Polybius and his monograph Περὶ τῆς περὶ τὸν ἰσημερινὸν οἰκήσεως that Geminus, *Isag.* XVI.32 assigns the theory.

But Strabo confuses the issue by linking this problem to the dispute over number of zones; because if the habitable equatorial strip is to be a third temperate zone, it will in fact divide Polybius' torrid zones into two, and give him a total of seven zones. Also it would not be 'better' than Posidonius' two 'zones under the tropics', because if a habitable equatorial strip is to be regarded as a zone, Posidonius also would have at least seven zones. The astronomical classification of five zones and the human geography of habitable and uninhabitable areas are distinct (see 44ff above, F209 comm.).

(α) 126–9 Polybius' temperate equatorial strip is supported (συνηγορεῖ, 125) by Posidonius too (καί, 125), using astronomical arguments like this: 'the fact that both (καί, 126; but du Theil's ἐκεῖ, 'there', 'in that region' makes much better sense) the oblique changes of course of the sun are more rapid, and in the same way also its movement from rising to setting; for in motions completed in the same time those over the greatest circle of circumference are more rapid.'

This seems to refer (a) to the annual movement of the sun on the ecliptic, which was thought to be slower in its oblique approach and retirement at the tropics, compared with a faster perpendicular crossing of the equator; Cleom. *De Motu* I.6, p. 52.3–20 Ziegler; F210. That this was a Posidonian assumption is also guaranteed by Cleomedes, F210.1–7. It also refers (b) to the daily motion from east to west of the sun, which is said to be more rapid at the equator than at the tropics, since the former circle is larger than the latter, yet accomplished in the same time (cf. Aujac, Budé, note *ad loc.*, p. 144). Strabo's sentence is unclear and confused, perhaps because the question whether there was a habitable equatorial strip did not interest Strabo as a geographer (II.5.4; II.5.34). An unusual sense is required for ὁμοταχῶν (128), which normally means 'of equal velocity' (e.g. Arist. *De Caelo* 289b 9; *Phys.* 237a 1). The argument is intended to imply that the sun passes more rapidly over the equatorial region than over any other area between the tropics, and that therefore the equatorial strip is more temperate.

(β) 130–5 Posidonius criticises Polybius for saying that the inhabited area under the equator is very high. He gives two different kinds of reasons: (i) there is no high point (i.e. peak) in a spherical surface because of its evenness. Cf. Strabo, II.5.5. This is a general theoretical answer. What provoked that kind of answer? Did Polybius suggest that the ground at the equator was high *by nature*? (ii) 'nor in fact (δή, 133) is the land under the equator mountainous, but rather flat, on a level with the surface of the sea.' This is a factual answer; but how did Posidonius believe that he had factual evidence for this? Strabo's reason does not seem to fit: 'For he says (accusative and infinitive) that the rains that fill the Nile come from the Ethiopian mountains.' Is the implication: 'and not from mountains on the equator'? But if Cleomedes is to be trusted (see F210.20ff), Posidonius used the case of the Ethiopian rains flooding the Nile as a parallel illustration for the equator (cf. also F222). Strabo's account once more obscures the argument. Had Posidonius heard of the sudd swamps south of Meroë and Khartum (Sen. *NQ* IV.A.2.3)?

(γ) 136–45 Strabo criticises Posidonius on this topic.

(i) Posidonius according to Strabo was inconsistent on this point, elsewhere suspecting that there were mountains at the equator, against which the clouds from both temperate zones on both sides strike and make rain (136–9). There is no other evidence for this.

(ii) 'Even granted that the equator is mountainous' (139f), there is another discrepancy, namely the theory of an equatorial ocean. But the object of Strabo's attack has become confused and returned to Polybius. If Posidonius had been the prime object, Strabo should have said: even granted that the country at the equator is flat and not mountainous.

141–5 'For the same men (οἱ αὐτοί must refer to Polybius and Posidonius) say that the ocean is confluent (with itself; i.e. flows in a continuous circle round the earth). So how do they place mountains in the middle of it, unless they mean by their statement islands? But however that may be (143 δήποτε is especially frequent in such expressions, see *LSJ* δήποτε 4, so Kramer is probably right to add ⟨δή⟩), it falls outside the sphere of geography; perhaps the examination of this question should be assigned to a man proposing a study of the ocean.'

141 It is implied that Posidonius believed in an equatorial ocean as well as a circumambient one. In fact only σύρρουν (141) is stated here, but the argument makes no sense in the context unless Strabo means confluent on the latitude of the equator. This was apparently a view held by οἱ φυσικοί: F210.44ff=Cleom. *De Motu* I.6.33. Macrobius too (F118) assigned an equatorial ocean to Posidonius. But there are good reasons for maintaining that while Posidonius believed in a circumambient ocean (σύρρουν . . . τὸν ὠκεανόν), he could not have held the theory of an equatorial ocean, which was the theory of Cleanthes and Crates: F118 comm.; F210; Strabo I.2.24; Geminus, *Isag.* XVI.21ff; Geminus in fact dismisses the theory. Strabo is also on doubtful ground in relation to Polybius; Plb. III.38.1 seems to leave the question of a circumambient ocean open.

Strabo's only interest in the question lies in the possibility of scoring a point against Posidonius and Polybius. He in fact dismisses the theory at II.5.5, as not being the concern of the geographer. The tossing of the question to a writer on ἡ περὶ ὠκεανοῦ πραγματεία (145) can hardly avoid being an allusion to Posidonius' title. It is probably not contemptuous, although the form of title was particularly well known from Pytheas whom Strabo loathed as a mountebank. Strabo had already distinguished Posidonius' Περὶ ὠκεανοῦ from pure geography (2f above) on the grounds of the 'physical' and mathematical form of part of its content. There were 'physical' explanations of the position of an equatorial ocean, such as nutriment for the sun, held by Cleanthes (see F118). For a more 'scientific' approach to the problem of a habitable equatorial zone, considered by Posidonius, linked to the explanation of the path of the sun through the ecliptic: Cleom. *De Motu* I.6; cf. F210. For the general view that this problem fell under the sphere of natural philosophy and mathematics: Cleom. F210.44ff; Geminus, *Isag.* XVI.23. Although Strabo admitted the necessity of physical and mathematical hypotheses (I.1.20; II.5.1), he wished to discuss only as much of this as would permit concentration on the real object of geography, the description of the inhabited world (II.5.34).

C. Eudoxus of Cyzicus and the circumnavigation of Africa (*146–293*)

The sequence of thought has moved from zones in general to the question of a temperate equatorial zone, which raises the question of an equatorial ocean, which in turn naturally leads to evidence for the circumnavigation of Africa. All these topics would have been proper for Posidonius' Περὶ ὠκεανοῦ. Again, a simple φησιν (147) is enough to indicate Posidonius as subject.

(a) Posidonius' account (146–232)

(a) 146–50 Doxography and criticism of earlier evidence.

146 Posidonius made a catalogue of those reputed to have circumnavigated Libya. This shows the orientation of Posidonius' interest in Eudoxus in Περὶ ὠκεανοῦ. The accounts of the first two voyages to India are background for the circumnavigation attempts.

(i) 147 He refers to Herodotus for thinking that some men sent by Darius completed the circumnavigation.

This is very confused. Hdt. IV.42–44 reported four distinct pieces of evidence:

(a) the expedition of Phoenicians sent by the Egyptian king *Necho* II (7th c. B.C.). This was supposed to be an east to west circumnavigation (said to be the easier, cf. Bunbury *History of Ancient Geography* I.291), passing the Pillars of Heracles after three years, having sowed and harvested en route. Herodotus believed in the circumnavigation, but not in the Phoenicians' story that in sailing round they had the sun on their right. Modern opinion is divided about the former: Hyde, *Ancient Greek Mariners* 234ff; Thomson, *History of Ancient Geography* 71f; Cary–Warmington, *Ancient Explorers*

87ff; Bunbury I.289ff; Berger, *Erdkunde* 62ff; Tozer, *History of Ancient Geography* 99ff; for ancient doubts: Hyde 237, 244.

(b) Carthaginians maintained circumnavigability (Hanno?); cf. Pliny *NH* 2.169; Thomson 73; Cary–Warmington 94; cf. Hdt. IV.196.

(c) Sataspes was given ships by *Xerxes*, on a plea from Sataspes' mother who was a sister of *Darius*; he failed and returned.

(d) Men sent by *Darius* discover that the greater part of *Asia* is surrounded by sea.

The circumnavigation referred to by Posidonius must be that of the Phoenicians sent by Necho, but the other references to Darius in this section of Herodotus confused his memory. It is likely that the mistake originates from Posidonius (again at line 235), since if Strabo had found Necho in Posidonius, he would not have changed it to Darius. It shows that neither Posidonius nor Strabo checked Herodotus, and that Strabo is simply following Posidonius at this point (cf. Aly, *Strabonis Geographica* 4, p. 414 n. 1). Jacoby (*Kommentar ad loc.*) suggested that Posidonius' doxography contained both the expeditions of Necho and Darius, and Strabo read Posidonius carelessly. But the subject at this point is the circumnavigation of Libya (146) in relation to a circumfluent ocean, although Posidonius' general subject no doubt was the surrounding of the whole inhabited world by ocean (230). This same objection would throw doubt on Schühlein's suggestion (op. cit. 38ff) that Posidonius named Darius deliberately and correctly, in that the subject was the unity of ocean, not simply the circumnavigation of Africa. So the following Heraclidean magus represented the circumnavigation of Africa, Darius' men the oceanic exploration of Asia, and so the two were complementary.

(ii) 148 Heraclides of Pontus in a dialogue makes a certain magus arrive at Gelon's court and say that he had circumnavigated Africa. Gelon was tyrant of Gela *c.* 491 and tyrant of Syracuse from 485 to 478. There is no other evidence for this story, and obviously no weight can be put on it. Posidonius probably knew Heraclides' work (F18.39; F110.9ff). It is interesting that he cites his authorities, but not the source. Wehrli (F69) following Bernays, *Gesammelte Abhandlungen* (1885) 1.42ff, assigns the reference to the *Zoroaster* (Plu. *Adv. Col.* 1115A), which is possible, but hardly certain.

150 Posidonius correctly dismisses (i) and (ii) as being ἀμάρτυρα, i.e. unsupported by evidence, and (iii) tells the story of Eudoxus of Cyzicus coming to Egypt in the reign of Euergetes II, as ambassador and herald for the games at the festival of Kore. For Ptolemy Euergetes II (Physcon) and Posidonius' interest in him: Frs. 56, 58. He reigned 146–116 B.C.

The Narrative (151–226)

(b) The first voyage to India (151–70)

The setting is drawn with considerable care. The character of Eudoxus as an explorer is stressed: he had particular interest in voyages up the Nile, being naturally curious of strange places, and not untutored in them.

153 **συσταθῆναι** is an odd word: joined up with the king and his court. Rougé, 'Prêt et société maritimes dans le monde romain', *Memoirs of American Academy in Rome* XXXVI (1980), 295f, claims that συσταθῆναι implies a joint commercial contract with Euergetes, which the latter eventually ratted on. Certainly a combination of exploration and commerce is typical of Greek adventure (cf. Pytheas); but συσταθῆναι occurs here in relation to the Nile explorations, rather than the later Indian venture.

156ff A curious tale, but full of detail: an Indian is picked up half dead by the garrison of the Arabian Gulf (i.e. Red Sea; a garrison against pirates, no doubt). Having been taught Greek, the Indian explained that his ship had lost its way, and his fellow sailors had died of starvation.

162 ὑποληφθέντα: 'Doubted' (Jones, Loeb) does not have much support from usage (*LSJ s.v.* III.2). 'Par reconnaissance' (Aujac, Budé) seems difficult. Perhaps 'supported'; cf. Str. XIV.2.5 . . . οἱ εὔποροι τοὺς ἐνδεεῖς ὑπολαμβάνουσι; or 'taken at his word'.

The Indian promised to act as guide for the route to India to a crew selected by the king. Eudoxus was one of them. For the significance of this see below.

164 ⟨**καὶ**⟩ Meineke is not necessary, but not unreasonable. Otherwise the sentence is very bald; cf. Jacoby's suggestions.

165ff They set sail with gifts and returned with spices and precious stones. The detail of the sources of such stones, washed down by rivers, dug from the ground, compressed from liquid, may be Posidonian; for πεπηγότας, 168, cf. παγῆναι F229.18 – the formation of the Stony Plain by compression. However, Strabo elsewhere in a non-Posidonian book (XV.67) describes the precious stones in India. But Eudoxus was deceived in his hopes (169); king Euergetes appropriated the whole cargo. See comment on 182 below.

(c) Second voyage to India (170–90)

Eudoxus was sent off again with greater equipment by Cleopatra, who had taken over sovereignty on the death of her husband Euergetes. On the way back he was carried south of Ethiopia by wind (the NE monsoon, probably). On making landings he won over the people with gifts in return for water and guides. He wrote down some of their words (177). He found a wooden prow from a shipwreck with a horse carved on it, and was told that this piece of wreckage came from some people who were sailing from the west. He took it with him. When he returned safely to Egypt, Cleopatra was no longer in charge, but her son (Ptolemy Soter II, Lathyros; see below). Again Eudoxus had all his cargo abstracted; for he was caught having appropriated a lot for himself.

This detail together with the unexpected royal appropriation of the cargo from the first voyage (διαψευσθῆναι δὲ τῶν ἐλπίδων . . ., 169) has been held to be a confusion created by ignorance on the part of either (or both) Posidonius and Strabo; because it is generally believed by scholars that the Ptolemies had a royal monopoly of the spice trade: Tarn, *Hellenistic Civilisation* 173ff, 225ff; Bouché-Leclerq, *Histoire des Lagides* III.243; Raschke, 'New Studies in Roman Commerce with the East', *ANRW* II.9.2, 658. In other words, the cargo was bound to go to Ptolemy in any case, and so disgruntled annoyance on the part of Eudoxus on that score is a distortion. Amusingly, both critics and supporters of the story claim benefit from this position in their argument. However, recently the supposed royal monopoly in spices has been denied by Rougé, op. cit. p. 295f, citing P. Berl. 5883 5853 (SB 7169), a mutilated papyrus of mid-second c. B.C., for a business group (*societas*) on a maritime expedition to spice countries. He argues that Eudoxus had such a commercial contract with Euergetes, which the latter broke; but for συσταθῆναι see 153 comm. However this may be, there is no mention of a royal monopoly either in the narrative, or in the considerable detail of Strabo's criticism; nor does its existence or non-existence seem crucial for the story. Eudoxus fell into disgrace and lost everything the second time, because he was caught misappropriating part of the cargo (182f); and after the first voyage, he had every right to be 'disappointed in his expectations' (169) if he received nothing; whether there was a royal monopoly or not, merchants could hardly be expected to undertake dangerous voyages without some reward.

183ff As for the prow, he showed it to ship masters in the market, who identified it as a type belonging to poorer fishing vessels from Gadeira, called 'horses' from the prow device, of the kind that went round the Mauretanian coast as far as the river Lixus (which was not far; it is now the Loukkos, not far down the coast from Tangier; XVII.3.2).

Some shipmasters actually recognised the prow as belonging to a boat that had sailed beyond the Lixus and not returned safely. This comment seems an obvious embroidery of the story. How could an Alexandrian captain know this? Perhaps disbelief is hinted by δή (188), which could derive from the Posidonian narrative. Did Posidonius get this from Cadiz? Scepticism on that detail does not necessarily invalidate the general identification of the type of boat.

(d) Third attempted voyage to India round Africa (191–219)

Eudoxus concludes that the circumnavigation of Africa is possible.

191–9 He went home (οἴκαδε, 192; presumably to Cyzicus), put all his property on a ship, called at Dicaearchia (Puteoli; for Dic. as a port with strong relations with eastern trade: Str. III.2.6; V.4.6), Massalia and along the coast to Gadeira, everywhere trumpeting (διακωδωνίζοντα) his purpose and doing business, fitted out a great ship and two tow-boats like pirate cutters, embarked chorus girls (always welcome in the east, *Periplus of Red Sea*, §49), doctors and other tradesmen, set sail on the high seas for India with steady westerlies.

This is a marvellous sentence with great speed and liveliness. Surely it is Posidonius rather than Strabo. The details are not only vivid, but also convincing.

199–208 His companions wearied of the voyage and forced him against his will to sail to land with a wind behind him, because he was scared of the ebb and flow of the tides (a point which would have interested Posidonius). He did in fact ground, but without completely breaking up, so he saved the cargo and most of the timber, from which he built a third cutter about the size of a penteconter, and sailed on until he encountered a folk speaking the same phrases as he had written down earlier (from east Africa, 177). At least he recognised that the people were ethnically similar to his former Ethiopians, while bordering on the kingdom of Bogus (i.e. Mauretania). Again this latitudinal ethnic extension of 'Ethiopians' is Posidonian (326ff). But Strabo too (XVII.3.5) refers to them generally as 'the so-called western Ethiopians'.

The kings of Mauretania from the period of the Jugurthine to the Roman Civil War appear to have been Bocchus I and possibly his sons Bogus (Bogud) and Bocchus II; sources are very confused and vague about them: Str. XVII.3.7; *RE*; *OCD svv.*; Carcopino, *Le Maroc antique* 28f; Gsell, *Histoire Ancienne de l'Afrique du Nord* VII.267ff: a Bocchus was still alive in 91 B.C. Gsell thought that Strabo's (or Posidonius') Βόγος is a mistake for Βόκχος (VI.91 n. 8), but this is quite uncertain in the general confusion.

209–19 Abandoning the Indian voyage, Eudoxus turned back. (He had to; he had lost his main cargo boat. The λέμβος was a light fast boat (such as a pirate or light war ship) hardly suitable for commercial purposes or heavy seas; Casson, *The Ancient Mariners* 167.) In coasting along, he saw and marked (for future reference?) a well watered, treed and uninhabited island (Madeira? (Hyde); but that would hardly be coasting; the Canaries?). He survived as far as Mauretania, disposed of the boats, went overland to Bogus, and proposed that he take on the expedition; but Bogus' friends turned the king against him by suggesting that the country might be open to intrigue if an ingress were opened up for invaders (cf. Laffranque, *Rev. Philos.* 153 (1963), 218). Discovering that the proposal to send him on the proclaimed expedition was an excuse for marooning him on a desert island, Eudoxus escaped to Roman controlled territory (Numidia, presumably), and crossed from there to Spain.

(e) Fourth attempted voyage to India round Africa (219–26)

Again Eudoxus fitted out a round ship (i.e. merchantman) and a long penteconter (i.e. battleship; cf. Hdt. I.163), to keep to the open sea with the former, and test the land with the latter (for this, Casson, *Ancient Mariners* 102; Berger, *Erdkunde*

571; Laffranque, *Rev. Philos. loc. cit.* 216f; Hyde, *Mariners* 246 has the ships the wrong way round). He put on board agricultural tools, seeds and builders, and set sail for the same circumnavigation, with the intention, if the voyage lengthened, of wintering on his formerly marked island, sowing and harvesting, and so completing the voyage he had decided on from the beginning. (It should be remembered that they expected to find the southern ocean not far south of Morocco, very much further north than it is.)

(f) Posidonius' conclusion (227–32)

227–9 From the beginning Strabo has used indirect speech throughout (146–226), implying that he reports the story directly from Posidonius. Now he quotes Posidonius in direct speech: 'I have come so far with the story of Eudoxus; what happened after that probably the people of Gadeira and Spain know.' This makes little sense unless Posidonius had heard the story himself at Gadeira at a time when further news of Eudoxus' last expedition was still possible. Therefore the dating of the voyage is of some interest.

Dating

Since Ptolemy VIII, Euergetes II (Physcon) died in 116 B.C. (Otto and Bengtson, 'Zur Geschichte des Niederganges des Ptolemäerreiches', *Abh. Bayer. Akad. N.F.* 17 (1938), 113f; Skeat, *Reigns of the Ptolemies* 35 n. 14; Samuel, 'Ptolemaic Chronology', *Münchener Beitr. z. Papyrusforsch. u. ant. Rechtsgesch.*, 43 (1962), 147f), Eudoxus' first voyage to India was completed before that date (169f). The second voyage took place after his death (170) equipped generously by his wife Cleopatra, who had succeeded to the kingdom (171f); but Eudoxus returned οὐκέτι τῆς Κλεοπάτρας ἡγουμένης, ἀλλὰ τοῦ παιδός (181).

From 116–107 B.C. Cleopatra ruled with her son Ptolemy IX, Soter II (Lathyros), but from 107 Lathyros was deposed to be king of Cyprus until 88 B.C., when he again became king of Egypt. Cleopatra continued to reign with her younger son Ptolemy X, Alexander I, until her death in 101, after which Alexander ruled with Cleopatra Berenice until 88 B.C. (Skeat, 35f). τοῦ παιδός therefore refers to Soter II Lathyros, not to Alexander, as Laffranque argued (*Rev. Philos. loc. cit.* 207), whose dating is vitiated by assuming that the reference of line 181 is to Cleopatra's death in 108/7. But (a) οὐκέτι . . . ἡγουμένης implies that Cleopatra was still alive but politically impotent at the time (contrast τελευτήσαντος, 170); (b) Cleopatra died in 101, not in 108/7 (Samuel, *op. cit.* 152); and a date after 101 for the second voyage to India would open up an unreasonable gap between the first and second voyages (*c.* 18 years), and create difficulties with regard to Eudoxus' age in relation to the later circumnavigation attempts (cf. Laffranque herself, *op. cit.* 208); (c) Cleopatra's intrigues were in favour of Alexander, and her tensions were with Soter; (d) Cornelius Nepos, as reported by Pomponius Mela (III.9.90 = F16 Marshall) and Pliny (*NH* 2.169), referred to Eudoxus fleeing from Lathyros. It is true that the account of Nepos (or his reporters) is badly garbled, telescoping the different voyages into one and assuming an east/west circumnavigation. But Nepos's evidence is independent of Posidonius and confirms the connection of the story with the circumnavigation of Africa and with the court of Lathyros.

Eudoxus' second voyage to India must then have taken place between 116 and 107 B.C. But in these years the intrigues and balance of power within the ruling dynasty were complicated and obscure (Otto and Bengtson, *Abh. Bayer. Akad. N.F.* 17 (1938), 112ff; Samuel, *op. cit.* 148ff; Will, *Histoire politique du monde hellénistique* II.369f; Volkmann, *RE* XXIII, 1738ff; Skeat, 35f). The continuing strained and explosive relationship between Cleopatra III and Lathyros make it virtually impossible to date with certainty within these limits the allusion of 181. Since there was considerable confusion on the death of Ptolemy VIII, who appears to have left the power to Cleopatra and whichever son she chose, and since at the beginning her preference for Alexander, the younger, was only overturned by the Alexandrian people in favour of Lathyros who was recalled from Cyprus (Will, II.370), the Eudoxus reference could be as early as 116/15 (cf. Otto and Bengtson, 194ff); but this does not leave much time for the voyage itself, and it could have been later. Papyrus evidence suggests brief shifts of power in 110/9 and in 109/8 (Samuel, *op. cit.* 149f). Various other guesses have been: 113/12, Bunbury II.75 n. 3 (cf. Müller, *GGM* I. *Proleg.* lvii); *c.* 111, Jacoby, *Kommentar* 176 (cf. Strack, *Die Dynastie der Ptolemäer* 185 and notes *ad loc.*, esp. 202f; Bouché-Leclercq, *Histoires des Lagides* II.94 n. 1); 108/7 Laffranque (*op. cit.*, but on false grounds, see above). Of the two later circumnavigation attempts, an interval must have elapsed after leaving Alexandria to plan, marshal support and equip (191–9; cf. Laffranque, *op. cit.* 207f). The reference to king Bogus of Mauretania is of little help (see above), even if grounded in fact. One should be careful to avoid circular argument over the dating of the Eudoxan circumnavigation attempts from Cadiz and Posidonius' journey to the west, but lines 227–9 suggest that Posidonius' visit probably took place at most a few years after the last expedition set sail, so the two dates should be complementary. The most plausible date for Posidonius' journey lies between 101–91 B.C. (Laffranque, *Poseidonios* 65–7; T14–24). Eudoxus arrived at Alexandria not long after 120 B.C., old enough to be θεωρός and σπονδοφόρος from Cyzicus. Since the first voyage was over by or before 116, a date about the turn of the century for embarcation on the fourth and last would fit the rather porous evidence best, and be in harmony with a Posidonian trip in the first decade of the century.

229–32 Strabo claims that Posidonius said that it is shown from all this that the inhabited world is surrounded in a circle by the ocean, and two lines of verse are quoted.

Belief in the unity of a circular ocean was held by

Eratosthenes (Berger, *Die geographischen Fragmente des Eratosthenes* II.A.8–13 (p. 91ff); Str. I.3.13), but apparently doubted by Hipparchus (Str. I.1.9 = F4 Dicks). Crates of Mallos elaborated the theory (Thomson, *History* 202f), but it was much debated. Polybius appears to have left the question open (III.38.1), and although there were influential doubters such as Ptolemy, who thought that the east coast of Africa and the Indian coast were joined in the south, shutting off the Indian Ocean (*Geogr.* VII.3), the theory found wide acceptance; e.g. by Strabo himself; Pomponius Mela, III.9.89ff; Pliny *NH* 2.167–71; Manilius, I.246; Macrobius, *In Somn. Scip.* II.9; Ps.-Arist. *De Mundo* 3.392b 20ff; Origen, *De Princ.* II.3.6 (cf. Redepennig, p. 174 n. 25, and Clem. *Ad. Cor.* XX.5.8); in general: Maass, *Aratea* (*Phil. Unters.* 12), p. 185ff; F214 comm.; Berger, *Erdkunde* 461, 568. Berger suggested that the anonymous verses (231f, 'No continental fetter shackles it, but without limit on it rolls; and so (τό 'wherefore') nothing sullies it') may have come from Eratosthenes' *Hermes* (so Schühlein, *Untersuchungen* 44, following Meineke, *Vindic. Strab.* 11; Scheppig, *De Posidonio Apamensi*, 41).

Curiously δεσμός recurs shortly afterwards (II.4.1) in a metaphor with reference to Polybius' (or Strabo's) criticism of Pytheas' tale of the insubstantial suspension of all elements round Thule (like a jellyfish) which ὡς ἂν δεσμὸν εἶναι τῶν ὅλων. In this same passage (II.4.2), Strabo reports Polybius as saying that Eratosthenes called Euhemerus a Bergaean, but believed Pytheas; cf. 233–7 here.

What is puzzling is why Posidonius should have believed that it is proved that the world is surrounded by ocean 'from all this'. It certainly is not the case that ἐκ πάντων δὴ τούτων . . . δείκνυσθαι (229f) if πάντων τούτων refers to the preceding account in Strabo. For, as Posidonius scrupulously recorded, there was no evidence that Eudoxus did circumnavigate Africa. If Strabo's report is complete, the only piece of evidence which could have been regarded as conclusive is the shipwrecked figure-head. Although with our superior knowledge of the extent of Africa and the coastal currents, we know that it was quite impossible that a wreck should be carried round from west to east, that was by no means evident to an ancient Greek, especially since the southern ocean was imagined to be much further north, and they were well aware of prevailing westerlies. A main point of the Eudoxus story is not whether the figurehead could in fact have been Gadeiritan washed round from the west, but that Eudoxus believed it to be so; cf. the story of figureheads of ships from wrecks identified as Spanish in the Arabian gulf at the time of Gaius Caesar's expedition there (Pliny, *NH* 2.168). Unfortunately it is not clear from the narrative whether Posidonius also believed this to be clinching evidence or not.

It is much more likely that ἐκ πάντων δὴ τούτων (229) referred in Posidonius to a much wider examination of which the Eudoxus story was only a part (cf. Schühlein, *Untersuchungen* 38f). After all, whatever is shown or not for the circumnavigability of Africa, still the question of the northern ocean remains, and there is no mention of that here. It looks as if Eratosthenes collected accounts of voyages which might contribute to evidence of a single circling ocean (Berger, *Erdkunde* 395; Schühlein, *Untersuchungen* 40). Posidonius appears to have taken this up, examined the credibility of some reports, and added more recent cases, above all the contemporary instance of Eudoxus (146ff), which clearly made a great impression. We are told only of this last case (at some length) by Strabo. It is likely that the historical evidence was cumulative rather than decisive for Posidonius; he would also note the evidence of Pytheas and Patroclus for the north (cf. Schühlein, 43; F206). Posidonius probably argued in addition from quite different physical grounds, namely the uniformity of tidal phenomena: F214; Schühlein, 38–44.

C. (2) Strabo's criticism of Posidonius (233–93)

(a) *General criticism* (233–7) Strabo is very sarcastic about this wonderful man Posidonius who rejected Heraclides' magus and Herodotus' expedition (of Phoenicians) from Darius (really Necho, 147 above) as being ἀμάρτυρα, and offers as convincing evidence this Bergaean tale (sc. of Eudoxus), whether made up by himself or swallowed as the invention of others.

Βεργαῖον refers to Antiphanes of Berge in Thrace, who became proverbial for tall stories; see line 290; I.3.1; in II.4.2 Strabo (with approval) quotes Polybius for a similar pattern of sarcasm in saying that Eratosthenes called Euhemerus a Bergaean and yet believed Pytheas (cf. Walbank, *Polybius* 126f). In fact Strabo confuses and obscures for us how far Posidonius believed in the Eudoxus evidence. The key word is ἀμάρτυρον (234; cf. 150; surely from Posidonius). The tales of Heraclides' magus and Herodotus were not subject to witnesses, whereas Eudoxus' adventures were; and such consultations of witnesses or reporters (e.g. at Cadiz) were important and recognised factors of historical evidence, cf. Laffranque, *Poseidonios d'Apamée* 182. But Posidonius was careful to record that the final evidence had not been reported, if it ever could be.

(b) *Detailed criticism* (237–88) Strabo indefatigably raises step by step each point in the tale for ridicule. Certain problems are aired, but hardly disposed of: e.g. how was an Indian found shipwrecked in the Red Sea (237–50)? But we are not told where the coastguard patrol picked him up (156f); it could have been at the entrance. Incidentally, either Strabo deliberately shortened the length of the Red Sea to 10,000 stades (codices' reading, 240), or the figure has been corrupted. The latter is more likely, since Strabo himself gave the usual length of 15,000 stades at I.2.28 (but cf. the

Eratosthenic account at XVI.4.4). The emendation follows the earlier passage.

The 'recognition' of the Gadeiritan figurehead (264) may involve a factual difficulty, but the point is that there is no reason why it should not have been believed and form a motive (cf. Pliny, *NH* 2.168; see above). It is likely that some parts of the story were embroidered (the Bogus affair? 279–83), or had unexplained gaps; e.g. how did Eudoxus extricate himself from Alexandria if in disgrace at having misappropriated royal property (261–73)? But Strabo is parading his own special qualifications here (271).

Some of the criticism involves unwarranted inference (that Eudoxus was ἀτιμωθείς (255) after the first voyage to India), or the merest quibbling on Strabo's part (why was being told that the figurehead came from the west significant for Eudoxus? He himself had to sail from the west to reach Alexandria again i.e. presumably by first reaching and rounding Cape Guardafui, 258–61), or a combination of quibbling and ignorance (why did Eudoxus fail to continue his journey having built a third boat after being shipwrecked on the east African coast (277f)? Obviously because it was the wrong kind of boat (see 204) for an open sea voyage of exploration).

Above all Strabo misses the point about the Indian voyages: how was Euergetes so short of competent pilots as to need a shipwrecked Indian taught some Greek, when that sea was well known (250–2)? Because what that survivor revealed was an overseas monsoon trade route.

Strabo concludes (283–5) by admitting that none of the events was impossible, but each difficult and a rare occurrence needing luck. But Eudoxus was always lucky – a final sarcasm on the original τυχεῖν of 156.

(c) *Strabo's reaction* (289–93) The most peculiar feature about the Eudoxus episode is the space that Strabo gives to it. In his Introduction, in which he reviews contributions to geography by his predecessors (Eratosthenes, Hipparchus, Polybius), the Eudoxus story occupies 41% of the section on Posidonius (148 lines out of 362), only for Strabo to dismiss it with scorn; which is an extraordinarily unbalanced account of Posidonian geography, or of the Περὶ ὠκεανοῦ. 289–93 suggest that he felt it to be a lapse into the uncritical and fabulous on the part of an author for whom he declared the highest admiration as a scientific geographer (T46). But there also seems to be real feeling behind the attack. The story puts Posidonius into the same category for Strabo as Antiphanes (line 236), Euhemerus (II.4.2) *and Pytheas*. But Pytheas appears to have raised Strabo's temperature in exactly the same way as Eudoxus (II.5.8; II.4.1–2; cf. T25, T46 comm., F208 comm.); in other words he had a complete distrust of the unfamiliar in travellers' tales, branding all such evidence as lies and sheer invention. As his judgement on Pytheas was distorted, so too is his reaction to Posidonius' account of Eudoxus. But his indignation preserves for us a feature of Περὶ ὠκεανοῦ. The tone and vivid detail of the Eudoxus explorations certainly at first seem different in kind from the technical and scientific account of zones for example. This is not to say that Περὶ ὠκεανοῦ was a popular work, but that Posidonius, the polymath, included different kinds of evidence: what he might regard as historical evidence as well as scientific. And the Eudoxus example is of particular interest to him as contemporary, and therefore at least to some extent subject to μαρτυρία.

Modern assessment

The reception of the story by modern scholars has varied from Strabonian scorn (e.g. Aly, *Strabonis Geographica*, Bd. 4, 111ff) to good-humoured scepticism (e.g. Thomson, *History* 175, 185); but a growing number of studies recognise the possibility of a genuine and important historical background. This is particularly true of the often ridiculed Indian-guided voyage to India. There were, of course, recognised trade routes to India, but passage by sea was dangerous because the long coastal route was infested by pirates (whose lighter boats could not venture far from the coast), and anyway was controlled by the Seleucids, the Arabs and the Indians. The only way to avoid this was by utilisation of open sea, which very much required expertise in navigational conditions of the area. The key was the secret of the monsoons (Casson, *Ancient Mariners* 178f, 185f; Hourani, *Arab Seafaring* 23–8), the south-west monsoon for the outward voyage, and the north-east for return (both of which were beyond the scope of Arab dhows (Hourani, 28; Raschka, 'New Studies in Roman Commerce', p. 937 n. 1143) and could be very hazardous for the inexperienced (Ascher, *J. Trop. Geog.* 31 (1970), 10ff; 34 (1972), 1ff)). The reward was the rich spice trade from India.

The discovery of the monsoon trade route was assigned by the *Periplus of the Red Sea* §57 to Hippasus, otherwise unknown, who has sometimes been given a later date; but Hippasus is only the name of the monsoon to Pliny (*NH* 6.100, 104), and he could have been as early as the Eudoxus expedition. But even if Hippasus were later than Eudoxus, one must not assume a single discovery of the monsoon route, and that everyone knew of it (cf. Raschke, *ANRW* II.9.2 (1978), p. 970 n. 1289). And if Strabo at II.5.12 (who in any case is at pains to contrast misgovernment and incompetence of the Ptolemies with the efficient benefits of the Romans, see XVII.1.12–13) stated that in the Prefecture of Egypt of Aelius Gallus (27–25 B.C., Jameson, *JRS* 58 (1968), 71ff; cf. Brunt, *JRS* 65 (1975), 242) 120 ships sailed from Myos Hormos to India, while before, under the Ptolemies, very few did (20 in XVII.1.13), Raschke (*op. cit.* p. 662) argued convincingly that the expansion of eastern trade in the later part of the 1st century B.C. was due to the economic climate and conditions rather than to the sudden discovery at that time of the monsoon route. Most recently Dihle, *ANRW* II.9.2 (1978), 548ff, has argued forcibly that the monsoon passage was already known during the whole of the 1st century B.C. This is almost certainly the importance of the Eudoxus voyages (see also Raschke, 660f; Otto and Bengtson, *Abh. Bayr. Akad. N.F.* 17, 197–218; Tarn, *Bactria* 368f; Hourani, *Arab Seafaring* 24f). It also explains why he was carried so far south on the return trip of the second voyage, which is precisely what one would expect from the north-east monsoon. The monsoon conditions, however, could be extremely dangerous, and one should be cautious over the extent of Eudoxus' use of the monsoon, or how far south on the coast of India he may have reached (Ascher, *J. Trop. Geogr.* 31 (1970), 10–26; 34 (1972), 1–7). The full exploration and exploitation of such routes could extend over a considerable period.

Posidonius, however, was interested in the Indian voyages only as a prefatory explanation for the circumnavigation attempts, since his context was the question of a circumfluent world ocean. It is also likely that Posidonius heard and checked the story in Cadiz rather than Alexandria (228f), which may explain the somewhat garbled account of Eudoxus' grievances against the Ptolemies. Also the other notorious target for criticism, the supposed Gadeiritan horse-prow turns into a red herring when we understand that its factual identity and source did not matter, but whether Eudoxus believed that it could have come from the west (see above). Posidonius saw that event as a motive for the eventual expeditions from Cadiz, and there is no evidence that he himself believed it to be true. It is hardly possible to doubt that the two Eudoxan expeditions set out from Gadeira. They must have been well known in Gadeira, involving Gadeiritan finance; it was precisely the ancient combination of trade and exploration (cf. 154ff) that is typified earlier by Pytheas from Massalia. Posidonius was in Gadeira at a time when these events were still fresh in the memory (228f). He does not say that Eudoxus circumnavigated Africa, but stresses the extent of his evidence (227f). He cannot therefore have used

Eudoxus as proof of the circumfluent ocean, but as part of contemporary belief concerning an open question capable of solution.

Eudoxus of Cyzicus: Select Bibliography

W. Aly, *Strabonis Geographica*, Bd. 4, 110ff.

E. J. Ascher, 'Graeco-Roman Nautical Technology', *J. Trop. Geogr.* 31 (1970), 10–26;

'Timetables of the Periplus and Pliny's Voyage to India', *J. Trop. Geogr.* 34 (1972), 1–7.

Berger, *Erdkunde der Griechen* 568–574.

Bunbury, *History of Ancient Geography* II.74ff.

Carcopino, *Le Maroc antique* 156–158.

Cary and Warmington, *Ancient Explorers* 98ff.

Casson, *Ancient Mariners* 178f; 185ff.

Dihle, 'Die Entdeckungsgeschichtlichen Voraussetzungen des Indienhandels der römischer Kaiserzeit', *Aufstieg u. Niederg. d. r. Welt* II.9.2, 546–580.

Dihle, *Innsbrucker Beiträge z. Kulturwiss.* 4 (1974), 11f.

Hourani, *Arab Seafaring* 24–27.

Hyde, *Ancient Greek Mariners* 200f; 245ff.

Jacoby, *Kommentar* 175ff.

Laffranque, 'Poseidonios, Eudoxe de Cyzique et la circumnavigation de l'Afrique', *Rev. Philos.* CLIII (1963), 199–222.

Otto and Bengtson, 'Zur Geschichte d. Niedergangs des Ptolemäerreiches', *Abh. d. Bayer. Ak. N.F.* 17 (1938), 194–218.

M. G. Raschke, 'New Studies in Roman Commerce with the East', *Aufstieg u. Niederg.* II.9.2, 604ff.

J. Rougé, 'Prêt et société maritimes dans le monde romain', *Memoirs of American Academy in Rome* XXXVI (1980), 295f.

A. E. Samuel, 'Ptolemaic Chronology', *Münchener Beitr. z. Papyrusforschung u. ant. Rechtsgesch.*, 43 (1962), 147ff.

F. Schülein, *Untersuchungen über des Posidonios Schrift* Περὶ ὠκεανοῦ, Diss. Erlangen, 1901, 38–44.

Skeat, *Reigns of the Ptolemies* 35f.

Tarn, *Bactria* 367ff; *Hellenistic Civilisation* 247ff.

J. H. Thiel, *Eudoxus of Cyzicus.*

Thomson, *History of Ancient Geography* 175, 185.

D. Changes in earth levels (*294–6*)

After criticism of Posidonius' treatment of Eudoxus, Strabo passes to what is right with Posidonius (ὀρθῶς κεῖται, 296), namely his account of the rising and sinking of the earth and its changes arising from earthquakes and the rest of such similar phenomena. Strabo adds: 'all of which (ὅσα) I *too* (καὶ ἡμεῖς) have enumerated' (296). This may refer to 1.3.5; 1.3.10, and in particular to 1.3.16–21, most of which Jacoby (*FGrH* F87) prints *en petit* as Posidonian. But καί (296) signals independence, and while 1.3.16 derives at least in part from Posidonius (see F231), Strabo goes on immediately to cite explicitly Demetrius of Scepsis (1.3.17) and Demetrius of Callatis (1.3.20; *FGrH* 85, F6) for their collections of instances. Eratosthenes too is involved in this area (e.g. 1.3.4). Schühlein too (55f) thought that the Demetrian collections may have come to Strabo through Posidonius. But while it is certain that Posidonius included in his works his own doxographies, and no doubt himself used earlier collections, like those of the Demetrii, is it likely that Strabo cites Demetrius (any Demetrius) if he is using and intending Posidonius? Jacoby, Reinhardt (*Poseidonios* 87ff) and Sudhaus (*Aetna* 59ff) outrun the evidence.

This passage does not necessarily show that Περὶ ὠκεανοῦ was the main source for Posidonian seismology, changes of earth levels, and related and consequent phenomena (295), such as appearance and disappearance of islands, changes of coastal levels, flooding and the like; F12 comes from Φυσικὸς Λόγος. But it is evidence that in Περὶ ὠκεανοῦ there was at least a compilation of fully documented accounts of the effect of such phenomena on the earth's surface.

In general: Frs. 12, 226–33; Berger, *Erdkunde* 567; Schühlein, 45–71.

297–305 Strabo appears to pick out two instances or samples from this section (πρὸς ὅ, 297, 'in relation to this'; καὶ, 303, 'also'), which are ludicrously superficial and inadequate to represent it. But Strabo was not interested in Posidonian physics and natural philosophy, but welcomed the topographical and ethnographical examples. Atlantis was a popular old literary chestnut, while the causes of the Cimbrian invasions of 115/14 B.C. were clearly still much debated (F272); both fitted in with Strabo's concept of geography.

(1) Atlantis (297–303)

Strabo approves (εὖ, 297) of Posidonius' bringing forward in relation to this (i.e. earthquakes, risings and subsidences; cf. Pl. *Tim.* 25c 6ff; *Crit.* 108e 8) Plato's point that the story of Atlantis (*Tim.* 24e ff; *Crit.* 108e) may actually not be fictional (cf. *Tim.* 26e 4f); according to Plato, Solon reported from information from the Egyptian priests that it once existed and then disappeared, no less than a continent in size (*Tim.* 24e 6f; *Crit.* 108e 6f). Posidonius thinks it is better to say that than that its inventor made it disappear, as the Poet (i.e. Homer) did with the wall of the Achaeans (*Il.* XII.1–33). Posidonius probably found this comment on Homer and the Achaean wall in Aristotle; cf. Str. XIII.1.36, ἣ οὐδ' ἐγένετο, ὁ δὲ πλάσας ποιητὴς ἠφάνισεν, ὡς 'Αριστοτέλης φησίν. Posidonius' statement is noticeably hesitant (ἐνδέχεται, 297; τοῦτο οἴεται βέλτιον εἶναι ἤ, 301f). Schühlein (47, 70) is perhaps right in thinking that this remark came towards the conclusion of the section in Posidonius, the possibility established in comparison (παρατίθησιν, 297) with Posidonius' earlier examples.

It is interesting that of all the treatment of seismic change in Περὶ ὠκεανοῦ, Strabo dredges up only this side reference to Plato, and that he praises support for its reality just after castigating Posidonius for not treating Eudoxus as fiction.

(2) The cause of the Cimbrian migrations (303–5)

'He conjectures (cf. T88) also that the migration of the Cimbri and their kin from their native land arose from an encroachment of the sea that occurred not all at once.'

This is an extremely puzzling sentence. In F272 (Str. VII.2.1–2) Strabo denies that the migration of the Cimbri was due to flooding of their land, and cites Posidonius with approval for criticism of the historians who maintained this view; Posidonius assigned the cause to the piratical character of the people themselves (F272.31ff).

Jacoby (*Kommentar* 179f; Aujac, Budé, I.2, p. 147 n. 3; cf. Reinhardt, *Poseidonios* 95) argued that there was no contradiction, but Posidonius held both views: the character of the Cimbrians was the basic reason, but flooding an immediate cause; the former was suitable for the *History*, the latter germane to Περὶ ὠκεανοῦ; and indeed cause of flooding is tied to the subject matter of F49.294–303 immediately before. But this is not derivable from Strabo's evidence. On the contrary, Strabo says explicitly that Posidonius censured (ἐπιτιμᾷ, F272.31) the latter view, regarded as γελοῖον (F272.8). Nor can we circumvent Strabo by suggesting that Posidonius later changed his mind in the *History* (character) from an earlier adherence in Περὶ ὠκεανοῦ to flooding, because it is not only Posidonius who is involved; Strabo approves of both (contradictory as they stand) Posidonian passages (ὀρθῶς κεῖται, F49.296; δικαίως, F272.31). The suggestion of *memoriae vitio* on the part of Strabo (Casaubon, Bake, p. 120) is surely desperate, and on this well-known subject, implausible.

The passage has therefore been emended to bring it into harmony with F272. In any case there has been some unease over the negative οὐκ ἀθρόαν (e.g. Berger, *Erdkunde* 567.1; Jones, Loeb *ad loc.*), suggesting a misplaced negative: ⟨οὐ⟩ κ.θ.ἐ. [οὐκ] ἀθρόαν (Schühlein, 96f). If the subject still concerns changes in the earth's levels caused by seismic action (294–303), then in this case the reference cannot be to gradual encroachment of regular tidal action, but rather to sudden inundation from the change of seabed level (ἐξαίρεσθαι τὴν γῆν, F49.294; cf. Frs. 226–8); and this is not countered by Jacoby's ridiculous argument, 'bei einer ἀθρόα ἔφοδος wäre das ganze volk vernichtet' (*Kommentar* 177); nor by Reinhardt's attempted parallel of the gradual emergence of a volcanic island (Str. 1.3.16, κατ' ὀλίγον ἐξαιρομένην, *Poseidonios* 97) which is no real parallel. Also the use of ἔφοδος in F272.24 seems to refer to the panic caused by a sudden cataclysm (but cf. Theophr. *Met.* 10a 28). On the other hand, the views criticised in F272 cover both a particular excessive flooding (F272.10f; which could also occur from a tidal source, see F218) and tidal action continuing over a period of time (F272.17ff). However, Meineke, following the lead of Corais, also posited a lacuna, to bring the whole expression in line with F272: ⟨κατὰ λῃστείαν⟩ γενέσθαι ⟨οὐ⟩ κ.θ.ἐ. [οὐκ] α.σ., and this is adopted by Sbordone *ad loc.*

Such an emendation would be satisfactory if the sentence were an isolated remark by Strabo here, and not connected with the preceding lines (294–303) on the effect of seismic change of levels in the ocean. This is argued by Schühlein (p. 96), pointing out that the next sentence, 305–8, ὑπονοεῖ δὲ . . ., clearly has nothing to do with the foregoing, and that therefore Strabo is making scattered superficial points. But εἰκάζει δὲ καὶ τὴν τῶν K . . ., 303, if καί means 'also', appears to link our sentence with the previous one on the sinking of Atlantis, as another instance of the effects of changing levels in the ocean; which would be odd if the sentence were to say that the migration was due to piracy and *not* to flooding. So the puzzle remains.

Nevertheless, since reconciliation between the two passages in Strabo seems impossible without emendation, I am driven to reading: ἐκ τῆς οἰκείας ⟨οὐ⟩ γενέσθαι κατὰ θαλάττης ἔφοδον [οὐκ] ἀθρόαν συμβᾶσαν, and assuming that although the context remains the same from 294 to 305, the sequence of thought is tenuous to vanishing point. After all the example of Atlantis must itself have been one of the most superficial side references in Posidonius' account of changing levels of the earth's surface. Strabo may have picked out at random two famous cases mentioned by Posidonius in this section, because Posidonius differed from and opposed the prevalent and established view. So Strabo introduces them negatively: Atlantis was *not* a fiction (298); the Cimbrian migration was *not* due to flooding of their territory (304f). See T88 and F272.32 for εἰκάζει.

E. Length of the inhabited world (305–8)

'He surmises (ὑπονοεῖ) that the length of the inhabited world, being somewhere about 70,000 stades, is half of the whole circle in respect of which it has been taken, so that, says he, sailing from the west with an east wind you would come to India within the same number of stades.'

Strabo defines the length of the inhabited world (1.4.5) as the distance from the extremities of India to the extremities of Iberia. He gives details of Eratosthenes' measurement by addition of stages (1.4.5–6) as 70,800 stades at the minimum, but with the addition of bulges and the like, rising to 77,800 (or perhaps 78,000, Aujac, *Strabon et la science* 186; cf. Thomson, *History* 165f). Hipparchus appears on the other hand to have concentrated on the breadth distance from south to north of the inhabited world (Aujac, *Strabon* 187). But Eratosthenes' distances were exaggerated (Thomson, *loc. cit.*), and the length was cut by Artemidorus to 68,545 (Pliny *NH* 2.242; Thomson, *History* 210; Bunbury, II.64f). This was also clearly the opinion of Posidonius, who already thought Eratosthenes' figure for the circumference of the earth too large (F202; F49.32ff). Strabo also reports (1.4.6) that Eratosthenes presented this mathematically (ὡς οἱ μαθηματικοί) as a proportion of a complete circle of a band of latitude (namely the master band established by Dicaearchus and adopted by Eratosthenes on, of the parallel supposed to run through the Pillars of Heracles, near Athens, and Rhodes; i.e. *c*. 36°). The inhabited world according to Eratosthenes would be more than a third of that. A figure for the circle of less than 200,000 stades is given, presumably approximated from the meridian, which is about right (actually 203,868) for the given latitude in ratio to Eratosthenes' figure of 252,000 for the earth's circumference.

Posidonius suggests that his 70,000 would be half of the whole circle, presumably for the Rhodes parallel again. This once more is approximately correct in ratio to Posidonius' figure of 180,000 for the circumference of the earth (as given in F49.34); for the Rhodes parallel at 36° would be 145,620.

It is interesting to note that the conjectural part (ὑπονοεῖ) of Posidonius' statement does not seem to be the figure of 70,000 (ὑπάρχον), although the figure is obviously round (που), but refers to that figure being half of the whole circle. Does that mean that Posidonius felt uncertain about calculating the parallel at 36° from the circumference figure (actually 180,000.cos 36°)? But he could arrive at an approximation. Or did he remain undogmatic about the actual circumference figure (F202 comm.)? Possibly one should not overstress ὑπονοεῖ. He was right in thinking that Eratosthenes' latitudinal distances were too great, but Eratosthenes happened to be nearer the mark in his fraction of known world to the unknown part from the Pillars westwards to India.

The figure of 70,000 was adopted by Strabo himself (II. 5.6), who however retained Eratosthenes' and Hipparchus' circumference figure, and by *De Mundo* 3.393b 22.

The idea that the earth being circular, it was theoretically possible to sail from the Straits of Gibraltar west to India if nothing got in the way, is as old as Aristotle (*Meteor.* 2.5.362b 15ff; *De Caelo* 2.14, 298a 10ff); in general: Elter, 'Das Altertum und die Entdeckung Amerikas', *RhM* 75 (1926), 241–65. Eratosthenes (1.4.6) uses the idea theoretically to define the complete circle of latitude. Posidonius with his interest in the circumfluent ocean, seems to be nearer belief in practical possibility. The distance shortens; you have merely to sail west with an east wind. εὔρῳ (308) would properly be an east-south-east (from the direction of the Indics, according to Timosthenes' windrose, F137 comm.), and presumably blew right round the globe. There is no need to change the text.

For Seneca (*NQ* 1. *Praef.* 13) it was a matter of *paucissimorum dierum spatium, si navem suus ferat ventus.*

F. Geographical divisions in relation to variations of fauna, flora, climate, race etc.: division by zones; division by continents. Human geography and environmental ethnography (309–56)

(1) Strabo blames Posidonius for both criticising and praising the usual division into continents (309–16)

But Strabo's language is misleading, perhaps deliberately so: 'Having tried to find fault with those who delimit (define, διορίσαντας) continents in the way they do (οὕτω) and not by certain parallels to the equator through which they were likely to show variations in animals, plants and atmospheric conditions, some connected with the frigid zone, others with the torrid, with the result that the continents are a sort of zones . . .' (309–13).

This implies that the question is how one divides continents, either οὕτω, i.e. by physical features like a river or isthmus, or by parallels of latitude, i.e. κλίματα. Although the latter would make complete nonsense of any continental division, Strabo apparently has this diaeresis in mind, since he concludes ὥστε οἱονεὶ ζώνας εἶναι τὰς ἠπείρους (313). It is obvious that Posidonius had two distinct types of division in mind: (i) by continents, (ii) by latitudinal κλίματα or zones. Strabo also implies that these would be exclusive alternatives, which is incorrect; Posidonius could both criticise and praise the existing (οὖσαν, 314) division into continents. Strabo even indicates how this could be so. At this point in Περὶ ὠκεανοῦ Posidonius seems to have turned from physical geography to geographical issues of a much wider kind, embracing regional environmental variations of fauna and flora, including human geography and ethnography. Posidonius claimed that such variations are more likely to be demonstrated (311), generically at least, from the environment of latitudinal position (cf. F49.56ff) than from arbitrary division into continents. On the other hand, continents have an influence in that variation of environment in separate land masses even in the same latitudinal band, produces special natural effects (326ff).

309 Fixing the boundaries of continents was an old problem; so esp. Str. I.4.7f.

309 οὕτω might mean 'simply', i.e. without further consideration of other kinds of division such as parallels; but it is more likely to refer to the common criterion of physical features. The boundary between Europe and Asia is variously given (Thomson, *History* 59, 254) as the R. Phasis, the Caucasus isthmus or the Don (i.e. the Tanais, Ptolemy). It was much argued whether the boundary between Africa and Asia was the Nile (e.g. Polybius, III.47.59; Thomson, 209) or the Red Sea (e.g. Ptol. II.1.6; IV.5.13; Thomson, 66, 271); so a special problem asked to which continent Egypt belonged, a question which particularly interested Strabo with his claims to a special knowledge of Egypt: I.2.25, 26, 28.

311 There is no need to change ἀέρων to ἀνθρώπων as suggested by Jacoby. ἀέρων is apposite to zonal divisions (cf. F49.84; F210.18), was long thought to have an effect on the characteristics of living things (e.g. Hipp., *Airs, Waters, Places*), and reappears in just such a trichotomy with plants and animals in Ptol. *Tetr.* II.2. Human beings are subsumed under ζῴων, but were no doubt especially in mind (cf. 317).

313 οἱονεὶ ζώνας κτλ. must be Strabo's comment, because of the confusion of zonal continents; but did Posidonius mean the three 'zones' by his παραλλήλοις τισὶ, or the commonly accepted seven κλίματα? He may of course have progressed from zones to κλίματα, but there is little doubt that he started at least with zones, for which there is some precedent in Hipp., *Airs*. The reference to 'frigid' and 'torrid' (312) indicates so; so does the interpretation of zones in terms of human geography, 49–61 above. The very similar theory in Ptol. *Tetr.* II.2 also makes clear that generic divisions were first fixed by the three zones (equator to tropic, tropic to 'Bears', 'Bears' or Arctic zone); so the Ethiopians occupy the zone from the equator to tropic (cf. 326ff). Modifications obviously followed: e.g. Posidonius' subtropical band (49ff), continental variation (326ff), particular natural conditions (Ptol. *Tetr.* II.2; cf. F169.84ff).

313–15 ἀνασκευάζει πάλιν καὶ ἐν ἀναλύσει δίκης γίνεται is a rather odd expression for Strabo. ἀνασκευάζειν may mean to destroy an argument (Str. I.2.18), or to build again, remodel (Str. XVI.1.5); both of these would demand an object. Perhaps in the context of δίκη, the verb may mean here 'reverse a decision or judgement' (cf. Vett. Val. p. 283.23, Kroll) which also requires an object; perhaps δίκην is to be supplied, which may account for δίκην in the codices after ἀναλύσει, which must be corrupt. Or it may be thought that ἀνασκευάζει πάλιν . . . ἐπαινῶν πάλιν . . . is surprising; so Jacoby doubted the second πάλιν; but perhaps the first conceals an accusative. ἀνάλυσις δίκης must refer to dissolving sentence, but are there any parallels?

θετικὴν ποιούμενος τὴν ζήτησιν. (i) 'making the enquiry a matter of debate', that is, suitable for a θέσις or maintaining a position in a debate, speaking first for and then against, *LSJ s.v.* III; Cic. *QF* III.3.4. This interpretation is supported by πρὸς οὐδὲν χρησίμως, with no practical purpose. (ii) Characteristic of θέσις, in the sense of arbitrary determination, convention; θέσει, as opposed to natural law or design, φύσει. This is a Stoic opposition (*SVF* III.308; cf. also Epicurus, D.L. X.76, p. 27 Us.); and compare Chrysippus in Gellius, VII.2.12 (*SVF* II.1000, p. 294.27): harm coming to men through themselves καὶ καθ' ὁρμὴν αὐτῶν ἁμαρτανόντων τε καὶ βλαπτομένων καὶ κατὰ τὴν αὐτῶν διάνοιαν καὶ θέσιν. So Strabo continues (315): *for* (γάρ) such dispositions do not arise from providence . . . but by accident and chance (κατὰ ἐπίπτωσιν καὶ συντυχίαν, 318). But πρὸς οὐδὲν χρησίμως counts strongly for (i). The interpretation of γάρ depends on the development of the argument.

(2) Strabo's criticism of natural and zonal variations (316–26)

Strabo offers an argument.

316–18 For such dispositions (i.e. animal, plant, climate) do not arise from providence (as Posidonius and Stoic physics would maintain), as neither do differences in respect of race (ἔθνη) or language, but by accident and chance.

318–21 And technical achievement (τέχναι), capacities (δυνάμεις), characteristics of behaviour (ἐπιτηδεύσεις), once a start has been made (ἀρξάντων τινῶν), prevail for the most part in any band of latitude, and in some cases even in spite of the latitude, so that some are endemic by nature, others by habituation and practice.

321 δὲ θέσει of codd. would mean 'by arbitrary convention' (cf. above); but it is clear from the combination with ἄσκησις, and from lines 323, 325 that δ'ἔθει (Kramer) is the correct reading.

322–5 For it is not by nature that the Athenians are lovers of literature (φιλόλογοι) and the Spartans not, or still nearer, (i.e. in latitude) the Thebans, but rather by habituation; and in the same way, it is not by nature that the Babylonians and Egyptians are lovers of science (φιλόσοφοι), but by practice and habituation.

325–6 The supreme excellence in horses, cattle or other animals is not created by locality only, but also by practice. But he (i.e. Posidonius) confounds this (with his zonal divisions).

So Strabo opposes the importance of habituation and practice to the natural effect of environment, which he conceives is Posidonius' theory.

(3) Strabo criticises Posidonius' support for continental variation from the basis of a Posidonian text (326–56)

326–337 'And when praising the sort of division of continents as is now held, he (i.e. Posidonius) uses as an example the fact that Indians differ from African Ethiopians (although being on the same latitude), for, he says, they (i.e. Indians) are more developed physically, less burnt by the dryness of the atmosphere.'

For such a distinction: Manilius, IV.724ff; Ptol. *Tetr.* II.2; Hipp. *Airs, Waters, Places* XII; Hdt. III.106; Frs. 280, 281; for the east–west differentiation: Str. XVII.3.10 – F23; Hipp. *Airs* V, VII. 'Therefore (διό), says he, Homer too, although calling all of them Ethiopians, split them in two (implying both that they were all the same ἔθνος by κλῖμα, and featured differences through continental division), "Some where Hyperion sinks, some where he rises" (*Od.* I.24), while Crates (F34f Mette) in introducing a second inhabited world, which Homer did not know, is a slave to a hypothesis; "he ought" says he "to have changed the line like this: "both Hyperion departing...", i.e. bending in his circle from the meridian."'

This is very obscure, and made worse by Strabo's following criticism.

The Homeric verses (*Od.* I.23–4) were clearly much interpreted and debated (Geminus, *Isag.* XVI.26ff), because the question of the extent of the Ethiopians through Libya (Africa) and Asia was a problem for geographers. Strabo, I.2.24–8 is a good illustration for Homeric 'geography' on precisely this point, although the discussion is somewhat confused.

Strabo (I.2.24) defended the Homeric lines, lambasting Crates and Aristarchus for misunderstanding them. This passage shows that the subject of εἰσάγοντα (333), which cannot be Homer, was Crates; and this subject must be supplied. Aristarchus in line 24 read οἱ μὲν δυσομένου Ὑπερίονος, οἱ δ' ἀνιόντος, but Crates ἠμὲν δυσομένου Ὑπερίονος, ἠδ' ἀνιόντος. Crates' position held that ocean divided the known inhabited world from an antipodal counterpart, and so assumed a second group of Ethiopians south of the equator in a corresponding area to those in the northern hemisphere (Thomson, *History* 202f). So for Crates the Ethiopians are 'split in two' by ocean stretching in an east–west direction at the equator over the torrid zone, and having Ethiopians on both north and south banks. Strabo adds an astronomical explanation for Crates' emendation, namely that all the Ethiopians lie within the two tropics, within which all the risings and settings of the sun take place. But then, as he says, what is the difference from Aristarchus' reading of the Homeric line, since for Crates too some Ethiopians will live at the rising and some at the setting sun (although strung along both sides of the ocean)? It is possible, however, that Crates, by his emendation of Homer, was objecting to the split in the Ethiopians being defined (οἱ μὲν . . . οἱ δ') by east and west. The distinctive split for him is north–south, while east–west is continuous (ἡμὲν . . . ἠδ'). According to Strabo, Aristarchus thought that Homer said (or wrote) διχθὰ δεδαίαται . . . οἱ μὲν . . . οἱ δ', but was simply mistaken through ignorance; the only Ethiopians are those next to Egypt, and they are not split in two. Strabo (1.2.25) objects that the Ethiopians are split, either by the Nile, or by the Red Sea (1.2.26), i.e. the common alternative continental boundaries between Africa and Asia. Strabo himself apparently believed (1.2.28) that the Ethiopians stretch along the whole oceanboard to the south through Africa and Asia, 'split in two' by the Arabian gulf (our Red Sea). Compare the Fisheaters on the band of latitude at the tropics (51–61, above).

The problem remains, however, what Posidonius meant by ἀπερχομένου, i.e. ἀπὸ τοῦ μεσημβρινοῦ περικλίνοντος. He ought to be objecting to an east–west distinction, and 'interpreting' by emendation a north–south division. He is possibly doing this by suggesting the removal of δυσομένου because of its association with the setting sun, i.e. the west, and by transferring the model from the diurnal path of the sun, which fixes an east–west line, to the annual path, where the ecliptic fixes north–south limits by the tropics (within which the Ethiopians of both hemispheres lie, according to Crates). The ecliptic cuts the meridian (i.e. the north–south great circle going through the celestial poles) at each tropic; in 'going away' (ἀπερχομένου) the sun is bending in its circle (περικλίνοντος) from the meridian, i.e. from the intersection of meridian and tropic of cancer, which is the zenith for the Ethiopians of the northern hemisphere (cf. II.1.20), towards the intersection of tropic of capricorn and meridian, which will be the zenith for the Ethiopians of the southern hemisphere, and from there in its continuous path (ᾗδ') it will again be rising (ἀνιόντος) towards the meridian and cancer again (Fig. 5). It seems from Str. 1.2.24 that Crates himself

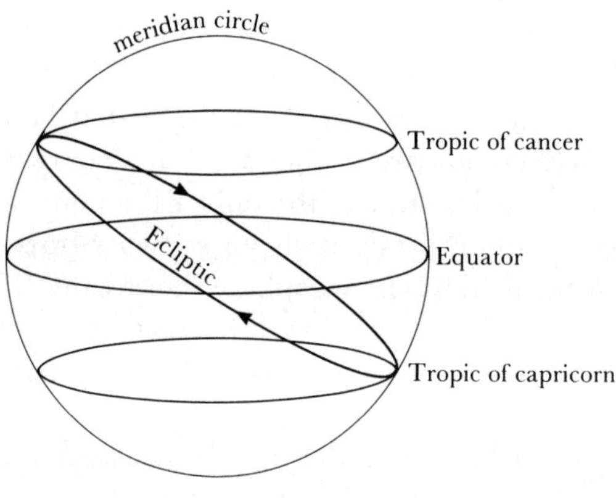

Fig. 5

visualised an annual ecliptic model defining the area between the two tropics. Posidonius develops this with rather fanciful logic, and perhaps with academic tongue in cheek; ἀπερχομένου is crashingly pedestrian and verges on a pun with Ὑπεριόν(τ)ος. Aujac (Budé, n. *ad loc.*, p. 148) suspects a confusion between meridian and equator (ἰσημερινός), but this is impossible; Strabo himself (350f) understands meridian. For a different interpretation: Dihle, *RhM* 105 (1962), 105f. See also F223.

338–56 If Posidonius was making a learned joke, Strabo certainly did not understand it, but laboriously takes Posidonius to task.

(i) 338–40 The Egyptian Ethiopians are themselves split in two (i.e. by the Nile, cf. 1.2.25; as distinct from a split between 'Egyptian' Ethiopians and 'Indian' Ethiopians); for some are in Asia (east of the Nile), some in Libya, with no distinction between the two.

(ii) 340–5 Homer did not split the Ethiopians because he knew that Indians were of a certain physical condition – in all probability he did not even know of the Indians at all (ἀρχήν), since not even Euergetes, adds Strabo sarcastically (see 250ff), according to the Eudoxus tale, knew anything about India, or even how to sail there. Homer's split was the one argued for by Strabo at 1.2.28, namely that the Ethiopians, stretched along the whole seaboard of ocean from east to west, were split by the Arabian Gulf (our Red Sea), which Homer knew about.

(iii) 346–56 In which case, Strabo had argued (1.2.24f), Crates' reading of the line makes no difference from Aristarchus in interpretation (see above). As for Posidonius' interpretative 'emendation', ἠμὲν ἀπερχομένου, that makes no difference either, because it is no different from ἠμὲν δυσομένου (Crates' reading). Strabo, interpreting μεσημβρινός as meridian in relation to the diurnal path of the sun, points out that the whole sector from the meridian (i.e. zenith) to setting (i.e. horizon) ('departing from the meridian') is called setting (δύσις, i.e. 'west'), just as the semicircle of the horizon (to the west, from north to south) is so called, e.g. Aratus, *Phaen.* 61: 'where the extremities of the west and east mingle with each other' (Fig. 6).

This must be a misunderstanding of Posidonius' meaning in giving a diurnal rather than an annual model (see above), but it confirms μεσημβρινός as meridian.

Posidonius was also interested in Aratus in relation to Homer (F48); but he was hardly alone in that. For the

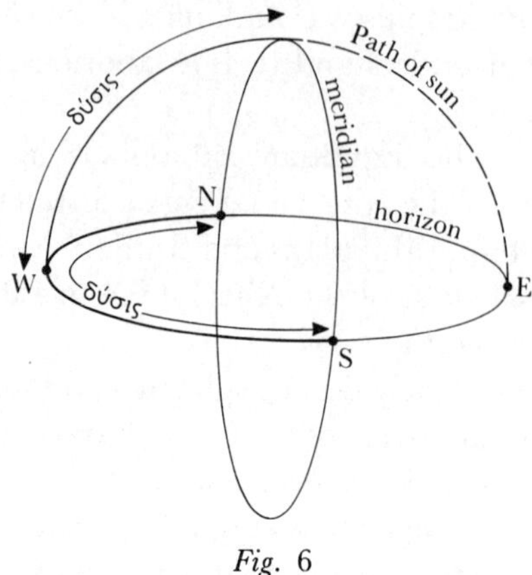

Fig. 6

combination of Crates and Aratus again in a Homeric context: Str. I.1.6; but we should not conclude that such passages necessarily derive from Posidonius; F216 comm. After all, the quotation of Aratus here is brought forward in criticism of Posidonius.

Although this section is obfuscated by Strabo's presentation and confused criticism, it is enough to give a tantalising glimpse of the scope and orientation of Posidonian geography in Περὶ ὠκεανοῦ. What began as a scientific attempt to define zones or geographical divisions has culminated in an account of human geography in relation to the vegetation, life and climate of the total environment. Echoes of Posidonius have been noticed in Vitruvius, VI.1.1–10, Manilius, IV.711–43 (especially 724ff for the Ethiopians and the Indian distinction; but the passage includes animals, plants, languages, customs, practices), Pliny *NH* 2.189–90 (Ethiopians again, animals, plants, human characteristics, customs and politics). But the most striking passage occurs in Ptolemy, *Tetr.* II.2: general ἐθνικὰ ἰδιώματα are established partly καθ' ὅλους παραλλήλους (latitudes) καὶ γωνίας ὅλας (i.e. compass points, east–west). Ptolemy makes clear that he refers to zones; so, οὓς δὴ καλοῦμεν κοινῶς Αἰθίοπας occupy the zone from equator to tropic. However, eastern sections are 'more masculine', since the orient partakes of the nature of the sun. The criteria cover human characteristics and plants, animals and climate. Nevertheless, within zones particular natural conditions have their own effect (φυσικῶς) on character and customs.

See in general: Reinhardt, *Poseidonios* 71ff, *RE* 675f; K. Trüdinger, *Studien zur Gesch. d. griech.-röm. Ethnographie* 118–26; Norden, *Die germ. Urgesch. in Tac. Germ.* 59ff, 107ff; F. Boll, 'Studien über Claudius Ptol.', *Jahrb. f. Philol. Supplb.* 21 (1894), 204ff; H. J. Mette, *Sphairopoiia* 73f; Jacoby, *Kommentar* 178; Berger, *Erdkunde* 557ff; Wilamowitz, *Gr. Leseb.* II.184; Aujac, *Strabon et la science de son temps* 267–73; K. Schmidt, 'Kosmologische Aspekte im Geschichtswerk d. Pos.', *Hypomnemata* 63 (1980).

Descriptive ethnography, embracing vegetation, fauna, climatic and physical features, customs and practices, had an early and long tradition in Greek historical and geographical writing; also works appeared declaring the effect of climate on character (e.g. Hipp. *Airs*; cf. Thomson, *Hist.* 106ff). But Posidonius apparently attempted an *explanatory* ethnography, depending on recognition of causes operating through the whole physical and animate features of a region. Ultimately this depended, at least partly, on the interrelation of celestial and terrestrial phenomena; hence human geography is a natural growth from the geographical establishment of astronomical zones, useful both πρὸς τὰ οὐράνια and πρὸς τὰ ἀνθρώπεια (44ff). Thus the scope of Posidonian 'geography' was extremely wide: the explanation of all terrestrial phenomena, in so far as this depended on geographical topography (310f). This latter *caveat* must be made, because for Posidonius not only were geographical factors in themselves highly complex (he certainly did not remain on generic levels such as 'the Ethiopians'), but were only partial and inadequate as evidence; cf. the role of physiognomy in F169.84ff comm. In any case, explanation of cause comes from natural philosophy (F18) in relation to the particular field, in this case geography.

G. Strabo sums up (357–62)

Such geographical scope and orientation is not for Strabo; but if Περὶ ὠκεανοῦ did culminate in such a concept of geography, it is more understandable why Strabo ends his general account with two specific criticisms; (i) the overdose of natural philosophy (ὅσα δὲ φυσικώτερα, 359) which must be examined elsewhere (i.e. not in a geographical work) or ignored (T76b); (ii) Posidonius' Aristotelianism in his addiction to argument from causes (T85). Strabo says that his School (οἱ ἡμέτεροι, 361; i.e. the Stoics, cf. I.2.3) shears off the latter, because of the concealment of causes. One must allow for Strabo's bias here; he has just been attacking Posidonian causal explanation in 316–26: much is due to accident, chance and arbitrary determination. But there is no doubt that Posidonius in his investigation of the sciences (of which geography was one) pursued more than any other Stoic the pattern of intermediate causation in attempting to establish the complete nexus; see Kidd, *Problems* 212f; id. *A & A* 24 (1978), 14f.

Strabo has been critical throughout (apart from 294ff): 'so much too in reply to (πρὸς) Posidonius' (357). But the next sentence shows how much he used him: 'For' (γάρ) has reference to τοσαῦτα; i.e. only so much now is given in reply, because there is much detail to follow also in the individual sections of the main work (357f). For τοσαῦτα expressing *limited* amount, compare its use after brief speeches in Thucydides (e.g. III.31) instead of the usual τοιαῦτα. This seems to be evidence that Περὶ ὠκεανοῦ also contained a good deal of what Strabo would recognise as geographical material (ὅσα γεωγραφικά). In the Introduction here, Strabo restricts himself to a survey of general themes or theories. The *Index of Sources* lists named references and appropriate discussion (τυγχάνει τῆς προσηκούσης διαίτης, 358); but Strabo no doubt also used him without acknowledgement.

F50 Pliny, *Naturalis Historia* 1.5

CONTENT

Pliny in his list of sources for *NH* Bk 5 names Posidonius 'qui περίπλουν aut περιήγησιν' (T56).

COMMENT

Pliny's reference has always been taken to be to the Περὶ ὠκεανοῦ, or to an extract from it: Reinhardt, *RE* 663; Jacoby, *Kommentar* 163; Malitz, *Die Historien des Posidonios* 57 n. 175; Theiler, *Poseidonios* II.4. But the assumption deserves examination. *Periplus* or *Periegesis* would be an odd title or designator for the Περὶ ὠκεανοῦ, and a still odder description of its contents (F49). Moreover Strabo (VIII.1.1; see T77 comm.) classifies earlier geographical works into (i) monographs such as Περίπλοι; (ii) general histories with topographical sections; (iii) scientific geographies. The Περὶ ὠκεανοῦ is firmly placed in category (iii) with Hipparchus, and thus fundamentally distinguished from category (i), which would be characterised by the works of Skylax, Agatharchides, Artemidorus and Arrian. There is no other titular reference to a separate *Periplus* monograph from Posidonius, but after all the title of the Περὶ ὠκεανοῦ only comes to us from Strabo (F49; and the Suda, T1a). It is highly likely that Pliny knew and used the Περὶ ὠκεανοῦ; F120 could derive from it (although it could have come from a meteorological work), and possibly F212. One would not expect him to be writing from confused ignorance of Posidonius' work (T56). So the question should at least be left open as to whether Posidonius wrote a separate chorographic monograph such as a *Periplus*. If so, did Strabo know of it? At x.3.5, on the improving accuracy of distances (see T78 comm.), a matter central to chorography, Strabo surprisingly couples Posidonius and Artemidorus, a typical *Periplus* writer. Pliny's fragment on India (F212), while possibly deriving from Περὶ ὠκεανοῦ, could have come from a *Periplus* type of monograph.

For the coupling of Περίπλους and Περιήγησις, cf. Athenaeus VII.278D: οἱ τὰς περιηγήσεις καὶ τοὺς περίπλους ποιησάμενοι.

F51 Athenaeus, VII.266E–F

CONTENT

Posidonius is referred to with Nicolaus for reporting in the *History* that the Chians were enslaved by Mithridates, and handed over in fetters to their own personal slaves to be settled in the territory of Colchis.

CONTEXT AND COMMENTARY

The context is important for the extent of Posidonian matter in this fragment. The passage continues: 'so truly did the deity vent his wrath on them for having been the first to use purchased slaves, when most men did their own work when ministering to their own needs' (5–7). The topic of slaves was begun by Democritus at 262B, and at 265B the statement that the Chians were the first Greek people to buy slaves is specifically quoted from Theopompus, *History*, Bk 17. Immediately after this quotation Democritus (i.e. Athenaeus) says: ἐγὼ δὲ τοῖς Χίοις ἡγοῦμαι διά τοῦτο νεμεσῆσαι τὸ δαιμόνιον· χρόνοις γὰρ ὕστερον ἐξεπολεμήθησαν διὰ δούλους. He then embarks on a long quotation (256D–266E) from Nymphodorus of Syracuse, τῆς 'Ασίας Παράπλους (second half 4th c. B.C.; *FGrH* III.572) on a Chian slave revolt led and maintained by a Drimacus, who after his death was given a ἡρῷον and the title ἥρως εὐμενής. Athenaeus mentions that in many other accounts he had seen, he was not named. All this shows that the remark about the animosity of τὸ δαιμόνιον in relation to the inauguration of bought slaves in F51.5–7 comes from Athenaeus and not from Posidonius (or Nicolaus). After the Nymphodorus extract there is a brief reference to Hdt VIII.105, followed by the Mithridatic anecdote from Posidonius and Nicolaus. So the Posidonian information is restricted to the first four lines of the fragment.

For the date of the Chian enslavement (86 B.C.) and Mithridates' grudge against the Chians, see App. *Mithr.* 46–7, Memnon 33, Magie, *Roman Rule* II.1108, nn.50–1. They were reinstated by Sulla at the end of the war (App. *Mithr.* 55).

Nicolaus of Damascus (*FGrH* 90) of the second half of the 1st c. B.C, was a court philosopher and historian of Herod the Great. The reference will have come from his *Universal History*, of which Bks 96–110 treated the Mithridatic War. He is grouped again with Posidonius in F288 as a detractor of Epicurus.

Posidonius was mentioned earlier in the slavery topic at 263C (F60), where reference is given to Bk 11 of the *History*. But we must not assume that the two references come from the same Book. F60 is a traditional instance on a different theme of slavery. F51 almost certainly occurred in one of the last books of the *History* dealing with the First Mithridatic War.

Date of the conclusion of the History

This is the latest datable event which can with certainty be assigned to the *History* from the surviving fragments. Moreover, Malitz (70) has pointed out the curious fact that Athenaeus no longer cites Posidonius for any subsequent event in the eighties and seventies, but only Nicolaus alone. This raises the question whether the *History* continued much after 86 B.C.

The Suda avers (T1a.6–8) that the *History* began where Polybius finished, comprised 52 books, and continued until 'the Cyrenaic war and Ptolemy'. There is no problem about the starting date of the *History*. But if the number of books is correct, the indications are that they are running out in the mid-eighties. The fragment from Bk 49 (F78) refers to the gourmet Apicius as being responsible for Rutilius' banishment in 92 B.C. The reference to Bk 47 (F77) concerns the high living of Ptolemy Alexander I; although he died in 88 B.C., he was of course politically prominent much earlier. But the precise contextual dating of either fragment is by no means certain. The scale of the earlier books also supports the view that the last 3–5 books of 52 could hardly have extended beyond the crowded events of the First Mithridatic War (Jacoby, *Kommentar* 156f; Malitz, *Die Historien des Poseidonios* 69ff; Laffranque, *Poseidonios d'Apamée* 118ff). Therefore those who argue that the *History* extended to a much later date, such as 63 B.C. (e.g. Strasburger, *JRS* 55 (1965), 42–4) have to emend the Suda figure significantly. Figures are corruptible and the Suda unreliable, but Strasburger in turn relies solely on hypotheses based on unattested evidence. That Posidonius wrote up Pompey in the *History* or elsewhere remains highly questionable (F79). And Athenaeus' silence after Bk 49 is strange. So far, the evidence, such as it is, favours the early date.

The Suda's end-point definition is hardly helpful, but however interpreted or emended, lends no support for 63 B.C. with Pompey's victory over the pirates and his settlement in the East. The history of Cyrenaica is complicated from the initial bequest to Rome in the will of Ptolemy Euergetes II (Physcon) of 155 B.C., nullified by his heir, and the effective bequest through the will of his successor, Ptolemy Apion, in 96 B.C. But although at that point the senate declared the cities free, Rome did not in fact annex Cyrenaica until 75/4 B.C. (Oost, *CPh* 58 (1963), 11–25; Harris, *War and Imperialism in Republican Rome* 154–8; Braund, *Papers of the British School at Rome* 51 (1983), 16–57). There was clearly continual local trouble in this period but hardly significant wars. Inscriptional evidence (Moretti, *RFIC* 104 (1976), 385–98; Robert, *REG* 1977, p. 444, no. 594, 1978, no. 561; Reynolds, *Mélange Guarducci* 622–30; Harris, *War and Imperialism* 154, n.5) records Libyan wars with Cyrene, which may tie up with Plutarch's story (*Mul. Virt.*, *Mor.* 255E–257E; Polyaenus VIII.38) of Artephila and the murderous brutality of the tyrants Nicocrates and Leander at Cyrene 'in the crucial times of Mithridates', which led to a Libyan war. There is no evidence of subsequent significant Cyrenaic wars, as distinct from unrest and disorders, up to and including the Roman annexation in 75, which was probably for financial reasons (Oost, *CPh* 58, 20f). So the Cyrenaic war has been connected with Lucullus' visit to Cyrene in early 86 B.C. (Plu. *Luc.* 2.3–4; Strabo, *FGrH* 91. F7 (Josephus *AJ* 14.114–18)). But Lucullus' purpose is not entirely clear. He had been despatched on a ship-gathering expedition for Sulla, and may have hoped to collect from Cyrene's capable port, Apollonia (for the harbour, Blackman, *International Journal of Nautical Archaeology*, 1982, p. 192f). Or he may have been called in, or stepped in, to put down trouble. Strabo refers to internal stasis through the spreading power of the Jewish section; but Plutarch alludes to turbulence from continual tyrannies and wars. Lucullus settled affairs and refashioned the constitution, but apparently collected no ships, no more than he did from Egypt, after an ambiguous reception from Soter II. 'The Cyrenaic war' would be a curious description of this event.

Ptolemy undefined (and emendation, T1a. 7–8 *app. crit.*, hardly helps) could refer to Alexander I (died 88 B.C.), Soter II (died 80 B.C.), Alexander II (installed by Sulla, but assassinated nineteen days after he murdered Berenice, 80 B.C.) or Auletes, who seized power after Alexander's assassination. Alexander I would fit in best with the rest of the evidence, although his death is rather early for the finish of the *History*.

On the whole the balance of evidence still points to the mid-eighties for the end-point (Jacoby, Malitz, Theiler). Theiler (*Poseidonios* II.78f), who links the Cyrenaic war to Lucullus, and Ptolemy to Alexander I, argues that Posidonius deliberately concluded the *History* with the death of Marius (T28) and the fall of Athens to Sulla (86 B.C.). This may be so, but then 'the Cyrenaic war and Ptolemy' is no description of that. If any credence at all is to be given to the Suda, we must keep open the possibility that the *History* did not have a definite concluding point of significance, but may have been unfinished like that of Thucydides, and petered out on some more transitory affair like 'the Cyrenaic war and Ptolemy'.

F52 Athenaeus, IX.401A

CONTENT

'The philosopher Posidonius mentions rabbits in the *History*: "We too saw a lot of them in our sail from Dicaearcheia to Neapolis. For there is an island a short distance from the mainland by the extreme end of Dicaearcheia with few inhabitants but a large number of these rabbits."'

CONTEXT

Athenaeus' discussion on the hare (λαγώς) as a delicacy began at 399D. Immediately before the fragment he quotes from Polybius 13.3.10 on the comparison between hares and rabbits.

COMMENT

1–2 Athenaeus gives no Book number. Jacoby (*Kommentar* 195) suggested that it was a side comment from part of Posidonius' Spanish history, because Spanish rabbits were notorious (Str. III.2.6; III.5.2; Pliny *NH* 8.217). But the possibilities of context are endless.

2–6 As Dicaearcheia is Puteoli, the sail was a brief rounding of the cape to Naples. But there was a regular coastal traffic from the port of Dicaearcheia. Also, on his return trip to Italy from Spain (T21, T22), Posidonius may have landed eventually at Dicaearcheia, which was a normal port for merchantmen from Turdetania (Str. III.2.6). Strabo's reference to Posidonius' return journey was in the previous chapter (III.2.5). The island was probably Nesis (modern Nisida) in the Bay of Naples, at that time volcanic (Lucan, *Phars.* 6.90), and later known for excellent asparagus (Pliny *NH* 19.146); presumably by then they had controlled the plague of rabbits (cf. Str. III.5.2). Polybius, 12.3.10 had already distinguished rabbits from hares (λαγώς), and noted them on Corsica with foxes and wild sheep. Varro, *RR* 3.12.6 has an account of hares and rabbits from different areas. Strabo (III.2.6; III.5.2) records that rabbits (he uses the diminutive λαγιδεύς) had become a serious plague in Turdetania, and had spread through the rest of Spain and as far as Massilia and the islands. He notes their destructiveness and the use of ferrets to control them. The problem became acute in the Gymnasiae (i.e. Balearic) Islands, where the local population appealed to Augustus for military help to put them down. The Spanish rabbits may have come from Posidonius, but not the Balearic story. Spanish rabbits, ferrets and the Balearic tale resurface in Pliny *NH* 8.217f, who also notes the succulence of their young. The Romans bred them in *leporaria* (Varro, *RR* 3.12.6–7), and Apicius (II.2.6) refers to rabbit rissoles (*isicia de caniculis*). See André, *L'alimentation et la cuisine à Rome*[2], n. 119. The ancient Neapolitans were well aware of them: there is a rabbit on a Roman wall-painting in the Museo Nazionale of Naples (Jashemski, *The Gardens of Pompeii, Herculaneum and the Villas destroyed by Vesuvius*, New York, 1979, fig. 166).

Posidonius lost no opportunity for personal observation of zoological or botanical detail; cf. F245.

F53 Athenaeus, IV.153C–D

CONTENT

History, Bk 2: (a) Roman triumphal banquets in the temple of Hercules. (b) Luxurious banquets among the Etruscans.

CONTEXT

Part of Athenaeus' list of banqueting customs. F57, F64 and F75 precede, and a note from Timaeus, *Hist.* I follows.

COMMENT

The two parts of the fragment were probably juxtaposed by Athenaeus, as it is unlikely that they had the same context in Posidonius, despite the arguments of Theiler (*Poseidonios* II.86f).

A. (1–6)

'In the city of Rome, whenever they hold a banquet in the temple of Hercules at the invitation of whoever is celebrating a triumph at the time, the provision of the banquet is also herculean. Honeyed wine flows (διοινοχοεῖται is a *hapax*) and the food is large loaves, boiled smoked-meat and roasted portions from the freshly sacrificed victims in abundance.'

It has been argued (Malitz, *Die Historien des Poseidonios* 64; Jacoby, *Kommentar* 163) that the first two books of the *History* contained an ethnography of Rome and Italy to which these two extracts belonged. It is likely that there was such an ethnography, although hardly occupying the whole of Bks 1 and 2, and Etruscan luxury was probably part of it. But the Roman sentence has little to do with luxury or the lack of it, in terms of early Roman simplicity (Frs. 256–7) or decadence, but is orientated by Roman triumphs celebrated in the temple of Hercules, a practice noted again by Athenaeus V.221F in connection with Marius. So it is possible that this passage too was prompted by a Roman triumph in the early part of the *History*. The legend of how the cult of Hercules came to Rome, leading to the Ara Maxima, is told by Livy, 1.7 (see Ogilvie, *Commentary on Livy*), and near it in the Forum Boarium was a circular temple of Hercules Invictus (or Victor, see *RE s.v.*) (Livy, 10.23.2; Pliny, *NH* 35.19) and a statue draped for triumphs (Pliny, *NH* 34.33). But two pieces of evidence involve a temple of Hercules and a triumph at a date about the beginning of the *History*. Plutarch (*Pr. Reip. Ger.*, *Mor.* 816C) records that Scipio was criticised in Rome because, when he entertained his friends at the dedication of the temple of Hercules, he did not include his colleague Mummius. Scipio Aemilianus celebrated his triumph over Carthage probably late in 146 B.C., the year when Mummius was consul (Broughton, *Magistrates* 1.467). Mummius himself after the reorganisation of Greece as proconsul in 145 returned to celebrate his triumph over the Achaeans and Corinthians, and built a temple of Hercules Victor on the Caelius (*CIL* I^2 626; Broughton, 1.470). Another notorious triumph of the time was that of Appius Claudius, cos. 143, celebrated on his own authority after a victory over the Salassi (Broughton, 1.471). Any of these might have provoked this comment.

B. (6–10)

"Among the Etruscans twice a day costly tables are spread, with flowered spreads and silver cups of all kinds, and a mass of comely slaves attend arrayed in costly garments.'

This presumably refers to the luxury of earlier Etruscan history. There is a parallel passage in Diodorus (5.40.3) which is clearly from Posidonius, and is firm evidence that Diodorus used Posidonius for Bk 5. As usual Diodorus repeats a number of phrases, but he also expands in his own fashion and is less succinct. See for comparison F67.28ff comm.; F274.7ff comm.; F59 comm.

F54 Athenaeus, IV.176B–C

CONTENT

'Posidonius, the Stoic philosopher, recounting in Bk 3 of the *History* the war of the Apameans with the people of Larissa, writes this: "Clutching belt dirklets and javelettes covered in rust and filth, with wee stetsons clapped on their heads and sun-shields that provided shade, yet did not prevent their necks from being ventilated, dragging along donkeys loaded with wine and food of all kinds festooned with flutelets and solo recorders, instruments of revelry rather than of war."'

CONTEXT

A section on musical instruments began at 174A. The discussion of the φώτιγξ (or cross-flute, πλαγίαυλος, cf. Theocr. 20.29) started at 175E; it was native to (ἐπιχωριάζει) Athenaeus' Alexandria. Quotations for the μόναυλος follow from Sophocles, Ararus, Anaxandrides, Sopater and from the work of Protagoras of Cyzicus entitled *On the Games at Daphne* (in Syria).

COMMENT

Bk 3 probably saw the opening of Posidonius' account of Syrian history (i.e. from 145 B.C.; Jacoby, *Kommentar* 164, 155).

In 145 B.C. Alexander Balas was defeated and assassinated, and the interfering Ptolemy Philometor dead, which left the Syrian throne clear for the moment for Demetrius II Nicator. This did not last long, for his cruel rule with his Cretan mercenaries gave fuel to his commander at Apamea, Diodotus (Tryphon), to set up Alexander's son, Antiochus VI Epiphanes, at first from a remote centre at Chalcis, but later gaining control of the Apamean area and of Antioch itself (D.S. 33.4a; Jos. *AJ* 13.131ff; App. *Syr.* 67; Str. XVI.2.10; Will, *Histoire Politique du Monde Hellénistique* II.378, 404ff; Bevan, *The House of Seleucus* II.223ff; Fischer, *Chiron* 2 (1972), 201–13). The struggle between Demetrius and Tryphon continued until Demetrius' ill-fated expedition against Parthia in 140. In this unsettled time no doubt various cities took the opportunity to move against each other. Diodorus (33.5) records such a case about this time with Aradus and Marathus. Larissa had originally come out on Tryphon's side (D.S. 33.4a) but Tryphon was also himself an Apamean citizen. So it may have been a case of local enmity which we cannot date precisely within this period.

Athenaeus as usual reads the *History* for the wrong reasons, in this case for the words φωτίγγια καί μοναύλια (Context). But there are historical and literary crumbs. Posidonius' picture of his own country-folk is not complimentary, and no doubt in deliberate contrast with the Larissaeans who had a strong martial reputation (D.S. 33.4a). This is historical explanation through character. The Apameans had degenerated through the decadent luxury with which Posidonius was later to characterise Syrian cities (F62). Their weapons were untended and rusty; their martial baggage consisted of drink, food and musical instruments, κώμων οὐ πολέμων ὄργανα (7f). Bar-Kochva (*The Seleucid Army* 99) misses the point in suggesting that this should be taken as a mark of contempt for the enemy.

The literary rewards of the striking original power and compressed vividness of Posidonius' prose style are immediate: the biting string of scornful diminutives, none of which occurs before Posidonius, the colourful vocabulary; one can actually see the ridiculous motley turnout of Falstaffian rabble in his sharp pictorial vignette of only five lines.

3–4 παραζωνίδια and πετάσια (Villebrun must be right) are invented diminutives for ridicule. λογχάρια may be too; Lucian uses it in *Hist. Conscr.* 25, but there is no sign of it before Posidonius.

5 προσκόπιον occurs nowhere else (another invented diminutive form?) but the context shows that it must have been some sort of visor or shade. But it was merely adopted for the comfort of shade from the sun, not for bodily protection of face or throat; the Apameans were more concerned that their throats should be cool than armed. καταπνεῖσθαι must be passive, since there is no evidence of middles of πνεῖν and its compounds, and so I cannot accept Gulick's 'but did not prevent breathing at the throat'. I take the literal sense to be 'not preventing their necks being blown upon' (by a cooling breeze presumably).

6 ὄνος could either mean donkey literally, or a vessel or flask popularly called 'donkey' (because of its donkey-eared handles), as in Ar. *Wasps* 616 (see MacDowell's note *ad loc.*). If the latter, οἷς (7) would refer to ὄνους, and we would have a picture of the bizarre festooning of unwarlike equipment on the men themselves. But MacDowell argued plausibly that the 'donkey' flask was a small vessel and Posidonius was clearly emphasising the quantity of food and drink. Therefore I think that donkey is intended, οἷς refers to βρωμάτων, γέμοντας means 'loaded with', not 'full of', and the picture is of the jangling cavalcade.

7 Two more invented diminutives (φωτίγγια καὶ μοναύλια) follow, with the succinct climax, κώμων οὐ πολέμων ὄργανα. A masterly piece of invective.

F55 Athenaeus, XIV. 649D; Eustathius, *Commentarii ad Homeri Iliadem* XX.321

CONTENT

Pistachios in Syria and Arabia.

CONTEXT

The character Ulpian of Tyre challenges the company for literary references to the pistachio nut. He produces a line from Nicander's *Theriaca*, where the spelling is doubtful, then passes to Posidonius.

COMMENT

Posidonius singled out the πέρσειον and the so-called βιστάκιον as fruit and nuts from trees growing in Arabia and Syria. πέρσειον (περσιον *AC*) is usually taken to be the fruit of the περσέα tree (Mimusops Schimperi). Joret (*REG* XII (1899), 43–7) argued that the persea could not be meant because the ancients (Theoph. *HP* 4.2.1; Pliny, *NH* 13.60) regarded it as an Egyptian tree. He suggested περσικόν in the sense of peach (Pliny, *NH* 15.44ff).

The pistachio is given a careful description by Posidonius (cf. F241): its fruit is in long entwined clusters, ash-coloured, like tear-drops (τοῖς δακρύοις, 4; or gum-drops? Hofmann suggested δακτύλοις, which can mean dates, or a kind of grape, Pliny, *NH* 14.15; but the relative ἃ favours δακρύοις), tight on each other like grapes in a bunch. They are greenish inside, less well-flavoured than the seeds of pine cones (Athen. II.57B–D; XIV.647F), but more fragrant. The style is rhetorical: ἧττον μὲν εὔχυμον, εὐώδη δὲ μᾶλλον. Ulpian continues with a passage which is reproduced by Eustathius (F55b.3–6). The pistachio seems to have been first called τέρμινθος (so

Theoph. *HP* 4.4.7); when its Syrian name was adopted, there was variation in the spelling of the first letter: π in Nicander's codd. and Dioscorides; φ or β by Athenaeus' Nicander; ψ by Ulpian in Athenaeus and in *Geoponica* 10.12.1; but Posidonius wrote βιστάκια.

The context in the third book of the *History* is not known, but an account of exotic fruit may have been connected with Syrian luxury.

F56 Athenaeus, VI.252E

CONTENT

Bk 4; Hierax of Antioch, influential parasite of Ptolemy VIII Euergetes, who later had him killed.

CONTEXT

Athenaeus' discussion of parasites began at 234C. F69 and F74 occur earlier in the list. Just before, there is an account from Nicolaus of Andromachus of Carrhae, the treacherous parasite of Licinius Crassus on his Syrian command of 53 B.C.; the fragment is followed by Nicolaus again on a parasite of Mithridates.

COMMENT

The chronological context must be after 146/5 B.C. (the starting point of the *History*, T1a.6) but before 140/139 (the eastern embassy of Scipio in Bk 7, F58). Ptolemy VI Philometor had died in 145 (F54, comm.), so this belongs to the earliest years of the sole rule of his brother Ptolemy VIII Euergetes. Philometor had been deeply involved in Syrian inter-dynastic politics (F54 comm.), in the course of which no doubt he picked up this favourite, who managed subsequently to transfer to Euergetes. Bks 3–5 appear to have dealt with early Syrian history, but our surviving sample is far too thin to be sure of scope. Perhaps Bks 3–7 concentrated on eastern history.

2–3 Hierax was a Syrian from Antioch, and his early professional history was lowly, as a recorder accompanist for burlesque shows. λυσιῳδοί referred to actors or actresses singing low songs in transvestite parts, named from a certain Lysis who wrote songs for the genre (Str. XIV.1.41; Athenaeus V.211A–C: XIII.620E; Maas, *RE* 3A 159, *s.v.* Simoidoi). Athenaeus' story of Diogenes of Seleucia (211A–C = Athenaeus *FGrH* 166, F1, from *On the Kings of Syria*) shows that this entertainment was popular in the Syrian court of Alexander Balas. It may be that Hierax was introduced at this point as another example of degeneration in Syrian cities and court. Such a clever and unscrupulous man went far, but came to a bad end.

5 Although Hierax rose to great power (τὰ μέγιστα δυνηθέντα) under Euergetes, it is quite uncertain whether he was the same as the general Hierax who by his talents and generosity saved Euergetes from the Galaestes disaffection (D.S. 33.22).

F57 Athenaeus, IV.152F–153A

CONTENT

The 'King's friend', from Posidonius' account of the Parthians in Bk 5 of the *History*.

CONTEXT

Part of Athenaeus' list of banquets and eating habits in Bk IV. F67 precedes, and F64, F75 and F53 follow.

COMMENT

The vividness of pictorial detail is typical: 'The so-called "Friend" does not participate at table, but sitting on the ground below the king, who reclines on a lofty couch (cf. F64.5f), is fed dog-like with scraps tossed by him; and often on any chance pretext he is dragged off from his groundling meal to be whipped with canes or bone-knotted thongs until blood-soaked (αἱμόφυρτος; cf. Plb. 15.14.2) he prostrates himself face down on the floor and does obeisance to his tormentor as his benefactor.'

This is not a pretty picture, and not intended to be. It is in sharp contrast to the usual honorific title of 'Friend', as when for example Athenion became a 'Friend' of Mithridates (F253.25), and even to the παράσιτοι of the Celts (F69; cf. F74). It is in equally strong contrast to the laudatory passage in Diodorus 33.18 (printed as F113 by Theiler), where Arsaces VI (Mithridates I) is praised for ἐπιείκεια and φιλανθρωπία, and for eschewing τρυφή and ὑπερηφανία. At this early stage in the *History* (Bk 5), it is likely that it is this same Mithridates, the real founder of the Parthian empire, whom Posidonius has in mind. Perhaps as elsewhere, he was developing his theme of kingship, and the relationship between ruler and subject.

8 **προπεσών** Kaibel is highly likely for προσπεσών *A*.

F58 Athenaeus, XII.549D–E

CONTENT

Ptolemy VIII, Euergetes II (Physcon); *History*, Bk 7.

'Like him too (i.e. Dionysius, son of Clearchus, of Heracleia) was Ptolemy VII (actually VIII, but the brief reign of Ptolemy VII in 145 B.C., was often ignored in ancient accounts), King of Egypt, who proclaimed himself Benefactor (Euergetes), but was named Malefactor (Kakergetes) by the Alexandrians. At all events, Posidonius the Stoic, who travelled with Scipio Africanus when he had been invited to Alexandria, and observed him, writes in Bk 7 of the *History* like this: "Because of luxurious living his body had been destroyed by fat and a vast belly that it would have been difficult to get your arms round; over this belly he put on an ankle-length tunic with sleeves down to the wrists. He would never go out on foot, unless because of Scipio." '

CONTEXT

Athenaeus XII is concerned with people notorious for luxury (τρυφή, 510B). This passage is preceded by Dionysius, the son of Clearchus of Heracleia; it is followed by a quotation from Euergetes' own Ὑπομνήματα, and then by Posidonius' reference to Ptolemy Alexander I (F77).

COMMENT

The contextual date in the *History* is fixed by reference to the celebrated diplomatic tour of Scipio with Sp. Mummius and L. Metellus Calvus (D.S. 33.28b; Justin 38.8.8–10; Plu. *Mor.* 200F; Cic. *Acad.* II.5; *Rep.* 6.11; Gruen, *The Hellenistic World* II.714f; Will, *Histoire Politique du Monde Hellénistique* II.427ff). The date has been controversial, generally assigned to 140/139 B.C. (Astin, *CPh* 54 (1959), 221–7; Broughton, *Magistrates* I.481 n. 2; cf. Otto-Bengtson, *Abh. Bayer. Ak.* 17 (1938), 38); but most recently Mattingley (*CQ* 36 (1986), 491–5) argues for 144/3 B.C.

Athenaeus makes the silly mistake of confusing Posidonius with Panaetius as Scipio's philosopher companion on this embassy (4), a mistake he repeats in T8. That Panaetius indeed accompanied Scipio is attested by Cic. *Acad.* II.5 and Plu. *Mor.* 200F and 777A (F254).

The King's gross physical appearance and pot belly

(Φύσκων was his nickname) is echoed by Trogus (Justin. 38.8.9: *sagina ventris*) and by Plutarch, who tells the anecdote of the embassy that Physcon could hardly keep up with the Romans δι' ἀργίαν καὶ τρυφὴν τοῦ σώματος, whereupon Scipio whispered to Panaetius: the Alexandrians have already benefited from our visit; because of us they have seen the King walk. Posidonius also marks for our notice the King's dress; so does Trogus (Justin. 38.8.10) who adds that it was a suggestive transparent garment. For the effeminate decadence of having long sleeves, see Alföldi, *Festschrift for A. M. Friend*, Princeton, 1955, 41–4. The King's physical deterioration was all the more striking in that he was just over forty at this date, and no doubt in high contrast to Scipio, perhaps three years older. He had returned to the throne of Egypt from Cyrene in 145 B.C. on the death of his elder brother Ptolemy VI Philometor, and through the murder of his nephew Ptolemy VII. Immediately, the cruelty of his subsequent persecutions (D.S. 33.6, 12–13, 22, 23; Fraser, *Ptolemaic Alexandria* I.121) earned him the hatred of the Alexandrians and the nickname Malefactor (3). But there is nothing to support the view (Otto-Bengtson, 38), that the political reason for the Scipio embassy was the Galaestes disaffection (D.S. 33.20, 22).

The form of the account of D.S. 33.28b is of much interest and may well derive from Posidonius. The emphasis is placed on the contrast between the frugal virtues of the Romans, and the degenerate luxury of Euergetes, and between Euergetes' standards of giving the Romans a good time, and their insistence on the practical inspection of the potential of the country, if well governed: διέλαβον μεγίστην ἡγεμονίαν δύνασθαι συσταθῆναι, τυχούσης τῆς βασιλείας ταύτης ἀξίων τῶν ἡγεμόνων. This sounds very like Posidonius' preoccupation with kingship, and with the contrast of early Roman virtues and later degeneracy through luxury. This may well have been how Posidonius portrayed the event in the *History* (cf. F253; F265); if so, that final comment above in

Diodorus probably came from Posidonius, and should not be interpreted with political inferences for the embassy.

10 διὰ Σκιπίωνα: Posidonius was probably punning with σκίπων, a staff or crutch. For the pun, cf. F239.11.

Compare the description of Ptolemy Alexander I, F77.

F59 Athenaeus, XII.542B

CONTENT

'Posidonius in Bk 8 of the *History* says of the Sicilian Greek Damophilus, who caused the outbreak of the slave war, that he was addicted to (a familiar of) luxury, and writes just as follows: "So he was a slave of luxury and malpractice, driven through the country in four-wheeled chariots at the head of horses, luscious attendants, and a concourse of bumsuckers and soldier-slaves. But later he came to a violent end with his whole household, treated with extreme violence by the slaves."'

CONTEXT

Luxury (τρυφή) in notable individuals is the theme of Athenaeus XII. This fragment is preceded by other examples in Sicily from Diodorus, Duris, Silenus of Caleacte and Callias. It is followed by Duris on Demetrius of Phalerum. So it is an isolated fragment.

COMMENT

The context is the outbreak of the first Sicilian slave war (?136–132 B.C.) (2), which was therefore treated by Posidonius in Bk 8 of the *History* (1). This passage must have occurred in an examination of the causes of the outbreak, seen in the atrocious social conditions exacerbated between master and slave. Compare D.S. 34.2.26, where the contemporary revolt led by Aristonicus after the death of Attalus III is mentioned, with which Posidonius must also have dealt. But the causes of Aristonicus' venture must have been very different from those described for the Sicilian revolt (Will, *Histoire Politique du Monde Hellénistique* II.419ff).

Posidonius' invective is biting. Damophilus, the wealthy landowner and owner of many slaves, is himself a slave to luxury and vice (3). The moral metaphor of slavery goes back to Plato as the mark of the tyrant (e.g. *Rep.* 587b 8–c 4; cf. *Phdr.* 238e 3). The choice and placing of words to create the incisiveness of Posidonius' compact sentence (4–6) is telling, and the emphatic repetition of stem with variation of prefix (ἐφυβρίστως . . . περιυβρισθείς, 7f) is characteristic (F253.66, 112f, 123–31; F240a.41). πανοικίᾳ (7) has been chosen for literary and sound effect, for it is not strictly true. Damophilus' daughter, whose kindness the slaves remembered, was conducted by them to safety (D.S. 34.2.13, 39).

Diodorus (34.2.10–14 (Photius), and 34ff (Excerpta)) had the story of Damophilus of Enna from his part in the beginning of the revolt until his capture and murder. At 34.2.34 (Excerpta) the following sentence occurs: ἐπὶ μὲν γὰρ τῆς χώρας ἵππους τε πολυτελεῖς καὶ τετρακύκλους ἀπήνας μετ' οἰκετῶν στρατιωτικῶν περιήγετο· πρὸς δὲ τούτοις εὐπρεπῶν παίδων πλῆθος, ἔτι δὲ κολάκων ἀνάγωγον παραδρομὴν ἔχειν ἐφιλοτιμεῖτο. This is unquestionably from Posidonius, although slightly rewritten so that the original incisiveness is diluted (28 words for 20; πρὸς δὲ τούτοις . . . ἔτι δέ). Compare F53.

This sentence forms the only secure link between Diodorus Bk 34 and Posidonius. Nevertheless, the strong likelihood remains that Diodorus used Posidonius for his whole account of the first Sicilian slave war (D.S. 34.2; 34.8–11). Even the truncated passages surviving from Photius and the Excerpta, compiled in the 10th c. for Constantine Porphyrogenitus, display a verve, vividness and social analysis that one would associate more with Posidonius than with Diodorus or other known historians. There is still no control over the possible extent and fidelity of this use, nor has there been any recent study on Diodorus and Posidonius on the scale of Jane Hornblower for Hieronymus of Cardia, and therefore there is still no alternative between printing the whole of Diodorus as Posidonius, or none of him apart from the sentence in §34. But see also Malitz, *Die Historien des Poseidonios* 144–58 (and in general, 134–69); Jacoby, *Anhang* F108; Theiler, *Poseidonios* F136b–f, F137, Frs. 142–6.

3 τρυφῆς οἰκεῖος glosses τρυφῆς δοῦλος, a slave to luxury, possessed by luxury; cf. Menander, *Aspis*, 89 for this use of οἰκεῖος. Was it confused with οἰκέτης in this usage?

F60 Athenaeus, VI.263C–D

CONTENT

'Posidonius, the Stoic, says in Bk 11 of the *History* that many who are unable to champion themselves because of the weakness of their intellect hand themselves over to the service of more intelligent people to get from them provision for their necessary wants, and themselves in return render to them through their own persons whatever service they are capable of. It was in this way that the Mariandynians submitted themselves to the Heracleots, promising to serve them permanently as long as the latter provided their needs, but with the additional stipulation that none of them be sold outside Heracleot territory, but only in their own land.'

CONTEXT

Athenaeus began the topic of slaves at 262B. F51 (266E–F) follows shortly and F262 (272E–F) forms a later parenthesis. Frs. 265–7 occur at the end of the theme.

The Posidonian fragment here is followed by a quotation from Euphorion (3rd c. B.C.; F87 Scheidweiler, 78 Powell, 73 Meineke) calling the Mariandynians δωροφόροι, explained by Callistratus (ὁ Ἀριστοφάνειος, i.e. pupil of Aristophanes of Byzantium, 2nd c., *FGrH* 348, F4) as taking away the bitter taste of the term οἰκέται (house slaves), just as the Spartans with the Helots, the Thessalians with the Penestae, and the Cretans with the Clarotae. There follow quotations on Cretan slaves from Ephorus (*FGrH* 70, F29), Sosicrates (*FGrH* 461, F4) and Dosiades (*FGrH* 458, F3), and on the Penestae from Philocrates (*FGrH* 601, F2). A paraphrase of Plato, *Laws* 6. 776bff on the subject is given at 264D–265B.

COMMENT

The Mariandynians, believed to be Thracian in origin (Str. XII.3.4), inhabited territory on the south shore of the Black Sea between Bithynia and Paphlagonia. On part of this territory the Megarian colony (Xen. *An.* VI.2.1; Strabo mistakenly says Milesian) of Heracleia was founded in the 6th c. B.C. When this arrangement between the Heracleots and Mariandynians was struck we do not know. It was unknown to Herodotus (I.28; III.90; VII.72) and to Xenophon (*An.* VI.2.1). The first statement appears in Plato, *Laws* 6.776d, where he couples the situation with that of the Penestae in Thessaly, and compares it with Helots in Sparta; but he distinguishes the position of the Helots as being more contentious and problematical. Aristotle, on the other hand, grouped Penestae and Helots together against the more liberal policy of the Cretans (*Pol.* 1264a 12–35); but Posidonius had probably not read the *Politics*. Strabo (XII.3.4) says that the Heracleots forced the Mariandynians to serve as helots (εἱλωτεύειν ἠνάγκασαν), but adds Posidonius' condition that they should not be sold beyond their boundaries; 'for they came to an agreement on this' (συμβῆναι γὰρ ἐπὶ τούτοις). He goes on to compare the Mnoan class in Crete, and the Penestae in Thessaly.

What is interesting is Posidonius' attitude and explanation. He singles out the Mariandynians as a case of voluntary subjection, where the agreement between master and servant is to the benefit of both, and arose initially from the needs of neighbouring Heracleots and Mariandynians. He probably distinguished this case historically from those where a conquering nation imposes serfdom by force on the vanquished original inhabitants, as with the Helots at Sparta; as Plato remarked, this only leads to continual trouble and tyranny. Posidonius' explanatory grounds depend on the realisation of differing intellectual capacity. All men are not alike; some need help, and must render service in return, as long as each recognises the needs and responsibilities of the situation. This is akin to Plato, but also to the Stoic philosopher king (F284.1ff), and deliberately opposed to the doctrine of the natural rights of power of a Callicles or Polus, or of Thucydides' Athenian empire, or of D.H. 1.5.2 with reference to Rome. So this is a philosophical view of history, the other side of Posidonius' interest in kingship (F253, F284.1–19). The stress on agreement and contract extends not only to the subject, but even apparently to a kind of conditional serfdom.

There is no means of knowing the context in Bk 11. Nor is there any evidence to interpret this passage as a Posidonian blueprint for the Roman empire (Capelle, *Klio* 25 (1932), 98–104; Walbank, *JRS* 55 (1965), 14), and such attempts should be treated with scepticism (Momigliano, *Alien Wisdom* 32; Gruen, *The Hellenistic World* 1.351).

7 μέν is odd. Is it a relic from the Posidonian context: he continued with another example?

10 μένειν, Gulick, makes sense, but is unnecessary.

F61a, b Athenaeus, XII.540B–C; Athenaeus, V.210C–D

CONTENT

Bk 14. The luxurious banquets for the masses given by Antiochus VII Sidetes, King of Syria.

CONTEXT

Athenaeus, Bk XII has the subject of luxury (τρυφή). F61a is oddly preceded by the example of the later Antiochus VIII Grypus from Bk 28 (F72a). In Athenaeus V where the doublets occur, F61b precedes F72b in the more natural order, and then at once F62b follows, which as F62a recurs in Athenaeus XII much earlier, because luxury in nations and luxury of individuals are treated in different sections. It looks as if Athenaeus, like Plutarch, kept notebooks or the equivalent of files.

COMMENT

The subject is Antiochus VII Sidetes, homonymous (1) with Antiochus Grypus just mentioned. The date must be in the 130s B.C. Sidetes (from Side in Pamphylia where he was brought up) returned to Syria after the capture of his brother Demetrius II Nicator by the Parthians in 140/39 (F64 comm.), possibly in time for Scipio Aemilianus' famous embassy to the east (F58; Syria came at the end of the tour, D.S. 33.28b.3); at any rate he attempted later in 134 to maintain contact by sending magnificent presents for Scipio, then at Numantia, with an embassy to Rome (Livy, *Per.* 57). He had immediately to deal with Tryphon, who collapsed and committed suicide in 138 (Jos. *AJ* 13.223–4; App. *Syr.* 68). He then set about pulling together the kingdom, and so turned to the Jews, eventually besieging and taking Jerusalem (probably 134–2; Jos. *AJ* 13.225–48; 1 Macc. 15–16; D.S. 34.1; Schürer–Vermes–Miller, *History of the Jewish People* I. 202, n.5). His final ill-fated expedition against Parthia was in 130 (F63). So these lavish popularising public feastings were probably held after Tryphon's collapse, or possibly after the taking of Jerusalem.

Antiochus Sidetes is a fascinating figure. Clearly capable, he was reorganising Syria after the disastrous interdynastic struggles which he had inherited. Moreover his handling of the Jews displayed diplomacy as well as firmness, so that even in Jewish sources like Josephus he earned the title of Pious (Εὐσεβής), and was noted for a sense of fairness (ἐπιείκεια) (*AJ* 13.242–8). Diodorus (34.1.5) called him μεγαλόψυχος ὢν καὶ τὸ ἦθος ἥμερος. This may be an exaggeration, but the sources all mark the contrast with his predecessors. It is therefore all the more galling that the account of Posidonius, himself originally a Syrian, in Bks 14–16 of the Syrian history of his time, is lost apart from the superficial snippets concerning luxury, which appealed to Athenaeus.

61a.3 The identification of Antiochus as the Seleucid who made the campaign into Media against Arsaces (Phraates II) probably comes from Athenaeus. It is not repeated in F61b, but recurs in F63 (cf. F64).

61a.3–10 As the coincidence of the doublet reveals, Athenaeus' quotation is literal, and displays a common feature of Posidonius' style, a love of vivid detail: 'He would give daily receptions for the masses. In them, apart from the heaps of food that were consumed and tossed out as scraps (ἐκφατνιζομένων), each diner would carry off whole joints of meat and fowls, and of sea creatures prepared uncarved, capable of filling a wagon. And after that, quantities of honey cakes and garlands of myrrh and frankincense with ribbons of compressed gold as long as a grown man.' The style is deliberately impressive both in vocabulary and arrangement. πλήθη (10) has been saved for the end for effect.

Compare the lavish banquets of Luvernius for the people (F67.37ff), and the liking for whole joints among the Celts (F67.8ff) and Germans (F73). See also F72.

F62a, b Athenaeus, XII.527E–F; Athenaeus, V.210E–F

CONTENT

Degenerate luxury in Syrian cities. Bk 16.

CONTEXT

See F61 context. F62a occurs in the section of Athenaeus, XII dealing with luxury in nations. F62b is grouped with F61b and F72b.

COMMENT

The date of reference should be late 130s or early 120s B.C.; see Frs. 61, 63, 65. The quotation from Posidonius is shown to be literal from the exact corresponsion of the doublets.

2 A picture of degenerate luxury in urban Syria is intended (ὡς ἐτρύφων).

3–4 The reason given is abundance (εὐβοσία) from the land. This is not quite the same as a klima ethnology. It merely suggests that the Syrians did not have to work for the necessities of life, and the leisure led to slackness, softness and luxury.

4 **ἀπό** on its own must be privative (LSJ I.10): free from the bother of the necessities of life. But this use is hard to parallel unless from later papyrological evidence. So Jacoby suggested ἀπο ⟨ύσης⟩. But ἀπό recurs in F62b. Perhaps it may remain in such a rhetorically contrived passage.

5–12 lists four instances or signs of degenerate luxury:

(1) They were for ever meeting for a continual life of feasting (5).

(2) The gymnasia, or centres for exercise, were turned into baths; i.e. for wet instead of dry sweats (Pl. *Phdr.* 239c 8); soft relaxing areas where even their unguents were expensive and perfumed, not practical for exercise (6–7).

(3) The Grammateia, local names for clubs possibly designated by letters like American college clubs, became their homes. They spent the greater part of the day there stuffing their bellies (γαστριζόμενοι) with food and wine, even carrying off a great deal back home as well (7–11). This is in sharp contrast to Posidonius' ideal picture of the frugal family life of the old Romans (F267).

(4) They were continually entertained by flute playing to the accompanying beat of the loud-twanging tortoise-shell (lyre) so that whole cities resounded with such noises (11–12). The language which has been rhetorically balanced throughout now becomes deliberately and climactically contrived, presumably to underline the irony. πρὸς χελωνίδος πολυκρότου ψόφον is a highly-coloured poetic phrase, and moreover in iambics. πολύκροτος is a poetic word, and so is 'tortoise' for the lyre, but normally χέλυς is used in earlier poetry. χελωνίς is a rare word and seemingly later Greek. S.E. *Adv. Math.* 1.246 records it as a local word used by Athenians and Coans for a footstool; χελωνίδες λίμναι is the name of a Libyan lake in Ptolemy; and Hesychius and Suda gloss it as the lintel of a door, probably from LXX Judith 14. So I doubt that it is a quotation from earlier poetry; more probably Posidonius made it up himself for effect.

F63 Athenaeus, X.439D–E

CONTENT

The death and drunken ambition of Antiochus VII Sidetes in *History*, Bk 16.

CONTEXT

In Athenaeus' list of notable hard drinkers and drunkards (πολυπόται, φιλοπόται), in particular among the Seleucid kings. At 438C he examples Antiochus II Theos from Phylarchus, followed (438D–439D) by Antiochus VI Epiphanes from the *Commentaries* of Ptolemy Euergetes, but mostly derived from Polybius. After F63 he turns (439E) to Antiochus III (the Great) from Polybius and then more examples from Polybius until 440B.

COMMENT

1–3 The subject is Antiochus VII Sidetes, having the same name (ὁμώνομος) as Antiochus VI Epiphanes dealt with immediately before. In 130 B.C. he invaded Media, but in the spring of 129 his army was defeated by the Parthians and he himself killed (Justin (Trogus) 38.10; D.S. 34/5. 15–17; Jos. *AJ* 13.249–53; App. *Syr.* 68; Debevoise, *A Political History of Parthia* 31–5; Bevan, *The House of Seleucus* II.243ff; Will, *Histoire Politique du Monde Hellénistique* II.413ff). The Parthian king was Phraates II. This gives a date point for Bk 16 (cf. F64).

4–6 Although Phraates' epitaph for Antiochus was hardly complimentary: 'Your boldness and drunkenness, Antiochus, caused your fall; for you expected to drink up the Arsacid kingdom in huge cups', he nevertheless treated his dead body with honour, took his niece (a daughter of Demetrius II) into his harem (Justin. 38.10.10), and kept his captured son Seleucus in regal dignity (Porphyr. *FGrH* 260, F32.19; see F64). The body was eventually returned in a silver casket (Justin. 39.1.6). This pattern had already been established in the honoured treatment of Demetrius II Nicator in his long captivity from 140/39, whom Phraates now regretted having set free (see F64 comm.).

The metaphorical use of ἐκπίνειν goes back to Pl. Com. 9.

F64 Athenaeus, IV.153A–B

CONTENT

The regal treatment at Parthian banquets of a royal Seleucid prisoner of war, as recorded by Posidonius in *History*, Bk 16.

CONTEXT

This is in Athenaeus' list of banqueting and eating habits. It occurs after F57 and is followed by F75 and F53.

COMMENT

The puzzle of this fragment lies in the contextual introduction: 'In Bk 16 (of the *History*) Posidonius, in the process of giving an account of Seleucus the King, how he invaded Media, made war on Arsaces, was taken prisoner by the barbarian and spent a long time with Arsaces treated royally, writes . . .'.

There appears to be confusion between content, name and chronology in the *History*.

(1) *Content*: the most famous Seleucid king to invade Media against Parthia and to be kept prisoner in a regal fashion was Demetrius II Nicator (Justin. 36.1.2–6; 38.9.2–3; Jos. *AJ* 13.184–6; 1 Macc. 14.1–3; App. *Syr.* 67; Debevoise, *Political History of Parthia* 22–5; Will, *Histoire Politique du Monde Hellénistique* II.407f; Gruen, *The Hellenistic World* 668; Bevan, *The House of Seleucus* II.232ff). Demetrius was indeed treated royally in Hyrcania by Mithridates I, and even given his daughter in marriage. This was not Seleucus. Also the invasion took place in 141/40, and Demetrius' capture *c.* 140/39 (*Cambridge History of Iran*, III(1).6). But these are early dates for Bk 16 (see F63 on the death of Antiochus VII Sidetes in 129). They would relate more naturally to Bk 5 (F57).

Theiler, however suggested that the circumstances and conditions of Demetrius' prisoner of war years might only have been mentioned by Posidonius after he had been set free by Phraates II in 129 (Justin. 38.10.7) to occupy the throne again until 125. But this would be surprising. It is of course possible that the Book number is wrong and should be 6 instead of 16. Intrusive iotas in numerals are not uncommon; cf. F7.

(2) *Seleucus*: The first Seleucus to be considered is the son of Demetrius and Cleopatra, who was assassinated by his mother in 125 B.C. immediately on assuming the throne as Seleucus V. He was probably taken prisoner with his father in 140/39, and no doubt was also treated royally. If it was he, and designated king, Posidonius must have been writing retrospectively in 125. But this Seleucus could hardly have been described as invading Media and making war on the Parthian king (1–2).

But apparently Antiochus VII Sidetes also had a son Seleucus (Porphyr. *FGrH* 260, F32.19 Euseb. *Arm. Chron.* 121.4 Karst). Antiochus Sidetes in his turn invaded Media in 129. It is noticeable that in the Athenaeus fragments it is Antiochus Sidetes who is defined as the Seleucid who invaded Media and made war on Parthia (F61a, F63). It seems that Antiochus had his family with him (Justin. 38.10.10). When Antiochus was defeated and killed (F63), Seleucus was taken prisoner and again treated royally by Phraates (Porphyr. F 32). This is more plausible chronologically for Bk 16, but Seleucus was never king. Jacoby therefore suggested τοῦ ⟨υἱοῦ τοῦ⟩ βασίλεως. But (a) the quotation refers to the King, not to the son of the King (5), and (b) it would be very odd if Posidonius' narrative (1–3) concentrated on this minor figure. It is safer to assume confusion on the part of Athenaeus, than to attempt to eradicate it.

5–8 The actual quotation at first looks like a general statement, but in the context must exemplify the regal treatment of the captive Seleucid. 'At banquets among the

Parthians, the King had his couch, on which he alone would recline, on a higher level and separated from the others, and his own table set as for a sanctified hero, full of native delicacies.' For the seating of the King, cf. F57.

F65 Athenaeus, XI.466B–C

CONTENT

Lysimachus the Babylonian invited to dinner Himerus, the tyrant not only of the Babylonians but of the people of Seleuceia as well, with 300 others; after the tables had been removed, he gave each of the 300 a four-mina silver goblet; he made libation and toasted all together. He gave the cups to be taken with them. Probably in Bk 16 of the *History*; see below.

CONTEXT

A miscellaneous section on drinking cups.

COMMENT

For Himerus (Euhemerus, Diodorus) see Justin. 42.1.3; Trogus, *Prol.* 42; D.S. 34/35. 21; Otto *s.v. RE* VIII.1638ff; Will, *Histoire Politique du Monde Hellénistique* II.416; Debevoise, *A Political History of Parthia* 35–9; Bevan, *The House of Seleucus* II.245ff; *Cambridge History of Iran* III (1).40. After Phraates II, King of Parthia, had defeated Antiochus VII Sidetes in 129 (F63), he was immediately deflected by the necessity of dealing with the Scyths, and left a favourite, Himerus, as his viceroy in Babylonia. We are thus in the immediate aftermath of F63, and so Müller was right to change codex A's Book number 26 to 16. Himerus was noted for extreme cruelty in dealing with the Babylonians and the population of Seleuceia, but was himself soon in trouble from the south from

Hyspaosines of Charax. The popular belief that Himerus made himself independent (Diodorus calls him King of the Parthians) is not borne out by coinage (Will, *Histoire Politique* II.416; *Cambridge History of Iran* III (1).283). Posidonius again seems to be dwelling on the corruption of luxury.

F66 Athenaeus, XIII.594D–E

CONTENT

In Bk 22 Posidonius described the lavish funeral given by Harpalus for his mistress Pythonice.

CONTEXT

Athenaeus is engaged with the topic of notorious ἑταῖραι, prostitutes and mistresses. The fragment is followed by Dicaearchus, *On the Descent into the Cave of Trophonius*, on the unexpected splendour of the monument to Pythonice outside Athens on the Sacred Way (594E–595A), and by the longer account by Theopompus in his *Letter to Alexander* (595A–C; *FGrH* 115, F253), denouncing the ἀκολασία of Harpalus, including the two monuments in Babylon and Athens, and the temple and altar to Pythonice Aphrodite, although he had erected no monument for the dead soldiers in Cilicia. Quotations from Philemon and Alexis follow.

COMMENT

A notorious *chronique scandaleuse* made much of by Theopompus. Harpalus, a boyhood friend of Alexander, was appointed head of administration and in charge of the royal treasury at Babylon when Alexander set off on the Indian campaign. He misappropriated large sums of money on high living, and in particular sent for a slave prostitute, Pythonice, from Athens, with whom he fell in love, and on her death squandered money on lavish monuments in Babylon and Athens. He replaced her with Glycera, another Athenian prostitute, and set up court at Tarsus in Cilicia with regal splendour. He appears to have been involved in an incipient satrap revolt, and on Alexander's return, took fright, fled with much of the treasury to Athens in 325/4, where he was arrested, not without scandal, allowed to escape, and was shortly assassinated in Crete (Badian, *JHS* 81 (1961), 16 ff).

We have one sentence from Posidonius' description of Pythonice's funeral procession in Babylon. But why did he introduce the story? Presumably it is another of his instances of the inadequate leader corrupted by weakness of character through power and luxury. But it must have been an analogy to a contemporary figure. The milieu would be Babylon or Cilicia, and so probably related to Syrian history. Jacoby (*Kommentar* 168) hesitantly suggested the period from *c.* 115 B.C. when Antiochus VIII Grypus and Antiochus IX Cyzicenus were contesting the throne (Trogus, *Prol.* 39); and certainly Cyzicenus appears to have surrendered to reckless luxurious habits (D.S. 34/5. 34). But in fact Athenaeus has left us no clues for context.

F67 Athenaeus, IV.151E–152F

CONTENT

History, Bk 23. Eating and drinking habits of the Celts. Wealth and prodigality of Luvernius. Posidonius' Celtic ethnography.

CONTEXT

Athenaeus in Bk IV is concerned with banquets and eating habits. The Galatae or Celts have already been reported on from Phylarchus (150D–F), followed by Thracian dinners from Xenophon (150F–151E).

COMMENT

A. Posidonius' Celtic ethnography

There are four main surviving Celtic ethnographies: Athenaeus (Frs. 67, 68, 69), Strabo, IV.4.2–6 (of which part of IV.4.5 and part of IV.4.6 are attested for Posidonius, Frs. 274, 276), Diodorus 5.25–32, and Caesar *BG* VI.11–28. To these may be added Ammianus Marcellinus 15.9, who claims to be using Timagenes. Diodorus 5.25–32 has almost universally been used as Posidonius; it is printed by Theiler as F169, by Jacoby as F116 *Anhang*, and discussed fully by Malitz, 169–98. Theiler also prints Strabo, IV.4.2, 4–6 as Frs. 33, 34. But there is a tendency to claim all these passages for Posidonius, as Tierney, 'The Celtic Ethnography of Posidonius' (*Proc. Royal Irish Academy* 60 (1960), 189–275). On this there is need for cautious scepticism, well argued by Nash (*Britannia* 7 (1975), 111–26).

Strabo certainly used Posidonius. Apart from the attested fragments, there is a close parallel to F67.39–41 in Strabo IV.2.3. There are no such clear verbal parallels in Diodorus with the attested fragments, but compare F274.7–9 with D.S. 5.29.5, and F67.28ff with 5.26.2. In general Diodorus seems to enlarge, compress and vary considerably in detail, which sometimes approaches conflict, F67.3ff and D.S. 5.28.4.

It seems beyond doubt that Diodorus, Strabo and probably Caesar read and used Posidonius. But what strikes the reader, despite common elements (which are hardly surprising in the Roman world of the time), is the completely different presentation of material in organisation, order, detail, language and emphasis in expansion or brevity by the four authors Strabo, Diodorus, Caesar and Athenaeus.

Diodorus seems generally to have used if possible a single

source as a base. If he used Posidonius, as is likely, his version is freely different from the attested controls in Athenaeus and Strabo. To add unattested material not only depends on circular hypothesis, but does not help greatly because of the differences of presentation, detail and organisation. This would suggest a somewhat loose version of Posidonius where details remain uncertain. But presumably Timagenes' *History* (*FGrH* 88.F2), which Ammianus used (15.9.2), a very different account from Posidonius (see F273 comm.), was available to Diodorus and cannot be discounted.

Strabo consulted and used a variety of sources; IV.2.3 refers to Caesar and Vercingetorix. Nash's principles stated in *Brit.* 112 should not be forgotten. It would be ludicrous to suggest that the only written or oral source on the habits of the Gauls available to intelligent writers in the latter part of the 1st c. B.C. was Posidonius. We have to allow for 'an author to have read (or listened) widely among sources on the same subject (some of whom will have made similar commonplace remarks) and to have written his account without direct reference to any of them'.

Caesar, who may well have read Posidonius, spent far longer in Gaul than Posidonius ever did (perhaps eight years before writing Bk VI of *BG*) and in areas unvisited by him. To suggest that Caesar in VI.11–28 simply rehashed material observed by Posidonius perhaps fifty years earlier (even if supplemented later) is improbable.

In the pursuit to add possible hypothetical material for Posidonius' Celtic ethnography, what has escaped notice is the nature of our cruel loss in the surviving evidence for Posidonius' *History*. It is the loss of context. Although ethnography may have been something new to Roman historiography, so that Posidonius' ethnographies were remarkable as such, it was hardly so in Greek historiography from Herodotus on. But the historical importance of Posidonius, was that he wrote ethnographies not for their own sake or for entertainment or even interest, but as his aetiological key to explain the behaviour and acts of a nation through its character. We have tantalising glimpses of this elsewhere (e.g. of the Cimbri, F272; or of the 'silly', gullible, greedy Athenians, F253); it is missing in the Celtic ethnography, because the authors who used, or may have used it had no interest in how it was applied. Athenaeus was merely concerned with subjects like food and drink and remarkable traits; Strabo was a geographer; Diodorus simply records ethnography for its own sake. Posidonius' portrait of this aristocratic society with its social code blending king, warrior class, bardic and druidical intellectual and religious sects, dependants and serfs, the complex Gallic character of naivety, cleverness, pugnacity, bravery, gusto, boastfulness, excitability and volatility of emotions, gullibility, proneness to excesses like drunkenness and love of barbaric splendour and display, must have been integral to his historical explanation of the Gallic wars of the later 2nd c., and of the contacts between Gauls and Romans. Of this potent historical brew, only the superficial froth has survived.

B. Introduction (1–3)

Gulick's translation in Loeb must be wrong in taking οὐκ ἀλλοτρίως . . . φιλοσοφίας with the following participial clause; it must go with συνέθηκεν: Posidonius, the Stoic, in the *History* which he composed in a manner consonant to the philosophy he had adopted, in recording many habits and customs from many people, says . . . On the significance of philosophical history and ethnography, see T80. Nevertheless, while this is an important statement, it is particularly inapposite patching by Athenaeus, for what follows contains nothing germane to Stoicism or even to a philosophers' history (see above, *A*). For ἀλλοτρίως with genitive, cf. Athen. XIII.607B = *SVF* I Persaeus F451.11f. If dialecticians meeting for a drinking party were to discuss syllogisms, one could object that they were acting in a manner alien to their present situation.

Norden, *Die Germanische Urgeschichte* 26, saw in πολλὰ παρὰ πολλοῖς ἔθιμα καὶ νόμιμα a deliberate allusion to the opening of the *Odyssey*, which seems fanciful.

C. Eating and drinking habits (3–36)

3–5 'The Celts serve their food with an underlay of hay and on wooden tables raised a little from the ground.' This is garbled. Does ὑποβάλλοντες mean that the straw was on the tables under the food, or that they were sitting on the ground on cushions of hay? Strabo, IV.4.3 says καὶ καθεζόμενοι δειπνοῦσι ἐν στιβάσι. On the contrary, D.S. 5.28.3 maintains that they sit on the ground on skins when eating.

Food (5–15)

5–7: a little bread and a great deal of meat boiled or roasted on charcoal or on spits. Strabo, IV.4.3 lays great emphasis on pork; for meat, see D.S. 5.28.4. Neither mentions bread, but Phylarchus (150D, *FGrH* 81, F9) stresses its quantity.

7 They are clean eaters, but with a lion's appetite. The cultivated Graeco-Romans snobbishly remarked on the cleanliness of barbarians: Strabo III.3.6 (Lusitanians); D.S. 5.33.5 (Celtiberians).

8–10 'They selected whole joints (cf. F73; D.S. 5.28.4) in both hands and gnawed bits off, or if a bit was hard to tear away, they sliced along it with a dirk which lies to hand with its sheath in its own box.' There is no mention of this detail elsewhere.

10–15 'Those who live by rivers or the sea offer fish baked with salt, vinegar and cummin, the last also sprinkled into drink. They don't use olive oil because of its scarcity, and they find its taste unpleasant because they are unused to it.' None of this occurs elsewhere.

Seating (16–23)

'In larger dinner parties, they sit in a ring with the mightiest in the middle, like a chorus leader, distinguished from the rest in his coolness in war (εὐχέρειαν, 18; or εὐχειρίαν, prowess?), or in family or wealth. The host sits next to him, and the rest in order of honour of rank on either side. Their shield-bearers stand behind, and the men-at-arms share in the feast, sitting opposite in a ring like their masters.' Again, this is unparalleled elsewhere.

Drink (24–36)

24–7 'The servants carry the drink round in vessels like carafes (ἄμβικοι), either of pottery or silver, and the platters on which they serve the food are of similar ware, but some also of bronze, others baskets of wood or wicker.' Again unique details. For ἄμβικοι see Jacobsthal, *Early Celtic Art* 109f; plate 206, p. 402. They appear to have been carafes or flagons shaped like distillation vessels or chianti bottles with thin tapering necks.

28–30 The drink among the rich was wine transported from Italy or the Massaliote region. On the transport of wine up the rivers and its high price, see D.S. 5.26.3, Cic. *Rep.* 3.9.16, and in general, Tchernia, *Le vin de l'Italie romaine* 88f, 91. Wine is drunk unmixed (so D.S. 5.26.3), but sometimes with a little water added.

31–2 'Among the poorer classes a beer is made from wheat (πύρινον, 31) with honey added.' This is odd. The beer was made from barley, and honey was used for a separate drink, mead, as D.S. 5.26.2 says: πόμα κατασκευάζουσιν ἐκ τῆς κριθῆς τὸ προσαγορευόμενον ζῦθος, καὶ τὰ κηρία πλύνοντες τῷ τούτων ἀποπλύματι χρῶνται. πύρινον (31) must be a mistake (by whom?), or is it simply used for grain? Barley beer was known from Herodotus' time (II.77, in Egypt); and Theophrastus (*CP* VI.11.2) used the word ζῦθος for it. Strabo (III.3.7) says that the Lusitanians drank ζῦθος.

The people drink beer neat. It is called 'corma'. This survives nowhere else, but Hesychius has a gloss: κορβᾶ. ἡ τοῦ κόρματος καὶ Κορύβαντος αἰτία (cf. F276?).

33–4 They sip (ἀπορροφοῦσι, swallow; Xen. *Cyr.* 1.3.10) from the same vessel (a loving cup), a little at a time, not more than a cyathos (i.e. a ladle-full, but also an Attic measure of about $\frac{1}{12}$ of a pint); but they do that rather often. Celtic drunkenness was notorious: D.S. 5.26.3.

34–5 The slave carries it round to right and to left. Gulick wished to emend: ἐπὶ τὰ δεξιὰ καὶ ⟨οὐ⟩ τὰ λαιά. But since precedence would be observed, after starting in the middle with ὁ κράτιστος (16–20), the cup(s) would surely go both right and left of him.

35–6 They say grace to their gods turning to the right. The Roman custom was to turn towards the east, to the rising sun (Plu. *Num.* 14.4; *Marc.* 6.6).

D. The wealth and prodigality of Luvernius (37–53)

This comes from the same Bk 23 of the *History* (53), still from the Celtic ethnography, but from a different section (ἔτι, 37).

37–8 Posidonius is describing the wealth of Luvernius, the father of Bituis, who was deposed by the Romans. The names, as one would expect, have variations: Strabo, IV.2.3 has Luverius. Bituis is usually Bituitus (Strabo; Livy, *Per.* 61; Orosius V.14.1; Val. Max. 9.6.3); he is Bitoitus in Appian, *Celt.* 12, and Betultus in *CIL* I^2 1.53. On the possible significance of the original names, Jullian, *Histoire de la Gaule* II.404.

The reference is to the defeat and annexation of the Averni, of the Massif Central, and Allobroges, of the upper Rhone valley and Savoie, in 121 B.C., after their protection of Saluvian refugees, by Cn. Domitius Ahenobarbus and Q. Fabius Maximus Allobrogicus, the nephew of Scipio Africanus. Bituitus (King of the Averni in Livy, *Per.* 61, of the Allobroges in App. *Celt.* 12) later featured in Domitius' triumph in 120 B.C. (Strabo IV.1.11; Livy, *Per.* 61; App. *Celt.* 12; Florus I.37.5; Orosius V.14.1; Val. Max. 9.6.3; Jullian, II. 548–50). This provides the historical context of Posidonius' ethnography in Bk 23.

39–41 There is a parallel passage for this sentence in Strabo, IV.2.3 (unattested). 'He says that attempting to curry popularity with the mob (Strabo: putting on a show of opulence for his friends (φίλοις: ὄχλοις Corais; φύλοις Jacob)) he was carried in a chariot through the countryside (ἐπ' ἀπήνης φέρεσθαι διὰ πεδίου, Strabo), and scattered gold and silver for the thousands of Celts who followed him (so more or less, Strabo).'

41–53 The following story of the lavish continuing banquet for all-comers and the compensation for the panting late Bard, occurs nowhere else. 'He fenced off an area twelve stades square in which he filled up vats with expensive wine and prepared such a quantity of food that for many days anyone who wished could enter and enjoy what had been prepared with a continuous service. After he had put a closure on the feast, a native poet arrived late (Kaibel's emendation, τῶν βάρδων καλουμένων ποιητῶν (47), is attractive (F69), but unnecessary), and on meeting him sang a song in honour of his eminence, but lamented his own late-coming; Luvernius was delighted, asked for a bag of gold, and threw it to him as he was running alongside. The man picked it up and started another song that the tracks of his chariot on the ground bore gold and bounty for men.' For Bards praising the king's wealth, App. *Celt.* 12 and F69.

Momigliano, *Alien Wisdom* 69f, can surely not be right in representing Posidonius' view of the Celts as a glorified Homeric, or even 'golden' age, which he viewed with approval. The original cutting edge of this story may lie in δημαγωγοῦντα τοὺς ὄχλους (39; so Malitz, 178f). This is another Posidonian 'king' and his bribery of the greedy masses, with close affinities to the Athenion fragment (F253;

and cf. F75). The humour of the mercenary Bard composing at the double is unmistakably ironic.

Although Gaul was still notorious to the Romans of the 1st c. B.C. for its wealth in gold (e.g. F273), archaeological finds of the late 2nd and 1st c. B.C. cannot be compared with the richness of those of the earlier period (Piggott, Daniel, McBurney (edd.), *France Before The Romans* 192). Posidonius was therefore harking back to a still more opulent and extravagant quasi-legendary period, even if only a generation earlier than Bituitus, before Roman constraint and exploitation in the 1st c. Stories of Gallic greed for gold were early: Livy, 5.48; 44.26; Plb. 1.66f; 2.17.11; 2.22.2; 4.46.3.

F68 Athenaeus, IV.154A–C

CONTENT

Celtic duels.

CONTEXT

F67 (*q.v.*) is followed by F57, F64, F75, F53, F73 (151E–153E). Then a gap is filled by Nicolaus of Damascus on Roman duels (μονομαχεῖν) during banquets, and Eratosthenes on Etruscans accompanying boxing bouts with the flute (153F–154A). Then comes F68.

COMMENT

This is part of the Celtic ethnography of *History*, Bk 23 (see F67). Lines 2–6 and 6–12 are distinguished and separated by τὸ δὲ παλαιόν (6), which implies that the first part describes practices still contemporary with Posidonius, while the latter part refers to more barbaric fatal practices of earlier times, perhaps discouraged by later Roman influence, as decapitation was (F274).

2–6 'The Celts sometimes engage in duels during dinner. After assembling fully armed they shadow fence and spar (ἀκροχειρίζονται, cf. Arist. *EN* 1111a 15) with each other, and sometimes even go the length of inflicting a wound, and roused by this, unless the bystanders stop it, as far as the kill.'

6–12 'In ancient times when whole joints were served, the best man would get the thigh; but if someone else claimed it, they would join in a duel to the death. Others would collect silver or gold from a public audience, or others a quantity of jars of wine, and securing the gift by pledge and distributing it to their nearest and dearest, would lie stretched out on their backs on their shields, while a man took his place by the victim and cut off his head.'

ἐν θεάτρῳ seems to indicate some sort of public occasion as distinct from a dinner party. τὸν λαιμὸν ἀποκόπτει suggests decapitation rather than cutting their throats; cf. S.E. *Adv. Math.* I.264, τὸν δὲ Πήγασον λαιμοτομηθείσης τῆς Γοργόνος ἀπὸ τῆς κεφαλῆς ἐκθορεῖν. This is followed by a similar tale of Romans by Euphorion of Chalcis.

7–8 Reproduced by Eustathius, τὸ μηρίον . . . θανάτου, F275.2–5. Diodorus (5.28.5) also notes the custom of Celts challenging each other to duels (μονομαχεῖν) during meals on any excuse (ἐκ τῶν τυχόντων). Diodorus couples this (5.28.6) with their belief in immortality and metempsychosis, said to be part of druidic philosophy by Strabo (IV.4.4), and by Caesar (*BG* VI.14).

F69 Athenaeus, VI.246C–D

CONTENT

Celtic parasites and Bards.

CONTEXT

The topic of parasites has been flourishing from 234C. F69 is immediately preceded by a reference from Ptolemy of Megalopolis, and is followed by F74.

COMMENT

Again part of the Celtic ethnography of *History*, Bk 23 (see F67). 'The Celts take round with them, even when engaged in war, boon-companions they call "parasites". They spout eulogies of them both before groups gathered together and before each of the audience individually. Their musical entertainment is provided by the so-called Bards; they are in fact poets who laud them in song.'

This seems garbled and compressed. Presumably παράσιτοι and Βάρδοι are different categories. μετ᾽ᾠδῆς distinguishes the Bards, who sing to musical accompaniment (ἀκούσματα, 6); compare D.S. 5.31.2: εἰσὶ δὲ παρ᾽ αὐτοῖς καὶ ποιηταὶ μελῶν, οὓς Βάρδους ὀνομάζουσιν. In Appian, *Celt.* 12 there seems to be only one type in the ambassador's retinue. παράσιτος, or favoured hanger-on (cf. F74), would hardly be of the same class as Bards.

There is no mention in the attested fragments of Druids, but this must be a mischance of the surviving tradition, for there can be little doubt that Posidonius knew of their importance, and included them in his ethnography. When the term first became familiar is unknown; D.L. 1.6 refers to Druids as ancient philosophers among the barbarians, paired with the Gymnosophists. This may be from Sotion (1.7). By the 1st c. B.C., a triple canon of intellectuals in Gallic society comprising poets, diviners and philosopher Druids was widely recognised.

Strabo, IV.4.4, listed three classes held in exceptional honour: Bards, Vates (Οὐάτεις), Druids. Bards are singers and poets; Vates are religious officials (ἱεροποιοί) and natural philosophers (φυσιολόγοι); Druids, in addition to φυσιολογία, practise moral philosophy (ἠθικὴ φιλοσοφία). They were thought to be the most just of men, and so were entrusted with legal and arbitration judgements. They say that men's souls are immortal and the cosmos too, although at times fire and water will predominate (cf. D.L. 1.6).

Diodorus (5.31.2–5) refers to Bards, ποιηταὶ μελῶν. To the accompaniment of musical instruments like lyres, they sing both panegyrics and obloquy. Druids are philosophers and religious theorists, specially honoured. Diviners (μάντεις, i.e. Vates) are also highly honoured. They are essential for sacrifices, and have an important part in war as well as in peace.

In Caesar, *BG* VI.13–16, apart from serfs, the two dominant classes are Knights (equites, a warrior class) and Druids (an intellectual priestly class). Druids are concerned with divine worship and sacrifices, are much honoured, concerned with legal and arbitration duties, instruct the young, are excused from military service and all taxes, and study Greek. They believe in metempsychosis. They theorise about the movements of the heavenly bodies, the size of the universe and of the earth, and about nature and the gods. Caesar has no mention of Bards or Vates. On this see Nash, *Britannia* 7 (1976), 121ff, and F67 comm. *A*. On the combination of divination and φυσιολογία in the Druids, Cic. *De Div.* 1.90.

The trio are still preserved in Amm. Marc. 15.9.8 with the corruption of Euhages for Οὐάτεις (or Vates). He claims to be taking his account from Timagenes' *History of the Gauls* (15.9.2; *FGrH* 88, F2).

So the likelihood is that Posidonius also recognised the three intellectual classes, and one would have expected him to be interested in the φυσιολογία of the Druids. One would have liked to know more.

F70 Athenaeus, IX.369C–D

CONTENT

'The Stoic Posidonius in Bk 27 of the *History* says about Dalmatia that wild turnips and carrots grew there.'

CONTEXT

Athenaeus' discussion on vegetables begins with turnips (γογγυλίδες) at 369A.

COMMENT

This fragment is not much help for the content of Bk 27. Jacoby (*Kommentar* 169) and Malitz (212) suggested that it may have been occasioned by the triumph of L. Caecilius Metellus Delmaticus over the Dalmatians in 117 B.C. (Livy, *Per.* 62; App. *Illyr.* 11; Broughton, *Magistrates* I.529). On the strength of this theoryTheiler changed the Bk number to 24, ΚΔ.

There appear to have been two main types of turnip, γογγυλίς (*Brassica rapa*) and βουνιάς (*Brassica napus*) or French turnip. Diphilus described the γογγυλίς as thinning, acrid and hard to digest, while βουνιάς was sweeter, more digestible and nourishing. See also Theophrastus *HP* VII.4.3. Speusippus (Περὶ ὁμοίων, Bk II) classified γογγυλίς with the radish (ῥαφανίς), rape turnip (ῥάφυς) and nose-smart (ἀνάρρινον). Athenaeus also quotes Crates on Cephisian turnips, and Nicander's *Georgics*. They were either roasted, pickled or boiled (Athenaeus); or boiled and eaten with salt and olive oil, or cooked with meat or bacon (Anthimus, 52); cf. Apicius III.13.1, 2; VI.2.3. Columella (2.22ff) however thinks of turnips as food for peasants and animals, and they were used medicinally for bladder complaints and dysentery (Gargilius Martialis, *Medicinae* 34).

For the carrot, see Andrews, 'The Carrot as Food in the Classical Era', *CPh* 44 (1949), 182–96. The ancient Mediterranean carrot was the white carrot (the Latin *pastinaca* could be applied to carrot or parsnip). Dioscorides, III.52W, says that the σταφυλῖνος ἄγριος has leaves like the γιγγίδιον (probably the shining leaved carrot), but broader and somewhat bitter, with an aphrodisiacal root, esculent when cooked. He contrasts the cultivated carrot (κηπαῖος) as better food, but weaker medicinally. So the σταφυλῖνος ἄγριος may be the wild carrot, but is more likely to be a primitive form of the cultivated carrot, *Daucus carota*. Compare Galen, *Alim. Fac.* II.65, and Numenius in Athenaeus 371C. The other word for carrot, δαῦκος, was a more generic term including the wild carrot, whereas σταφυλῖνος on its own referred to the cultivated carrot. Carrots seem to have been widely used as a cathartic medicine, but see also Apicius, III.113–15. Athenaeus' discussion on the σταφυλῖνος is in IX.371B–E.

F71 Athenaeus, XV.692C–D

CONTENT

Perfume at royal symposia in Syria. Bk 28.

CONTEXT

The discussion has centred on perfume from 686C. This passage is preceded by quotations from Philonides' *On Perfumes and Wreaths* and from Aristotle's *Probl. Phys.*; it is followed by a short passage on the introduction of wreaths at Rome.

COMMENT

1 **ἀναγιγνώσκων:** 'when reading Bk 28 of Posidonius' *History*'. If this is to be believed, then the *History* was available to Athenaeus, and he read it, not extracts.

3 The royal court referred to in the context of Bk 28 is probably that of Antiochus VIII Grypus between 121–115 B.C.; see F72.

4–8 The ἥδιστον (1), or very nice observation on perfume, was probably not the expensive Babylonian perfume (Forbes, *Studies in Ancient Technology* III^2.26ff), but the method of distribution: 'When wreaths are given to the diners, attendants enter with little pouches (ἀσκίδια) of Babylonian perfume, and keeping their distance (πόρρωθεν is stressed by position) as they go round, they bedew the wreaths of the reclining guests from them, sprinkling nothing else than those as they pass.' This must have required considerable skill. Another example of Posidonius' eye for curious detail. παραρραίνειν occurs nowhere else, but Posidonius loved compound verbs.

F72a, b Athenaeus, XII.540A–B; Athenaeus, V.210E

CONTENT

Bk 28. Lavish entertainment of Antiochus Grypus at Daphne.

CONTEXT

See F61, Context.

COMMENT

Antiochus VIII Grypus (Hook-nose) had come to the Seleucid throne in an exceedingly unsettled and turbulent period even for the Seleucids. His father, Demetrius II Nicator, returned from captivity in Parthia, had been finally defeated by the Egyptian-supported pretender, Alexander II Zabinas, shut out by his mother, Queen Cleopatra Thea, and murdered in 126/5 B.C. Demetrius' elder son, Seleucus V, was thereupon assassinated by Cleopatra on assuming the throne, and Grypus was recalled by his mother the Queen to be King. He immediately had to deal with Alexander established at Antioch, who, now without the support of Egypt, was eliminated in 123. But Grypus, still a very young man, remained dominated by Cleopatra until her attempt to murder him in 121 rebounded in her own throat, whereupon Grypus became sole ruler (Justin (Trogus) 39.1.4ff; D.S. 34/5. 22, 28; Jos. *AJ* 13.267ff; App. *Syr.* 68–9; Bellinger, 'The End of the Seleucids', *Transactions of the Connecticut Academy of Arts and Sciences* 38 (1949), 51ff; Will, *Histoire Politique du Monde Hellénistique* II.435f, 445ff; Bevan, *The House of Seleucus* II.247ff). From 121 to *c.* 115/114, when the next dynastic challenge appeared from Antiochus IX Cyzicenus (the son of Antiochus Sidetes and Cleopatra), Grypus reigned in comparative peace, and therefore it is likely to be in this period that the lavish festival receptions described took place at Daphne, so giving a chronological bracket for Bk 28.

2 Daphne was the royal park about four miles from Antioch, dedicated to the royal gods, especially Apollo, by Seleucus I, where games were celebrated by the Seleucid monarchs (Bevan I.213f).

4–9 The literalness of the quotation is guaranteed by the exact repetition of the doublet, and characterised by Posidonius' gift of vivid detail. Not only were gifts distributed to all of whole joints of meat (4; for ὁλομελῶν βρωμάτων cf. F61a, F67.8, F73), but also of live geese, hares and gazelles (later thought to be 'barbaric' by Dio, 77.1.2), golden crowns (F61a.8), and quantities of silverware, servants, horses, camels (5–7). The final vignette is splendid: 'Each guest had to mount the camel, drink a toast, then take the camel, what was on the camel, and the attendant slave' (9–10). The repetition of κάμηλος is surely humorous.

F73 Athenaeus, IV.153E

CONTENT

'Germans, as Posidonius reports in Bk 30 (of the *History*), eat meat roasted in joints for luncheon and drink milk, and their wine unmixed.'

CONTEXT

Athenaeus is in the process of reviewing national eating and drinking habits: the Celts (151Eff, F67), Parthians (152F–153B, F64), Syrians (153B, F75), Romans and Etruscans (153C–D, F53 and Timaeus), Indians (153D–E, from Megasthenes), Germans (F73), Campanians (153E), Romans (153F–154A, Nicolaus of Damascus), Etruscans (154A, Eratosthenes), Celtic feast duels (F68), etc.

COMMENT

This seemingly straightforward fragment has engendered much speculation. Whom did Posidonius designate Γερμανοί?

Diodorus (5.32.1–5) in his Celtic ethnography (F67 comm. *A*) merely talks of Celts and Galatae, adding that the Romans called the whole lot Galatae. But in this group he includes the northern European lands and the stretch to the east as far as Scythia. Moreover, he clearly includes the Cimbri among them (5.32.4). Appian, *Illyr.* 4 too called the Cimbri Κελτοί, and so it appears did Strabo, VII.1.2ff. There is every reason to think that Posidonius did so too (F272).

Strabo, IV.4.2, at the beginning of his Celtic ethnography (F67, comm. *A*), distinguishes Γερμανοί as a group and Γερμανία from the Gauls (or Celts), perhaps influenced by Caesar. But he says that they are similar in nature (φύσει) and in political organisation, and that the two groups are kin to each other, live in neighbouring countries separated by the Rhine (again, this looks like Caesar), but are in most things similar except that Germany is further north. But he does not seem to regard them as ethnically different (VII.1.2); indeed he uses them as a kind of more primitive, barbaric, untamed version of Celts, and so useful as a guide to earlier Celtic ethnography, much in the way that Caesar used the Suebi for his Germani.

In Spartacus' army in 73–71 B.C. there is some evidence of a contingent of Germani as distinct from Gauls (Livy, *Per.* 97; Plu. *Crass.* 9.7) but no further details are known.

Caesar seems to have been the first to distinguish Germani from Galli geographically and collectively as the people who live beyond the Rhine (*BG* I.1). He probably also distinguished them ethnically, as he recognised Germani who had become naturalised *cis Rhenum* (*BG* II.3–4).

There have been three main views on Γερμανοί in F73.

(1) Posidonius did not in fact use the term, which is a later substitution by Athenaeus for Κιμβροί (Müllenhoff, *Deutsche Altertumskunde* II.161f, 188). This is unlikely (cf. Norden, *Germanische Urgeschichte* 72ff; Jacoby, *Kommentar* 169f). It is against Athenaeus' common practice, and it makes nonsense of Athenaeus' context. Athenaeus had already given a separate entry from Posidonius for the eating habits of Κελτοί (see Context above), and Posidonius probably regarded the Cimbrians as Celts. Γερμανοί comprise a separate and distinct tribal entry from Posidonius.

(2) It is a national term like Κελτοί, but Posidonius like others of his time was vague over the terms Κελτοί, Γαλαταί, Γερμανοί and used them interchangeably, or at least as all part of the same group. This is true of Κελτοί and Γαλαταί; but Γερμανοί are distinguished from Celts. Certainly Γερμανοί cannot be the equivalent of or an alternative for Κελτοί, because of the argument from context above. The Γερμανοί of Bk 30 must be different from the Celtic ethnography of Bk 23 (F67, 151Eff). But then who were they, if the Celts were thought to stretch from the Atlantic and North Sea to Scythia? Posidonius may have intended a subdivision or offshoot of Γαλαταί (so Jacoby, 170), perhaps a supposed wilder, more barbaric northern section, like Strabo, IV.4.2 (see above); it would thus be a vague group term, but not a specific one like Cimbri. But Diodorus had no word of them,

and the use of Germani as a collective term before Caesar has been doubted. On the other hand, such a term, Germani, may have been in use in the seventies of part of Spartacus' force (see above).

(3) Celts and Germani may be terms used at different levels; i.e. Γερμανοί is not, like Κελτοί, an ethnic collective term for a geographical group of tribes, but the name of a particular tribe of which Posidonius had heard (so Malitz, 205). This is in line with Tacitus' later analysis in *Germ.* II.5: 'The name Germania is of recent application. The first people to cross the Rhine and oust the Gauls and now called Tungri, were then called Germani. And so it was the name of a tribe (*natio*), not that of a nation (*gens*), that gradually strengthened in common use.' So, although archaeological and linguistic evidence (Wells, *The German Policy of Augustus* 14–31; Keller, *The German Language* 46ff) shows a semi-nomadic more primitive culture in the northlands spreading to Bohemia, Prague and Bratislava distinct from the La Tène oppida culture of the Celts, a group of peoples who spoke a different language from the Celts (Caesar *BG* 1.47.4; Tac. *Germ.* 43.1), yet these 'Germanic' peoples had no common word to name their own tribes collectively (Keller, 47). Germani in the collective sense (a word of uncertain Celtic or Germanic origin, Keller) was given them by Gauls and Romans, perhaps, as Tacitus suggested, from a particular tribe.

It is still more speculative to guess where Posidonius thought the Germani were. The Rhine is the most common suggestion (e.g. Malitz, *Die Historien* 205; Jacoby, *Kommentar* 169; Unger, *Philologus* 55.112f). But milk-drinking is the mark of a semi-nomadic people, and the Rhine was settled on both banks by Celtic La Tène culture, so that Caesar's definition of Germani was more convenient than accurate; rivers, as main highways, unite rather than divide. Also, this sentence is reproduced by Eustathius (F277b) in his commentary on *Il.* XIII.6, where he is dealing with Posidonius' interpretation involving the European Mysians or Moesians by the lower Danube (F277a). It is also coupled by Eustathius with Pindar F166f (Bergk) on Centaurs. This suggests a more eastern, nomadic and perhaps rather vague semi-legendary location. Bk 30 probably dealt with the Cimbrian migrations, and the Germani may have been a tribe they were supposed to have come in contact with. Since they were also wine-drinkers, it is unlikely that they were based in the far north, as Malitz pointed out (205); certainly not the Cimbri themselves in their native Jutland homeland.

F74 Athenaeus, VI.246D

CONTENT

Bk 34. Posidonius recorded the name of a certain Apollonius who had become a parasite of Antiochus Grypus, King of Syria.

CONTEXT

The discussion on parasites began at 234C. F74 immediately follows F69 on Celtic parasites.

COMMENT

Nothing more is known of this Apollonius, but he must have belonged to the last years of Grypus' reign. See F72 in Bk 28, and compare F75.

F75 Athenaeus, IV.153B–C

CONTENT

How Heracleon of Beroea, the lieutenant of Antiochus Grypus, fed his army. Bk 34?

CONTEXT

Part of Athenaeus' list of banqueting and eating habits. F57 and F64 precede, and F53 follows.

COMMENT

Heracleon of Beroea in Syria belongs to the end of the reign of Antiochus Grypus. Here we are told that he repaid his benefactor the King for his advancement by almost driving him from the kingdom (2–4). Josephus (*AJ* 13.365) claims that he was responsible for the assassination of Grypus, and Trogus (*Prol.* 39) suggests that he seized the throne. This was in 96 B.C. Heracleon's moment of power must have been brief, because Grypus was succeeded by his eldest son Seleucus VI, who was quickly followed by yet another interdynastic struggle between Antiochus X (the son of Antiochus Cyzicenus), Demetrius III, and the twins Antiochus XI and Philippus I, all sons of Grypus (Will, *Histoire Politique du Monde Hellénistique* II.446f). The picture of how Heracleon fed his army probably refers to the period when he was still Grypus' commander.

Codex A gives τετάρτῃ for the Bk number, which is chronologically impossible; so is 14 (see F63) and 24 (see F72). 44 (Müller) seems rather late. 34 ($\overline{\lambda\delta}$, Bake) is most likely.

Once more we are left with the superficial scrap from Athenaeus' interests. Heracleon kept strict discipline (5–8). His troops were seated on the ground in the open air in battalions of 1000. The men were given a large loaf (black (μέλας) bread, Wilamowitz; but cf. F53.5), meat and an ordinary wine diluted with cold water served by men wearing their swords. Strict silence was observed.

F76 Athenaeus, XI.494F–495A

CONTENT

Bk 36: 'There were also onyx cups and combinations of these up to a capacity of about a pint; and also very large "Panathenaica", some of about 1½ gallons, some even larger.'

CONTEXT

A list of cups under their names.

COMMENT

The κοτύλη was a liquid measure of *c.* ½ pint. χοῦς = 12 κοτύλαι, so δίχους holds about 12 pints, the capacity of one of the court water clocks at Athens (Arist. *Ath. Pol.* 67.2). The name Παναθηναϊκά (4) may have been derived from the sacred oil vessels which were prizes at the Panathenaea.

The description has been associated with Syria, and Malitz (298) referred to the notorious valuable cups filched at a later date by Verres from Antiochus in Sicily (Cic. *2 Verr.* IV.62). But Posidonius is emphasising the capacity of the drinking vessels rather than their value, probably in an attack on heavy drinking. This could still apply to Syria, of course (cf. F63), but we have no evidence for Posidonius' context.

4 συνδέσεις is without parallel, but might mean 'combinations (of bowls)'. Theiler's συνθέσεις (collections) is attractive.

F77 Athenaeus, XII.550A–B

CONTENT

'Ptolemy Physcon's son Alexander also increased in girth, the one who killed his mother when she was joint ruler with him. At all events Posidonius in Bk 47 of the *History* speaks thus of him: "The ruler of Egypt, hated by the mob, but fawned on by his entourage, lived in great luxury, not even able to relieve himself (walk) unless (he went) supported on either side by a couple of men. But he would leap down from a lofty couch into the dances at drinking parties barefoot and perform them more energetically than the experts."'

COMMENT

This follows immediately an account of the luxury of Ptolemy Euergetes II on which Posidonius is quoted (F58).

Ptolemy Alexander I, younger son of Euergetes II and Cleopatra III, after alternating with his older brother, Soter II, ruled jointly with his mother until the death of Cleopatra in 101 B.C. (Samuel, *Ptolemaic Chronology* 152). He then appears to have ruled in Egypt with Cleopatra Berenice whom he married after his mother's death, until his own death in battle in 88 B.C. (Samuel, 152). The death of Cleopatra III does not seem to have been so clear as the murder of Berenice by her stepson, Alexander II, in 80 B.C., but the imputation of matricide also occurred in Trogus (Justin. 39.5.1) and in Pausanias (1.9.3, but garbled); it does not seem to be mentioned in Porphyry (*FGrH* 260, F2.8). It is likely that Posidonius' description applies to Alexander in the gross fruits of power in the late nineties or early eighties. For dating and the termination point of the *History*, see F51. Posidonius' theme may have been the corrupted degeneracy of the ruler in Egypt, and so provoked towards the end of Alexander's reign.

7 **ἀποπατεῖν,** Capps, 'to relieve himself', is both funnier and more cutting than Kaibel's περιπατεῖν. It also makes more sense physically. ἐπορεύετο should then probably be bracketed.

The extract displays the scathing vividness of Posidonius' prose style.

F78 Athenaeus, IV.168D–E

CONTENT

Posidonius mentions in Bk 49 of the *History* a certain Apicius who had overshot all men in prodigality. This was the Apicius who was responsible for the exile of Rutilius, the man who had published a *History of Rome* in Greek.

COMMENT

The context in Athenaeus is a long list of examples of ἀσωτία or prodigality. The context in Posidonius is not so clear. It could come from a context deploring contemporary corruption of old Roman virtues (F265–6; cf. D.S. 37.3–5), but Athenaeus links it to Apicius' connection with the trial of Rutilius in 92 B.C., which is likely to have come from his source, Posidonius (so Jacoby, *Kommentar* 171). Posidonius in turn probably used as his source Rutilius, whose *History* he must have read and probably mentioned at this point, which would explain Athenaeus' reference to it here. Athen. XII.543B has a reference from Rutilius on Sittius as an example of Roman luxury, and then goes on to mention Apicius as having been referred to earlier (no doubt this passage). If therefore, the context in Posidonius was the trial of Rutilius, this passage gives a date for the content of Bk 49. On the possible significance of this for the termination point of the *History*, see F51.

For this Apicius see Nicolet, *L'Ordre Équestre* II.779, no. 26. He is to be distinguished from the Tiberian gourmet of the same name (Athen. I.7A–B; Pliny, *NH* 9.30; 10.68; Sen. *Helv.* 10.8–9; Martial, III.22). This one was also a gourmet, probably a Knight and possibly a Marian (Nicolet), since he was chosen to prosecute Rutilius before the equestrian tribunal (D.S. 34.31) in 92 B.C. Rutilius had clearly offended in his clearing up of Asia as Scaevola's legate in 94/3 B.C. (D.S. 37.5), was prosecuted *repetundarum*, and went into exile to Smyrna. Also, as a practising Stoic, he was known as one of the three men (Scaevola, Aelius Tubero) who tried to live by the sumptuary lex Fannia (Athen. VI.274C–E; a passage following a Posidonian context: F262–6). As such he would incur the enmity of the likes of Apicius.

On Rutilius and his connection with Posidonius, see T13.

F79 Strabo, XI.1.6

CONTENT

Did Posidonius write a monograph on Pompey?

CONTEXT

F206.

COMMENT

In its context this is a very vague, ambiguous and uncertain statement. Strabo criticises Posidonius for misjudging the length of the southern neck of the Caucasian 'peninsula' between the Caspian and Black Seas. He should have known better because Pompey was a friend and called on him before setting off on his Caucasian campaign. Strabo proceeds: 'Add to that, he actually wrote τὴν ἱστορίαν . . . τὴν περὶ αὐτόν.'

(1) Since the nearest masculine singular preceding this reference is Pompey, the question arises whether Strabo is citing a monograph on Pompey. Reinhardt not only accepted this but contributed to the content of the work (*RE* col. 638–40); but the theory has met with scepticism (Jacoby, *Kommentar* 157; Aly, *Strabonis Geographica* Bd. 4.94ff; Malitz,

71–3; Theiler, II.59f). In any case Strabo cannot be citing the title of the book, for which we would expect περὶ with the genitive. The sentence should mean: 'Add to that, that he actually (καὶ, or 'also') wrote up his investigations about him' (cf. F49.227f). It might still be a general allusion to investigation into Pompey elsewhere; but where? Not in the *History*, because the evidence indicates that it concluded before the sixties (Jacoby, 157; Malitz, 73). Posidonius must have been about seventy by the completion of Pompey's Asiatic campaigns. Besides, the field was occupied by the well-known monograph by Pompey's historian, Theophanes of Mytilene (Cic. *Arch.* 24). Posidonius might have written an encomium of Pompey at some point, but there is no other reference whatsoever to such a work on Pompey, and doubt must remain as to whether it ever existed.

(2) But then to what could αὐτόν refer? Reinhardt argued that the sentence was a climax to Strabo's attack on Posidonius for not consulting Pompey. But Aly (*Strabonis Geographica* Bd. 4.408 n. 8) showed that προστίθει δὲ τούτοις is a feature of Strabo's style, where he tacks on to a list a new suggestion which need have nothing to do with a previous item (cf. I.2.29; VI.4.1). He therefore referred αὐτόν back beyond the Pompeian section to τὸν 'Ωκεανόν at the end of XI.1.5 (F206.21), understanding the work to be Περὶ ὠκεανοῦ. This is an interesting suggestion, but although Strabo's grammatical leaps are often wide, this is particularly difficult to accept. More importantly, it makes no sense of καί in the sentence.

(3) Schwartz in *Philologus* 86 (1931), 391 n. 22, emended to περὶ αὐτῶν referring to the Iberians and Armenians mentioned just before (F206.25), and understanding the work to be the Περὶ ὠκεανοῦ. This has been adopted by Theiler (II.59f), but the emendation is weak. Of course, if the measurement reference comes from *On Ocean*, Posidonius wrote about Iberia and Armenia, but that makes no sense at all of καί.

The Greek strongly favours a reference to Pompey, but the difficulties under (1) remain.

F80 Aelian, *Tactica* 1.2

CONTENT

Posidonius wrote a handbook on tactics.

CONTEXT

Aelian gives a list of previous writers on tactics: Aeneas, Cineas, Pyrrhus of Epirus and his son Alexander, Clearchus, Posidonius and many others.

COMMENT

There is no doubt that Posidonius of Apamea is meant: ὁ Στωϊκός (1), and cf. F81. Nor is it surprising that Posidonius wrote a book on tactics. Apart from the evidence of his enormous range of interests, Posidonius is known to have held that the arts and sciences (τέχναι, *artes*), while in a different category from philosophy, were a proper field of study, at times a necessary one, for the philosopher in his comprehension of the world and human activity, and in respect of his contribution to human society (Frs. 90, 284). Also in a more particular sense, a study of tactics would be germane to Posidonius the historian; cf. Lucian, *Hist. Conscr.* 37.

For the arguments that the Τακτικὰ Κεφάλαια of Asclepiodotus may be an epitome or abridgement of Posidonius' work: T41 comm. Aelian seems to have used the former without acknowledgement, while listing the latter as an authority. If the Τακτικὰ Κεφάλαια is an abridgement of Posidonius, it should give us some idea of the character of Posidonius' handbook. For it would then have included a historical study of the composition, equipment and drill manoeuvres of the hellenistic phalanx (T41 comm.). But the language and composition of Τακτικὰ Κεφάλαια is so stark that it must be Asclepiodotus' own notes, and not abstracts taken from Posidonius (contrast Geminus in F18). Also even if we grant that Τακτικὰ Κεφάλαια is an epitome of some kind of Posidonius, we cannot conclude that it represents the whole scope of Posidonius' book, although it may do.

F81 Arrian, *De Tactica* 1.1–2

CONTENT

Posidonius wrote and left behind a kind of handbook on tactics.

CONTEXT

The opening of Arrian's monograph is missing; the text begins in mid-sentence with a list of previous writers on the subject. They are: ⟨Pyrrhus of Epirus⟩ and his son Alexander, Clearchus, Pausanias, Evangelus, Polybius, Eupolemus, Iphicrates and Posidonius.

COMMENT

Arrian used Aelian and probably Asclepiodotus' Τακτικὰ Κεφάλαια, which he does not mention. For the relationship of Posidonius to this: F80, T41.

Arrian's description of Posidonius' work is curious: καὶ τέχνην τινὰ τακτικὴν συγγράψας κατέλιπεν. The term συγγράμματα (treatise) is used for Pausanias, the vague ἄλλα for Evangelus and Polybius, and συγγέγραπται ἄλλα of Eupolemus and Iphicrates. Posidonius is the only one credited with a Τέχνη, but it is qualified by τινα, a sort of handbook. Also what is the significance of συγγράψας κατέλιπεν? Does this mean it was found in his papers, in his Nachlass, in an unfinished state (τινα)? If so, is this what Asclepiodotus may have used as a base for his Τακτικὰ Κεφάλαια (T41 comm.)? There is simply not enough evidence to take any of these questions further; nor do we know whether Arrian was acquainted at first hand with Posidonius' work.

Arrian characterises all the books of his predecessors as not useful, because they were written as if for experts; so the names of equipment and formations are given as if they were familiar terms, but they cannot be understood if not explained (2–6). Arrian will remedy this lack of clarity (6f). This ought to mean that he believed Posidonius' handbook to be of a technical nature not intended for laymen.

F82, F83 Cicero, *Ad Atticum* II.1.2; Cicero, *De Officiis* III.10

LETTERS

The first letter was a personal one to Cicero (T34). The second is more interesting in that the remark from it probably came to Cicero in a ὑπόμνημα from Athenodorus Calvus on material from Posidonius on the topic of the apparent conflict between *honestum* and *utile* from certain Commentarii and other sources. See F41 comm. for details. So it is uncertain whether this letter had been 'published', or become generally known in some other way.

DUBIA

F84 Ps.-Plutarch, *De Placitis* II.9; *Moralia* 888A

CONTENT

A reference to void is assigned to Bk I Περὶ κενοῦ.

COMMENT

Diels (*Dox. Gr.* p. 9) argued that Posidonius wrote no such book, deleted reference to it and substituted Eusebius' wording which has no mention of the Περὶ κενοῦ. He is followed by Mau, *Plutarchi Moralia* V.I.2.

The arguments against the title are as follows:

(1) Of the three surviving reports of this fragment of Aetius, two have no reference to the book title, namely Stobaeus, *Ecl.* I.18.4b and Eusebius, *Praep. Evang.* XV.40. This is hardly a conclusive argument. Although the wording is very similar in all three authors, the reports are by no means identical even in the Posidonius sentence. Stobaeus inserts τὸ ἐκτὸς τοῦ κόσμου which is not in the other two. Eusebius has διάβασιν for διάλυσιν. One of the most important codices of Eusebius (*B*) reads Ποσειδώνιος καὶ Πλάτων and omits οὐκ ἄπειρον . . . Ἀριστοτέλης. Stobaeus has no reference at all to Aristotle who appears in the doxography of the other two. It is well known that some compilers and copyists have a liking for bibliographical records and others do not. For example in the tradition of Diogenes Laertius, manuscript *F* made a practice of suppressing bibliographical references preserved by *B* and *P*. Where did the title in Ps.-Plutarch come from? A reference to Περὶ κενοῦ might be a guess (but why?), but the

reference to Bk I of a title which did not exist could only be deliberate (and meaningless) falsification. It is simpler to assume that Ps.-Plutarch found a reference to a work entitled *Void* by Posidonius.

(2) D.L. VII.140 says that Posidonius talks about void in Bk 2 of the Φυσικὸς Λόγος. If Posidonius had written a special book on *Void*, Diogenes would have referred to it; therefore no such book existed. This is a non-sequitur. It assumes (a) that Posidonius could not have written on the same subject in different books, an assumption not only unlikely, but factually disproved by the surviving fragments with book titles; (b) that if Posidonius wrote a book entitled *Void*, Diogenes (or his source) must have known and used it.

(3) Diels was also misled by the report on Aristotle in Ps.-Plutarch where he thought that the manuscripts read εἶναι κενόν. Such a manifestly false statement encouraged him towards major surgery and the healthy goal of Eusebius. But the manuscripts have μηδὲν εἶναι κενόν which is unexceptional.

There appear therefore to be no firm grounds for rejecting the title offered by Ps.-Plutarch.

For the content of the fragment, see F97.

F85 Sextus Empiricus, *Adv. Mathematicos* VII.93

CONTENT

'And as light, says Posidonius in expounding Plato's *Timaeus*, is grasped by sight that is luminous and sound by hearing that is airy, so too the nature of all that there is (ἡ τῶν ὅλων φύσις) should be grasped by the *logos* that is kin to it.'

CONTEXT

The subject from VII.27 has been the criterion. At 89 the question is raised as to who introduced the enquiry (σκέψις) into the criterion. A historical survey follows, the first part of which (89–140) covers the φυσικοί from Thales to Democritus. The general point is at once made that it was through mistrust of the senses that reason was recognised as the critical factor of truth. So Anaxagoras declared reason in general (κοινῶς) to be the criterion (91). Sextus immediately passed to the Pythagoreans, who occupy 92–109. They denied (92) that it was reason in general (κοινῶς) that was the criterion, but τὸν ἀπὸ τῶν μαθημάτων γενόμενον, 'as Philolaus too kept saying, and they say that since it (i.e. reason) is contemplative (θεωρητικόν) of the nature of all that there is (τῆς τῶν ὅλων φύσεως), it has a kind of kinship (τινὰ συγγένειαν) with that, since like is naturally grasped (καταλαμβάνεσθαι) by like'. This is illustrated by quoting Empedocles F109 DK, without acknowledgement (92). The Posidonian fragment follows immediately. Then Sextus passes at once to the point that since the principle (ἀρχή) of the structure τῶν ὅλων is number (ἀριθμός), so the *logos* that is the criterion τῶν πάντων could be called number. This is clearly (cf. 94) continued Pythagorean exposition. The analogical argument from Plato's *Tim.* recurs in the later section on Plato (119), but with a different Platonic conclusion, and no reference to Posidonius.

COMMENT

A. Title

τὸν Πλάτωνος Τίμαιον ἐξηγούμενος. Fabricius assumed that this indicated a book, Ἐξήγησις τ. Πλατ. Τιμ., and Bake (*Posidonii Rhodii Reliquiae Doctrinae* 238) adopted the title. This view held sway until it was attacked in detail by Reinhardt,

Poseidonios 416ff. The immediate subsequent debate (1926–34) was reviewed by Schroeder, *Galeni in Plat. Tim. Comm. Frag., CMG, Suppl.* I (1934), but Reinhardt's denial has been generally accepted (e.g. by Jaeger, Wilamowitz, Edelstein, Cherniss, Pohlenz, Laffranque, Theiler). Two types of later attempted defence may be illustrated by Taylor and Abel. Taylor, *Commentary on Plato's Timaeus*, 35 n. 1, argued that the whole section 89–140 of Sextus derived from a Stoic commentary on the *Tim.*, and from whom other than Posidonius, as indicated by 93. But this is challengeable all along the line; and even if Taylor's first premisses were granted, it would not follow that even a quite extensive Posidonian commentary on or interpretation of *Tim.* must come from a book with that title. Abel, *RhM* 107 (1964), 371ff, attempted to prove that ἐξηγούμενος is the equivalent of ἐν τῇ ἐξηγήσει. . . . But his parallels will not hold (cf. Theiler, II.404). ἐξηγούμενος can simply mean 'expounding'. Reinhardt was right; there is no sure evidence that Posidonius wrote a separate Commentary on *Tim.* Nor of course is there any evidence that he did not.

But the controversy over the book title is of minor importance. There is no doubt that Posidonius was particularly interested in *Tim.*, for surviving attested reference is frequent: Frs. 28, 31, 49, 141, 149, 205, 291. Also it is clear that this was not restricted to incidental reference, for F141 shows an example of extended exegesis not only involving scholarly interpretation of considerable detail, but active reinterpretation in the light of his own philosophy. But it is not easy to proceed further with any confidence. The form in which such commentary survived remains open to conjecture. It is still possible that Posidonius wrote some kind of extended commentary on *Tim.* or parts of it, for this seems to have been popular since Crantor (Dillon, *The Middle Platonists* 43), and about Posidonius' time, *Tim.* was a particularly restive and popular hobby horse; Eudorus of Alexandria, for example, seems to have published a commentary (Dillon, 116), not to mention Cicero's translation. But if so, Plutarch does not appear to have known it directly, for his information seems to come second-hand, possibly from Eudorus (F141 comm.). Also one reference at least (F28) comes from Περὶ ψυχῆς, and more could have been incorporated there, or elsewhere. Lasserre argued (*Accademia Toscana di Scienze e Lettere, Studi* 83 (1986), 71–127) that traces of an Epitome of a Posidonian Commentary may be found in PGen inv. 203. But his arguments are highly speculative.

B. Extent of fragment and influence

The minor question of form of transmission has been replaced by Reinhardt and Theiler with theories of the widespread influence of the content of Posidonius' commentary on subsequent thought, extending beyond the Timaeus literature (e.g. Reinhardt, *RE* 692). In particular, Reinhardt (*Kosmos und Sympathie* 188–92) constructed a vitalistic theory of sense perception for Posidonius from the supposed influence of this passage in Sextus on later passages in Galen, *De Plac.* (641ff M = 472ff De L; 625ff M = 460f De L) combined with Plotinus and Cic. *ND* II. This was attacked by Cherniss with material from Jones (*AJPh.* 54 (1933), 154ff). Reinhardt defended his theory of vision in detail adducing other passages such as Plu. *De Fac.* 922D in *RE* 726–33. Finally Theiler not only accepted Reinhardt's position, but elevated Galen, *De Plac.* 625.4–627.4 M (460.28–462.24 De L) and S.E. *Adv. Math.* VII.116–19 to the status of fragments (F395b, F462).

It is important first to estimate the extent of this fragment. Reinhardt appears to have assumed that it began with 92, the section which opens the account of the Pythagoreans and introduces Empedocles F109 DK as an illustration of like being apprehended by like (see Context above). Theiler actually begins his fragment (F461) in the middle of a sentence of 92: θεωρητικόν τε . . . 'and they (i.e. Pythagoreans) say that since it is contemplative . . .' (see Context). But there is nothing to indicate that this must be Posidonius. The general argument is continuous. The Pythagoreans limited the kind of reason as criterion (and 92 is itself linked to the preceding introductory sections, κοινῶς), on the principle of like being kin to and therefore apprehending like, compare Empedocles, and compare Posidonius on *Tim.* referring to the nature of the whole being apprehended by kindred reason. But applied to the Pythagoreans, this means that soul is ἀριθμός (see Context). Now the Posidonian interpretation of *Tim.* refers to his own philosophy. What follows continues with the Pythagoreans, for Posidonius did not hold either that the principle of the structure of things was number, nor that the soul was ἀριθμός. In the same way, it is perfectly natural in any account of the Pythagoreans on this topic to refer without benefit of Posidonius to Empedocles and the 'like to like' theory. The language of the half sentence before the Empedocles quotation would of course suit Posidonius, but it is hardly unique to him, and is just as much Pythagorean or common currency: for θεωρεῖν, cf. Philolaus, B 11 DK; for τῆς τῶν ὅλων φύσεως, D.L. VIII.34 (from Aristotle, *On the Pythagoreans*); συγγένεια in relation to ὅμοιον ὁμοίῳ goes back at least to Plato (e.g. *Prot.* 337d 1), and καταλαμβάνειν is hardly exclusively Stoic. On the link between *Tim.* and Empedocles on theory of vision: Taylor, *Commentary* 278–81 ('Plato is deliberately ascribing to Timaeus the theory of Empedocles'). Above all, explicit juxtaposition and connection of the Empedocles 'like by like' F109 with *Tim.* is traceable at least to Aristotle, both in connection with the psychogony and structure of soul in *Tim.* 35ab (Arist. *De An.* 404b 8ff), and for theory of vision, *Tim.* 45 (Arist. *De Sensu* 437b 11ff), and no doubt became commonplace in the *topos* of subsequent debate. So the mere juxtaposition of luminous organ of sight, airy organ of hearing etc, and Emp. F109 in Galen's theory of sense perception (*De Plac.* 460.28ff De L = F395b Theiler) is hardly conclusive evidence for Posidonius, especially since Galen himself explicitly refers both to

Plato (*De Plac.* 464.16ff De L). In fact, when Galen criticises the orthodox Stoic visual theory of βακτηρία, he does so with Aristotle's instantaneous ἀλλοίωσις (*De Plac.* 474 De L), not with Posidonius. Cherniss was surely right that Galen's theory was based on Plato, refined by Aristotle and his own better knowledge of the brains and nerves. Nor is the occurrence of terms such as φωτοειδές or αὐγοειδές a mark of Posidonian authorship. αὐγοειδές or the like in this context is widespread (and cf. *SVF* II.859f), and φωτοειδές in Plu. *QC* I.8.4, 626C is referred to Plato, and obviously is a common term in debate. Plu. *De Facie* is not evidence for Posidonius (Cherniss, Loeb *passim*), and Nemesius *De Nat. Hom.* 6–7 derives from Galen.

In other words there is no reason to extend the Posidonian fragment in the sense of information on Posidonian philosophy, beyond its immediate reference, and consequently the subsequent structure of Posidonian influence, as argued by Reinhardt, which depends on both 92 and 93, collapses. It would be more consistent to argue that the whole Pythagorean section, or indeed the whole historical section, 89–140 derives as a historical doxography from Posidonius (cf. Schmekel, *Die Philosophie der mittleren Stoa* 405ff; Taylor, *Commentary* 278–81; Burkert, *Lore and Science* 54ff; Mansfeld, *The Pseudo-Hippocratic Tract* Περὶ Ἑβδομάδων 66ff, 156ff). But apart from parallels in arithmology from such sources as Philo, Theo of Smyrna, and Anatolius, there is no more certain evidence for that than for a separate *Commentary on Timaeus* from ἐξηγούμενος. There would be severe difficulties in thinking that the whole section was orientated or coloured by Posidonius himself; in particular in the very paragraph (119) which Theiler prints as his F462, presumably because in that section on Plato the analogical argument based on *Tim.* is repeated (so also Burkert, 56 n. 19). But this cannot be the same as 93, because the *Tim.* is interpreted differently: although the premisses of the analogy are similar to 93, the conclusion is different: '. . . so the soul too must be incorporeal (ἀσώματος) in grasping (λαμβάνουσα) the incorporeal forms, like those in numbers (ἀριθμοῖς) and those in the limits of bodies'. This is no Posidonian reinterpretation, because although τὰ πέρατα τῶν σωμάτων is reminiscent of F141 (*q.v.*), he certainly did not believe the soul to be incorporeal, nor akin to incorporeal form whether in number or limit. Furthermore, Posidonius believed that mathematical limits existed in reality, not as intellectual concepts (Frs. 16, 92, 141), so the account in §§99–104 is equally inapposite.

C. Posidonius

So no peculiar or distinctive theory of visual perception, or sense perception in general can be derived for Posidonius from this fragment. The acceptance of the premisses of the analogy appears to show that he accepted what had come to be recognised as the Platonic theory of sense perception from *Tim.* The conclusion is reinterpretation shaped for his own philosophy (cf. F141). As ἡ τῶν ὅλων φύσις is for him λόγος or the divine active creative reason (cf. F5), so it is apprehended by the kindred reason in us: F187.6ff, τὸ μὴ κατὰ πᾶν ἕπεσθαι τῷ ἐν αὑτῷ δαίμονι συγγενεῖ τε ὄντι καὶ τὴν ὁμοίαν φύσιν ἔχοντι τῷ τὸν ὅλον κόσμον διοικοῦντι. Cf. also F186.13ff. It is tempting to identify this with the ὀρθὸς λόγος which Posidonius recorded as a κριτήριον held by the older Stoics, and perhaps by himself (F42). But if so, it should be noted that this apprehension or κατάληψις is *distinguished from* sensation in the argument, as being an analogy from it. Nevertheless, it does stress, however vaguely, the importance for him of ὀρθὸς λόγος in a theory of knowledge, as in other parts of his philosophy (Kidd, 'Posidonius and Logic' 273, 276; and 'Orthos Logos').

See also F291.

Baltes, *Philologus* 122 (1978), 183–96, discusses the history of the relationship of the elements to the senses, and argues that Posidonius' equation derives from the Old Academy.

F86a

An examination of Ps.-Plutarch *Pro Nobilitate* 18 (Bernardakis) reveals that the reference and quotations are from Aristotle's Περὶ εὐγενείας. The alleged discourse (διαλεγόμενον) of Posidonius with or to Tubero (πρὸς Τυβέρωνα) is too vague in content and uncertain in source to permit any hypothesis of a separate work. The details are discussed at T12.

F86b

A late collection of scholia (see F113) attribute to a Posidonius a work on τὸ παλμαστικόν (or παλμικόν), that is, divination or augury through involuntary twitching, as a subsection of οἰωνιστική. The Suda (T1a.15ff) assigns such a work to another undefined Posidonius. The Suda entry on Posidonius is extremely garbled, and Posidonius of Apamea with his strong interest in divination could have written on augury. But even if he did, the evidence for a book Περὶ οἰωνιστικῆς is flimsy, and such a book must remain no more than a possibility.

See F113.

F86c

Posidonius certainly knew Plato's *Phaedrus* well, and indeed embedded a reinterpretation of the Platonic charioteer and horses simile (*Phdr.* 246a 6ff) into his own psychology (F31). Two surviving passages (F24, F290) smack of straight exegesis, and so have roused suspicions of a Commentary on the *Phaedrus* (e.g. by Zeller, III.1.599 n. 3). But at least one of these fragments (F24) comes from another book, and so too may the other, more puzzling passage (F290). There is no evidence that Posidonius wrote a separate Commentary.

F86d

The reference to 'the philosopher from Rhodes' (ὁ ἐκ Ῥόδου φιλόσοφος) in Proclus' *Commentary on the Parmenides* VI T.vi,25 (p. 25 Cousin) led Zeller to speculate (III.1^{6}.581 n. 1, 599 n. 3) whether Posidonius or Panaetius had written a commentary on *Parmenides*. The reference is far too vague to permit any such speculation. Proclus, *In Tim.* I.20.2, 85.28 Diehl, cites Aristocles of Rhodes, presumably the contemporary of Strabo (XIV.2.13), for comments on Plato. See Wenzel, *RE* II.935f; Usener, *RhM* 25.614; 28.433. But Aristocles' remarks are those of a grammaticus, not a philosopher. The comments from 'the philosopher from Rhodes', whoever he was, were certainly of a philosophical nature. Posidonius (or Panaetius) may indeed have commented on *Parm.* (although no other reference to the dialogue survives in the fragments); but there is no evidence whatsoever that he wrote a Commentary on it.

F86e

Because of the Posidonian references to the famous M. Claudius Marcellus of the later 3rd c. B.C., the conqueror of Syracuse, in Plutarch's *Life*, and because these events lay well outside the chronological scope of Posidonius' *History*, it has been argued that Posidonius wrote a separate monograph on Marcellus (Toepelmann, *De Posidonio* 39; Mueller, *FHG* III.270; Wilamowitz, *Glaube der Hellenen* II.403). Jacoby (*Kommentar* 189–90) accepted that this was an open possibility, but inclined to a special excursus or appendix to the *History*. Malitz (361f) adopts much the same position. Reinhardt (*RE* 569) and Theiler (II.89f) were more sceptical.

There is really no evidence for such a monograph, of which there is nowhere mention. Of the four references in Plutarch, *Marc.*, the longest is a graphic story of Nicias of Engyium in which the mention of Marcellus is of minor importance (F257 comm.); the second ventures comment on the name Marcellus (F261), in line with Posidonius' known general interest in Roman proper names (F264); another merely offers the nickname of Marcellus as the Sword of Rome (F259); and the last records the inscription on his statue at Lindos in Rhodes (F258). The Posidonian derivation of other elements in Plutarch's *Life*, such as the death of Archimedes (Gigon, *Romanitas et Christianitas* 162ff) are problematical and unproven (Theiler, II.90). This is not enough to assume a special monograph on Marcellus (or Marcelli), whether in 51 B.C. (T1a, F258 comm.) or at some other time, nor even for an extended excursus or appendix in the *History*.

Posidonius, because of the Marcellan connection with Rhodes (F258), or because of his personal acquaintance with contemporary leading members of the family (F258 comm.), may have derived from them information about their famous ancestors, particularly with regard to Sicily and Spain, and may even have attempted to correct in passing the more hostile tradition against them stemming from Polybius (F271 comm.). But such incidental remarks could easily have been incorporated into his accounts of Spain (F271 comm.; Theiler, II.89) and Sicily (F257 comm.).

PART III

FRAGMENTS NOT ASSIGNED TO BOOKS

DIVISIONS AND CONTENT OF PHILOSOPHY

F87 Diogenes Laertius, VII.39

CONTENT

Divisions of philosophy.

CONTEXT

At the beginning of Diogenes' general (ἐπὶ κεφαλαίων) exposition of Stoic doctrines, after his biographical introduction. It is followed by the similes of philosophy and its parts (F88).

COMMENT

1 φησιν *B* is not impossible. In §38 Diogenes made specific reference to Zeno for what is to follow; but the following sections adopt plurals so *PF* are probably right.

4 **τῇ**: so exactly Frs 42.3, 5.7, 6.2, 13.2, 20.5, 12.4 (sometimes without any article: Frs. 39.4, 40.3, 4.4, 16.2, 6.4, 13.3, 99a.2, 20.2, 25.2, 3); and cf. F44.1 (ἐν τῇ Περὶ λέξεως εἰσαγωγῇ); στοιχειώσει: Fr 14.

εἰσαγωγῶν: introduction. Could all of these instances refer to more elementary or popular works?

5 **ὁ Ἔφιλλος**: The reading remains uncertain: Crönert, *Kolotes und Menedemos* 80, n. 395; Zeller, III.1.48, n. 2; Pohlenz, *Die Stoa* II.91; v. Arnim, *RE* I, col. 2894f; *SVF* III, Apollod.; Pease, *Cic. ND*, p. 455; Traversa, *Index Stoicorum Herculanensis*, Genoa, 1952, 69f, 75f. It seems dangerous to base too much on

Cic. *ND* I.93, where the reading is also quite uncertain: *Zeno* (the Epicurean) *quidem non eos solum qui tum erant, Apollodorum* †*sillim* (*A*; silum *C*: sillum *NO*: sive *dett.*) *ceteros, figebat maledictis* ... The cast of Cicero's sentence would suggest that the name concealed by sillim refers to a person different from the preceding Apollodorus. Cicero's Apollodorus may not be the same as Diogenes'. The latter was almost certainly Apollodorus of Seleuceia on the Tigris, the pupil of Diogenes of Babylon (D.L. *Epitome*, Διογένης· Ἀπολλόδωρος· Βοήθος· Μνησαρχίδης· Μνησαγόρας· Νέστωρ· Βασιλείδης· Δάρδανος· Ἀντίπατρος . . .; cf. Traversa, *Ind. Stoic. Herc.* col. LI, where he again appears as a pupil of Diogenes immediately before Boethus). He is thus rather early to be classed by Cicero as a rough contemporary of Zeno the Epicurean. Cicero may be referring to the Stoic, Apollodorus of Athens, who was a pupil of Antipater (*Ind. Stoic. Herc.* col. LIII; v. Arnim *RE* I, col. 2895).

If there was more than one Apollodorus (and the name was common), ὁ Ἔφιλλος could be a nickname, perhaps derived from some eye defect; cf. ἔπιλλος, ἔφηλος.

Diogenes' list in this fragment is not in chronological order, since Diogenes of Babylon should appear before Apollodorus and Eudromus, but authors whose books are cited are named first (but cf. F89).

Tripartition

Tripartition of philosophy became a commonplace in hellenistic philosophy. A general survey of ancient classifications of philosophy is given by S.E. *Adv. Math.* VII.2–23 (F88) and Seneca, *Ep.* 89.9ff. Sextus sees an implicit tripartition in Plato (cf. Zeller, II.1.583ff; so also Cic. *Acad.* I.19, *fuit ergo iam accepta a Platone*); cf. Atticus F1 (Eus. *Praep. Evang.* XI.508d–510a), Baudry (Paris, 1931), Des Places (Paris, 1977). In D.L. VIII.6 there is a kind of tripartition for Pythagoras, who is reported to have written συγγράμματα τρία, παιδευτικόν, πολιτικόν, φυσικόν. The tradition continues that those three books were bought by Plato (Iambl. *Vit. Pyth.* 199; D.L. III.9; VIII.84; Burkert, *Weisheit und Wissenschaft* 209). Sextus, however, expressly singles out Xenocrates, the Peripatetics and the Stoics for the tripartition. For Xenocrates: Heinze, *Xen.*, p. 1; Ueberweg-Flashar III.46f; Zeller, II.1.1011, 3. Cicero, *De Fin.* IV.4, suggests that Zeno adopted the tripartition from *veteres Academici*. Chrysippus (Plu. *De SR, SVF* II.42) assigned it to οἱ ἀρχαῖοι. It is noticeable that Sextus immediately elaborates on Stoic similes (F88). The evidence for Zeno and the early Academy is strongest in the ancient evidence; but no doubt such analyses were discussed contemporaneously in all the Schools. The tripartition is already in Aristotle, *Top.* A14, 105b 19–25. For Stoics, also Aetius, *Plac.* I Prooem. 2 (*Dox. Gr.* 273, 11ff, *SVF* II.35). Ariston of Chios was thought to deviate from Stoic practice by dismissing physics and logic (Sen. *Ep.* 89.13; S.E. *Adv. Math.* VII.12); in this he was compared with Cynics (D.L. VI.103; *SVF* I.354ff).

The expression, τὸν κατὰ φιλοσοφίαν λόγον (1) has a parallel in Cic. *Acad.* I.19: *philosophandi ratio triplex*. Cleanthes, who is noticeably missing from this list, is said in D.L. VII.41 to have named six parts (dialectic, rhetoric, ethics, politics, physics, theology); Diogenes adds: ἄλλοι δ' οὐ τοῦ λόγου ταῦτα μέρη φασίν, ἀλλ' αὐτῆς τῆς φιλοσοφίας, ὡς Ζήνων ὁ Ταρσεύς.

What did Posidonius call the divisions? Possibly γένη, although Diogenes writes ἄλλοι, not οἱ ἄλλοι. Almost certainly not εἴδη like Chrysippus, nor μέρη. As he refused these terms for faculties of soul (Frs. 145, 146), he is not likely to have applied them to philosophy, when he was so much concerned to represent the divisions as being ἀχώριστα and organically related (F88) (in spite of Sextus' μέρη at F88.12).

The divisions were again sub-divided. See F89 for ethics and physics. Posidonius is not mentioned specifically for a subdivision of logic.

The doxography may have come from Posidonius, T101/102 comm.

F88 Sextus Empiricus, *Adv. Mathematicos* VII.16–19

CONTENT

Posidonius' simile for philosophy and its divisions.

CONTEXT

Chs. 1–26 discuss briefly views on the parts of philosophy, their relative importance and teaching order.

COMMENT

A similar ȝῷον comparison occurs in D.L. VII.40, but there ethics (τοῖς σαρκωδεστέροις) and physics (τῇ ψυχῇ) have changed places. The Diogenes simile is introduced only by εἰκάȝουσι (sc. οἱ Στωϊκοί), and therefore we have no right to emend Diogenes to agree with the passage from Sextus as Bake (p. 40) does. Diogenes also gives the egg simile and a field simile comparable to Sextus' παγκάρπῳ ἀλωῇ. The field appears again in Philo (*SVF* II.39), and, this time as a vineyard, in Origenes (*SVF* II.40).

Clearly the field simile was the most common one before Posidonius, and the most important evidence for his own philosophy is his criticism of his predecessors for giving the impression that the parts of philosophy were separable, and not organically related. Walls are certainly separate from plants (κεχώρισται) and plants, at least theoretically (θεωρεῖται) from fruit. The words are carefully chosen, and the criticism seems to me likely to derive from Posidonius, not from Sextus (as Heinemann believed).

The egg simile which occurs immediately before Posidonius in Sextus raises problems. It seems an organic simile itself, and is in fact entirely ignored by Posidonius' criticism. Perhaps it was not a simile employed by the old Stoa, but was even later than Posidonius (Zeller, III.1.64 n. 1 against Ritter, III.432). It is not mentioned by Philo, but that proves nothing. His field simile comes naturally enough in his *De Agric.* (but also in *De Mut. Nom.* 74). On the other hand an egg may not have satisfied Posidonius. In particular, logic as the shell, was too similar to the wall of the field; and in criticism it is not surprising if he specifically attacked the more vulnerable simile.

For Posidonius' use of the ζῷον idea in general, see Rudberg, *Forschungen zu Poseidonios* 172ff. The specific point made in this passage is the organic relationship of the three parts of philosophy, and not an account of their relative value or importance, as Zeller (III.1.598) suggested, arguing for the pre-eminence of ethics in Posidonius' philosophy. But we should avoid value judgements here. So D.L. VII.40: . . . καὶ οὐθὲν μέρος τοῦ ἑτέρου προκεκρίσθαι (ἀποκεκρίσθαι Cobet) . . . ἀλλὰ μεμῖχθαι αὐτά.

Perhaps Posidonius was also saying something about the relative *function* of the different parts of philosophy; so, no doubt, Heinemann, *Poseidonios' Metaphysische Schriften* II.483, referring to ethics as 'das einigende Band des Systems'. Soul was not only a unifying factor, but indeed was what holds body together (F149); it is the source of movement (F139; a common idea, of course: Arist. *De An.* Bk I); in F21 Posidonius allies himself with the common Stoic doctrine that psyche is the human counterpart of the organising cosmic nous. But how all this would relate to the function of ethics is not clear; nor is the function of physics as blood and flesh; indeed, it is doubtful whether it was clear to the ancient commentators, since Diogenes reverses the roles of ethics and physics not only in the organism simile, but also in the egg simile.

It is more interesting to turn to logic. It is certain that

Posidonius was trying to avoid the view that logic was merely a defensive mechanism, as might have been assumed from the wall comparison in the field simile. He stresses that it is an organic part of philosophy like the other two divisions. Therefore it should not merely be thought of as an organon (as by Aristotle and the Epicureans). What then is its function? The image of bones and sinews seems a dynamic one; they are operational equipment for the movement and functioning of the organism. They are in fact commonly connected with movement: Pl. *Ph.* 98–9; cf. *Laws* 644e: ζῷα as puppets of the gods, ταῦτα τὰ πάθη ἐν ἡμῖν οἷον νεῦρα ἢ μήρινθοί τινες ἐνοῦσαι σπῶσί τε ἡμᾶς. . . . They also help to maintain the posture and condition of the organism; if they collapse, so will the ζῷον (Pl. *Tim.* 84eff; and perhaps *Laws* 945c).

It follows that logic was of great importance for Posidonius' whole system of philosophy, and that Reinhardt, for example, was wrong to ignore it. I have developed the question of what might be meant by an organic Posidonian logic in 'Posidonius and Logic' (*Les Stoïciens et leur logique*). Faust, in his good exposition of the organic role of Stoic logic in *Der Möglichkeitsgedanke*, vol. I.243–9, especially p. 247 (*Synthesis* Band VI, Heidelberg 1931), presents it simply as Stoic opposed to Peripatetic and Epicurean logic; and this may be generally so. Again Ammonius (*In Arist. Anal. Pr.* p. 8.20ff Wal = *SVF* II.49) names no names when criticising Stoic logic for being a part of philosophy rather than an organon as with the Peripatetics. This may refer to a period earlier than Posidonius, in which case, as elsewhere, Posidonius would be enlarging and deepening an idea which had already occurred in the Stoa; but it may very well reflect later debate sharpened by Posidonius' simile. If the simile is to be taken seriously, it was Posidonius who stressed this role of logic, which is reflected in the aetiological methodology which permeates the whole of his philosophy. It is all the more infuriating that so little has survived on logic from Posidonius. But if the details are now lost, there is revealed a new relationship between philosophy, logic and the sciences. For Posidonius logic is no longer the organon, but an organic part of philosophy; it is the sciences which are the tools for the philosopher, the organa for his philosophy. For this see Kidd, *A & A* 7ff.

F89 Diogenes Laertius, VII.84

CONTENT

Subdivisions of ethics.

CONTEXT

Unlike Zeno and Cleanthes, the older Stoics, Posidonius, whose name occurs at the end of a named list of Stoics beginning with Chrysippus, subdivided the ethical part of philosophy as follows: (1) impulse, (2) good and evil, (3) emotions, (4) virtue, (5) end, (6) first value, (7) actions, (8) appropriate acts, (9) exhortations and dissuasions. Chrysippus and the Stoics named after him also subdivided logic and physics. The passage begins immediately after Diogenes' account of Stoic logic, and is followed directly by his exposition of ethics, beginning with ὁρμή.

COMMENT

Zeller, III.1.210 n. 1, and Dyroff, *Die Ethik der alten Stoa* 1–15, wished to punctuate after παθῶν (3), to indicate that the last six items on the list should be regarded as subdivisions of the first three. They thus distinguished between διαιροῦσιν (1) and ὑποδιαιροῦσιν (5), and between the form εἰς τὸν τόπον introducing the first three items, and περί used thereafter. Zeller held that it remained quite uncertain how then the subdivisions should be related to the three main divisions.

Dyroff argued that if items (4) and (5) were subclassified under (1), and items (6), (7) and (8) under (2), this order would foreshadow exactly Diogenes' order of presentation of Stoic ethics that follows at 85ff (Dyroff, 7). He also maintained that it made sense of the use of τε and καί in the passage.

Such an interpretation raises two main difficulties. It appears to me (as it seems to have appeared to Zeller) factually not to make much sense.

A developed presentation, which is what follows in Diogenes, is a quite different thing from a logical classification of the main and subordinate topics in Stoic ethics. In the case of the latter, to make ἀρετή and τέλος subdivisions of ὁρμή would be an oddity, and indeed in general I think that Zeller's instinct was right to find no relationship for the last six items as subheadings.

In the second place, I cannot see how the suggested interpretation can be derived from the Greek, with or without the spurious help of punctuation. οὕτω δ' ὑποδιαιροῦσιν (5) must refer to all that has gone before; therefore it takes up διαιροῦσιν (1) by reminding the reader that the ethical divisions are in fact subdivisions of one of the divisions of philosophy as listed at VII.39 (F87). The variation in the presentation of the long nine-item list in the first sentence does not seem to me surprising. If Diogenes meant what Dyroff suggests, he was not merely writing badly, he was not writing grammatical Greek. He could distinguish clearly enough, when he wished, between generic and specific division (VII.132).

Nor is Dyroff's classification borne out by other evidence. The tripartition in Epictetus III.2.1ff is different: (1) ὁ περὶ τὰς ὀρέξεις καὶ τὰς ἐκκλίσεις (τόπος) (which includes πάθη); (2) ὁ περὶ τὰς ὁρμὰς καὶ ἀφορμὰς καὶ ἁπλῶς ὁ περὶ τὸ καθῆκον; (3) ὁ περὶ τὴν ἀνεξαπατησίαν καὶ ἀνεικαιότητα καὶ ὅλως ὁ περὶ τὰς συγκαταθέσεις.

The order followed by Arius Didymus in Stob. *Ecl.* II.57–

116 W, τὰ κεφάλαια τῶν ἀναγκαίων δογμάτων ἀναλαβών, is again dissimilar. Nor can I agree with Dyroff that Cicero's presentation at *De Fin.* III.16ff is in many ways similar (cf. Hirzel, *Untersuchungen zu Ciceros Philosophischen Schriften* II.568ff). Even Diogenes' own classification of Chrysippus' ethical books (as far as it goes, which is not far) does not fit.

I therefore take Diogenes' list simply as a list of ethical subdivisions; and in view of the variety of the other evidence, and the badly written character of the paragraph as a whole, I would not put too much weight on the passage as exclusive and accurate evidence.

To whom does οὗτοι (11) refer? At first sight to Zeno and Cleanthes; but the μέν (9)/δέ antithesis presumably refers οὗτοι to the preceding list beginning with Chrysippus. If so, is Posidonius still included? If he is, he also subdivided (as one would expect) logic and physics. Diogenes gives such subdivisions at VII.41 (logic), and at VII.132 (physics), but names no names in either passage, so that we know no details. If οὗτοι refers to the list of names from Chrysippus to Posidonius, but not to Zeno and Cleanthes, did the latter two not subdivide logic and physics at all, or merely in a simpler fashion than the later Stoics? And does the previous phrase applied to Zeno and Cleanthes, ἀφελέστερον περὶ τῶν πραγμάτων διέλαβον, mean that they divided ethics more simply, or that they had simpler classifications of philosophy in general? For example, Diogenes says (out of context) in VII.41, that Cleanthes said that there were six parts: dialectic, rhetoric, ethics, politics, physics, theology. One can only, once again, deplore the vagueness of Diogenes' evidence. The ambiguity of οὗτοι, rather than indifferent eyesight, may have led *F* to write οὕτω instead. But οὕτω does not really make sense.

Seneca, *Ep.* 95.65–7 (F176) offers another classification for Posidonian ethics: *praeceptio*, *suasio*, *consolatio*, *exhortatio*, *causarum inquisitio* (*aetiologia*), *ethologia*. But we should regard these as methodological concepts different in kind from the subjects of ethics given by Diogenes.

It is particularly infuriating that Diogenes was not more precise when dealing with the corresponding passage on the subdivisions of physics at VII.132–3, which have a strong Posidonian flavour. The division into species gives prominence to limits (πέρατα) which is Posidonian (Frs. 16, 196). The triple generic classification includes ὁ αἰτιολογικὸς τόπος (T85, Frs. 18, 176), and its subdivision (133) is also markedly Posidonian. The subject of κόσμος is subdivided into topics for physical philosophers and scientists, which is precisely the Posidonian division of F18, and all are covered in Diogenes' following detailed section on the universe with specific reference to Posidonius. But Diogenes' account of Stoic logic, ethics and physics appears to have quite different origins (T66 comm.).

Giusta, *I Dossographi di Etica* (Turin, 1964, vol. I), argued for a common source for D.L. VII.84–116, Cic. *De Fin.* III. 16–59, and Arius Didymus (Stob. *Ecl.* II.57–116 W). This hypothetical common source, a body of *vetusta placita* for ethics comparable to the *vetusta placita* for physics so plausibly established by Diels (*Dox. Gr.*), Giusta thought comprised a collection of δόξαι for all the Schools presented by topic. Giusta further argued that the collector was Didymus himself, and that the classification is also apparent in that of Eudorus, the Academic of Alexandria, given in Stob. *Ecl.* II.42ff. Giusta tabled his supposed order of Topics (p. 150) as: (1) Introduction: definition of ethics and its fundamental terms, together with the parts of ethics; (2) τέλος, including οἰκείωσις on the one hand, and εὐδαιμονία on the other; (3) virtues and vices; (4) ἀγαθά and κακά; (5) καθῆκον; (6) ὁρμή; (7) πάθη. While Giusta reveals some broad affinities of treatment in the different presentations, he fails in my opinion to show anything like the concurrence of detail required to substantiate his thesis (so also Kerferd, *CR* 17 (1967), 156ff; Boyancé, *Latomus* 26 (1967), 246ff). In any case his master order of ethical presentation hardly corresponds to the ethical classification of D.L. VII.84, a passage which Giusta did not examine in great detail (p. 215).

S.E. *Adv. Math.* VII.12 gives a classification by Ariston of Chios.

10 ἀρχαιότεροι: cf. F42.

F90 Seneca, *Epistulae* 88. 21–8

CONTENT

A division of *artes* and their relation to philosophy.

CONTEXT

The general context of this Letter is to distinguish philosophy and goodness from learning and erudition, the 'liberal arts'. Seneca earlier contrasts with the philosopher the grammaticus (§3), the musicus (§9), mathematician (§10), and astronomer (§14). He debars (§18) even from this company the painter, sculptor and physical trainer. So, he argues (§20), the 'liberal arts' contribute *ad instrumenta vitae*, but not to virtue. They prepare the soul for the reception of virtue. As the primary course in grammar prepares the way for the 'liberal arts', so in their turn the 'liberal arts' prepare and set the soul going in the direction of virtue.

COMMENT

The meaning of the fragment has been disputed, so an analysis of what is said is necessary; cf. also Stückelberger, *Senecas 88 Brief*.

§§**21–3** Posidonius distinguishes four *artes* (τέχναι). Each is in turn identified, and in the case of the first three, the limitations of each are added.

(1) *vulgares et sordidae* (βαναυσοι?, βαναυσικαί?); defined

as manual work of artisans, for equipping us with the necessities of life. Limitations: *nulla decoris, nulla honesti simulatio* (i.e. no moral pretensions).

(2) *ludicrae* (θεατρικαί?; γλαφυραί, Theiler, II.383); these are aimed at the pleasure of eye and ear; exampled by mechanical coups d'oeil or coups de théâtre. Limitation: they depend for their effect on not knowing causes.

(3) *pueriles* (παιδικαί? cf. παιδικὰ μαθήματα, Plb. 9.26a 4 referring to sciences) identified as what the Greeks call ἐγκύκλιοι, Romans *liberales*. The limitation implied is: *aliquid habentes liberalibus simile*.

(4) *liberales* (ἐλευθεραί?) defined as those whose concern is virtue. Seneca adds that he would more truly name them *liberae*.

It is vital to understand what Posidonius meant to include under these four headings, but in particular the content of the last two. There is no guarantee that the comments derive from Posidonius, or whether they are Seneca's, but if the latter they are presumably intended to clarify what Posidonius intended. The last two sections make no sense unless this is the case.

The first group raises no problems. Its contents are clear from the description. The terms of valuation are common from at least Aristotle; the limitation, that they have nothing to do with morality, not only fits in with Seneca's thesis (Reinhardt, *Poseidonios* 50), but with Posidonius' classification, which is presumably why Seneca chose it.

The second class is more vague; Spiel- und Luxuskünste (Reinhardt), the Fine Arts (Edelstein, in a note); both thinking of the earlier passage in Seneca's argument (§18), where he refuses to include (as was usual at the time) among the 'liberal arts', *pictores . . . non magis quam statuarios aut marmarios aut ceteros luxuriae ministros*, later characterised as *voluptatibus nostris ingenia accommodantes sua*. But if so, the examples of mechanical theatrical devices are odd. Reinhardt thinks this is Seneca again, but it neither fits in particularly with his previous argument, nor was Posidonius uninterested in technical inventions (F284). Perhaps we should not be too precise here. Like the Line in *Rep.* VI, this classification is clearly of ascending order, of which the lower items for the most part clarify the higher. The two details of significance are what distinguishes these τέχναι from philosophy: (1) that their object is to delight the senses, and (2) that they do not know causes. The commonly accepted view of the next two sections was put first by Reinhardt (*Poseidonios* 50), and apparently followed by Pohlenz (*Die Stoa* II.105), and by Laffranque (p. 363). According to Reinhardt, the third section refers to 'die Kunste des Unterrichts und der Erziehung' ('technique intellectuelle élémentaire', Laffranque), 'endlich die vierte Art: – doch die bleibt ungenannt.... Was ursprunglich dastand, kann jedoch kein Zweifel sein: genannt waren die Fachwissenschaften, Geometrie, Astronomie, Medizin, usw.' This cannot be the case. The third section is quite clearly identified as ἐγκύκλιοι in Greek and *liberales artes* in Latin. For the ἐγκύκλιος παιδεία see Marrou, *Histoire de l'Éducation dans l'Antiquité*[6], 266ff. While the contours of this term for 'general education' remained vague, the main items included under it did not, especially at the time of our reference. The variable items sometimes included medicine, architecture, law, military science (Marrou[6], 569, nn. 4 and 5), but the mainstay of this educational system was what became in the Middle Ages the Seven Liberal Arts (Trivium: grammar, rhetoric, dialectic; Quadrivium: geometry, arithmetic, astronomy, music). Marrou argues that these contents probably hardened in the middle of the 1st c. B.C., between Dionysius Thrax and Varro. Reinhardt's 'Fachwissenschaften' and Laffranque's 'les mathématiques' have their natural home in the third, not the fourth section. This also *must* be the case in the context of this letter. What Posidonius named *pueriles artes, nostri*, says Seneca, *autem liberales vocant*. But Seneca's own argument up to the point of the mention of Posidonius was to attack the 'liberal arts' in relation to philosophy. The letter begins *de liberalibus studiis*, and included under this label for attack are the mathematician (§10) and the astronomer (§14). Some of the confusion has arisen because Seneca and Posidonius use *liberales artes* to designate different things. Posidonius' use is the peculiar one; Seneca, since he was writing for a Roman audience, employs the normal (*nostri*) designation; but in commenting on Posidonius' term *pueriles*, he clarifies exactly what is meant by this (what is normally called 'liberal arts'). At the beginning of the letter (§2) he even looks forward to Posidonius' terminology, where he remarks that all other *studia*, apart from *sapientia* (i.e. philosophy, *studium* VERE *liberale*) are *pusilla et puerilia*. When Seneca writes *pueriles . . . aliquid habentes liberalibus simile*, here *liberalibus* must of course refer to the Posidonian use; so this must be following Posidonius' statement – it is not Seneca's comment.

What then are the *artes liberales*, so called by Posidonius, of the fourth group? The only clue we have is: *quibus curae virtus est*. This in itself shuts out the sciences, which could never be so classified. What follows in Seneca indicates that Posidonius meant philosophy.

§§**24–8** An objection is put forward (*inquit*, 16). The subject cannot be Posidonius, as Susemihl, *Geschichte der griechischen Literatur* II.135, 179 suggested, as the sense shows. In any case, *inquit* is a common feature of Seneca's style, when he wishes to raise an objection (F170.13). The objection is: should not the 'liberal arts' join physics, ethics and logic as a part of philosophy? In natural philosophy, a decision is taken on the evidence of the mathematician. So mathematics is a part of what it helps. *Liberalium* here is used in the current Roman sense, which would indicate that the objection does not come from Posidonius, but is brought forward by Seneca. The counter-argument maintains with examples that what helps something is not a part of that thing. It includes a ζῷον simile, food as an aid to the body, which might be Posidonian. One should note that this argument depends on the assumption that mathematics does help philosophy, which in any case is explicitly stated by Seneca. §26 distinguishes the fields of the natural philosopher (*qua* φυσικός) and the mathematician (or scientist) in terms which when compared with Geminus' report of Posidonius (F18), can leave no doubt that Posidonius is the source. This is followed by a further differentiation between the competence of philosopher and mathematician on mirrors which another fragment (F134.55ff) indicates is still Posidonius. §28 contains Roman legal terminology (and therefore probably Seneca), but the conclusion follows from the preceding (Posidonian) arguments that there is no other *ars* of morals than *scientia bonorum ac malorum inmutabili*. This must be referred back to Posidonius' *artes liberales*. It is difficult to know whether the terms here are Posidonian or Senecan, since Posidonius' arguments refer more to the φυσικός than to the ethical philosopher. However that is more natural when dealing with the relation between philosophy and science. F88 would indicate that for the art of philosophy, Posidonius would wish to include all three organically related parts, physics, logic and ethics, even when he had in mind a master art of ethics (and this would be Stoic in any case, as Chrysippus is said to have preceded ethical questions with physics (Plu. *De SR*)). It would not have been unnatural for Posidonius so to characterise his *liberales*, since the context of the classification is so clearly ethical.

It should be clear from the analysis that the reply given in Seneca to the objector is in line with, and may possibly be derived from, Posidonius' arguments attested elsewhere. It is therefore false to take this passage as Seneca's criticism of Posidonius, which is what Reinhardt maintained (*Poseidonios* 549ff), a view derived from his misconception of the classification of arts.

Seneca then goes on in §§29–35 to develop a similar argument in the purely ethical field as to the relationship between the 'liberal arts' (in the commonly accepted use of the terms) and philosophy, parallel to the physical arguments just used. It is possible that these arguments too may be in agreement with statements of Posidonius; they are certainly within the same context as what has already been said. But we have no evidence that this is Posidonius as distinct from Seneca. Reinhardt in *RE* 645–6 also adduces D.L. VII.132–3 and Strabo, II.5.2. These passages deserve consideration in this context, although there is no indication in either of a Posidonian source.

The philosophical Schools debated the educational position of the sciences of the ἐγκύκλιος παιδεία. Some regarded them as propaedeutic (like Plato); others denounced them as useless, as Epicurus (D.L. x.6), the Cynics and the Sceptics. Stoics differed on the question, and sometimes an individual Stoic changed his mind, as Zeno, who in his Cynic *Republic* days rejected such studies (D.L. VII.32 = *SVF* I.259), but later granted light from μαθήματα (floril. Monacense; Bonhöffer, *Die Ethik des Stoikers Epictet* 127 n. 10). Ariston of Chios sneered at those engaging in them, comparing them to the suitors making do with the servant girls when they couldn't have Penelope (*SVF* I.349–50). On the other hand, Chrysippus granted that τὰ ἐγκύκλια μαθήματα rendered a service (εὐχρηστεῖν) (D.L. VII.129 = *SVF* III.738).

There is little doubt that Posidonius was particularly interested in the relationship betwen the sciences and philosophy. Stoicism, as a study of an organic material cosmos, had always had a fundamental interest in natural philosophy, in the sense of the φυσικὸς τόπος of philosophy. But Posidonius, more than any other Stoic, seems to have been aware of the assistance the sciences could give to that part of philosophy. Sometimes, apparently, he is prepared to emphasise the indispensability of this assistance (especially, F134.57–60; but even in Sen. *Ep*. 88.25: *necessaria*). Because philosophy and the sciences were so much alike in some respects (*aliquid habentes liberalibus simile*, F90.13; cf. F18), it was all the more important to clarify their essential difference, which is what happens in Frs. 90 and 18. It remained true for Posidonius as for Plato, that the sciences relied on philosophy to supply their ἀρχαί, but the philosopher necessarily used them as tools, as the mathematician used necessarily the instruments made by the carpenter (F90.24f). Perhaps we can say that as Posidonius exalted logic, the organon of Aristotle, to be an integral part of philosophy (F88 comm.), he made the sciences the 'tools' of philosophy (*ad instrumenta vitae*, Sen. *Ep.* 88.20). This has been discussed at greater length by Kidd, 'Philosophy and Science in Posidonius', *A & A* 24 (1978), 7–15.

F91 Diogenes Laertius, VII.40–1

CONTENT

Order of teaching.

CONTEXT

Preceded by similes on the relationship between the three parts of philosophy (F88); followed by a remark on a six-fold classification by Cleanthes.

COMMENT

As some Stoics say, no part of philosophy is preferred to another; they are mixed up. And they would teach them mixed up. But others arrange them: logic, physics, ethics (Zeno, Chrysippus, Archedemus, Eudromus). Diogenes Ptolemaeus put ethics first, Apollodorus put ethics second, and Panaetius and Posidonius begin with physics.

The writing is unclear. In line 1, προκεκρίσθαι of the codices (which should be kept, Kidd, 'Posidonius and Logic' 274), means that no part is preferred to another, but all are mixed up. But from relative value, Diogenes passes to order of teaching (παράδοσιν, 2), and this is confirmed by the language of 7–11.

Who are τινες of line 2? One would have imagined that the idea behind it was especially applicable to Posidonius (F88 comm.); this is not countered by line 9, since we have passed from relative value to teaching order.

It is not clear what order Posidonius followed after physics. If we could trust Diogenes, the implication would be that, as Apollodorus is singled out as putting ethics second (instead of in the usual third place), Posidonius continued with logic, ethics.

But we cannot trust Diogenes. S.E. *Adv. Math.* VII.22–3 has: οἱ δὲ ἀπὸ τῆς Στοᾶς καὶ αὐτοὶ ἄρχειν μέν φασι τὰ λογικά, δευτερεύειν δὲ τὰ ἠθικά, τελευταῖα δὲ τετάχθαι τὰ φυσικά.

The context in Sextus is order of teaching. Moreover, Sextus goes on to give the Stoics' reasons for that order.

In Plutarch, *De SR*, ch. 9, *Mor.* 1035A, Chrysippus is said to have recommended the teaching order: logic, ethics, physics, and Plutarch quotes a passage from Chrysippus' Περὶ βίων, Bk 4 to this effect. It should also be remembered that Sextus and Diogenes differed over the order of physics and ethics in the similes (F88).

Genuine confusion or misunderstandings could arise. For example, Plutarch goes on (1035Bff) to accuse Chrysippus of inconsistency when he maintained that all ethical questions have their ἀρχή in physics; and again (1035E), Plutarch alludes to a statement of Chrysippus that one should interrupt the initial study of logic with questions related to the other parts. Plutarch gives the impression of being somewhat rhetorical in this chapter, but differences of order or classification might depend on whether a Stoic was talking about teaching order or relative value of the different parts; or between theory and practice; or depending on which subject, or book, he was writing. There were also differences between different Stoics, and perhaps individual Stoics changed their minds. Also in a School which put so much emphasis on the interdependence of the parts of philosophy, one would not expect them to hold rigidly to an order of teaching, although one would expect them to have views on such an order. See also, Goldschmidt, *Le Système Stoïcien* 61–7.

Diogenes gives a book reference for Zeno, but not for Chrysippus. Plutarch seems much more decisive for a Chrysippean order of logic, ethics, physics; and one would expect Sextus to take Chrysippus' evidence as canonical. This would be a possible method of reconciliation between the reporters.

But it appears that we have no evidence for Posidonius apart from the datum that he began with physics. Again this is teaching order, and we have no right to deduce from this that he regarded physics as the most important part of philosophy *in value* (as Laffranque, 363). For example, Sextus says that physics was taught last by the Stoics, θειοτέρα γάρ ἐστι. The ζῷον simile (F88) should indicate that Posidonius did not wish to elevate one part of philosophy over another.

The problem presumably did not exist for Ariston of Chios, for whom ethics was the only study. Cleanthes is not mentioned, but in the sentence after this passage, he is said to have divided philosophy into dialectic, rhetoric, ethics, politics, physics, theology. This is a sequence of logic, ethics, physics, but is not given as a teaching order.

10 Phanias: T43. The doxography may then have derived from Posidonius.

PHYSICS

F92 Arius Didymus, *Epitome* Fr. 20 (Stobaeus, *Eclogae* I.133 W; *Dox. Gr.* 458)

CONTENT

Substance and matter

'Posidonius said that the substance of the whole, and (i.e. ?) matter was without quality and without shape, in so far as in no way has it a form detached of its own, nor quality by itself either, but always is in some form and quality. (For?) He said that substance differs from matter, being the same in reality, in thought only.' (There is a textual crux in the last sentence.)

CONTEXT

The extract occurs in Stobaeus in a section Περὶ ὕλης, defined as: τὸ ὑποκείμενον πάσῃ γενέσει καὶ φθορᾷ καὶ ταῖς ἄλλαις μεταβολαῖς. After entries under Hermes, Thales, Pythagoras, Heraclitus, Plato (with reference to *Tim.*) and Aristotle, all dealing specifically with ὕλη, and raising problems of lack of quality, shape, and the corporeality of matter, Stobaeus turns to the Stoics. Zeno relates πρώτη ὕλη to οὐσία ἡ τῶν ὄντων πάντων; for Chrysippus: τῶν κατὰ ποιότητα ὑφισταμένων πρώτην ὕλην.

Both Zeno and Chrysippus distinguish between a generic (πᾶσαν) ὕλη (which seems to be πρώτη ὕλη), and specific ὕλη (κατὰ μέρη); the former is eternal and not subject to increase or decrease, the latter is subject to διαίρεσις and σύγχυσις. Through ὕλη runs ὁ τοῦ παντὸς λόγος. Then follows a short section suggesting that the earlier physiologoi said that ὕλη was not amorphous but σῶμα; then a sentence that the Stoics declare ὕλη to be body (σῶμα). That short section is assigned by Diels to Aetius. He thinks that the Arius extract continues with the Posidonius fragment. After Posidonius there is a final reference to Plato from *Parm.*, of which the subject is οὐσία.

COMMENT

Some commentators have seen in this fragment an entirely new position, unorthodox and heretical to the earlier Stoic view of the two ἀρχαί or principles, and consequently difficult to reconcile with F5: so especially Edelstein, *AJPh* 57 (1936), 290f, and Reinhardt, *RE* col. 642f. Rist (*Stoic Philosophy*), takes a different view (p. 203ff). But it is not clear how what is said here differs from normal Stoic doctrine, nor indeed whether it does.

It might be thought that the opening particle, ἔφησε δὲ ὁ Π., was contrasting Posidonius with what went before; but we can hardly be certain that δέ is adversative here. If there was a contrast, what would it be? In Stobaeus the previous statement is that the Stoics call ὕλη σῶμα. Whatever the last sentence in the Posidonius fragment means, it is no evidence that Posidonius did not think that matter was body, and it is hardly credible that he should not have thought so. Suppose with Diels the fragment to follow in Arius Didymus immediately after the references to Zeno and Chrysippus; although there is different information in the Posidonius material, it is not immediately obvious that it is opposed to what Zeno and Chrysippus are reported to have held.

The first sentence is a statement about the substance of the whole, and matter. The verb ἔχει is singular, therefore they comprise a single reference, or one of them is the main subject. The section in Stobaeus is on ὕλη, but there has already been an equation between ὕλη and οὐσία under Zeno; οὐσίαν is subject of the next sentence, and the reference to Plato which follows refers to οὐσία. I suggest that they are equated in this passage, and that the καὶ joining them is explanatory, 'that is'. This equation is normal in the evidence. The terms οὐσία and ὕλη are often further qualified, because as D.L. VII.150 reports, both terms are used in a generic cosmic sense (τῶν πάντων) or in a specific sense (τῶν ἐπὶ μέρους). So οὐσία is τῶν ὄντων πάντων (Zeno, Stob. *SVF* I.87; D.L. VII.150 = *SVF* II.316), or τὴν ἄποιον οὐσίαν (D.L. VII.134 = *SVF* II.300), or ἡ πρώτη οὐσία (Galen = *SVF* II.323); all parallel to τὴν τῶν ὅλων οὐσίαν here. Also ὕλη in this equation was sometimes called πρώτη ὕλη by Zeno and Chrysippus (D.L. VII.150 = *SVF* I.87; Stob. *SVF* I.87; *SVF* II.317; Galen *SVF* II.323; Origenes *SVF* II.318; Simplicius (ἡ πρωτίστη ὕλη) *SVF* II.326), to distinguish it from specific instances of ὕλη (e.g. Chalcidius *SVF* I.86). What is meant by these terms is put beyond doubt by D.L. VII.134 (*SVF* I.85; II.300) (F5), namely the passive principle in Stoic physics. All the other contexts fit. Posidonius states that this principle, or the substance of all things, or matter, or prime matter, is without quality and without form. This again is common ground: for ἄποιος: *SVF* II.300 (D.L.), 301 (S.E.), 309 (S.E.), 313 (Plu.), 315 (Plotinus), 318 (Orig.), 323 (Galen), 326 (Simplicius); ἄμορφος: *SVF* II.299 (D.L.), 314 (Plotinus); ἀσχημάτιστος: *SVF* II.311 (S.E.), 318 (Orig.).

Posidonius proceeds to explain his statement (or perhaps qualify it – καθ' ὅσον) about unqualified cosmic substance and matter: it has no form or quality peculiar to itself, it always is in a certain form and quality. This in turn is explained: for (δέ) substance and matter differ conceptually only, in *fact* they are the same; matter is always the substance of something.

It is these statements which led Edelstein to think that Posidonius had a heretical conception of matter. 'The Posidonian definition of the first principle of the universe is original with him' (*AJPh* 57.291). Reinhardt agreed (*RE*, col. 642f): 'P. lehrte, nach Aetius (a slip for Arius), nicht nur etwas anderes, sondern etwas, was sich gegen eben diese gemeinstoische Lehre richtete.' But what does Posidonius say that is against normal Stoic doctrine? I know of no passage where a Stoic says that ὕλη, the passive principle of the universe, could exist on its own, unqualified in some way. Even when an ἐκπύρωσις takes place, there is no unqualified matter. Zeus (θεός, the active principle) exists then ἐπὶ μιᾶς τῆς τοῦ αἰθέρος οὐσίας. That is, although there are then no specifically qualified individual things, there is still Zeus-qualified *aether*, or the two ἀρχαί combined in their most general cosmic state (Plu. *Comm. Not.* 1077Df (*SVF* II.1064)).

The fragment gives the impression not that Posidonius is wishing to criticise Zeno or Chrysippus, but that he is attempting to clarify a Stoic dogma that had come under attack from opponents. For this reason the lack of context is especially to be regretted, and one can only proceed with caution and hesitation.

There is certainly trace of criticism of the Stoic doctrine of principles, and in particular on the relation between ὕλη and οὐσία, ὕλη and λόγος, ὕλη as an unqualified substance. See, for example, Plotinus, *Ennead.* VI.1.25–8; Plutarch, *Comm. Not.* 1085B–1086B; Alex. Aphr. *SVF* II.306. The Stoics indeed had inherited the problems of matter, substance, form, and corporeality. Plato had raised similar problems over the ὑποδοχή in *Tim.* 50–2, and Aristotle had discussed the relation between ὕλη and οὐσία in *Met.* Z. ch. 3 (especially 1029a 20ff), distinguishing the two, and enquiring what ὕλη could be if stripped of all quality. (See also Arist. *Phys.* 191a 7.) The Stoics differed from Aristotle in equating ὕλη and οὐσία, and also in insisting that ὕλη was σῶμα (on this problem, C. Bäumker, *Das Problem der Materie*, Munster, 1890, pp. 326ff). The latter position was derived from their dynamic view of the principles: only the corporeal can act or be acted upon (Plu. *Comm. Not.* 1073E; S.E. *Adv. Math.* VIII.263 (*SVF* II.363)). ὕλη σῶμα was orthodox doctrine (so Stobaeus immediately before the Posidonian fragment (*SVF* II.325, see also *SVF* II.305, 310, 312, 326). It then followed that ὕλη was an ἄποιον σῶμα (Simplicius, *SVF* II.326), which required explanation. Aristotle had already asked the question, but Plutarch (and no doubt others) put it to the Stoics again in *Comm. Not.* 1086A. He seems to offer a simple dilemma: ἄποιος means either (a) stripped of all quality (but in what sense, if any, could such a thing be then a body?); or (b) possessing all qualities; but to say that none means all is an odd way of speaking. (a) might be thought to imply that there exists separately such an unqualified body. In fact the Stoics maintained that there did not, it is ἀχώριστον from the active qualifying principle (e.g. *SVF* II.307, 308). But some Stoics may have been puzzled how to explain the position and extricate themselves from the attack, and so may have been tempted to make an explanation in physical terms. In a passage in D.L. (VII.150) where the terms ὕλη and οὐσία are employed, we find Antipater and Apollodorus using the term πεπερασμένη, and the latter also the word παθητή. The criticism of Plotinus (see above) would suggest that some Stoics may have used the term ἀντιτυπία, as if they had thought of matter simply as a space filler characterised by resistance. None of this is attested for Zeno or Chrysippus, and there is no sign that the actual doctrine of ὕλη as a principle changed, but Posidonius may have been the first to show clearly, that the explanation lay in a logical distinction rather than in a physical analysis. This would be in accord with his assessment of the organic importance of logic for philosophy (F88). Plutarch's dilemma is too simple. In a sense (a) is acceptable, as in another sense so is (b); as Diogenes can say loosely: τὰ δὴ τέτταρα στοιχεῖα εἶναι ὁμοῦ τὴν ἄποιον οὐσίαν τὴν ὕλην (D.L. VII.137).

This is loose because Zeno and Chrysippus appear to have made a distinction between ὕλη and πρώτη ὕλη (Chalcidius, *SVF* I.86). But whenever or however ὕλη occurs it is always as qualified substance, whether one has in mind cosmic or particular substance. Indeed since 'being' is grounded for the Stoics in the corporeal, with the unity of matter is linked the unity of substance. There is one world, and one world substance. Matter is not a substance, it is, in occurrence, substance (so Bäumker, *Das Problem*). Matter and substance can only be distinguished conceptually. The same holds for the two principles, active and passive, or the relationship between ὕλη and λόγος/θεός. Neither 'exists' on its own, they are only logically distinguishable. Some at least of the criticism of Alexander of Aphrodisias and of Plotinus is due to misinterpretation. Posidonius with his stress on the ȝῷον simile, was concerned no doubt with opposing dualistic interpretations (as Reinhardt, *RE*, col. 643), but he was hardly unorthodox to do so.

Posidonius, of course, is not wanting to deny the existence of ὕλη; and Reinhardt is at least confusing when he wrongly emends the last sentence of the fragment with the comment (as something new in Stoicism) (*RE*, col. 643): 'zwischen οὐσία und ὕλη ist ein Unterschied, die οὐσία ist real, die ὕλη dagegen, d.h. das Korrelat zum Logos und Demiurgen, ist nur in unserer Vorstellung: διαφέρειν δὲ τὴν οὐσίαν τῆς ὕλης, τὴν οὖσαν κατὰ τὴν ὑπόστασιν ⟨τῆς⟩ ἐπινοίᾳ μόνον.'

On the contrary, ὕλη is 'real', it is σῶμα, it exists as οὐσία in everything as qualified material substrate. ὕλη and οὐσία always in fact concur. They can of course be distinguished by definition (cf. Chalcidius *SVF* I.86). But does Posidonius also mean that the concept of ὕλη as an ἀρχή, that is, as a separate ἄποιον that is the principle of being qualified, is nothing more than a logical concept? If so, this may have some bearing on the choice between the readings σώματα and ἀσωμάτους in D.L. VII.134 = F5.12. But on this, see F5 comm.

It must be stated, however, that sometimes Stoics, or their reporters appear to have been incautious in their accounts of generation, and it is not easy to know what value or emphasis to put on these. D.L. VII.136 is a good example of this.

Two passages remind one strongly of the Posidonius fragment:

(a) Origen, *SVF* II.318: κατὰ τούτους [sc. τοὺς Στωϊκοὺς] δὲ ἡ οὐσία (equated earlier with πρώτη ὕλη) ἐστὶν ἄποιός τε καὶ ἀσχημάτιστος κατὰ τὸν ἴδιον λόγον, ἀλλ' οὐδὲ μέγεθος ἀποτεταγμένον ἔχουσα, πάσῃ δὲ ἔκκειται ποιότητι καθάπερ ἕτοιμόν τι χωρίον.

(b) Galen, *De Sequela, Scripta minora*, vol. II.36 (Müller): . . . ἀναμνησθῶμεν δὲ περὶ τῆς κοινῆς οὐσίας ἁπάντων σωμάτων, ὡς ἐκ δυοῖν ἀρχῶν ἡμῖν ἐδείχθη σύνθετος ὑπάρχειν, ⟨ὕλης τε καὶ εἴδους⟩, ὕλης ⟨μὲν⟩ ἀποίου κατ' ἐπίνοιαν, ἐχούσης δ' ἐν ἑαυτῇ ποιοτήτων τεττάρων κρᾶσιν, θερμότητος ψυχρότητος ξηρότητος ὑγρότητος. This is said of Plato, but this is the essay where Galen refers to Posidonius extensively at the end (F35).

The final sentence of the Posidonius fragment can hardly stand. Hirzel (*Untersuchungen* II.759, n. 1) criticised the sense of the reading of the codices: 'Der Gedanke konnte aber doch dann nur der sein, dass das Sein der οὐσία als eines κατὰ τὴν ὑπόστασιν nur auf der ἐπίνοια beruhe, hypothetisch sei.' Apart from the sense, the Greek is hardly tolerable. Hirzel's emendation at least restores sense, indeed, if my interpretation is correct, is exactly the sense required. For his reading he compares Stob. *Ecl.* II.64 W: ἀρετὰς δ' εἶναι πλείους φασὶ καὶ ἀχωρίστους ἀπ' ἀλλήλων καὶ τὰς αὐτὰς τῷ ἡγεμονικῷ μέρει τῆς ψυχῆς καθ' ὑπόστασιν. See in general Hirzel, *Untersuchungen* II.756ff, and compare Mansfeld, *Mnem.* 31 (1978), 170f.

τὴν τῶν ὅλων οὐσίαν: cf. F85 (ἡ τῶν ὅλων φύσις); F186 (τὴν τῶν ὅλων ἀλήθειαν).

ὑπόστασις/ἐπίνοια: F16 (ἐπιφάνεια).

F93a Simplicius, *In Aristotelis De Caelo* IV.3, 310b 1

CONTENT

Elements; natural places and relationship.

CONTEXT

Immediately after the reference to Posidonius at the end of the fragment, Simplicius records a note of Alexander's on what he has been saying. It is possible, although no more than that, that the information on Posidonius came from this source through Geminus; see F18 comm.

COMMENT

Aristotle at this point of *De Caelo* is discussing natural places of elements in terms of weight and lightness in relation to form. 'That which produces upward and downward movement is that which produces weight and lightness, and that which is moved is that which is potentially heavy or light, and the movement of each body to its own place is motion towards its own form' (310a 31ff). He remarks in passing that this is the way to interpret that statement of οἱ ἀρχαῖοι that 'like moves to like' (310b 1f). The base of his subsequent theory is the following sentence: 'Since the place of a thing is the boundary (πέρας) of that which contains it (τοῦ περιέχοντος), and what contains (περιέχει) all things that move up and down is the extremity (ἔσχατον) and the centre (μέσον), and this (boundary, τοῦτο) becomes in a sense (τρόπον τινα γίγνεται) the form of that which is contained (τὸ εἶδος τοῦ περιεχομένου), it is to its like that a body moves to its own place' (310b 7ff).

Simplicius in F93a.24ff distinguishes this system of the

division of the four elements εἰς τὰ εἰδικὰ καὶ ὑλικά, from a second (ἄλλος) to which Aristotle refers elsewhere (but where precisely is now unknown), and Theophrastus, and which Posidonius took from Aristotle and Theophrastus and uses everywhere.

(a) The *De Caelo* system of division εἰς τὰ εἰδικὰ καὶ ὑλικά. The base of this system is that: τὸ περιέχον τρόπον τινα εἶδος γίνεται τοῦ περιεχομένου.

For πῦρ, the εἶδος is τὸ ἔσχατον ἄνω, the upper limit or boundary;
for ἀήρ, the εἶδος is πῦρ;
for γῆ, the εἶδος is τὸ μέσον (i.e. the centre, the other limit);
for ὕδωρ, the εἶδος is γῆ (*its* περιέχον).
So πῦρ and ἀήρ are light; γῆ and ὕδωρ are heavy.

(Shown diagrammatically in Fig. 7.)

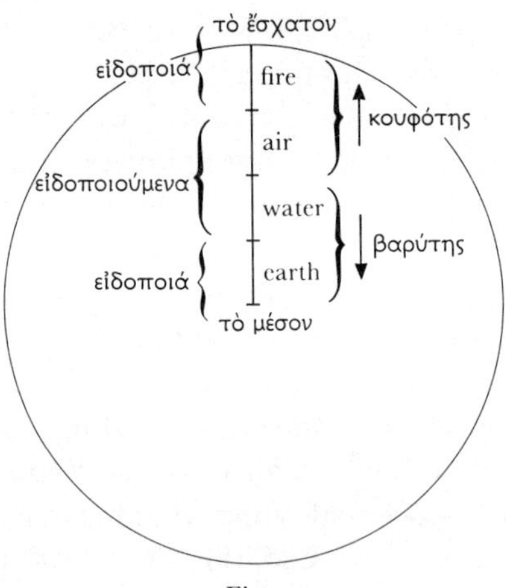

Fig. 7

So, εἰδικά and εἰδοποιά are: τὸ ἔσχατον, πῦρ, τὸ μέσον, γῆ. ὑλικά and εἰδοποιούμενα are: ἀήρ, ὕδωρ (τὰ μέσα, i.e. the 'intermediate' elements).

(b) The second division is less explicit, but in addition to matter, form, weight and lightness, adds hot and cold. Hot and cold can only apply to elements, and so the governing factors of ἔσχατον and μέσον appear to be eliminated. The analysis is:

τὰ μὲν βαρέα καὶ ψυχρὰ ὕλης λόγον ἔχειν,
τὰ δὲ κοῦφα καὶ θερμὰ εἴδους (λόγον ἔχειν);
(which might be represented diagrammatically, as in Fig. 8).

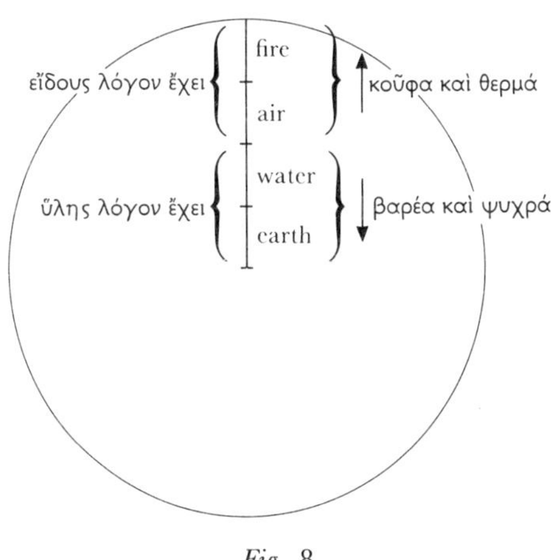

Fig. 8

It is obvious that this analysis differs from the former in the characteristics of earth and air. Earth, instead of being εἰδοποιόν at least in relation to water, is now associated with ὕλη. Air, instead of being an εἰδοποιούμενον in relation to fire, εἴδους λόγον ἔχει. At least the plural form of the Greek would lead one to include air in this category with fire.

As far as form and matter go, system (b) fits in well with Stoicism; thus *SVF* II.439 (Galen, τὴν μὲν γὰρ πνευματικὴν οὐσίαν τὸ συνέχον, τὴν δὲ ὑλικὴν τὸ συνεχόμενον· ὅθεν ἀέρα μὲν καὶ πῦρ συνέχειν φασί, γῆν δὲ καὶ ὕδωρ συνέχεσθαι; cf. *SVF* II.440). So also Nemesius (*SVF* II.418): δραστικὰ μὲν ἀέρα καὶ πῦρ, παθητικὰ δὲ γῆν καὶ ὕδωρ; and compare Plu. *De SR* 1035F (*SVF* II.449); *Comm. Not.* 1085C (*SVF* II.444). Plutarch as he continues his own argument in *De SR* (1054B) uses the expressions: εἰδοποιεῖν ἕκαστα καὶ σχηματίζειν (εἰδοποιεῖν again in Simplicius *SVF* II.378, 393). ἀήρ is κούφη and ἀνωφερής in Plu. *De SR* 1053E (*SVF* II.434) . . . τοῦ μὲν ὕδατος τῇ γῇ μᾶλλον προσνεμομένου, τοῦ δ' ἀέρος τῷ πυρί.

The application of (b) to Stoic evidence in general breaks with Simplicius' classification of hot and cold. For Aristotle the common quality to active elements is heat, since fire represented hot/dry, air hot/moist, water cold/moist, earth cold/dry. But in general Stoic theory the qualities assigned to the elements were fire hot, air cold, water moist, earth dry. That Stoics maintained that the principle of cold was ἀήρ is shown by Plu. *De Prim. Frig.* 948Dff (*SVF* II.430); Plu. *De SR* 1053F (*SVF* II.429); *SVF* II.431 (Galen); D.L. VII.137.

There is no other evidence that Posidonius abandoned the orthodox Stoic equation of air and cold (F94). Perhaps we are simply to understand that Posidonius applied that part of the Aristotelian system of natural places which related to weight, lightness, form and matter, but not the theory of potentiality and actuality whereby natural places were governed by the form of that which is contained (the theory of extremity and middle, and the Aristotelian interpretation of like to like). Nor is it clear what Simplicius means by universal (πανταχοῦ) application on the part of Posidonius.

Reinhardt argued (*RE*, col. 661; *Kosmos und Sympathie* 347 n. 1; *Poseidonios* 148f, 225, 345 n. 2; followed by Pohlenz, *Die Stoa* II.108), that Posidonius had a new and unorthodox theory that the active and creative elements, τὰ γονιμὰ καὶ ποιητικά, were the warm and moist, while τὰ φθαρτικὰ καὶ παθητικά were the cold and dry. However, none of the passages on which he relies (e.g. Ptol. *Tetr.* I.5.1 (p. 19 Boll and Boer); Cicero, *ND* II.23ff; Vitr. VIII.3.28) name Posidonius, and it is uncertain how the subject of these passages relates to natural places. Indeed the most certain evidence of this passage is the association of Posidonius with Aristotle and Theophrastus, for which see T100.

For a general attack on 'natural places': Plu. *De Facie*.

F94 Plutarch, *De Primo Frigido* 16. 951F

CONTENT

Posidonius said that the cause of coldness was that the marsh air was fresh and moist.

CONTEXT

Earlier in the essay Plutarch examined the Stoic theory that the principle of cold is air (948Dff). He proceeds to argue, after Empedocles, that water may be the principle of cold. It is in the middle of this argument that the fragment occurs. Plutarch finally argues on his own behalf that earth may be the principle of cold.

COMMENT

Since Plutarch is arguing for water being the principle of cold, he naturally makes much of Posidonius' νοτερόν and πρόσφατον in the sense of ἀήρ fresh from the marsh water. ἕλειον too shows that Posidonius is referring to very wet mists. However, οὐκ ἔλυσε τὸ πιθανόν is no evidence that Posidonius was trying to combat the argument that water is the principle of cold, but merely that Plutarch regards this reference from Posidonius as not damaging his argument. While the words, τῆς ψυχρότητος αἰτίαν, might give the impression that Posidonius was talking about the general principle of cold, the particular instance of marsh mists suggests that the context of the reference is geographical, and is hardly decisive for the principles of elements.

F210 gives another geographical employment of moist air and coolness.

F95 Arius Didymus, *Epitome* F18 (Stobaeus, *Eclogae* 1.13.1c = 1.138.14W; *Dox. Gr.* 457)

CONTENT

Cause is defined as cause of something, through which it is this something, or as the first activator, or as the originator of action. Cause is, and is corporeal; that of which it is the cause neither is, nor is a body, but is accidental and a predicate.

CONTEXT

Stobaeus' section is concerned with different philosophers' definition or description of cause. After Plato, Pythagoras and Aristotle follows the fragment from Arius (if Diels is correct), in which Posidonius' views are given after Zeno and Chrysippus.

COMMENT

There are elements common to all three Stoics, namely defining αἴτιον as δι' ὅ, characterising cause as ὂν καὶ σῶμα and thus distinguishing cause from οὗ αἴτιον. In the Zeno entry there is an additional explanation and illustration of αἴτιον and οὗ αἴτιον (4–9); to Chrysippus is assigned a definition of αἰτία; for Posidonius, besides the normal label for cause as δι' ὅ, there is added ἢ τὸ πρῶτον ποιοῦν, ἢ τὸ ἀρχηγὸν ποιήσεως.

Either the three terms for cause in Posidonius are alternatives or they refer to three different causes. Edelstein (*AJPh* 57.301ff) argued the latter, identifying the three labels respectively with matter, soul and god, and relating this theory to the tripartite division in Frs. 103 and 107.

There are great difficulties in such an interpretation. Apart from the fact that there is no other evidence for it although Edelstein maintained that this was a heretical view of cause, it seems difficult to derive from the context. For one must ask what the difference would be between τὸ πρῶτον ποιοῦν and τὸ ἀρχηγὸν ποιήσεως, and how these are different from δι᾽ ὅ.

δι᾽ ὅ as an expression is itself vague (Frede, *Doubt and Dogmatism* 220). Stobaeus begins his chapter with it as a working definition of αἴτιον. αἴτιόν ἐστι δι᾽ ὃ τὸ ἀποτέλεσμα ἢ δι᾽ ὃ συμβαίνει τι. ἀρκεῖ γὰρ ὑπογραφικῶς. Indeed, in the entry under Aristotle δι᾽ ὅ is related to τέλος (p. 138.12W). And compare *SVF* II.501, line 22, where δι᾽ ὅ is equated with τέλος, ὑφ᾽ οὗ with αἴτιον (Sextus). In general see Proclus, *Comm. in Alc.*, Cousin II.337f for differentiation of causes by prepositions. But S.E. *PH* 14 suggests later general agreement on cause as δι᾽ ὃ ἐνεργοῦν γίνεται τὸ ἀποτέλεσμα (Frede, *Doubt and Dogmatism* 218). In Stoicism the expression δι᾽ ὅ as defining cause must refer to the efficient cause (in general *SVF* I.89–90; II.336–46). Even so it appears from Clement (*SVF* II.347) that δι᾽ ὅ might be regarded as an inadequate description on its own.

τὸ πρῶτον ποιοῦν would naturally refer to the 'first' cause (πρώτη αἰτία Arist. *Met.* 984a 3), as an efficient cause (τὸ αἴτιον καὶ ποιητικόν Arist. *De An.* 430a 12). Of course πρῶτος in a given context could refer to something more immediate (as Arist. *EN* 1112b 19; or τὰ πρώτως ἀφορμὴν παρεχόμενα of procatarctic causes, *SVF* II.346). But on its own one would surely take the expression as in Arist. *De Gen. et Corr.* 324a 24ff, where τὸ πρῶτον ποιοῦν is compared to τὸ πρῶτον κινοῦν (ἡ γὰρ ἀρχὴ πρώτη τῶν αἰτιῶν); cf. Aristocles in Eus. *Praep. Evang.* XV.14.1, οὗτοι (Stoics) ἄμφω (ὕλη and θεός) σώματά φασιν εἶναι, ἐκείνου (Plato) τὸ πρῶτον ποιοῦν ἀσώματον εἶναι λέγοντος. So again, οἱ Στωϊκοὶ τὸ πρῶτον αἴτιον ὡρίσαντο κινητόν, just following in the same section in Stobaeus (*SVF* II.338). How then would the reference of τὸ πρῶτον ποιοῦν differ from that of τὸ ἀρχηγὸν ποιήσεως? ἀρχηγός refers to an originator, or common ancestor, or founder (cf. Arist. *EN* 1162a 4; Arist. Fr. 94R[3] (84R[2], Περὶ εὐγενείας Fr. 4 Ross)). In connection with cause, Posidonius may have thought of the word from Pl. *Crat.* 401d: τὸ οὖν αἴτιον καὶ τὸ ἀρχηγὸν αὐτῶν (sc. τῶν ὄντων) εἶναι τὸ ὠθοῦν (etymologising), cf. Pl. *Soph.* 243b–d.

So τὸ ἀρχηγὸν ποιήσεως may simply be a more colourful title for τὸ πρῶτον ποιοῦν; cf. Ps.-Arist. *De Mundo* 399a 26: διὰ τὴν πρώτην καὶ ἀρχαιόγονον (ἀρχέγονον Wendland, Wilamowitz, Furley) αἰτίαν.

Seneca in *Ep.* 65 is quite explicit: *Stoicis placet unam causam esse id quod facit* (§4). He has already explained what is meant by this; *causa autem, id est ratio, materiam format et quocumque vult versat, ex illa varia opera producit. esse ergo debet, unde fiat aliquid, deinde a quo fiat. hoc causa est, illud materia* (§2). He turns to the common illustration of the statue: *ergo in statua materia aes fuit, causa opifex. eadem condicio rerum omnium est; ex quo constant quod fit, et ex eo quod facit.* Everything consists of that which is made and of the maker (§3).

So he accuses Aristotle and Plato that their *turba causarum* embraces too much or too little. Too little if they are including under cause everything without which the object cannot be made (ὧν οὐκ ἄνευ); such a list would have to include e.g. time, place, motion (§11). *sed nos nunc primam et generalem quaerimus causam.* (One is almost tempted to read *generabilem*, but *generali* recurs (§14), and anyway change is unnecessary; cf. *Ep.* 58.12 where the subject is *quod est* (τὸ ὄν): *hoc ergo est genus primum et antiquissimum et, ut ita dicam generale.* Posidonius, as usual, was more vivid, and used the word ἀρχηγόν, originator, first founder.) *haec simplex esse debet; nam et materia simplex est. quaerimus quid sit causa? ratio scilicet faciens, id est deus. ista enim, quaecumque rettulistis non sunt multae et singulae causae, sed ex una pendent, ex ea, quae faciet* (§12).

Of course, the one cause could have different forms; so e.g.

σπέρμα, φύσις, ψυχή, θεός in S.E. *Adv. Math.* IX.196 (*SVF* II.337). There could also be and was a subclassification of cause (προκαταρκτικά, συνεκτικά, συνεργά, ὧν οὐκ ἄνευ, συναίτια; *SVF* II.346, 348, 351, 354, 355). For such a classification from Posidonius himself, and for his philosophical use of it: Frs. 190, 170. But these distinctions do not seem to be relevant here, where both the context of Arius, and the context of Stobaeus (p. 137,10f W; p. 139.12 W), favour simply a general definition of the term αἴτιον.

I therefore take ἢ[1] and ἢ[2] in line 15 to express alternatives rather than as disjunctives (cf. Stobaeus' ἢ at the beginning of the chapter, p. 137.10 W; Pl. *Laws* 663a 7). If so, there is no evidence of an unorthodox view on Posidonius' part. Indeed, it would be possible to suppose that Posidonius may have been reinforcing Stoic doctrine against criticism, for example that δι' ὅ was not a sufficient description of cause for the Stoa (cf. Clem. *Strom.* VIII.9 = *SVF* II.347). Or he may have selected additional labels to advise against entertaining *quocumque remoto quid effici non potest* (Sen. *Ep.* 65.11); cause is the efficient cause, the first activator, the originator of action (so Sen. *Ep.* 65.12).

Indeed, the context of Arius is more concerned with comparing the status of αἴτιον and οὗ αἴτιον. What is meant by calling the latter συμβεβηκὸς καὶ κατηγόρημα is illustrated in the Zeno entry. There, that of which cause is a cause is indeed a predicate expressed in Greek by verbs: φρονεῖν, ζῆν, σωφρονεῖν; see also *SVF* II.349. On the category difference between ὀνόματα and κατηγορήματα: Zeller, III.1.90 n. 3; Watson, *The Stoic Theory of Knowledge*; Bréhier, 'La Théorie des Incorporels dans l'Ancien Stoïcisme', *Arch. f. Gesch. d. Phil.* 22 (1909) 114–25; Rist, *Stoic Philosophy*, ch. 9. The κατηγορήματα did not exist, but subsisted (ὑπάρχειν, l. 4), in the category τι. So perhaps Posidonius in l. 14: αἴτιον δ' ἐστί τινος. For ὑπάρχειν, in relation to predication: Long, *Problems* 88ff; Kerferd, *Les Stoïciens et leur Logique* 269f.

Since clearly every piece of information in each entry is not reproduced in all three entries, there is no reason to introduce a statement on αἰτία for Posidonius, because Chrysippus had one. Therefore, the emendation of Reinhardt (*RE*, col. 643–4) seems unnecessary.

For further elaboration of cause see F190.

F96 Arius Didymus, *Epitome* Fr. 27 (Stobaeus, *Eclogae* 1.20.7 = 1.177.20 W; cf. 1.17.4; *Dox. Gr.* 462)

CONTENT

Destruction and generation.

It is necessary to lay out the structure of this difficult fragment:

A. Description (1–10)

(1) There are four φθοραί and γενέσεις (1).

(2) Main characteristics: ἐκ τῶν ὄντων εἰς τὰ ὄντα (2–4). Generation and destruction from what is not, or into what is not is denied (whether by Posidonius and/or Stoics is not clear from the reading).

(3) Classification of destruction as change into being (4–7):

- (a) dismemberment (διαίρεσις)
- (b) alteration (transmutation?) of one substance into another (ἀλλοίωσις)
- (c) fusion (σύγχυσις)
- (d) dissolution from a whole (ἀνάλυσις), breaking up (of a whole); cf. *SVF* II.413.

(4) Subclassification (7–9)

ἀλλοίωσις is related to substance;

(a), (c) and (d) have reference to qualities supervening on substance (οὐσία).

(5) Generation is analogous (9f).

B. Explanation (τὴν γὰρ οὐσίαν κτλ.) (10–24)

(1) Substance does not admit of increase or diminution by addition or subtraction, but only of transmutation (like number and measure).
But individually qualified particulars (like Dion and Theon) also admit of increase and diminution.
That is why also the predominant quality of each thing persists from generation to destruction (as in Dion and Theon (stock names in Stoic logic, *SVF* II.397), and in the case of animals, plants and things like that that admit destruction) (10–16).

(2) In individually qualified particulars he (or they) says there are two receptive parts, in respect to the reality of substance and quality; it is the latter that admits of increase and diminution (16–20).

(3) (a) The individually qualified particular is not the same as its constituent substance;
(b) nor is it different either;
(c) but it is all but the same in that its substance is a part of it and occupies the same space. (For things that are said to be different from others must both be spatially separate and not be viewed as part and whole.) (20–4).

CONTEXT

The fragment occurs in a section in Stobaeus (I.20) entitled Περὶ γενέσεως καὶ φθορᾶς which is mostly concerned with whether the cosmos is destructible (as in the entries under Zeno, Cleanthes, and Chrysippus, p. 171 W). The fragment is followed by a reference to criticism by Mnesarchus, the pupil of Panaetius, on the difference between τὸ κατὰ τὸ ἰδίως ποιόν and τὸ κατὰ τὴν οὐσίαν (p. 179 W). The fragment recurs in Stobaeus at the end of I.17 (Περὶ μίξεως καὶ κράσεως). This is the chapter which contains Chrysippus' classification of μεταβολή as παράθεσις, μῖξις, κρᾶσις, σύγχυσις (p. 154 W; *SVF* II.471).

COMMENT

A. 1 (1)

The only other Stoic classification which survives of generation and destruction is recorded by Philo, *De Aet. Mund.* 79ff, a tripartition (διαίρεσις, ἀναίρεσις, σύγχυσις) assigned to Boethus (*SVF* III. Boeth. 7).

There is an implicit division of διαίρεσις and σύγχυσις attributed to Zeno and Chrysippus in Stob. *Ecl.* I.11.5a (p. 132.26ff W; Ar. Did. F20, *Dox. Gr.* 457 Diels. See also F92). Chrysippus' quadripartition mentioned above (*SVF* II.471) is different, since μῖξις and κρᾶσις show that Chrysippus here is classifying types of *mixture*.

Philo also outlines a Peripatetic quadripartite τρόποι τῆς φθορᾶς which he distinguishes from the Stoic (v. Arnim, *Quellenstudien zu Philo von Alexandria*, ch. I; *Philol. Studien*, vol. II, Berlin 1888).

A. 2 (2–4)

Edelstein believed that this statement must refer to Posidonius, and therefore that the emendation of Usener ἀπέγνω ὡς ἂν (or ἀπέγνωσεν ὡς Heeren) was necessary, because not all Stoics may have denied destruction into non-being, when the destruction of the world took place (Zeller, III.1.154.1). But in Stoic materialism, οὐσία was ἀΐδιον (e.g. Stob. *Ecl.* I.2.5a, 132.26ff W) φθορὰς γίγνεσθαι ἔκ τινων μερῶν (sc. τῆς πρώτης ὕλης) εἴς τινα, Stobaeus. Again in Philo, *De Aet. Mund.* 78, εἰ, φασί (sc. οἱ περὶ τὸν Βοηθόν), γενητὸς καὶ φθαρτὸς ὁ κόσμος, ἐκ τοῦ μὴ ὄντος τι γενήσεται, ὅπερ καὶ τοῖς Στωϊκοῖς ἀτοπώτατον εἶναι δοκεῖ (*SVF* III.165.26f; cf. 266.1). *SVF* III.266.20f: ἄπαγε, δεήσει γὰρ πάλιν εἰς τὸ μὴ ὂν γίνεσθαι τὴν φθορὰν παραδέχεσθαι. So the plural ἀπέγνωσαν ὡς ἀνύπαρκτον cannot be dismissed, and καθάπερ εἴπομεν πρόσθεν may introduce a more general reference. Since however the next sentence again certainly deals with Posidonius, one would expect that the subject does not change here. Plurals and singulars are very uncertain in the codices; compare lines 2 and 17.

A. 3(4–7)

Of the four terms, two, διαίρεσις and σύγχυσις are common in other Stoic evidence. They occur in the division assigned to Zeno and Chrysippus by Arius Didymus in Stob. *Ecl.* I.11.5a. In Boethus' tripartition, διαίρεσις refers to dismemberment of a conglomerate (ἐκ διεστηκότων), exampled by herds, choruses, armies. The term is thus the opposite of παράθεσις in Chrysippus' classification of mixture (*SVF* II.471). σύγχυσις is explained in Philo as a fusion of several substances into a new whole in which the old properties have vanished. It is also defined in Chrysippus' account of mixture (*SVF* II.471): τὴν δὲ σύγχυσιν δύο ⟨ἢ⟩ καὶ πλειόνων ποιοτήτων περὶ τὰ σώματα μεταβολὴν εἰς ἑτέρας διαφερούσης τούτων ποιότητος γένεσιν, ὡς ἐπὶ τῆς συνθέσεως ἔχει τῶν μύρων καὶ τῶν ἰατρικῶν φαρμάκων. The latter example is also given in Philo, cf. Stob. *Ecl.* I.17. Such chemical compounds (cf. Sambursky, *Physics of the Stoics* 11ff) are distinguished from κρᾶσις, where, although the mixture is complete, the elements remain distinguishable (*SVF* II.472 (Philo), 473 (Alexander)).

According to Philo, Boethus added ἀναίρεσις τῆς ἐπεχούσης ποιότητος, annihilation of the prevailing quality. Posidonius distinguished ἀνάλυσις and ἀλλοίωσις. Of ἀνάλυσις the only guide is that it was ἐξ ὅλων, i.e. the breaking up or dissolution of a whole, and that the name ἀνάλυσις was current. Also ἀνάλυσις was classified by Posidonius with διαίρεσις and σύγχυσις as involving addition and subtraction (taking away) and so different in kind from ἀλλοίωσις (A.4). Perhaps it referred to the opposite process to σύγχυσις.

Reinhardt (*Kosmos und Sympathie* 6f) cannot be right in thinking that the Posidonian element stopped at κατ' ἀνάλυσιν (7, A.3); what follows (7ff, A.4) is closely linked to the preceding sentences in verbal reference.

ἀλλοίωσις, alteration of substance or transmutation, is clearly a key term for Posidonius, for he distinguishes this kind of change from the others (A.4) and the subsequent argument is concerned with this. Zeller (III.1.96 n. 4) thought that the reference was to the change e.g. of water to air, but what follows in this fragment shows that Posidonius had more than this in mind. The relation of ἀλλοίωσις to substance (οὐσία, A.4), and the insistence that substance is not susceptible to increase and diminution by addition or subtraction (B.1, B.2) is reminiscent of Ar. Did. on Zeno and Chrysippus (F20, *Dox. Gr.* 457, Stob. *Ecl.* 1.11.5a; see Pos. F92). There Zeno says of οὐσία as πρώτη ὕλη: ταύτην δὲ πᾶσαν ἀΐδιον καὶ οὔτε πλείω γιγνομένην οὔτε ἐλάττω· τὰ δε μέρη ταύτης οὐκ ἀεὶ ταὐτὰ διαμένειν, ἀλλὰ διαιρεῖσθαι καὶ συγχεῖσθαι. As for Chrysippus: τῶν κατὰ ποιότητα ὑφισταμένων πρώτην ὕλην· ταύτην δὲ ἀΐδιον, οὔτε αὔξησιν οὔτε μείωσιν ὑπομένουσαν, διαίρεσιν δὲ καὶ σύγχυσιν ἐπιδεχομένην κατὰ μέρη, ὥστε φθορὰς γίγνεσθαι ἔκ τινων μερῶν εἴς τινα κατὰ διαίρεσιν κτλ.

But Posidonius in this context is clearly different. In his case διαίρεσις and σύγχυσις are related to τοὺς ποιοὺς λεγομένους (8), not to οὐσία (A.4). Furthermore, it is difficult to see how ἀλλοίωσις could apply to οὐσία in the sense of prime matter, which he believed could only be conceptually distinguished (F92). Therefore οὐσία refers to something else. For Posidonius οὐσία existed as individually qualified entities τὰ ἰδίως ποιά, which are precisely the subject of the rest of the fragment from line 12 (B.1) on. But such ἰδίως ποιά are subject to two kinds of change and destruction: (a) through admitting increase and diminution; (b) final destruction as that ἰδίως ποιόν (12–16). The implication seems to be that Posidonius thinks he can explain (διό, 13) why such an individually qualified entity can also persist (καὶ παραμένειν,

14) while being subject to change (a) (cf. Simplicius, *SVF* II.395, τὸ ἰδίως ποιόν . . . τὸ αὐτὸ ἐν παντὶ τῷ τοῦ συνθέτου βιῷ διαμένει, καίτοι τῶν μορίων ἄλλων ἄλλοτε γιγνομένων τε καὶ φθειρομένων), until it itself perishes (or comes into being) through ἀλλοίωσις, whereby the dominant characteristic of the enformed οὐσία changes. This is a substantial change whereby one ἰδίως ποιόν becomes a different ἰδίως ποιόν; the οὐσία persists, but the qualified entity transmutes κατ' ἀλλοίωσιν. The οὐσία becomes something else. At first in B.1 this is expressed by the general Stoic terms, τὴν ἑκάστου ποιότητα (14). This must be distinguished from τοὺς ποιοὺς λεγομένους τοὺς ἐπὶ τῆς οὐσίας γινομένους (8f) to which διαίρεσις etc. apply, but not ἀλλοίωσις. Compare Galen (*SVF* II.494) defining ἀλλοίωσις in a general non-Posidonian way: ἀλλοίωσιν δὲ ἢ μεταβολὴν κατὰ τὸ ποιόν, ἢ ἀλλαγὴν τῆς προϋπαρχούσης ποιότητος.

B. 2(16–20)

This is now explained by claiming that any ἰδίως ποιόν can be regarded as having two aspects susceptible to change (δεκτικά, 17): οὐσία and quality (16–18). But it is only the latter which is susceptible to change by increase and diminution (18–20); therefore it is *its* οὐσία which is subject to ἀλλοίωσις. But the οὐσία of a particular ἰδίως ποιόν is that particular predominant and individuating qualified matter which makes it what it is; if that suffers ἀλλοίωσις, change into something else, which is the only change such οὐσία can undergo, it is destroyed (cf. Pl. *Laws* x.893d–894a). Since this seems to be part of Posidonius' argument, I would read φησι in line 17 (as Heeren) instead of φασι of the codices. Since I do not see how ἀλλοίωσις can apply to οὐσία simpliciter but to the peculiar qualified οὐσία of an ἰδίως ποιόν, which is what anyway Posidonius seems to be saying here, I do not think that there is an opposition of οὐσία and ἰδίως ποιόν as do Theiler (*Poseidonios* II.143) and Rist (*Stoic Philosophy* 159). There is no reason to emend with Theiler to ἑκτικὰ ὅρια in line

17 (cf. Plu. *Comm. Not.* 1083CD, ὡς δύο ἡμῶν ἕκαστός ἐστιν ὑποκείμενα κτλ.

B. 3(20–4)

The explanation in B.2 is in a sense identifying the ἰδίως ποιόν with its οὐσία, so Posidonius now has to point out that although in one sense they are not different and indeed occupy the same space (and therefore by Stoic logic are the same), they are also distinct in that the essentially qualified οὐσία of the ἰδίως ποιόν is a constituent of the ἰδίως ποιόν which has other constituent qualities as well. In line 22, τὴν οὐσίαν FP should be retained.

A. 5(9–10)

The classification was given for φθορά, but γένεσις is analogous. γένεσις and φθορά are two ways of looking at the same process. Posidonius' theory of ἀλλοίωσις is very different from Aristotle's, who in the first book of *De Gen. et Corr.* (cf. *Phys.* 224a 21–226b 17) distinguishes ἀλλοίωσις (qualitative change) from γένεσις and φθορά or substantial change. ἀλλοίωοις is grouped with αὔξησις and φθίσις (change of quantity) and with φορά (change of space) as γένεσις ἡ κατὰ μέρος (*De Gen. et Corr.* 317b 34f). Aristotle, however, suggested that any philosophers who held that there was only one elementary substance must maintain that γένεσις and ἀλλοίωσις were the same (*De Gen. et Corr.* 314a 8ff, 314b 2ff).

Long and Sedley in *The Hellenistic Philosophers*, vol. I give a different interpretation of this passage; for an attack on the general Stoic position, see Plu. *Comm. Not.* 1083A–1084A with Cherniss's notes.

F97a, b Aetius, *Placita* II.9.3 (*Dox. Gr.* 338.17); Ps.-Plutarch, *De Placitis* II.9, *Mor.* 888A; Stobaeus, *Eclogae* I.18.4b (160.13f W). Also in Eusebius, *Praep. Evang.* XV.40

CONTENT

Posidonius said that the void outside the cosmos was not infinite but sufficient for the dissolution (or, if emended: the void outside the cosmos is not infinite in so far as it is sufficient for the dissolution).

CONTEXT

Both Ps.-Plutarch and Stobaeus precede the statement with a sentence on Pythagoreans on void; then that the Stoics say void is what the cosmos dissolves into at the ekpyrosis, and that it is infinite. Ps.-Plutarch continues with a book reference to Posidonius (F84), followed by the statement that Aristotle and Plato denied void. Stobaeus continues with Plato on place (τόπος) and void.

COMMENT

The Stoics denied void within the finite cosmos (e.g. *SVF* I.95; II.502), but argued that there must be void outside the cosmos, and that this vacuum was infinite (ἄπειρον). This evidence occurs in all the sources: Arius Didymus 25 (Stob. *SVF* II.503); Aetius again (*Dox. Gr.* 316; *SVF* I.95, II.609); *SVF* II.534–46 (including Plutarch, Alexander of Aphrodisias, Diogenes Laertius, Cleomedes); Sextus Empiricus (*SVF* II.524); Philo (*SVF* II.619). See in general Cleomedes, *De Motu* I.1.2–8. There is only one apparent dissident voice, Achilles,

Isagoga in Aratum 8 (p. 38 Maass, *SVF* II.610); οὐ μὴν ἄπειρόν (sc. τὸ κενόν) φασιν, ἀλλὰ τοσοῦτον ὅσον χωρῆσαι λυθὲν τὸ πᾶν. φασιν must be wrong, but the question must be asked whether the statement could derive from Posidonius (who was known to Achilles; Frs. 128, 148, 209).

Stoics and Peripatetics carried on a continual controversy on the topic of void. Aristotle had denied that there was κενὸν ἔξω τοῦ οὐρανοῦ (*De Caelo* 279a 11f; cf. *Phys.* 206a 17; 206b 20ff; 207a 8ff; 212b 8). Cleomedes, *De Motu* I.1.5–6 preserves and attempts to rebut later Peripatetic arguments against the Stoa. These include: (a) if void were infinite, matter pouring into it (at the ekpyrosis or at any other time since absolute or natural places would not hold in an infinite vacuum) would scatter to infinity; (b) an infinite void would imply ἄπειρον σῶμα, i.e. an infinite cosmos. Nevertheless, the Stoics did hold to a finite cosmos and an infinite void outside it, even to the extent of differentiating explicitly between τὸ ὅλον (the cosmos) as finite and τὸ πᾶν (cosmos and κενόν) as infinite (*SVF* II.522 (Aetius), 524 (Sextus), 525 (Plutarch), III Apollod. 9 (D.L.)).

There was however a tendency to confuse void (κενόν) and place (τόπος). Aristotle said (*Phys.* 213b 31) that those who believe in void think of it as a place without any body in it (δοκεῖ δὲ τὸ κενὸν τόπος εἶναι ἐν ᾧ μηδέν ἐστι). So Stoics defined τόπος as τὸ ὑπὸ σώματος κατεχόμενον, and κενόν as τὸ μὴ κατεχόμενον but ἁπλῶς δὲ σῶμα δέχεσθαι οἵου τε ὄντος or τὸ οἷόντε ὑπὸ ὄντος κατέχεσθαι, μὴ κατεχόμενον δέ (e.g. Cleomedes, *De Motu* I.1.2; I.1.4; Sextus, *SVF* II.505; D.L. VII.140, *SVF* II.543; Alexander in Simplicius (*SVF* II.535)). As τόπος was clearly finite, this laid Stoics open to the kinds of attacks relating to finite cosmos and infinite void found in Cleomedes and in Alexander (in Simplicius *SVF* II.535). Cleomedes, when expounding the Stoic position, keeps switching from place to void, e.g. I.1.2; and again: ὁ τοίνυν ἐν τῇ ἐκπυρώσει ὑπὸ τῆς οὐσίας χεομένης καταλαμβανόμενος τόπος νῦν κενός ἐστιν, οὐδενός γε σώματος αὐτὸν πεπληρωκότος (I.1.3, p. 6.15ff Ziegler); and especially I.1.4, p. 8.1–14 Z. Arius Didymus F25 (Stobaeus, *Dox. Gr.* 460f, *SVF* II.503) gives the same sort of account, and while maintaining unswervingly the infinity of void on the part of the Stoics, clearly has some trouble with the finite/infinite problem. He concludes: κατὰ γὰρ τὴν αὑτοῦ (sc. τοῦ κενοῦ) ὑπόστασιν ἄπειρόν ἐστι· περατοῦται δ' αὖ τοῦτο ἐκπληρούμενον· τοῦ δὲ πληροῦντος ἀρθέντος οὐκ ἔστιν αὐτοῦ νοῆσαι πέρας.

In such a situation it is possible, either that a Stoic might re-examine the accepted tradition, or that confusion might arise in a reporter over ambiguity of reference. In the first case, Posidonius might have been impressed by Aristotelian or Peripatetic arguments, or by others which we do not know, to withdraw from the dogma of the infinity of void. But on balance it seems to me unlikely. The Peripatetic arguments, which after all appear to be the key arguments according to Cleomedes, are directed not simply against void as infinite, but that it should be accepted that there is void outside the cosmos at all; and this Posidonius did not deny. Granted such a void, it would be a very peculiar concept to hold that it was finite, although not of course that the space to be occupied by substance at the ekpyrosis was finite. On the other hand, one would not expect Posidonius to be puzzled by such ambiguities (like the ambiguity of 'space' in English), because the Stoa was careful to distinguish by definition the concepts of κενόν, τόπος and χώρα (*SVF* I.95; II.504). Moreover, it is very strange that in the longest continuous argument on this subject, that by Cleomedes, *De Motu* I.2–8, there is no record of such an important deviation, although Cleomedes seems to have been using a reference book specially related to Posidonius (*De Motu, ad fin.*, T57). Nor is there any mention in the range of reporters referred to above that any Stoic denied the infinity of void. A garbled report then is more probable; perhaps based on a similar limitation made by Posidonius to that made in F92 (καθ' ὅσον), where I have argued against some commentators that Posidonius is making no heretical statements, but holding to an unqualified cosmic substance, *in so far as* (καθ' ὅσον) it has no quality of its own, but in fact it always occurs in a qualified form. If ἀλλ' ὅσον in F97 is changed to καθ' ὅσον the sentence makes sense: Posidonius said that the void outside the cosmos was not infinite in so far as being sufficient for the dissolution, i.e. in the aspect of τόπος for the ἐκπύρωσις (although τὸ κενόν as such remains infinite). The error occurred from the form οὐκ ἄπειρον which invited ἀλλ' ὅσον.

The use of διάλυσιν is slightly odd. Both Ps.-Plutarch and Stobaeus in the sentence immediately preceding this fragment use ἀναλύεται of the Stoics and ἐκπύρωσις. ἀνάλυσις is the normal term with the doxographers: *Dox. Gr.* 471.20; 468; Stob. *SVF* II.413. Cleomedes uses ἀναλύεται (*De Motu* I.1 = *SVF* II.537); so also Philo, *De Aet. Mund.* 101ff (*SVF* II.619), . . . ἀναλυόμενον . . . ἀναλύεται . . . ἀναλυθείσης (where Bernays emends ἀναλύεται of the codices to διαλύεται). Spoerri (*Späthellenistische Berichte* 112) pointed out that ἀνάλυσις was used especially of change into a single element (*Dox. Gr.* 653.22; 276a.13; 278.12; 284a.13; 558.18; 589.23f), while διάλυσις should refer to a break up into several elements (*Dox. Gr.* 651.21; 652.10). There are, however, exceptions: Stob. *SVF* II.413.13, 17; *Dox. Gr.* 475.17. Eusebius' report of this sentence has τὴν διάβασιν ('the transition'?), a use I have not met elsewhere.

It would therefore be precarious to use διάλυσις as an argument that Posidonius did not hold the orthodox doctrine of ἐκπύρωσις. In spite of Spoerri's hesitations (*Späthellenistische Berichte* 111ff), D.L. VII.141–2 is strong evidence that Posidonius was orthodox on this topic (F13 comm.), and it is difficult to see to what else this fragment refers. See also F99b comm., and Hoven, *Stoïcisme et Stoïciens face au problème de l'au-delà* 33f.

F98 Arius Didymus, *Epitome* Fr. 26 (Stobaeus, *Eclogae* 1.8.42 = 1.107.17 W; *Dox. Gr.* 461)

CONTENT

Time.

CONTEXT

The Stobaeus doxography on 'time' runs from *Ecl.* 1.8.40–2, pp. 102–6 W. It begins with very brief notices: Thales, Periander, Euryphon, then (placed under Aetius by Diels, *Dox. Gr.* 318) Pythagoras, Eratosthenes, the Stoics, οἱ πλείους, Xenocrates, Chrysippus, Hestiaios, Straton, Epicurus, Antiphon and Critolaus. These are followed by larger notes under Aristotle (Ar. Did. F6), the Aristotelians (Ar. Did. F7), Zeno (Ar. Did. F26), Hermes (ἐκ τῶν πρὸς Τάτ), then Apollodorus, Posidonius and Chrysippus (Ar. Did. F26). The order is odd at this point in putting Chrysippus after Apollodorus and Posidonius.

COMMENT

The arrangement of this fragment on time is surprising. All the other Stoic entries in Stobaeus start with a definition of time. This one begins with the concept of the infinity of time (1–3), into which is introduced in a general way the factor of limit, the present (3). Then follows a definition of time (4–5), after which is raised the question of time*s* (πότε) in the form of past, future and present, where the concept of before and after is shown to depend on a limit, in this case not 'the present', but a dividing limit like a point (5–9). Finally this precise conceptual limit or 'now' is distinguished from a loose usage of 'now' as the least perceptible time constituted about the dividing limit of future and past (9–12).

Although it is dangerous to read too much into a doxographical note, this passage seems to display not the disjointed statements common to such entries, but a sequence of thought based on the particular problem in time of the finite limit on an infinite continuum.

A major problem of interpretation which also relates to the sequence of thought, lies in the manuscript corruption at line 5.

1–3 'Some things are wholly infinite, like the whole of time taken together, others in some respect: past and future time are each limited only in respect of the present.'

The Stoic arguments on time, and not least those of Posidonius, may have been influenced by Aristotle's discussion of the topic, for which see especially *Phys.* Δ, chs. 10–14 (Sorabji, *Time, Creation and the Continuum*, 21ff; but see the doubts of Sandbach, *Aristotle and the Stoics*, 50f, and Schofield, 'The Retrenchable Present', *The Bounds of Being*). That the continuum of time, taken as a whole, is infinite is Aristotelian (*Phys.* 218a 1), and was agreed by Chrysippus (*SVF* II.509 = Ar. Did. F26, Diels) and by the Stoa in general. Chrysippus (*loc. cit.*) said that past and future were infinite, Posidonius that they were limited by the present. D.L. VII.141 (*SVF* II.520) states that past and future are infinite, the present (τὸν ἐνεστῶτα) finite. Aristotle had already pointed out that 'now' is a limit (πέρας) (*Phys.* 218a 24). The problem lies in what is meant by 'the present'. The word given to Posidonius here is the vague τὸν πάροντα. The statement is still ambiguous and inaccurate, and is refined below. Criticism of the Stoa on whether time is limited or unlimited, and on the problem of making the present the limit of past and the beginning of future is to be found in S.E. *Adv. Math.* X.189ff, 200ff; Plu. *Comm. Not.* ch. 41.

3–5 'Time is an interval (or extension, διάστημα) of movement, or a measure of quick and slow.'

That time is an interval of movement is the stock Stoic definition and goes back to Zeno (Stob. *Ecl.* I.104.7 W = Ar.

Did. F26, *Dox. Gr.* 461 = *SVF* I.93). It may be partly derived from Aristotle. Movement implies bodies, space and time (cf. S.E. *Adv. Math.* x.121, 169), and Aristotle's definition of time was the numerical aspect of movement in respect of the before and after, ἀριθμός ἐστι κινήσεως κατὰ τὸ πρότερον καὶ ὕστερον (*Phys.* 220a 24). The Stoics changed from number to extension or interval of movement. Possibly this was due to the close analogy with space (cf. Chrysippus, Ar. Did. F26, p. 461.27 Diels = *SVF* II.509, p. 164.20 Arn.; also Simplicius, *In Phys.* p. 786.12f Diels on Archytas (probably Ps.-Archytas; there is a hyper-doricism); Bréhier, *La Théorie des incorporels*; Goldschmidt, *Le système stoïcien* 33–45; but see also Sorabji, *Time* 22–6, Sambursky, *Physics of the Stoics* 101), thus contributing to the confusion of the 'spatialisation' of time. Perhaps it was also related to their wish to stress the concept of time as a continuum. Aristotle also held time to be continuous (συνεχές), and related movement and time to magnitude (μέγεθος, *Phys.* 219a 11ff, 220b 28ff), and himself once used the term διάστημα (*Phys.* 223a 1). For the Stoics time, like space and λεκτά, was incorporeal (ἀσώματος, D.L. VII.141; S.E. *Adv. Math.* x.218ff).

The report of Posidonius' definition of time is interesting for an omission. Chrysippus had expanded Zeno's διάστημα κινήσεως to διάστημα τῆς τοῦ κόσμου κινήσεως (*SVF* II.510) or to τὸ παρακολουθοῦν διάστημα τῇ τοῦ κόσμου κινήσει (*SVF* II.509). This addition of 'interval of movement *of the world*' became the standard Stoic definition (Stob. *Ecl.* I.105.9f W = Ar. Did. F26 = *SVF* III. Apoll. 8; D.L. VII.141; S.E. *Adv. Math.* x.170), but Posidonius appears to ignore it here. If Chrysippus' intention was to establish fixed points on the continuum by means of the cosmic cycle (Rist, *Stoic Philosophy* 276ff), or by using Stoic physics to show the unity and thus the knowability of time (cf. Goldschmidt, *Le système stoïcien* 34), Posidonius resorted to other reference points than cosmic ones (see below).

Time as a measure of velocity (quickness and slowness) is

also Aristotelian (*Phys.* 218b 15, 220b 32ff, 222b 30ff), and was adopted as part of the standard Stoic definition (Zeno: Stob. *Ecl.* 1.104.8 W = Ar. Did. F26 = *SVF* 1.93; Chrysippus: Stob. *Ecl.* 1.106.6 W = Ar. Did. F26 = *SVF* II.509).

5 After βραδύτητος (5), codices *FP* in Stobaeus give the following: καί πως ἔχει τὸν ἐπινοούμενον κατὰ τὸ πότε τοῦ χρόνου κτλ, which is grammatically unintelligible.

Heeren emended to ὅπως ἔχει τὸ ἐπινοούμενον, linking with the preceding words, a solution adopted by Diels and Wachsmuth, and apparently generally accepted without comment. Oddly, in the Stobaeus entry under Zeno (*Ecl.* 1.104.9 W = Ar. Did. F26 = *SVF* 1.93) μέτρον καὶ κριτήριον τάχους τε καὶ βραδύτητος is followed by ὅπως ἔχει and then apparently a lacuna. If Heeren is correct, the addition would be both difficult and of considerable importance. Literally it should mean: measure of fast and slow according to the state of that which is being conceived (the conception of any given moment?).

Without further evidence this is hard to interpret, but it would seem to lay some stress on the subjective element in the consciousness of time. Aristotle had briefly raised the question (*Phys.* 223a 21–9) whether time depends for its existence on a mind (ψυχή). Heeren's emendation would suggest that Posidonius had been grappling with problems which foreshadow in part Augustine's rejection of time as objective. Augustine, holding like the Stoics that past and future do not (now) exist, and that the present has no duration, defined the past by human memories and the future by human expectations; so that time became an extension of the mind itself (*Confessions* XI.10–28, and esp. 26–8; cf. Bergson, *Time and Free Will* 120: duration and succession belong not to the external world, but to the conscious mind). But Heeren's Greek raises severe difficulties, which have hitherto been innocent of comment. It is true that elsewhere Posidonius contrasts κατ' ἐπίνοιαν (or ἐπινοίᾳ) (conceptually) with καθ' ὑπόστασιν (in reality), Frs. 92, 16; but τὸ ἐπινοούμενον is strange. What is 'the thing being conceived'? What is it a conception of? And how would it relate to fast and slow? Also what could ὅπως ἔχει mean with reference to a conception? It remains doubtful whether Heeren's emendation is translatable.

Bake (p. 51) put a stop after βραδύτητος and continued: καὶ πῶς ἔχει τὸ ἐπινοούμενον κατὰ τό ποτε τοῦ χρόνου; *et quomodo se habeat id quod cogitatur, quantum ad quando temporis*; which is equally obscure in both languages.

Schofield has proposed to me: (a) . . . βραδύτητος. καὶ πῶς ἔχει τὸ ἐπινοούμενον κατὰ τὸ πότε; τοῦ χρόνου κτλ, translating: 'What about time conceived in terms of when? Part of time is . . .'; this makes good sense, but τὸ ἐπινοούμενον is still strange, and the sudden rhetorical question in a doxographer surprising; or (b) the same punctuation as above, but reading πως ἔχειν, and translating: 'And he said that a conception in terms of when has some standing'; but I find πως ἔχειν in this sense difficult, and my doubts persist over τὸ ἐπινοούμενον.

Harold Cherniss in conversation suggested the following: βραδύτητος. καί πως ἔχειν τὸν ἐπινοούμενον κατὰ τὸ πότε τοῦ χρόνου· τὸν μὲν εἶναι παραληλυθότα κτλ. 'And (he said that) time conceived (i.e. that depends on mental concepts) is so and so in respect of temporal position (the 'when' of time): part is past, part is future and part is present . . .'.

He pointed out that ὁ ἐπινοούμενος (χρόνος) is recorded as a term used by Epicurus; *PHerc.* 1413, 10, VIII (Arrighetti, *Epicuro*[2] 402; Cantarella and Arrighetti, 'Il libro "Sul tempo" dell' opera di Epicuro "Sulla natura"', *Cronache Ercolanese* II (1972), 25), ἀνάγκη τὸ[ν ἐπι]νοούμενον [κ]α[ὶ] παρεπ̣όμε[νον δια]λαμ[βάνειν χρ]ό̣ν[ον], where the prefix of the verb is guaranteed by *PHerc.* 1413, 11, II (Arrighetti, *Epicuro*[2] 404; *Cron. Erc.* II.26), ἀφήσομεν [οὖν ἡ]με[ῖς] τὸ ἐπινοη[θὲ]ν ε[ἶναι] χρόνον. ὁ παρεπόμενος χρόνος is presumably Epicurus' σύμπτωμα συμπτωμάτων . . . παρεπόμενον ἡμέραις τε καὶ νυξὶ κτλ (S.E. *Adv. Math.* X.219). What Epicurus may have meant by ὁ ἐπινοούμενος χρόνος is a matter for argument and conjecture (Arrighetti, *Epicuro*[2] 665; *Cron. Erc.* II.42f;

Isnardi Parete, 'χρόνος ἐπινοούμενος *e* χρόνος οὐ νοούμενος', *Parola del Passato* 31 (1976), 168–75), but is irrelevant, since Posidonius is unlikely simply to have taken over a concept from Epicurus, of whom he was severely critical (Frs. 22, 46, 47, 149, 160). But the papyrus does supply evidence that τὸν ἐπινοούμενον of Stobaeus' manuscripts could have been used by Posidonius of time (χρόνον).

Does it make sense? The position is certainly different from that of Heeren, and the sequence of thought much clearer. The standard definitions are given (interval of movement, measure of velocity). These may be taken as objective or at least they are colourless. Posidonius would then be going on to say that there is a time which depends on mental concepts (ὁ ἐπινοούμενος). For time in the sense of past, future, present, is subjective in the sense of involving a concept of before and after, since even the present 'is constituted from a part of the past and a part of the future about the dividing limit (διορισμόν) itself' (7f); and it is important how we conceive (10) this limit. So finally a distinction is drawn between a conceptual 'νῦν' and a minimal perceptible 'νῦν' (9–12), that is, a conceptual limit and the 'specious present'.

καί πως ἔχειν τὸν ἐπινοούμενον κατὰ . . . is still surprisingly abrupt and clumsy Greek, and τὸν ἐπινοούμενον as a semi-technical term makes unusual demands of the reader in a collection of this kind, but Cherniss's emendation makes excellent sense with minimum alteration to the text, and may be preferred.

5–9 The tripartition of time recurs in Zeno (Ar. Did. F26, p. 461.5f Diels, *SVF* I.93) and in Apollodorus (Ar. Did. F26, p. 461.9f Diels, *SVF* III. Apoll. 8). But Chrysippus had a problem with 'the present' (S.E. *Adv. Math.* X.197ff), because a continuum was taken to imply infinite divisibility (S.E. *Adv. Math.* X.123–41). So Chrysippus 'says most clearly (Ar. Did. F26, p. 461.29ff Diels = *SVF* II.509) that no time is entirely present. For since the division of things that are continuous goes to infinity, in accordance with this division (i.e. of a continuum) all time too has its division to infinity; so that there is no present at all in a strict sense, but only in a loose sense.'

Nevertheless, Chrysippus said that the present ὑπάρχει, while past and future merely subsist (ὑφεστάναι) (cf. also Plu. *Comm. Not.* 1081F). This position naturally met with criticism: esp. Plu. *Comm. Not.* ch. 41, 1081cff, with Cherniss's notes; and S.E. *Adv. Math.* x.169ff. For what Chrysippus may have meant by the present 'existing', although there is no present 'in a strict sense', see Goldschmidt, *Le système stoïcien*[4], 36ff, 247; 'ὑπάρχειν et ὑφιστάναι dans la Philosophie Stoïcienne', *REG* 85 (1972), 331–44 (esp. 340ff); Long, 'Language and Thought in Stoicism', *Problems in Stoicism*, 89–93.

Although Posidonius agreed with Chrysippus that the 'present' is partly past and partly future (7), he is more interested in the dividing limit (διορισμός) (8) of past and future, which is likened to a point (σημειώδης) (9). Aristotle too had defined the 'now' as ὅρος τοῦ παρήκοντος καὶ τοῦ μέλλοντος (*Phys.* 223a 6) and compared it to a point (στιγμή, 219b 16ff, 222b 30f; σημεῖον, *Phys.* 262b 2ff, *De Caelo* 283a 11), which holds together and marks off length (τὸ μῆκος) by being the beginning of something and the end of something (*Phys.* 220a 10ff; cf. 222a 10ff). So Archedemus (Plu. *Comm. Not.* 1081E = *SVF* III, p. 263.31–7 Arn.) regarded 'now' as a kind of juncture and connection (ἁρμήν τινα καὶ συμβολήν) of what is past and what is coming to be. Plutarch criticises this position as annihilating the whole of time 'for, if now is not time but a limit of time and if every part of time is such as now is, all time in its entirety obviously has no constituent part at all but is wholly resolved into limits and connections and junctures'.

This fragment shows how Posidonius broke that dilemma. He did not do it by regarding the point as substantial. It is true that he believed that some mathematical limits (e.g. surface) were substantial as well as conceptual (F16), but he can hardly have thought so of the point, which has no dimension (F199; cf. S.E. *Adv. Math.* IX.376). Nor indeed did διάστημα in the sense of 'extension of movement' imply substantiality for him any more than the 'extension' of space. The substantial limit that contained a body was in Posidonius' view its shape, not its place (F196).

9–12 He extricated himself from the dilemma by distinguishing two senses of 'now', one conceptual and one temporal:

' "Now" and similar expressions (τὰ ὅμοια) are conceived of as time in a broad loose sense (ἐν πλάτει) and not in a rigorous precise sense (κατ' ἀπαρτισμόν). And he says that "now" is used (λέγεσθαι) also in respect of (or, if κατά is deleted, "for") the least perceptible time (τὸν ἐλάχιστον πρὸς αἴσθησιν χρόνον) constituted about the dividing limit of future and past.'

11 It is by no means certain that κατά should be deleted with Wachsmuth. καὶ κατά *may* be an orthographical doublet. καί (also) would imply that there are 'broad' usages of νῦν in Greek other than 'least perceptible time'; as indeed there are, since 'now' in the temporal sense may have a wide temporal band (as οἱ νῦν). The sentence makes sense with both or either of the words καὶ κατά, and so the manuscript evidence should be retained.

For 'now' as the dividing limit which is like a point, Posidonius followed the lead of Aristotle, who had declared that 'now' as a point merely marks off and potentially divides time, but cannot itself be a part of time (*Phys.* 218a 6, 219a 30ff). So for Posidonius, his διορισμὸς σημειώδης, which is the key for 'before and after', cannot itself be conceived of as time in any strict (i.e. philosophical) sense at all (9–10). It can only be a conceptual limit or marker. On the other hand, if 'now' is used in a temporal sense, as Posidonius does use it for 'least perceptible time', that is different, and is a loose (i.e. imprecise) usage.

Chrysippus too had the distinction between κατ' ἀπαρτισμόν and κατὰ πλάτος (Stob. *Ecl.* 1.106.17f W = Ar. Did.

F26 = *SVF* II.509, p. 164.25 Arn.). But Chrysippus' context is the infinite divisibility of a continuum, so that any talk of 'present' (ἐνεστάναι χρόνον) must be in a loose, and never in a precise sense, for strictly speaking, 'no time is entirely present'. There is no sign here (in spite of Goldschmidt, *Le système stoïcien* 37) that Chrysippus had reached Posidonius' analysis. Chrysippus' preoccupation with the 'existence' or rather 'reality' of the present, developed along different channels of argument (Long, *Problems in Stoicism* 89–93).

Posidonius' analysis is in response to the problem of time viewed as a continuum. On the one hand the concept of before and after in a continuum derives from the limit of the point. Time itself is not the sum of these, as Plutarch suggested, because the limit is a timeless concept. On the other hand, time as an interval can be recognised as the least perceptible interval of which we are aware. Since the continuum is continuous and infinitely divisible, there is no atomic instant or unit of time, so this 'least perceptible' is necessarily imprecise, and is in fact the 'specious present'. This bears a remarkable similarity to the position of E. C. Clay and William James, who held that the philosophically correct use of the present is confined to a durationless instant, which is the conceptual boundary between past and future. But 'the prototype of all conceived times is the specious present, the short duration of which we are immediately and incessantly sensible' (James, *Principles of Psychology* vol. I, p. 631). As far as I know, Posidonius was the first to approach the problem of time in just this way.

F99a Diogenes Laertius, VII.142–3

CONTENT

'That the universe is a living creature (animal, ζῷον) that is rational (λογικόν), animate (ensouled, ἔμψυχον) and intelligent (νοερόν) is said by Chrysippus in *On Providence*, Bk 1, Apollodorus in *Physics* and Posidonius; ζῷον because it is an animate substance with sensation. For animal (ζῷον) is superior to non-animal; nothing is superior to the universe; therefore the universe is an animal. And it is ἔμψυχον (ensouled) as is clear from our (human) soul(s) being a fragment (ἀποσπάσματος) from that source. But Boethus denies that the universe is an animal.'

CONTEXT

The passage occurs towards the end of Diogenes' extended report on the Stoic universe (137–43). It is preceded by F13 and followed by F4.

COMMENT

1 The characterisation of the universe in the first line goes back to Zeno (*SVF* I.111), although he is not mentioned here. An animate universe was accepted as standard Stoic doctrine in the doxographies (Ar. Did. F29 Diels = *SVF* II.528, p. 169.15 Arn.). Compare Plato, *Tim.* 30b for a very similar precursor. F23 makes it probable that the Posidonian reference came from Περὶ θεῶν, possibly from Bk 3 (see F21).

4–7 The terms ζῷον and ἔμψυχον are explained. It is impossible to say whether this is also to be referred to Posidonius, but the passage is clearly related to the previous section in Diogenes.

4 **οὕτως** makes very difficult Greek, and ὡς (Reiske, or οὖν ὡς Diels) is to be preferred. αἰσθητικήν: *SVF* I.114.

5f The syllogism also goes back to Zeno: S.E. *Adv. Math.* IX.104 = *SVF* I.111; and for Cleanthes, S.E. *Adv. Math.* IX.88. It was still being used by Cicero, *ND* II.21; and since Posidonius defended such syllogisms from Zeno (F175), it is possible that he may have used it too.

6f The argument for ἔμψυχον is neither syllogistic, nor by analogy (cf. F21), but depends simply on Stoic physics (*SVF* I.134, 135, 459; II.774); but δῆλον is so optimistic that presumably it is abbreviated from a longer argument. The human soul as an ἀπόσπασμα in this sense recurs in M. Aur. V.27 in relation to δαίμων, which may remind one of Posidonius' phrasing of the δαίμων within us (F187.6f). There is a similar manner of expression in Xenophon, *Mem.* I.4.8, which Cicero recalls in *ND* II.18 (Jaeger, *Hermes* 50 (1915), 545). But if Posidonius is involved in any of this, it is not in any distinctive role, but as an authority for standard Stoic doctrine.

7f Boethus also denied that the cosmos was destructible (F99b). The two denials may be linked.

The evidence for Posidonius on the universe

Frs. 4, 6, 8, 13, 14, 20, 21, 23 are also relevant.

It is remarkable that all the evidence for Posidonius on this topic occurs in Diogenes Laertius, and within a self-contained unified report on the Stoic κόσμος (VII.137–43). Moreover, in this section, which abounds in references, Posidonius is actually referred to more often than anyone else, nine times, against Chrysippus (six), Antipater and Apollodorus (three times each), Zeno and Cleanthes (twice each), and Apollophanes, Panaetius and Boethus (once each). Four separate works of Posidonius are mentioned (Φυσικὸς Λόγος, Περὶ κόσμου, Μετεωρολογική, Περὶ θεῶν) compared with three or four (depending on the identity of two books on Physics) for Chrysippus, and one each for Zeno, Antipater, Apollophanes and Apollodorus. Also we find features such as long lists of references (e.g. F13), and lists referring to a general topic rather than to a particular statement (F6, F13), which are most unusual in Diogenes' reports outside the Stoic doxography (see Mejer, 'Diogenes Laertius and his Hellenistic Background', *Hermes, Einzelschr.* 40 (1978), 6). Above all, in this section, Posidonius may be specifically grouped with

Chrysippus (F21, F23), or singled out as the sole reference for common Stoic doctrine (F8, F14). In other words he is represented in this doxography as a prime authority for the standard Stoic philosophy on the universe.

The opening classifications for Diogenes' whole section on Stoic physical philosophy (VII.132–3) also have strong Posidonian associations. The first division into species (εἰδικῶς) runs: (1) bodies, (2) principles, (3) elements, (4) gods, (5) limits, place and void, where the prominence of πέρατα seems Posidonian (F16, F196). Then a generic (γενικῶς) triple classification is given as (1) universe (κόσμος), (2) elements (στοιχεῖα), (3) ὁ αἰτιολογικὸς τόπος, for which cf. T85, F18, F176. The subject of κόσμος is subdivided as (a) topics with which scientists (οἱ ἀπὸ τῶν μαθημάτων) are also concerned, relating to fixed stars and planets, e.g. the size of the sun and moon, and their revolutions, and (b) topics for physical philosophers (οἱ φυσικοί). But this is exactly the Posidonian division of F18. Moreover, the topics listed under (b), physical philosophy, also correspond to F18, and all are covered in Diogenes' following detailed section on the universe with specific reference to Posidonius. The topics are: (1) ἡ οὐσία of the universe (so, Frs. 4, 8, 20, 14); (2) whether the universe is γενητός or ἀγένητος (so, F13); (3) whether it is ἔμψυχος or ἄψυχος (so, F23, F99a); (4) whether it is φθαρτός or ἄφθαρτος (so, F13); (5) whether προνοίᾳ διοικεῖται (so, F21). The subdivision of ὁ αἰτιολογικὸς τόπος (§133) is also markedly Posidonian.

The whole of the foregoing evidence suggests that Diogenes' source for this topic wrote at a time comparatively near to Posidonius himself, whether this source was Diocles of Magnesia (D.L. VII.48; Mejer, *Hermes*, *Einzelschr.* 40 (1978), 5–7; v. Arnim, *SVF* I.XXX–XLIII) or not; and it could be argued that the source was based on a Posidonian exposition. This is not, however, comparably the case with other sections of Diogenes' account of Stoic philosophy; see T66 comm.

F99b Philo, *De Aeternitate Mundi*, ch. 15, II.497 M (VI.96.19 Cohn; p. 24f Cumont)

CONTENT

'Boethus of Sidon and Panaetius abandoned the doctrines of conflagrations (ἐκπυρώσεις) and regenerations (παλιγγενεσίας) and deserted to a more divine opinion on the indestructibility of the whole universe (κόσμου).'

COMMENT

1 ὁ σιδώνιος *M*: ὁ ἰδώνιος *U*: ἡ σιδώνιος *HP*: καὶ Ποσειδώνιος *v* Turnebus.

It was Turnebus in 1552 who began the trouble with the conjecture καὶ Ποσειδώνιος, which influenced Bake (p. 50, 53–8) and Hirzel (*Untersuchungen* I.226–30). Bernays in his edition (*Abhandlungen der Berliner Akademie* 1876, p. 248; 1882, p. 72) established the correct manuscript tradition, and Hirzel (*Untersuchungen* II.1.138 n. 1) retracted. But Turnebus' conjecture continued to trouble Edelstein (*AJPh* 57.294f) and misled Bréhier (*Histoire de la Philosophie* I.2.404) into entertaining doubts about the possibility that Posidonius too rejected the orthodox Stoic view of the destructibility of the cosmos. The emendation is nowadays generally and rightly set aside; see Hoven, *Stoïcisme et Stoïciens face au problème de l'au-delà* 33f.

It is true that there were stories that reservations about the doctrine were made by Zeno of Tarsus (*SVF* III. Zen. Tars. 5) and by Diogenes of Babylon (*SVF* III. Diog. Bab. 27). There is better evidence that it was strongly doubted by Panaetius (Frs. 64–9, van Straaten) and by Boethus of Sidon (*SVF* III. Boeth. 7) whose arguments are given by Philo in ch. 16 of *De Aet. Mundi*. And Cicero can imply such doubt in *ND* II.85 (but cf. 118, where Panaetius again is cited for this). But the positive evidence for Posidonius indicates decisively against Turnebus, that he did maintain an orthodox position, that the universe was destructible: F13, F97 comm.

F100 Scholia in Lucani Bellum Civile, Pars I, *Commenta Bernensia* IX.578.

CONTENT AND CONTEXT

Lucan describes the seat of god as the elements. The scholiast quotes Posidonius: 'God is intelligent *pneuma* pervading the whole of substance', and interprets substance (οὐσία) as the elements (earth, water, air, heaven).

COMMENT

The characterisation of god as πνεῦμα νοερόν seems to be stressed as particularly Posidonian, cf. F101 (for πνεῦμα, Frs. 139, 286). In fact, surviving evidence does not record the early Stoics defining god as πνεῦμα (Heinemann, *Poseidonios' Metaphysische Schriften* II.29ff; Dragona-Monachou, *Existence of Gods* 164). Zeno referred to god as νοῦς κόσμου πύρινος or as fire (*SVF* I.157), or as *aither* (*SVF* I.154), or as λόγος (*SVF* I.160); and Cleanthes is said by Cicero (*ND* I.37 = *SVF* I.530) to have called god κόσμος, or the mind and soul of the universe, or *aither*. *Spiritus* is referred to Zeno by Chalcidius (*SVF* I.88), and to Cleanthes by Tertullian (*SVF* I.533), but these may be later misapplications (Heinemann, II.29f).

On the other hand, although Posidonius is the only Stoic who is expressly named for this phraseology, the dogma that god was *pneuma* pervading the whole of substance was later applied to Stoics in general (οἱ Στωϊκοί): *SVF* II.1035 (Clement); II.310 (Alexander); II.1033 (Theophilus); II.1027 (Stob. *Ecl.* I.1, p. 37.23 W = Aetius, *Dox. Gr.* 306); II.1051

(Origenes); S.E. *Pyrrh.* III.218. Whether this was through the influence of Posidonius or not, it indicates that Posidonius was presenting standard Stoic doctrine, although he may have expressed it in his own way.

That god is intelligent substance pervading the whole of being is of course common doctrine from the start: F5; *SVF* I.158; I.155; I.161; II.310; II.475; II.1021; II.1027; II.1042. *Pneuma* is defined as a peculiar combination of fire and air (*SVF* II.310; cf. II.841). To say that god is πνεῦμα is not to deny that he was also fire (πυρῶδες, F101; cf. F17) and *aither* (F24; F127). But in the physical structure of the Stoic universe, fire and *aither* have a natural location in the outermost heaven or circumference (F93), and if Posidonius chose the more neutral term, *pneuma*, for the material aspect of god, it was probably to stress the immanent pervasiveness of god through the whole of being. This view was important for him (F92, F101). The principles of god and matter were only distinguishable in thought; in reality they always co-existed as everything there actually is.

For god in relation to the elements: *SVF* II.310; II.414; Cic. *ND* II.71. But Dragona-Monachou (*Existence of Gods* 166–8) pointed out that the Posidonian πνεῦμα νοερόν is completely absent from Cicero, *ND* II.

F101 Aetius, *Placita* I.7.19 (Stobaeus, *Eclogae* I.1.29b = I.34.26 W = *Dox. Gr.* 302.19)

CONTENT

Posidonius said that god is intelligent and fiery *pneuma*, without form, but changing into what he wishes and assimilating to everything. That is, god has no shape of his own, but always has a shape or shapes as being co-extensive with the objects that he gives form to and creates.

CONTEXT

In the same section of Stobaeus, but later (*Ecl.* I.37.20 W), there is a separate entry under οἱ Στωϊκοί (*SVF* II.1027).

COMMENT

πνεῦμα νοερὸν καὶ πυρῶδες: F100 comm.

οὐκ ἔχον . . . συνεξομοιούμενον πᾶσιν: It was this phrase in particular which led Edelstein to believe that 'the definitions of the second principle of the universe are also original' (*AJPh* 57 (1936), 292). But this is misleading (cf. Dragona-Monachou, *Existence of the Gods* 165f), and requires examination.

ἀμόρφους. This is supported explicitly by F5 (D.L. VII.134), and supposedly for the Stoa in general. In fact there is little other evidence. Ps.-Gal. *Hist. Phil.* 16 (*Dox. Gr.* 608.16ff = *SVF* I.153) contrasts Plato and Zeno: Plato thought that god was incorporeal, Zeno that he was corporeal, 'without any mention of his shape' (μορφῆς). In surviving arguments it is Stoic ὕλη which is attacked for being both ἄποιος and ἄμορφος (e.g. Plu. *Comm. Not.* ch. 48; F92 comm.). Lactantius (*SVF* II.1057) says *Stoici negant habere ullam formam deum*; but since his reading of Greek authors seems to have been minimal (Ogilvie, *The Library of Lactantius*; cf. F155), one would like to know where he found the evidence for his statement. However, we have no reason to doubt that this was a Stoic view, but it may have been Posidonius who pressed this aspect of god. It is not contradicted by the well-known story that Stoics believed that god was spherical in shape (*SVF* II.1059, 1060), because that refers to god as cosmos.

μεταβάλλον δὲ εἰς ὃ βούλεται καὶ συνεξομοιούμενον πᾶσιν. This has been seen as a paradox, that god, being without shape, changes into and becomes assimilated to everything (Reinhardt, *RE* 643; he advocates the Proteus simile in *Kosmos und Sympathie* 294, 42). Compare Plutarch's attack on ὕλη as ἄποιον σῶμα in *Comm. Not.* 1086AB (F92 comm.). But it is an expression of the standard interpretation of god as ὕλη πως ἔχουσα (*SVF* II.320; cf. τὸν ἐκ τῆς ἁπάσης οὐσίας ἰδίως ποιόν, D.L. VII.137 = *SVF* II.526; cf. *SVF* II.528).

Edelstein objected (*AJPh* 57 (1936), 292): 'Posidonius does not mention such a creative power of God. The action of God apparently is restricted to the ruling of the world. He can only become accommodated to that which exists'. (cf. Reinhardt, *RE* 643). In the first place, since Posidonius believed in ἐκπύρωσις (F13), he also believed in regeneration and the creative power of θεός/λόγος, although this is not mentioned here. But Edelstein clearly felt that the phrase was passive in expression. Perhaps it may be contrasted in form with Alexander's σχηματίζοντα καὶ μορφοῦντα καὶ κοσμοποιοῦντα (*SVF* II.310); but it can be paralleled, e.g. by Origenes' ἀλλοιωτὸν καὶ μεταβλητόν (*SVF* II.1053), and by Ps.-Gal. *Hist. Phil.* 16 = *Dox. Gr.* 609.1f: οἱ Στωϊκοὶ δὲ ἰδίαν μὲν ἰδέαν οὐκ ἔχειν διηνεκῶς, πνεῦμα δὲ πυρῶδες ὁμοιούμενον πᾶσι ῥᾳδίως, οἷς ἂν προσρυῇ.

It is true that Plutarch in his argument against Chrysippus in *De SR* 1054AB, appears to associate συνεξομοιοῦσθαι with passivity, and therefore ill assorting with an active principle. Reitzenstein (*Die hellenistischen Mysterienreligion* 135) suggested that the verb was associated with the Mysteries, but in fact, it is a colourless scientific term (Theophr., *De Causis Plant.* 1.9.3; Soranus, 1.88; Galen, *De Usu part.* 14.7). It could be middle. But that the whole phrase is essentially in tune with an active principle is shown by εἰς ὃ βούλεται. The multiform activity of god is in accord with his wish.

βούλεται does not refer to the installation in the universe of *omnes motus voluntarios* (Cic. *ND* II.58, as Reinhardt, *Kosmos und Sympathie* 294f), but we should rather compare (as Heinemann, *Poseidonios* II.231) πρὸς τὴν τῶν ὅλων διοικητοῦ βούλησιν (D.L. VII.88 = *SVF* III.4) and κατὰ τὴν τοῦ Διὸς βούλησιν (Plu. *Comm. Not.* 1076E = *SVF* II.937). So Seneca, *Ep.* 65.2: *causa autem, id est ratio, materiam format et quocumque vult versat, ex illa varia opera producit* (*SVF* II.303); *De Mundo* 400b 12: θεός . . . πάντα κινεῖ καὶ περιάγει, ὅπου βούλεται καὶ ὅπως, ἐν διαφόροις ἰδέαις τε καὶ φύσεσιν . . . All this is in line with the Posidonian stress on the immanent pervasiveness of god as a first principle (F100 comm.), possibly in order to counter any misapprehension of a separate active enforming principle (πῦρ τεχνικόν). If there is a paradox, it is between the changing assimilations to everything of the divine first principle and its everlasting permanence. Since it is active and persists for ever, god in Stoic physical philosophy must be expressed in physical terms (cf. F5) applicable to itself alone: *pneuma* without form. And yet, that god is without form is also a logical supposition, in the sense that he never exists separately on his own, but only as ὕλη πως ἔχουσα, as what there is, even in the ἐκπύρωσις when everything else perishes except god-enformed matter; see F92 comm.

This is, in substance, orthodox Stoicism; and F101 is repeated exactly in Ps.-Plu. *De Plac.* I.6 = *Dox. Gr.* 292a 23–293a 1, but assigned to the Stoics in general. But the stress and the underlying arguments (with F92) are Posidonian; the difference in emphasis is shown in the later passage in Stobaeus' section assigned to the Stoics (*SVF* II.1027). Posidonius' approach may have been stimulated by criticism of the Stoic presentation of ἀρχαί as σώματα ἄποια καὶ ἄμορφα: F92.

F102 Joannes Lydus, *De Mensibus* IV.71.48 (p. 122.15ff Wuensch)

CONTENT

In a note on the etymology of Zeus, Posidonius is mentioned with Crates of Mallos, Chrysippus, and unnamed others. Posidonius is said to have associated the word Zeus (Δι-) with the Greek word to administer, control or govern (διοικεῖν). Zeus is he who administers everything.

COMMENT

Lydus seems to have been using doxographies here, cf. D.L. VII.147, Stob. *Ecl.* I.31.11ff W = Ar. Did. F30, *Dox. Gr.* 465.

The whole cluster of etymologies has Stoic associations. Crates of Mallos was influenced by Stoic etymology, and although his own suggestions of διαίνειν (wet) and πιαίνειν (fatten) are not recorded elsewhere for Stoics, the added phrase, τὸν εἰς πάντα διήκοντα (2) is common; for Posidonius: F100, F21; and in general: D.L. VII.147.

The Chrysippean version, that everything is because of him, τὸ δι' αὐτὸν εἶναι τὰ πάντα (4), recurs in D.L. VII.147, Δία μὲν γάρ φασι δι' ὃν τὰ πάντα, and in Stobaeus, *loc. cit.* (*SVF* II.1062).

The derivation from δεῖν, i.e. binding (δεσμεύειν) or holding together (συνέχειν) (5f), also sounds Stoic, and indeed Posidonian, see F149. For the association of Ζῆνα with ζῆν (to live, 6): D.L. VII.147.

The etymology assigned to Posidonius, τὸν πάντα διοικοῦντα, is also given to Chrysippus by Philodemus (*SVF* II.1076). But the word and concept are commonly associated with god in Stoicism; e.g. D.L. VII.88 . . . ὁ ὀρθὸς λόγος, διὰ πάντων ἐρχόμενος, ὁ αὐτὸς ὢν τῷ Διί, καθηγεμόνι τούτῳ τῆς τῶν ὄντων διοικήσεως ὄντι; and slightly later in the section: πρὸς τὴν τοῦ τῶν ὅλων διοικητοῦ βούλησιν. But διοίκησις in the sense of the government and control of reason was of special importance in Posidonius' philosophy: Frs. 33, 147, 169.3, 185, 187.8. The idea goes back to Plato, *Phdr.* 246, ψυχὴ . . . πάντα τὸν κόσμον διοικεῖ.

F103 Aetius, *Placita* I.28.5 (Ps.-Plutarch *De Placitis* I.28, *Moralia* 885B; Stobaeus, *Eclogae* I.5.15 (I.78.15 W); *Dox. Gr.* 324); Ps.-Galen, *Hist. Phil.* 42 (*Dox. Gr.* 620.20–2); Joannes Lydus, *De Mensibus* IV.81.53.

CONTENT

Posidonius is recorded in the doxographies as saying that fate (εἱμαρμένη) is 'third from Zeus; for first there is Zeus, second nature (φύσις), and third fate'.

CONTEXT

In S(tobaeus) the passage occurs in a section, Περὶ εἱμαρμένης καὶ τῆς τῶν γινομένων εὐταξίας. (Ps.-)G(alen)'s section is Περὶ εἱμαρμένης, and (Ps.-)P(lutarch)'s Περὶ οὐσίας εἱμαρμένης. In L(ydus) the context is a doxographical note on ἀνάγκη and εἱμαρμένη. In S the entry is followed by Zeno (*SVF* I.176), Antipater (*SVF* III. Ant. 35) and Chrysippus (*SVF* II.913), all on εἱμαρμένη. In G and P the order is: Heraclitus, Plato, Chrysippus, Stoics, Posidonius: the same names reappear in L. The doxographical context is fate; but there is no context for Posidonius.

TEXT

1 τρίτην SPL: τρίτον G. ἀπὸ Διός SPG: ἀπόδοσιν ποιεῖται L (apparently a corruption at some stage of ἀπὸ Διός). πρῶτον SPG: πρώτην L.

2 δεύτερον SP: δευτέραν L; εἶτα G. τρίτον P: τρίτην SL: εἶτα G. The variations are insignificant; they all appear to mark a sequence. But cf. F107.

COMMENT

It is important not to overreach oneself in the interpretation of this fragment, considering the paucity of the evidence and the lack of context.

A Normally Stoic evidence does not treat Zeus, nature and fate as a sequence of powers, but as different aspects of the same thing; although distinguishable, they have the same reference, namely to the divine reason in its function in nature. Indeed the terms are frequently equated; fate and god: *SVF* I.102; II.1076; II.928; II.931. God, nature and fate: *SVF* II.937; II.945; II.1024; II.913; I.176. God and nature: *SVF* I.158. The only hint of a hierarchical relationship between providence and fate before Posidonius is ascribed to Cleanthes by Chalcidius (*SVF* I.551); but this is highly suspect (Dragona-Monachou, 'Posidonius' "Hierarchy" between God, Fate and Nature', *Philosophia* 4 (1974), 287; cf. id. *Philosophia* 3 (1973), 297).

B This fragment however does indicate an order. But there has been much disagreement over what kind of order is meant, and over the reference of the three terms.

(a) Some interpretations argue for a hierarchy of separate entities, e.g.:

(i) a heretical foreshadowing of the Neoplatonic triad (so, Jaeger, *Nemesios* 97–133), or of Middle Platonic triads (such as that of Harpocration of Argos, cf. Dillon, *The Middle Platonists* 259f). There is no evidence for this, and it is not supported by the named fragments.

(ii) Edelstein (*AJPh* 57 (1936), 292f, 301–5), relying only on attested fragments, offered an ingenious theory that the three terms represent three distinct hierarchical powers as causes: god, soul, matter. He argued that they could be distinguished existentially, with god a punctual existence, soul (φύσις) as two-dimensional, and matter (εἱμαρμένη) as three-dimensional. This does not seem to me to be borne out by surviving fragments on cause (F95 comm.) and soul (F141 comm.). It is doubtful whether Posidonius recognised punctual existence (F98, F16 comm.), and it seems to be contrary to Posidonius' views on matter and substance (F92) and on god (F101). For further criticism: Dragona-Monachou, *Philosophia* 4 (1974), 288f; Rist, *Stoic Philosophy* 203ff.

(iii) Rist too (*op. cit.* 202–11) argued for a hierarchy involving physical distinction. God is the soul, and nature the body of the universe; god/soul as the perimeter of heaven holds the body of nature together. But then fate is represented as the 'errant' cause of necessity which fits neither the other two nor Stoic Posidonius. Also Rist emphasises separation, where Posidonian physics (F92, F101) stresses the inseparable permeation of the two principles. See also Dragona-Monachou, *Philosophia* 4. 289f.

(b) Because of these difficulties Graeser, *Plotinus and the Stoics* 110 rejected all theories of a hierarchy of powers, and suggested that the triad is relevant only to Posidonius' methodology of divination. This line of argument has been most convincingly developed by Dragona-Monachou, 'Posidonius' "Hierarchy" between God, Fate and Nature', *Philosophia* 4 (1974), 286–301, which also contains a full review of the state of the problem. She argues that F107 is primary, and that F103 is a muddled derivative. This may be correct.

(c) However, Frs. 103 and 107 show what may or may not be significant differences. F103 is introduced by the phrase τρίτην ἀπὸ Διός, which emphasises the sequence, and looks remarkably like an ape of Pl. *Rep.* x.597e; but it remains uncertain whether it comes from Posidonius or from a doxographer. Again the sequence of terms in the two fragments is different. This may merely be careless confusion in the doxographical tradition, but there is no variation in the four reporters.

It is worth asking briefly whether, if a hierarchical order is to be rejected, sequence in some other sense may be applicable to Posidonius' physical philosophy. A major difficulty is the fluidity of use of the terms themselves. It is not clear without context what Posidonius may have meant by φύσις, for example.

(i) In a cosmic sense, Zeus could be thought of as primary, if φύσις and εἱμαρμένη have reference to the *cosmos* which is destructible and has to be regenerated by god-in-matter. But such 'cosmic' sequence is far-fetched, and it is difficult to put φύσις and εἱμαρμένη in sequence.

(ii) More promising is logical sequence. Since god *is* the providential governing factor (F21), he is logically prior to the other two aspects of his function operating in the universe, where nature is the realm where he operates as the cohesive force (D.L. VII.148), and fate is the law of his operation as linked chain of cause and effect (D.L. VII.149; *SVF* II.913, 917, 918, 976; I.98). There is no question of physical distinctions and hierarchies, since the subject is three aspects of what there is; but there may be logical priority between the ruling principle, its natural function, and the law of its operation.

(iii) Reference may be to an explanatory presentational sequence. It is noticeable that the order of presentation of Diogenes' report on Stoic physics (D.L. VII.148–9), runs: god: φύσις: εἱμαρμένη: μαντική. All are linked, and especially the last item with what goes before: 'And what is more, they say that divination exists in all its forms (πᾶσαν), if actually providence (πρόνοιαν) exists' (see F7, F27). God, nature and fate are all aspects of providence.

So the triad can be used as an explanatory tool or device for the explanation of (a) the providential government of the universe which is the working of god-in-matter permeating as providential intelligence through the whole universe (F21), *and so* also for (b) the science of divination (cf. F107).

But (a) is also important, indeed the base of (b), so it is

doubtful whether Dragona-Monachou (*Philosophia* 4. 292) is right in saying that (a) is 'of no particular significance independently of it' (i.e. divination). It does have significance for the explanation of providence in physical philosophy, but not as a triad of separate distinct powers. Posidonius liked triads, but they were not necessarily hierarchical entities (F87, F95).

F104 Cicero, *De Fato* 5–7

CONTENT

Cicero argues against the thesis of Posidonius that everything happens by fate; cf. F25.

CONTEXT

The passage occurs immediately after a huge lacuna in which Hirtius had spoken in defence of the Stoic doctrine of fate, and Cicero had begun to reply. Cicero is still speaking.

COMMENT

A. (1–4)

Cicero grants, or at least does not exclude the possibility, that between some events there may be involved a *naturae contagio*, but not a *vis fatalis*.

Naturae contagio, a natural contact, the 'contagion' of nature (*contagio* can be used for contagious diseases), is one of Cicero's expressions for the Stoic (*SVF* II.534, 546, 1013, 1211) technical term, συμπάθεια (F106).

The instances given in the compact list (1–3) are clearly stock:

(a) Antipater of Sidon throughout his whole life only had a fever on the day he was born and one other he died of on his birthday (see Val. Max. 1.8.16);

(b) those born at the winter solstice were especially connected with astrology;

(c) for the case of the brothers falling ill at the same time, see F111; Augustine found a more complete version of this story in a part of *De Fato* now lost;

(d) the inspection of urine and the colour of nails was used both in astrology and medicine.

All these instances were clearly (cf. Val. Max. and F111) interpreted in relation to fate and divination; but Cicero is saying that there could be natural physical connections or influences in these cases open to more scientific explanations, such as those given in medicine.

B. (4–19)

But *all* cases cannot be so explained. Some cases can involve elements of chance (*fortuita*); and others even seem to have been invented (*comminisci*) by Posidonius; in any event they are ridiculous.

The (Posidonian) instances are:

(a) (7–10) Daphitas, who for a joke asked the oracle at Delphi whether he should find his horse (he did not possess one). The oracle replied that he would meet his death thrown from a horse. King Attalus of Pergamum had him hurled from a rock called the Horse (Val. Max. 1.8.8).

(b) (10f) Philip of Macedon (Val. Max. 1.8.9), warned by the same oracle to look out for a chariot, was killed by a sword which had a chariot engraved on it.

(c) (11–14) Then there is the anonymous sailor (Cicero waxes sarcastic) of whom death by drowning was predicted (and so presumably he avoided going to sea). He drowned in a burn.

(d) (14–19) Icadius appears to have been a notorious Rhodian pirate (see Festus, ed. Lindsay, pp. 94, 332); if he was crushed by a rock in a cave, that was a matter of chance if anything is (18f).

The reader is expected to know the details of these cases. They had probably already surfaced in an earlier part of *De Fato* now lost. They had become common debating τόποι, but are referred particularly to Posidonius. Probably the instances in A came from him as well.

C. (19–24)

Cicero offers an argument, which will have a wide application (*atque hoc late patebit* (20)): if there were no such thing as fate (no *nomen*, no *natura*, no *vis*), and if most or all things that happened were to take place accidentally, at random, by chance, would they turn out otherwise than they turn out now? This seems to be a rhetorical question, because he concludes: what is the point then of cramming in fate, when the explanation of everything can be referred to nature and chance, without fate?

D.

Does Cicero's argument give a clue to Posidonius' defence of fate? Perhaps he argued exactly the opposite. Things would happen differently if everything did not happen by fate. But that things will happen the way they will (i.e. not accidentally) is shown by divination.

Divination can be seen to be a science by its results, i.e. the fulfilment (ἔκβασις) of the prediction; so F7 (cf. Cic. *De Div.* I.12, 15, 35, 71, 124, 126). It could only be a science if everything did happen by fate. This in turn depends on the complete permeation of providence through the whole of nature (F7, F21). Therefore divination is both the result and the proof of god, nature, and fate (cf. F103, F107, and D.L. VII.148–9; see Cic. *De Div.* I.9–10).

If this is so, it shows the close connection for Posidonius of providence, the behaviour and interconnection of natural events, and natural law (or fate), see F103. It also explains his strong interest in and insistence on divination, and the details of its ἐκβάσεις. Related also is his indefatigable interest in the scientific investigation of natural order. Cf. in general Dörrie, 'Der Begriff "Pronoia" in Stoa and Platonismus', *Freiburger Zeitschr. f. Philos. u. Theol.* 24 (1977), 60–87.

The debate concentrated on supposed particular instances. Cicero thinks that it is enough to show *some* chance outcomes in order to break the complete chain of fate. From the other side, Quintus in *De Div.* I.71 claims that it is enough to establish *one* event so clearly foretold that it excludes the hypothesis of chance.

For Cicero's tactics of argument, where by partial concession he can concentrate on the extreme example, cf. F106, which also employs rhetorical ridicule of examples.

F105 Seneca, *Epistulae* 113.28

CONTENT

One should not put one's trust in the armour of Fortune.

CONTEXT

Seneca in this Letter has been attacking the Stoic theory that the virtues are ζῷα (*SVF* III.305–7). At §27 he says that he does not wish to learn whether courage is an animal, but that no animal can be happy without courage, unless he is fortified *contra fortuita . . . et omnes casus*. Courage is an impregnable rampart for human weakness. He who girds himself with it survives safely in the siege of life; for he then uses his own strength, his own weapons (*telis*). This naturally leads into the Posidonian *sententia*.

COMMENT

Fortuna = τύχη, that is to say, chance or luck. But since for the Stoics everything happens by fate (F25), strictly speaking there is no such thing as chance. In fact Stoics define τύχη as αἰτία ἄδηλος ἀνθρωπίνῳ λογισμῷ (*SVF* II.965, 966, 967, 970, 971). So τύχη does not exist in an objective sense, but only in a subjective one. *Fortuna*/τύχη is that aspect of εἱμαρμένη which is inexplicable or unexpected to a man, both in a bad sense of unexpected misfortune, or in the opposite sense of good luck. So in the bad sense, ὁ σοφὸς ὑπὸ τῆς τύχης ἀήττητός ἐστι (*SVF* I.449, Persaeus), and in the good sense, τὸν σπουδαῖον οὐδέν φασι δεῖσθαι τῆς τύχης (*SVF* III.52).

Stoics continued to use the word whether in argument with opponents, or in concession to ordinary usage. So Posidonius in the Athenion fragment (F253.38) can write of the crowd running together at the spectacle of the sumptuous arrival of Athenion, τὸ παράδοξον τῆς τύχης θαυμάζοντες; and of the gold and silver mines he writes rather fancifully that every hill is bullion piled up ὑπό τινος ἀφθόνου τύχης (F239.6). Both passages are very rhetorical (cf. οὐκ ἀπέχεται τῆς συνήθους ῥητορείας, F239.2). So is the passage quoted by Seneca here. *Fortuna* is personified. 'You will never be able to think that you are safe with the armour of Lady Luck. Fight with your own armour (i.e. virtue, ἀρετή). Luck does not provide armour against herself. You may be equipped against your enemies, but defenceless against her.'

The context is ethical. Posidonius may have used τύχη in relation to the 'intermediates', the physical and external advantages and disadvantages which are not under our own control (ἐφ' ἡμῖν); so F170.31, *a fortuitis* (with reference to wealth and health). But that passage is itself difficult and obscure (F170, comm. *ad loc.*), and shows signs of Senecan influence. Certainly *fortuna* and *fortuita* are favourite topics for Seneca; see *Concordantiae Senecanae* (Busa and Zampolli) *s.vv.* Compare for both context and metaphor *Ep.* 74, where (§16ff) Seneca has been talking about the limitations of *commoda* (i.e. προηγμένα, F170 comm.), and of the calamities that can fall in this sphere. So (§19) *adversus hos casus muniendi sumus; nullus autem contra fortunam inexpugnabilis murus est; intus instruamur. si illa pars tuta est, pulsari homo potest, capi non potest.*

F106 Cicero, *De Divinatione* II.33–5

CONTEXT

In the second book of *De Div.* Cicero takes up the question whether divination exists at all, or whether there is any need for it. At §28 he attacks the method of divination by inspection of entrails. At §33 he denies that 'signs' from entrails have anything to do with scientific observation. What relationship (*cognatio*, cf. Posidonius' use of συγγένεια, see F108) can they have with *rerum natura*? But even supposing the universe is a unified harmonious whole, what connection can there be between entrails and making a financial gain, or between the entrails and the universe, and a fortune and the laws of nature? Cicero proceeds to attack the Stoics, among whom Posidonius is named, on this particular point.

COMMENT

The structure of argument is similar to F104. Cicero is willing to concede, or at least leave open, the possibility that the explanation for some events may be referred to a natural connection in the nature of things. What he has in mind is the Stoic doctrine of συμπάθεια, so labelled at line 17. He has various translations of this expression: *contagio* (1) which implies infectious or influential contact between natural phenomena and events (cf. F104.3); *cognatio naturalis*, or a natural relationship between remote (*distantium*) things (13), for which the Greek would be συγγένεια (F108.6 for Posidonian background); *coniunctio naturae* (natural coupling), *concentus* (concord), *consensus* (unanimity) (16). It must be stressed that συμπάθεια is not assigned to Posidonius in particular but to the Stoics in general (2), and Posidonius is only named after Chrysippus and Antipater (25f). Cicero may still have used Posidonius for the background for this passage (cf. 10–12).

Cicero's concession, however, to one aspect of συμπάθεια is limited (13f), and intentionally destructive of the full doctrine. By singling out one example, the prediction of financial gain from the inspection of entrails, where he asserts that the supposition of natural connexion is ridiculous, he breaks the chain of fate which Stoics maintained held between all events. Cicero's dramatic opponent, Quintus, had said (*De Div.* I.71, 124–5) that it was enough to establish *one* event so clearly foretold as to exclude the hypothesis of chance; Cicero counters that one example to the contrary destroys universal συμπάθεια. Hence his ridicule of the core of the doctrine (28f), that a sentient divine power permeated through the whole universe leads to the choice of victim. For divination, συμπάθεια, fate and providence were inseparably linked for the Stoa (F103, F104). Again *vis sentiens atque divina* is assigned specifically to Chrysippus and Antipater as well as to Posidonius. Both phrase (including *quae toto confusa mundo sit*) and context (in relation to leading one to choose a victim) are repeated from Quintus in *De Div.* I.118. For the divine power, see also *De Div.* I.12, 110, 120.

Cicero was right to attack the *vis sentiens atque divina.* Stoic divination depended fundamentally on the postulates of their physical philosophy (F7, F103). But Stoics and Posidonius also claimed that 'technical' or 'scientific' divination (τέχνην F7, *artis* Cic. *De Div.* I.11f) could be 'scientifically' checked by observation (*De Div.* I.34, 126; II.47) of the results (ἐκβάσεις, F7; cf. *De Div.* I.12, 15, 35, 71, 86, 109) that followed the 'signs' (σημεῖα, *signa*).

The supposed instances of *contagio naturae* which Cicero offers from the Stoic collection (2–12) vary considerably in character, and he himself appears to progress from the ludicrous to the serious. He opens with a scathing double diminutive, the liverkins of mousies (*musculorum iecuscula*) which are said to have become larger in winter. This popular lore (e.g. Pliny *NH* 11.196; 29.59; Plu. *QC* 670B; Aulus Gellius, 20.8.4) is elsewhere connected with the moon, so it is tempting to read *luna* instead of *bruma* (3). But Cicero appears to be grouping winter phenomena first (2–6), followed by a class of lunar phenomena (7–12), so perhaps the slip originates with Cicero, rather than from a copyist. Similar lore (Pliny *NH* 2.108; 18.227; Ps.-Arist. *Probl.* 20.21) is the case of the dry pennyroyal (βλήχων) which blooms and scatters its seed on the very day of the winter solstice. Quite different, however, is the case of sympathetic concinnation of the strings of a musical instrument (also noted in Ps.-Arist. *Probl.* 19.24; A. Gell. 9.7). Then come two lunar phenomena; in zoology, oysters and shellfish are said to wax and wane with the moon (Arist. *PA* 680a 31–4; *HA* 544a 18–21; Pliny *NH* 2.109, 221; S.E. *Adv. Math.* IX.79); and in botany, trees are thought to be seasonably cut down in winter with an old moon, since they are dried up without sap (Theophr. *HP* 5.1.3; Pliny *NH* 16.193). Both popular beliefs started life in the Aristotelian stable, then passed probably through Stoicism into popular science. Finally comes the reference (10–12) to the lunar periodicity of tidal phenomena, which can only derive from Posidonius. The last item may well indicate that Cicero found the whole list in Posidonius. He accuses him elsewhere of ridiculous examples (F104). The mixed character of the list shows how difficult it was to distinguish genuine scientific explanation from popular conjecture.

Cicero's style is that of rhetorical ridicule throughout. Even supposing (and he is not prepared to suppose) that there is a natural connection between a victim's liver and coming into a minor windfall (*lucello* and *quaesticulus* (18) are again scornful diminutives), what about the other complicating factors, such as finding the victim with the appropriate entrails? And as for the more choice (*melius*, 30) assertion that at the moment of sacrifice a 'sign' occurs by a change in the entrails, no granny (*aniculae*, 33) would swallow that.

F107 Cicero, *De Divinatione* 1.125

CONTENT

'Therefore I think we should, as Posidonius does, trace the whole influence and rationale of divination first from god, about whom enough has been said, then from fate, and then from nature.'

CONTEXT

Quintus in *De Div.*, Bk 1 distinguishes two main types of divination, technical (soothsayers, astrologers, oracles) and natural (dreams, frenzy) (11f); but the principal line of argument is directed to proving that divination exists in both categories. At §124 he reiterates his belief that divination exists even if sometimes a prophecy is mistaken. It is only necessary to find very few, indeed one instance of agreement, excluding chance or accident, between prediction and event to establish 'that divination undoubtedly exists, and everyone should admit its existence'. F107 follows, with *quocirca*, therefore. . . . Indeed it becomes necessary to establish an all-embracing natural law, if the case is to rest on one or a few instances from observation.

COMMENT

The best examination of this fragment is by Dragona-Monachou, 'Posidonius' "Hierarchy" between God, Fate and Nature', *Philosophia* 4 (1974), 286–301, who also reviews previous literature. She argues convincingly that the triple division does not refer to different categories of divination, but to those aspects of Stoic physical philosophy from which the justification of the whole of divination is derived. The sequence is a presentational or explanatory sequence, and is not dictated by a hierarchy of powers. This is clear because the presentation in *De Div.* I assumes general Stoic doctrine, and does not restrict itself to supposedly peculiar Posidonian views. And when Cicero refers back to this passage in *De Div.* I.27 he simply says, *duxisti autem divinationem omnem a tribus rebus, a deo, a fato, a natura*, without any reference, or without any suggestion that this is unusual in Stoicism. The inference would be that Posidonius gave explicit expression to the implications of the relationship between standard Stoic physical philosophy and divination (see D.L. VII.148–9). But this may have gained greater emphasis with Posidonius, since Panaetius had apparently doubts about divination (D.L. VII.149 = F73 van Str.; Cic. *De Div.* I.6 = F71 van Str.).

For the relationship between F107 and F103, see F103.

a deo de quo satis dictum est. *De Div.* I.82–3 gave the argument for divination based on the existence of gods and their providence. This is assigned to the Stoics in general, and to Chrysippus, Diogenes and Antipater in particular; Posidonius was not named. In §110 the argument is applied to 'natural' divination where human minds are moved by *contagione divinorum animorum*. Cf. §§117–20 where *vis quaedam sentiens, quae est toto confusa mundo* (118) is Posidonian as well as referred to Chrysippus and Antipater (F106). But the divine justification applies also to 'technical' divination, since the *divina mens* sends *signa* for interpretation.

The singular *deus* is merely characteristic of Posidonius' thought (Frs. 100–3), not because of the mention of Socrates' δαιμόνιον in §122ff (as Dragona-Monachou, *Philosophia* 4. 298).

a fato The justification through fate follows immediately in §§125–8. Reason compels us to admit that everything happens by fate (cf. F25), which is an order and series of causes, whereby nothing has happened which would not have happened, and nothing will be whose efficient causes are not contained in nature. So it can be marked by observation what result follows what cause for the most part. Man is not god, so he cannot see all the causes and may make a mistake. But since the evolution of time is like the unwinding of a rope, both 'natural' and 'technical' diviners, although they may not discern the causes themselves, can mark the signa of the causes and so predict (cf. F109). In the same way as you can predict future positions of the heavenly bodies, so divination is a form of prediction related to future events that are not yet present. It depends on the assumption of a continuum of the orderly unfolding of everything that happens, i.e. fate.

There is obviously a continuous argument in progress, and since Posidonius is mentioned again under the third heading of *a natura* (130), it is possible that Cicero based all these sections (125–30) on him (so Long, *CR* 26 (1976), 75). But in the justification *a deo*, Cicero, while using Posidonian material, also indicates a wider Stoic reference (see above). It may be safer to assume that Cicero was working within a Posidonian framework (F107), and that all the material of these sections may not necessarily derive from Posidonius (cf. F108), although it may have done so. To put it slightly differently: Cicero gives the impression that the arguments follow Posidonius *and the Stoics in general* (apart from Panaetius).

a natura: F110.

F108 Cicero, *De Divinatione* 1.64

CONTENT

Posidonius is quoted for an example confirming that men about to die can have the power of prophecy. He gave a threefold explanation of divine dreams.

CONTEXT

At §11f Cicero distinguished between two kinds of divination, that depending on art (i.e. scientific) and that which depends on nature. Dreams are a category of the latter. From §39 Cicero devotes himself to dreams with many examples. Chrysippus and Antipater are mentioned for collections (39), and so are Stoics in general (56). But there is also a mass of Roman examples. Cicero does not seem to be drawing on Posidonius here. At 60f, Plato, *Rep.* IX.571 is quoted, and Epicurus (62) is contrasted with Plato. In 63, the power of divination of the soul in sleep, when withdrawn from the body, leads to the topic of such powers at the approach of death. Posidonius is merely cited for a famous instance of this. But his general classification of how divinatory dreams happen, does not fit into the context of the argument, and has the appearance of an inset here, rather than part of the thread of Cicero's development. Therefore Posidonian influence should at this stage be confined to this section.

COMMENT

A. (1–4)

The *example*: a certain Rhodian on his death-bed named the sequence of dying of six of his contemporaries.

For Posidonius using a historical Rhodian example (as distinct from mythical and literary examples), cf. the pirate Icadius in F104. The story had become famous, *illo etiam exemplo... quod adfert confirmat*: divination was confirmed by its results or fulfilment (ἐκβάσεις), see F7, Cic. *De Div.* I.12; and the reality of divination in turn confirmed fate (F104), and the existence of god and providence (Cic. *De Div.* I.9–10).

B. (4–9)

Three-fold explanation of how divinatory dreams occur, *deorum adpulsu*.

deorum adpulsu: (a) This is the 'natural' category of divination (*naturae*), as distinct from technical (*artis*) (*De Div.* I.11). (b) For Stoics and for Posidonius, the propositions that divination exists and that gods exist are interdependent (*De Div.* I.10).

(1) (5f) The mind of its own nature (*ipse per sese*) foresees, inasmuch as it is imbued with kinship with the gods (*deorum cognatione*).

This became something of a commonplace, Pease, *Ciceronis De natura deorum, ad loc.* But there is a very close parallel assigned to Aristotle by S.E. *Adv. Math.* IX.21 (F10 Rose): ὅταν γάρ, φησίν, ἐν τῷ ὑπνοῦν καθ' ἑαυτὴν γένηται ἡ ψυχή, τότε τὴν ἴδιον ἀπολαβοῦσα φύσιν προμαντεύεταί τε καὶ προαγορεύει τὰ μέλλοντα. τοιαύτη δέ ἐστι καὶ ἐν τῷ κατὰ τὸν θάνατον χωρίζεσθαι τῶν σωμάτων. (See also §§20–2, which also contain the example of Hector foretelling the death of Achilles, cited by Cicero immediately after the Posidonian extract.) If Posidonius was following Aristotle here, it was in conscious opposition to Plato, *Tim.* 71d–72b. But Sextus' report on Aristotle refers solely to the context of how the conception of gods arose in human beings (IX.20), and it is clear from Aristotle's essays *On Dreams* and *On Divination in Sleep* that he held very different views on divinatory dreams from Posidonian Stoicism (Dodds, *Greeks and the Irrational* 120). We know, however, that this concept was of great importance for Posidonius. *Cognatio* = συγγένεια; and human reason (νοῦς) is a *daimon* in us which is συγγενής to the reason which governs the universe (F187.6ff), and so it can understand the latter because of its kinship (F85).

(2) (7–8) 'The air is full of immortal souls, in which appear as it were clear marks of truth.'

Edelstein (*AJPh* 57 (1936), 300, n.57) suggested that these immortal souls may be the fixed stars. He compared *De Div.* I.130 (F110), and one could add that in Aristotle F10 (cited above B (1)) the alternative source of divination giving rise to a concept of gods is said to be the heavenly bodies. But this interpretation cannot be right, because the *immortales animi* must be different from *ipsi di* of line 9, and it would be a strange expression to say that the air is full (*plenus*) of the fixed stars.

There seems little doubt that the reference is to δαίμονες,

divine go-betweens between gods and men, or to surviving human souls of the dead (ἥρωες), or to a combination of both. Nothing further can be inferred from this passage. Although the survival of the soul after death is taken for granted in the previous section (63), analysis of the context (see above) does not permit us to assume that to be Posidonian (cf. Hoven, *Stoïcisme et Stoïciens face au problème de l'au-delà* 58).

But daemonic theories were widespread at the time; cf. in very similar form, Alexander Polyhistor (1st c. B.C.) on the Pythagorean version (D.L. VIII.32), and Philo of Alexandria, *De Somn.* I.134. They were much elaborated by Plutarch in his myths in *De Sera Numinis Vindicta, De Genio Socratis* and *De Facie*, and continued to flourish in the 2nd c. A.D. (Maximus of Tyre, Albinus, Apuleius (cf. Augustine, *De Civ. Dei* VIII.22–4)). Above all, belief in δαίμονες and ἥρωες was stated to be standard Stoic doctrine by D.L. VII.151, and facets surface in Epictetus (Bonhöffer, *Epiktet und die Stoa* 84) and in M. Aurelius (e.g. II.13). All theories preserve a double factor: (a) a part of the human soul is a δαίμων; (b) there are independent δαίμονες which have contact with and look after men. Both factors are peculiarly apposite to Stoicism, which regarded the rational aspect of the human soul as a fragment (cf. M. Aur. V.27) of the divine reason, and secondly saw the universe as a continuum permeated by god or λόγος. Posidonius expressly referred to human νοῦς as the δαίμων within us akin to that of the universe (F187.6ff), and wrote a book entitled *On Heroes and Daemons* (F24). The conclusion seems to be inescapable that this is the reference here.

For sober examinations of the much discussed passage, S.E. *Adv. Math.* IX.72–4, see Hoven, *Stoïcisme et Stoïciens* 63f; Dragona-Monachou, *The Stoic Arguments for the Existence . . . of the Gods* 173f.

But there cannot be a reference to the immortality (*immortales*) of human souls as such in any strict sense. Posidonius believed in ἐκπύρωσις (F13), so only god-qualified matter undifferentiated in its purest form was ἄφθαρτος.

The 'clear marks of truth' that appear on these souls, would be meaningless ('ganz rätselhaft', Reinhardt, *RE* 802; 'ungeschickt', Pohlenz, *Die Stoa* II.118), unless Posidonius made use of some such imagery as the marks on the soul-daemons of Plutarch, *De Sera* 564DE. But that Posidonius regarded this as imagery is shown by *tamquam* (8). In Stoicism a 'clear mark of truth' would be provided by a cataleptic presentation.

(3) (9) 'The gods themselves speak with men who are asleep.' Again there is no clarification of what Posidonius had in mind. He may have been thinking of dream oracles and incubation (see Pease, *ad loc.*; Iamblichus, *De Myst.* III.2).

F109 Cicero, *De Divinatione* II.47

CONTENT

Posidonius investigated the causes of meteorological phenomena as prognostic signs.

CONTEXT

At §42 Cicero in criticism of Quintus passes from divination by means of entrails to divination through portents. Meteorological phenomena such as lightning seemed to present greater opportunities for observation, and to offer a field more open to reason and conjecture. But while these events happen from natural causes, that does not mean to say that they are signs of future events (§44). At §§46–7 Cicero refers back to *De Div.* I.13ff where Quintus quoted from Cicero's *Prognostica*, a verse translation of the Προγνώσεις διὰ σημείων, or Weather Signs, which forms the second part of Aratus' *Phaenomena*. Quintus argued that weather 'signs' are a good example of divination, in that you can observe force and effect without necessarily understanding the causes.

COMMENT

Cicero argues against Quintus on two counts:

(a) Weather signs are not a good example of divinatory phenomena, by illustrating observation of effect without understanding cause, because not only Boethus the Stoic, whom Quintus had mentioned (*De Div.* 1.13), but also Posidonius did investigate the causes of weather signs.

(b) But even if it is true that meteorological phenomena are capable of being observed for result without knowledge of causes, this is irrelevant for divination of portents, because the two are totally dissimilar (*dissimile totum*, §47). What opportunity is there for long-standing observation in the case where Natta's statue and the brazen tablets of the laws were struck by lightning (quoted by Quintus, *De Div.* 1.19, from Cicero's poem *Consulatus*, and therefore not from Posidonius)?

The defence of divination based on the argument that we merely need to observe the agreement between sign and event without understanding the cause or explanation runs through much of Quintus' exposition in *De Div.* 1; e.g. 1.12ff, 35, 71, 86, 109, 124f, 127. The thesis, put in that form, does not sound characteristic of Posidonius with his aetiological enthusiasm. That Posidonius investigated the causes of meteorological phenomena is well attested (Frs. 15, 129–38). He did emphasise results (ἐκβάσεις, F7), but in the sense that divination is confirmed as a τέχνη by its results, which is a different matter.

The context here, and the term *prognostica*, indicate that Posidonius not only enquired into causes, but connected meteorological phenomena with 'signs', and so with a form of divination and probably with portents. This appears to be confirmed by F132, although the reference there (F132.20ff) may be drawn from the *History* (see comm. *ad loc.*).

F110 Cicero, *De Divinatione* 1.129–30

CONTEXT

F107.

CONTENT AND INTERPRETATION

1–3 'From nature comes another (*alia*) particular rational explanation (*ratio*) which teaches how great the power of the soul is when separated from the physical senses, which especially happens to men who are sleeping or inspired.'

The reference is still to F107 (§125), where the authority of Posidonius is invoked for justifying divination from god, fate and nature. The topic of god had been dealt with before §125, and fate was the subject of §§125–8 (F107 comm.). Quintus now turns to 'nature', and *alia* means other than that provided by fate.

An example follows, which is not printed in the text of F110. It is in the form of a comparison (*ut . . . sic*): as gods communicate with each other without sense organs, so human souls freed from the body in sleep or mental excitement, discern what they cannot see when they are thoroughly mingled with the body (cf. F108).

3–7 Quintus continues: 'It is perhaps difficult to translate *that* (*quidem* – as compared with the principle of fate) principle of nature to the category of divination we say proceeds from art (*ex arte*, i.e. 'technical' divination as opposed to 'natural'), but that too Posidonius grubs up (*rimatur*) as far as he can: he thinks that there are certain signs of future events in nature (*in natura*).'

Quintus' references for the 'natural' justification of divination apply to the category of divination he calls 'natural' as distinct from 'technical' (see F108). But Posidonius' triple justification of divination was intended to apply to the whole of divination (*vis omnis*, F107; cf. *divinationem omnem*, *De Div.* II.27; F7), and the justification from god and fate covered both natural and technical divination (F107 comm.). If Cicero had a difficulty with the range of application of explanation from nature (implied by *rimatur*, 6), Posidonius it appears was determined to retain the overall justification.

What is the meaning of *natura* throughout the passage? One would expect that the meaning in lines 1, 4, 7 should be the same. In line 1, *natura* should mean 'natural' with reference to 'natural' divination as distinct from 'technical' (*ex arte*, 5). This is borne out by the example of the human soul's communion when separated from the body in sleep or frenzy (F108), and by the difficulty of applying this divinatory principle of function to technical divination (4–6). Then what are the signs of the future 'in nature' that technical divination can mark? Probably *natura* means basically not 'Nature' but 'natural structure', the natural ἕξις or properties or make-up of a thing or things (i.e. φύσις). The 'nature' which is important in 'natural' divination is the 'nature' of the soul, which in sleep, *ipse per sese* (F108.6; cf. the example here; and the example of the magnet, *De Div.* I.86), by its own nature, communes with other such 'natures'. So in technical divination, Posidonius believes that there are signs in the nature of things. Lines 8–14 offer an explanation (*etenim*), and although the example comes from Heraclides Ponticus (cf. F18.39), the citing of it probably derives from Posidonius and his interest in meteorology and the observation of stars (F204, F205). From the observation of signs of the 'nature' of the Dog Star at rising, prognostications of health and sickness are made. So in 'art' there is no 'direct contact' (*naturae contagio*) with nature, but an examination of the signs of the nature of things, signs given by the gods and produced in the natural continuum of cause and effect. The expert observes stars and entrails for the signs in their condition, assuming that the unrolling of the rope of events is marked by signs shot through the continuum of nature. Cicero (or Quintus) describes technical diviners as those *qui novas res coniectura persequuntur, veteres observatione didicerunt* (*De Div.* I.34; cf. *SVF* II.1207–16). But Stoic divination could never rest on observation; it is a logical derivation from the hypotheses of their natural philosophy. Posidonius appears to have seen that; but there is little evidence that he was able to distinguish clearly between scientific and other forms of prediction.

F111 Augustine, *De Civitate Dei* V.2; V.5

CONTENT

Posidonius commented on the astrological explanation of the illness of twins.

CONTEXT

At the beginning of Bk V Augustine claims that the greatness of the Roman empire is due neither to chance (*fortuita*) nor to fate (*fatalis*). He interprets fate (*fatum*) as *cuiusdam ordinis necessitas*, but in ordinary usage he says that this is taken to imply the influence of the position of the stars at the moment a child is born or conceived. Since Augustine had himself once believed in astrology, he is now much exercised in attacking it in his defence of the will of God in Christianity. He distinguishes between the stars foretelling (portending, giving *signa*, *significare*) and stars influencing (causing, *facere*, an active force) (cf. F112). He seems to imply that *mathematici* held the latter view, *philosophi* the former (at F111.40f Posidonius appears in both categories). He then raises the problem of twins. How can they and their lives be so different, although only a very brief interval separates their birth, and they were conceived at the same moment?

COMMENT

The context naturally leads Augustine to what was obviously a well-known case which he picked up from Cicero, almost certainly from a missing part of *De Fato*, where the reference to sick brothers in §5 (F104) looks back to a fuller discussion in the earlier lacuna (see Hagendahl, *Augustine and the Latin Classics* 526f).

If the original reference to Hippocrates (1) was to *Epid.* 1.20, where a case history is given of two brothers who fall ill on the same day, there are minor discrepancies. *Epid.* says nothing about twins, and indeed refers to 'older' and 'younger' brothers; and the first crisis took place on successive days, although the relapse and final crisis occurred on the same days. But Augustine understood from Cicero (F111.4 and v.5 *init.*) that Hippocrates inferred from the similarities that they were twins. It seems to have been a well-known case, referred to as οἱ δύο ἀδελφεοί, and well documented – their sick bed was near the summer cottage of Epigenes.

Augustine contrasts the medical explanation of very similar physical constitutions and temperaments of health (7f) with the astrological account of Posidonius, who kept maintaining (*solebat asserere*, 6f) that the brothers had been born and conceived under the same constellation, and so assigned their common illness to the influence and arrangement of the stars (*ad vim constitutionemque siderum*, 8f) when they had been born and conceived.

Augustine goes on to say that there are perfectly good medical and environmental reasons which can explain both similarities and differences in twins. However, astrologers face a dilemma. On the one hand, if the explanation depends solely on astrology, all babies born at the same moment under the same arrangement of stars should have identical lives (F111.12–19). On the other hand, astrologers even if they could explain similarity in twins could not explain differences. Posidonius and the others try to do this (*conantur*, 22, must include Posidonius) by reference to the small interval of time elapsing between the birth of twins; but then they cannot have it both ways (22–34).

After discussing Nigidius Figulus (v.3) and Esau and Jacob (v.4, very dissimilar twins), Augustine returns to the Hippocratic passage in v.5. He reiterates that Posidonius (F111.40ff) stressed not only the time of birth, but in addition that of conception (cf. 6); but then if they are identical in being conceived at the same moment, how can the differences be explained? So there is an inconsistency between the explanation of natal horoscopes (22ff) and of conceptual horoscopes (40ff). Hagendahl (*Augustine* 528) suggests that the arguments advanced by Augustine against the astrologers may also come from Cicero's *De Fato*. Cf. also S.E. *Adv. Math.* v.1–105; Favorinus in Gell. xiv.1. It is very difficult to know from this evidence how far Posidonius was prepared to take astrological explanation. There seems little doubt that he was prepared to see 'signs' in the stars, but Augustine clearly places him in his second category as thinking that the stars exercised an active force (*facere*, Context; *vim*, 8) or influence (cf. F112). Stoics, however, while making some concessions to Chaldean astrology, also imposed limitations and reservations; cf. Diogenes of Babylon in Cic. *De Div.* ii.90. Posidonius by the very distinction between natal and conceptual horoscopes pointed to problems. He clearly took into account other factors, such as environment in physiognomy (F169). His whole enquiry into causes in physical philosophy (F18) puts his interest in astrology into context. See also F112, T74.

F112 Boethius, *De Diis et Praesensionibus* (from a commentary on Cicero's *Topica*, vol. v.2, pp. 394–5, ed. Orelli-Baiter)

CONTENT

Boethius classifies Posidonius with Firmicus Maternus as a chief authority on astrology.

CONTEXT

Boethius comments on Cic. *Top.* 77, where Cicero reviews *divina testimonia*, enumerating things in which are embodied certain works of the gods. F112.2–17 refers to Cicero's *primum ipse mundus* ⟨*eiusque omnis ordo et ornatus*⟩, i.e. the starry order of the heavens (*mundus*). F112.17–19 comments on Cicero's *aerii volatus* ⟨*avium atque cantus*⟩, 'the flight of birds through the air and their songs'.

COMMENT

Commenting on Cicero's divine evidence in the heavens (*mundus*) of the orderly progression of the stars, Boethius says that if something unusual happens, the outcome is foretold by astrologers (*mathematicis*) from the testimony of heaven (2–6).

At this point he brings in Plato (6–8), seemingly with a reference to *Tim.* 40c 9–d 2: . . . καὶ πάλιν ἀναφαινόμενοι (sc. the visible gods, i.e. the stars) φόβους καὶ σημεῖα τῶν μετὰ ταῦτα γενησομένων τοῖς οὐ δυναμένοις λογίζεσθαι πέμπουσι . . .

He interprets this (9) by making a distinction between (a) understanding that the stars *faciunt*, i.e. have a positive influence over what happens (which he denies), and (b) believing that they contain signs whereby one may tell the future (9f). This is precisely the distinction made by Augustine (F111, context and comm.). The latter alternative, that the stars merely give signs (*significant*, 10), is what Plato (?) says (*ait.* Or Cicero? But *significant* does not appear in this section of the *Topica*, although a little later in connection with dreams Cicero has *a dormientibus quoque multa significata visis*).

But otherwise, those who hold interpretation (a), i.e. 'who think that these stars have this power consciously to make harmful decisions, would do great injustice to heaven' (in ascribing the causes of crime to it) (11–15).

'But it is in the treatment of this sort of thing that the talk of Posidonius and Julius Firmicus (Maternus), or of the rest of the astrologers, holds sway.' (16f).

Boethius then passes to Cicero's second category, divination from birds (17–19).

So to Boethius as to Augustine, Posidonius represented the stronger version of astrology, which stressed the influence of the stars as well as seeing them as signs or portents. This is confirmed by the classification with Firmicus. Boethius gives no indication of attempting to understand this within a Stoic context. Indeed imputing crimes to heaven would be in direct opposition to Posidonius' views on providence; in general F111, T74.

F113a, b Ps.-Nonnus Abbas, *Ad S. Gregorii Orationem I Contra Iulianum* 72 (Migne 36.1024); Suda, *s.v.* Διαίρεσις οἰωνιστικῆς. Οἰωνιστική, 163

CONTENT

Posidonius wrote on that type of divination or augury which is based on involuntary twitchings of various parts of the body.

COMMENT

At some point in the 6th century, scholia explicating the allusions to pagan mythology were added to four homilies of Gregory of Nazianzus, one of which was the first invective against Julian (*Or.* 4). We do not know who the author was, for the attribution to Abbas Nonnos, i.e. Nonnus of Panopolis in cod. BM Add. 18231 (971/2 AD) is incorrect, and does not appear in the Syriac and Armenian translations. The scholia were translated into Syriac probably still in the 6th c., and then revised in 623/4 by Paula, Bishop of Edessa (Brock, *The Syriac Version of the Pseudo-Nonnos Mythological Scholia* 7–12). A translation of the Syriac version is given by Brock, p. 117. A further translation was made into Armenian, possibly in the 7th c. (Brock, 12ff). This particular scholium turns up again in the Suda (F113b), and appears once more in Eudocia Violarium LVII (p. 72.7–10, Flach; now generally attributed to Konstantinos Palaiokappa) with minor variations.

In the Gregorian version the whole scholium (of which the Posidonian part is the final section) is entitled Περὶ τῆς οἰωνιστικῆς (*On Augury*) (cf. Pl. *Phdr.* 244d, where the term οἰωνιστική is used as a generic term for technical divination), and the subsections on which there are notes are: τὸ ὀρνεοσκοπητικόν, τὸ οἰκοσκοπητικόν, τὸ ἐνόδιον, τὸ χειροσκοπητικόν and τὸ παλμαστικόν. The Suda gives the technical term for augury by twitch as τὸ παλμικόν and in Eudocia Violarium it appears as τὸ παλματικόν; all derive from παλμός signifying vibration.

Bouché-Leclercq (*Histoire de la Divination* 1.160–5) notes that one of the commonest examples of this category of divination was sneezing; buzzing in the ears was another feature (cf. F113b.3). He maintains that the part dealing with the involuntary twitchings of other parts of the body was a later development. There is a collection Περὶ παλμῶν from the Erythraean Sibylla (Suda, *s.v.* Σίβυλλα), and a Περὶ παλμῶν μαντική by Melampus (3rd c. B.C.) for a Ptolemy (ed.

by Diels, *Abh. Berl. Akad.* 1907). Melampus' name is added to that of Posidonius in the Armenian version of the Ps.-Nonnus scholium.

The Suda (T1a) assigns the authorship of τὸ παλμικὸν οἰώνισμα to another Posidonius. Yet Posidonius of Apamea with his strong interest in divination could have written on this subject.

F114 Cleomedes, *De Motu* II.1.68

CONTENT

Differences in apparent size and distance of sun.

CONTEXT

Cleomedes' chapter is engaged in a general attack on the Epicurean theory that the sun is as big as it looks. For Posidonius as *a* source as distinct from *the* source: F115.

COMMENT

The sun looks bigger and further away through dank thick air, smaller and nearer through pure air. So if we could, says Posidonius, look through solid walls and other bodies, like Lynkeus in the story, the sun would appear very much bigger through them and seem at a much greater distance.

Although Posidonius is quoted only for the Lynkeus simile, the content of the simile shows that he must have at least concurred with the previous sentence. Not only apparent size but also apparent distance is involved. The paragraph in Cleomedes begins with distance (p. 124.9ff Z). When high in the sky the sun looks nearer, when setting it appears further. Apparent difference in size is added, and the cause (αἰτία) stated to be the quality of the ἀήρ. All this looks like garbled

Posidonius, especially when compared with F119 (Str. III.1.5, *q.v.*), which provides the link between Cleomedes' size and distance of the setting sun and thick mist, because Posidonius (F119) was attempting to explain sunset phenomena over Ocean. But cf. Arist. *Meteor.* 373b 13f.

It is impossible to be sure of the provenance of this passage. It could have occurred in a work, Περὶ μεγέθους ἡλίου (Cleomedes I.11.65; F19), or in a meteorological work, or in Περὶ ὠκεανοῦ (cf. F119). It is unlikely that the purpose was simply anti-Epicurean, as Cleomedes' context suggests (but cf. Frs. 22, 46, 47, 149, 288; and see F19), nor is it likely merely to reflect observational curiosity. It could be connected with an investigation for d_s and R_s (see F115). The discrepancy and unreliability of visual phenomena might have been a prelude to what he believed to be the safer ground of mathematical theory. It also throws doubt on the ascription to Posidonius of any theory relying on the measurement of the apparent diameter of the sun (see F115).

I take it that the reference to Lynkeus is a joke with a serious purpose. For Posidonius' liking for similes: T105 comm.

F115 Cleomedes, *De Motu Circulari* II.1.79–80

CONTENT

Method of estimating size of sun.

CONTEXT

This chapter of Cleomedes is concerned with combatting the Epicurean statement that the sun is as big as it looks, i.e. a foot wide. There is an earlier reference to Posidonius in the chapter (F114) related to this question in that it deals with apparent difference of size of the sun under different conditions; but it is unsafe to assume that the whole chapter is derived from Posidonius, since Cleomedes himself, introducing the chapter (1.2.65 = F19) says that he is to bring forward the evidence of a number of writers on this subject, of whom Posidonius is one. F115 is followed in Cleomedes by another method of estimating the sun's magnitude which may or may not be by Posidonius.

Related fragments: Frs. 9, 19, 114, 116, 120.

COMMENT

Symbols used in this note are as follows:

d_e – diameter of earth; r_e – radius of earth; c_e – circumference of earth; d_s – diameter of sun; r_s – radius of sun; c_s – circumference of sun; C_s – circumference of orbit of sun; R_s – radius of orbit of sun from earth. d_m – diameter of moon, etc.

The argument of Posidonius as given by Cleomedes is as follows:

What we are to be given is a method (ἔφοδος) which reveals τὸ ἀξίωμα (the rank) of the sun's magnitude.

A (a) Syene (Aswan) lies on Cancer.

(b) At the summer solstice at mid-day the sun casts no shadows within a band of 300 stades in diameter. This seems to be given as an empirical fact of observation, ὧν οὕτως ἐν τοῖς φαινομένοις ἐχόντων (6); i.e. the phenomenal datum.

B A hypothesis (ὑποθέμενος): ὁ ἡλιακὸς κύκλος is 10,000 times greater than ὁ τῆς γῆς κύκλος. The argument which follows shows that ὁ ἡλιακὸς κύκλος must refer to C_s (not to c_s), while ὁ τῆς γῆς κύκλος must refer to c_e.

C A and B prove that d_s is 10,000.300, i.e. 3,000,000 stades.

D This is because:

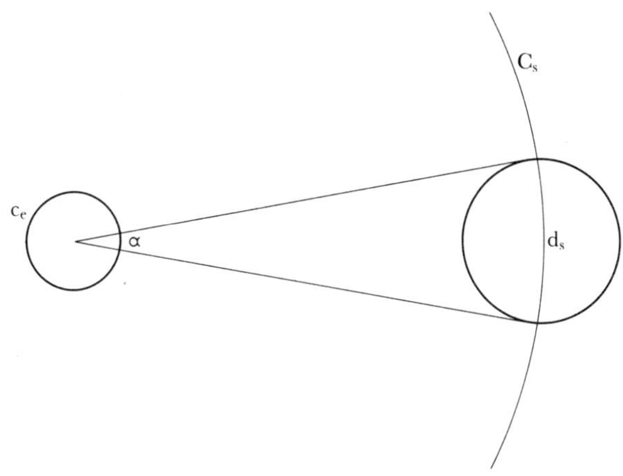

Fig. 9

$$\frac{d_s}{\alpha}=\frac{C_s}{c_e}, \text{ i.e. } \frac{d_s}{300}=10{,}000 \quad \therefore\ d_s=3{,}000{,}000 \text{ (Fig. 9)}$$

E This is the result, *on that sort of hypothesis*, i.e. that $C_s = 10{,}000\ c_e$. It is πιθανόν that the ratio should be *not less than* 10,000, since the earth is proportionately like a dot compared with the sun. But it is admissible (contingent?) that we are ignorant as to whether it is bigger or again smaller.

A (a) was a common assumption.

A (b) appears not infrequently elsewhere. Cleomedes mentions it twice earlier (II.1.76, p. 140.7ff Z; I.10.53, p. 98.4f Z), the first passage having reference to Eratosthenes, and arrived at through gnomons. Strabo, II.1.35 tells us that Eratosthenes took difference of latitude to be observable within 400 stades, in a passage of Hipparchean criticism of Eratosthenes, with Hipparchus seeking a more accurate approximation. Again Strabo says that measurements were made through gnomons or διοπτρικά. Of course these figures were only round approximations; for the difficulties of gnomon readings and the limitations of their accuracy see Heidel, *The Frame of Ancient Greek Maps* 125, and Dicks, *Hipparchus* 130. Geminus seems to have accepted 400 as a round number (*Eisagoge* XVI.16, p. 170 Manit. cf. V.66, p. 66 Manit.); Pliny, *NH* 2.182 settles for between 300 and 500 stades. Cf. also Mart. Capell. VI. 595; Macrobius, *Sat.* VII.14.16; *In Somn. Scip.* I.15.18; Proclus, *De Sphaera* 11, 12.

It has been suggested by Neugebauer that the figure of 300 stades diameter for vertical solar rays may have been reached by calculation rather than by experimental observation. For given the ratio established by water clock (see Cleomedes in the following paragraph, p.148.2ff Z, and *K* below) that

$$d_s = \frac{C_s}{750},$$

then in Fig. 9, the arc α can be expressed as

$$\frac{\alpha}{c_e} = \frac{d_s}{360^\circ}.$$

If c_e for Posidonius be taken as 240,000 (see F202), then

$$\alpha = \frac{240{,}000}{360} \cdot \frac{360}{750} = 320 \text{ stades} \approx 300 \text{ stades.}$$

But the derivation in this argument of 300 stades from

$$d_s = \frac{C_s}{750}$$

is doubtful, because

(a) the relationship does not fit the 10,000 factor of this argument, nor resultant figures for d_s, C_s, R_s (see below);

(b) the evidence of Strabo and Cleomedes on gnomon measurement is backed by the accepted variations throughout the literary evidence between 300 and 500 stades, which would be consistent with the inaccuracy of gnomons, but not with the above equation.

(c) Posidonius here seems to be concentrating on method and trying to do without figures. d_s can be estimated without an estimate of c_e. Also, if one substituted Posidonius' other estimate for $c_e = 180{,}000$ in the above equation, 300 stades would be a very bad approximation. (The figure would be 240 stades.)

It must be stressed that the most important element of this procedure is the method, not the figures. This is underlined, not only in the introduction to the passage, but especially also in *E*. Of course *B*, the hypothesis of the 10,000 factor, is arbitrary, although the belief is stated that it is a minimum (*E*). Nevertheless the figure is almost certainly derived from Archimedes, *Sand-reckoner*, where $D_s < 10{,}000\ d_e$ (see Heath, *Aristarchus* 348). But figures seem to be given only to fill the equation, and the result is 'on that sort of hypothesis' (*E*). Further scientific investigation may supply a more accurate approximation for the figures, but that is not Posidonius' concern. This whole approach is very typical, and is exactly paralleled by his method for estimating the circumference of the earth, for which see F202 comm.

It is possible, of course, by accepting Cleomedes' report (F202) that for Posidonius $c_e = 240{,}000$ stades, to arrive at the following results:

$$C_s = 10{,}000 c_e = 2{,}400{,}000{,}000 \text{ stades (minimum).}$$

$$R_s = \frac{C_s}{6} = 400{,}000{,}000 \text{ (minimum).}$$

Cleomedes now goes on (p. 146.18 Z–p. 150.23 Z) to another method of estimating the size and distance of the sun, this time based on lunar calculations. Since such a method may be implied by Macrobius for Posidonius (*In Somn. Scip.* 1.20.8–10, F116), Cleomedes' report of the second method deserves examination.

F (p.146.18ff Z) The moon is said to measure out twice the shadow of the earth on total eclipses, since a lunar eclipse lasts at most the same time as the immersion or the exit. (The model Cleomedes has in mind is shown in Fig. 10.)

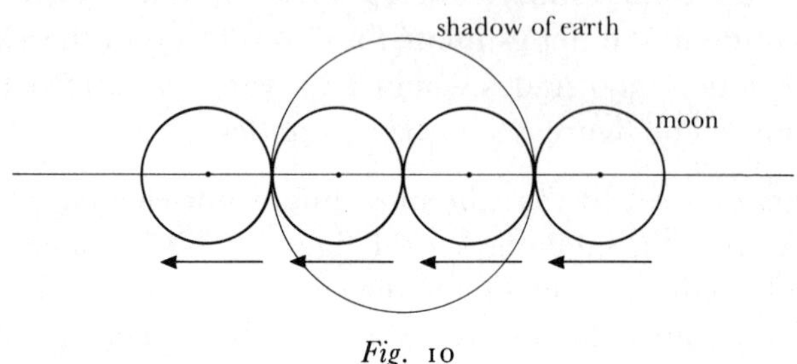

Fig. 10

i.e. $d_m = r$ earth's shadow; or, r earth's shadow $= 2r_m$.

This assumption was familiar from Aristarchus, *On the Sizes and Distances of the Sun and Moon*, hypothesis 5 (Heath, *Aristarchus* 352). It does not seem to have been universally accepted. Hipparchus put the shadow at $2\frac{1}{2}$ lunar diameters (Ptol. *Alm.* IV.9; I.327.1–4 Heiberg), and Plutarch at 3 lunar diameters (*De Facie* 923B, p. 56 Cherniss; *De An. Proc.* 1028D), perhaps through a misunderstanding of the temporal calculation.

G (p. 146.26f Z) It is πιθανόν to assume that the earth is twice the moon.

This assumes that $d_e = d$ of the shadow into which the moon passes. In other words a cylindrical shadow is assumed instead of a cone. D.L. VII.144 (F9) reports that Posidonius had assumed a conical shadow of earth (as indeed Aristarchus, *On Sizes and Distances*; Cleomedes himself later II.2 (p. 170.11ff Z); Pliny *NH* 2.51; Plu. *De Facie* 923B, 932E). Perhaps this should not be pressed since the ancients assumed or ignored parallax for convenience (see for Hipparchus, Swerdlow, 'Hipparchus on the Distance of the Sun', *Centaurus* 14 (1969), 287ff).

The general assumption of relative size is contrary to orthodox Stoic belief; they held that the moon was bigger than the earth (*SVF* II.666). According to Stobaeus, so did Posidonius (F122); but Ps.-Plut. *De Plac.* (*Dox. Gr.* 357) does not mention Posidonius, and it is likely that Stobaeus made a mistake here.

H (p. 146.27f Z) $c_e = 252{,}000$ stades, according to Eratosthenes' method. This would suggest that Cleomedes is not reporting Posidonius, but one cannot be sure. Posidonius may have used Eratosthenes' figures on other occasions (F202).

$\therefore$ *I* (p. 148.2 Z) $d_e > 80{,}000$ (actually 84,000).

$\therefore$ *J* (p. 148.2 Z) $d_m \approx 40{,}000$.

(This would do of course for Posidonius' figures of $c_e = 240{,}000$, $r_e = 40{,}000$.)

K (p. 148.2ff Z) $d_m = \frac{C_m}{750}$. This has been established by waterclocks.

There is a similar equation for the sun: $d_s = \frac{C_s}{750}$.

This measurement of the apparent d_s (0;28, 48°) is again very similar to Aristarchus, who gave 1/720 C_s, or 0;30° (Archimedes, *Sand-reckoner*, II. p. 222.6f Heiberg). Aristarchus himself in *On Sizes and Distances* gives 2° (1/15 of a sign), for which see Heath, *Aristarchus* 311f. Later similar approximations were: Archimedes (*Sand-reckoner*) between 1/164 and 1/200 of a right angle, i.e. between 0;27° and 0;32, 55°; Hipparchus (Ptol. *Alm.* IV.9, p. 327.1–3 Heiberg) that d_m was contained about 650 times in the circle described by it, i.e. ≈ 0;33, 14°; Martianus Capella (VIII.860) as 1/600 of its orbit, i.e. = 0;36°.

The same account of the waterclock occurs earlier in Cleomedes (II.1.75, p. 136.24ff), where the Egyptians are said to have thought up the method first. And it appears elsewhere (P.Oslo 73, Proclus *Hyp.* IV.73–5; also Macrobius, *In Somn. Scip.* I.21.9ff). The method consisted of timing the rising of the solar disc in relation to a total daily outflow of water. It was rightly criticised by Ptolemy (*Alm.* V.14; I. p. 305 Manit.; *Tetrab.* II.2; p. 110 Boer, p. 231, Loeb) and by Proclus (*Hyp.* IV.80–6). Since the method seems to demand an accuracy of 1/1000 in measurement of daily outflow, it is clear that 1/750 is an approximation, or more likely a rounding to a numerically desirable figure (perhaps aided by the result obtained by Aristarchus more easily by a diopter?).

The assumption that the apparent diameter of moon and sun can be taken as the same was also made by Aristarchus.

L (p. 148.6ff Z) $R_m = 1/6\ C_m$.

A common approximation, e.g. Archimedes, *Sand-reckoner* II.3 (II. p. 234, 28f Heiberg).

M (p. 148.8ff Z)

$$\therefore\ R_m = \frac{750}{6} \cdot d_m = 125 \cdot d_m$$

$$= 125 \cdot 40{,}000$$

$$= 5{,}000{,}000 \text{ stades.}$$

But this is the figure for R_m that was assigned to Apollonius of Perge (Hippol. *Refut.* IV.8, p. 66 Duncker; see Heath, *Greek Mathematics*, II.195).

Archimedes had calculated 5,544,130 stades. But these figures are about twice the correct distance, and had been corrected by Hipparchus. In his *On Sizes and Distances* (of the Sun and Moon) (Ptol. *Alm.* V.11) Hipparchus arrived at the estimate $R_m \approx 67\frac{1}{3}\ r_e$ (Swerdlow, *Centaurus* 14 (1969), 287ff).

The association of this whole procedure with Aristarchus, Eratosthenes and Apollonius suggests that it is before Hipparchus.

Cleomedes now continues with a derived argument for the sun.

N (p. 148.12ff Z) Again (πάλιν), a simpler (ἁπλούσ-τερον) hypothesis: the planets move in their orbits with equal velocity.

O (p. 148.14ff Z) Moon completes orbit in $27\frac{1}{2}$ days. Sun takes a year.

∴ *P* (p. 148.17f Z) $C_s = 13\ C_m$,

but *K* (p. 148.19ff) (i.e. diameter of both sun and moon 1/750 of their orbit circumferences).

∴ *Q* (p. 148.18f Z) Sun is 13 times larger than moon.

∴ *R* (p. 148.22 Z) $d_s = 13.40{,}000 = 520{,}000$.

∴ *S* (p. 148.23ff Z) The orbit of the sun, corresponding to the zodiac, if divided into 12, each 1/12 will be 32,500,000

$$\left(\frac{750}{12}\cdot 520{,}000\right)$$

∴ *T* (p. 148.26ff Z) $R_s = 2.32{,}500{,}000$ $(R_s = \frac{1}{6}C_s = 2/12 \cdot C_s)$

$$= 65{,}000{,}000.$$

U (p. 150.11ff Z) $C_s = 390{,}000{,}000$.

What appears to be a kind of confirmation follows:

V (p. 150.14ff Z) If divide each 1/12 by 30, each μοῖρα

$$(1^\circ) = \frac{32{,}500{,}000}{30} = 108\tfrac{1}{3}.\ 10{,}000.$$

W (p. 150.17ff Z) $\frac{1}{2}^\circ = \frac{1}{720} \cdot C_s$

but the sun is 1/750 of its orbit (*K*)
therefore $d_s < \frac{1}{2}^\circ$ of C_s.

X (p. 150.20ff Z) $\frac{1}{2}^\circ$ of $C_s = 54\frac{1}{6}.10{,}000$; but $d_s = 520{,}000$ (see *R* above).

Comparison of method A–E with method N–T

A–E establishes estimates:

(i) $d_s > 3{,}000{,}000$.

(ii) $C_s > 10{,}000\ c_e > 10{,}000.240{,}000 > 2{,}400{,}000{,}000$.
(or $> 10{,}000.180{,}000 > 1{,}800{,}000{,}000$).

(iii) $R_s > 400{,}000{,}000$ (or $> 300{,}000{,}000$).

N–T establishes estimates:

(i) $d_s = 520{,}000$.

(ii) $C_s = 390{,}000{,}000$.

(iii) $R_s = 65{,}000{,}000$.

i.e. *N–T* reduces the figures of *A–E* by roughly 1/6, but not evenly.

The only arguments in favour of a Posidonian source for *F–X* are:

(1) that the passage follows immediately a named Posidonian account of a method for estimating the size of the sun. Other Posidonian evidence shows that he was in general interested in comparing alternative theories e.g. Frs. 18, 49, 138, 210, 219; Kidd, *A & A* 24 (1978), 14.

(2) Macrobius, *In Somn. Scip.* 1.20.9 (F116), says Posidonius based his estimate on lunar eclipses. But there are difficulties over this passage (see above).

Arguments against ascription of *F–X* to Posidonius are:

(1) Posidonius is not mentioned anywhere throughout the passage. The only name given is that of Eratosthenes.

(2) The figures established by *N–T* are wildly below what are stated as hypothetical *minima* in *A–E*. This would seem to be a strong argument.

(3) The figures established by *N–T* depend on a previous set of hypotheses and calculations on the moon (*F–M*), which are stated as dependent on an Eratosthenean figure (*H*), use an assumption made by Aristarchus, but not accepted later

by Hipparchus (*F*), and result in a figure ascribed elsewhere to Apollonius (*M*), which is difficult to understand after Hipparchus.

Three more arguments should not be pressed, namely:

(4) The calculation *N–T* depends heavily on (*K*, *PQ*), and is checked by (*VWX*),

$$d_s = \frac{C_s}{750}$$

which will not fit the relationship of figures in *A–E* (see comment on *A*(b)). See also F114.

(5) The assumption of a cylindrical shadow of earth (*G*) seems to contradict F9 (D.L. VII.144). But see comment on *G*.

(6) *FG*: that the earth is larger than the moon appears to be contradicted by F122. But this is almost certainly not so; see comment on *G*, and F122.

(7) Cleomedes continues after *X* with an attack against *N–T* (p. 150.24ff Z), by denying *N* (i.e. equal velocity of planets), using terms which remind one of Posidonius; e.g. τὴν σελήνην ἀερομιγὲς ἔχουσαν τὸ οἰκεῖον σῶμα, cf. Frs. 10, 122.

(8) The only other named reference to Posidonius giving figures for R_s and R_m is Pliny *NH* 2.21.85–7 (F120), where $R_m \approx 2{,}000{,}000 \quad R_s \approx 500{,}000{,}000$.

These figures may be garbled; but R_s makes sense as a round figure above the minimum figure of *A–E*; while R_m makes sense after Hipparchus. Neither make sense in comparison with *F–T*.

(9) Macrobius (*loc. cit.* F116) maintains that Eratosthenes in *On Dimensions* says that the size of the sun is 27 times the size of earth; while Posidonius' estimate was many many times greater.

This would seem to mean that for Eratosthenes

$$d_s = 27d_e = 27.84{,}000 = 2{,}268{,}000$$
$$c_s = 27c_e = 27.252{,}000 = 6{,}804{,}000$$

Whereas for Posidonius in *A–E*

$$d_s = 3{,}000{,}000, \quad d_e = 80{,}000 \quad \therefore\ d_s = 37\tfrac{1}{2}d_e.$$

This is hardly many many times greater. Much ingenuity has been spent by Hultsch, *Poseidonios über die Grösse und Entfernung der Sonne* (see also Heath, *Aristarchus* 340f) to improve Macrobius' embarrassing statement by assuming that he was referring to volume, not diameter or circumference (but see Tannery, *Mémoires scientifiques* I.391f). It seems to me much more probable that Macrobius had in mind *B*, i.e. Posidonius' hypothesis that ὁ ἡλιακὸς κύκλος is 10,000 times greater than ὁ τῆς γῆς κύκλος. He then confused C_s and c_s (see comment on *B*). If so, Macrobius' statement, however mistaken, makes sense for *A–E*.

It makes no sense whatever for *N–T*, where $d_s = 6\tfrac{1}{2}d_e$. This latter ratio is roughly that of Aristarchus (*On the Sizes and Distances*, Prop. 15, Heath, *Aristarchus* 403), which again raises suspicions similar to those of argument (2) above.

The cumulative affect of these arguments would suggest that we should hesitate to accept *F–X* as Posidonian.

See also Neugebauer, *History of Ancient Mathematical Astronomy* II.655f.

F116 Macrobius, *Commentarii in Ciceronis Somnium Scipionis* I.20.8–10

CONTENT

Size of sun and method of measurement.

CONTEXT

Macrobius is commenting on *Somn. Scip.* IV.2 (Cic. *Rep.* VI.17) where the sun is mentioned; and in this section, clearly on the phrase: *tanta magnitudine, ut cuncta sua luce lustret et compleat.*

In general: F115.

A. Size

According to Macrobius, Eratosthenes in *On Dimensions* says that the size of the sun is 27 times the size of earth; Posidonius' estimate was many many times greater.

If we assume for Eratosthenes that $c_e = 252{,}000$ stades, and that therefore $d_e = 84{,}000$ st., then $d_s = 27\ d_e = 27 \times 84{,}000 = 2{,}268{,}000$, and $c_s = 27\ c_e = 27 \times 252{,}000 = 6{,}804{,}000$. But for Posidonius $d_s = 3{,}000{,}000$ (F115), $d_e = 80{,}000$ (F202) $\therefore d_s = 37\frac{1}{2}d_e$. On these calculations it is ludicrous to say that Posidonius' estimate was many many times greater than that of Eratosthenes.

Hultsch (*Poseidonios über die Grösse und Entfernung der Sonne*), attempted to relieve the embarrassment of these statements by interpreting Macrobius as referring to volume, not diameter or circumference (cf. *In Somn. Scip.* 1.20.32; also Heath, *Aristarchus* 340f, Stahl, *Macrobius' Commentary* 170, n.13; but see Tannery, *Mémoires Scientifiques* 1.391f). It seems more probable, however, that Macrobius' reference derives from Posidonius' hypothesis that ὁ ἡλιακὸς κύκλος is 10,000 times greater than ὁ τῆς γῆς κύκλος (F115.7f). There, of course, the earth's circle refers to circumference, while the sun's circle refers to orbit. But a confusion could easily have arisen between C_s and c_s.

B. Method

Macrobius implies that Posidonius' estimate of the size of the sun was based on lunar eclipses. For this see commentary on F115, for possible reference to Cleomedes, II.1.80–2, pp. 146.18–150.23 Z, where reasons are given for doubting Posidonius as a source. There may be nothing more behind this than using lunar eclipses to prove that the sun is greater than the earth, as Cleomedes, II.2.94 (p. 170.11–27 Z).

Macrobius' criticism that lunar eclipses and the size of the sun have been argued in a circular fashion, receives some confirmation from Cleomedes, II, although our evidence for Eratosthenes and Posidonius is not sufficiently clear.

F117 Diogenes Laertius, VII.144

CONTENT

Shape of sun.

CONTEXT

The paragraph in Diogenes is complex. (a) Posidonius, Περὶ μετεώρων Bk 7 is quoted for the composition of the sun (F17); (b) *Physics*, Bk 6 for its size (F9); then (c) this fragment on shape on the authority of οἱ περὶ Ποσειδώνιον; Diogenes then adds information on (a), followed by further matter on (b). So the arrangement is (a-b-c-a-b).

COMMENT

Why is the formula οἱ περὶ Π. used? For this form of expression see T45. The formula may have sole reference to Posidonius, or refer only to his followers, or include both Posidonius and his followers. It is odd coming after two precise references to books of Posidonius. Either it is used simply as an elegant variation for 'Posidonius', or Diogenes may have used it here because his source was rather vague in ascription, and Diogenes remained unsure whether to assign it to Posidonius himself or to his pupils or circle.

After Aristotle, *De Caelo* II.4; II.11, a spherical sun was reported by the doxographers as common Stoic belief (*SVF* II.652 (Ar. Did.), 653 (Achilles), 654 (Aetius), 667 (Aetius) 681 (Aetius)), as also a spherical cosmos (*SVF* II.547, 681,

1009 (Aetius), 1143 (Philo)). It seems that the Presocratics differed on the shape of the sun (Aet. *Plac.* II.22), but the Pythagoreans are reported as holding that the sun was spherical (Aet. *Plac.* II.22.5, *Dox. Gr.* 352). One wonders whether this last item may have come from Posidonius, for whose interest in Pythagoras and Pythagoreans as precursors of his own theories see T91, T95 (and see Index *s.vv.*). Indeed, it is remarkable how all the evidence comes from the doxographies. And when Diogenes reports on the Stoic spherical cosmos, it is Posidonius who is cited (F8), coupled with οἱ περὶ Ἀντίπατρον.

Posidonius used the assumption of the sphericity of the sun in his method for measuring the circumference of the earth (F202), and for assessing the size and distance of the sun (F115).

F118 Macrobius, *Saturnalia* I.23.2; Cornificius Longus, F.6, *Grammaticae Romanae Fragm.* p. 476 Funaioli

CONTENT

Posidonius and Cleanthes maintain that the sun's path does not deviate from the torrid zone, because under it runs Ocean which circles and divides the earth.

CONTEXT

The general context of *Sat.* I.17–23 deals with the form of syncretism whereby all the gods are manifestations of a single divine power, the sun. At this point *Il.* I.423, Ζεὺς γὰρ ἐς Ὠκεανὸν μετ' ἀμύμονας Αἰθιοπῆας, is interpreted by Cornificius allegorically. Zeus represents sun for which the water of ocean serves as if it were food (1–2). So Homer meant that the sun follows ocean, expressed in the solar and geographical theory of Cleanthes and Posidonius (2–5), which is in line with the commonly agreed physical theory that heat is nourished or sustained by vapour (5–6). Macrobius goes on to find further support from Plato, *Phdr.* 246E (wrongly ascribed to *Timaeus*).

COMMENT

Despite Bake (p. 101) and Reinhardt (*Kosmos und Sympathie* 353ff) this fragment cannot be accepted as it stands as Posidonius' view.

Distinguish two theories:

A. The sun is nourished by vapour from ocean.

B. The sun's path on the ecliptic is to be explained by an equatorial ocean.

Posidonius probably held *A*, but did not hold *B*.

A. It seems that this theory was pre-Aristotelian (Heraclitus?: Aetius II.20.16, *Dox. Gr.* 351; cf. Ps.-Plut. *Plac.* II.17, 889D), since Aristotle, *Meteor.* 354b 35ff, while admitting that sun causes evaporation which subsequently drops as rain, delivers a scathing attack on theory *A*, and seemingly also on theory *B* (. . . καὶ διὰ τοῦτ' ἔνιοι καί φασι ποιεῖσθαι τὰς τροπὰς αὐτόν, 355a 1); cf. also his commentators, Alexander, *In Meteor.* II.2, p. 72.18–22; 73, 1–9 Hayduck, and Olympiodorus, *In Meteor.* II.1, p. 130 Stüve.

After Aristotle the theory in the Stoa was explicitly assigned to Cleanthes by Cicero (*ND* II.40 (*SVF* I.504); III.37 (*SVF* I.501)), and by Aetius (II.20.4 = Stob. *Dox. Gr.* 349). The phrase in the last reporter, ἄναμμα νοερὸν τὸ ἐκ θαλάττης, was taken up by Chrysippus and became orthodox Stoicism (*SVF* II.650, 652, 655, 656; Plu. *De SR* 1053A). *Etym. Gud. s.v.* ἥλιος (*SVF* I.121) alone assigns it to Zeno, which has every appearance of a throwback. Cicero is probably right in making Cleanthes the champion of this theory which fits well with his interest in the sun as the ἡγεμονικόν of the cosmos (*SVF* I.499; which it was not for Posidonius, F23). The metaphor underlying this peculiar physical theory presupposed that the sun and stars were ζῷα, which was indeed generally held by Stoics (e.g. Plu. *De SR* 1053A; *Comm. Not.* 1084E), but again in this connection is assigned by Cicero to Cleanthes (*animantia*, *ND* II.39ff); indeed so is the more general theory of heat as the *vis vitalis* in the universe (*ND* II.24), despite Reinhardt's attempts to confine it to Posidonius.

The theory was further elaborated to distinguish sea water as the nourishment of the sun, fresh water for moon, earth moisture for stars (Cicero, *ND* III.37 (Cleanthes again); II.118; Plu. *De Is. et Os.* 367E (*SVF* II.663); Porphyry, *De Antr. Nymph.* 11). Posidonius (F10, D.L. VII.145) probably held that theory, although we cannot perhaps be certain how far Diogenes' reference to Posidonius stretches. Cicero may well have found the references to Cleanthes in Posidonius. The general doctrine is also found in Pliny *NH* 2.46, Lucan, *Phars.* X.258, and Seneca *NQ* II.5. Servius *Ad Verg. Aen.* (*SVF* I.659) refers to *physici* like Macrobius.

B. The sun follows the path of its nutrient, i.e. an equatorial ocean.

Although Aetius (II.23.5 = *Dox. Gr.* 353) refers in general to Stoics, Cicero (*ND* III.37) firmly assigns this doctrine again to Cleanthes; and Cicero's line and a half of verse might be a translation, for Cleanthes liked poetry (cf. *SVF* I.502). But the interesting evidence is Geminus, *Isagoge* XVI.21ff. Cleanthes is again singled out for the view that ὑποκεχύσθαι μεταξὺ τῶν τροπικῶν τὸν ὠκεανόν. Geminus adds that Cleanthes was followed by Crates of Mallos who interpreted Homer as implying ocean in between the tropics. But, says Geminus, such an arrangement ἀλλοτρία ἐστι καὶ τοῦ μαθηματικοῦ καὶ τοῦ φυσικοῦ λόγου. Then Geminus seeks to disprove an equatorial ocean by researches showing that most of the area between the tropics was inhabited and not seabound. But this latter position is exactly that of Posidonius (Frs. 210, 211, 49), from whom Geminus in all likelihood took this whole account. Indeed Cleomedes, *De Motu* I.6.31–2 (F210) gives Posidonius' views on an inhabited torrid zone, to which *is opposed* (33) the opinion of οἱ φυσικοί that there is a great sea there.

From this it surely follows that Bake (p. 101) must be wrong in assigning theory *B* to Posidonius, and that Reinhardt (*Kosmos und Sympathie* 353ff) was still more misguided to use the whole of *Sat.* I.23.1–9 as a base on which to construct for Posidonius a theory of solar eschatology (criticised on other grounds by Jones, *CQ* 27 (1932), 132ff). Nor is it necessary to suppose with Berger (*Fragmente des Eratosthenes* 23) that the Posidonius referred to by Macrobius was Posidonius of Alexandria, fellow pupil with Cleanthes of Zeno (T1a). It is possible that Cornificius (in his *De Etymis Deorum*) was inspired by the allegorising Crates (for whose orb with equatorial ocean see Thomson, *History of Ancient Geography* 203), whose theories were certainly known also to Strabo (I.2.24; cf. I.2.27, 28), although, of course, Cleanthes allegorised (*SVF* I.502, 503, 535), as did other Stoics (*SVF* II.662). But the combination of the evidence of Geminus, Cleomedes, Cicero and Strabo indicates that Macrobius mentioned Posidonius because he was a common source for the whole discussion. Posidonius' own teacher Panaetius accepted an equatorial ocean (linked with the Academic Eudorus in *In Arati Ph.*, Anon. I, Maass p. 97, F135 van St.). Posidonius surely must have discussed the theory in his Περὶ ὠκεανοῦ and, with his interest in the doxographical development of a theory, probably retailed Cleanthes' views (cf. Index *s.v.* Κλεάνθης), possibly even including *Il.* I.433 (cf. the reference to Cleanthes in F166), and perhaps mentioning also Crates (Index *s.v.* Κράτης). Macrobius' indirect vague information led him to believe mistakenly that Posidonius not only cited Cleanthes' theory, but also endorsed it; cf. Strabo, F49.141. The theory remained popular, however: e.g. Lucretius V.523–6; Philo, *De Prov.* II.64 (*SVF* II.1145); Seneca *NQ* VI.16; VII.21.2; Macrobius again *In Somn. Scip.* II.10.10. Posidonius did however believe in a circumambient ocean (F49.141–232), which is distinct from an equatorial ocean, but easily confused with it.

Select Bibliography

Bake, *Posidonii Rhodii Reliquiae Doctrinae* 101.
Berger, *Fragmente des Eratosthenes* 23.
Bouché-Leclercq, *L'Astrologie Grecque* 75 n. 1.
Boyancé, *Études sur le Songe de Scipion* 89f.
Dreyer, *History of Planetary Systems from Thales to Kepler* 159.
Gilbert, *Griechische Meteorologie* 683.
Mansfeld, *The Pseudo-Hippocratic Tract* Περὶ Ἑβδομάδων 127.
Pease, *Ciceronis De natura deorum libri* 635.
Reinhardt, *Kosmos und Sympathie* 353ff.
Thomson, *History of Ancient Geography* 168, 202f.
Zeller, *Die Philosophie der Griechen* III.1.192f.

F119 Strabo, III.1.5

CONTENT

Criticism of popular accounts of sunset phenomena, and an explanation for such phenomena.

CONTEXT

Strabo has just given Artemidorus' account of the Sacred Cape, with criticism of Ephorus to the effect that there are only rocking stones there, no temple of Heracles. This is the reference of line 1. Strabo now proceeds to controvert Artemidorus' statement on ocean sunsets by Posidonius' criticism of popular tales.

COMMENT

A. Posidonius says that the tale of many people is false that:

(a) the sun *is* larger when it sets on the ocean horizon, sinking with a sizzling noise (3–6);

(b) night follows immediately on sunset (7).

Note that the evidence only gives Posidonius' criticism of οἱ πολλοί, not of Artemidorus. Strabo later (21f) links Artemidorus with (a) and (b), further specifying (a) with 'a hundred times larger'.

B. Posidonius' criticism of (b) (7–12):

(i) Darkness follows not immediately but a little later as with any other sea. This would appear to be a statement of observation (cf. 19f).

(ii) An explanation is added (γάρ): when the sun sinks behind hills, more daylight elapses after sunset from diffused light, while after oceanic sunsets there is less twilight (but not immediate darkness) as on great plains.

This would appear to imply a theory of twilight dependent on contours, since sea and plains are linked together against mountainous country.

C. Posidonius' criticism of (a) (12–20):

There is only an *appearance* (φαντασία) of increase of size of sun at sunset and sunrise at sea.

Explanation: because of increase of exhalations from the water the light is refracted through this to give a broader flatter image, as when a setting or rising sun or moon is seen through a dry thin cloud (when the star may also appear reddish). This is a different theory from that of *B*, since it applies only to a watery horizon. On the other hand the addition of cloud refraction can make the application general. This is perhaps the point of ξηροῦ (17). The explanation is further widened to explain not only apparent difference of size, but also of colour (although this is not necessary for Strabo's purpose). For the latter cf. Arist. *Meteor.* 342b 5ff; and in general, Arist. *Meteor.* 373b 13f.

D. Posidonius says that he exposed the false statement by personal observation at Gadeira (19f). Strabo uses this to establish Posidonius' credentials against Artemidorus (20 ff). Posidonius was there, whereas we cannot accept Artemidorus' statement as deriving from autopsy. For he betrays himself by saying that (i) no one sets foot on Sacred Cape after dark; (ii) night follows sunset immediately. Nor could the observation have been made anywhere else on the coastline; for Gadeira is on the coast, and we have Posidonius' autopsy for that.

E. The analysis shows not an attack on Artemidorus by Posidonius, but a critical testing and explanation of commonly reported phenomena (which Artemidorus had accepted). For Artemidorus (of Ephesus, fl. 100 B.C., to be distinguished from his namesake of Parium, F134): T78, Frs 217, 223, 246, 247, and Berger, *RE* II.1, col. 1329f, Thomson, *History of Ancient Geography* 210.

As for the stories, Cleomedes calls them old wives' tales from Spain (*De Motu* II.1.89, p. 162.14ff Z), and it is natural to connect them with that locality (e.g. Juv. XIV.280), where Posidonius (and Artemidorus) may have heard them. But they probably go back at least to Pytheas (Geminus, *Isag.* VI.9, cf. Tac. *Germ.* 45.1). Strabo (F49.289) certainly thought Pytheas a liar; whether Posidonius did or not, it may have been an added incentive to check. But Posidonius wastes no time over the absurd tale of the sun sizzling as it sinks into Ocean. He is interested in horizon distortion. Cleomedes connects this with polemic against Epicurus (*loc. cit*) but that need not have been Posidonius' motive (F114).

F. Posidonius' method appears to be based on observation followed by scientific explanation.

For the theory under *B*, it is noticeable that neither Posidonius nor Strabo takes account of difference of duration of twilight according to latitude and season (cf. Aujac, *Strabon et la Science* 137f). This is perhaps consequent on observation from a single coastal base (Gadeira), for a limited period (30 days). Yet Posidonius should have observed differences from his travels in the north-west; cf. Hipparchus (Str. II.1.18; II.5.42).

For the theory under *C*, see F114; for a comparable theory, F134 (and cf. Sen. *NQ* I.6.5). It is to be noted that Posidonius recognised the problem of horizon distortion through refraction. For relevance to measurement of circumference of earth: F202.

G. Text

15–16 δι' αὐλῶν *codd.*, does not make sense. Aristotle (*GA* 780b 19ff) used δι' αὐλοῦ βλέπων for a kind of telescoping effect, a device to see further. The effect Posidonius is describing is of objects seen through water or mist, hence δι' ὑδάτων *Anon. Jenens.*, or perhaps δι' ἀτμῶν. But Voss's δι' ὑάλων (through glass vessels filled with water) is neater and receives support from Sen. *NQ* I.6.5 (*per vitream pilam aqua plenam*) where just such a method and effect are described in a passage of similar context which may relate to Posidonius.

F120 Pliny, *Naturalis Historia* II.21.85–7

CONTENT

Distance from earth of cloud belt, moon and sun.

CONTEXT

In §§83–8 Pliny gives several instances of estimations of the distances of the planets from the earth, and indignantly criticises the whole procedure.

COMMENT

In general, F115.

A. General

Only 1–6 relate to Posidonius: cloud belt 40 stades; moon 2,000,000; sun 500,000,000. This is followed by another estimate of the cloud belt of 900 stades. The rest of the passage is Pliny's criticism, which has been included to show the context and value of his report. It is marked by an irrelevant moral indignation (for which see also II.1.3), and an abysmal ignorance of any mathematics involved (see Beaujeu, Budé vol. II, p. 174).

B. The figures

The context shows that it is unlikely that Pliny understood any figures he may have found from Posidonius, but this does not mean that they may not derive from Posidonius, although probably not directly (cf. Beaujeu, Budé vol. II, XV–XVIII).

Since Posidonius was interested in atmospheric phenomena, he may well have attempted to estimate the extent of this 'turbulent' region. Codices and modern editors divide between the reading *minus* and *non minus XL stadiorum*. The best codices omit *non*, and Capelle ('Der Physiker Arrian und Poseidonios', *Hermes* 40 (1905), 619 n. 3) and Kroll (*Die Kosmologie des Plinius* 23), argued persuasively that a contrast was intended between the short cloud belt which clings close to the earth, and the vast distances of sun and moon. The large number (*plures*, 6) who, according to Pliny, gave the distance as 900 stades, are unknown to us. There is a passage in Stobaeus (*Ecl.* I.31.8, p. 246 W), supposedly from an Arrian, which puts the distance at 20 stades. A very similar passage occurs in Geminus (*Isagoge* 17, p. 180 Manit.) where the figure is unfortunately corrupt. Capelle (*Hermes* 40) attempted unsuccessfully to relate these two passages to Posidonius (see also Capelle, 'Berges- und Wolkenhöhen bei griechischen Physikern', *Stoicheia* v (1916); Reinhardt, *Poseidonios* 181 n.2). Since there was clearly interest in the cloud belt since at least Aristotle (*Meteor.* 340a b; cf. his commentators, e.g. Alexander, *In Meteor.* p. 16.12ff Hayd.; Philoponus, *In Meteor.* p. 28.27ff Hayd.), there were no doubt several guesses as to its extent, so figures should not be doctored for assimilation.

We have no other explicit information for Posidonius' estimate of the distance of the moon from earth, but 2,000,000 stades (since this is clearly a round number, despite Pliny's protestations, there is no need to add on 40 for the cloud belt) would make sense after Hipparchus (F115 comm.).

Since it is possible to calculate from F115 a figure for the distance of the sun of not less than 400,000,000 stades, Pliny's 500,000,000 could have been given as a very round figure for the distance *from earth*. It would be nonsense as a distance from the moon. Therefore *inde* (4) is a foolish insertion. The rest of the paragraph shows that it could well be due to Pliny himself, although it may already have been present in his source.

The connection of the magnitude of the sun's distance with the fact that the sun does not burn up the earth could be Posidonius, cf. F219.

It should be noted that in this fragment there is no difference in the characteristics of *aer* between cloud belt and moon, and between moon and sun.

F121 Scholia in Aratum 881

CONTENT

Parhelion, or mock sun.

CONTEXT

None. Since Aristotle, *Meteor.* III.2–6 grouped together halo, rainbow, rods (ῥάβδοι) and parhelia as atmospheric phenomena admitting of the same explanation, and since Seneca *NQ* I.2–13 does the same, it is likely that Posidonius followed the same plan. F121 should accordingly be compared with Frs. 133 and 134, and with Arist. *Meteor.* III.6, Sen. *NQ* I.11–13, and Pliny *NH* 2.99.

COMMENT

Posidonius said that parhelion was a spherical cloud near the shining sun, taking its light from the sun; it does not shine by its own light, but by that of the sun, as the moon does too (F123). He said that it was in sun form through its being round and illuminated by sun. It becomes like it through following the sun, inasmuch as it is seen at the side of the sun (1–6).

Seneca is very close to this in I.11: *quidam definiunt, nubes rotunda et splendida similisque soli. sequitur enim illum nec unquam longius relinquitur quam fuit cum apparuit.* Seneca's *sequitur* seems to fix the sense of παρεπόμενον (5); in fact parhelia occur at definite distances (22° and 46°) from the sun. The sentence in the scholium seems to invite the meaning of 'being consequent on'. Aristotle makes no mention of the shape of the cloud, being more interested in its consistency. Roundness is being stressed to distinguish it from rainbows (F134) and perhaps from ῥάβδοι. ἡλιοειδές (3) is a striking adjective for a scholiast (but cf. p. 503.7 Maass; Olymp. (schol.) *In Phaed.* p. 239.20 Norvin), whose εἶπε seems to stress its Posidonian origin. Did he have in mind Plato, *Rep.* 508b 3, 509a 1 where φῶς and ὄψις are ἡλιοειδεῖς?

Lines 6–13 are concerned with two questions, the colour and position of parhelia, both of concern to Aristotle and Seneca. But such arguments as there are in the scholium are tangled and garbled, and we must assume that they hardly represent Posidonius' full account.

Parhelion is λευκός (so also Aristotle; *candida, splendidae* Sen. 1.13). Aristotle says this is due to the air being even (ὁμαλός) and dense (πυκνός) (377b 16ff; *coactus et limpidus*, Sen. 1.12; *densae, leves, planae*, Sen. 1.13); this is to contrast with the varying consistency of clouds which produce ῥάβδοι of different colours (377a 2–b 15). We do not know how Posidonius explained it; line 7 is no explanation. But line 13, concerning the obliquity of the sun's rays (which makes little sense in its context), may have originally been the same explanation of colour as Sen. 1.13.2: *ob hoc omnia eiusmodi simulacra candida sunt et similia lunaribus circulis, quia ex percussu oblique accepto sole respondent.*

The phenomenon appears ἐκ πλαγίων (so Aristotle 372a 11, 377b 30; *oblique* Seneca; *ex obliquo* Pliny). Aristotle now has a twofold classification: (a) position; not above, nor below, nor opposite (and hence at sunset and sunrise) (372a 12f; 377b 29); (b) distance; not very close, nor very far off; because if near, the sun breaks up the condensation, if too far, the sight rays are too weak for reflection (377b 31ff). This scheme is briefly repeated in Pliny. Posidonius seems to have condensed: (i) clouds under the sun are quickly broken up; (ii) clouds far distant cannot reflect the rays. So parhelia happen at sunset and sunrise. Seneca is very similar to this (1.13.2), but adds *propior* (i.e. too near) to (i).

Parhelia happen on each side of the sun often (line 14). So Seneca 1.13.1, *solent et bina fieri.* (Pliny raises the number to three.) This is quite true. The parhelic circle passes through the sun and parallel to the horizon. Where this cuts the inner halo of the sun, two parhelia can appear; where it cuts the outer halo two more may appear, although this is less frequent (Fig. 11).

Aristotle says that parhelia are reflections (ἔμφασιν) having no substance or reality (ὑπόστασιν). Aristotle does give a purely optical explanation of all these phenomena. Cf.

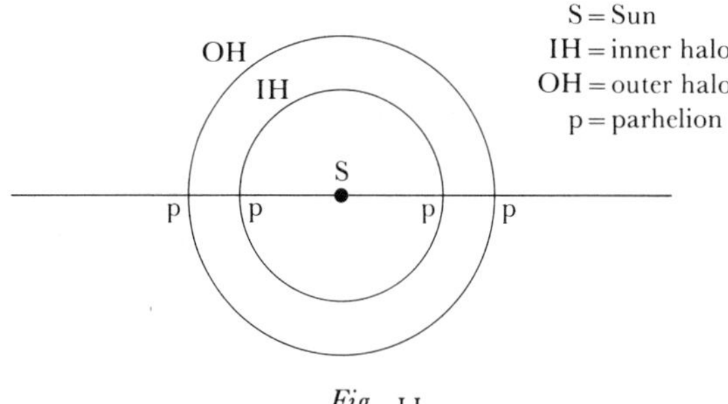

Fig. 11

Olymp. *In Meteor.* III.2, p. 210.22ff (on haloes). Does this sentence imply that Posidonius did not? He certainly did not regard rainbows as having ὑπόστασις, but only as reflected images (F134). Seneca is also insistent at *NQ* I.15.6f that while comets really have flame (*certa illis substantia est*), yet *nobis non placet in arcu aut corona subesse aliquid corporis certi . . . simulacra ista sunt et inanis verorum corporum imitatio*. But he does not mention parhelia there, although he calls them *imagines solis* at I.11.3. There are two odd pieces of evidence. Aetius (Ps.-Plut. *Plac.*) III.6 singles out ῥάβδοι and ἀνθήλιοι (a solar image on the parhelic circle opposite the sun) as μίξει τῆς ὑποστάσεως καὶ ἐμφάσεως; and scholia on Aratus 811 (p. 488.14ff Maass) has a triple classification of κατ' ἔμφασιν (rainbow, halo), μικτά (parhelia), and καθ' ὑπόστασιν (comets). So someone regarded parhelia as κατ' ἔμφασιν καὶ καθ' ὑπόστασιν. But it is difficult to be certain about Posidonius from this fragment. At least he appears to have held a theory of reflection (ἀνάκλασιν, 10), no doubt, from the example in that line, similar to Aristotle and Seneca. The two latter regarded the optical direction as proceeding from the sight rays to the reflector and thence to sun and back, while Posidonius' rays appear to come from the sun, but the passage is too fragmentary to be certain. The evidence shows that all theories were based purely on reflection and not on refraction (also F134). The phenomenon clearly aroused much interest. Aetius (Ps.-Plut. *Plac.*) III.5.11 records that Anaxagoras explained it in the same way as rainbow; there is another summary of Aristotle's theories in Arius Did. F14, *Dox. Gr.* 454f; Cleomedes, *De Motu* II.6.24 (p. 224 Z) attempts to explain anthelion.

It is interesting that for Posidonius only a scientific interest in the phenomenon is recorded; there is no surviving trace of two main sources of interest in the ancient world. One of these was as a meteorological weather sign, e.g. Arist. *Meteor.* 377b 24ff; Theophrastus, *De Signis*, F6.1.22 Wimmer; Aratus, *Phaen.* 148–59; Seneca *NQ* I.13.3. The second was as a portent. Seneca (*NQ* I.11.2) and Pliny (*NH* 2.99) remark on their occurrence in the historical tradition, for which cf. Livy 22.1.10; 28.11.3; 29.14.3; Cic. *Rep.* I.10.15; Dio Cassius 45.17.5; 47.40.2 (and Constantine's sign, Eusebius, *Vita Const.* I.40–1; Lactantius, *De Mort. Persec.* 44.5). But Cicero, *ND* II.14 mentions the portent of *sole geminato* in a passage associated with Cleanthes, which may derive from Posidonius.

See vol. I, Introduction, xxiv for the text of this fragment.

F122 Aetius, *Placita* II.25.5; 26.1; 27.1 (Stobaeus, *Eclogae* I.219.16 W; *Dox. Gr.* 356–7)

CONTENT

Moon: composition, size, shape, and phases.

CONTEXT

This whole fragment is continuous in Stobaeus. It comes after entries on the moon assigned to Zeno and Cleanthes, and is followed by Chrysippus. Codex *P* has as its lemma Ποσειδωνίου καὶ Στωϊκῶν, but that would be odd in the sequences of entries.

Diels in *Dox. Gr.* removed the Zeno, Cleanthes and Chrysippus entries to become Arius Didymus F34, and he separated the Posidonius fragment into three separate entries as follows (*Dox. Gr.* 356–7):

(1) Ποσειδώνιος . . . ἀέρος (line 2) = Aet. *Plac.* II.25.5, balanced by Ps.-Plu. *Plac.* II.25 (891B) = οἱ Στωϊκοὶ μικτὴν ἐκ πυρὸς καὶ ἀέρος.
(2) μείζονα . . . ἥλιον (lines 2–3) = Aet. *Plac.* II.26.1, with a lemma supplied by Diels; Ποσειδώνιος καὶ οἱ πλεῖστοι τῶν Στωϊκῶν, and balanced by Ps.-Plu. *Plac.* II.26.1 = οἱ Στωϊκοὶ μείζονα τῆς γῆς ἀποφαίνονται ὡς καὶ τὸν ἥλιον.
(3) σφαιροειδῆ . . . μηνοειδῆ (lines 3–5) = Aet. *Plac.* II.27.1, with Diels' lemma: Ποσειδώνιος καὶ οἱ πλεῖστοι τῶν Στωϊκῶν, and balanced by Ps.-Plu. *Plac.* II.27.1 = οἱ Στωϊκοὶ σφαιροειδῆ εἶναι ὡς τὸν ἥλιον.

However, in Stobaeus all references are under Posidonius, and in the Ps-Plutarch *Placita* all are under Stoics. Therefore we have no real grounds for splitting the assigned authorship; whether the ascription is correct throughout is another matter, cf. Diels, *Prol.* 68, n. 1, and see below.

COMMENT

A. Composition

Mixture of fire and air. So ἀερομιγής F10. According to Stobaeus in this same context (see Context above), Zeno thought the moon πύρινον δὲ πυρὸς τεχνικοῦ (*SVF* I.120), Cleanthes πυροειδῆ (*SVF* I.506), and Chrysippus an ἔξαμμα (*SVF* II.677; cf. the use of ἄναμμα νοερόν for the sun, Frs. 17, 118). From this Bonhöffer, *Epiktet und die Stoa* I.50.1 mistakenly maintained that for the old Stoa moon as πῦρ νοερὸν καὶ τεχνικόν was orthodox. But Stobaeus elsewhere (*Ecl.* I.130 W) makes it clear that for Chrysippus moon διὰ πυρὸς καὶ ἀέρος συνέστηκε (*SVF* II.413). This seems to have become accepted as standard for οἱ Στωϊκοί: Ps.-Plu. *Plac.* II.25.5; Plu.

De Facie 921F ἀέρος μῖγμα καὶ μαλακοῦ πυρός (see following and Cherniss *ad loc.*); Philo (*SVF* II.674); ἀερομιγής, referred to οἱ Στωϊκοί by both Ps.-Plu. and Stob. in Aet. *Plac.* II.30.5, *Dox. Gr.* 361, *SVF* II.669; cf. Cleomedes, *De Motu* II.3.99, p. 180.4ff Z. The intended contrast with the εἰλικρινὲς πῦρ of the sun (F17), could presumably easily be exaggerated, as Plutarch's ἀέρος ζοφεροῦ καὶ πυρὸς ἀνθρακώδους (*De Facie* 922A).

For a general survey, see Gilbert, *Griechische Meteorologie* 698f, Reinhardt, *Poseidonios* 202, Pohlenz, *Die Stoa* II.48, 111.

B. Size

Greater than earth, like the sun. This is the only evidence to this effect. The parallel passage in Ps.-Plu. *Plac.* II.26.1 (*SVF* II.666), assigned to the Stoics in general, is again the only direct evidence for them. Plu. *De Facie* 940C (cited by Reinhardt, *Poseidonios* 201 n. 1) in a Stoic context, may refer to the sun, not the moon. Certainly, Pliny (*NH* 2.49) stupidly maintains this view. Cicero does not, but in *ND* II.103, has a theory whereby moon is smaller than earth, comparable to Cleomedes, *De Motu* II.1. p. 146.18–27 Z, which in part derives from Aristarchus, *On the Sizes and Distances of the Sun and Moon*, Hyp. 5 (see F115, notes *F* and *G*; cf. Plu. *De Facie* 923B). Cleomedes, *De Motu* II.3, p. 178.10ff also holds to the smaller moon theory of οἱ ἀστρολόγοι. It is difficult to think that anyone interested in meteorology, as Posidonius was, would advocate the large moon after Aristarchus and Hipparchus. Hence Stobaeus or his source has been thought to be mistaken (Diels, *Dox. Gr.* Prol. 68, n. 1; Hirzel, *Untersuchungen* I.193, n. 1; Reinhardt, *Poseidonios* 201, n. 1. Stobaeus was accepted by Bake, p. 72; and by Gilbert, *Griechische Meteorologie* 699). It should be stressed that this is the only evidence. Cf. F115, notes *F* and *G*.

C. Shape

Spherical. Against Cleanthes' πιλοειδής (Stob. see above,

SVF I.506; Cleanthes thought the stars were κωνοειδεῖς, *SVF* I.508). The spherical shape is already in Chrysippus (Stob. *loc. cit.*, *SVF* II.677), and generally in the Stoa (Ps.-Plu. *Plac.* II.27.1, *SVF* II.667). Also spherical were sun (F117), earth (F18.20; F49.7) and cosmos (F8; F49.7).

D. Phases

Why πολλαχῶς? The four terms are standard (Geminus, *Isag.* IX.5–12 (126.5ff M); Plu. *De Facie* 929BC; Cleom. *De Motu* II.4.100, pp. 180.26–182.7 Z). διχότομος, half moon: Arist. *De Caelo* 291b 21, 292a 4; *GA* 777b 21f; Aristarchus, *Hyp.* 3; ἀμφίκυρτος, gibbous: Arist. *De Caelo* 291b 20, Theophr. *De Signis 56;* μηνοειδής, crescent: Theophr. *loc. cit.*

There is more evidence for Posidonius' interest in the effects of different phases of the moon: Frs. 217, 218, 219, 138, 106; also F291.

E.

This fragment could ultimately have derived from *Physics*, Bk 6; see F10.

F123 Cleomedes, *De Motu* II.4.105

CONTENT

The moon in solar eclipses.

CONTEXT AND COMMENT

While the immediate context is concerned with solar eclipses, the general context in Cleomedes deals with theories of lunar illumination (II.4.100ff). Three theories are distinguished:

(1) (p. 180.23ff Z) that of Berossus, that the moon is half fire (ἡμίπυρος) and generates its own light. This is quickly

dismissed on the ground that the moon in the earth's shadow (in eclipse) would then be brighter, not disappear; compare the objection of Plu. *De Facie* 932C, F125.17–20.

(2) Illumination by reflection from the sun, as with mirrors (p. 182.16ff Z) (see F124).

(3) Combustion produced by a mixture of lunar and solar light, so that the moon changes its character (ἀλλοιοῦσθαι) by the sun's rays, and by this mixture has its own peculiar light by participation (like the glow of red-hot iron) (p. 182.20ff Z) (see F124).

Cleomedes thinks that (3), the σύγκρασις theory, is sounder than (2), the ἀνάκλασις theory (p. 184.4ff Z), for two reasons: (a) reflection is impossible from a rarified body (ἀπὸ δὲ μανῶν σωμάτων ἀδύνατον ἀνάκλασιν γίνεσθαι, p. 184.12f Z), which soaks up light as a sponge water (p. 184.18 Z). The moon being a compound of fire and air is rarified. (b) The reflection theory cannot explain the wide arc of the moon's illumination (p. 184.18ff Z).

Cleomedes therefore adopts the σύγκρασις theory of illumination (p. 188.2ff Z) and now faces three objections to it. They all concern what happens in eclipses.

The first problem (p. 188.11ff Z) asks why in lunar eclipses (when the moon enters the shadow of the earth) the moon immediately vanishes, immediately to reappear on emerging. Such immediacy of phenomena is typical of mirror reflection, Sen. *NQ* 1.4.2. Cleomedes answers that the same happens in the illumination of air. When a light is taken into a dark house, the air is at once illuminated; when the light source is quenched, the air is at once dark. So with the sun, moon and earth's shadow. Such immediacy of illumination of darkness is typical of λεπτομερῶν σωμάτων (28). The third problem posed is how the moon can occult the sun although it is smaller (p. 190.17ff Z).

The second problem is F123 (p. 190.1ff Z). Why in solar eclipses do not the sun's rays, reaching through the whole of the moon, send light, as happens through clouds which are thicker than the moon? Posidonius says that not only the surface of the moon is illuminated by the sun, as solid bodies have their surface alone illuminated, but as the moon is a rarified body, it has sun's rays penetrating to a very great extent, but not completely; for it has a very large diameter, and the sun is a considerable distance from it. Cloudy air easily allows rays to penetrate, since it has no depth. Perhaps one could say not unreasonably that there is a peculiar character to the moon's density (πύκνωμα), through which the sun's rays cannot escape (ἐκπίπτειν). This last sentence may well be a comment by Cleomedes, see Plutarch's objection, F124.

There is therefore a strong possibility that Posidonius held Cleomedes' σύγκρασις theory of illumination; it fits his theory of lunar composition (F122), and he is cited as a counter to an objection to the theory. And yet, although the solution of all three problems is supposed to remove objections to the σύγκρασις theory, none of the methods of solution depends on or involves that theory. There is no phrase in F123 which suggests the peculiar combination of lunar and solar light, and indeed, if one did not know the context, the language would convey a simple theory of penetration of solar rays.

There may have been different variations of the theories. For example Macrobius, who maintained (like Geminus, *Isag.* IX.1–2) that the moon had no light of its own (*In Somn. Scip.* I.19.10), seems to combine a reflection theory with a Posidonian semi-penetration theory of solar light (*op. cit.* I.19.12–13). He compares the earth, which becomes bright from the sun without reflecting light, with the moon, which, like a mirror, reflects the light that it receives. This is because the earth is more compressed and does not allow any light to penetrate beyond the surface; but the moon, although denser than the other celestial bodies is much purer than earth, and permits the light to penetrate to such a degree that it sends it forth again. When a ray of light is poured into the body of the moon, and is reflected, it gives forth light but no heat.

Perhaps then the only certain evidence is for Posidonius on eclipses (which is the immediate context in Cleomedes). On the other hand, Posidonius held that the moon was a star (F127), and so presumably had some light of its own (it was fiery as well as airy). See also F124.

For size of moon, see F122; for distance of sun from moon, F120.

But see F121: as with a halo cloud, the moon does not shine by its own light, but by that of the sun.

F124 Plutarch, *De Facie* 929D

CONTENT

The moon in solar eclipses.

CONTEXT AND COMMENT

This is clearly a reference to the same Posidonian theory of moon in solar eclipse as in F123. Furthermore the general context in Plutarch is concerned with lunar illumination, as in Cleomedes. But the arguments are different. Plutarch, holding that the moon is earthy in structure, argues for a reflection theory, as Cleomedes, believing in a rarified moon, argued against reflection for σύγκρασις. Again the question arises, how much is to be assigned to Posidonius.

The argument up to F124 goes like this:

929B A previous reference to Anaxagoras that the sun imparts brilliance to the moon is to be developed by investigating how this happens. Two views are examined in order to be discarded.

Moon is not illuminated by sun

(a) like glass or ice by illumination or shining through; or

(b) by 'conlumination' or joint shining, as torches, the light increasing.

Neither can be the case, for we would have a full moon at the beginning of the month no less than at the middle of the month if (929C),

(i) moon does not keep out or block off the sun, but lets through the light because of her fine structure; or if

(ii) she shines by a compounding of light and joins (i.e. with the sun) in setting herself alight.

For (γὰρ) the moon's ἐκκλίσεις and ἀποστροφαί cannot be blamed (as might be the case when she is at half or gibbous or crescent) when she is in conjunction (with sun). Then she is in direct line with the light giver, takes and receives the sun, and so it would be reasonable for the moon to be visible and the sun to shine through (i.e. (ii) or (i) above). But that is not the case; what happens is an eclipse.

Then follows F124 (929D): as for what Posidonius says, that the sun's light does not reach us through the moon, because of the moon's depth, that is transparently refuted. There is much greater depth of air, yet it is entirely illuminated by sun's rays.

Plutarch then proceeds to argue for the reflection theory of Empedocles.

It is clear that (a) = (i) and that (b) = (ii). Both theories seem intended to be refuted by the argument introduced by γὰρ in 929C. (b, ii) is obviously the same theory as Cleomedes' σύγκρασις theory, and in *De Facie* 930F–931, Plutarch seems to assign this theory to the Stoics. The only other parallel with a named reference (cf. Cherniss, *De Facie*, p. 101, n. g) is Aetius II.29.4, *Dox. Gr.* 360a 3–8, b 5–11, under οἱ νεώτεροι τῶν Πυθαγορείων. Cherniss (*op. cit.* p. 101, n. h) assigns it to Posidonius on the grounds of *De Facie* 929D (F124). This may be true, but is not obvious. 929D could apply to any theory except that of Berossus cited by Cleomedes (see F123). In fact neither in this fragment, nor in F123 is there any trace of σύγκρασις language, there is only penetration language, which could apply to (a, i); and any holder of (a, i) would have to explain solar eclipse on Posidonian lines. I am not arguing that Posidonius held (a, i) any more than he held (b, ii); simply that the evidence does not seem entirely clear what theory of lunar illumination he did adhere to. 929D (F123) looks rather like an additional afterthought in argument by Plutarch. The evidence of Plutarch and Cleomedes shows that an explanation by Posidonius of solar eclipse was well known, and that it was used by theorists on lunar illumination for their own purposes.

As for Plutarch's criticism of Posidonius on βάθος, much depends on whether Posidonius meant by that word depth or density. Yet F123.9–11 would indicate the sense 'depth', and although βαθύς can mean thick, βάθος in Greek always seems to refer to depth. If then the last sentence of F123 is Cleomedes' comment, it was he who reinterpreted βάθος by πύκνωμα, or density.

F125 Plutarch, *De Facie* 932B–C

CONTENT

Solar eclipse is explained as the shadow of the moon.

TEXT

It is unfortunate that there is a lacuna in the middle of the fragment (line 15); but the following γὰρ clause shows that the sense must be that of Cherniss's suggested supplement.

CONTEXT

The general context in Plutarch is a comparison of (a) darkness of night and (b) darkness of solar eclipse. Both are due to occultation of sun: (a) through occultation by earth,

(b) through occultation by moon. Plutarch argues that the darkness of eclipses is not so deep as the darkness of night, because the occulting bodies, although of the same substance, are not equal in size. Plutarch gives certain authorities that the moon is smaller than earth, including Aristarchus (based on *On the Sizes and Distances of the Sun and the Moon*, Prop. 17; Heath, *Aristarchus* 409f) and Aristotle (F210 Rose, 738 Gigon; Cherniss, *De Facie ad loc.* compares Ps.-Alex. *Probl.* 2.46, in Rose, *Arist. Pseudepigraphus* 222; and Philoponus, *In Meteor.* p. 15.21–3 Hayduck; but the latter is on the same grounds as Aristarchus: Cleomedes, *De Motu* 146.18–27 Z, and F115, notes *F* and *G*). Then follows the definition of Posidonius with Plutarch's criticism. Görgemanns (140–6, 148) has shown that the reference to Aristotle came from Plutarch.

COMMENT

According to Posidonius, what happens in solar eclipse is a conjunction of the moon's shadow with whatever parts of the earth fall under that shadow; for only those experience eclipse whose visual rays towards the sun are caught and blocked by the moon's shadow. Plutarch criticises *ad hominem*. Posidonius said the moon was a star, and so has light which cannot produce shadow.

Posidonius' statement is commonplace; e.g. for ἔκλειψις (in this case, lunar eclipse) as στέρησίς τις φωτός, Arist. *PA* 90a 15ff, 93a 23, 93a 37ff. See in general Geminus, *Isag.* x for the shadow and the limitation of different visual points on the earth; cf. Cleomedes, *De Motu* II.3.95 (172.9ff Z), II.3.98 (178.13–24 Z), II.4.106 (192.14–20).

Plutarch's objection might apply to the theory of Berossus in Cleomedes, *De Motu* II.4.100 (p. 180.23ff; especially p. 182.10–14 Z), but it is unlikely that it held much force against Posidonius. For an answer to a similar *aporia*: Cleom. *De Motu* II.4.100, p. 188.11–28 Z, where however lunar and not solar eclipse is in question (see F123). Posidonius did think moon a star (F127). The real issue between him and Plutarch (in Plutarch's eyes) lies in the composition of the moon. Plutarch believing it to be earthy, criticises here a star-like composition, in F124 a theory of air composite. So earlier (Context) Plutarch assumes that moon and earth are of the same substance. Nothing can be inferred from this fragment about the relative size of moon and earth for Posidonius; F122.

17 ἀντιφράττειν appears to be accepted as a technical expression in this context; cf. *De Facie* 929C, Geminus, *Isag.* X.I.

F126 Diogenes Laertius, VII.146

CONTENT

Lunar eclipses and lunar latitude.

CONTEXT

This section in Diogenes is concerned with eclipses. Solar eclipse was mentioned first with a reference to Zeno, Περὶ τοῦ ὅλου; F126 follows on lunar eclipse. The last sentence of the fragment, assigned to Posidonius and/or his pupils, has in fact nothing to do with eclipses, although Diogenes appears to have thought it did.

COMMENT

The first part of the fragment explains lunar eclipses as the moon falling into the earth's shadow. So eclipses take place only at the time of full moon. Every month there is a full moon with the moon's position opposite the sun; but there is not an eclipse every month, because the moon moves obliquely to the orbit of the sun and her latitude diverges too far to the north or to the south. But when the moon's latitude comes right on the solar orbit and the ecliptic and she then is diametrically opposite the sun, then there is an eclipse.

This is a perfectly correct and simple account of the cause of lunar eclipse with nothing remarkable about it. Cf. Geminus, *Isag.* XI. It may have come partly from Zeno, whose work 'On the Whole' is referred to for solar eclipse (see above), and who is named by Stobaeus (*Ecl.* I. p. 213.26 W = Arius Did. F33, *Dox. Gr.* p. 467) for lunar eclipses at the full moon. It is possible, however, that the elaboration concerning lunar latitude may have been due to Posidonius, since it is latitude of the moon which links the eclipse sentence to the last sentence assigned to Posidonius and his pupils.

The final sentence can have nothing to do with eclipses. (The following note derives mainly from conversations with Dr. O. Neugebauer.) For it says that the moon's latitude is right at the ecliptic in Libra and Scorpio and in Aries and Taurus; which would imply a stable nodal line for the moon which obviously is not true. If, however, a line is drawn as diameter through these points mentioned in the ecliptic, it can be seen to be a nodal line at right angles with respect to Leo 0° as northernmost point: see Fig. 12.

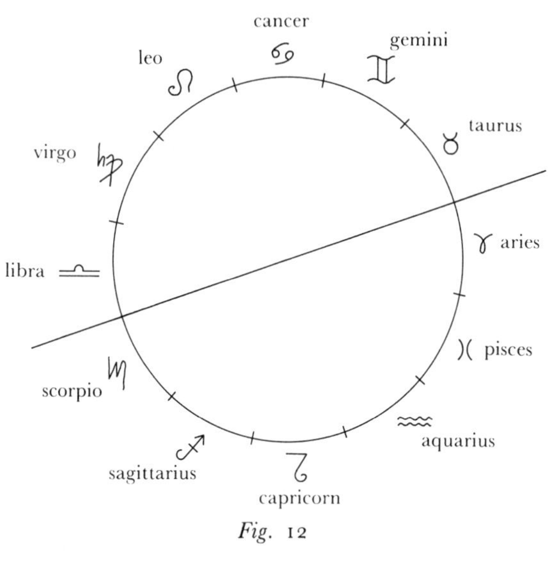

Fig. 12

This shows that we are dealing with lunar latitudes in the form of angular measurement known as 'the steps' (βαθμοί), expressed as fractions of the ecliptic: 'sign' (ζῴδιον), 'step', 'part' (μέρος) representing 1/12, 1/24, 1/48 of the ecliptic, or in Babylonian units, 30°, 15°, 7;30°. See Neugebauer and Van Hoesen, *Greek Horoscopes* 154. It was a peculiarity of this system to use the starting point of Leo 0° (not equinoxes or solstices) for lunar latitudes and the distance of the moon from the nodes. So Vettius Valens, *Anth.* I.18 (Kroll, p. 31) measures the 'steps' of moon, starting from Leo to Libra (καταβαίνει βόρεια; continuing Scorpio to Capricorn, καταβαίνει νότια; Aquarius to Aries, ἀναβαίνει τὰ νότια; Taurus to Cancer, ἀναβαίνει τὰ βόρεια. He then defines βαθμός as 15° and ζῴδιον as 30°). Cf. Theon of Alexandria, *Commentary to the Handy Tables*, Halma HT I.54; 55.16 for step notation for solar declinations and lunar latitudes. In astrological versions the language changed to ταπεινοῦσθαι, ὑψοῦσθαι (Vett. Valens III.4, p. 140.4–28 Kroll; cf. Cleomedes, *De Motu* I.4, p. 34.23–36.1 Z). Arcs of 1/24 and 'signs' of 30° can be traced before Posidonius to Hipparchus, but they do not seem to occur in Aristarchus or Archimedes. Ptolemy ignores this primitive system.

So Diogenes has tacked on to an account of lunar eclipses a fragment dealing with the steps of the moon, clearly without understanding it.

Posidonius used 'steps' again in his theory of measuring the circumference of earth. See F202.

Χηλαῖς (line 8) has been persistently mistranslated as Cancer in translations of Diogenes since Yonge (Bohn, 1895). As The Claws of Scorpio it represents Libra. But this use shows that Diogenes' source is early.

For οἱ περὶ τὸν Ποσειδώνιον: T45, Frs. 89, 117, 141a, 180, 195, 288.

F127, F128 Arius Didymus, *Epitome* F32, Stobaeus, *Eclogae* 1.24.5 (p. 206.18 W, *Dox. Gr.* 466); Achilles, *Isagoge* 10

CONTENT

Definition of star.

CONTEXT

In Stobaeus the previous entry refers to Eudoxus and Aratus, *Phaen.* 10–12 (where both ἄστρα and ἀστέρες occur). Chrysippus on rising and setting of ἄστρα follows. Chapter 10 begins Achilles' account of stars; he goes on to comment on οὐδέποτε στάσιν ἔχον. Later in ch. 14 he discusses the difference between ἀστήρ and ἄστρον.

COMMENT

Both passages obviously refer eventually to the same source in Posidonius.

Diodorus is the mathematicus from Alexandria. He was possibly a pupil of Posidonius; Diels, *Dox. Gr.*, Prol. 19–22. See also F130.

A. ἄστρον and ἀστήρ

Achilles has ἀστήρ, Arius ἄστρον. Arius contains additional information that Posidonius called sun and moon ἄστρα, and that there is a distinction between ἀστήρ and ἄστρον. Diodorus however is reported for this distinction in Achilles, *Isag.* 14, p. 41.17ff Maass. Διόδωρος δὲ καὶ οἱ ἄλλοι μαθηματικοὶ ἰδίως καὶ κοινῶς τὰ ȝῴδια ἄστρα καλοῦσι καὶ ἀστέρας παρατιθέμενοι Πλάτωνα μάρτυρα ἄστρα τοὺς ἕπτα πλανήτας ἐν τῷ Τιμαίῳ εἰρηκότα. τὸν Κύνα μέντοι ἀστέρα ὄντα ἐν τῷ βίῳ ἄστρον λέγομεν. ἀλλ' ὁ μὲν ἀστὴρ καὶ ἄστρον, οὐκέτι δὲ τὸ ἀνάπαλιν.

This has raised needless difficulty. Just before the Diodorus reference, Achilles himself distinguishes between ἀστήρ as a single star and ἄστρον as a constellation (τὸ ἐκ πολλῶν ἀστέρων σύστημα, p. 41.13–15; so later p. 42.3–4: εἴη οὖν ὁ μὲν ἀστὴρ σῶμα ἡνωμένον, τὸ δὲ ἄστρον ἐκ διεστώτων καὶ ὡρισμένων; so also schol. on Pindar *O.*1.6, and Suda, *s.v.* ἀστήρ). He gives as an example of the distinction Arat. *Phaen.* 11f (which preceded F127 in Stobaeus, see Context above; so the source for both passages is close even here).

The Diodorus reference must not be taken as a further illustration of that distinction, but in opposition to it (Διόδωρος δὲ καὶ οἱ ἄλλοι μαθηματικοί . . .), because the distinction star/constellation makes nonsense here. It would be meaningless to say that every star is also a constellation, but not *vice versa*. Also sun and moon are not constellations (and F125 (Plutarch) backs ἄστρον here). Greek usage in any case does not maintain such a distinction; e.g. ἀστήρ seems to be used for the Great Bear in A.R. I.108; while ἄστρον is commonly used for a star (e.g. Geminus, *Isagoge* XII.27; XIV.2f).

Edelstein (*AJPh* 57.297) suggested that ἀστέρες was reserved for the fixed stars. Perhaps there is some evidence for this e.g. in Plu. *Comm. Not.* 1075D (*SVF* I.510 (Cleanthes)); cf. *SVF* II.579, 681, 682. But these passages may be countered by the use of ἀστήρ in *SVF* II.674, 676, 677, 1009 (p. 300.20 Arn.). It would be a distinction hard to maintain in general; e.g. Geminus uses ἀστέρες of both fixed stars and planets (*Isag.* XII.22; XIV.1), and ἄστρα for planets (*Isag.* XII.27) and fixed stars (XIV.4).

Perhaps Posidonius meant that ἀστήρ properly used without additional qualification such as πλανήτας (Geminus, *Isag.* XII.22) or κινουμένων (Geminus, XIV.1) should refer to fixed stars, while ἄστρον was a more general or generic term covering any celestial body (bodies) whether fixed or planetary. Geminus, XIV.2f does seem to use it as a general term. Posidonius could not have meant to restrict ἀστέρες to fixed stars, and ἄστρα to planets, as Edelstein (*AJPh* 57.297) appears to suggest. That would still make nonsense of the proposition that every ἀστήρ is an ἄστρον, but not *vice versa*. But as Diodorus said, in everyday life (ἐν τῷ βίῳ) no distinction was made. Achilles himself, *Isag.* 10–13 makes none; cf. Atticus, F6.4 Baudry (Eusebius, *Praep. Evang.* XV.806d). So Diels, *Dox. Gr.*, Index II, *s.v.* ἄστρον: *sed nullo fere discrimine utroque nomine utuntur doxographi*. We should certainly not try to derive any theory from the distinction (as Edelstein) nor from Posidonius' using the term ἄστρον specifically (ἰδίως) for sun and moon. This was common in the Stoa; e.g. Zeno, *SVF* I.120 (Arius); Cleanthes, *SVF* I.499 (Eusebius), 510 (Plutarch); Chrysippus and Stoics in general, *SVF* II.668 (Plutarch), 650 (D.L.), 672 (Plutarch), 527 (Arius). For Posidonius again see F125, F217.35.

It is more likely that Posidonius used ἄστρον (F127) in this fragment than ἀστήρ (F128) because: (a) ἄστρον was the more general term, whatever the details of the distinction; (b) Achilles up to this point used ἀστέρες not ἄστρα, so ἀστήρ is his word for which he gives Diodorus' (and Posidonius') definition. Only in ch. 14 does he come out with the distinction; (c) the general term is governed by the specific application (ἰδίως, F127.3), which in turn is partly controlled by Plutarch's evidence in F125.

B. The characteristics of ἄστρον

The above argument would suggest that there should be no differences in the characteristics presented by the two fragments, and indeed there are none. Edelstein was wrong to see a distinction and build a theory on the different wording of ἐξ αἰθέρος συνεστηκοτός (F127.2) and οὐράνιον τῆς αὐτῆς μετειληφὸς οὐσίας τῷ ἐν ᾧ ἐστι τόπῳ (F128.2). The difference of expression may be due to Diodorus, but the sense is the same; Plutarch, *De Facie* 928CD (*SVF* II.668). The two fragments are parallel, and the information they give appears orthodox Stoicism.

σῶμα θεῖον: Zeno, *SVF* I.165; Cleanthes, *SVF* I.530; in general, Cicero, *ND* II.39; *SVF* II.92, 613, 1027.

ἐξ αἰθέρος συνεστηκός (F127), **οὐράνιον . . . τόπῳ** (F128): cf. Plu. *De Facie*, 928CD (*SVF* II.668); Cic. *ND* II.39; D.L. VII.137 (*SVF* II.580); cf. Geminus, *Isag.* XVII.15.

λαμπρόν (Frs. 127, 128) **καὶ πυρῶδες**: *aether* for the Stoa was a kind of fire; cf. *SVF* II.682 (Achilles); αὐγοειδεῖς (*SVF* II.788, Galen). Cf. F101, god is πνεῦμα νοερὸν καὶ πυρῶδες.

οὐδέποτε στάσιν ἔχον ἀλλ' αἰεὶ φερόμενον ἐγκυκλίως: cf. *SVF* II.1009 (p. 300.20 Arn., ἀεὶ θέοντας); explained by Achilles with reference to fixed stars as well as to planets (p. 39.10ff Maass); also *SVF* II.688 (Philo), Cic. *ND* II.54. So also F18.

For stars as ζῷα: F149.

F129, F130 Aetius, *Placita* III.1.8 (Ps.-Plutarch, *De Placitis* 893A; Stobaeus, *Eclogae* I, p. 227.1W, *Dox. Gr.* p. 366); Macrobius, *Commentarii in Ciceronis Somnium Scipionis* I.15.3–7

CONTENT

The Milky Way.

CONTEXT

Both fragments are part of doxographies. The doxography in Macrobius is given in full. In Aetius the Posidonius entry is the last in a section on Milky Way, preceded by Pythagoreans (two theories), Metrodorus, Parmenides, Anaxagoras, Democritus, and Aristotle. The report is identical in Ps.-Plu. *Plac.* and Stobaeus, except for a different expansion of Aristotle's theory.

COMMENT

A. The doxographies

At first sight the two doxographies look quite different; the only common ground appears to be Democritus and Posidonius.

The Aetius doxography appears at first to have greater affinities with Aristotle's *Meteorologica.* The first Pythagorean theory related to the myth of Phaethon (Aet. III.1.2) occurs in Arist. 345a 15. The second (Aet. III.1.2) explaining the phenomenon as an optical effect is mentioned in Arist. 345b 10. For Metrodorus on the passage of the sun (Aet. III.1.3) cf. Arist. 345a 16. Anaxagoras' theory that the Milky Way shines because it lies in the path of the shadow of the earth at night (Aet. III.1.5) is developed by Arist. 345a 26ff. Democritus is mentioned by Aristotle (345a 26) but his theory is not examined. Finally Aristotle's own theory is given by Aetius (III.1.7). On the other hand Macrobius' doxography consists of Theophrastus, Diodorus (of Alexandria) and Democritus, whose Milky Way theory of joint light through the density of many small almost continuous stars shining together is recorded by Aetius (III.1.6) but not by Aristotle.

But the matter is not so simple, when one looks at Macrobius more closely, and other related material. Macrobius begins by refusing to detail fabulous explanations. Stahl (*Macrobius' Commentary on the Dream of Scipio, ad loc.*) suggests here Hyginus, *Astron.* II.43; Philo, *De Prov.* II.89; Porphyry, *De Antro Nymph.* 28 (under Pythagoras). But the omission would also include members of Aetius' list which reappear in Manilius and Achilles, *Isagoge*; e.g. the Pythagorean

Phaethon story (Aet. III.1.2; Arist. 345a 15f; Manilius *Astron.* I.735–49) and the stories of Oinopides (Achilles, *Isag.* 24, p. 55.18ff M; cf. Arist. 345a 16; Metrodorus *ap.* Aetius, III.1.3) and of Eratosthenes (μυθικώτερον in Achilles, 24, p. 55.9ff M; Manilius, I.750–4). When we turn to Theophrastus in Macrobius, the theory (whether actually held by Theophrastus or not) that the Milky Way is the seam where the two hemispheres of the celestial sphere are joined together, reappears once more in Manilius (I.718–28), and in Achilles (24, p. 55.17f M). So the theory of Democritus recurs in Manilius, I.755–7 and in Achilles 24, p. 55.24ff.

So when we allow for what has been omitted, but referred to implicitly by Macrobius under *fabulosa*, we appear to have a body of varying but common elements in Manilius (Diels, *RhM* 34 (1879) 490), Aetius, Achilles and Macrobius, which are more similar than seemed at first sight to be the case. Both explicit doxographies, Aetius and Macrobius, conclude with Posidonius; Manilius and Achilles are very similar to Macrobius. Macrobius includes Diodorus of Alexandria who was later than Posidonius (see F128). Yet Diodorus seems to have had some close affinities to Posidonius (see F128; Diels, *Dox. Gr.*, Prol. 19–22), and may have been influenced by him or even been a follower of some sort. So we must entertain the possibility that the doxography or part of it may be traced back to a Posidonian doxography (T101/102 comm.).

B. Posidonius

(1) Constitution

πυρὸς σύστασιν (F129). Diels (*RhM* 34 (1879) 488f) pointed out that this is not unlike *Arist. Meteor.* 345b 32ff, εἴρηται γὰρ πρότερον ὅτι τὸ ἔσχατον τοῦ λεγομένου ἀέρος δύναμιν ἔχει πυρός, ὥστε τῇ κινήσει διακρινομένου τοῦ ἀέρος ἀποκρίνεσθαι τοιαύτην σύστασιν οἵαν καὶ τοὺς κομήτας ἀστέρας εἶναί φαμεν. The brevity of the Posidonian reference should make us cautious, but there is no hint of Aristotelian characteristics such as air, setting on fire, dry exhalations, and similarity to comet phenomena. Also, Posidonius' definition of the fiery constitution, a flow or steam (*infusionem*) of stellar heat (F130), sounds different from Aristotle. There seems a stress on consistency, with the interesting gradation, finer than star, denser than light (F129). It also seems different from Diodorus' *densetae concretaeque naturae* of fire. Posidonius' *infusionem* (F130) appears to have more affinity with μανωτέραν of F129. At any rate Posidonius (like Aristotle) regarded Milky Way as a substantial phenomenon, καθ' ὑπόστασιν, not optical, as in the theory recorded by Aet. III.1.2, *Dox. Gr.* p. 365.3–6, and Arist. *Meteor.* 345b 10. Compare Frs. 121, 133, 134.

(2) Purpose

ideo (F130.17) only makes sense if taken to anticipate *ut* (line 18): so designed to curve obliquely to the zodiac that, since the sun by never leaving the boundaries of the zodiac has left the remaining part of the sky without a share in its heat, this circle, passing athwart the path of the sun, tempers the universe with its warm band.

If we could be sure that the construction of this sentence conveys accurately Posidonius' statement and intention, it would show an interest in Milky Way as an instance of cosmic design or purpose. For this see Reinhardt, *Poseidonios* 250.

(3) Position

The Milky Way intersects the zodiac (F130.21f; so also Achilles, *Isag.* 24, p. 56.3ff M) at Capricorn and Cancer (so Macrobius, *In Somn. Scip.* I.12.1, and also Porphyr. *De Antro Nymph.* 28; but actually at Gemini and Sagittarius, cf. Stahl, *ad loc.*). It is uncertain whether this latter detail comes from Posidonius or Macrobius. But for an interesting use of this intersection in myth see Plutarch, *De Genio* 590F.

(4) Influence

Most people agree with Posidonius' definition (F130.16). Compare for Posidonius' influence in meteorology F132 (rainbow) and F131.

Gilbert (*Griechische Meteorologie* 662) argued that Posidonius departed from an orthodox Stoic view which was to be discovered in Aetius' introduction to the section on Milky Way (III.1.1), κύκλος νεφελοειδὴς ἐν μὲν τῷ ἀέρι.... With this he compared Achilles, *Isag.* 24, p. 55.28 M, μήποτε μέντοι ἄμεινον αὐτὸν λέγειν ἐκ νεφῶν ἢ πίλημά τι ἀέρος διαυγὲς εἶναι κύκλου σχῆμα ἔχον, and Geminus, v.68, συνέστηκε δὲ ἐκ βραχυμερείας νεφελοειδοῦς.

Gilbert's suggestion seems very far from certain. The interesting thing is that there is no certain evidence on Milky Way for the Stoa apart from Posidonius. There is nothing in Diogenes Laertius, nothing in Seneca's *Naturales Quaestiones*, and no entries in *SVF*. As far as we know the Stoics ignored the phenomenon. But to whom does Macrobius refer when he says that most people have agreed with Posidonius?

F131a, 131b Scholia in Aratum 1091; Parisinus graecus 2422, fol. 143, cap. 1.1–3

CONTENT

Theory of comets.

TEXT

Neither text is good on its own. The Aratus scholium depends on *M* alone without benefit of the Escorialensis (vol. I, *Introd.* xxivf). The Parisinus codex was edited first by Graff in 1864, listed by Tannery, *REG* XI (1898) 96ff, and catalogued and described as a 16th-century codex by Cumont in the *Catalogus Codicum Astrologorum Graecorum*, VIII.1, cod. 7, p. 65 (in 1929). Unknown to Bake (p. 76), it remained unknown to the editor and emenders of the Aratus scholia (Maass, Diels, Rehm), and apparently to Posidonian scholars. It is now however possible by juxtaposing the texts, which obviously come from the same source, to improve the text of both.

CONTEXT

None. But for the doxographical section before Posidonius, compare Arist. *Meteor.* I.4 and 6–7, to which there is a direct reference (343b 8ff) in F131a, 21ff. In general cf. Sen. *NQ* VII (and F132); Aet. *Plac.* III.2 (also Diels, *Dox. Gr.*, Prol. p. 230f); Arrian *ap.* Stob. *Ecl.* I.28.2, p. 229f W (see also Capelle, 'Der Physiker Arrian und Poseidonius', *Hermes* 40 (1905), 626ff).

COMMENT

A The fragments consist of two sections. The latter states Posidonius' theory without criticism, and the presentation in both fragments agree closely. The first section is a doxography where views are presented and criticised; but only one part has survived common to both fragments, that on the Pythagoreans. This fragmentary doxography has clear relations with Arist. *Meteror.* I.6.

(1) An introduction. Only in F131b.2–6. That comets arise from dry exhalations as a material cause was the theory of Aristotle: Arist. *Meteor.* I.7.344a 9ff; I.4.341b 6ff; Aetius, III.2.3.

(2) Pythagoreans: comets are planets (both F131a and F131b); so also Arist. *Meteor.* 342b 30; Aetius, III.2.1, lines 6–10. Compare Seneca, *NQ* VII.17, where ascribed to Apollonius of Myndus.

Criticism (a): some comets seen outside zodiac (both F131a and F131b); so also Arist. *Meteor.* 343a 23ff; Seneca, *NQ* VII.18.

Criticism (b): if it had been a planet, expert scientists would have observed its revolutions. Anyway no single phenomenon, but many; not seen in one form (τύπῳ *M*; place (τόπῳ) Maass), but κομῆτες above stars, πωγωνίαι below, ξιφηφόροι in between. This criticism occurs only in F131a and nowhere else. It replaces in the Aristotelian account (342b 36) the theory of Hippocrates and Aeschylus (Heath, *History of Greek Mathematics* I.182ff) that the 'tail' is produced by reflection of sun to our vision on moisture which a planet draws to it. There is a trace of this under Pythagoreans in Aetius, III.2.1, lines 10–13 (Diels, *Dox. Gr.*, Prol. 231). In the classification of comets in this section of F131a πωγωνίαι are common from Aristotle on, but ξιφηφόρος is not; the nearest allusion is *xiphiae* in Pliny, *NH* 2.89. Compare however Posidonius' *clipei* (F132.21). This insertion may be due to him.

(3) Democritus and Anaxagoras: an optical effect produced by conjunction of planets; so also Arist. *Meteor.* 342b 27; Aetius, III.2.2. The same theory is presented in Seneca *NQ* VII.11. This section does not occur in F131b.

Criticism (a): comets occur outside the zodiac; cf. Arist. *Meteor.* 343a 23ff; Seneca *NQ* VII.11–12.

Criticism (b): as many as three comets are seen at the same time; cf. Arist. *Meteor.* 343a 26; Seneca, *NQ* VII.12.1.

Criticism (c): a named reference to Arist. *Meteor.* 343b 8ff.

(4) Posidonius: comets are not planets nor stars nor optical illusions caused by them, but have their ἀρχὴ γενέσεως when a denser bit of ἀήρ is shot under pressure into the αἰθήρ and is bound in the whirling revolution of the αἰθήρ; as their sustenance (τροφή) flows in they are borne on to spin faster; and so they are seen to expand and decrease, as at one point they grow greater as the sustenance increases, at another as sustenance fails they contract.

That this is similar to Aristotle's theory can be seen from *Meteor.* 344a 16ff; 341b 36ff. A similar theory is presented by Seneca *NQ* VII.4–8 (cf. *turbines* (4), *elisus* (6), dry exhalations (7), *alimenta* (8)) under the name of Epigenes, but reintroduced as Stoic 19.2–21.1 (see F132). It is basically the theory known to Diogenes (D.L. VII.152); something similar is recorded under Arrian by Stobaeus, *Ecl.* I, p. 230.16–20 W.

Posidonius continues: That is why they form above all in the north, where the ἀήρ is thicker and condensed (So Arrian, Stob. *loc. cit.* p. 229.19 W; Seneca, *NQ* VII.21.1; but apparently not so Aristotle, e.g. *Meteor.* 343a 35ff; nor *De Mundo* 395b 14ff). Changes of weather coincide with their conflagration and destruction; droughts or, the opposite, violent rain storms occur at their dissolution, as their formation occurs in the atmosphere (so again Arist. *Meteor.* 344b 20ff).

B (a) Three basic theories are tabulated: (1) planets; (2) optical effect created by planets; (3) Posidonius. There is a similar tripartition scheme in Arist. *Meteor.* substituting Aristotle's own theory for that of Posidonius. Seneca *NQ* VII also presents a tripartite arrangement, but this time criticises all three types and adds a new solution of his own. Probably then the three types of solution had become commonplace (but cf. the straggling doxography in Aetius, III.2).

(b) Although a tripartite presentation may have become common, this one is based on Posidonius (and not e.g. Aristotle; neither is Seneca's for that matter). Therefore the preceding doxography may also derive from Posidonius. Posidonius was addicted to doxographical reviews before presenting his own account. Here Posidonius' theory is not criticised; the preceding ones are. The criticism of F131a.7–12 occurs nowhere else, nor does the name ξιφηφόροι for a type of comet. Aristotle is named (see Index *s.v.*). The deliberate pun at F131a.16 is also characteristic of Posidonius (cf. Frs. 58.9f, 239.11).

(c) In this meteorological phenomenon, Posidonius is basically in agreement with Aristotle, although he expresses his theory in his own way (cf. F133; contrast F134; cf. also F121).

(d) In the classification of atmospheric phenomena into optical, substantial, or a mixture of the two (κατ' ἔμφασιν, καθ' ὑπόστασιν; Frs. 121, 133, 134) Posidonius agrees with Aristotle that comets are καθ' ὑπόστασιν.

(e) For the influence of Posidonius' theory: F132.

132 Seneca, *Naturales Quaestiones* VII.19.1–21.2

CONTENT

Occurrence of comets; theory of comets.

CONTEXT

For general context, see F131 under Context.

In Seneca Bk VII of *NQ* is devoted to comets. Before this fragment opens Seneca reviewed three types of theory:

(1) Comets are produced through whirlwinds (*turbines*) in the atmosphere, where dense air from dry exhalations has been squeezed up (*elisus*) and fed (*alimenta*) until dissolution (chs. 4–8). This is represented as the theory of Epigenes, possibly the latest expounder, but is basically the theory of Aristotle and Posidonius (see F131, comm. *A*4).

(2) Comets are an optical illusion produced through conjunction of planets (chs. 11–12). Seneca does not name the author, but it derives from Democritus and Anaxagoras; see F131, comm. *A*3, where the criticism is also similar to Seneca's.

(3) Comets are planets (chs. 17–18). Apollonius of Myndus is attacked by Seneca for this theory, probably because he, like Epigenes above, was the latest exponent; but it is the same theory as that assigned to Pythagoreans by Aristotle and Posidonius; see F131, comm. *A*2.

For tripartition in comet theory: F131 *B*(a).

Seneca now turns in chs. 19–21 (F132) to Stoic theories, after which he gives his own. So ch. 19 *init.*: *Zenon noster . . .*; ch. 20 *init.*: *in hac sententia sunt plerique nostrorum . . .*; ch. 21 *init.*: *placet ergo nostris . . .*; ch. 22 *init.*: *ego nostris non assentior.*

COMMENT

A. Stoic theories

Seneca in ch. 19 again classifies these into three, corresponding to the three main theories presented and criticised in chs. 4–18 (see Context).

(a) F132.1–6. Zeno thought comets to be a conjunction of stars. So *quidam* (some Stoics) think them a *speciem* and to have no real existence. This is the theory attacked in chs. 11–12, that of Democritus and Anaxagoras in F131 and Aristotle; it is the κατ' ἔμφασιν theory.

(b) F132.6–8, *quidam . . . exire*. Certain (Stoics) say that comets exist (i.e. καθ' ὑπόστασιν), have their own orbits, and after fixed periods come into human view. This is the planetary theory (chs. 17–18), held by Apollonius of Myndus and the Pythagoreans (F131 and Aristotle). What Stoics held it? Perhaps Diogenes of Babylon: Aetius, *Plac.* III.2.8: Διογένης ἀστέρας εἶναι τοὺς κομήτας. For ἀστέρας: Frs. 127, 128.

(c) F132.8–10, *quidam . . . dissipantur*. Certain (Stoics) say that they indeed exist (i.e. καθ' ὑπόστασιν again), but are not to be called stars (or planets), because they dissolve, do not last long, and are broken up in a short space of time. Further details of this theory only emerge gradually. Most Stoics hold it (line 11). *Ignes sunt aeris triti et impetu inter se maiore collisi* (line 17). The duration of their fires depends on their *alimentum* (line 19f). They are created from dense air (line 40). They occur most frequently in the north (line 41). These details show that this is indeed the theory of Posidonius (F131, comm. *A*4), entertained earlier by Seneca under the name of Epigenes (see Context (1)).

B. Posidonius

The third Stoic theory is undoubtedly that of Posidonius, and when Seneca says that most Stoics hold it, he must mean most Stoics of his own day. There is no sure trace of it before

Posidonius in the Stoa. Chrysippus does not appear to have been interested in the problem. The reference in D.L. VII.152, although printed in *SVF* II.692 as Chrysippan, almost certainly derives from Posidonius.

But Seneca's presentation is very strange. He does not name Posidonius as the author of the theory anywhere, although he must surely have known that it was his. He does indeed bring in Posidonius' name, but incidentally. *Hoc loco sunt illa a Posidonio scripta miracula* (20f). Seneca does not agree with Posidonius here, and he actually uses him to deride the theory as pandering to the general love of the miraculous. Here is where the marvels written up by Posidonius come in, the columns (no doubt the portent of 63 B.C.; cf. Manilius I.841; perhaps copied by Lucan, VII.155 as a portent for the army of Pompey before Pharsalus; but κίων already in Heraclides Ponticus, Aetius, III.2.5 (F116 Wehrli)), the blazing shields (surely the one Pliny, *NH* 2.100 found reported for the consulship of Marius and Valerius Flaccus). The derision in Seneca's following lines (22–31) is patent, and *posset* (28) may be right and refer to Posidonius. But where did these references come from? The *History* is a reasonable guess, rather than the *Meteorology*. And the second mention of Posidonius refers to an observation that at an eclipse of the sun, a comet was once seen, which had not been visible owing to its nearness to the sun. The context was more likely to be solar eclipses than theory of comets.

Seneca's main evidence here is for the popularity of Posidonius' theory among the Stoics of the time. Seneca wishes to discredit it, and advance his own theory (ch. 22), that comets are true celestial bodies, but to be distinguished from planets through the different nature of their orbits. Seneca, for once, was right.

F133 Alexander, *In Meteorologica* III.3 (372a 29), pp. 142.21–143.11 Hayduck

CONTENT

Posidonius followed Aristotle's theory of halo. Almost everyone else differed.

CONTEXT

See F121 Context; cf. also F134; Arist. *Meteor.* III.3; Seneca *NQ* I.2.

COMMENT

For Aristotle's theory it is better to read *Meteor.* III.3 than Alexander's paraphrase. Aristotle held an optical theory of reflection (cf. 19ff) whereby our vision reflects from a mist cloud to the luminary, whether this be sun, moon or star (cf. 3ff). The round halo effect is due to the characteristics of the cloud, in that the condensation of air and vapour is uniform and the particles small (cf. 2, 6ff). If perpendiculars are dropped from the ring to the direct line from viewer to luminary, these perpendiculars will be equal (cf. 8ff). The reflecting particles are continuous but individually so small as to be invisible, but because they are continuous they appear in aggregate as a single substance; yet because the individual reflectors are so small, we have a reflection of colour (brightness) rather than shape (cf. 24f). Aristotle certainly thought that the direction proceeded from sight rays to mist cloud to luminary (19–21), rather than the other way round, what Alexander calls κατὰ δὲ τὸ ἀληθές (21–4).

It is uncertain how much of all this Posidonius agreed with, because Alexander seems to separate Posidonius from the rest on the question of a reflecting theory and some other optical theory (28ff). This other theory happens by some other kind of κλᾶσις than ἀνάκλασις (reflection), as when objects are seen through water. We should probably read at line 28, ἀλλὰ κατὰ κατακλάσεις ὄψεων. Compare Aetius (Ps.-Plu. *Plac.*) III.18 also on halo, τῆς ὄψεως κατακλωμένης καὶ εὐρυνομένης. Also Scholia in Aratum 811, p. 488.21ff Maass: ἡ τοίνυν ὄψις . . . λείοις δὲ καὶ ὁμαλοῖς προσφερομένη (οἷά ἐστι τὰ ἔσοπτρα καὶ τὰ ὕδατα) ἤτοι ἐνδοτέρω διαδύεται οἱονεὶ ἐγκατακλωμένη ἢ, εἴπερ τοῦτο ἀδυνατεῖ ποιεῖν δι' ἀντιτυπίαν τῶν σωμάτων, ἀνακλᾶται . . . This looks like a theory of refraction approaching the true explanation of refraction of light from ice crystals in the atmosphere usually assigned first to Descartes. Cf. Olympiodorus, *In Meteor.* III.2, p. 210.15ff Stüve: ἐνταῦθα δὲ γενόμενος ὁ Ἀφροδισεύς, οὐκ οἶδα τί παθών, τὴν μὲν ἶριν λέγει γίνεσθαι κατὰ διάκλασιν, τὴν δ' ἅλω κατὰ ἀνάκλασιν.

Later ancient theories seemed to divide then between mirror reflection theories (Aristotle and Posidonius) and water refraction theories. Seneca (*NQ* I.2) appears to have had a theory of his own based on a circular wave theory of light (expanding like waves in a pool from a stone; for a comparable sound theory: Vitruvius, V.3). He is however very unclear. Some of his language (*figurari* §7; *lumen immissum* §11) suggests some kind of physical alteration in the condensed moist air from the light. But he cannot mean this because he insists at I.15.6 that the phenomenon is due simply to optical reflection (i.e. κατ' ἔμφασιν not καθ' ὑπόστασιν). If Posidonius followed Aristotle, he too would have maintained so (compare on this matter F121 and F134).

There is again no mention for Posidonius (cf. F121) of halo as a weather sign (as Arist. *Meteor.* 372b 18ff; Seneca, *loc. cit.*; Geminus, *Isag.* XVII.47), or as a portent (as Pliny, *NH* 2.98). Nor do ancient authorities in general discuss the fact that there can be two haloes, inner and outer (at 22° and 46°), which pluralise the parhelia (F121).

For difficulties in Greek reflection theory, see also Beare, *Greek Theories of Elementary Cognition* 66, 84.

F134 Seneca, *Naturales Quaestiones* I.3.14 ff

CONTENT

Theory of rainbow. See also F15.

CONTEXT

For general context with halo and parhelion, see F121 under Context.

Seneca begins his account of rainbow at *NQ* I.3, following the treatment of halo. Certain preliminary suggestions are raised about the effect of peculiarities of cloud (§1), and of the sun on drops of water (§2). Certain drops may transmit light, others are too compact, so one might have an effect of light and shade, but how to explain the different colours (§3–4)? §§5–8 present for examination what appears to be the theory of Aristotle (for which see Arist. *Meteor.* III.4–5). This explains rainbow on the basis of optical reflection between sun and rain cloud, where the separate raindrops in the cloud act as a group of reflecting mirrors. Seneca raises objections in §§9–10. Why then do we not see a large number of different reflected images of sun, and how still does one explain the different colours? At least (§11) he agrees that rainbow is *imago solis . . . roscida et cava nube concepta*. The variation of colour is due to the double source of sun and rain cloud (§12). There are two elements: sun and cloud, that is, object (*corpus*) and mirror (*speculum*) (§13). F134 now begins, and it is followed by more arguments by Seneca in chs. 6–8 concerning size, shape, optical illusion and reality, colours, position, time and season, where there are no allusions to Posidonius.

COMMENT

A. Analysis

3.14 There are two causes, sun and cloud.

4 Mirror reflection theory in general. Since the phenomenon occurs opposite the sun, it must happen by reflection (since it cannot be due to light shining *through* the cloud directly to the observer). This is proved geometrically by mathematicians. (What mathematicians? Oltramare suggested Euclid's *Katoptrika*, but the only geometrical proofs extant occur in Aristotle, *Meteor. loc. cit.* Typically however, Seneca sheers off mathematics.) (§1). Evidence for mirror theory is the rapidity of emergence and fading of the phenomenon (§2. For this as a characteristic of mirror reflection cf. Cleomedes, *De Motu* II.4.104, p. 188.8ff Z: F123). Such a reflection could be caused, according to Artemidorus of Parium, by a concave mirror formed like a ball cut in half; so a rainbow would be an optical effect when a round hollow cloud is looked at from the side. (This appears to be identical with the theory assigned to Posidonius at 5.13 below.)

5 Objections to mirror theory. Are we dealing with merely optical reflection, or is the effect on the cloud that we see substantial (§1)? (Seneca later makes it clear that he (like Aristotle) holds the former opinion; see especially 1.6.3; 1.15.6.) §§2–9 have been omitted. The sequence of thought is not clear, but Seneca raises questions such as: rainbows and sun are not at all like each other; air does not seem to be like a mirror in texture.

5.10 A counter objection by Posidonius to those who hold that the cloud *is* coloured: Posidonius, who is among those who hold to the mirror reflection theory, objects; if the cloud were coloured, the colour would persist, whereas it vanishes as you approach. Seneca (§§11–12) disagrees with this argument, but approves of Posidonius' sententia.

§§13–14 The sententia of Posidonius, with which Seneca agrees. Rainbows arise in a cloud shaped like a hollow round mirror, whose form is that of a ball cut through the middle. (This seems indistinguishable from the opinion of Artemidorus of Parium cited at 4.3 above; it is repeated at ch. 8.4

under the title of *nostri* (i.e. Stoics).) This cannot be proved without the aid of geometry, whose proofs leave no doubt that a rainbow is an *effigiem solis*, but *non similem*. For certain mirrors can distort reflections.

B. Posidonius' theory

(1) Posidonius has a theory different from Aristotle; cf. F133. Seneca agrees basically with Posidonius (5.13), but expresses differences of opinion (5.11–12). Therefore the whole of Seneca's account (1.3–8) cannot be taken as deriving from Posidonius.

(2) Posidonius differs from Aristotle in taking the cloud as a whole as the reflector instead of the individual moisture drops in it. For Posidonius, the effect is produced not only from the moisture in the cloud, but from its general shape, like that of a distorting mirror. Perhaps for this reason, our evidence shows Posidonius more concerned with shape than with explanation of colour, which concerned Aristotle more (*Meteor.* 373b–374a). This is also borne out in Posidonius' definition of rainbow preserved from the *Meteorology* (F15). This definition is reproduced almost exactly in Ps.-Arist. *De Mundo* 4.395a 33ff. For whatever reason, a very similar definition is preserved in Arius Didymus F14, *Dox. Gr.* p. 455.15f under Aristotle.

(3) On the other hand, Posidonius agrees with Aristotle (so also Seneca) in regarding rainbow as an optical phenomenon only, and not substantial. The cloud is not coloured (1.5.10); i.e. it is κατ' ἔμφασιν and not καθ' ὑπόστασιν. For this: Aetius, *Plac.* III.5. Both Aristotle and Posidonius accept a mirror reflection theory; but what we would call a refraction effect Aristotle explains by the multiplicity of tiny mirrors in the individual raindrops, Posidonius by the distorting effect of the whole mirror cloud. This fragment should perhaps make us hesitate as to how far Posidonius followed Aristotle in the explanation of halo; see F133. Olympiodorus, *In Meteor.*

III.2, p. 210.15ff Stüve, records a refraction theory distinct from the more usual reflection theories: ἐνταῦθα δὲ γενόμενος ὁ Ἀφροδισιεύς, οὐκ οἶδα τί παθών, τὴν μὲν ἶριν λέγει γίνεσθαι κατὰ διάκλασιν, τὴν δ' ἅλω κατὰ ἀνάκλασιν. See F133.

(4) Geometry necessary for proof of the theory. Compare for the role of geometry in mirror theory F90.33ff. The theory is the responsibility of the philosopher; science is a tool which helps to work out the details. For Posidonius on the relationship between philosophy and the sciences, see F18, F90, and notes on F202. Note that here it is said that geometry is *necessary* for the proof.

(5) How influential was Posidonius' theory? Artemidorus of Parium, also quoted for it by Seneca, is attacked vigorously for a theory of comets at *NQ* VII.13, but otherwise we know nothing of him (Kauffmann, *RE* II.1 col. 1333f; Reinhardt, *Poseidonios* 164.1). At *NQ* I.8.4 the theory is held by *nostri*, 'we Stoics'. No doubt all sorts of variations occurred. Aetius, III.5, seems to record the drop theory rather than the cloud theory (although the order of colours is different from Aristotle's); Arius Didymus F14 is nearer Posidonius, but puts it under Aristotle. Pliny (*NH* 2.150) is vague, but has *cavae nubi*. Seneca was clearly influenced by Posidonius, but had views of his own. Plutarch has a cloud reflection theory rather than one based on drops, but associates it with the mathematicians (*De Facie* 921A (with Cherniss's notes); *De Iside* 358F; *Amatorius* 765E–F). *De Mundo* (*loc. cit.*) reproduces Posidonius. Aetius assigns a reflection theory first to Anaxagoras (III.5.11).

(6) Posidonius probably discussed rainbows in *Meteorology*. See F15.

In general: Gilbert, *Griechische Meteorologie* 614–16; Reinhardt, *Poseidonios* 162–6.

F135 Seneca, *Naturales Quaestiones* II.54.1–55.3

CONTENT

Theory of thunderstorms.

CONTEXT

The fragment begins: 'Now I return to the view of Posidonius . . .'. Since earlier in Bk II in the account of thunder and lightning, Posidonius was not mentioned for a theory, but only incidentally for the report of an isolated phenomenon (II.26.4), and since a very similar theory was described earlier (II.12.4–6) under the name of Aristotle, all editors (Gercke (Teubner), Oltramare (Budé), Corcoran (Loeb)), assume that Seneca is referring back to Aristotle's theory. This would indeed be a curious procedure, and it can be shown to be unlikely from an analysis of the development of Seneca's theme in Bk II. It is also of some importance to attempt to establish an earlier area of Posidonian opinion on this subject in Bk II, if it exists.

Seneca begins his exposition of thunder and lightning at II.12:

Ch. 12

General classification: sheet lightning (*fulguratio*), forked or lightning bolts (*fulmina*), thunder (*tonitrua*) (§1).

A. General agreement that (a) these occur in clouds and issue from clouds; (b) that lightning is either fire or presents the appearance of fire (§2)

B. What is disputed:

(1) Fire is in the clouds, *or*

(2) It is produced for the occasion, and did not exist before. (For this division cf. Arist. *Meteor.* 370a 25.)

Subdivisions of (2):

(a) Due to sun's rays (ascribed by Arist. 369b 13 to Empedocles).

(b) Anaxagoras: from the aether (cf. Arist. 369b 13). (§3).

(c) Aristotle: very close to Arist. *Meteor.* II.9 (§§4–6).

The doxography of ch. 12 has strong affinities with Arist. *Meteor.* II.9.

Chs. 13–14

Criticism of theories that fire is stored up in the clouds, or falls from *aether*.

Ch. 15

Some Stoics: that air is kindled by motion, and noise is produced by scattering and tearing apart of clouds (cf. *SVF* II.703–5).

Chs. 17–20

An Ionian doxography: Anaximenes, Anaximander, Anaxagoras, Diogenes of Apollonia. This is different from the Aristotelian one in ch. 12. Anaxagoras occurs a second time. It has rather more affinities with Aetius, *Plac.* III.3.

Chs. 21–30

Theories of lightning and thunder, but not ascribed by name.

Chs. 21–6 A theory of *fulmina* and *fulguratio* with objections which are answered. Posidonius is mentioned incidentally in ch. 26.

Chs. 26–30 A theory of thunder (*tonitrua*). Ch. 30 contains an elaboration by Asclepiodotus.

These theories cannot be those of Seneca, who only gives his at II.57.

Chs. 31–53

A digression on *mira fulminis* and dealing with portents, divination and effects.

Chs. 54–55.3

A *return* to Posidonius. After a brief recapitulation of the general cause of such phenomena, the subject is clearly thunder (*tonitrua*).

Ch. 55.4

Clidemus on *fulguratio* (cf. Arist. *Meteor.* 370a 12. The theory is similar to that given in Aetius, III.3.2 under Anaximenes).

Ch. 56

Heraclitus on *fulguratio*. A few philological remarks on the words employed.

Ch. 57

quid ipse existimem quaeris; adhuc enim alienis opinionibus commodavi manum. dicam. Seneca's own opinion comes only now.

It will be seen from this analysis that Posidonius on thunder in chs. 54–55.3 should refer back to the unnamed treatment of thunder (chs. 26–30) which was interrupted by the intervening digression. If Seneca means that he is returning to Posidonius' view, the statement can only have that reference. And the likelihood is that the whole of the unnamed theory from ch. 21–30 is then to be taken as derived from Posidonius (how accurately or faithfully is another matter). The trouble with this theory is that Seneca begins ch. 21 with the words: *dimissis nunc praeceptoribus nostris incipimus per nos moveri . . .* Nevertheless Seneca does present theories in chs. 21–30 which are not his theories (ch. 57 *init.*). I can only suggest that up to ch. 21, Seneca has accepted doxographies from elsewhere (ch. 12 Aristotle? chs. 17–20 Posidonius? Gilbert, *Griechische Meteorologie* 635 n. 2, would take the Posidonian influence back to ch. 12, but this seems to me to go too far. His general remarks on structure appear however to have been undeservedly ignored). Then, he operates a development or procedure of argument that is his own, but on a base of

Posidonian theory (21–30). What indications there are in chs. 21–30 seem to support this. The theory (21–3) that *fulmina* and *fulguratio* are fire produced by friction in clouds is certainly Posidonian (*atterendi* F135.12; *terit* F135.13), and with the emphasis on friction closer to Posidonius than to Aristotle. Then Posidonius is named in ch. 26. In ch. 27 there is a triple classification of thunder:

(a) *grave murmur*; a rumble like an earthquake. This is *spiritus* rolling about in clouds, cf. *pervolat*, F135.11.

(b) A sharper sound, *fragor*; when a dense cloud bursts, cf. *rumpit nubes* F135.11.

(c) Thunder also happens when *inclusus aer cava nube et motu ipso extenuatus diffundatur*, cf. F135.6–7.

Ch. 28 deals with problems about collisions of clouds; cf. F135.15ff. Ch. 29: sound as *ictus aer*: not unPosidonian in any case; but if Axelson (*Senecastudien* 42f) is right with his suggested emendation for F135.13 of *icti aeris sonitus*, the parallel would be still closer. Asclepiodotus (ch. 30) was *auditor Posidonii*: T41 a & b. Seneca's own opinion (ch. 57f) is really just that of Posidonius again, apart from his own moralising contribution (ch. 59) on delivery from fear of thunderbolts and death.

One thing that can be certain from the analysis is that the long digression with its emphasis on portents and divination (chs. 31–5) is not Posidonius. On the other hand ch. 53.3 which dismisses the digression in order to return to the business in hand, strongly reminds one of Posidonius: *fortasse enim libebit ostendere quam omnia ista a philosophia parente artium fluxerint* (cf. F248, F90). *illa primum et quaesivit causas rerum et observavit effectus et, quod in fulminis inspectione longe melius est, initiis rerum exitus contulit.*

COMMENT

The Posidonian theory (ch. 54) (F135.1–14)

Seneca opens with an introduction (ll.1–3) which is taken straight from Aristotle (Arist. *Meteor.* 365a 14ff; 369a 13ff); already given and named as Aristotle by Seneca II.12.4. This is the general dichotomy of the different effects of wet and dry exhalations. This is what made all editors look back to ch. 12, but it is clearly meant here as a résumé which Posidonius too accepted, because the dry exhalations are *fulminibus alimenta*, while the topic for the Posidonius piece is clearly *tonitrua*.

However it is clear that the basis of Posidonius' theory (3–6) is Aristotelian, namely that the cause of thunder is dry exhalations from earth being shut up in clouds and forcing exit (cf. in general Arist. *Meteor.* II.9 and Seneca II.12). *fumosus* (cf. *fumo similis*, II.12.4) translates καπνώδης whereby Aristotle himself distinguished dry from wet (ἀτμιδώδης) exhalations (e.g. *Meteor.* 360a 10).

§2 **(6–9)** adds something new which is not in Aristotle. Quite apart from exhalations, in the air itself, whatever is rarified at once becomes dried and heated. This too, if enclosed, equally seeks escape, and emerges noisily. But for this addition cf. Seneca II.27.4 and Context above. Posidonius adds a distinction of noise (ll.9–10). If it bursts out altogether there is a more violent sound than if the air emerges bit by bit and gradually. This is quite different from Aristotle's explanation (369b 1) that different kinds of ψόφοι occur because of the unevenness (ἀνωμαλίαν) of the clouds, and because of the hollows in between where the density is not continuous (so Seneca's version of Aristotle at II.12.6; but cf. Arist. *Meteor.* III.1, 370b 5ff).

10–12 emphasise *spiritus* (πνεῦμα), i.e. a moving current of air, and how this is a most powerful type of friction. Again the emphasis on friction (*atterendi . . . terit*) is much more stressed than in Aristotle. These powerful currents (a) burst the clouds (cf. Seneca II.27.3) or (b) fly through them (Seneca II.27.1–2; see Context above).

12–14 The final definition; thunder is nothing else but the sound produced by turbulent air; the sound can only happen while the air produces friction or bursts out. *citi aeris* has been doubted and emended. Axelson (*Senecastudien* 42f) proposed reading . . . *icti aeris sonitus, feriri nisi dum* . . . supposing this to be supported by *is quem desideras ictus* of 15f; mistakenly, since the first objection dismisses blow as the cause (see below). *icti aeris* would certainly suit ch. 29 where sound is *ictus aer* (see Context above), but this is not enough reason to change the text. *citi* (< *cieo*) fits the context of the present chapter exactly with its emphasis on the movement of air. Bake, p. 81, prints *sicci* without explanation. There is also no cause to read *teritur* with Gercke and Axelson. See Oltramare *ad loc.*; air produces the friction.

The objections

Three objections to the theory follow, each introduced by *inquit*, and answered. This is very much in Seneca's style in *NQ*. The objections are no doubt made by him, but the replies may be based on Posidonius (cf. F90).

(1) The phenomenon may be caused simply by collision of clouds, i.e. by a *blow* (*ictus*), not by friction of air. This seems to have been a Stoic theory: Aetius, *Plac.* III.3.12, οἱ Στωϊκοὶ βροντὴν μὲν προσκρουσμὸν νεφῶν. The answer is that there is nothing hard in clouds to produce a noise from a blow (15–18).

(2) As fire plunged into water hisses while being extinguished, so the noise comes from fire in a wet cloud. This introduces a fire theory in place of an air theory. Compare the criticism of this kind of view in Arist. *Meteor.* 369b 13ff, and especially 370a 7. For such a theory: Aetius, *Plac.* III.3.5 (Archelaus). The answer given is that fire is produced, but is

not the cause. Air movement and friction are the cause of the fire (19–22).

(3) The effect could be produced by a shooting star falling into a cloud and being extinguished. Compare the theory of Anaxagoras (Arist. *Meteor.* 369b 15) that part of upper *aether* has descended into the lower atmosphere. Answer: this may be a concomitant phenomenon, but it is occasional and accidental and therefore cannot be the cause.

Relations to previous theories and influence

Posidonius' theory is clearly similar to that of Aristotle, but is independent of him, see above.

It also seems to be different from Stoic theories:

(a) Zeno (D.L. VII.153 = *SVF* II.704) appears to put emphasis on the rubbing action of clouds.

(b) Chrysippus (Stob. *Ecl.* I.29.1, p. 233 W = Aet. III.3.13 = *SVF* II.703) has more emphasis on the movement of pneuma.

(c) The Stoics (Aet. III.3.12 = *SVF* II.705, see above) talked of collision of clouds.

This evidence includes cloud banging and rubbing and bursting and even the forceful movement of pneuma, but there is no mention of the rarefaction of πνεῦμα or ἀήρ, and nothing about pneuma being enclosed in the clouds and through expansion forcing a way out.

There are later explanations similar to Posidonius in Arrian, *ap.* Stobaeus, *Ecl.* I, p. 235 W, Ps.-Arist. *De Mundo* 4.395a 11ff, and cf. Anon. II *Isag.* p. 127.5ff Maass. See Capelle, *Hermes* 40 (1905) 620ff, Gilbert, *Griechische Meteorologie* 634ff. But one cannot be certain (as Capelle and Gilbert appear to be) that the classification of different kinds of thunder and lightning that follows in Arrian and *De Mundo* derives from Posidonius.

F136 Seneca, *Naturales Quaestiones* IVb.3.1–2

CONTENT

Theory of hail.

CONTEXT AND COMMENT

This is a baffling fragment, whose peculiar difficulties arise because the preceding context is missing, and the internal context is befogged by Seneca's attitude.

A. This part of *NQ* was probably originally the last part of the first book of the work (Oltramare, *Notice* 193). It was no doubt concerned with what Aristotle called (*Meteor.* I.9) the phenomenon of water above the earth in the atmosphere that lies between the celestial and terrestrial spheres. Traditionally from Aristotle on (*Meteor.* I.9–12; Aetius, *Plac.* III.4; Stob. *Ecl.* I.31) this involved an examination of cloud, moisture, rain, snow, hail in that order. Only hail survives in Seneca, beginning with the Posidonian fragment; therefore we miss the account of the related phenomena, and perhaps even earlier remarks on hail.

B. In the fragment itself Seneca writes with kittenish playfulness which seems to involve an attitude to Posidonius, but since his motives are not clear, neither is the emphasis nor interpretation that we should put on his words.

(1) **1–2** Why does Seneca protest that the first statement on hail is bold or shocking? It would appear to lie in the comparison with how ice is formed *apud nos*. Most editors interpret *apud nos* by 'on earth' as compared with up in the sky. But there is nothing shocking about the way ice forms on earth.

Perhaps then it is the idea of the whole frozen cloud. But this does not seem to have been an unusual concept in meteorology (unless to a very lay audience) (cf. Anaxagoras,

Arist. *Meteor.* 348a 15, Aetius III.4.2; Chrysippus, Stob. *Ecl.* I, p. 245 W = *SVF* II.701; Arist. *Meteor.* 347b 23; cf. Arrian *ap.* Stob. *Ecl.* I, p. 247 W; *De Mundo* 394a 33ff; Anon. II, *Isag.* 8, p. 127 Maass). Such a comparison is certainly denied by Aristotle (*Meteor.* I.11.347b 28ff) on the grounds that there is nothing corresponding to hail in evaporation ἐνταῦθα (i.e. on earth); but that would hardly provoke Seneca's statement; i.e. we don't have frozen clouds on earth. But what is the point of that? Perhaps *apud nos* has a social reference: 'among us Romans'. It is significant that Seneca winds up the discussion on hail (ch. 13) with a prolonged sermon against the effete liking for the luxury of iced water. Usually this appears to have been effected by snow added as a sherbet, but the addition of ice (*glacies*) is quoted as the acme of depraved luxury (13.8). The difficulty with this theory is that while the Romans were able no doubt at considerable expense to store snow and ice in ice houses, they had no means of *making* ice (*quo apud nos glacies fit*). It might however be thought that the snow compressed by slaves (*stiparemus nivem*, 13.3) produced a kind of ice. But a further block to connecting *apud nos* to the outburst in ch. 13 is that the latter chapter refers to society in Seneca's time, while the boldness of the statement on hail appears to be thrown back to Posidonius. Also *tamquam interfuit* (10–11, 'as if he had been there', i.e. up in the sky) tells against such a theory. It remains unclear why Seneca shies at the statement.

(2) **3–7** Why the elaboration of Seneca's claim that he is only a hearsay witness? And it is elaborate.

(i) He is to be regarded as a witness *secundae notae*. The metaphor appears to come from marks grading vintage in the wine cellar (Hor. *Odes* II.3.8; *Sat.* I.10.24; Cic. *Brut.* 83.287; quickly widened in reference: Curius *ap.* Cic. *Fam.* VII.29.1; Columella, 9.15; Seneca himself *NQ* II.2.4; *Ben.* III.9.1).

(ii) He embarks on a second comparison with historians, and even quotes *penes auctores fides erit* from Sallust, *Iug.* 17.

Does Seneca mean to convey:

(a) that he does not believe the statement himself, so all he can do is to retire behind an authority, and the reader is warned (in which case Seneca is sceptical of Posidonius), or

(b) is Seneca implying that although he believes this description of hail, he does not think that his readers will believe *him*, so he brings forward an authority who will give weight to the statement (in which case he is putting stress on Posidonius' testimony)?

If Seneca is merely saying, '*I* have never seen a frozen cloud', he is making a very laboured joke.

(3) 7–11 At first sight here Seneca does seem to be stressing Posidonius' authority (7–8; i.e. 2(ii)(b) above). But the end of the sentence appears to return to heavy sarcasm and scepticism (see 2(ii)(a) above): *tamquam interfuerit*, as if he had been there himself. Is this a hit at the dogmatic tone of Posidonius' theory? Or is it a general quip at Posidonius' stress on autopsy?

For what is Posidonius being cited as authority? What seems to produce the reaction in Seneca (whatever it is) is conveyed by his stress in the words: *tam in illo quod praeteriit quam in hoc quod secuturum est* (8–9). Oltramare (*ad loc.*) translates *tam . . . praeteriit* by 'aussi bien pour ce qu' il a passé sous silence', and he supposes an important omission by Posidonius in the earlier lost part of the book. This is a fantastic interpretation. As *quod secuturum est* refers to the immediately following statement on hail, so *quod praeteriit* refers to the past statement at the beginning of the fragment. It may be the juxtaposition of the two statements which is causing Seneca's elaborate gyrations. His embarrassment and denial of responsibility may well have derived from the uncertainty of how to proceed from the first statement (frozen cloud) to the second (watery cloud). See below.

The theory

The statements stripped bare of Seneca's elaborations are:

(1) Hail is formed once a whole cloud has frozen.
(2) Hail is formed from a watery (*aquosa*) cloud only just turned to liquid. To this we might add for consideration D.L. VII.153 (F11):
(3)(a) Hail is frozen cloud, crumbled (διαθρυφθέν) by wind.
(b) Snow is moisture (ὑγρόν) from a frozen cloud.
(3)(b) is certainly ascribed to Posidonius. (3)(a) because of the association between snow and hail may also be in the same ascription, but it cannot be taken for granted that it is. (2) is indubitably assigned to Posidonius by Seneca. (1) might conceivably be a hesitant statement from Seneca, but *tam in tam in illo . . . secuturum est* (ll. 8–9) is strong evidence for ascribing it also to Posidonius (see Context above).

Can (1) and (2) be reconciled? Only if we assume a process:

(a) initially, a cloud totally frozen;
(b) later, the cloud begins to melt, thus breaking into frozen drops.

The reason for stage (b) is probably supplied by Seneca's next sentence (3.3): *quare autem rotunda sit grando, etiam sine magistro scire possis, cum adnotaveris stillicidium omne glomerari.* One of the problems for theories of hail was how to explain the roundness common, although not universal in hailstones. Some suggested (e.g. Epicurus, Aet. III.4.5; Sen. IVb.3.5; argued against by Arist. *Meteor.* I.12, 348a 25ff) that the stones were rounded by the friction of their fall. Posidonius seems to have suggested that their shape was determined by the process of liquefaction in the cloud having started, and so round ice drops are produced before they start to fall. But of course the cloud would have been completely frozen before this process started. No one denied that hail is ice, or ice fragments (cf. Arist. *Meteor.* I.12, 347b 37), and came from a cloud; the different theories were concerned with the process of the ice formation in relation to the cloud. Did the freezing take place in the cloud, then how were the discrete stones formed? Or if moisture drops fell from a cloud, how was this 'rain' subsequently frozen?

See in general the doxographies and arguments in Arist. *Meteor.* I.11–12; Aetius, *Plac.* III.4; Ar. Did. F35 (Stob. *Ecl.* I, p. 245 W); Arrian *ap.* Stob. *Ecl.* I, p. 247 W; *De Mundo* 394a 33ff; Anon. II. *Isag.* 8, p. 127 Maass; and Gilbert, *Griechische Meteorologie* 503ff.

Relation to other theories

The Posidonian theory in Seneca would seem original; at least it survives nowhere else. It is certainly different from Aristotle, indeed reverses the process which Aristotle outlined of a cold wet cloud descending to a warmer area, with the result that the warm air compressed the wet cloud thus freezing the drops in it before they fell. Posidonius' process is from freezing to semi-liquefaction. Gilbert (*Griechische Meteorologie* 507) thought that Posidonius reversed Chrysippus' theories of snow and hail, but his argument is vitiated from the start through ignoring the last statement (2) in the Seneca fragment. Also we have even less information on Chrysippus than on Posidonius (only in Ar. Did. F35 = Stob. *Ecl.* I, p. 245 W = *SVF* II.701). Hail is defined as the breaking in pieces (διάθρυψιν) of frozen rain (ὑετοῦ πεπηγότος). But the genitive may be objective, and the sense taken to be consisting of frozen rain (the cloud being broken into that). Chrysippus' διάθρυψιν recalls διαθρυφθέν of (3)(a) (above, D.L. VII.153). But the crumbling of the cloud by wind (ὑπὸ πνεύματος) in that sentence, looks different from Posidonius' theory. The same sort of vocabulary (ἀπόθραυσιν, θραυσμάτων) occurs in the definitions of snow and hail in *De Mundo* 394a 33ff, where the underlying theories are quite certainly different from Posidonius.

The 'rain' language of Chrysippus occurs again in Anon. II, *Isag.* 8, p. 127 Maass: hail is 'a frozen shower' (ὄμβρος πεπηγώς) and snow, 'rain drizzle (ὑετῶν ψακάς) in a frozen cloud'. Posidonius' theory appears to have had no influence.

Source

Seneca's evidence could have come from one of Posidonius' books specifically on meteorology, but it could equally well have come from the *Physics* (see F11).

F137a, b Strabo, I.2.21; Eustathius, *Commentarii ad Homeri Iliadem* XXI.334

CONTENT

Compass card of winds and Homer.

CONTEXT

Strabo is engaged in a defence of Homer's geographical knowledge. Eratosthenes was critical of Homer's description of winds (notably *Il.* IX.5, cf. F137a.9) as inaccurate. Strabo's defence is that for people in Thasos, Lemnos and Imbros, Zephyrus (west wind) does seem to come from Thrace (i.e. Chalcidice), as at Athens it seems to come from the Scironian Rocks and is called Scirones. Strabo now uses Posidonius on winds as a stick with which to beat Eratosthenes.

COMMENT

Posidonius is first mentioned at line 10; since he is there said to criticise the theories given in 1–9, the whole passage should be taken as Posidonius' account of two conflicting tendencies and classifications of wind compass card systems, of which he supports the second. Both sides (and Posidonius) appeal to Homer as evidence. It is the Homeric evidence which interests Strabo in order to criticise Eratosthenes.

The quarrel between the two schools of thought centred on

(a) the number of points on the card, the first group tending towards economy, the second towards plurality; (b) direction of some of the winds. That (a) was debated is also shown explicitly by Pliny, *NH* 2.119, Seneca, *NQ* v.16, and implicitly by Arist. *Meteor.* II.4–6, *De Mundo* 4.394b 20ff, Agathemerus, II.6–7, Galen, XVI, p. 396ff Kühn, Gellius, II.22.

Group A (1–9)

Some say that there are two cardinal winds, Boreas and Notus; the rest differ by slight inclination.

The compass card is described in Fig. 13.

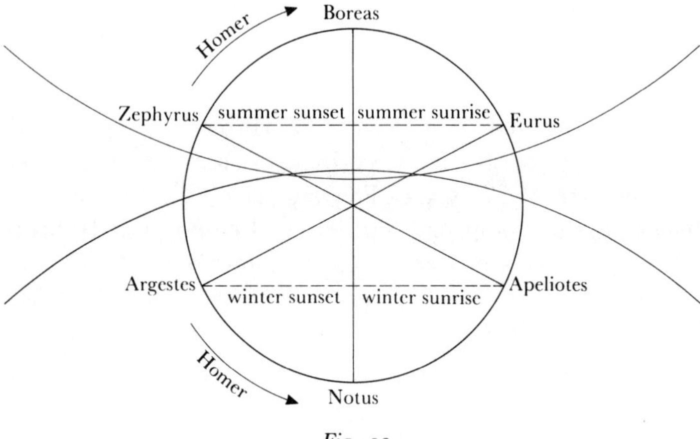

Fig. 13

They support their claim by an appeal to Thrasyalces and Homer. The former is presumably Thrasyalces of Thasos (appropriate for Strabo on *Il.* IX.5; see Context above) mentioned again by Strabo, XVII.1.5 (F222) as a physical philosopher earlier than Aristotle, who took a theory of the risings of the Nile from him. Nothing more is known of Thrasyalces on winds, and no particulars are given in this passage. Homer is used for swinging Argestes towards Notus and Zephyrus towards Boreas (*Il.* IX.5, the evidence for the latter, being the bone of contention between Strabo and Eratosthenes). All this shows that the compass card of Fig. 13 should not be ascribed to Thrasyalces and Homer (as Aujac, *Strabon et la Science*, Figure VIII, B). Homer seems to have adopted a four point description (NSEW; *Od.* v.295f; Strabo, I.2.20; but cf. *Il.* xx.225). Thrasyalces may have been used by these later theorists like Homer for all we know. Posidonius did not consider him an expert on winds (10–11). It is not known who the τινες are whom Posidonius (and Strabo) criticise. Curiously, in the extant evidence it is Aristotle who talks of the prevalence of north and south winds (*Meteor.* II.4, 361a 5; cf. 363a 3ff), and who at the end of his more refined compass card, mentions a more general classification into northerly and southerly winds; west winds, as colder, being included with north, and east winds, as warmer, being classified with south (*Meteor.* 364a 18ff). Aristotle, of course, belongs to Group B, but his remarks on a more general north–south orientation may have been taken up again in the 1st c. B.C. Pliny (*NH* 2.119) remarks that there was a reaction against the common 12-point card (developed, he says, from an original 4-point system; cf. Homer). But Pliny's reduction is to 8 (so also Agathemerus II.6). Seneca (*NQ* v.16) besides 12-point systems, describes a 4-point card by cardinal points EWNS. So also *De Mundo* 4.394b 20ff, having accepted apparently the Timosthenes 12-point card (see below), proceeds to group under the four cardinal points NSEW, the two adjacent winds to each cardinal wind being grouped with it. This is similar to Varro *ap.* Seneca *NQ* v.16. Strabo himself (I.2.28) used a 4-point cardinal direction system of winds. So there is plenty of evidence for a simplification to 4 points, but not for the 2 point simplification of Fig. 13.

The other oddity about Group A is the axis of Eurus/Argestes. This occurs thus nowhere else. Whenever Argestes is cited for a compass card it is invariably put at summer sunset; Eurus (unless for the very few occasions where it appears at equinoctial sunrise) is always diametrically opposite Argestes at winter sunrise (see the table in Gilbert, *Griechische Meteorologie* 550f). Since the Group A axis can only have been adopted to explain Homer's ἀργεσταο Νότοιο (7f), this suggests that Group A were not scientists or philosophers at all but literary critics. This suspicion is strengthened by the remark (2) that the other winds differ from north and south only by a small inclination. The gap is closed by swinging Argestes south and Zephyrus north (and so Eurus and Apeliotes correspondingly) because of Homer; but scientifically the ἐγκλίσεις remain marked because of defining them (as usual) by summer and winter sunrise and sunset.

Group B (10ff), supported by Posidonius

Posidonius names three authorities. Of these Bion, ὁ ἀστρολόγος, has been identified with Bion of Abdera (cf. D.L. IV. 58), a mathematicus of the Democritan school, and thought by Hultsch (*RE* III.1 Bion (11), col. 485ff) to have flourished at the beginning of the 4th century B.C. He is however mentioned after Aristotle and Timosthenes, and nothing is known concerning winds of any Bion. We can however construct the compass cards of Aristotle and Timosthenes (Figs 14 and 15).

(1) Number of compass points

Aristotle operated basically on an 8-point system with two additional northerly winds (NNW Thrascias, and NNE Meses); a system which he saw as reducible to 4 and even further to 2 (northerly and southerly winds). D'Arcy Thompson (*CR* 32 (1918) 49ff) argued however that Aristotle's compass card was basically duodecimal in structure. Timosthenes used a regular 12-point card. Posidonius at first mentions only 6 (Caecias, Lips, Eurus, Argestes, Apeliotes, Zephyrus) which are enough to correct the Eurus/Argestes axis. To these would be added Aparctias, Notus. But he also

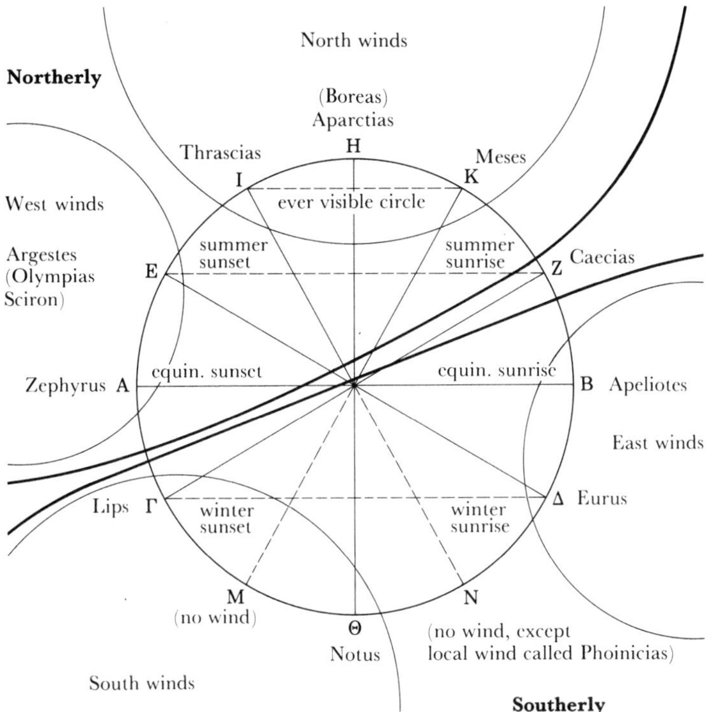

Fig. 14 Aristotle. *Source*: From Arist. *Meteor.* II.6. The circle is the circle of the horizon. There are three classifications: (a) a detailed 10-point classification, reduced to (b) 4 (NESW winds), reduced further to (c) 2 (northerly and southerly). Directions are based fundamentally on summer and winter risings and settings. The structure is meteorological.

uses Leuconotus, a wind not mentioned by Aristotle, and at a point where Aristotle expressly says there is no wind. Also Posidonius, if criticising Group A numerically, would not be interested in Aristotle's further reductions to 4 and to 2. Therefore it seems that Posidonius has chiefly in mind here the compass card of Timosthenes. Also Pliny cannot then be following Posidonius in claiming (*NH* 2.119) that the 8-point card had become common. That it had become common is shown by the 8-sided Tower of Winds of the 1st century B.C. in Athens; cf. also Vitruvius 1.6.4ff. It was a natural and

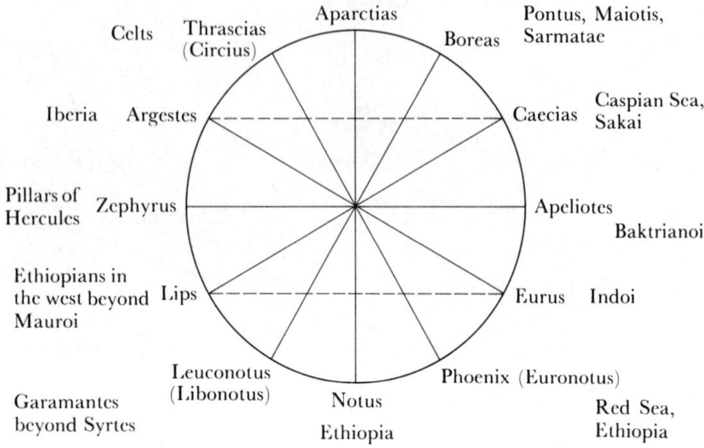

Fig. 15 Timosthenes of Rhodes (fl. under Ptolemy II Philadelphus, c. 280–270 B.C.). *Source*: from Agathemerus, II. 7 (*Geographi Graeci Minores* II. 473, Müller). The structure is geographical rather than meteorological, and is based on a fixed point, most likely Rhodes.

convenient classification to begin with the 4 cardinal points (north, south, equinoctial sunrise and sunset) and then add the 4 solstitial orientations. One could either stop there or add the extra four northerly and southerly winds; so basically Gellius II.22 and Galen, XVI, p. 396ff Kühn. Ps.-Hipp. *Sevens* 3 modified the 8-point rose to 7 (Mansfeld, *Ps. Hipp.* Π. Ἑβδ. 146ff).

(2) Wind direction

Both Aristotle and Timosthenes correct the Eurus/Argestes axis, but this does leave the Homeric interpretation of ἀργεστᾶο Νότοιο more acute. It was probably Posidonius who set out to solve that (compare for his interest in Homeric interpretation and evidence, Frs. 216, 277a, 222); the oratio obliqua of 16ff could refer to his views. He connected Homer's ἀργεστᾶο Νότοιο with Leuconotus, no doubt thinking of the roots ἀργ- and λευκ-. The wind Argestes is equated with Homer's δυσαῆ Ζέφυρον (an association of δυσαῆ with ἀργαλέον?). At any rate the exegesis could well be Posidonian.

(3) Grouping

Seneca (*NQ* v.15) assigned to Varro a method of classification whereby he simply quartered the heavens into EWNS, and then partitioned each quarter into 3, by assigning to each cardinal wind 2 subsidiary winds. A similar method seems to be followed by *De Mundo* 4.394b 20ff. There is no evidence of this for Posidonius, and since Seneca explicitly ascribes it to Varro, no assumptions should be made for Posidonius. Direction was still indicated by solstitial sunrise and sunset.

(4) Regional application

In an orientation system based on winds there is a problem of regional reference. On the one hand it was probably methods which defined winds by local geography (like the Scironian wind at Athens) that Eratosthenes was attacking in Homer (Strabo, I.2.20). Orientation by sunrise and sunset provided a general frame of reference which was convenient and apparently never abandoned (δι' οὗ (i.e. the zodiac) φερόμενος ὁ ἥλιος τρέπεται καὶ διδάσκει διαφορὰς κλιμάτων τε καὶ ἀνέμων, Strabo, I.1.21), but it raised the problem for regional application that the apparent path of the sun varies with latitude. It may have been for this reason that Timosthenes further defined his compass card by geographical references which showed that it was based on Rhodes (e.g. W – Zephyrus – Pillars of Hercules; see Fig. 15). D'Arcy Thompson (*CR* 32 (1918), 52f) argued that Aristotle's card can be shown to be particularly appropriate for the latitude of Athens. Eratosthenes, who admired Timosthenes while trying to improve on his positions (Strabo, II.1.40), was interested in finding a frame of general reference (ὡς καθόλου οὖν δέχεται (Strabo I.2.20)) which could have more accurate particular application. It appears from Galen (XVI, p. 403ff Kühn) and Vitruvius (*loc. cit.*) that he tried to work out a geometrical method by shadows whereby his compass card could be related to any particular latitude (cf. Thalamas, *La Géographie d'Ératosthène* 180ff). In fact, as D'Arcy Thompson showed (*CR* 32 (1918) 52), the variation within the Greek world of the time was not very significant, so perhaps it is not surprising that we find no further trace of this in Posidonius or elsewhere. On the other hand, writers on the subject (and presumably Posidonius) continued to be careful to distinguish between winds which were καθολικοί and τοπικοί (e.g. Galen, xvi, p. 400 Kühn; Gellius, II.22.19ff).

Bibliography

Aujac, *Strabon et la science de son temps* 259ff.
Beaujeu, *Pline L'ancien, Histoire Naturelle*, II. 195–201.
Capelle, *N. Jahrb. f. d. Klass. Altertum*, 15 (1905), 542ff.
D'Arcy Thompson, 'The Greek Winds', *CR* 32 (1918), 49–56.
Gilbert, *Griechische Meteorologie* 539ff.
Kaibel, 'Antike Windrosen', *Hermes* 20 (1885) 579–624.
Mansfeld, *The Pseudo-Hippocratic Tract* 'Περὶ Ἑβδομάδων', 146–55.
Nielsen, 'Remarques sur les Noms Grecs et Latins des Vents et des Régions du Ciel', *Class. et Med.* 7 (1945), 1–13.
Rehm, 'Griechische Windrosen', *Sitz.-Ber. d. Kön. Bayer. Akad. d. Wiss.* Munich, 1916, 3.
Reinhardt, *Poseidonios* 119.
Steinmetz, *De Ventorum Descriptionibus*.

F138 Aetius, *Placita* III.17.4 = Stobaeus, *Eclogae* I.38.4 = I, p. 253.1 W = *Dox. Gr.* 383

CONTENT

Winds are moved by the moon; the winds move the seas in which tides take place.

CONTEXT

This section on tides in Aetius has entries in the following order: (1) Aristotle and Heraclides (2) Euenios of Messene or Dicaearchus (3) Pytheas (4) Posidonius (5) Plato (6) Timaeus (7) Crates (8) Apollodorus of Corcyra (9) Seleucus. Ps.-Plut. *Plac.* has items: 1, 3, 5, 6, 9 (and therefore not the Posidonius item). Stobaeus (codd. *F* and *P*) has only items 1 and 5. The other entries, including Posidonius, come from cod. Laur. VIII.22, sometimes known as the florilegium of St John Damascenus. It is not easy to see any reason for the order of items, unless in terms of theories 1–4 are to be grouped and 5–9.

COMMENT

If this is a theory of tides it is very vaguely stated (ἐν οἷς τὰ προειρημένα γίνεσθαι πάθη). Furthermore Priscianus Lydus (F219) appears to advance a theory from Posidonius whereby tides swell directly from heat from the moon (and perhaps indirectly from the sun). Strabo, who is full of Posidonius' researches into the corresponsion of moon and tides (Frs. 214–18), omits any mention of how this is effected.

It was, of course, well known that Posidonius regarded the moon as the cause of tides; but he was not the only one to do so, nor the first. We may disregard Arist. *Mir.* 54.834b 3f, ὁ πορθμὸς ὁ μεταξὺ Σικελίας καὶ Ἰταλίας αὔξεται καὶ φθίνει ἅμα τῷ σεληνίῳ. This is hardly credible for Aristotle. (See F220 for the difficulties over evidence for Aristotle on tides. Whatever views Aristotle might have held, they were not lunar like those of Posidonius, who criticised him (F220). And see below for the relationship of Aristotle in Aetius, III.17.1 to Posidonius.) Tides in the Mediterranean, as distinct from channel currents (Straits of Messina, Euripus), were difficult to observe (but cf. Hdt. VII.198.1), and more informed statements were forthcoming once the Greeks ventured into the Persian Gulf and Indian Ocean with Alexander (Nearchus, Onesicratus; Duhem, *Le système du monde* II.270), and into the Atlantic, as Pytheas and Euthymenes of Marseilles.

Pytheas probably observed high tides (Pliny, *NH* 2.97), and could have noticed a connection with the moon (so Aetius, III.17.3; but the enlargement that the tides were related to the waxing and waning of the moon is absurd. Also the same statement is ascribed to Euthymenes by Ps.-Galen, *Hist. Phil.* 88). At any rate Eratosthenes (Str. 1.3.11) compared the currents in the Straits of Messina with the diurnal cycle of tides and moon. Seleucus who came from the Persian Gulf and was an older contemporary of Hipparchus, gave a detailed account of the diurnal irregularity of the tides of the Indian Ocean, which was known and approved of by Hipparchus (F218; F214; Aetius, III.17.9). All this was before Posidonius. Strabo makes it clear, however, that different theories were still debated in his day (and cf. Lucan, *Phars.* 1.412–17: wind *or* moon *or* sun). The evidence (Frs. 214–19) shows that Posidonius gave a much more detailed account, not only of diurnal lunar effect, but also of monthly and annual cycles, which clearly gained favour (Strabo, F217; Manilius, II.89–92; Pliny, *NH* 2.212ff; Seneca, *NQ* III.28.6 (but cf. III.14.3); Cleomedes, *De Motu* II.1.85; II.3.98).

According to Strabo then, Posidonius' contribution was to work out in greater detail the corresponsions between moon and tides. But it is unlikely that Posidonius was content with that. (1) The philosopher was not confined to ultimate causes but his function included examination of alternative theories of science (F18), and in general to work out in theory the intermediate causation (T76b; Kidd, *Problems* 210f; *A & A* 24 (1978), 14). (2) It would not be uncharacteristic for him to have considered in the atmosphere a medium between moon and water. Twice in Cleomedes (II.1, p. 156.10–16 Z; II.3, p. 178.1–5 Z) in passages where Posidonius is not named, but which are very reminiscent of him, the moon's effect on both atmosphere and tides are mentioned together. In Aetius, Aristotle (III.17.1) is given the theory that the sun moves winds, which push the Atlantic to create flood tides. It is true that this statement has quite uncertain authenticity; but there is a clear parallel with the Posidonius entry. Further (Aetius, III.17.9) Seleucus, who accepted Aristarchus' heliocentric theory (Plu. *Plat. Qu.* 1006C), is credited with elaborating his lunar tide theory by the effect on the ocean of winds created by the revolution of the moon and the rotation of the earth. (3) It would not be surprising to have two different theories from Posidonius on how the moon caused tides (Aetius and Priscian); compare for example, his different theories on how the inhabited part of the torrid zone was cooled (F210, F49).

(4) It is probably due to Strabo and his dislike of physics and aetiology in Posidonius (T76a & b) that we have no fuller account of the theorising behind Posidonius' tidal observations. But in doxographies where theories are compared, it is another matter. The statement, however, in Aetius is so bare ('ein magerer Ersatz', Jacoby, *Kommentar* 201), that it must remain obscure and uncertain. It must also be admitted that in the accounts of Posidonius' observations on tides and moon, there is no mention of wind; indeed when it is mentioned in F218, it is as a cause of river flooding which is not tidal. Also the cast of the sentence in Aetius is vague, and may have originated from some statement on moon/wind movements which could have an effect on wave motion, as indeed the sea can rise through volcanic action (see Frs. 227, 228).

F139 Diogenes Laertius, VII.157

CONTEXT AND CONTENT

At §156 Diogenes begins a general Stoic account of soul in what is, although extremely concise, a clear and continuously developed line of thought. Nature (φύσις) is artistic fire proceeding methodically to generation (πῦρ τεχνικὸν ὁδῷ βαδίζον εἰς γένεσιν), which is precisely breath of fiery and artistic form (ὅπερ ἐστὶ πνεῦμα πυροειδὲς καὶ τεχνοειδές);

and soul is nature with the characteristic of perception (αἰσθητικήν). Soul is that breath which is congenital with us (τὸ συμφυὲς ἡμῖν πνεῦμα); therefore it is a body (σῶμα, material) and endures after death. It is perishable, but the soul of the universe (τῶν ὅλων), of which the souls in animate beings are a part, is imperishable. Then comes F139 giving special references: Zeno of Citium, Antipater in his books *On Soul* and Posidonius say the soul is warm breath (πνεῦμα ἔνθερμον). For it is by this that we have the breath of life in us (εἶναι ἔμπνους, are alive, animate), and by its agency we move (κινεῖσθαι). This is followed by another detailed reference, this time to the destructibility of individual souls: Cleanthes says that *all* souls persist until the Conflagration (ἐκπυρώσεως), Chrysippus that only the souls of the wise do. Diogenes then passes to an account of parts of the soul.

COMMENT

It is clear from the structure of the whole passage, that Diogenes intends the whole of his account until F139 to refer to all Stoics in general (including Posidonius), to which he appends, as commentary, two sets of references. The second records Cleanthes' and Chrysippus' disagreement over a refinement of the general doctrine of destruction of individual souls mentioned earlier. The first merely gives authority for a particular phrasing of definition in line with his general account above. We should certainly not regard τὸ συμφυὲς ἡμῖν πνεῦμα in the general account and πνεῦμα ἔνθερμον in the Posidonian references as opposing definitions. Stobaeus (*SVF* III.305) records them neatly together, τὸ γὰρ συμφυὲς πνεῦμα ἡμῖν ἔνθερμον ὂν ψυχὴν ἡγοῦνται, as normal Stoic doctrine.

It is interesting that the two names other than Posidonius given as references for πνεῦμα ἔνθερμον are Zeno and Antipater. Antipater was a teacher of Posidonius (T11), who would have been able to cite his work, and Zeno was upheld by him as holding correct views (e.g. F166.20f), defended (F175), and even perhaps reinterpreted (T99). This note could have come ultimately from a Posidonian doxography, perhaps at the beginning of his Περὶ ψυχῆς, see F28.

The information is normal Stoic doctrine, frequently attested. For πνεῦμα ἔνθερμον: *SVF* II.773 (Nemesius); 779 (Aetius); 787 (Galen); for ἔμπνους, *SVF* II.792 where it is connected with the argument that ψυχή is a σῶμα (for which, *SVF* I.137; II.780, 790–800; III.305). κινεῖσθαι is connected with ἔμψυχα, *SVF* II.988, and with ψυχή as σῶμα, *SVF* II.387; 801; I.136; I.145. πνεῦμα itself is ἀὴρ κινούμενος, and hence κινοῦν ἑαυτὸ πρὸς ἑαυτὸ καὶ ἐξ αὑτοῦ, *SVF* II.471. Also for the relation of πνεῦμα to the elements, συγκείμενόν πως ἐκ πυρός καὶ ἀέρος: *SVF* II.786, 787; III (Boethus) 10. See F93.

Therefore Posidonius followed stock Stoic views in this definition of the substance of soul. That need not have prevented him from putting forward other forms of definition, as F141 appears to preserve a definition of the form of soul. And it is probable that a combination of two such accounts was the source of Diogenes' ἰδέαν τοῦ πάντῃ διεστῶτος πνεύματος, which he stupidly assigns to Plato (D.L. III.67; see F141).

What is certain from this fragment is that Posidonius regarded soul as material in the normal Stoic meaning of the term (σῶμα), and could therefore not have regarded it as a 'mathematical' in any special ontological sense of the term. See F141.

F140 Macrobius, *Commentarii in Ciceronis Somnium Scipionis* I.14.19

CONTENT

Posidonius said that the soul was 'form' (*ideam*).

CONTEXT

Macrobius *In Somn. Scip.* 1.14 examines the nature of the soul. At §19 without warning, and immediately after a passage discussing the relation of soul to stars and the heavenly bodies, a doxography on definitions of the soul is inserted: *non ab re est ut haec de anima disputatio in fine sententias omnium qui de anima videntur pronuntiasse contineat.* The transition itself is clumsy and the following conclusion (§20) maladroit. The doxography seems in the wrong place, and is surely culled from some external source (Flamant, *Macrobe et le Néo-platonisme latin à la Fin du IVᵉ Siecle* 507). See Flamant, *op. cit.*, pp. 508–11 for discussions on the origins and source of this doxography, which cannot now be determined. The most recent name on the list is Posidonius.

COMMENT

The list itself is long but terse in the extreme in information, containing 21 names in 14 lines. The order is certainly not chronological, nor according to 'School' divisions. It has been noticed (e.g. by Schedler, *Die Philosophie des Macrobius* 39; Flamant, *Macrobe et le Néo-platonisme* 509) that names are grouped first according to those who, in the compiler's version, hold the soul to be immaterial in some sense (Plato, Xenocrates, Aristotle, Pythagoras, Philolaus, Posidonius, Asclepiades), followed by theories related to a single element (Hippocrates, Heraclides Ponticus, Heraclitus, Zeno, Democritus, Critolaus, Hipparchus, Anaximenes, Empedocles, Critias) or to two elements (Parmenides, Xenophanes, Boethus) or three elements (Epicurus).

Posidonius appears in the first group, so it seems that for the doxographer *ideam* represented either something like Platonic Form, or 'form' in some other immaterial, possibly mathematical sense. Macrobius in 1.14 appears to have been addressing himself to the nature of individual soul rather than cosmic soul, but since the doxography is quite distinct and external, that is irrelevant to its information. In fact the doxography is evidence for nothing except that a doxographical tradition knew that Posidonius used the term ἰδέα in a definition of soul. See F141 for the sense of such an expression.

F141 Plutarch, *De Animae Procreatione in Timaeo* 22.1023B–D; *Epitome* 1030F–1031B

CONTENT

Posidonian interpretation of Pl. *Tim.* 35a b gives rise to a definition of soul.

TEXT

The *Epitome* contributes nothing to the original text, apart from ἀεικίνητος (14).

CONTEXT

The first part of Plutarch's essay is concerned with the interpretation of the psychogony of Pl. *Tim.* 35a 1–b4. Plutarch offers his own explanation and criticises the Xenocratean definition that soul's essence is number itself moved by itself, and the interpretation of Crantor that the soul is a mixture of the intelligible nature and the opinable nature of preceptible things. In ch. 21 he attacks the view that the constituents of soul include the indivisible in the sense of shape and the divisible interpreted as corporeal matter; because he maintains that it is after the generation of the soul that Plato introduces τὴν περὶ τῆς ὕλης ὑπόθεσιν. At this point (ch. 22) he introduces the Posidonians as liable to similar criticism (F141a.1).

COMMENT

The most detailed and acute examination of this difficult and obscure passage is to be found in Cherniss, Plutarch's *Moralia* XIII, Part 1, pp. 217–25. See also, Merlan, *From Platonism to Neoplatonism*[2] 34–40 (bibliography, p. 57f); Thévenaz, *L'Âme du Monde* 63–7; Rist, *Stoic Philosophy* 205f; Laffranque, *Poseidonios* 431f.

It is important to realise the inherent complexities of the context. It is a report interpreted, in some places already misinterpreted, by Plutarch of οἱ περὶ Ποσειδώνιον, on a passage in which Posidonius himself is said (F141.2f) to be interpreting Plato. So we have Plutarch and his source to grapple with, as well as Posidonius' context of which we know very little.

A. (1–8)

1 **τοῖς περὶ Ποσειδώνιον.** The form of the phrase is ambiguous. It may mean either (i) 'Posidonius', or (ii) 'the followers of Posidonius' (Laffranque, 379 n. 37), or (iii) 'Posidonius and his followers'; for the evidence for this, see T45. From comparison with the use of οἱ περὶ τὸν Κράντορα at 1012F (cf. 1012D), Cherniss (p. 218) argued for (iii), and ἔλαθε τούτους (9) strongly supports this. There is a strong presumption that Plutarch used some intermediary sources for this essay, such as Eudorus (1013B, 1019E, 1020C), who may also have reported Posidonius (cf. F149), although there could easily have been some other 'Posidonian' source more immediately identified with οἱ περὶ Ποσειδώνιον. We are clearly engaged in contemporary debate. Plutarch nowhere else uses the οἱ περί formula for Posidonius. Although in comparison with the other Stoics, Posidonian references in Plutarch are few, and he does not surface at all in the 'Stoic' essays, we can not assume that Plutarch did not consult on occasion his work on specific issues (see Frs. 124, 125). And even if in this case there is an intermediary, that does not

preclude the basic information from being correct, although obviously there is an additional hazard. Plutarch is more reliable as a quoter, than as an interpreter.

2 'They did not withdraw far from matter (τῆς ὕλης).' The Posidonians are equally open to Plutarch's objections to material interpretations of soul. There is no need to introduce τὴν ψυχὴν from the *Epitome*; ἀπέστησαν is intransitive.

2f 'But having accepted that "the being of the limits" (τὴν τῶν περάτων οὐσίαν) was the meaning of "divisible in the case of bodies", and having mixed these with the intelligible . . .' The reference is to the interpretation of *Tim.* 35a 2–3: τῆς αὖ περὶ τὰ σώματα γιγνομένης μεριστῆς (οὐσίας). Cf. καὶ περὶ τὰ σώματα γίγνεσθαι λεγομένην μεριστήν κτλ. 1014D, where Plutarch already rejects the Posidonian interpretation. This shows that Plutarch at least believed that the definition of soul which follows arose in the context of interpretation of the *Timaeus*. It does not follow that it occurred in a *Commentary* on the *Timaeus* (see F85). Nor is there evidence to show that it did not.

3 τὴν τῶν περάτων οὐσίαν. Merlan (*From Platonism to Neoplatonism* 38) understood this simply to mean, 'bodies': 'οὐσία is the πεπερασμένον without its limits [i.e. ὕλη]; "the substance of limits" is anything which has received, or can receive a limit.' Cherniss (p. 218f) proved this to be mistaken, and that Plutarch clearly in the context refers to τὰ πέρατα, which is the antecedent to ταῦτα (4); cf. τοῖς τῶν σωμάτων πέρασιν (10) (indeed, 9–13 makes no sense on Merlan's view); and ch. 23 *init.* (1023D) which in a common attack against Posidonians and Xenocrateans represents the Posidonian ingredient as τοῖς πέρασιν and the Xenocratean as τοῖς ἀριθμοῖς. For the form of the phrase, cf. F141.18. So Posidonius' version of the Platonic 'divisible being that comes to pass in bodies' is 'the being of (the) limits', which was regarded by Plutarch as material (and so open to objection). This makes excellent sense for Posidonius (cf. Cherniss, p. 219), since although orthodox Stoicism held that limits existed in thought only (κατ' ἐπίνοιαν, Proclus, *In Euc. Def.* 1, p. 89F = *SVF* II.488), Posidonius believed that they existed in reality also (καθ' ὑπόστασιν, see F16); and for him οὐσία that exists in reality differs from matter only in thought (F92). As Plutarch appears to know all this for Posidonius, although he was well aware of the usual Stoic dogma on limits (*Comm. Not.* 1080E) our confidence in his report here should increase. Also that Posidonius chose πέρατα in his mathematically orientated re-interpretation of Plato is entirely consonant with his sharp distinction between limit and what is limited, and the association of σχῆμα and limit in the question of what imposes or is the cause of definiteness, limitation and inclusion (F196).

4 τῷ νοητῷ, the intelligible, presumably represents Plato's indivisible being. But what would that represent in a Stoic context?

4–6 '... they declared the soul to be form (ἰδέαν) of that which is everywhere (πάντῃ) extended, constructed (constituted, συνεστῶσαν) according to number which encompasses (περιέχοντα) concord (ἁρμονίαν)'.

ἰδέαν: Plutarch incredibly, in order to score a debating point, interprets ἰδέα as a Platonic Form in 13–17. His own report refutes him; συνεστῶσαν (5) could not apply to a Form, nor could it have its being in a category intermediate between νοητά and αἰσθητά (6–9). Cherniss pointed out (p. 220) that ἰδέα occurs in *Tim.* 35a 7 in the sense of 'entity', which may have been the genesis of its appearance in subsequent definitions (cf. Speusippus, F40 Lang; Iamblichus, *De Comm. Math. Scientia* 40.20 Festa; see below). Here Cherniss (p. 220) takes it in the sense of 'rational configuration', i.e. τὸν λόγον τοῦ σχήματος; see F196.4. It must refer to mathematical form. That Plutarch was quite aware of this is indicated by the beginning of the criticism in ch. 21 (1022E), ὡς μορφὴν καὶ εἶδος. That Posidonius in fact used the term ἰδέα is supported by Macrobius (F140). τοῦ πάντῃ διαστατοῦ: tridimensional extension. For πάντῃ: Arist. *De Caelo* 268a 7ff and a 24ff and Simpl. *De Caelo* 8.17ff; Proclus,

In Tim. II, p. 152.24ff D; Philo, *De Op. Mundi* 36, p. 11, 9f Cohn; Pl. *Tim.* 36e 2. The reference is to geometrical shape or configuration of body. For what Posidonius meant by terms such as 'surface', 'shape', 'limit': Frs. 16, 196.

κατ' ἀριθμὸν . . . περιέχοντα: the soul is a composition of constituents (συνεστῶσαν) formed according to a definite precise pattern (ἀριθμός in mathematics represents exact number as distinct from indefinite plurality), containing in it concord of ratios (ἁρμονία) i.e. order.

Accounts of the soul in mathematical terms, whether in relation to *Timaeus* or not, certainly go back to the Old Academy, indeed to Plato (Arist. *De An.* 404b 18ff). Aristotle (*De An.* 414b 20ff) *compares* the defining of soul with the defining of σχῆμα, but Xenocrates had an arithmological definition, self-moving number (ἀριθμός, e.g. Plu. *De Anim. Procr.* 1012D). According to Iamblichus (Περὶ ψυχῆς, Stob. *Ecl.* 1.364.4f W = F40 Lang), Speusippus had a geometrical definition, ἰδέα τοῦ πάντῃ διαστατοῦ, which is identical to the first part of Posidonius' account. After Posidonius, the practice continued especially with Platonists and Pythagoreans, as is shown by two passages from Iamblichus (discussed by Merlan, *From Platonism to Neoplatonism* 17ff), (a) Stob. *Ecl.* 1.364ff W and (b) *De Comm. Math. Scientia*, ch. IX, p. 40f Festa. Iamblichus does not mention Posidonius, and the passages are not evidence for him, but they help to bring out part of the individuality of Posidonius' definition. In the Περὶ ψυχῆς (for details: Festugière, *La Révélation d'Hermès Trismégiste* 3.179ff) Iamblichus reviews accounts of soul as a μαθηματικὴ οὐσία. One class refers to σχῆμα, πέρας ὂν διαστάσεως, καὶ αὐτὴ ⟨ἡ⟩ διάστασις (p. 364.2f); the Platonist Severus (?2nd c. A.D.) is mentioned (cf. Proclus, *In Tim.* II, p. 152.24D, διάστημα γεωμετρικὸν ἐπὶ τὴν οὐσίαν αὐτῆς ἀναφέρειν, ὡς Σεβῆρος) and Speusippus (364.2–5). A second class of definitions is based on ἀριθμός, and includes a motley collection of Pythagoreans, Xenocrates, Moderatus (in relation to ratios, λόγοι, see Festugière, *Révélation* 182, n. 1),

Hippasus (acousmatic) and Plato (364.7–18). From this class Iamblichus pulls out a sub-class based on ἁρμονία μαθηματική, and instances Moderatus; τὴν τὰ διαφέροντα ὁπωσοῦν σύμμετρα καὶ προσήγορα ἀπεργαζομένην ἀναφέρει εἰς τὴν ψυχὴν Μοδέρατος (364.19–23). In *De Comm. Math. Scientia* IX, p. 40 Festa, Iamblichus again distinguishes three branches of mathematics: geometrical, arithmetical, harmonic. He refuses a definition of soul relating to one class only. So he rejects in the first class ἰδέα τοῦ πάντῃ διαστατοῦ (Speusippus), in the second class ἀριθμὸς αὐτοκινητός (Xenocrates), and in the third ἁρμονία ἐν λόγοις ὑφεστῶσα (Moderatus?). He wants to combine all three: κοινῇ δὲ συμπλέκειν πάντα ἄξιον, ὡς τῆς ψυχῆς καὶ ἰδέας οὔσης ἀριθμίου καὶ κατ' ἀριθμοὺς ἁρμονίαν περιέχοντας ὑφεστώσης, πάσας τε συμμετρίας κοινῶς . . . (p. 40.19ff Festa). This is evidence not for Posidonius, but for his originality in combining in his definition all the categories of mathematics; geometrical σχῆμα, ἀριθμός and ἁρμονία. One can be sure that this was not for any scholastic reason, but it fits well with his passion for the completeness of an account in the unity of all sciences, here expressed in mathematical form. One can regretfully only speculate on how he may have developed and explained this formula. But according to F196, shape (σχῆμα) for Posidonius was the containing limit (cf. soul to body, F149), the cause of definiteness, limitation and inclusion. Perhaps then in soul it is that factor which furnishes identity. ἀριθμός, or the preciseness of number, would be associated with intelligibility; also for the association for Posidonius of ἀριθμός with substantial change (ἀλλοίωσις in his use of the term), see F96.12 and comm. ἁρμονία as the concord of ratios would represent the principle of order, and through its particular association with the mathematical science of astronomy, perhaps also with motion. It is clear that Posidonius, like most other commentators on Plato from Aristotle on, was not simply interpreting *Tim.*, but reinterpreting it in the light of his own philosophy. And a prime factor in this was mathematical, physical (and metaphysical) concept of shape and limits. Rist (*Stoic Philosophy* 204ff) developed this by linking for Posidonius world soul with the οὐρανός the ἐσχάτη περιφέρεια, as the ἡγεμονικόν of the cosmos (cf. F23), and further suggesting that τὰ νοητά, the Platonic Forms, thereupon become God's concepts (already in Schmekel, *Die Philosophie der mittleren Stoa* 430; cf. for criticism Jones, 'The Ideas as the Thoughts of God', *CPh* 21 (1926) 317ff). But this remains speculative; see comm. on next sentence (6–9).

6–9 'For they said that, as the mathematicals (τὰ μαθηματικά) have been ranked between the primary intelligibles (νοητῶν) and the perceptibles (αἰσθητῶν), so it is appropriate for the soul, which has the permanence of the intelligibles and the passivity (τὸ παθητικόν) of the perceptibles to have her being in the middle'.

8 προσῆκον: Festugière (*Révélation* 180, n. 2) appears to take προσῆκον with τὸ παθητικόν ('comme il convient'). It is tempting to read προσήκειν (Bernardakis), but perhaps it is unnecessary (cf. Philo, *De Vita Mosis* II.69 = IV.216.18–19 Cohn, cited by Cherniss).

This is the really difficult sentence. The indirect speech should indicate that Plutarch is still reporting Posidonius (or the Posidonians), and γάρ shows that it is an explanation of the previous sentence. But an explanation of what? The argument is analogical, although paratactic in form: as mathematicals have an intermediate position, so the soul has her being (οὐσία) in the middle. But what does 'in the middle' mean? It does not make much sense to a Stoic, or for Posidonius, to say 'in the middle position of being, between intelligibles (νοητά) and perceptibles'. It makes sense only for Platonists and Plato, i.e. purely as a commentary on *Tim.* But then there is a misfit between the two sentences. The definition is a reinterpretation of *Tim.* in the light of Posidonius' own structure of thought; the 'explanation' does not seem to be an explanation of that reinterpretation, but a straight interpretative explanation of Plato.

Either (1) Plutarch has conflated an account by Posidonius, where both reinterpretation and comment on *Tim.* have been involved; or (2), the argument of the explanation has been abbreviated. Posidonius was appealing to the authority of Plato, where mathematicals hold a middle position, not for the middle position of soul, but for its definition as a mathematical, or even for the soul having characteristics both of permanency and of affection or passivity (παθητικόν). But this runs counter to the structural spine of the argument, which goes from the 'mathematicals' to the positional οὐσία of soul, and takes the opposing characteristics of soul for granted. However, the assumed characteristics are themselves Platonic, so perhaps the argument ran: the soul, too, having these characteristics, has its being in the middle, *and therefore* is a mathematical, as I, Posidonius too, like Plato interpret it. The trouble with this is that although Posidonius interpreted soul in mathematical terms, it is doubtful whether he, or any Stoic, could mean by that a 'mathematical' in the full ontological sense of an intermediate being between intelligibles and sensibles; cf. F139. The 'intermediate' for Posidonius was not soul, but the science of mathematics itself (Kidd, 'Philosophy and Science', *A & A* 24 (1978), 7ff). I take it that the formula given here may be Posidonius' definition of the form of the soul, while F139, πνεῦμα ἔνθερμον, is his description of its substance. But soul itself was simply σῶμα, a material body, and not some mysterious intermediate 'mathematical' (F139). One would incidentally like to know where Posidonius found out about 'mathematicals' in Plato. Was it from Aristotle, which is our source? This sentence remains intractably Platonic, not Stoic. For this reason, parts of Rist's account (see above) seem to me uncomfortably Neoplatonic rather than Posidonian.

It is just possible that (3), the sentence embodies someone else's, or even Plutarch's explanation foisted on the Posidonians. Plutarch was not overscrupulous in such matters. It is certainly the case that reinterpretations and straight interpretations (or explanations) of Plato became confused with each other in the tradition. Diogenes Laertius (III.67) actually assigns ἰδέαν τοῦ πάντῃ διεστῶτος πνεύματος of the soul to Plato. Wherever Diogenes found this, it is clearly Stoic, and probably derives ultimately from Posidonius' tangling with *Tim.*

B. (9–19)

Plutarch's criticism hinges apparently on the assumption that the Posidonian version is simply an interpretation of Plato, and he answers it from Plato or from his own interpretation of *Tim.*

(i) 9–13 'The Posidonians failed to see that god (i.e. in *Tim.*) later, after he had produced soul, used the limits of the bodies for the shaping of matter (ἐπὶ τὴν τῆς ὕλης διαμόρφωσιν) by limiting and circumscribing its dispersiveness and incoherence with the surfaces from the triangles fitted together.' This betrays a certain understanding of the Posidonian position, but argues that it is misplaced at this point in *Tim.* It depends also on Plutarch's own literal interpretation of the 'creation' in *Tim.* It is related to the attack on materialist interpretations of the psychology of the previous chapter.

(ii) 13–17 An absurd criticism of Posidonians for calling the soul an ἰδέα, by interpreting ἰδέα as Platonic Form. For the incoherence of this and the probability that it was conscious misinterpretation, see ἰδέα, line 4, above.

(iii) 17–19 A reminder of a previous objection against Xenocrates (1013C–D), that Plato did not posit the substance of soul as number either (οὐδὲ, i.e. as he did not call it ἰδέα), but as being ordered by number.

This serves as a transition to ch. 23 where Plutarch contends that it is an argument against both Posidonians and Xenocrateans, that neither in πέρατα (i.e. Posidonius) nor in ἀριθμοί (Xenocrates) is there any trace of the δύναμις by which the soul naturally κρίνει τὸ αἰσθητόν. νοῦς and τὸ νοητόν have been produced by ἡ τῆς νοητῆς μέθεξις ἀρχῆς (he refers to ταῦτα τῷ νοητῷ μίξαντες F141.4), δόξας δὲ καὶ πίστεις καὶ τὸ φανταστικὸν καὶ τὸ παθητικὸν ὑπὸ τῶν περὶ τὸ σῶμα ποιοτήτων, τοῦτ' οὐκ ἄν τις ἐκ μονάδων οὐδὲ γραμμῶν οὐδ' ἐπιφανειῶν ἁπλῶς νοήσειεν ἐγγιγνόμενον. In other words in Plutarch's view, the Posidonians have the worst of all positions, they are subject both to his attack against materialist interpretations, such as those of the supporters of Crantor, and to his criticisms of mathematical versions, such as those of Xenocrateans.

F142 Galen, *De Placitis* v.454–5, p. 432.9–15 M, p. 312.29–34 De Lacy

CONTENT

That there are three faculties of soul with which we desire, are angry and think is agreed by Posidonius and Aristotle. The doctrine of Hippocrates and Plato is that these are separately located and our mind not only has in it many faculties, but is basically a composite of parts which are different in kind and in their being.

CONTEXT

Galen is beginning (432.1 M, 312.22 De L) an argument against Chrysippus that it is not in a single part of the soul nor by virtue of a single faculty of it that both judgements (κρίσεις) and emotions (πάθη) occur. He enlists the authority of Aristotle, Posidonius, Hippocrates and Plato.

COMMENT

This fragment makes explicit that Galen believed that the views of Posidonius and Aristotle on the faculties of soul were different (τὸ μὲν . . . τὸ δέ) from those of Hippocrates and Plato. While Posidonius distinguished three faculties, for Plato they were separately located parts essentially different in kind. The inference must be that Posidonius disagreed with Plato on the addition contained in the τὸ δέ sentence. This is confirmed by F146. Galen cites *both* groups here to enlist maximum support. He himself holds the theory of spatial separation as well as plurality of faculties.

Galen is quite specific on the number of faculties, namely three; see also F143. They are expressed in terms (ἐπιθυμοῦμεν, θυμούμεθα, λογιζόμεθα) which are clearly derived from Plato, but Posidonius had his own interpretation (F31, comm.). It may be characteristic that they are expressed by verbs (so also Frs. 143, 145), since they represent ὀρέξεις or ὁρμαί, each with its own οἰκείωσις (Frs. 158, 160) towards a proper distinctive goal.

For διαφερόντων ταῖς οὐσίαις (l. 6), cf. F146.

F143 Galen, *De Placitis* v.480, p. 461.4–6 M, 336.24–6 De Lacy

CONTENT

That we think, are angry, desire with different faculties is a doctrine common to Aristotle, Plato and Posidonius.

CONTEXT

An examination of Plato, *Rep.* IV on the three parts of the soul (460.9ff M)

COMMENT

Galen at this point merely wishes to stress that the human soul consists of three δυνάμεις. The question as to whether these are also separately located parts differing in essence is put off until Bk VI 326.26ff De L). Therefore in this context it is understandable that Galen lumps Aristotle, Plato and Posidonius together instead of distinguishing them as in F142. However, in the next sentence (336.26–32 De L), in terms similar to F142, Galen goes on to associate the postponed argument on separately located parts with Hippocrates and Plato, as distinct from Aristotle and Posidonius.

In the context (336.16–23 De L), Galen is very positive that there are three faculties of soul in all, and only three, and this must apply to Posidonius. Distinguish however from 'divisions' of soul, F147.

F144 Galen, *De Placitis* V.481, pp. 462.12–463.3 M, 338.11–16 De Lacy.

CONTENT

In so far as he posited three faculties of soul, Posidonius parted company with Chrysippus and followed Aristotle and Plato to a greater extent.

CONTEXT

The same as F143. Galen has just quoted Plato, *Rep.* IV.435c 9–d 3 to convey Plato's hesitation in that context to argue for separate parts of soul.

COMMENT

Once more Galen is careful to distinguish between parts

(μέρη) (338.4 De L) and faculties (δυνάμεις) and quite definitely and conclusively restricts Posidonius to the faculty theory. The δυνάμεις are qualified as ἑτερογενεῖς (l. 4), which was used of the specifically Platonic position in F142.5, but Galen here is dealing with common ground between Plato and Posidonius; ἑτερογενεῖς is an ambiguous word, and in Posidonius' case may mean no more than ἑτέροις ἀλλήλων (F145).

οὕτω γοῦν . . . ὑπολαβών: It seems to be implied not only that Galen is comparing Posidonius with Aristotle and Plato, but that Posidonius himself took the basis of his psychology from them. In any case this seems virtually certain from F31. As in F143, Aristotle is put before Plato (l. 6), as having the greater similarity to Posidonius.

That F183 follows this fragment is interesting for the structure of F31 (comm. *E* on F31). F183 explains μᾶλλον (l. 6) with reference to difference in virtues, although there is general agreement in psychology.

F145 Galen, *De Placitis* v.493, p. 476.2–6 M, 348.17–20 De Lacy

CONTENT

Galen will not yet in this Book (v) criticise Aristotle and Posidonius for agreeing that we think, are angry, desire with different faculties, rather than with species or parts of soul.

CONTEXT

Still the same as Frs. 143, 144.

COMMENT

Again there is explicit restriction of Posidonius (and Aristotle) to a δύναμις theory, and rejection for them of distinctions of form (εἴδη) or parts (μορία). This is all the more reliable because Galen says that he himself intends later to argue against Posidonius for parts (μέρη) of soul that differ from each other in form (κατ' εἶδος) (476.6–8 M, 348.20–2 De L). But Posidonius' δύναμις theory is sufficient to belabour Chrysippus.

οὐδέπω, 476.6–8 M, 348.20–2 De L clearly show that οὐδέποτε *H* is wrong. For the implication of οὐδέπω: F143.

Frs 142–6 supply sufficient evidence that Posidonius wished to make this to him important distinction from Plato. They need not require us to assume that Posidonius always scrupulously used the word δύναμις instead of μέρος, if he was not wishing to make that particular point, but F187.19 is not good evidence for this (Rist, *Stoic Philosophy* 212 n. 3), since it is a comment by Galen who has just mentioned Plato. But μέρους in Clement's definition of τέλος (F186.15) seems inaccurate. There is no contradiction with F147, which is quite a different classification.

F146 Galen, *De Placitis* VI.515, p. 501.7–14 M, 368.20–6 De Lacy

CONTENT

Posidonius and Aristotle are distinguished from Plato and Chrysippus in a classification of theories on the form or composition of soul.

CONTEXT

Galen has been comparing Plato's metaphorical imagery for the parts of soul in *Phdr.* 253c–254a and *Rep.* IX.588c 6–d 8. Galen supports Plato's use of the terms εἴδη and μέρη (500.16–501.7 M).

COMMENT

A triple classification of psychological analysis is given:

(1) Plato, because he thinks the faculties of soul are separate in physical location (e.g. *Tim.* 44d, 69d 7–70a 7) and differ very greatly in essence (ταῖς οὐσίαις), reasonably terms them forms or species (εἴδη) and parts (μέρη) (ll. 1–3).

(2) Aristotle and Posidonius refuse the terms 'forms' and 'parts' of soul, and say that they are faculties or capacities or powers (δυνάμεις) of a single substance (οὐσία), with its base in the heart.

(3) Chrysippus not only pulls anger and desire into a single substance (οὐσία), but also into a single faculty (δύναμις).

Galen goes on (501.14–502.4 M) to state his view that these are in order of correctness, the error of (2) being to suppose that the three faculties belong to a single οὐσία. The general position is clear and consistent with Frs. 142–5; the details are obscure.

The distinction between 'parts' and 'faculties' is clear. Posidonius presumably wished to deny that soul was an aggregate of parts, but was rather a single substance (and for all Stoics soul was a substance) that thinks, desires and is angry.

But what is meant by μία οὐσία in l. 5 and is it the same or a different sense from ταῖς οὐσίαις πάμπολυ διαλλάττειν of l. 2? μία οὐσία cannot mean one essence, because ἐπιθυμεῖν, θυμοῦσθαι and λογίζεσθαι differ from each other (Frs. 144, 145), have different οἰκειώσεις, different ends (Frs. 158–61), are not simply relative aspects of a single δύναμις such as the rational as Chrysippus suggested; on the contrary, Posidonius' rational and irrational faculties are opposed to each other (F31). Then μία οὐσία can only mean 'one substance' (i.e. based at the heart, l. 5), agreeing thus far with Chrysippus against the local separation of Plato. But 'substance' has no meaning in l. 2, where sense demands 'differ in essence'.

One wonders whether the confusion derives from Galen, who seems to understand μία οὐσία as 'one essence', and objects that the three δυνάμεις cannot come from a single οὐσία (502.1–4 M). But it is normal Stoic doctrine to hold that a single substance (μία οὐσία) could have a plurality of capacities or faculties (δυνάμεις) depending on how it was qualified or disposed (e.g. *SVF* II.826). There would have been no difference between Chrysippus and Posidonius on that point. It is possible that confusion arose between Posidonius' objections to Plato and Chrysippus. The objection to Plato was clearly on local separation, which in Posidonius' opinion made soul an aggregate of parts. (Pohlenz, *Die Stoa* I.227; II.114 wrongly ascribes localisation to Posidonius.) The objection to Chrysippus was not over μία οὐσία, which was a point of agreement, but because Posidonius believed that Chrysippus reduced the activity of soul to μία δύναμις, one capacity, the rational, whereas there was a separate δύναμις or δυνάμεις (F148), two of them in fact (Frs. 142–5).

For similar problems relating to virtue(s): F182 comm.

Posidonius' disagreement with Chrysippus is fundamental, not only for his theories of πάθη, but for his whole ethical philosophy; see Frs. 30, 150, 187; Kidd, 'Posidonius on Emotions', *Problems* p. 202ff.

7 For Chrysippus θυμός was a species of ἐπιθυμία.

F147 Tertullian, *De Anima* 14.2

CONTENT

Posidonius had a division of soul arising from the two categories ἡγεμονικόν and λογικόν, resulting in a division of (possibly) 17.

CONTEXT

In ch. 14 Tertullian maintains that the soul is a single, simple entity entire in itself, incapable of being put together or of being divided. Yet philosophers have divided it into parts; whereupon the doxography of F147 follows.

COMMENT

A much chewed passage: Waszink, *Tertullian, De An.* 212–14; Pohlenz, 'Tierische und Menschliche Intelligenz bei Poseidonios', *Hermes* 76 (1941), 12 n. 1 = *Kl. Schr.* I.303, n. 1; *Die Stoa* II.112; Reinhardt, *Poseidonios* 352–6; Schindler, *Die stoische Lehre von den Seelenteilen* 53ff; Holler, *Seneca und die Seelenteilungslehre der Mittelstoa* 54ff; Diels, *Dox. Gr.* 205f; Laffranque, *Poseidonios* 380f.

The doxography

Waszink (Introduction, p. 21*ff, esp. p. 30*), following the lead of Diels, has shown that the likely source of the doxography for Tertullian was Soranus' Περὶ ψυχῆς, and that Soranus may have gained the information from the *Vetusta Placita*, probably through the intermediary of Aenesidemus. The form of criticism by presenting variation of 'dogmatic' opinion in a numerically mounting series is Sceptic; cf. the doxography in S.E. *Adv. Math.* X.313–18, where starting from the view that all things come into being from one thing (Hippasus, Anaximenes, Thales), the numerical progression of ἀρχαί proceeds in order through two, four, five and six until we finally reach ἐξ ἀπείρων (infinity) with Anaxagoras, Democritus and Epicurus. So here the pattern is an increase from two parts (Plato) to seventeen for Posidonius. It does not inspire confidence. Apart from difficulties with other members, e.g. Zeno and Panaetius, the structure of polemic is biased to present the largest possible number at the end of the series. Also the text is defective, or at least the transmission of tradition has become muddled and confused.

Posidonius

(a) The text

The problem with regard to Posidonius is obvious; the solution is not. The simple arithmetic in 5–9 does not seem to work out.

'. . . but the soul is divided into twelve parts (*cod. A*, the best evidence; another tradition preserved in Mnesartius (*B*) and Gelenius (*Gel.*) has 10) by certain Stoics, and into two more by Posidonius, who starting from two labels, "governing" (which Stoics call ἡγεμονικόν) and "rational" (called by them λογικόν), proceeded to cut up the soul into seventeen.' Fourteen (or twelve) does not correspond to seventeen.

There have been two basic methods of solution.

(1) Waszink accepts the text of *codex A*, and therefore *duodecim* (6) and *decem septem* (9), and believes that Tertullian's Latin can distinguish between the two totals. He translates: '. . . and into two more parts by Pos. ⟨= 14⟩, who ⟨, however,⟩ when starting from two different notions (ἡγ. and λογ.) goes further still (*exinde*), and ⟨even⟩ divides the soul into seventeen parts.' (Cf. Schindler, *Die Stoische Lehre* 60). But this is achieved by emending the translation by the inserted words without emending the Latin, and involves an unexpected use of *exinde* which should mean either 'from there' i.e. proceed to . . .; or 'thus' (οὕτως, so Pohlenz). Also the sense is odd, to say that he divided the soul into seventeen parts. But the real difficulty remains in the text.

(2) There is a corruption in the figures. Some scholars (see *app. crit.*) have altered seventeen (in line 9) to *duodecim* or *decem et quattuor*, depending on whether they accept ten or twelve in line 6. But the manuscript tradition at 9 is solid for *decem* (*et*) *septem* and it is not easy to see how *septem* arose. Alternatively, one can assume a lacuna after *duodecim* at line 6, where ⟨*et in*

quindecim⟩ has fallen out (so Reinhardt). But in this case it is rather odd to say that certain Stoics divided the soul into twelve and into fifteen parts.

Neither solution is fully convincing. I suspect that this is because there is an inherent confusion, which is more deeply set than has been so far admitted. For example, *duas amplius* (7) seems to refer (a) to two more parts, added to the figure of the preceding Stoics; but (b) it also appears to foreshadow the two *tituli*, which are however categories of classification, rather than simple parts themselves. Even if that point were to be disregarded for polemical rhetoric, λογικόν would already have been included in any Stoic list, and Posidonius' innovation of the irrational powers of soul is still excluded. So to what does *duas amplius* refer? On the other hand, it does not help to emend *rationali* . . . λογικόν to *irrationali* . . . ἄλογον with Stein, Laffranque and Philippson on the grounds that ἡγεμονικόν and λογικόν refer to the same part, because that wrecks the ἡγεμονικόν/λογικόν classification. It is clear that those who see a confusion between two previously existing separate systems of division into parts and classification of division are correct, but the confusion and incoherence is in Tertullian himself, and/or his immediate source, and therefore may be understood but not emended.

(b) Interpretation

The most reliable information is that Posidonius adopted a classification of powers of soul (he did not like the use of 'part', F146) based on rational/irrational and governing/subordinate. This fits well with the evidence from Galen; e.g. for rational, irrational: Frs. 142–6, 148, 158–60; for rule and obedience: Frs. 31, 187.

It is also likely that Posidonius increased the number of powers recognised by previous Stoics, although the details remain uncertain. The Chrysippean eight-part division is well-attested, comprising the five senses, the generative power (σπερματικοὶ λόγοι), power of speech (τὸ φωνητικόν), and power of reasoning (τὸ λογιστικόν) (D.L. VII.157; cf. VII.110; *SVF* II.827–30). It is certain from the Galenic evidence that Posidonius under the rational/irrational classification would list three; λογιστικόν, θυμοειδές, ἐπιθυμητικόν (e.g. F160). Under ἡγεμονικόν would come a wider range, cf. Sen. *Ep.* 92.1: *partes ministras, per quas movemur alimurque, propter ipsum principale nobis datas* (cf. also *SVF* II.830). So probably the five senses, and ἡ κινητική, θρεπτική, αὐξητική, σπερματική and φωνητική. Perhaps also representation from the still more basic powers such as, ἑλκτική, καθεκτική, ἀλλοιωτική, ἀπωστική (cf. Reinhardt, *Poseidonios* 105). But this is very speculative, and Pohlenz (*Hermes* 76, 12) is rightly sceptical of the use of Nemesius, *De Nat. Hom.*, ch. 26 as Posidonian by Reinhardt (who adds ch. 15 as well) and Schindler (see also Waszink p. 213f), especially in such detail as ἡ σφυγμικὴ δύναμις.

F148 Galen, *De Placitis* V.467, p. 445.13–15, 446.10 M, p. 324.9–11, 20 De Lacy; *De Placitis* IV.349.4 M, p. 248.10 De Lacy

CONTENT

Posidonius recognised irrational powers of soul.

CONTEXT

See Frs. 31, 34.

COMMENT

Under the 'rational' classification of divisions of soul (F147), Posidonius recognised distinct (ἑτέρα) irrational powers. Although sometimes these were expressed simply as an irrational power, he in fact commonly distinguished two (e.g. Frs. 142–5). In this he differed sharply from Chrysippean Stoicism (Frs. 144, 146, 33), but believed that he was following the earlier Stoa of Zeno and Cleanthes (F166.20ff). It was not a division of parts, but a recognition of distinct δυνάμεις (F146). He presented against Chrysippus a proof for such irrational powers (F34). Since they were distinct, they had their own proper function and training (Frs. 31, 160, 161, 169). He believed that all ethical problems depended on the recognition of this psychology (F150).

F149 Achilles Tatius, *Introductio in Aratum* 13

CONTENT

The topic arises from ζῷον defined as ἔμψυχος οὐσία, ensouled being or substance. Then comes a doxography as to whether the stars or heavenly bodies are ζῷα (cf. Frs. 127, 128). The Epicureans say that there are no such things as ζῴδια (i.e. signs of the zodiac, related to the form of the Greek term ζῴδια), because they are ⟨not⟩ held together by bodies (σωμάτων), but the Stoics maintain the opposite. Posidonius said that the Epicureans do not know that it is not bodies which hold souls together (συνέχει), but souls bodies, just as glue controls (masters, κρατεῖ) both itself and what is outside it. Then follow some arguments used by the Stoics (οἱ Στωϊκοί) to prove (πρὸς ἀπόδειξιν) that the stars are living beings (ζῷα), arguments related to substance (πυρώδη), movement, and κρίσις.

The doxography

For the doxography cf. Frs. 129, 130. Diels argued (*Dox. Gr.* 22, cf. Dillon, *Middle Platonists* 129) that Achilles used Eudorus, from where he derived material from Diodorus, the mathematicus from Alexandria, who in turn was probably influenced by Posidonius; see Frs. 127–30, comm. It is not impossible that the doxography may thus be traced back to Posidonius. For Posidonian criticism of Epicurus and Epicureans: F22, Frs. 46, 47, F160, Frs. 288, 289.

COMMENT

Reinhardt (*Kosmos und Sympathie* 210) called this 'das Poseidonische Argument', but it is Stoic in general, and indeed the concept goes back at least to Aristotle, *De An.* 411b 6: τί οὖν δή ποτε συνέχει τὴν ψυχήν, εἰ μεριστὴ πέφυκεν; οὐ γὰρ δὴ τό γε σῶμα. δοκεῖ γὰρ τοὐναντίον μᾶλλον ἡ ψυχὴ τὸ σῶμα συνέχειν (cf. Heinemann, *Poseidonios' Metaphysische Schriften* II.33; Jones, 'Posidonius and Solar Eschatology', *CPh* 27 (1932), 115). It was central to the Stoic doctrine of πνεῦμα. Soul is πνεῦμα ἔνθερμον (F139), and τὴν μὲν πνευματικὴν οὐσίαν τὸ συνέχον, τὴν δὲ ὑλικὴν τὸ συνεχόμενον (*SVF* II.439); or, τὸ μὲν πνεῦμα καὶ τὸ πῦρ συνέχειν ἑαυτό τε καὶ τὰ ἄλλα (*SVF* II.440; cf. Plu. *Comm. Not.* 1085D = *SVF* II.444). Closer still to the Posidonian expression of the concept is S.E. *Adv. Math.* IX.72, οὐδὲ γὰρ πρότερον τὸ σῶμα διακρατητικὸν ἦν αὐτῶν (i.e. ψυχαί), ἀλλ' αὐταὶ τῷ σώματι συμμονῆς ἦσαν αἴτιαι, πολὺ δὲ πρότερον καὶ ἑαυταῖς. Reinhardt, however, went much further, and starting from the base of the rest of the Sextus context (71–4) (*Kosmos und Sympathie* 75, 210, 308), adding other dubious unnamed passages from Plutarch, Julian, Macrobius and the Hermetic corpus, constructed an eschatological theory for Posidonius which was demolished by Jones (*CPh* 27 (1932), 113–35).

For more judicious examinations of S.E. *Adv. Math.* IX.71–4: Hoven, *Stoïcisme et Stoïciens face au problème de l'au-delà* 62–4, 74ff; Dragona-Monachou, *Existence of the Gods* 173f.

Nevertheless, Posidonius may have shown particular interest in soul as the containing concept. We know that he had original views in mathematics on limit and what 'contained' or 'formed' a figure. In opposition to Euclid, he defined shape (σχῆμα) as containing limit, separating the *logos* of shape from quantity, and making it cause of definiteness, limitation and inclusion (F196). It is possible that this line of thought may have been translated to arguments on soul, and affected his interpretation of soul as συνέχον and ἑκτικόν. For a speculative development of this line of thought: Rist, *Stoic Philosophy* 204ff; but see F141 comm. But the idea of an outside container (οὐρανός on Rist's theory), clearly does not fit, or at least is inadequate (cf. Rist, *Stoic Philosophy* 208f), with the simile of glue in this passage, which is more in line with the normal Stoic theory of the permeation of πνεῦμα. The simile is certainly from Posidonius, who had a fondness for them, and forms an interesting parallel with Aristotle, who in *De An.* defined soul as the form of body. In a materialist philosophy such as the Stoa, a model for the principle of ἑκτικόν becomes glue. Such a model need not by any means emphasise dualism.

The statement about the Epicureans as given by Achilles' text (7–8) is odd. Sandbach has suggested to me ⟨οὐ⟩ συνέχεται, which makes more sense.